MW00785215

Metaphysics

"The influence of Alexander Baumgarten's philosophy in the eighteenth century, and on Kant's system in particular, cannot be overestimated. Its structure is a major catalyst for the form and content of much of even Kant's critical work, and especially of its metaphysics. This new English edition of Baumgarten's metaphysics is therefore essential reading for all scholars interested in the most substantive work of the period." **Karl Ameriks, McMahon-Hank Professor of Philosophy, University of Notre Dame, USA**

"Alexander Gottlieb Baumgarten's *Metaphysica* was both a refined restatement of the German rationalism of Leibniz and Wolff and an original work of philosophy. Not merely the textbook for Immanuel Kant's lectures on metaphysics and anthropology, it fundamentally shaped Kant's 'Critical Philosophy' and through that most of later German philosophy. This lucid translation finally makes Baumgarten's seminal work available in English. Including Kant's annotations in his own copy of the *Metaphysica* along with an illuminating introduction and extensive notes and glossary, this volume will be indispensable for all future students of Kant and German philosophy." **Paul Guyer, Jonathan Nelson Professor of Humanities and Philosophy, Brown University, USA**

"A splendid and permanent contribution to the study of modern philosophy. The well-researched and fully accurate English translation of Baumgarten's work takes proper account of contemporaneous Latin usage as well as key philosophical concepts, especially the concepts underlying the development of metaphysical thinking in eighteenth-century Germany after Leibniz. The translators' historically contextualizing introduction, textual annotations, and ancillary translations of Kant's notes on the *Metaphysica* will thus be remarkably useful to anyone who wants to understand what goes on in a highly significant phase of early modern philosophy. It almost goes without saying that Kant scholars should find this book indispensable. It is, for example, the ideal accompanying volume for graduate seminars on *The Critique of Pure Reason* that seek to come to grips directly with Kant's own understanding of metaphysics." **Jeffrey Edwards, Associate Professor of Philosophy, Stony Brook University, USA**

"Of all the philosophical works of Kant's predecessors and contemporaries that have remained untranslated into English in their entirety, Alexander Baumgarten's *Metaphysics* is likely the most important for an understanding of Kant's theoretical philosophy. But Fugate and Hymers' volume goes well beyond what we could have reasonably hoped for. It provides not only a meticulous translation of Baumgarten's

Metaphysics and lengthy notes on the translation, but also an overview of Baumgarten's life and philosophy, an assessment of the relations of this philosophy to the philosophies of Wolff, Leibniz, Meier, and Kant; a translation of all of Kant's *Erläuterungen* (elucidations) of Baumgarten's text; and an extensive glossary and index. Fugate and Hymers have simply produced an exceptional volume that will be of great value to Kant scholarship, and we can only hope that they will engage in similar translation projects in the future." **Julian Wuerth, Associate Professor of Philosophy, Vanderbilt University, USA**

"Baumgarten's manual was enormously influential and widely discussed in Kant's time in matters such as metaphysics, cosmology, and psychology. Kant used it repeatedly in many of his courses and annotated it extensively. This volume offers the first full translation of Baumgarten's *Metaphysics* (in its fourth, 1757 edition) in English, inclusive of Kant's hand-written elucidations. It is a very welcome addition to the primary sources available to scholars. The current state of debate makes this a timely contribution that will help anyone interested in Kant to gauge in a more accurate and historically informed fashion the extent of his relation to his eighteenth-century German predecessors. Fugate and Hymers' rich, attentive and scrupulous critical notes never make the reader feel unassisted in this undertaking." **Alfredo Ferrarin, Associate Professor of Philosophy, University of Pisa, Italy**

Metaphysics

A Critical Translation with Kant's Elucidations, Selected Notes, and Related Materials

Alexander Baumgarten

Translated and Edited with an Introduction by
Courtney D. Fugate and John Hymers

B L O O M S B U R Y
LONDON • NEW DELHI • NEW YORK • SYDNEY

Bloomsbury Academic
An imprint of Bloomsbury Publishing Plc

50 Bedford Square	1385 Broadway
London	New York
WC1B 3DP	NY 10018
UK	USA

www.bloomsbury.com

First published in paperback 2014

First published 2013

Translated Material, Introduction and Bibliography © Courtney D. Fugate and John Hymers, 2013, 2014

This translation is based on *Metaphysica Alexandri Gottlieb Baumgarten, Professoris Philosophiae*. Editio IIII. Halae Magdeburgicae. Impensis Carol. Herman. Hemerde.1757

All rights reserved. No part of this publication may be reproduced or transmitted in any form or by any means, electronic or mechanical, including photocopying, recording, or any information storage or retrieval system, without prior permission in writing from the publishers.

No responsibility for loss caused to any individual or organization acting on or refraining from action as a result of the material in this publication can be accepted by Bloomsbury Academic or the authors.

British Library Cataloguing-in-Publication Data
A catalogue record for this book is available from the British Library.

ISBN: HB: 978-1-4411-3294-9
PB: 978-1-4725-7013-0
ePDF: 978-1-4411-9674-3
ePub: 978-1-4411-9622-4

Library of Congress Cataloging-in-Publication Data
A catalog record for this book is available from the Library of Congress.

Typeset by Fakenham Prepress Solutions, Fakenham, Norfolk NR21 8NN
Printed and bound in Great Britain

Also available from Bloomsbury

The Continuum Companion to Kant, edited by Gary Banham,
Dennis Schulting and Nigel Hems
Difficult Freedom and Radical Evil in Kant, Joel Madore
Kant's 'Critique of Aesthetic Judgement', Fiona Hughes
Kant's 'Groundwork for the Metaphysics of Morals', Paul Guyer

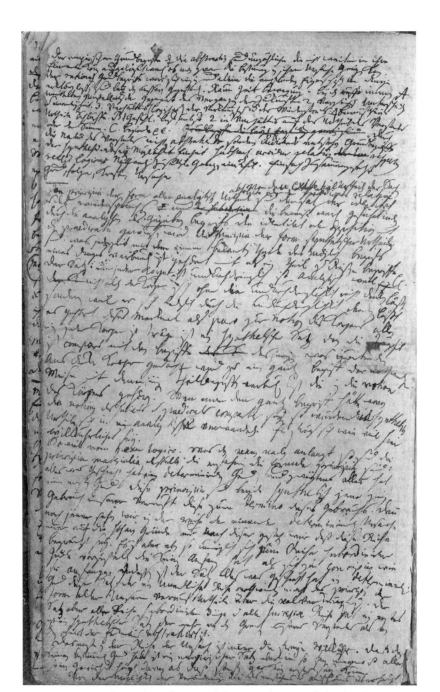

Figure 1. Pages V and VI of Kant's copy of the *Metaphysics*, with his handwritten notes. See Introduction, section 3 for a translation of the notes.

METAPHYSICA

ALEXANDRI GOTTLIEB
BAVMGARTEN
PROFESSORIS PHILOSOPHIAE

HOC ERIT IN VOTIS

EDITIO IIII.

HALAE MAGDEBVRGICAE
IMPENSIS CAROL. HERMAN. HEMMERDE
1757.

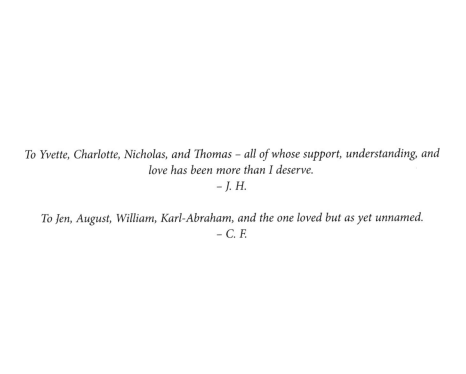

To Yvette, Charlotte, Nicholas, and Thomas – all of whose support, understanding, and love has been more than I deserve.
– J. H.

To Jen, August, William, Karl-Abraham, and the one loved but as yet unnamed.
– C. F.

Contents

Detailed Table of Contents

List of Illustrations

Acknowledgments

Our translation of Alexander Baumgarten's *Metaphysics* is a joint project many years in the making, one which has benefited from the help of a number of people whom we would now like to thank. We are grateful to Catarina Belo for reading and commenting on very early drafts of the prefaces, Hanno Birken-Bertsch for help with issues concerning German and for supplying us with primary sources we could not otherwise obtain, Robert Dobie for being a helpful Latin resource, Frederick Van Fleteren for help with the proofreading and for his advice, Eric Watkins for allowing us to consult an advanced draft of his translation of sections of the *Metaphysics*, Pieter d'Hoine for advice with the Greek on page 108, Bob Zunjic for additional materials, and finally the various anonymous readers of our proposals and drafts from whom we have profited immensely. Of course, we take full responsibility for the final product. We are grateful to Karl Krueger, director of the Krauth Memorial Library at the Lutheran Theological Seminary in Philadelphia, for full access to the fourth edition, to the library at the University of Mannheim for providing us with a copy of the third edition, and especially to the University of Tartu Library (Tartu, Estonia) for permission to reproduce pages from Kant's own copy of the *Metaphysics*. We also thank Walter de Gruyter for permission to use volumes 15, 17, and 18 of the *Akademie* edition of Kant's writings. Finally, John Hymers would like to acknowledge Richard Nigro, former Provost at La Salle University, and Tom Keagy, Dean of Arts and Sciences at La Salle University, for a research grant to help complete the work, and Marc Moreau for encouraging and facilitating that process.

Courtney D. Fugate is Assistant Professor at the American University of Beirut, Lebanon.

John Hymers is Assistant Professor of Philosophy at La Salle University, USA, where he teaches modern philosophy.

Part One

Introduction to the Translation

Introduction

This volume contains only the second modern translation of Alexander Gottlieb Baumgarten's *Metaphysica*, the other being recently published in German by Günter Gawlick and Lothar Kreimendahl (frommann–holzboog, 2011). It is constructed as a critical translation. The base text is the fourth edition, published in 1757, which has been compared with all other editions, including the condensed German translation composed by Baumgarten's student and colleague, Georg Friedrich Meier. All significant variants have been noted, while the text as a whole has been supplemented by numerous historical notes and references to the writings of Wolff and Leibniz. A complete translation of the *Erläuterungen* (elucidations) that Immanuel Kant penned in his edition of the *Metaphysics* has also been included and these are inserted as close as possible to their original positions in the text. Finally, to facilitate a better understanding of how Kant used the *Metaphysics*, and in particular how it relates to the handwritten notes collected in the *Akademie* edition of Kant's writings, we have included a photographical reproduction of some of the pages from his personal copy along with a translation of the notes penned on those pages.

Alexander Gottlieb Baumgarten was arguably the most influential German philosopher in the period between Christian Wolff and Immanuel Kant. His writings formed the terminological and conceptual bridge between the older Leibniz–Wolff tradition and the Kantian revolution that began in 1781. This is due partly to his direct philosophical and personal influence on other important figures in German philosophy, and partly to the widespread adoption of his works as lecture manuals. Baumgarten is also important for having made original contributions to the field of philosophical aesthetics that prepared the way for the emergence of the German tradition in literary and art criticism.

The *Metaphyics* is the scientific foundation for all Baumgarten's later writings, and consequently the definitions and arguments it contains are the key to unlocking his influential *Aesthetica* (1750 and 1757) and *Ethica Philosophica* (1740), among other writings. Apart from this, the *Metaphysics* is arguably the single most important textbook on the topic published in the German tradition prior to Immanuel Kant. It went through seven Latin and two German editions over a span of twenty-seven years and formed the basis of Kant's lectures on metaphysics, anthropology and religion over four decades. At several places in his writings, Kant makes it clear that he regarded the *Metaphysics* as the most perfect textbook of traditional metaphysics and as the chief source of the views of many of the metaphysicians of his generation. This is in part due to the fact that the *Metaphysics* provided by far the richest, clearest, and most systematic attempt at constructing a complete metaphysical system of the kind envisioned by Leibniz and Wolff. In addition to this, the development of many key arguments and concepts in Kant's own pre-critical and critical philosophy are documented in Kant's handwritten comments on Baumgarten's text and in many respects cannot be understood apart from it. Naturally, this is even more the case with the transcripts of Kant's lectures, many of which have been available in English for some time. Finally, Moses Mendelssohn, Thomas Abbt, George Friedrich Meier, Johann Gottfried von Herder, Johann August Eberhard, and Salomon Maimon are only a few of the other philosophers for whom Baumgarten's compendium served as a model of philosophical instruction.

1

Alexander Gottlieb Baumgarten (1714–62) and Georg Friedrich Meier (1718–77): A Historical Sketch[a]

A. Alexander Baumgarten

Alexander Baumgarten was born in Berlin on 17 June 1714 to Jacob Baumgarten, a Protestant evangelical preacher, and Rosina Elizabeth, née Wiedemannin. The fifth of seven sons, Alexander's early life was not easy, although the strong unity of his family and the support he would later receive from the Pietistic community assured him a certain degree of privilege. His mother died when he was three, and his father adopted, rather strictly it would seem, the educational theory espoused in John Locke's *Some Thoughts Concerning Education* (1693). Whether this meant that the young Alexander was denied fruit, made to sleep on a hard bed, and forced to wear wet shoes—something that might in part explain his later frail health—has not been recorded. But it does indicate that he was raised not only in a pious, but also in an "enlightened" household, one in which reason was highly prized in religious and secular matters alike, in which Latin was taught early, and, as Meier confirms, in which much of Alexander's education would be handled by his elder brothers. This was indeed fortunate, because Jacob Baumgarten died when Alexander was only eight, and his future development, from the focus of his early education to his eventual choice of a profession, indeed even his interest in the philosophy of Christian Wolff, turned out to be the direct result of the guidance of his oldest brother, Siegmund Jacob.

Once orphaned, the brothers were left little more than a large provision of books (which their father's will forbade them to sell) and their father's command to accept no charity and for each to study theology at the recently founded University of Halle. While the two oldest brothers joined the *Pädagogium*, a boys' school for noble and middle-class families directed by the Pietist August Hermann Francke (1663–1727), Alexander remained at home under the care of his grandmother and a friend of his father's. At this time his education was placed in the hands of Martin Christengau, the rector of a school in Frankfurt on the Oder, from whom Alexander learned not

[a] The details of this biographical sketch are drawn principally from: Georg Friedrich Meier, *Alexander Gottlieb Baumgartens Leben, beschrieben von Georg Friedrich Meier* (Halle: Hemmerde, 1763); Thomas Abbt, *Leben und Charakter Alexander Gottlieb Baumgartens*, originally 1765, in *Vermischte Werke* (Berlin and Leipzig, 1783), 213–44.

only the appropriate arts and sciences, but also Hebrew (indeed sufficiently to lecture on the subject later), and, most importantly given his work in aesthetics, the appreciation of fine art, especially of Latin poetry. According to his biographer, the young Baumgarten's enthusiasm for the latter was so great under Christengau that for several years he composed Latin poems daily, even translating the Sunday sermons into Latin verse.

In 1727, Alexander left the care of Christengau and traveled to Halle, where he was taken into the home of Francke and attended classes at the latter's famous *Waisenhaus*, or orphanage, where his two oldest brothers now oversaw the instruction of Latin. Here his education in theology and philosophy was largely provided by Siegmund Jacob Baumgarten. This close relationship with his oldest brother was extremely significant for Alexander's overall development. For, although Siegmund Jacob had grown up in the very institutions created by Francke, and had literally been fed at the latter's table, he was no party to the Pietistic opposition to Wolff or to its suspicions regarding rationalism in general. Indeed, Siegmund Jacob not only recommended that his younger brother study the writings of Wolff, but himself went on to become one of the foremost proponents of Wolff's philosophy.

This influence continued when Alexander undertook his studies at the University of Halle in 1730, where Siegmund Jacob had recently been appointed as professor of theology. Along with continued instruction in philosophy and theology from his brother, Alexander studied theology under Johann Justus Breithaupt and Gotthilf August Francke (August Hermann's son). Both Breithaupt and the elder Francke were close allies of Phillip Jacob Spener (who is often said to be the father of Pietism) and long-time enemies of Christian Thomasius, with whom they originally founded the university in the early 1690s. Moreover, both were instrumental in securing the edict by which Christian Wolff was stripped of his titles and compelled to flee the king's lands in 1723. Joachim Lange, another of Baumgarten's teachers in theology, was also a younger member of the anti-Wolffians, and is now remembered chiefly for the scathing popular attacks that served as the main propaganda in the campaign against Wolff.[a] In addition, Alexander studied philology under Christian Benedikt Michaelis and Johann Heinrich Michaelis, as well as Syrian, Arabic, Greek, ancient history and numismatics under the polymath Johann Heinrich Schulze. When he finally undertook the serious study of Wolff's philosophy, Alexander visited the University of Jena, where he also heard the lectures of Johann Peter Reusch, Jakob Carpov, Heinrich Köhler, and Georg Erhard Hamberger.

Upon his return to Halle, Baumgarten set about examining Wolff's philosophy in its own terms by following the method of study prescribed by Wolff himself. Accordingly, he first studied the latter's Latin mathematical works with the goal of acquiring skill in the methods of proof. He then studied Wolff's Latin logic, while, most remarkably, lecturing on Latin poetry and logic at Francke's *Waisenhaus*. Since Baumgarten had to make use of a more appropriate textbook for his lectures,[b] this gave him an opportunity to make a detailed comparison between Wolff's conception

---

[a] Baumgarten probably makes reference to Lange in the preface to the third edition. Please see p. 77.
[b] This was Johann Gottlieb Heineccius' *Elementa Philosophiae Rationis et Moralis* (1728). Heineccius was a famous jurist, and professor of philosophy and jurisprudence in Halle.

of philosophy and of philosophical method with that accepted in Halle at the time.[a] Baumgarten continued this study by venturing to teach Wolff's logic itself in a group that convened at his brother's home, although this was still officially under ban. These lectures seem to have been far more successful than expected, for as his biographer reports, Baumgarten "attempted to teach philosophy in secrecy, but his study became full of those who asked after reason."[b]

Finally, in 1735 and at the direction of his brother and grandmother, Baumgarten defended his dissertation *Meditationes philosophicae de nonnullis ad poema pertinentibus* (*Some Reflections Concerning Poetry*),[c] supported by Christian Benedikt Michaelis, to take up the post of doctor in philosophy at the University of Halle. His first lectures were held on Wolff's logic, which by now could be taught without its being officially noted. In the following year, Baumgarten studied Wolff's metaphysics with the help of Georg Bernhard Bilfinger's *Dilucidationes philosophicae de Deo, anima humana, mundo et generalibus rerum affectionibus* (*Philosophical Elucidations Concerning God, the Human Soul, the World and the General Affections of Things*), holding his first lectures on the subject in the winter of that year. This timing is significant for two reasons. First, even if it was possible to lecture on Wolff's logic, the same was not true of Wolff's metaphysics. It is to this that we owe the very existence of the *Metaphysics*, which was composed in the process of delivering these lectures. Secondly, this timing raises the question as to how much of Wolff's metaphysics Baumgarten had read when the work was first composed. Wolff's comparatively very short German metaphysics had long been in print, but was likely of little use to Baumgarten. Of the Latin writings, the *Ontology*, *Cosmology*, and the two parts of the *Psychology* had been published by 1734. The first part of the *Natural Theology*, however, did not appear until 1736, around the time the lectures were delivered, while the second part only appeared afterward in 1737. Since it is unclear how available Wolff's writings might have been in Halle, where of course their sale was still at least officially banned, Baumgarten's reliance on these later works, and perhaps even the slightly earlier ones, remains unclear.

Baumgarten continued to lecture on many subjects at the University of Halle, from Isaiah and Hebrew grammar, to natural theology, logic, metaphysics, natural law, philosophical ethics, and the history of philosophy. This lasted until 1739, when he was ordered by the king, and despite the protests of his students, to occupy the post of full professor of philosophy at Frankfurt on the Oder, which had remained vacant since the departure of Heineccius, who himself, somewhat ironically, had been ordered to move to the University of Halle in 1733. Baumgarten remained in Frankfurt for the remainder of his career, teaching, among other things: the lectures on aesthetics, which would later form the basis of Georg Friedrich Meier's highly influential *Anfangsgründe aller schönen Wissenshaften* (*Elements of all Beautiful Sciences*, 3 Vols., 1748–50) as well as his own *Aesthetica* (2 Vols., 1750 and 1757); the lectures

---

[a] Meier, *Baumgartens Leben*, 14.
[b] Meier, *Baumgartens Leben*, 15.
[c] Translated as *Reflections on Poetry*, with the original text, introduction and notes by Karl Aschenbrenner and William B. Holther (Berkeley and Los Angeles: University of California Press, 1954).

on metaphysics, which would form the basis of Meier's *Metaphysik* (4 Vols., 1747–9); the lectures on logic, which would form the basis of Meier's *Vernunftlehre* (1752), an abridged version of which was used by Kant as the textbook for his own lectures, as well as of Baumgarten's own *Acroasis logica in Christianum L. B. de Wolff* (*Discourse on Logic According to Christian, the Baron of Wolff*, 1761), which was found in Kant's library at the time of his death; and the lectures on ethics and practical philosophy, which would form the basis of his *Ethica philosophica* (*Philosophical Ethics*, 1740) and *Initia philosophiae practicae primae acroamatice* (*Introductory Lectures on First Practical Philosophy*, 1760), both of which were also used by Kant.

Troubled by ill health even before his move to Frankfurt on the Oder, Baumgarten's later life was spent in an almost constant battle with what, given Meier's description, was likely severe tuberculosis. The end of his struggles came in 1762, just after Baumgarten had seemingly regained his health sufficiently to begin his summer lectures. As his health again declined, and his fate became clear, Baumgarten made all the appropriate arrangements and retired to spend his final days in peace with his family and friends. When finally asked how he would like to be buried, Baumgarten responded as only a German professor could: "the more academically, the better"[a] —by which he meant according to all customs and ceremonies of the university. According to his biographer's detailed record of these final days, Baumgarten claimed to have returned to the simple piety of his youth, which he discussed and illustrated almost continuously, and to no longer see any significance in metaphysical knowledge. He died aged 48 on 27 May 1762.

B. Baumgarten and Pietism[b]

From this sketch it is clear that Baumgarten was closely associated with Pietism in Halle, and particularly with August Francke, who was by far the strongest, most active and most politically engaged of the group, eclipsing in some ways even Spener himself. Yet it must be recognized that Pietism was not a philosophical, but a religious movement. It focused on the practical rather than the theoretical side of learning and in this respect stood opposed to orthodox Lutheran scholasticism. For this reason, Pietists were keen to replace what they saw to be an oppressive and spiritually sterile obsession with scholastic correctness and method, particularly in theology, with a freer, more eclectic approach which judged a doctrine by its practical effects rather than its adherence to a specific school of thought. This meant giving individuals, particularly university professors, a certain amount of freedom to teach according to

---

[a] Meier, *Baumgartens Leben*, 25.
[b] In this sketch we have profited greatly from the research of John Holloran, *Professors of Enlightenment at the University of Halle 1660–1730* (Dissertation, University of Virginia, 2000). We have also made free use of information gleaned from Johann Christoph Gottsched, *Historische Lobschrift des wieland hoch- und wohlgebohrenen Herr Christians des H. R. R. Freyherrn von Wolff* (Halle, 1755). In English, the best accounts of German Pietism are: F. Earnest Stoeffler, *German Pietism During the Eighteenth Century*, in the series Studies in the History of Religions, Supplements to Numen, 24 (Leiden: Brill, 1973), and *The Rise of Evangelical Pietism*, in the same series, Supplements to Numen, 9 (Leiden: Brill, 1971).

the dictates of their own judgment, with the only restriction being that this did not have a negative effect on the character of their students. It also meant that the divisions between faculties, as instantiated at the University of Halle, were now seen as reflecting limits in a professor's authority to criticize the work of his colleagues. Consequently, as long as philosophers, for example, restricted their teachings to the judgment of philosophical matters, i.e. of matters to be judged by natural reason, they were in principle free from interference from the theology faculty, and vice versa. This opposition to internal controversy indeed became the central focus of official university politics.

Now in all these respects, Pietism bore strong affinities with early modern rationalism, and it is this that explains the early alliance in Halle between Francke and Thomasius. Both movements rejected the authority of tradition and emphasized the autonomy of an individual's judgment, and both were focused on the practical benefits to be gained from doing so. But as Pietism itself was initially neither a philosophical nor even a theological position, this left it an open question as to how its goals would become specifically articulated in these disciplines. Was there, for instance, one particular philosophy that was more in line with the aims of Pietism? Or one that was particularly incompatible with it? From the start there were some Pietists, such as was perhaps Baumgarten's father, who embraced the broad kind of rationalism found in Locke,[a] Thomasius and others, and who thus saw the appeal to healthy reason as an appeal to a kind of natural inner revelation regarding how we should conduct our worldly affairs. Others, however, such as those who would flourish in the theology faculty in Halle, saw in the very same appeals the dangerous seductions of the vanity of human reason.

When Wolff came on the scene, what was merely an annoying tension at the university, now broke out into open battle. The reasons for this are complex, but they are in part traceable to the central aims of Wolff's philosophical activity. Above all else, Wolff sought to do two things. First, he sought to unify all genuine knowledge under the heading of philosophy; for according to his new definition of philosophy, it was nothing but demonstrated knowledge of the reasons and causes of things. Even mathematical knowledge, which Wolff defined as the knowledge of quantities, and historical knowledge, which he defined as knowledge of bare fact, were thus to be circumscribed and grounded by this new discipline. Secondly, in a complementary move, Wolff sought to show that there is but one correct method that must be observed in all knowledge, and that this is the method grounded in the primary philosophical science, namely, metaphysics. Thus Wolff's logic, which is intended to be a universal instrument for the acquisition and demonstration of knowledge, is itself grounded in and thus inseparable from his metaphysics.

In view of this, it is understandable that many Pietists saw in Wolff not only the vanity of human reason, but also a new attempt to expel academic and disciplinary freedom from the university. For if Wolff's innovations were successful, then this would mean that the philosophical faculty, traditionally the lower faculty, would

---

[a] It must be remembered that in the early modern period "rationalism," understood as the view that in worldly matters one's own reason is the only true guide, was a category and a cause that embraced what are now called rationalists as well as empiricists.

become the indispensable prerequisite and gauge of all departments of knowledge at the university. It is here that rationalism's belief in a universal method based in human reason becomes most clearly incompatible with the Pietists' desire for freedom of judgment and for doctrines to be measured by their moral or spiritual impact, rather than their supposed scholarly correctness. Of course, there were other doctrines that troubled the Pietists, such as Wolff's supposed determinism and his belief that morality did not require revelation. But while irritating, these were in many ways of secondary significance, and likely only received so much attention because the only way to oppose Wolff's innovations, given the very academic freedoms the Pietists wanted to protect, was to go outside of the university and its restrictions, and to convince the king that Wolff was teaching atheism or something equally detrimental to religion.

However, with Wolff's expulsion in 1723, those more moderate Pietists who were inclined toward rationalism generally found in him a new symbol for academic freedom. Indeed, the expulsion propelled the already ascending Wolff to the status of an intellectual celebrity throughout Europe. And it was thus not long before many of the younger Pietist academics—like Martin Knutzen (1713–51), Kant's famous teacher in Königsberg—broke away from the older generation and began to develop ways in which Wolff's doctrines could be adapted to their own purposes. Much as Aristotle's writings did for the Catholic Church, Wolff's writings now provided the Pietists with a powerful tool for articulating theological doctrines, while the Pietists' development of Wolff's philosophy in turn gave rise to a form of rationalism more clearly compatible with their spiritual concerns. Such was Wolff's success that even the later allies of Lange, such as Adolph Friedrich Hoffmann, and their descendants, such as Christian August Crusius, were forced to fight Wolff using the philosophical instruments he himself invented.

Now, it is to this new generation of philosophy that Baumgarten's *Metaphysics* belongs. Consequently, as Clemens Schwaiger has noted, there are several respects in which the differences between the doctrines of the *Metaphysics* and those found in Wolff's writings can be understood as seeking a middle ground between Wolff and Pietism.[a] Three areas in particular stand out. The first is Baumgarten's treatment of freedom (*Metaphysics*, §719–32), which according to Schwaiger's analysis can be seen as trying to enrich Wolff's theory with a sufficiently complex account of motivation, and particularly of the possibility of motivational indifference (*Metaphysics* §651–4) and weakness of will, to counter Lange's charges of fatalism. A second and closely related area is that of empirical psychology, which we find far more articulated in Baumgarten than in Wolff's writings. It would seem that the emotional and psychological side of Pietism provided Baumgarten with a fertile source, which would later in turn provide Kant with the essential structure of his own anthropology. A final area of possible influence, also noted by Schwaiger, is Baumgarten's focus of moral theory

---

[a] For the following points see: Clemens Schwaiger, *Alexander Gottlieb Baumgarten – Ein Intellektuelles Porträt* (Stuttgart-Bad Cannstatt: frommann-holzboog, 2011), esp. ch. 4 and 7; see also his "The Theory of Obligation in Wolff, Baumgarten, and the Early Kant," in *Kant's Moral and Legal Philosophy*, edited by Karl Ameriks, Otfried Höffe and translated by Nicholas Walker (Cambridge: Cambridge University Press, 2009), 58–73.

on the concept of obligation, which likely also provided an essential stimulus to the development of Kant's theory of obligation in the 1760s.

C. Georg Friedrich Meier[a]

Georg Friedrich Meier was born in Ammendorf near Halle on 29 March 1718 and died 27 June 1777. He attended the University of Halle in 1735, where he studied logic, metaphysics, natural right, philosophical morals, Hebrew grammar and Isaiah under Alexander Baumgarten, as well as all of the regular theological courses under Siegmund Jacob Baumgarten. According to Meier's own report, his relationship to the brothers was very close: "Because I saw both of the Baumgartens daily, and won their love through academic disputations and answers, they became my true benefactors and the advancers of my career. They deemed me worthy of their personal company, and I have them chiefly to thank for my good fortune."[b] Indeed, just as he had with his own brother, Siegmund Baumgarten guided the young Meier to the study of philosophy, eventually convincing him and his father that he should make this his career. After a short and successful period of lecturing at Siegmund Baumgarten's home, Meier defended a dissertation in 1739 to earn the right to lecture at the University of Halle. Thus when Alexander Baumgarten was called away that same year to Frankfurt on the Oder, Meier assumed his teaching duties in Halle, where he would remain until his death.

This short sketch is indicative of the general philosophical relationship between Baumgarten and Meier. For, although Meier was extremely prolific over his career— his biographer lists among his writings some 63 books, several of which run to three or more volumes, along with numerous essays, prefaces and Latin disputations—his own philosophy consists largely, although not entirely, of popularizations, expansions and applications of what he learned from Alexander Baumgarten's textbooks and lectures. For instance, Meier's *Beweis der vorherbestimmten Übereinstimmung* (*Proof of Pre-established Harmony*, 1743) clarifies and expands upon Baumgarten's discussion in *Metaphysics* §448–65,[c] his *Versuch eines neuen Lehrgebäudes von den Seelen der Thiere* (*An Attempt at a New Doctrine Concerning the Souls of Animals,* 1749) uses Baumgarten's theory of the lower cognitive faculty, and particularly of the analogy of reason (*Metaphysics* §640, 792–9), to argue that animals have a form of reason, while his *Betrachtungen über die Schrancken der menschlichen Erkenntnis* (*Reflections Concerning the Limits of Human Knowledge,* 1755), explains in detail the ways in which the metaphysics of the kind taught by Baumgarten is not only consistent with, but even presupposes that there are essential limits to human knowledge. Many of

---

[a] Many of the details of this sketch are from Samuel Gotthold Lange, *Leben Georg Friedrich Meiers* (Halle: J. J. Gebauer, 1778). A fuller biography is found in Riccardo Pozzo, *Georg Friedrich Meiers "Vernunftlehre." Eine historische-systematische Untersuchung* (Stuttgart-Bad Cannstatt: frommann-holzboog, 2000).

[b] *Leben Georg Friedrich Meiers*, 35–6.

[c] On this see Eric Watkins, *Kant and the Metaphysics of Causality* (Cambridge: Cambridge University Press, 2005), 73–80.

these works are rich in content, and their study promises to provide a deeper insight not only into Baumgarten's achievement, but also more generally into the nature of pre-Kantian metaphysics.

For present purposes, however, the two most important of Meier's productions are his translation of Baumgarten's *Metaphysics* in 1766 and his own four volume *Metaphysics*, which can be read as a direct commentary on Baumgarten's earlier work. As Meier tells us in the preface to the former, the project of translating the *Metaphysica* into German was one initiated by Baumgerten himself. This is also indicated by the fourth edition's inclusion of German glosses for all of the major terms. These glosses, however, serve more as a signal of the difficulties faced by any future translator than as a guide; for in the majority of cases Baumgarten offers a list of possible translations or a descriptive phrase, rather than an authoritative solution. It is not surprising, then, that in many cases Meier does not follow any of Baumgarten's proposals.

Whatever stage the translation might have reached under Baumgarten, the fruits of these labours were lost when he died. Meier tells us that he finally translated the work simply in order to facilitate his own lectures, and that the omission of many passages and the overall reorganization of the text were undertaken merely for pedagogical reasons. Still, in many cases, as the reader will see, these changes do provide an insight into Baumgarten's meaning, or at the very least offer us an authoritative interpretation. For an explanation of our use of Meier's translation in constructing this volume, see "Text and layout" in "Notes on this translation" below.

2

The Philosophical Context of the *Metaphysics*

A. Leibniz and Baumgarten

Baumgarten is often referred to as the most Leibnizian of Wolff's disciples. However, both sides of this description require careful consideration. First we should ask: In what sense is Baumgarten particularly Leibnizian? And secondly: In what sense is he particularly Wolffian? We address the first question in this section, and the second in the next.[a]

There is no question that Baumgarten's *Metaphysics* is generally Leibnizian in character. At the time of his death, Baumgarten's library contained a relatively large number of Leibniz's writings, including the *Ars combinatoria*, the *Monadology*, the *Theodicy*, the correspondence with Clarke, the volumes of the *Acta Eriditorum* in which some of Leibniz's most important essays appeared, as well as many collections of his mathematical, historical, and legal writings.[b] Additionally, in the preface to the third edition of the *Metaphysics*, Baumgarten notes his acceptance of what he takes to be two cardinal Leibnizian doctrines, namely, the principle of reason and the existence of monads. Baumgarten also embraces the system of pre-established harmony in its universal form, while expanding his treatment well beyond anything found in Leibniz's writings. Finally, Baumgarten also accepts the distinctively Leibnizian doctrines of monads as living mirrors of their worlds, of metempsychosis taken in the broad sense (i.e. palingenesis), and of the *exsilium mortis* (i.e. the banishment of death; cf. §779).

However, Baumgarten's reliance on Leibniz can easily be overstated. First, and most generally, the doctrines of the *Metaphysics* are generated according to a systematic method unlike anything found in Leibniz's writings (only Leibniz's *Monadology* comes anywhere close). In this respect, the *Metaphysics* fully bears out Meier's observation about Baumgarten: "His mind was above all systematic. Everything that he thought became system."[c] This persistent view to consistency and the overall architectonic of the system leads Baumgarten to adjust and ramify principles and often to universalize doctrines found not only in Leibniz, but in other philosophers as well.

For this reason, whenever a doctrine of Leibniz is integrated into the *Metaphysics*, the reader will often find it presented, justified, or used in a wholly new manner. One example of this is Baumgarten's treatment of pre-established harmony (§448–65).

[a] See also Schwaiger, *Alexander Gottlieb Baumgarten—Ein Intellectuelles Porträt*, 25–6.
[b] See *Catalogus librorum a viro excellentissimo amplissimo Alexandro Gottlieb Baumgarten* (1762).
[c] Meier, *Baumgartens Leben*, 37.

Leibniz tells us that he introduced the doctrine originally to explain the possibility of human freedom and the apparent coordination between substances that could not in principle really influence one another.[a] In the *Metaphysics*, by contrast, Baumgarten introduces the system of pre-established harmony only after he has developed, based upon the principle of ground, sufficient ground and various corollaries, the concept of a nexus of influence, and has proven that in this world and in every world there exists a universal nexus of influence (§356, 357). The system of pre-established harmony is only then introduced as one of an indeterminate number of seemingly possible systems for accounting for this nexus of influence, the others being the general systems of occasionalism and physical influence, along with the many particular mixed systems. Thus, in a manner completely distinct from Leibniz, Baumgarten first proves the necessity of universal influence, and only afterwards proves that this influence must be ideal rather than real.[b]

Another point of difference regarding the same doctrine concerns the grounds Baumgarten provides for its acceptance. Leibniz held physical influence to be impossible because it contradicted the true nature of a substance, and rejected occasionalism because it presupposed a continuous miracle. He presented pre-established harmony primarily as a hypothesis, but suggested it might be something more than this given the failure of the other systems and its agreement with the doctrine of freedom. Baumgarten, by contrast, holds pre-established harmony for a proven theorem. On his analysis, there are of necessity only three possible general systems, namely, general pre-established harmony along with the general systems of physical influence and occasionalism. The two latter, however, turn out to be contradictory, while all systems, including particular systems consisting of a mixture of pre-established harmony, physical influence and occasionalism are such that a world in which they were true would be less perfect than one in which pre-established harmony was true, which means that they are not true of this, the best of all possible worlds.

As the reader will further discover in the *Metaphysics* itself, Baumgarten is Leibnizian in regard to many doctrines, but he is no slavish follower of Leibniz, nor is he even really Leibnizian in spirit. In formulating his philosophical system, Baumgarten exhibits considerable independence, developing his doctrines according to a set of motivations and historical circumstances foreign to Leibniz, and, as we will see, to Wolff as well.

---

[a] See "A New System of The Nature and Communication of Substances," *Journal des savants*, June 27 1695, G 4: 477–87. A good history of this doctrine, along with a summary of sources, is found in Mario Casula, "Die Lehre von der prästabilierten Harmonie in ihrer Entwicklung von Leibniz bis A. G Baumgarten," in *Akten des II. Internationalen Leibniz-Kongresses*, Hanover, 17–22 July 1972 (Wiesbaden: Franz Steiner, 1975), Vol. 3, 397–414.
[b] For more on this see Watkins, *Kant and the Metaphysics of Causality*, 73–8.

B. Wolff and Baumgarten

I. Wolff's method

By contrast with Leibniz, who was more problem-oriented than methodical, Wolff approached philosophy generally, and metaphysics in particular, almost entirely from the standpoint of the wider concern of developing a single universal doctrine of scientific method. Of course Leibniz was also deeply interested in such issues, and indeed it was he who brought to Wolff's attention the importance of syllogistic reasoning after the latter had rejected it as sterile.[a] Yet Wolff's pursuit of a universally useful method preceded his correspondence with Leibniz, and had its origins in his early examination of the writings of Descartes and Johann Christoph Sturm, von Tschirnhaus' *Medicina mentis* (1687), and Barrow's *Lectiones Geometricae* (1670), all of which he found wanting in regard to a criterion for the discovery of real definitions.[b] Moreover, even more so than von Tschirnhaus', Wolff's interest in method is distinctively focused on its practical significance, such that his main goal is to put in the hands of the educated public a method for discovering and ordering knowledge in a most efficient and thus most useful way for common life. Wolff's desire is to reform intellectual society as a whole by showing, for instance, that truths like those found in agriculture or jurisprudence, and even theology, can be discovered and demonstrated through a single universal and reliable method easily adopted and clearly applied. For this reason, he is in many ways nothing else than the strongest German voice in the chorus of modern philosophers calling for the increased rationalization not only of scientific practice, where very much still nevertheless had to be accomplished, but also in politics, jurisprudence, medicine, agriculture—indeed in all possible departments of knowledge.

As Wolff explains in the first chapter of his *Preliminary Discourse*, this universal method presupposes a threefold division of knowledge into the historical, mathematical, and the philosophical. Historical knowledge, as Wolff defines it, includes all knowledge acquired through experience, and is in the strict sense limited simply to that which is presented immediately therein. It thus concerns the mere knowledge of fact or existence (DP §7), and not the reasons for such. Mathematics, by contrast, concerns knowledge or calculation of the quantitative features of what is known historically, and is thus restricted, as all mathematics is, to what can be derived from definitions and axioms exclusively by means of the principle of contradiction. Unlike historical knowledge, mathematics thus concerns reasons for things, though only in their quantitative determinations, and is fully demonstrated.

By contrast with both, philosophy is in general the "knowledge of the reason of those things that are or occur," (DP §6) or, somewhat more famously, the "science of the possibles, insofar as they can be" (DP §29).[c] According to Wolff this is merely a

---

[a] Gottsched, *Historische Lobschrift*, 21–2.
[b] Gottsched, *Historische Lobschrift*, 16–17.
[c] In his German Logic, Wolff defines it somewhat differently as "a science of all possible things, how and why they are possible" (§ 1). This difference is noticed by the editor of Wolff's *Gesammlete kleine philosphische Schriften*, Vol. 2 (Halle, 1737), 5–7. He, however, claims that this is only a difference in wording.

nominal definition; what philosophy really is must be determined by consideration
of what is possible, what "science" precisely means, and how far the limits of human
knowledge extend.[a] Now, as a science, philosophy shares with mathematics the
feature of being demonstrated knowledge. More precisely, science is the "proficiency
<*habitum*> of demonstrating assertions, this is, of inferring them by means of legit-
imate arguments <*consequentiam*>[b] from certain and immovable principles" (DP §30;
cf. *Acroasis logica* §32 quoted below in the note to *Metaphysics* §1). Now since any
piece of scientific knowledge requires "certain and immovable principles" from which
it can be demonstrated, and these in turn presuppose still others, the very possibility
of scientific knowledge requires that there be a very first science, i.e. a first philosophy.
Such first philosophy, or ontology, is thus the "certain and immovable" *conditio sine
qua non* for the use of the demonstrative method in all further science (WO §6), and
we know it to be really possible because it is actual (WO §3). So philosophy, which is
really nothing but the collection of all demonstrated knowledge of the reasons of real
things, has its methodological basis in ontology, and the whole of this philosophical
knowledge constitutes one great deductive or scientific system in which each science
must be placed between those relatively more basic ones from which it draws its
principles and those to which it in turn provides principles.[c]

   Wolff himself informs us that he arrived at his conception of philosophical
method through reflection on mathematical method, and recommends the study of
mathematics as the best way of learning philosophical method. For this reason, Wolff
termed his the "mathematical method," while others interpreted him simply to mean
that the method of mathematics should be applied to philosophy. It is important to
notice, however, that this interpretation does not properly reflect either the depth or
the breadth of Wolff's actual claim. First, this interpretation does not reflect the claim's
depth, because according to Wolff the very principles of demonstration employed by
mathematics have their proper foundation in ontology. Thus in truth, mathematics
draws all of its certainty from ontology, which provides it with principles (WO,
Preface): "The whole of mathematics is grounded in Euclid's *Elements*. These, however,
rest in turn on ontological truths, which Euclid accepted as axioms. [...] Accordingly
it is obvious that the entirety of mathematics amounts to ontological principles, and
thus it receives its light from this."[d] Thus rather than treating philosophy mathematically, Wolff intends to show that the method employed in mathematics is successful
precisely because it accurately draws upon the metaphysical first principles according
to which all knowledge must be treated in order to become science. Secondly, the
suggestion that Wolff treats philosophy using the mathematical method also does not
reflect the breadth of Wolff's claim, because mathematics employs only a few of the
principles that belong to a properly developed doctrine of metaphysics. Perhaps most
importantly, in addition to the principle of contradiction, philosophy employs the

[a] *Gesammlete kleine philosphische Schriften*, Vol. 2, 6–7.
[b] By *consequentiam* Wolff means the interconnection of premises and conclusions, thus by means of
    syllogisms or arguments.
[c] The other details of Wolff's method, such as his doctrine of nominal and real definitions, are of
    course important, but their explanation is beyond the scope of this introduction.
[d] *Gesammlete kleine philosophische Schriften*, Vol. 2, 140–1.

principle of sufficient ground to make deductions regarding not only quantities, but also the real properties of possible and even existing things. Consequently, it demonstrates and makes use of many principles, such as those of efficient and final causes, which have no place in mathematical science.

II. The "holy marriage" of philosophy and experience

The practical focus of Wolff's method is evinced in the emphasis he places on the role to be played by ontology in guiding and guaranteeing empirical research. Ontology, according to Wolff, is the most important of the sciences precisely because it is the key to practical success in all further sciences no less than in morality and religion. Indeed, Wolff's Latin *Ontology* contains a wealth of propositions devoted to explaining the empirical use and function of specific metaphysical concepts for acquiring knowledge of the world. This is because ontology, according to Wolff, is nothing other than the clear and distinct representation of the most general principles in human knowledge, i.e. the very laws of thought regarding beings. Now, as these are at the same time the most general principles of the beings thereby thought, a science of such concepts provides us with a complete conceptual scheme under which empirical experience—if it is to become philosophical knowledge or science—must be carefully and methodically subsumed.

For instance, to reach the distinct knowledge that the sun is the cause of a rock's growing warm, one must be able to show with certainty, i.e. to demonstrate, that this and nothing else must be thought under the heading, in this relation, of a cause. How can this be done? According to Wolff we need above all else to have a definition of cause and effect, and the major premise that everything that happens has a reason, or in this case that every effect has a cause.[a] With the former as our criterion for identifying possible reasons for a given event we can then eliminate all other possibilities, for instance the surrounding air etc., until the only remaining option is the light falling from the sun. Now since it is demonstrated in ontology that everything that happens has a cause, and we have shown by experience that if the sun is not the cause then the warming would have no cause, we must conclude that the sun must be its cause. Thus by taking an ontological principle as our major premise, we are able, it would seem, to extract certainty from experience, assuming that our enumeration of possible causes was exhaustive.[b] This example might seem trivial given the progress of science since Wolff's time, but in the specific German context in which he was working, the idea that by means of a complete metaphysical system one could demonstrate all fields of human knowledge in such a simple and clear way was radically new. As Gottsched reports, prior to Wolff:

> Almost everywhere people held [metaphysics] to be a most dispensable part of learning, and believed that it was nothing other than a nest of scholastic nonsense, or a dictionary of certain barbaric and artificial terms, which one only needed in

---

[a] Cf. *Gesammlete kleine philosphische Schriften*, Vol. 2, 49–50.
[b] Cf. *Gesammlete kleine philosphische Schriften*, Vol. 2, 49–50: "Philosophy must therefore provide us with the universal grounds (general principles) for judging, which we employ as the major premise in an argument regarding a thing that is present to us …"

the language of the schools, and perhaps in theology. One did not then see, or so to say forgot, that it also provides certain universal major concepts, principles and propositions that must serve as certain grounds and themes in all remaining sciences, and indeed were presupposed even by the mathematical sciences.[a]

In this respect, Kant's later view that empirical knowledge is guided by certain fundamental concepts of objects in general, i.e. the categories, is directly dependent upon the influence of Wolff, even if Wolff did not invent this general idea.

The empirical bent of Wolff's thought is also clear from the emphasis he in turn places on experience as the foundation, guide and guarantee for metaphysics. To demonstrate that the sun was the cause of the rock's warming in the example above, we had to possess certain universal concepts and principles—universal laws of *thinking* that are at the same time laws of *beings*—to serve as the major premises in our demonstration. But how are we to acquire these? Wolff's answer is initially surprising: "In the abstract disciplines themselves, such as *first philosophy*, the fundamental notions <*notiones*> are derived from experience, which establishes historical knowledge" (DP §12).

How can this be possible if every proposition belonging to a science must be demonstrated and certain? Wolff's answer has two interconnected parts. The first consists in his essentially Leibnizian conception of sense perception as a confused representation of its object. According to Wolff, although sense experience is confused, and although even clear judgments of experience are always singular judgments, i.e. judgments concerning individual objects, and thus are not universal, nevertheless sensible representations in principle represent these individuals *in their complete determinacy*, although confusedly (cf. Baumgarten, *Metaphysics* §425 and 517). Consequently, representations of individuals contain—in a manner yet to be determined—those same universal or ontological concepts and principles that apply to every being as such. These concepts are initially noticed and separated from the rest so as to produce a clear representation. They are then explicitly employed as themes in our reflection on the content of our representations in various particular circumstances. This reflection in turn leads to judgments, or clear representations, of the parts of the original representation, of its necessary relations to others, etc., and thereby to a distinct conception. In this way, Wolff understands the progress from pre-scientific knowledge to science as an accumulation and then an analysis of reflective judgments regarding experience. Furthermore, those who are capable in this way of analyzing experience so as to elicit more general principles, to reflect on them, to abstract them, and thereby to render the confused content of sense perception distinct, possess an acquired acumen for seeing the universal in the particular. In this way, experience provides the indispensable basis of all abstract concepts by providing the material from which they can be abstracted analytically.

The second part of Wolff's answer lies in his unique conception of a natural ontology <*ontologia naturalis*>. Since ontology concerns the most *universal* principles of beings, these are also present in *every act of thought* about a being. Furthermore,

---

[a] Gottsched, *Historische Lobschrift*, 46–7.

since we have the capacity to reflect and abstract, we can, by means of these, reflect upon and abstract these same principles from our own mental acts. On this basis, Wolff claims that:

> Commonplace and confused ontological notions constitute a particular species of natural ontology. Whence (WO §19) natural ontology can be defined as the collection of confused notions corresponding to the abstract terms with which we express general judgments about a being, acquired by the common use of the mind's faculties. (WO §21)

This idea of a natural ontology has two further important consequences for Wolff's philosophy. First, it allows him to explain his own ontology as merely a more fully analyzed version of everyday conceptions and to interpret previous philosophy, from Aristotle and the Scholastics to Descartes and Leibniz, as just so many expressions of the progression of reason in the analysis of its own confused principles (cf. WO §22). Wolff's own scientific ontology, as he explains it, thus arises from this natural one through the latter's cultivation by the intellect and reason, and thus relates to it as the artificial <*ontologia artificialis*> relates to the natural (WO §23). Secondly, this conception of a natural ontology provides Wolff with two external tests for the distinctness and adequacy of a conception, which he locates in its ability to explain through clear concepts the usage of previous philosophers and the standard significance of philosophical terms. This explains why Wolff quite often includes in his writings short historical overviews of how a given term has previously been employed and defined, and why he is often eager to demonstrate that a given definition agrees with common usage.

Thus whether we consider the matter from the side of the beings, or from the side of the mental faculties involved in representing these, through his conception of natural and artificial ontology, Wolff defends the existence of an innate basis for the development of even our most abstract concepts. And it is precisely this innate basis and the natural tendency of reason to cultivate this natural ontology that enables historical or empirical knowledge to provide a foundation for philosophy, although the latter is nevertheless fully demonstrated knowledge, i.e. knowledge in which every proposition is rationally proven. Experience provides all content for thought, but it is the intellect and reason that first render this content distinct. This does not violate the philosophical method, because the fundamental propositions drawn from experience do not serve philosophy as principles in the sense of universal propositions from which its truths are to be demonstrated, but rather as materials from which universal principles are abstracted. And the possibility and truth of just such a process is demonstrated within philosophy itself.

Now, this dual relation of experience and philosophy—that they mutually support and guide one another—is what Wolff refers to as their "holy marriage" <*sanctum connubium*> (DP §12), and it genuinely belongs to the core of Wolff's entire conception of philosophical method. From this flows not only much of Wolff's manner of presenting his philosophy, but also the limits he places on its content. In particular, it stands behind many of Wolff's departures from Leibniz, the most important of which of course concern the theory of monads and doctrine of pre-established harmony.

The reason for this is that, according to Wolff's method, there must always be an experiential basis, or some given sensible material, from which we abstract concepts or universal propositions. Thus in the case that no corresponding experience is possible or has been located, the concepts or principles in question may not be admitted into philosophy. They are mere hypotheses, which may be studied, and which do have some limited uses, but insofar as they remain undemonstrated, must not be employed in philosophy as basis for the derivation of further propositions (DP §128, 129). It is thus specifically because of the merely hypothetical character of Leibniz's doctrines regarding monads and pre-established harmony that Wolff makes no use of them in their universal forms. And where he does employ them, he does so only in specific or limited cases in which he believes an empirical basis can be given for that limited use. Thus Wolff accepts the existence of monads as the basis of physical nature, but makes no claim regarding their internal character, as did Leibniz. Likewise, Wolff makes use of monads in his psychology in order to explain the unity and simplicity of souls, but only because this has a basis, he believes, in empirical psychology. The same is true of pre-established harmony, which Wolff only employs in explaining the interaction of the mind and the body.[a]

III. Wolff and Baumgarten's *Metaphysics*

The reader of the *Metaphysics* who is familiar with Wolff will notice many points of agreement, but an almost equal number of departures. As the historical record informs us, Baumgarten composed the metaphysics in a climate that would have favored his own careful critical review of each particular doctrine in Wolff's writings. This is also what Baumgarten himself claims, and it is confirmed by a closer examination of the *Metaphysics*. Here are just a few of the more obvious similarities and differences between their philosophies:

---

[a] This is well expressed by Wolff himself in *Gesammlete kleine philosphische Schriften*, Vol. 2, 67ff: "§17 *The goal of the author in improving philosophy.* Whoever considers what has been presented to this point, will not bring into question the fact that philosophy will first become useful in life when such definitions and propositions as I have sought are brought forth within it. It is therefore no surprise that those who conduct their philosophy in the usual way bring forward hardly anything other than what one will have hopefully learned to forget in the future, or what is helpful only for vain and empty quibbling. Through this the whole of philosophy has become an object of contempt. Since I have taken it upon myself to free it from this contempt, I have believed that in order to make it useful, I must do so by investigating the most hidden grounds of things, and also work out precise definitions and precisely determined principles. This is the goal towards which I strive, when I desire to bring philosophical truths to a harmonic system, and this desire is one aimed at finally improving and increasing the prosperity of the future state for which the human race has endeavoured. My intention is therefore distinct from that of the great Leibniz. Due to the surpassing acuteness of his mind, and his not unsuccessful investigations into the most hidden of things, he attempted to untie the most difficult of knots, which in all times had confounded the greatest geniuses, namely the interaction between the soul and the body, and likewise the first origins of things. For this reason, the well-known doctrine of pre-established harmony and the theory of monads have today been reawakened. I hold pre-established harmony to be the best among the other views. However, because I count it among the philosophical hypotheses, I do not use it as a ground from which to prove something else [...] I have more serious reasons for not accepting Leibniz's monadology. What I have, however, taught concerning the simple things in general, is that which one abstracts from our souls as a genus from a species [...]."

(a) Baumgarten accepts Wolff's general understanding of philosophy, philosophical method and the threefold division of knowledge. Yet he rejects Wolff's *definition* of philosophy. For Baumgarten philosophy is best defined not as the "science of the possibles, insofar as they can be," but as the "science of the qualities in things that are to be known without faith" (*Acroasis logica* §35). The precise nature of this difference is difficult to reconstruct. In his *Philosophia generalis* §28, Baumgarten seems obliquely to suggest that Wolff was erroneously led to his definition through a desire for novelty and an ignorance of history. Still this does not explain precisely what is wrong with Wolff's definition. Two reasonable possibilities suggest themselves. The first would be that Wolff's definition is simply inadequate to capture Wolff's own conception of philosophy as distinct from mathematics. This would explain why Baumgarten restricts philosophy to qualities, rather than quantities. The second possibility would be that Baumgarten thought Wolff's definition a potential source of confusion over the relationship between philosophy and one specific kind of historical knowledge, namely revealed religion. According to Wolff's definition, philosophy would seem to encompass everything treated by the philosophical method. Yet certain parts of traditional theology aim to clarify revelation using philosophical concepts and methods, and for this reason would seem to belong to philosophy, just as the knowledge deduced from other forms of historical knowledge, such as empirical experience, is regarded by Wolff as belonging to philosophy. Baumgarten's definition clearly excludes this possibility by restricting philosophy not only to those things that can be known philosophically, but to those that can be known entirely independently from faith. Consequently, unlike Wolff, Baumgarten stresses that not all philosophical knowledge belongs to philosophy (*Philosophia generalis* §13).

(b) Baumgarten rejects Wolff's definition of substance as "an enduring and modifiable subject," replacing it with the conception of something that is able to exist even when it is not the determination of another (see Baumgarten's Second Preface, and *Metaphysics* §191 below).

(c) Baumgarten develops the mathematics of intensive quantities, which is not found in Wolff, thereby introducing throughout the work a line of thought concerning the maximum that appears to be inspired by Nicholas of Cusa's use of the same as a manner of glorifying God.

(d) While Baumgarten retains the chapter on empirical psychology, and even expands it in several ways not found in Wolff, he otherwise eliminates the empirical focus of Wolff's metaphysical writings. Thus in contrast to what is found in Wolff, the *Metaphysics* contains not a single proposition devoted to the empirical instantiation of metaphysical principles. This focus seems to be replaced by an increased emphasis on the role of metaphysics for the glorification of God. Likewise, although Baumgarten was surely sensitive to the common use of terms, and no doubt embraced the central reason behind Wolff's belief in essential correctness of their use, he places no especial emphasis on this in the *Metaphysics*.

(e) Unlike Wolff, Baumgarten embraces the major doctrines of Leibniz, and he does this not for the reasons given by Leibniz, nor because he is willing to accept hypotheses into philosophy, nor, finally, because he has located a new empirical foundation to convert them from hypotheses into theorems. Rather, Baumgarten does this effectively by strengthening the strictly systematic structure of the work, and by more rigorously drawing out the consequences of what was already given, to show that the basis that Wolff thought to be insufficient to prove Leibniz's doctrines is sufficient after all.

C. The *Metaphysics* as a source for Kant

For many, the main interest of the *Metaphysics* will lie in the light it can shed on the philosophy of Kant. And in this respect, the work will surely not disappoint. That Kant held Baumgarten's writings in the highest respect is abundantly clear. Beyond simply employing his *Metaphysica*, *Ethica philosophica* and *Initia philosophiae practicae primae* in his lectures on metaphysics, ethics, anthropology and natural theology, Kant publicly referred to Baumgarten as the "Corypheus of the metaphysicians,"[a] as an "excellent analyst" (A 21n/B 35n) and indeed as among the "greatest analysts" of German philosophy, along with Moses Mendelssohn and Christian Garve.[b] In the announcement for his own lectures for the academic year 1765–6, Kant explained that he chose the *Metaphysics* as his textbook because of its "richness and the precision of its method" (AA 2: 308). Finally, when Kant himself proposed in 1787 that a colleague write a metaphysics textbook founded on the *Critique of Pure Reason*, he advised that the categories and predicables be treated "just as they can be found in Baumgarten."[c] Even granting that Kant regarded this part of the project as strictly analytical, this shows his perfect confidence in Baumgarten's delineation of concepts, and illuminates one respect in which certain parts of the *Metaphysics* still find a place in the critical philosophy.

I. Kant and dogmatism

Nevertheless, it is obviously true that Kant charges the metaphysical tradition, of which he takes Baumgarten to be a chief representative, with failing to investigate the most important issue, namely, as to how metaphysical knowledge would really be possible. However, Kant tends to distribute this single charge over two related but distinct questions, namely: (1) How is metaphysics possible as a science that goes beyond experience? (2) How is experience itself possible? Or more precisely, how are those synthetic principles required for any experience in general guaranteed *a priori*? Leaving the first question aside momentarily, it is important to recognize that

---

[a] *Nova Dilucidatio* AA 1: 408. That this occurs in the context of Kant's criticism of Baumgarten's principle of consequence does not take away from the fact that Kant considers Baumgarten one of the foremost metaphysicians of the time.
[b] Letter to Marcus Herz, 24, November 1776, AA 10: 198.
[c] Letter to Ludwig Heinrich Jakob, 11, September 1787, AA 10: 493.

the followers of Baumgarten such as Eberhard were largely right to cry foul at Kant's suggestion that no one in their tradition had ever seriously considered this second question. Indeed, Wolff had written copiously about experience, and provides a very straightforward explanation of its possibility. Experience is possible (a) because it is actual, i.e. because we have actual knowledge such as mathematics and physics (DP §37), (b) because confused knowledge, or knowledge of the senses, implicitly contains a complete representation of its object, which can be rendered explicit and distinct through analysis and demonstration, and (c) because this latter is guaranteed by the pre-established harmony between the body and the mind. In turn, (c) can be demonstrated either metaphysically by means of its fitness to the most perfect world, as in Baumgarten, or from (a). So as Arthur Lovejoy once noted, Wolff in some ways already possesses a rather strong regressive argument for proving the possibility of experience that in many ways resembles Kant's own regressive argument.[a] Even if it is granted that few today would be satisfied with Wolff's explanation, to say that the entire question had never been raised before Kant is utterly false. In regard to experience, at least, Wolff and Baumgarten fall into the same general and rather large group of philosophers who take the existence of mathematics and the physical sciences to be self-evident, and who are interested in explaining its possibility only to the extent that this might tell us something about the nature and limits of such knowledge.

Likewise, Kant's charge with respect to question (1) can be easily laid aside if it is taken as suggesting that Baumgarten and his followers were epistemologically naïve or irresponsible. According to Baumgarten, all finite things, and consequently human intellect and reason, have both contingent and essential limits (*Metaphysics* §249). For this reason, sensation is always burdened with confusion, and no matter how far we analyze our perceptions through the intellect, there will always remain an admixture of confusion. "Nature makes no leap from obscurity to distinctness" (*Aesthetica* §7). Not only this, but because there are essential limits to human intellect and reason, there will be many things permanently beyond its sphere (*Metaphysics* §631, 633, 648). Such, for example, is the complete knowledge of any individual thing as such (i.e. its complete real essence), since this would require a distinct knowledge of all other things in the universe. And human knowledge is, in fact, distinct from divine knowledge not only in degree, but in kind, for the former is at most indeterminately infinite (i.e. progressively unbounded), always containing some confusion, while the latter is really infinite (i.e. complete within itself) and essentially pure. Furthermore, because human knowledge can only be rendered entirely distinct through abstraction, i.e. by leaving out what is sensible, such knowledge is not of real or individual things, and also is essentially less vivid or powerful (*Metaphysics* §624–39). Baumgarten's development of aesthetics was indeed at least in part motivated by his view that human knowledge remains essentially mixed with sensation, and thus cannot be improved without the improvement of sensibility as such. Finally, in the third preface to the *Metaphysics*, Baumgarten twice pauses to point out that he regards supreme

---

[a] Arthur O. Lovejoy, "On Kant's Reply to Hume," reprinted in *Kant: Disputed Questions*, edited by Molke S. Gram (Chicago: Quadrangle Books, 1967), 284–308. See also the footnote to §91 below.

certainty to be impossible for human beings and that he always emphasizes the
essential distinction between human and divine knowledge.

Meier is no less clear regarding the importance of knowing the limits of human
knowledge. As he writes in *Reflections Concerning the Limits of Human Knowledge*
(1755):

> A person [engaged with knowledge beyond the sphere of human reason] does not
> want their time and effort to have passed away uselessly, and will not be pleased
> to admit to not possessing sufficient understanding to know such matters, and is
> ashamed to recognize their own ignorance. On this basis, such a person makes
> for themselves a pipe dream, which one takes to be the sought after insight, and
> thereby gets entangled in a labyrinth of a hundred artificial terms and overly subtle
> distinctions, seizing upon a mere shadow of knowledge, instead of knowledge
> itself. More than this, this person neglects to search out the knowledge that is
> within their capacities, and behaves just like the dog in the fable, which when
> swimming through a stream with a piece of meat in its mouth, tried to snap up
> the shadow of the meat in the water, and thereby lost the piece of meat that it had.
> Therefore, if one could accurately determine the limits of human knowledge, then
> one would ward off many useless, vain and harmful endeavours of humanity, and
> thereby indeed further human knowledge in an exceptional way. No competent
> person will accordingly hold it for a useless and unnecessary employment, if one
> endeavors to investigate the limits of human knowledge more precisely than this is
> for the most part usually done. One can remark that the great English philosopher
> Locke had it perfectly right, when he said that: The one who knows the very least
> among all human beings is the one who does not know that there is very much
> that they do not know. And one can make this expression still more general, and
> say that the one who knows the least of all among human beings is the one who
> does not know the limits of human knowledge. (6–7)

As far as content is concerned, this passage could just as easily be from any of Kant's
critical writings.

Thus neither Baumgarten nor Meier suggests that we are able to possess absolute
knowledge or that one should not seek to cultivate a very deep sense of cognitive
humility. Hence, if Kant is in fact right that a failure to observe the limits of human
knowledge lies at the heart of the kind of metaphysics we find in Baumgarten and
Meier, then the problem is not, as is often suggested, that they simply failed to consider
the limits of human knowledge or that they possess no positive account for the possibility of the knowledge they do claim to posessess. Kant's argument must rather be
that the theory they do have is wrong in significant ways. Adjudicating this issue,
therefore, requires a balanced assessment of the arguments on both sides. It is our
hope that this translation will help to dispel at least some of the misconceptions about
pre-Kantian metaphysics that are, unfortunately, far too common, and facilitate just
such an assessment.

However, if Kant's charge with respect to question (1) is that the dogmatists have
failed to explain how the metaphysics of transcendent objects is possible, then he
seems to have a much stronger case. Wolff's proof of the reality of his metaphysics

in general rests on the certainty of the existence of our empirically based knowledge. All concepts that arise for us are generated from sensible experience and separated from it by means of abstraction, which merely leaves out the unresolved component. What guarantees that objects that cannot in principle be perceived can nevertheless be treated using these very same concepts? How do we know that a principle that is valid in respect to experience is such also with respect to objects beyond this? More specifically, how do we know that ontological concepts apply to things in themselves unrestrictedly or to beings simply as beings, and not merely to objects insofar as they can be given in experience? Even here Wolff and Baumgarten have something inter-esting to say in response,[a] but it seems nothing amounting to the kind of explanation Kant's philosophy demands. And granting this, one might further suggest that since part of their account of the possibility of experience invokes just such transcendent metaphysics, to this extent it too must be found defective. Still, given Baumgarten's and Meier's emphasis on cognitive humility, one could nevertheless argue that they never claimed absolute certainty regarding the universal validity of their metaphysical projects in the first place.[b]

II. Some examples of Kant's use of the *Metaphysics*

Kant penned several hundreds of pages of elucidations and notes in the margins and interleaved pages of his own copy of the *Metaphysics*, many of which show a direct line of development of both terminology and of ideas from Baumgarten to Kant. When combined with Kant's extensive lectures on the *Metaphysics*, these materials provide the scholar not only with a rich picture of Kant's intellectual development, but also suggest a multitude of new ways to approach his central doctrines and their relation to the wider philosophical tradition. Despite many years of work with this material by scholars, very much remains to be discovered. The following is intended simply to provide just a few select examples of how this can be done, and thus to provide, if necessary, some evidence for the value of this work for Kant scholarship.

a. Nature

In the *Critique of Pure Reason*, Kant writes:

> Nature taken adjectivally (*formaliter*) means the connection of the determina-tions of a thing according to an inner principle of causality. By contrast, by nature taken substantively (*materialiter*) one understands the collection of appearances insofar as these are in thoroughgoing connection by virtue of an inner principle of causality. In the first sense, one speaks of the nature of fluid matter, of fire, etc. and

---

[a] This is already evident from Wolff's refusal to admit Leibniz's doctrines in their universal form, due to the lack of an experiential foundation. The deeper point of disagreement between Kant and Wolff on this point seems to concern the nature of experience itself.

[b] One might even go further and observe that the Christian metaphysical tradition, particularly in thinkers like Nicholas of Cusa, often cultivated an extreme form of cognitive humility that is not taken into account by Kant. Cusa's writings in particular were evidently known to Baumgarten, as the *Catalogus librorum a viro excellentissimo amplissimo Alexandro Gottlieb Baumgarten* (1762) lists the Henricpetrina edition of Cusa's *Opera*, 3 Vols. (Basil, 1565).

employs the word only adjectivally; by contrast, if one speaks of things of nature, then one has in mind a subsisting whole. (A 418n/B 446n)

As unusual as it might first appear, this definition is no merely occasional utterance: Kant repeats it in *Prolegomena* §14–17 to structure the chapter headed "How is pure natural science possible?" Then in §36 of the same work he uses it to formulate the two chief questions regarding the possibility of physics, namely "How is nature possible in a general and in a *material* sense?" and "How is nature possible in the *formal* sense?" Kant again uses it in the B-deduction, at CPR B 163–5, to explain in what sense the intellect prescribes laws to nature. The same definition also opens the very preface to the *Metaphysical Foundations of Natural Science* (AA 4: 467).

As if that were not proof of its significance, Kant also uses it extensively in his moral philosophy: He draws upon it in *Groundwork* II in order to derive the natural law formulation of the categorical imperative (AA 4: 437), and arguably the others as well. It forms the basis of the construction of the Typic in the second *Critique* (AA 5: 70), and he uses it to formulate his conception of the moral world as a "supersensible nature" (AA 5: 43). Kant also later employs it throughout the *Religion*, first implicitly (AA 6: 154–7) and then explicitly (AA 6: 190–4) to explain that both his morality and the religion to which it leads are not supernatural, but indeed natural, concluding with the startlingly non-Leibnizian statement that freedom and the moral world in fact belong to the realm of *nature*, not to that of grace. Finally, Kant uses his peculiar definition of nature to emphasize the same point later in *The End of All Things*, where he explains:

> Natural (*formaliter*) means what follows necessarily according to laws of a certain order *of whatever sort*, hence also the moral order (hence not always the physical order). Opposed to it is the non-natural, which can be either supernatural or contranatural. (AA 8: 333n; emphasis added)

This definition of nature thus clearly has a deep significance for the way we understand Kant, if only because its basic role spans both his theoretical and practical philosophies. But where does it come from? How can Kant think he is justified in using such a seemingly unusual conception of nature, with introducing a distinction between two forms of nature found in no previous writer, and at no point explaining where it comes from in any of his published writings?

This is in fact rather typical of Kant's use of concepts that he spent many years developing in his metaphysics lectures and notes. And in this case one has only to examine the handwritten notes to find that this complex definition of nature arose from Kant's continuous refinement, over several years and in several phases, of the definition of nature found in §430 of Baumgarten's *Metaphysics*:

> The NATURE (cf. §431, 466) of a being is the collection of those of its internal determinations that are the principles of its alterations, or, in general, of the accidents inherent to it. Hence, to the nature of a being pertains its (1) essential determinations (§39), (2) essence (§39), (3) faculties, (4) receptivities (§216), and (5) all the powers with which it is equipped (§197).

A full explanation of this definition is not possible here. But three points are significant for present purposes. First, it must be noted that Baumgarten, and so Kant, would have understood this as a general metaphysical definition, and thus to be of application to *any* being to which belongs such a structure. And since, as a quick check shows, this structure is nothing but the structure of a finite substance, such a nature will belong to every substance as such. Consequently, a nature is ascribed by Baumgarten to physical bodies, spirits, and indeed anything that possesses just such an internal principle of the actuality of its own accidents. Secondly, this definition for Baumgarten is the one that fixes all proper senses of nature and natural in all further contexts. Thus the actions of spirits are just as natural as those of bodies, if indeed they follow from such an internal principle; likewise, supernatural events are possible in both bodies and spirits if something happens in them that does not flow from their own internal principle of activity. Thirdly, and most significantly, this means that the use of the term "nature" that is typical of modern physics—namely, as referring to the whole of the physical world—is both derivative and not particularly correct. For Baumgarten, indeed, the physical world constitutes a whole of nature governed by universal laws only because the beings within it share at least one common inner principle of the actuality of the world's alterations or accidents. So properly speaking, one should not speak of "physical nature," but rather of "the nature of the physical world," and one should not speak of the events in nature as natural as such, but rather as natural insofar as they follow from the nature of a particular whole of physical bodies. Since the definition in §430 quoted above is broadly Aristotelian in character, one can say that with this last set of ideas, what Baumgarten effectively does is to fuse an Aristotelian view of nature (as, e.g. the nature of water) and the understanding of nature typical of modern physics, by speaking of the latter as constituting a nature unified by universal laws, thus in the modern sense, because it has and follows a single common nature in the Aristotelian sense.

Now the phases of Kant's reflection on this passage can be defined by the following central notes: Phase 1 (1764–9): 4095–7. Phase 2 (middle to late 1770s): 4838–40, 5406–11, 5430, 5432 and 5433. Phase 3 (after 1779 but before the critical writings): 5707 and 5708. In the first phase, the notes already show Kant making changes to the definition in order to fit his pre-critical distinction between logical and real grounds. Thus he retains the essentials of Baumgarten's definition, but replaces the talk of an internal principle of the inherence of accidents with that of a real, rather than merely a logical, principle of such. Then, in the second phase, when he is formulating the critical philosophy, Kant begins to introduce the distinctions found in his mature definition between nature used in an adjectival/*formaliter* sense and nature in a substantial/*materialiter*.

These notes reveal two things. First, they reveal why in the critical writings Kant uses the Latin phrases *natura materialiter/formaliter spectata*, although they are not found in Baumgarten, namely, because he arrived at these concepts while re-working Baumgarten's Latin formulations. Secondly, they reveal that Kant introduces these terms in order to relate the key aspects of Baumgarten's original definition to his new critical vantage point. Thus, nature in a formal sense refers precisely to Baumgarten's sense of nature in §430, which Kant now identifies with the structure belonging to

every object insofar as it is an object of the intellect, whereas natural in a material
sense he identifies with this same nature applied, however, to the whole of all appearances, which in the new critical standpoint is just the intellect applied to what
is presented through the forms of intuition.[a] Consequently—and this is a major
result—Kant is now prepared to apply nature to anything that can in principle be a
real object of the intellect, and thus uses his notion of nature in a general way just
as does Baumgarten. However, unlike Baumgarten, because the only real object to
which this structure can really be applied theoretically is the realm of appearances,
the term nature no longer has significance in such an application to spirits or other
non-sensible beings.

We can now see the precise source of Kant's definition above:

> Nature taken adjectivally (*formaliter*) means the connection of the *determinations*
> *of a thing according to an inner principle of causality*. By contrast, by nature taken
> substantively (*materialiter*) one understands the collection of appearances *insofar*
> *as these are in thoroughgoing connection by virtue of an inner principle of causality*.
> (A 418n/B 446n; emphasis added)

Still left from Baumgarten is Kant's identification of nature in the primary sense with
the general or formal sense, which is a reformulation of *Metaphysics* §430, as is the
identification of the modern use of the term nature (physical nature) as an application
of this to a single whole. Indeed, Kant still speaks very much in a way parallel to
Baumgarten, when he claims that appearances constitute a nature only because they
have a nature, i.e. insofar as they necessarily—if they are to be objects of knowledge at
all—must be determinable by the intellect and its categories.

Finally, this set of observations provides a way of understanding Kant's application
of the term nature in his moral philosophy as mentioned above. Namely, although
the intellect has no valid theoretical object aside from the whole of appearances, from
a practical standpoint the intellect, according to Kant, has very many objects, and
indeed is capable of making use of its categories in regard to both freedom and the
moral world. Thus, since physical nature for Kant can first be called a nature at all
because the intellect can be applied to it, then to the extent it is possible to apply it on
moral grounds to moral objects, there is *equal ground* for calling the latter natural in

---

[a] Two notes in particular reveal Kant making this connection. The most explicit, R5707, reads: "All
possible objects of experience have their nature, in part their particular nature, in part the common
nature along with others things. Nature taken substantively means: the collection of all objects
of experience. Nature rests on the powers (fundamental powers) and in general the lawfulness of
appearances. [...] Things are not in themselves appearances, but rather only because there are beings
that have sense; just as they belong to a nature because we have understanding. For the word nature
does not mean something in things in themselves, but rather only the order of appearances of such
through the unity of the concepts of the understanding or the unity of consciousness in which they
can be combined. We do not have understanding because there is a nature; for we can in no way
come to know the rules (laws) from experience; their necessity consists precisely in that they can be
known *a priori*. For the same reason, we can have *a priori* knowledge of appearances and of nature, in
which they [i.e. the appearances] are connected, because the form of our sensibility, as a principle of
possibility, lies at the ground of the first [i.e. the appearances] and the form of our understanding, as
a principle of possibility, lies at the ground of the second [i.e. nature]" (AA 18: 248). See also R5608
(AA 18: 248–9).

a well-defined sense. And Kant, evidently, exploits this possibility when he speaks of the moral world both as a supersensible nature, rather than a supernatural world, and refers to it as an archetypal nature (AA 5: 43).

b. Natural and artificial metaphysics

We noted in our discussion of Wolff above that he relies heavily on the conception of a natural ontology that provides a genetic ground for reason's reflective formulation of a scientific ontology. In his prolegomena to the *Metaphysics* (§3), Baumgarten generalizes this conception so that he can now speak of a *natural metaphysics* <*metaphysica naturalis*>, which he distinguishes from an artificial or scientific metaphysics in a way exactly parallel to Wolff. The former exists in human reason as a genetic ground from which develops, through reflection and abstraction, the latter as a fully scientific doctrine.

As several texts reveal, Kant adapts this generalized version of the distinction to articulate his own understanding of the nature, genesis and goal of metaphysical knowledge, and to explain the special role to be played by his critical philosophy in making possible a safe transition from natural to scientific metaphysics. In both the *Prolegomena to Any Future Metaphysics* (no doubt titled after Baumgarten's "*Prolegomena Metaphysicorum*") and in the expanded introduction to the B-edition of the *Critique of Pure Reason*, Kant asserts that metaphysics has always existed and will forever exist in human reason as a natural predisposition <*Naturanlage*>, which he glosses *in Latin* as "*metaphysica naturalis*" (CPR B 21). Kant also distinguishes this, just as does Baumgarten, from the same metaphysics when it has been brought by reason into the form of a science. Yet, in a quite different manner, Kant emphasizes that essential to this natural metaphysics is an *inexorable tendency* to develop itself into such a scientific doctrine. In Wolff and Baumgarten, this development was also regarded as natural and indeed perhaps even as inevitable throughout history, but this was stressed only insofar as it provided a way of linking both common knowledge and traditional metaphysics with their own results. Kant, however, focuses on just this aspect because it explains in his view the historically verifiable tendency of reason to strive to transform this natural metaphysics into a scientific one, despite its always having been unsuccessful. Going beyond anything in Baumgarten, Kant then explains that if left to develop by itself in a normal way, natural metaphysics unavoidably generates an equally natural dialectic of reason (*Prolegomena* AA 4: 362).[a] Kant thus situates the problem of the *Critique*, in terms of these questions: "How is metaphysics as a natural predisposition possible?" "How is metaphysics possible as a science?" And he answers these by asserting that a critique of reason alone, as a kind of second order metaphysics ("metaphysics of metaphysics") will necessarily supply a transition from metaphysics as a mere disposition, to metaphysics as a genuine science that will finally satisfy its drive to self-development (CPR B 22–3; *Prolegomena* AA 4: 362ff.).

---

[a] Kant speaks at length of the further aspects of Baumgarten's conceptions of natural and scientific metaphysics in a way that further confirms his adoption of this terminology in the Mrongovius metaphysics lecture notes (AA 29: 782–4).

Kant thus invites us to understand the entire critical project as an expansion of §3 of Baumgarten's *Metaphysics*, pointing to this text in particular to explain the dynamic or transitional role played by transcendental critique. But more than this, in these and other texts, the most interesting of which are the drafts for his essay on the progress of metaphysics,[a] Kant further indicates that the true goal of the natural metaphysics first described by Baumgarten is ultimately the realization of reason's *moral* vocation. As Kant explains, the natural disposition gives rise to dialectical speculative metaphysics that naturally evokes the transcendental critique that both provides a foundation for natural science, and frees the ideas of reason from everything empirical so that they are subsequently able to assume their true moral function (*Prolegomena* AA 4: 362–3). Baumgarten's natural metaphysics, on this reading, become for Kant the generative foundation for reason's self-cultivation by means of transcendental critique up to the point of producing a genuinely scientific metaphysics of natural science and of morals. Instead of a theoretical-dogmatic doctrine, the outcome will be a practical-dogmatic one, which will put an end to all traditional disputes by putting reason into a state of perpetual peace with itself, and establish for all time the unavoidable moral doctrines that belong to *wisdom*, i.e. the true science of reason *in sensu cosmico*.

c. Absolute

In the *Critique of Pure Reason*, Kant pauses for three full pages at the beginning of the Transcendental Dialectic to discuss the meaning of the term "absolute" (A 324ff/ B 380ff). This is clearly an important term, not only for Kant's conception of dialectics generally, since these are always generated in reason's search for the *absolutely* uncon-ditioned, but also for Kant's conception of synthetic judgments *a priori* and even the categorical imperative, which are both said to have *absolute* necessity and universality as essential characteristics. Thus if Kant uses the term "absolute" in a unique sense, then this has far ranging consequences; and if this use differs significantly from that of his predecessors, this also may tell us something about the nature of the Kantian turn.

In the passage in question, Kant does not refer explicitly to Baumgarten, but rather to those who use the term "merely to indicate that something is valid of a thing considered in itself and therefore internally," thus in abstraction from its relations to other things (A 324/ B 381). As examples of this use, Kant notes that on this meaning, absolute possibility refers merely to a thing's internal possibility, while absolute necessity refers merely to its internal necessity, which is something "with which we cannot connect the least concept." By contrast, Kant tells us that the manner in which the term is best used is almost the exact opposite of this; something is considered absolutely when it is considered as valid in all possible relations. Thus the opposite of the absolute is not what is external, but rather what holds only in some particular relation. According to this Kantian meaning, then, absolute possibility and absolute necessity both refer respectively to what is possible and necessary in every possible relation.

To Kant's contemporaries the source and significance of this claim would have been far more obvious than today. Anyone who had read the *Metaphysics* would have been

---

[a] AA 20: 259–351.

familiar with Baumgarten's definition: "Whatever is considered, but not in a nexus with those things that are posited externally to it, IS CONSIDERED IN ITSELF (intrinsically, simply, absolutely, *per se*)" (§15). They would also be familiar with the content of §102, which equates absolute necessity with what is necessary in itself, which is to say with that the opposite of which is intrinsically impossible. Indeed, the reader of the *Metaphysics* would quickly recognize that this contrast between something considered it itself, i.e. absolutely, and what is considered in a nexus with other things, that Kant is remarking upon, runs throughout the entire *Metaphysics*, and provides a basis for the distinction between, among others, absolute and hypothetical possibility (§15, 16), impossibility (§17), determinations (§37), necessity (§102), contingency (§104), existence (§109), perfection, and imperfection (§121–3). They would also likely notice that for Baumgarten the very conception of God is that of an *absolutely* necessary being, and that the proof of his existence as well as of his attributes is dependent upon the correctness of this determination.

Rejection of this use of the term "absolute" by Kant thus signals much more than a change in terminology; it signals a radical departure from a most basic element of Baumgarten's metaphysical system, and thereby from the whole Wolffian tradition. Now, what is the basis of this particular departure? Is it motivated by the critical turn, or is it perhaps part of a change of mind that led to the critical turn?

The answers to these questions, although they cannot be investigated in detail here, can clearly only be found, if at all, in Kant's notes and lectures on Baumgarten's textbook. For Kant indeed criticizes this use of "absolute" for the first time while lecturing on Baumgarten, and develops his own understanding of this concept in notes in which he is directly reformulating passages of the *Metaphysics*. But we can still broadly learn something without such a detailed investigation by noting that in Baumgarten absolute concepts are not constructed as terminal concepts as they are for the critical Kant, i.e. they are not concepts that first arise for reason through its need to presuppose an infinite but also complete set of conditions, or to provide the final ground of such a series. The absolutely necessary, in particular, is not for Baumgarten the concept of a being necessary in every possible relation, as in Kant, but rather that of a being necessary *apart from* every possible relation. So the concept is not generated in any kind of infinite progression or regression to final conditions. Yet although for Baumgarten such absolute concepts are not generated in this way, due to their intrinsic independence, they are nevertheless capable of and do serve precisely as final conditions for such progressions (see, e.g. *Metaphysics* §381, 854).

Something in the 1760s, however, clearly brought Kant to the conclusion that such absolute concepts could have no significance at all when understood objectively, or as internal properties belonging to objects in themselves, and thus to the rejection of their primary sense in Baumgarten (this is reflected in Kant's claim, quoted above, that we cannot connect the least concept with such internal necessity). And this in turn must have led him to search for their true source in the "subjective" constitution of human reason, and finally in reason's need for a terminal point in the series of its *own* conditions. Only then, however, could Kant have recognized these to be intrinsically dialectical concepts, since only then did he understand such concepts to presuppose the completion of a series of conditions that, in another relation, must be maintained as infinite. But if Kant's transformation of the traditional conception of "absolute" is a precondition for the development of the antinomies, then it also predates the critical standpoint. This further suggests that this conception may provide an important clue to Kant's original motivations for developing the critical philosophy.

From this we have an interesting story regarding one aspect of Kant's intellectual development. But can this assist us in our pursuit of a better comprehension of Kant's critical doctrines? With an understanding of the depth of thought that is, as it were, concentrated in Kant's use of the little word "absolute," we are now in a position to detect subtle nuances or layers of meaning in passages from Kant's mature works.

Just one possible example: In the *Metaphysics of Morals*, Kant explains that virtue consists of strength in control of oneself, and thus "in the state of *health* proper to the human being." That is to say, strength is not to be measured by brute and momentary power, but by measured and constant power in reference to a holistic goal. Extending this comparison, Kant then remarks that this is true, "since health consists in the balance of all one's bodily forces, while lack of health is a weakening in the system of these forces; and it is only by reference to this system that *absolute* health can be estimated" (AA 6: 384). The deeper point here, suggested by the term "absolute," is that virtue as strength must be measured through its relation, not to the ability to perform a few specific moral actions, but rather in reference to the system of all possible ones. One might then wonder: To what extent does this intrinsic holism perhaps affect the way Kant understands the proper development of virtue?

d. Anthropology

Kant's lectures on anthropology as well as his published *Anthropology from a Pragmatic Point of View* (1798) were largely built upon the Empirical Psychology chapter of the *Metaphysics*.[a] Indeed, the structure of the entire first part of the *Anthropology*, which makes up seventy percent of the book, is almost directly lifted from Baumgarten's text. Additionally, Kant adopts numerous definitions and Latin terms from this without comment and with almost no alteration. To this extent, Kant can genuinely be called a disciple of Baumgarten. That this has long been known, but has as yet had virtually no impact on the study of Kant's own empirical psychology (something in which there is wide interest today), again underscores the importance of a reliable translation of the *Metaphysics*.

Of course, while Kant's reliance on Baumgarten is interesting in itself, his many departures are perhaps even more so. Kant's anthropology provides us, indeed, with what is in effect his single most sustained critical commentary on a central aspect of traditional metaphysics. That Kant no longer regards anthropology as part of this discipline, although its inclusion was for Wolff and Baumgarten a direct result of the "holy marriage" of empirical and rational knowledge, and that he places it instead in the service of the metaphysis of morals, as well as all the numerous adjustments Kant makes to individual concepts—all these things provide a further rich source for

---

[a] Despite this fact, there is *not a single reference* to Baumgarten in the entire volume of the Cambridge Edition that contains Kant's anthropological writings.

interpreting the meaning of Kant's critical philosophy and its break with traditional metaphysics.

* * * * *

These are just a few ways in which we have found Baumgarten's *Metaphysics* enlightening when read alongside Kant's notes, lectures, and published works. We hope that the following pages will prove useful to others in adding to such discoveries.

3

Kant's Handwritten Notes to the *Metaphysics*

One of the principal aims of this volume is to facilitate a deeper understanding of Kant's intellectual development. As we have seen, knowledge of Baumgarten's *Metaphysics*, paired with an examination of Kant's handwritten notes, can provide a rare and powerful insight into his working methods, the stages through which he developed certain concepts, as well as the principal historical sources of ideas that emerge otherwise unexplained in his mature writings.

Unfortunately, however, many of the original documents have been lost since their transcription into AA, and those still extant remain unavailable for first-hand inspection to the majority of Kant scholars. To help mitigate this last deficiency, we have reproduced three sets of pages from Kant's 1757 edition of the *Metaphysics*, which we believe conveys more about Kant's use of the book than can any description.[a] We have also provided a translation of all the notes penned on these pages, so that the reader can gain an impression of the variety of topics Kant discussed in such notes and of the general way they are placed on the page. On the third set of pages in particular (XVII and XVIII), we have for this purpose graphically indicated the location of the specific notes.

To understand the way in which such handwritten materials were transcribed into AA, and how they are presented in this volume, a few particulars need be explained. First, in setting up the volumes for AA that concerned Kant's textbooks, the general editor Erich Adickes divided the notes into those that he deemed to be entirely incomprehensible apart from the text and those that he thought could potentially stand apart. The former were restricted mainly to corrections, insertions and reformulations of specific lines or paragraphs of the text itself. In AA such notes are termed "*Erläuterungen*" ("elucidations") and are printed separately from the rest, which are termed "*Reflexionen*," although Adickes clearly recognized that even the more independent notes often bear such a close relationship to the main text that they are incomprehensible without it. All of the elucidations to the *Metaphysics* printed in AA have been translated in this volume and inserted as close to the place indicated there as possible. Unfortunately, we were only able to gain permission to reproduce pages bearing examples of the notes, not the elucidations. We should also point out that a translation of many of Kant's notes to the *Metaphysics* can be found in *Notes and Fragments*, edited by Paul Guyer and translated by Curtis Bowman, Paul Guyer, and Frederick Rauscher (Cambridge: Cambridge University Press, 2005), 68–404.

[a] See pp. vi, vii, and 36–9 of this book.

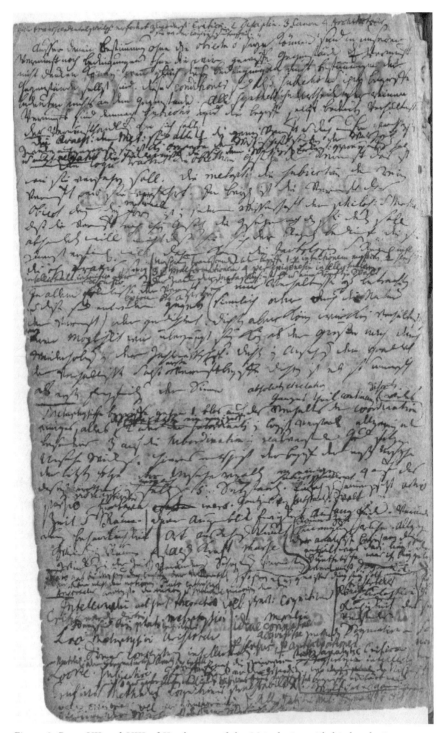

Figure 2. Pages VII and VIII of Kant's copy of the *Metaphysics*, with his handwritten notes. Preface to the first edition.

AVDITORI BENEVOLO.

Q uem enim potius, quam TE, compellarem, dum ad paginas TIBI paene dixerim soli conscriptas more consuero praestandum est? Non est, TIBI cur excusem prodire denuo metaphysica post infinitum numerum simili titulo notatorum, in quo quota sint a decantatissimis illis Aristotelis non magis noui, quam quotus ipse mortalium sim ab orbe condito, TVIS praecipue TVIS vnice commodis data, dicata, dedicata quae sint, prima se dicere satagant. TE quum appello, coronam excitatissimorum ad a... dua

R4291
R4915
R5682
R4916
R4292
R4917
R4918
R5683
R4919
R4920
R4293
R4921
R4922
R4912
R4465
R4923
R4466
R4913
R4912

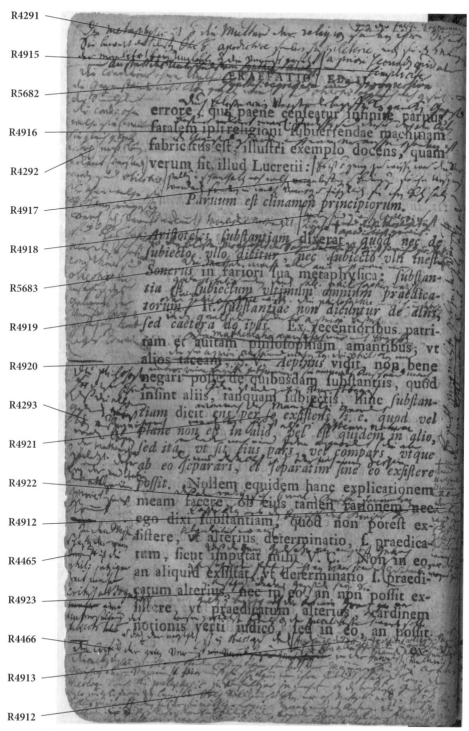

Figure 3. Pages XVII and XVIII of Kant's copy of the *Metaphysics*, with his handwritten notes. Preface to the second edition.

PRAEFATIO ED. II.

exsistere, licet nullus sit determinatio, s. praedicatum. Primum de multis substantiis cum S. V. Aepino concedo, hinc secundum non possum de singulis ponere. Tertium autem omnibus et solis substantiis convenit, hinc a me, tanquam character, quem definitiuum aiunt, sumitur, per quem explicem tritum illud *per se subsistere.* Idem clare distincteque percepturus *Cartesius* in *Responsionibus IIII. Operum* p. m. 107. addit: h. c. absque ope ullius alterius substantiae posse exsistere, et in *principiis philo.* P. I. n. 15: *Per substantiam nihil aliud intelligere possumus, quam rem, quae ita existit, ut nulla alia indigeat ad existendum. Et quidem substantia, quae nulla plane re indigeat, unica tantum potest intelligi, nempe deus. Alias vero omnes non nisi ope concursus dei existere posse percipimus. Atque ideo nomen substantiae non convenit deo et illis univoce* e. c. Aperte si loqui voluisset, dicendum ipsi utique fuisset, ex sua definitione, praeter deum non esse substantias. Nam neminem putarim *Antonio le Grand* concessurum, lapidem ex hac esse notione substantiam, quando ille *Inst. Phil. Cart.* p. m. 28: *substantia,* inquit *est res, cui nulla alia substantia opus est ad exsistendum, ut deus lapis caelum.* Propo potius alieo, iarisque connexis ratiocinationibus ex substantiae descriptionibus eiusmodi deduci

R4294
R4467
R4468
R4924
R4469
R4925
R4926
R4927
R4470
R4472
R4471

Another important aspect of the presentation of these materials in AA is the dating system developed by Adickes. In this volume, we have reproduced most of the information provided in AA at the head of the individual elucidations and notes, although we have omitted some of the finer details, which would be of concern only to one handling original manuscripts. To facilitate the use of this material, we have translated the combination of Greek letters and superscripts Adickes used to distinguish the thirty-three layers of texts he identified into their corresponding dates. In addition to these letters, Adickes had a system to represent his degree of confidence in assigning a note to a certain period or layer of texts, and this has been retained in our translation. The way in which the system works in this volume is as follows: A single date, or a set of two dates connected by a single dash, indicates the confident ascription of a note to that period. More than one date or set of dates connected by a dash, either followed by question marks or not, indicates periods of equal certainty. If several dates or sets of dates connected by a dash are enclosed in braces, then this indicates that they are all equally less certain than what precedes the braces. Finally, the addition of question marks, one and then two, indicates further levels of uncertainty. To give an example: 1769 (1770–2? 1775–6?) (1764?) 1776–8?? In this case, 1769 is the most likely dating, 1770–2 and 1775–6 are less likely, but equally so, while 1764 is still less likely and 1776–8 is far less likely than the rest, but not impossible. The reader more concerned with these finer details will want to consult Adickes introduction to AA 14 and Guyer's introduction to *Notes and Fragments*, the latter of which also considers the relevance of this dating system now that in most cases the originals have been lost.

In translating the elucidations and notes, we have provided the numbers for AA in this form: "E140" means *Erläuterungen* number 140, whereas "R3927" means *Reflexionen* number 3927 in AA. When Kant writes in a language other than German, usually Latin, we often put the original in angle brackets <>, as we do when we want to display the German for the sake of clarity. For the most part, we have not attempted to correct Kant's often fanciful punctuation and grammar, or to provide guesses at the continuation of his often elliptical sentences. We leave these to the reader.

Page V

R3927, 1769? 1771–2??
Of the empirical fundamental concepts, innumerable through abstraction, that cannot be further resolved into their elements, even though one can indeed show the determination in their cause. Of the rational fundamental concepts, wherein the perceived attributes of things can be uniquely and solely explained, in regard to external objects [these] are: space, time, motion. In regard to the inner: A1. Immediate representation of the present, past, and future. 2. Comparison, distinction and sameness. 3. Relation (logical) of combination and opposition. 4. Consciousness, judgments, syllogisms. B1. Feeling, pleasure, displeasure. 2. In relation to the judgment of the understanding or the senses. C. Desires etc. etc. (*crossed out:* Fundamental concepts, that are common to both sensations) Through the nature of the understanding, the fundamental concepts of synthesis arise not by abstracting <*abstrahendo*>, but rather by judging <*iudicando*>. Existence, possibility, unity, substance, accidents, relation,

(*crossed out:* the lo) real and logical respect <*respectus realis, logicus*>, necessity, contingency. Whole, a part. Simple, composite, ground, consequence, power, cause.

R3928, 1769.

The principles <*principia*> of the form of all analytic judgments (of the existential judgments of things absolutely <*absolute*> or of the predicates relatively <*relative*>) are the principles of identity and contradiction, and (*crossed out:* the subjective) the proofs are carried out by demonstrating through the analysis <*analysin*> of the given concept its identity or opposition with the predicates. The principles <*principia*> of the form of synthetic judgments are: what is always combined with a known part of the possible concept of a thing belongs as a part to this concept etc. etc. The proposition: every body is impenetrable is analytic, because not only can one not think of body without impenetrability, but rather because it can be thought solely through impenetrability; this mark belongs as a part <*pars*> to the notion of body, however: every body is inert, is a synthetic proposition; for inertia is a copart <*compars*> along with the concept (*crossed out:* of b[ody]) of that which is thought under the expression "body," and it belongs to a complete concept that is combined in a necessary way with those same partials concepts that belong to the notion of body. If one had the entire concept of which the notions of the subject and the predicate are coparts, then the synthetic judgments would be transformed into analytic ones. The question arises as to just how arbitrary this may be.

So much for the logical nexus <*nexu logico*>. As for what concerns the real nexus <*nexum realem*>, its material principles <*principia materialia*> are the experiences, the formal principles <*principia*> are: everything that happens has a determining ground, and secondly: everything has a first ground. These principles <*principia*> are both synthetic, the former for the use of our reason, the latter for the boundary <*termino*> of this use. For according to the former, we look always to the higher ground in the series of mutually determining causes, and according to the latter we see that this series is bounded. It is, however, just as impossible to represent a series of subordinate grounds that has no beginning as it is to conceive how it begins. Nevertheless, the proposition that everything that happens has a determining ground, this proposition, which necessitates an infinite series, is the principle <*principium*> of the form of all our rational judgments regarding real connection. However, the proposition: every series of subordinate things and every successive series has a first cause is a synthetic proposition that is abstracted more from the boundaries of our understanding than from the object of knowledge.

The first in the series of causes is always free choice. That this has no determining ground is an empirical proposition, but to this extent it is uncertain; its certainty, however, depends upon that otherwise there could be no first [cause].

Of the possibility of alteration, i.e. of coming into being and passing away in general.

Page VI

R3708, 1762–3? (1769?) 1780–9??
Only rational concepts can be defined, empirical ones never. The concept of the latter serve only to designate the subject of synthetic judgments, never, however, for analysis.

R3935, 1769.
The proposition: all events (individually) have consequences, and all events combined in turn have consequences, are not the same.

All rational synthetic propositions are subjective, and vice versa, only the analytical are objective. The principle of identity and contradiction <*principia identitatis et contradictionis*>.

The synthesis of reason (rational) or of experience (empirical).

The former is either of coordination: whole and part, number and unity; or of subordination: ground and consequence.

(*crossed out:* Empirical) The second of coordination according to space and time.

R3936, 1769? end of 1769 – autumn 1770?
Everything is considered either distributively or collectively. The former indicates a universal concept, insofar as it is a common mark of what is inferior; the second indicates the collecting together of many. Now, because the collection of all cannot always happen, the collective allness <*omnitudo collectiva*> is sometimes fictional.

The subjective principles <*principia subiectiva*> contradict themselves if they are taken to be objective. E.g. everything has a ground, contradicts this proposition: nothing is necessary through itself, etc., etc.

R3937, 1769.
One should think something is absolutely necessary, because everything that is necessarily is, but not everything can be hypothetically necessary. However, one can think nothing absolutely necessary. One must think of the world as bounded, but one cannot also think the boundaries.

Those synthetic propositions are objectively valid that do not cancel (*crossed out:* to through), according to their own nature, those same conditions of comprehensibility that they set, such as those of the interaction of substances <*commercio substantiarum*>.

R4158, end of 1769 – autumn 1770? (1769?).
One cannot think a subject otherwise than through its predicates and predicates not otherwise than in their subject. Hence the necessity of representing substances, which (*crossed out:* a) is more a subjective necessity of the laws of our understanding than it is an objective one.

All judgments arise as the understanding attends to its own actions or in general to representations. If these are representations of sensation and of their relations, then they are empirical and correct; if they are representations [breaks off]

R4856, 1776–8? 1770–1??
In every relation within which we would like to make something understandable, both members must be known. Now, the object (*crossed out:* known the) is unknown, although the sensation is known. Therefore it cannot be rendered understandable. By contrast with this, sensation and the feeling of pleasure are both within us, and therefore determined and understandable through itself.

R4857, 1776–8? 1770–1??
Pleasure and displeasure alone make up what is absolute, because they are life itself.

Page VII

R3938, 1769.
Apart from those determinations without which the object cannot exist, there are yet other determinations in our reason without which we cannot think certain objects by means of reason, even when these conditions are not determinations of the objects themselves. These conditions <*conditiones*> are therefore subjective, and their concepts stand for nothing in the objects. According to this all synthetic judgments of pure reason are subjective, and the concepts themselves stand for relations between the actions of reason.

R3939, 1769.
Logic treats of the objective laws of reason, i.e. how it should proceed. Metaphysics [treats of] the subjective [laws] of pure reason, how it proceeds. In both, reason is the object, for the (rational <*rationale*>) form is in every science of philosophy and mathematics. That reason explicates, according to its own laws, the laws according to which it ought to think, means that reason provides the rules that it will discover first of all. From this comes the tautologies and rules that exist without being practically employed <*ohne Praxis seyn*>.

R3940, 1769.
In all knowledge of reason there are only relations to consider, and these are either given (sensibly or through the nature of reason) or invented. However, we can invent no relation (of) that whose possibility we can be convinced of except according to magnitudes through repetition in arithmetic. To invent in regard to the quality of relations, and therefore to invent (first) rational concepts, is just as impossible as [would be the invention] of the first sensations of the senses.

R3941, 1769.
Metaphysical concepts relate (1) merely to the relation of coordination: (absolute and relative <*absolutum et relativum*>, whole, part, the continuous, the discrete <*continuum, discretum*>) (many) some, all (the first, last, a single one); (2) or to that of subordination in a logical sense: universal or particular; (3) to subordination in a real sense: ground, consequence, cause, effect. From this springs the concept of the first cause, the last consequence, the cause of all, of some. (4) to existence: necessary, contingent (possible); (5) substance. (subject, predicate) Simple, composite, action, passion (power, receptivity

<vis, receptivitas>), spontaneity <spontanea>, (crossed out: constrained <coacta>) inert. (Whole of substances. World.) Time and Space. Duration, moment, eternity, beginning, end. Alteration, persistence. Place, extension, point. (Space and Time:) Motion, rest. Omnipresent. Effect in space: occupation, power, mass. Effect in time: alteration, creation, annihilation.

R4446, around 1771? (1769 - autumn 1770?)

The intelligible is either theoretical (metaphysical) or practical (moral) knowledge <Intellectualia vel sunt theoreticae (metaphysica) vel practicae (moralia) cogitiones>	Dogmaticians <docmatici> Aristotle Plato Romans Scholastics <Scholastici> Rasmus
Critique before the doctrine	Rawness of … Understanding

(later addition: Ideas for Plato are intuition <intuitus>.) ⎛(later addition: Dogmatic Method <methodus Dogmatica Skeptical <Sceptica> Critical <Critica>. Descartes Hume⎞

The metaphysical locations of Aristotle <Loci Metaphysici Aristotelis>

The domain of intellectual concepts <domus conceptuum intellectualium>.

⎛ inborn ideas <ideae connatae>;
acquired <aqvisitae>:
through the senses, through anticipations <per sensus, per anticipationes>. ⎞

(later addition: Natural or supernatural sources of intellectual knowledge <cognitionen>.)

Locke. Subjective <subiective> habituation. (later addition: He took the principle of becoming <principia fiendi> for that of being <essendi>.)

⎛ (later addition: instead analytic) The physiology of the intellect <physiologia intellectus>, where (crossed out: whose phen) the origin of one's concept is explained. Wolf does not have this at all. ⎞

Crusius* Method of pre-established knowledge <Methodus cognitionis praestabilitatae>.

either through epigenesis or through preformation <vel per epigenesin vel per praeformationem>.

*(later addition: is not to be used, because we do not know what God has disclosed to us)

(later addition: All have treated metaphysics dogmatically, not critically.)

(later addition: Criterion <Criterium> of the truth: the holding as true <das vor Wahrhalten>.)

R4447, 1771–8.
Plato did well in indicating the origin of the concepts of perfection. But not of the notions <notionum>. Plato enthusiast, Aristotle analyist. The objective and subjective principles of D [breaks off].

R4453, 1771–8.
The questions <quaestiones> of metaphysics are all raised through common reason and through our most important ends; it is no organon of science, but rather of wisdom and is used negatively to abolish the obstacles that oppose the most important knowledge.

R4858. 1776–8.
Above all, transcendental philosophy requires critique (to distinguish it from the empirical). 2. Discipline. 3. Canon. 4. Architectonic.

R4859, 1776–8.
Origin of transcendental concepts (1) through mystical intuition <per intuitionem mysticam>. (2) through sensitive <sensitivum> (influence <influxum>). (3) through preformation <per praeformationem>. (4) through intellectual epigenesis <per epigenesin intellectualem>. (intellectual things <intellectualia> intuitively or discursively.)
The end of metaphysics is God and a future world.
Epicurus nothing a priori.

Pages VII–VIII

R4448, 1771–8.
The analytical concept of the thing contains whatever lies therein; the synthetic whatever must be ascribed to it insofar as it should be a certain thing.*
    *Appearance, concept, notion, idea <apparentia. conceptus. notio. idea>. The idea of that through which things are a priori possible according to the rules of a perfect will. Images. Concepts. Ideas. Plants. Origin: minerals. Ends.

Page VIII

R4449, around 1771.
History of the distinction between the sensitive <sensitivis> and the intellectual <intellectualibus>. Egyptians. Pythagoras. Heraclitus (Eleatic). Plato (innate ideas) and Pythagoras make the intellectual things* <intellectualia> into particular objects of possible intuition; his school, the academic philosophers, exoterically skeptical and esoterically dogmatic. Intellectual intuition <intuitus intellectualis>, from which everything descends. Aristotle taught the sensitive (categories <categorien>), but did not remain with it. Epicurus: a philosopher of sensations. Aristippus: merely the feeling of the pleasant.
*(added later: intellectual things or objects with respect to the form of knowledge <intellectualia vel quoad obiecta formam cognitionis>)
(added later: either mystical or logical intellectual things <intellectualia vel mystice vel logice talia>)

(*added later:* intellectual knowledge, but about objects of the senses, and not innate notions <*circa obiecta sensuum, neque notiones connatas*>)

(*added later:* either through an intellectual intuition or an intellectual concept <*vel per intuitus vel conceptus intellectuales*>. The latter either metaphysical: Locke—Leibniz. Or physiological: Aristotle and Epicurus.)

R4450, around 1771.
Aristotle was mistaken because he made a division in logic of universal concepts though which one can think things: this belongs to metaphysics. Logic has to do with concepts, whatever they are, and treats only their relation.

R4451, 1771–8.
Theosophical and mystical principles.
Pythagoras, the Eleatic school: Parmenides, Plato treat of intellectual things; Plato through innate ideas and intuition <*per ideas connatas et intuitivas*>, the others through discursion <*per discursivas*>, but the sensible <*sensitiva*> only as appearance <*apparentias*>. Aristotle teaches everything from the senses, but nevertheless treats intellectual things <*intellectualia*>, which he holds to be sensible <*sensitiva*>.

R4452, around 1771.
The true concepts of reason relate only to the relation of things in general. The objects are sensitive; only (*crossed out:* their) the use of reason in regard to these happens according to merely intellectual laws; if the objects are intellectual, then this is enthusiastic.

R4445, around 1771.
(*added later:* The possibility of such a science. In regard to that which is not intuited.)
Prolegomena. Some sciences contain merely a use of the understanding in regard to diverse objects of inquisitiveness and advancement, and logic is the universal organon of these, namely the instruction for its use.

Other sciences have the determination of the understanding itself as their goal, namely according to its faculty as well as its highest ends, or the objects to which the understanding and the will are limited through the highest laws of nature. Therefore (*crossed out:* is) are all other sciences organs of skillfulness, and most ultimately of prudence, metaphysics [however, is the organ] of wisdom.

The use of metaphysics in regard to the theoretical is purely negative; it does not disclose the knowledge of things and is not dogmatic; for where should it (*crossed out:* its) get the (*crossed out:* attrib) knowledge of things without the senses. Mathematics makes arbitrary concepts of magnitudes as hypothetical conditions, from which consequences can be drawn (*crossed out:* A categorical science) through mere repetition. As for the question, however, what a thing is, we can invent no concepts and also no relations. They must relate to what is given, at least as grounds of their use. Metaphysics prevents only the false use of reason, which oversteps its limits and considers intellectual things <*intellectualia*> to be objects, since metaphysics is indeed only used as the way of knowing <*modo cognoscendi*> those things that can be sensibly given <*sensitive dabilium*> and in any case as a the limitation of these, insofar as reason wishes to use the sensitive <*sensitiva*> beyond its limits. Pure reason is only dogmatic in regard to the objects of the will, in regard to speculation, however, (merely spectating) cathartic. In metaphysics there are no hypotheses, because first the possibility of a highest ground of reason would be entirely without rule and because metaphysics places limits precisely on reason in its purest use.

Aristippus: our judgments of that which is pleasant (*added later*: likewise everything that expresses mere appearances) are always true, however the object may be composed, because pleasantness means something that is in us; but the judgment: this or that object exits, (*crossed out*: is) are uncertain, because the object is distinct from us.

Page XVII

R4465, around 1771.
In the sciences of pure reason, philosophy is presently more critical than dogmatic, (*crossed out*: more) an investigation of the subject (*crossed out*: than) and through this of the possibility of thinking an object.

R4466, around 1771.
The critique of pure reason [is] an exercise in theoretical philosophy preliminary to metaphysics.

R5682, 1780–9? 1776–8??
Instead of the distinction between synthesis and analysis: regressive <*regressive*> synthesis and progressive <*progressive*> synthesis.

R5683, 1780–9? 1776–8??
The mere possibility of the proposition that a God exists is sufficient for religion, and this possibility is apodictically certain.

R4291. 1770–1? 1773–5? 1776–8?
Metaphysics is not the mother of religion, but rather its bulwark (*added later*: against false sophistry). It proves the existence of God not apodictically <*apodice*>, but rather in a supplementary way <*suppletorie*>, in that through reason it replaces the lack of morality in the unbeliever.

R4292, 1770–1? 1773–5? 1776–8?
The conditions <*conditiones*> without which objects cannot be given are objective, even if according to laws of sensibility. The conditions <*conditiones*> without which they (if they are given at the same time) cannot be known (understood) are objective. Those without which they cannot be completely understood <*eingesehen werden*> (known through reason)*, are merely subjective; but these subjective conditions <*conditiones*> are objective in respect to the use of reason in regard to experiences (*crossed out*: cond) (appropriate laws <*leges convenientiae*>).

(later addition: possibility, necessity)

R4293 1770–1? 1773–5? 1776–8?
Philosophy has this particularity, that universal thoughts can be drawn up first of all, in contrast to mathematics [where this can only be done] at the very end. For this reason, in meditation the universal project *<proiet>* comes first of all.

R4915. 1776–8? around 1771?
qualifiedly *<secundum quid>* or unqualifiedly *<simpliciter>* a priori

R4916, 1776–8.
Through merely pure concepts of reason no object at all can be known to be determined. However, these are indeed the ways of knowing the object, not as it appears, but rather as it is.

R4917, 1776–8.
It is not enough to know what the representations contain within themselves, nor to what inducements and conditions they owe their origin, but rather in what faculties and capabilities they are located.

R4918. 1776–8.
Distinction between Copernicus and Tycho.

R4919, 1776–8.
The method constitutes everything, not as one has thought, but rather as one should think. To know how to philosophize or to know (*added later:* a) philosophy. Philosophy must mainly consist in the sources of a priori knowledge.

R4920, 1776–8.
Mathematics proceeds only with concepts that it can make intuitive a priori. Philosophy can only subsume them under pure concepts and can never make them intuitive.

R4921, 1776–8.
An idea is in every instance a concept of reason, according to which the manifold can be ordered. It is therefore a system of nature *<systema naturae>* either arranged according to an idea (that, however, is only didactic) or according to a design *<dessin>*.

R4922, 1776–8.
That the radius may be drawn six times around the circumference of circle cannot be derived from the concept of the circle.

R4923, 1776–8.
That the pure fundamental principles are of empirical use in regard to experience and not of transcendental use in regard to ideal objects. They are valid in relation to the manner in which the boundaries for our practical knowledge should be determined by speculative [knowledge].

R4912, 1776–8.
Metaphysics is not for children and youths, but rather for adults. It is a way of revising reason. One must already be familiar with it in order to be able to estimate its validity. The theologian needs no metaphysics; the simpler, the more on empirical fundamental principles [the theologian's doctrine is based]: the more useful. The theologian can know the concept of divine perfections without metaphysics. Only at the close of studies does the theologian need metaphysics. Logic and morals provide the beginning. Learning the practical method of morals also comes last. The logician, metaphysician and moralist at the same time receive true importance through this for the very first time.—and yes, there is no possible examination for this.

(One will not resent this judgment if it comes from a man who, as he is paid to teach metaphysics publicly, wishes to convince himself that he is (*crossed out:* for something) good for something after all.)

R4913, 1776–8.
The Academy of Sciences: a college of revision. Encouraged by the honor of all the writings that it improves. In it notices are read out loud.

R4914, 1776–8.
There are practical laws of reason, since, namely, one should follow no other rule than that according to which it is possible to employ reason. These are rules of judgment in service of speculative reason; e.g. the sight of a miracle goes beyond all reason in its evidentiary force, but not the account [of one]. Hence it is a rule for reason, i.e. of its use, not to believe accounts of miracles, because even if something true were introduced through a miracle, afterwards it should not be believed because of this account, but rather from itself, because otherwise it could again be overthrown by new accounts.

Page XVIII
R4467, around 1771.
(*crossed out:* Speculation) Rational learnedness and Rational wisdom: the first is speculative and (*crossed out:* concerns) is a skillfulness for solving the questions <*quaestionen*> of reason; the second is a determination of the worth of these exercises of the understanding and of their boundaries. Philosophy contains the former; the philosopher, who contains the end of philosophy in himself, is the latter. He is not a craftsman of reason, but rather a legislator of human reason.

R4468, around 1771? 1776–8??
That reason requires discipline. That, if it is not trained, but rather wildly shoots out its branches, it brings forth blossoms without fruits.

That therefore a master of discipline is necessary (not a disciplinary master), who governs it. That without this discipline it does not harmonize with religion and morals, dominates the discussion, and, as it does not know itself, confuses the understanding that is healthy and practiced in experience.

R4469, around 1771.
The skeptical method is the best and only one that drives back objections through retorsion.[a] Does there then arise from this a universal doubt? No, rather through this the presumptuousness of pure reason in regard to the conditions of the possibility of all things is driven back. Through it all judgments of healthy reason in regard to the world and what is practical receive their great esteem. Healthy, or practical, reason will never permit itself to be persuaded that there is no God, only if it does not seek subtly to win [his] position for itself.

R4470, around 1771.
The first question is: how can concepts (*crossed out:* of things) arise within us that become known to us through no appearances of things themselves, or propositions that no experience has taught us.

R4471, around 1771.
Many kinds of knowledge belong to philosophy as means and as the cultures of our insight, but they do not belong to this as integral parts. Philosophy itself is the science for determining the ends and boundaries, or circle, for all these uses of reason. The former are a part of scholarship, the latter of wisdom. A wise person and a philosopher are not one and the same. The latter concerns only the knowledge and judgment of essential ends, the former the exercises and is practical. Philosophical spirit and the spirit of philosophy.

R4472, around 1771.
Empirical (fundamental) propositions are always synthetic. Universal ones are never empirical. Hence the former are always universal only to a certain degree <*in tantum*>. One makes new propositions from empirical ones through analysis <*per analysin*>.

R4294, 1770–8? (1769?).
All sciences and arts teach skillfulness, philosophy alone [teaches] the fundamental principles and rules of the use of all skillfulness according to the final context <*Beziehungen*> of understanding and the will, while it establishes the object itself and its relation to the human being.

---

[a] Retorsion is a kind of reply that indicates that the one who objects must be able to answer the same or a similar question. See R3892 for a clear instance of Kant's usage.

R4924, 1776–8.
Dogmatic transcendent doctrine is sophistical, namely that of reason overstepping its limits. The disciplinarian of the sophist is the teacher of morals, or indeed the satirist.

R4925, 1776–8.
Philosophy is the legislation (nomothetic) of human reason. The art of reasoning is the doctrine of the skillfulness of reason according to rules (not laws).

In knowledge, the philosopher is just as much an ideal as is the wise person in the use of his free will. He is the model of every use of reason.

R4926, 1776–8.
We can appeal to common human understanding if we wish to determine the rules and the incentives of our conduct, and therefore that which actually concern us. If, however, we wish to progress further, as concerns our duty, and lose ourselves in theoretical claims, then we appeal in vain to common human understanding.

R4927, 1776–8.
Philosophy is actually nothing other than a practical knowledge of man; everything else is knowledge of nature and a craft of reason; but the authoritative dignity over human reason and all crafts, insofar as they are subordinate, belongs to philosophy. O! It is to be regretted that we have let this sense disappear. Without such a distinguishing title this knowledge <*Kenntnis*> is not separated from others, and there is no actual doctrine of philosophy.

4

Notes on this Translation

A. The Latin text of the *Metaphysics*

The Latin text of Alexander Baumgarten's *Metaphysics* appeared in seven editions, each consisting of precisely 1,000 paragraphs organized into four parts. Baumgarten himself prepared the first four editions, and these are the most important. Not only do they contain Baumgarten's own evolving vision of the work, but those variations found in these four editions, which in general are substantial, are also the most philosophically significant. Beyond these seven editions, a final one can also be mentioned: the version found in the *Akademie* edition of Kant's works.

The first edition appeared in 1739. It is the smallest of the editions, with its thousand paragraphs running a mere 292 pages. It is the only edition to number the paragraphs using Roman numerals, and it contains the fewest number of sections. It is also distinguished by the number of typographical errors it contains, about which Baumgarten complains bitterly in the prefaces to both the first and the second editions. Indeed, the publisher needed to include a two-page list of errors at the end of the first edition, and cursory inspection of the text indicates this to be insufficient.

Although the preface to the first edition hints at polemic with elliptical references to unnamed opponents, the preface to the second edition takes specific issue with an early review of the work, contesting its interpretation of such terms as confusion, perfection, and substance. Appearing four years later in 1743, the second edition greatly expanded, and sometimes rewrote, the paragraphs of the first edition, which now stretch to 336 pages. For instance, §190 is a scant 15 words in the first edition, but 112 in the second edition. As well, the second edition divides up many of the longer sections of the first edition, and thus introduces many new sections. Baumgarten sharpens his concept of substance (see §191, 389, and 390), and becomes more confident in his treatment of pre-established harmony, changing it from a "hypothesis to a theorem," as he tells us in the new preface (p. 90 below). Another feature typical of the second edition is Baumgarten's treatment of the "mathematics of intensive quantities" (see especially §160–90, but also throughout the book), which, he also tells us in the preface to the second edition, he sets in italics "so that they would be that much more easily distinguished from the rest, should someone wish either to inspect these alone or to skip them entirely" (ibid.). He sectioned off and rewrote half of §776–81, which now becomes section four of the rational pyschology, "The immortality of the human soul." A new §515 greatly expands upon the perfections of thinking, and §742 adds a discussion and refutation of the atomist concept of "thinking matter." Finally, the second edition introduces a synopsis, which will remain in every subsequent edition and offers Baumgarten's complex vision of the book's structure.

As of the third edition, the form of the book is almost completely set. And like the second edition, its preface is largely concerned with repelling attacks on the work's core theses. Thus, this third preface contains a long passage on an attack against Leibniz and Wolff that offends Baumgarten personally, a passage, incidentally, quoted by Moses Mendelssohn at length (please see our footnotes to the third preface). Rather interesting is the preface's discussion of apagogic demonstration, which helps us to understand a strategy that Baumgarten uses repeatedly in the text proper. We will have reason to return to this below. Also noteworthy is Baumgarten's extended defense of the principle of sufficient ground, which takes up the bulk of the preface. Concerning the text proper, the third edition continues the second edition's trend toward expansion and re-writing, now running an even 360 pages. It also further divides the book into more sections, a practice that ends with this edition. Finally, it removes the italics from the mathematics of intensive quantities.

In the fourth edition Baumgarten neither adds new section headers nor provides a new preface. However, he changes a few passages and appends some short passages, mostly in the form of appositives and clarifications, often parenthetically. The fourth edition's major contribution are the German glosses that Baumgarten adds directly after many paragraphs, which serve to further define the technical Latin terms (we only note these rarely where they help us translate a term). These glosses—along with Wolff's German texts—were important in the history of German-language metaphysics in general. The small changes and the substantial glosses allow the book to reach a length of 406 pages, a length which will remain constant throughout the final three editions.

The fifth, sixth, and seventh editions add nothing of note to the book. The changes in the final three editions are almost entirely typographical errors, although some of the paragraph references are changed, and a handful of errors that slipped through previous editions are corrected. They are each essentially reprints of the fourth edition, as the identical pagination indicates.

Since Kant used the *Metaphysics* as a text book for three courses, and since a significant number of Kant's published reflections refer to the *Metaphysics*, the *Akademie* edition of Kant's collected works, under the general editorship of Erich Adickes (1866–1928), includes a Latin critical edition of Baumgarten's *Metaphysics* edited by Emil Thomas (1858–1923). The Akademie edition presents the *Metaphysics* in two separate volumes; most of the *Metaphysics* is found in Volume XVII. However, §504–699, which comprise the bulk of the Empirical Psychology (Part III, Chapter 1), are located in Volume XV, which deals with Kant's anthropology. This edition is critical, but in a limited sense; using the fourth edition as the baseline—the edition that Kant used—it draws only from that and the second, third, and fifth editions. It ignores the vast differences with the first edition, and does not trace the changes between any of the various editions, since it is only concerned with producing the best possible version of the fourth edition.[a] Thomas usually corrects the fourth by finding precedence in the second and/or third editions, but once in a while he looks to the fifth, or inserts his own readings. Adickes supplements these with his own preferences a handful of times. The vast majority of the edition's changes are superficial—this edition is seemingly fixated on punctuation, and on commas in particular. And at least one-third of the corrections concern the index, none of which we entertain. However, it does catch a handful of errors in the fourth edition, especially references to paragraphs. Moreover, Thomas and Adickes make a few helpful suggestions, especially in §660.

Abbreviations of the Latin editions

Our translation uses numbers to differentiate the various original editions, and AA for the edition found in the *Akademie Ausgabe*:

1   *Metaphysica per Alexandrum Gottlieb Baumgarten, Professorem Philosophiae.* Halae Magdeburgicae. Impensis C. H. Hemerde. 1739.

2   *Metaphysica per Alexandrum Gottlieb Baumgarten, Professorem Philosophiae.* Editio II. Halae Magdeburgicae. Impensis Carol. Herman. Hemerde. 1743

3   *Metaphysica Alexandri Gottlieb Baumgarten, Professoris Philosophiae.* Editio III. Halae Magdeburgicae. Impensis Carol. Herman. Hemerde. 1750.

4   *Metaphysica Alexandri Gottlieb Baumgarten, Professoris Philosophiae.* Editio IIII. Halae Magdeburgicae. Impensis Carol. Herman. Hemerde. 1757.

5   *Metaphysica Alexandri Gottlieb Baumgarten, Professoris Philosophiae.* Editio V. Halae Magdeburgicae. Impensis Carol. Herman. Hemerde. 1763.

6   *Metaphysica Alexandri Gottlieb Baumgarten, Professoris Philosophiae.* Editio VI. Halae Magdeburgicae. Impensis Carol. Herman. Hemerde. 1768.

7   *Metaphysica Alexandri Gottlieb Baumgarten, Professoris Philosophiae.* Editio VII. Halae Magdeburgicae. Impensis Carol. Herman. Hemerde. 1779.

AA   *Metaphysica Alexandri Gottlieb Baumgarten, Professoris Philosophiae.* Editio IIII. Halae Magdeburgicae. Impensis Carol. Herman. Hemerde. 1757. Reproduced in *Kant's gesammelte Schriften*. Hg. von der Preußischen Akademie der Wissenschaften. Bd. XVII. Dritte Abtheilung: Handschriftlicher Nachlaß Bd. IV: Metaphysik. Erster Theil. Berlin, Leipzig 1926; Bd. XV. Handschriftlicher Nachlaß Bd. II, erste Hälfte: Anthropologie. Berlin Leipzig 1913.

B. Overview of other translations of the *Metaphysics*

In 1766 Baumgarten's student Georg Friedrich Meier produced the first German translation of Baumgarten's *Metaphysics*; for generations, this was the only access to the book for students and researchers without Latin. Johann August Eberhard

---

[a] In the introduction to their translation, Gawlick and Kreimendahl note that the work itself contains many errors which, in some cases are carried over from the fourth edition, and, in others, added by the editors (lxxxii).

re-worked this translation and published a new edition in 1783. After Eberhard, no new translations or editions emerged for about two centuries, until the decades surrounding the turn of the millennium witnessed an upsurge in translations of the *Metaphysics*. However, with one exception, none of these are complete, and most are not substantial. A number of partial translations emerged in German and French between 1974 and 2004, none of which translated more than about a tenth of the work.[a] Karl Ameriks and Steve Naragon translated various passages of the *Metaphysics* in notes to support their translation of Kant's *Lectures on Metaphysics* (1997). In 1998, Ursula Niggli published her German translation of Baumgarten's three prefaces, complete with helpful notes and charts detailing Baumgarten's changing organization of the *Metaphysics* over the first four editions. Since Meier did not try his hand at the prefaces, her volume filled an important gap in Baumgarten scholarship. In 2004, Dagmir Mirbach re-worked Eberhard's edition and added some critical apparatus. But more importantly, in 2007 Mirbach published her epochal German translation of Baumgarten's *Aesthetics*, whose notes contain a wealth of translated passages from the *Metaphysics*. Then, in 2009, Eric Watkins published a translation of important sections of the Metaphysics in his *Kant's Critique of Pure Reason: Background Source Materials*, echoing the late twentieth-century tradition of partial translation. Finally, Günter Gawlick and Lothar Kreimendahl's German translation appeared in 2011 with Latin facing pages, relatively late into our work on this translation.

From this list, we most seriously consulted Meier, Eberhard's Meier, Ameriks and Naragon, Niggli, Mirbach's *Aesthetica*, Watkins, and Gawlick and Kreimendahl. Not all of these works require close discussion in these pages, but Meier and Eberhard, Watkins, and Gawlick and Kreimendahl certainly do.

Meier's work, and Eberhard's edition, are invaluable for understanding the text of the *Metaphysics*, since they have a disciple's insight and verve. As part of a project initiated by Baumgarten himself, G. F. Meier (1718–77) translated the work into German and published it in 1766.[b] Johann August Eberhard, a famous opponent of Kant, then reissued it in 1783 as part of an attempt to defend and revive the Leibnizian tradition. The changes and additions that Meier and Eberhard made to Baumgarten's text are both historically and philosophically significant and their inclusion adds considerably to the value of this translation in at least two ways. First, they clarify Baumgarten's meaning, which is couched in notoriously crabbed Latin[c] and presented through arguments that often lack premises that Meier, being a close friend and student of Baumgarten, would have been in a unique position to supply. Secondly, Meier is an important philosopher in his own right, and the changes he makes to the text reflect an ongoing critical development of the Leibnizian tradition.

---

[a] See G/K (lxxxc) for a list of these works.

[b] See Meier's preface to his translation, p. 73.

[c] Meier found Baumgarten's Latin to be difficult; please see the preface to his translation below. Lewis White Beck also refers to the "deadly monotony of Wolff's and Baumgarten's [Latin]." Cf. *Kant's Latin Writings. Translations, Commentaries, and Notes*, edited and translated by Lewis White Beck in collaboration with Mary J. Gregor, Ralf Meerbote, and John A. Reusche (New York: Peter Lang, 1986), 14. It is not clear to us that this constitutes a good criticism, or that it is true of Baumgarten.

Nevertheless, Meier's work has the serious drawback of being a radical re-working of the text. Among other things, Meier re-orders paragraphs, concatenates arguments, paraphrases greatly, and completely skips the mathematics of intensive quantities. Thus in no way can this work be considered a translation in the modern sense. For these reasons, Meier can only be used as a guide to what Baumgarten wrote in the *Metaphysics*; to read Meier is to read for the sense of Baumgarten, but not to read Baumgarten. The project of completely and accurately translating Baumgarten in German—or any language—thus remained unfulfilled until the twenty-first century.

Previous to our translation, Watkins was the first to render the *Metaphysics* into English in something approaching an integral text, and not just a series of endnotes. It would have constituted a major contribution to Baumgarten scholarship for this reason alone, but it is also had the virtue of making evident Baumgarten's place in Kant's thought—a place that hitherto many readers could only grant by accepting the authority of secondary sources. We consulted it quite early in our process, and thanks to his generosity, before it was even published. Nevertheless, his translation contains only a fragment of the total work. Baumgarten, true to the exacting methodology of the rationalist tradition, constructed his work as a single argument sustained *more geometrico* from beginning to end. Thus its 1,000 paragraphs are intended to hang together as a unity of logically interdependent definitions and proofs, no single paragraph of which can be understood without following up on Baumgarten's many references to previously established propositions. Omitting over three-quarters of the text, Watkins' translation suits its purpose but cannot substitute for a full translation, which it does not pretend to do.

Although Watkin includes many preliminary sections for the purpose of providing the reader with a general sense of the text, his selection reflects the passages cited by the editors of the Cambridge translations of Kant's *Lectures on Metaphysics* and *Critique of Pure Reason*. If we set aside the fact that the internal integrity of Baumgarten's argument does not come into view through this method, we still must note that these editors' citations are only episodic and, particularly in the case of the *Critique of Pure Reason*, are not based upon anything approaching a careful comparison with Baumgarten's original. Limited also by considerations of space, Watkins' selection ends up omitting a very large number of passages that are of immediate relevance to Kant's work. To take a single instance, Watkins' text omits all discussion of identity and diversity, (§265–79) which includes the proof of the identity of indiscernibles, a topic Kant discusses in detail in the Amphiboly chapter of the *Critique of Pure Reason*. This passage by Kant not only includes Latin glosses based upon terms taken directly from Baumgarten, but can in fact be shown by examination of the *Nachlass* to have originated in Kant's careful commentary on precisely these passages. The same can be said of Baumgarten's discussion of efficient causality, which Watkins' selection also omits, among other important passages.

By contrast with Watkins' translation, that of G/K is complete, including even the three prefaces and a critical edition of the Latin text. We have also found it in general to be highly reliable, although some of their choices we find to be less than optimal. The first is their rendering of *singuli* as "*Einzelne* [individual]." While *singuli* can indeed secondarily mean "singles" or "individuals," it primarily functions as a distributive numeral, and hence is best translated as "every" or "every single." Baumgarten has the adjective *singularis* at his disposal for "single" or "individual," which G/K correctly translate as *Einzelne* (e.g. §148); Baumgarten can also use *unicus* (e.g. §283), which G/K also translate as *Einzelne*. Nevertheless, in a crucial passage like §21, where Baumgarten defines a sufficient ground of something as the ground of each and everything within it, G/K have it as the ground of "the individual [*des Einzelnen*]" in this thing, which entirely misses the distributive point. The same mistake, with equally serious consequences, occurs in §22, 48, 75, 92, 172, 267, 376 and in very many others. Moreover, even though *singuli* never appears in the singular case in the *Metaphysica* (thus underscoring its distributive function), G/K often render it in the singular case (e.g. §21, 48, 172). Yet, there are cases in which G/K translate *singuli* with *jene* [each] (e.g. §47), which is our preferred reading. Corrupting, as it does, the very definitions of the principle of sufficient reason (or ground) and the principle of complete determination, as well as a host of other fundamental passages, this inconsistency in our view weakens the translation as a whole.

Another issue is their position that "*q. a.*" means "*quae antecedit/antecedent.*" This is certainly incorrect, and their alteration of the sentence structure to support this reading compounds the error further. The incorrectness of this rendering can be seen both from the context and from a comparison with parallel passages in Meier's translation. This abbreviation always occurs as the final step of a *reductio*, and thus if one omits it or renders it in another way, then the argument patently lacks a conclusion. Consider just the following two passages:

> Baumgarten: §20 *Omne possibile aut habet rationem, aut minus, §10. Si habet rationem, aliquid est eius ratio, §8. Si non habet, nihil est eius ratio, §7. Ergo omnis possibilis ratio aut nihil est, aut aliquid, §10. Si nihil foret ratio alicuius possibilis, foret ex nihilo cognoscobile, cur illud sit §14, hinc ipsum nihilum repraesentabile et aliquid, §8, nihil aliquid, §14, 8. Hinc quoddam possibile impossibile, §7, 8 q. a. §9. Ergo omnis possibilis aliquid est ratio ...*

> Fugate/Hymers: Everything possible either has a ground or does not (§10). If it has a ground, something is its ground (§8). If it does not have one, nothing is its ground (§7). Therefore, the ground of every possible thing is either nothing or something (§10). If nothing were the ground of some possible thing, it would be knowable from nothing why that thing is (§14), and hence the nothing itself would be representable and something (§8), and nothing would be something (§14, 8). Hence something possible would be impossible (§7, 8), which is absurd (§9). Therefore, something is the ground of every possible thing...

In their critical version of the Latin, G/K change Baumgarten's "*Hinc quoddam possibile impossibile, §7, 8 q. a. §9*" to read "*...impossibile (§7, 8 q. a. §9).*" translating it then as "*...unmöglich (§7, 8 als Voraussetzung für §9)* [...impossible (§7, 8 as presupposition of §9)]." But, in all similar cases Baumgarten means the abbreviation to be a continuation of the sentence, not something specifically referring to the citations. So the placement within the braces by G/K seems unwarranted.

Another example where the meaning of "*q. a.*" is especially clear from the context is the following:

> Baumgarten: §112 *Omne ens contingens habet modos. Pone enim alicui enti contingenti nullos modos inesse, omnes affectiones eius sunt absolute necessariae, §57, 107, hinc et existentia eius absolute necessaria est, §55 q.a. §109.*

> Fugate/Hymers: Every contingent being has modes. For suppose that no modes belonged to some contingent being, then all of its affections would be absolutely necessary (§52, 107), and hence its existence would be absolutely necessary (§55), which is absurd (§109).

Here, again, G/K change the last part to read "*hinc et existentia eius absolute neces-saria est* (§55, q. a. §109)," and translate it as "*folglich ist auch seine Existenz absolut notwendig* (§55 *als Voraussetzung für* §109)." In both of the cases above, as well as in the third introduction and in §§23, 271, 272, 361, 742, the translation of "*q. a.*" as anything other than "which is absurd" <*quod absurdum est*> clearly makes little sense.

This interpretation is in our view definitively confirmed by a comparison with parallel passages translated by Meier (note that he does not translate all of them). For instance, in his translation of §20 considered above, Meier has the relevant part as: "*und einiges Unmögliche wäre möglich §7. 8. welches ungereimt ist. §9* [and something impossible would be possible §7. 8. which is absurd. §9]." And for §112 he has the last part as: "*und seine Würklichkeit wäre auch schlecterdings nothwendig §.41. welches ungereimt ist* [and its actuality would also be absolutely necessary (§41), which is absurd]". Indeed, in all other passages translated by Meier "which is absurd" occurs in exactly the place where "*q.a.*" falls in Baumgarten's original. As Meier is second to none in his familiarity with Baumgarten's work, his translation must be granted rather high authority.

Finally, we would be the first to stress that no translation is perfect, and that rendering a text for the first time into a language is especially difficult. There are indeed extremely few first attempts, even by excellent translators, which do not contain mistakes. This is just part of the difficulty of translating any complex philo-sophical text. We hope that we have been able to avoid many errors by learning from the efforts of previous translators, and by the extreme care we have taken in trying to comprehend Baumgarten's meaning and the structure of his individual arguments (often looking to Meier, Kant, Wolff, and Leibniz). Moreover, we independently trans-lated Baumgarten's original into English and then compared it line-by-line several times with a completely independent translation of Meier's version, thereby giving sufficient authority to Meier's interpretation while at the same time not allowing it to cloud our approach to Baumgarten's Latin.

Partial list of works and translations consulted

Works that we used more systematically are found instead in our list of abbreviations, which concludes our introduction.

Baumgarten, Alexander Gottlieb. Ästhetik. Latin–German. Translated and edited by Dagmar Mirbach, 2 Vols., Hamburg: Felix Meiner Verlag, 2007.

Baumgarten, Alexander Gottlieb. *Die Vorreden zur Metaphysik*. Translated and edited by Ursula Niggli, Frankfurt am Main: Klostermann, 1998.

Kant, Immanuel. *Anthropology, History, and Education*. Edited by Günter Zöller and Robert B. Louden, translated by Mary Gregor, Paul Guyer, Robert B. Louden, Holly Wilson, Allen W. Wood, Günter Zöller, and Arnulf Zweig, Cambridge: Cambridge University Press, 2007.

Kant, Immanuel. *Lectures on Metaphysics*. Translated and edited by Karl Ameriks and Steve Nargon, Cambridge: Cambridge University Press, 1997.

Kant, Immanuel. *Notes and Fragments*. Edited by Paul Guyer, translated by Curtis Bowman, Paul Guyer and Frederick Rauscher, Cambridge: Cambridge University Press, 2005.

Kant, Immanuel. *Religion and Rational Theology*. Translated by Allen W. Wood and George di Giovanni, Cambridge: Cambridge University Press, 1996.

Watkins, Eric. *Kant's "Critique of Pure Reason": Background Source Materials*, Cambridge: Cambridge University Press, 2009. 84–131.

Wolff, Christian. *Erste Philosophie oder Ontologie: Latin—Deutsch*. Translated from Latin to German by Dirk Effertz, Hamburg: Felix Meiner Verlag, 2005.

Wolff, Christian. *Logic, or Rational Thoughts on the Powers of the Human Understanding; with their Use and Application in the Knowledge and Search of Truth*, translator anonymous (1770), reprinted Hildesheim: Georg Olms Verlag, 2003.

Wolff, Christian. *Preliminary Discourse on Philosophy in General*. Translated by R. J. Blackwell (Indianapolis and New York: Bobbs Merrill, 1963).

C. This translation

I. Text and layout

The text in the main body is the fourth edition. We have exhaustively compared all seven Latin editions, as well as AA. Text that we have established as varying from the fourth edition is located at the end of the book in the endnotes. In this volume we have ignored most orthographical differences if they seem to be typographical; when we were uncertain, we included them. As well, we have not listed any differences between the first edition and the rest if they are noted in the Errata to the first edition. Please see the beginning of the Variants section for a detailed key to our procedure for noting these differences.

We list Meier's changes, emendations, elucidations, or expansions to Baumgarten's text in smaller print directly after the paragraphs to which they pertain. If these are changes, we first include an indication of the text that was changed, followed by a bracket, which in turn is followed by the changed text. The nature of any other text introduced by Meier or Eberhard is indicated clearly with such phrases as "*Eberhard adds*," or "*Meier inserts*." Multiple changes are separated by double bars, ||.

We use footnotes in various manners. They (i) indicate our own editorial or scholarly observations; (ii) they contain supporting texts by Wolff, Leibniz, and other writers or philosophers; (iii) they contain the elucidations that Kant penned in his personal copy.

We modernize all of Baumgarten's references by placing them in parentheses. We add breathing marks and accents to his Greek quotations, and translate them in the footnotes. We generally follow his orthography—for instance, we capitalize and italicize whatever he does, and we follow the complex structure of his synopsis literally. However, we have ignored his use of wide spacing, which in some editions is almost too subtle to be noticeable. We follow a similar procedure when quoting Wolff or any other author.

We have translated the index of the fourth edition, but have re-ordered it alphabetically according to the English. Our glossary is based on, but not limited to, the headwords in the index.

Please see the beginning of the section on Kant's Handwritten Notes above for a detailed key of our procedure there.

II. Vocabulary

It is our view that the basic unit of meaning in a text of this kind is the argument. Each term used by Baumgarten is either defined or has its complete meaning fixed through its logical relation to other terms. Baumgarten himself aimed not primarily at beauty or readability, but at correctness of argumentation. For this reason, we have attempted to translate every term, as far as was possible, based upon a clear understanding of the specific structure of the argument in question as well as its function in regard to the surrounding text. We have sought readability as far as possible, but only on the condition that the basic structure of the paragraph and the ordering of its main ideas be preserved, since this is often directly connected to the flow of an argument. Because of the importance of Baumgarten's work for understanding the genesis of Kant's philosophy, we have attempted as far as possible to translate Latin terms that have established German equivalents in keeping with the standard English translations of his works, most particularly with that of the *Critique of Pure Reason*. However, in a small number of cases we have chosen to depart from this in order to preserve distinctions that exist in Latin, but which fall away in the German. The reader can consult our extensive glossaries at the back of the book.

The glosses that Baumgarten added in the fourth edition were helpful but not decisive. We have not translated these glosses, at least not as glosses. They are German translations of Latin, and are usually literal. Were we to translate them, most glosses would be identical to those words being glossed in the paragraph. However, at times the glosses are helpful, and in these cases, we have referred to them in the footnotes; please see §209 below for an example.

Sometimes we have also been forced to depart from our standard translation; when we have done so, we have indicated the Latin word in angle brackets < > behind the English. We have also used angle brackets to indicate Latin words where they are etymologically or morphologically helpful for grasping the English translation. An example of both breaking from our standard translation and etymological assistance can be found in §341, where we gloss "end" with *finis* and "limited" with *finita*. This permits us to use a non-standard English translation ("limited" instead of "finite") to continue the flow of an argument otherwise more obvious in Latin, and at the same time underscore the meaning of "means" as something having an end (i.e. goal driven) and being bounded by the same (i.e. limited). Also, in rare occasions, Latin's otherwise smaller vocabulary is richer than that of English. A notable example of this is §291, in which we are forced to use one word, "measure," both as a noun and a verb, for four separate but related Latin words: *metimur*, *mensuratam*, *mensura*, and *dimensio*; here, glosses in angle brackets were essential.

With our glossary in mind, and Baumgarten's habit of carefully defining words, an extensive discussion of word choice is not necessary. However, certain words deserve our attention here, especially words that appear throughout the translation and not just in one location, like "measure" above.

Consectaria/logical consequences

This word connotes the further effects of something, i.e. those effects that follow logically or rationally from a given cause. For Baumgarten, no event is sterile (i.e. without consequence) and these consequences each have consequences, and so on. These are the *consectaria* or logical consequences. "Consequences" would be the natural choice, but this creates a problem with Baumgarten's *consequentia* and with the fact that we have chosen "consequence" to translate *rationatum*.

Fallacia, illusiones, praestigia/deceptions, delusions, illusions

These all refer to what could loosely be called "illusions," but which we distinguish as follows: *fallacia* are those "deceptions" depending on or arising from the senses (§545); *illusiones* are "delusions" arising when the mind's faculties are incorrectly used in perceiving the correspondences and differences in things, i.e. when there is failure of wit or acumen respectively (cf. §576); and *praestigia* are "illusions" which deceive the senses (cf. §547).

Medium, remedium/means

Both of these words are clearly related. Baumgarten prefers *remedium* instead of *medium* in the first two editions; as of the third, he prefers *medium* (cf. §341). However, he employs *remedium* alongside *medium* in Part IIII in every edition (cf. §882–8, and 944). Following Baumgarten's own German gloss of *remedium certum* in §885, "*ein gewisses Mittel* [a certain means]," we translate *remedium* in all its forms as "means," except in one instance when it appears as a gloss to §341, where we use "remedy." The changes in the various editions are preserved in our endnotes, and we liberally gloss these terms when helpful.

Monadatum

This word means "a being composed of monads." There is no word in English with this meaning, so we have kept the Latin term, which we also pluralize in the Latin way as "monadata."

Principium, principiatum/principle, founded

Principium becomes "principle," and its cognate *principiatum* becomes "founded," i.e. that which depends on a principle.

Ratio/ground, reason, relation

Perhaps the hardest word to translate is *ratio*, which in Latin has an extensive range of thematically-united meanings. We have elected to translate *ratio* as "ground," "reason," and "relation" depending on context. We gloss these words when necessary, but usually the context clarifies the proper choice.

Rationcinia, ratiocinatio/reasoning, argument

Baumgarten considered *ratiocinia* to be perceptions of reason that are expressed formally, or symbolically, in syllogisms; i.e. they are the mental counterparts, so to say, of syllogisms (cf. §646). *Rationcinatio*, which we also translate as "reasoning," rarely occurs in the *Metaphysics*. However, it also occurs in some passages we translate from Wolff (e.g. WPE §366, part of which we translate in support of *Metaphysics* §646 below).

Respectus, relatio/respect, relation

We translate *respectus* as "respect" and *relatio* as "relation." Both words depend on the concept of determination <*determinatio*>. If the determinations of something can only be thought of in a nexus, i.e. if the determinations are connected or related, these are called relations. Baumgarten uses *respectus* for a relation in the broad sense, i.e. a determination understood within either an internal or external nexus. In everyday English, this meaning is preserved in phrases like "in that respect" and in the related adverb "respectively." On the other hand, *relatio* refers strictly to a determination understood in an external nexus. Hence, an instance of a *respectus* that is not a *relatio* is that of one mental faculty to another, since their nexus is not external. Please see §37 below.

Scientia, cognitio/science, knowledge

The obvious English cognate for *scientia* is science, which we often use for this word (for instance, in the prolegomena to each of the four parts of the *Metaphysics*). However, in certain contexts we translate it as knowledge, largely to accommodate a larger tradition that refers to the "free knowledge, "middle knowledge," and so on, of God. Please see §875ff. for this usage. In general, however, we reserve "knowledge" for *cognitio*. This constitutes a departure from our general goal of accommodating our translation to the current practice with regard to Kant's writings. In the latter, *Erkenntnis*, which is the German equivalent to *cognitio*, is generally rendered as "cognition." The usual argument for this is that in Kant *Erkenntnis* seems to have a far wider range of meanings than we generally associate with the English term "knowledge," and it is thus better rendered by something less determinate like "cognition." We are not entirely convinced by this. In particular, we believe that the verb "to know" is in fact used in common speech in a wide range of ways, and thus that the suggestion that it has only a very strict meaning originates from a particular philosophical program. On the other side, in thinkers like Leibniz, Wolff and Baumgarten, there is a very clear sense in which one having even the merest of sensible representations possesses a kind of implicit knowledge in the strictest sense. Taking this into account, it is our view that the violence that must be done to the English in order to use "cognition" and its cognates for *cognitio* outweighs the possible benefits.

Tollo, tollere/remove, deny

Any reader of Hegel knows how difficult this word is to render in English. However, here we are not faced with the typical (post-)Hegelian issues, because Baumgarten only uses it in its negative sense. Hence, we use either "remove" or "deny," depending on context. We usually gloss it when using it as "deny" to differentiate it from *nego/negere*, whose primary meaning is "to deny" in our text. That Baumgarten intended *tollo* to stand as *nego* can be seen in those passages where he clearly uses the terms synonymously (e.g. §451).

Unicum/unique, one, only one

This simple and versatile adjective requires different translations for the English ear depending on context. We translate it variously as "unique," "one," and "only one."

Volo, volitio and nolo, nolitio/to will, volition and to refuse, nolition

These terms are elegantly related in Latin, but we cannot always render this relation as nicely in English. Latin can simply negate any form of *volo, volere* ("to will") with an "n," but in English this is not always possible. Thus, we translate *volitio* as "volition" and *nolition* as "nolition," where volition indicates rational desire, and nolition indicates rational aversion. However, although we translate *volens* as "willing" and *voluntas* as "will," we can't use *nilling for *nolens* or *nill for *noluntas*; hence *nolens* becomes "refusing" and *noluntas* becomes "refusal," from *nolo, nolere* "to refuse."

III. Abbreviations used in this volume

AA (Volume: Page Number)	Immanuel Kant, *Kants gesammelte Schriften*, 29 Vols., issued by the Prussischen Akademie der Wissenschaften (Vols. 1–22), the deutchen Akademie der Wissenschaften (Vol. 23), and the Akademie der Wissenschaften zu Göttingen (Vols. 24–9), Berlin: Walter de Gruyter, 1902–.
Acroasis logica	Alexander Gottlieb Baumgarten, *Acroasis Logica in Christianum L. B. De Wolff*. 1761. Hildesheim: Georg Olms Verlag, 1973.
AT (Volume: Page Number)	René Descartes, *Oeuvres de Descartes*, edited by C. Adam and P. Tannery, new edition, 12 Vols., Paris: Vrin, 1964–76.

CPR (A-Edition/ B-Edition)	Immanuel Kant, *Kritik der reinen Vernunft*, AA 3–4.
DP	Christian Wolff, *Discursus Praeliminaris de Philosophia in Genere in Philosophia Rationalis sive Logica Methodo Scientifica Pertractata*, in WLL 1–69.
G	Gottfried Wilhelm Leibniz, *Philophische Schriften*, edited by C. I. Gerhardt, 7 Vols., Berlin: 1875–90.
G/K	Alexander Gottlieb Baumgarten, *Metaphysica/Metaphysik: Historisch-kritische Ausgabe*. Translated, introduced and edited by Günter Gawlick and Lothar Kreimendahl, Stuttgart-Bad Canstattt: frommann-holzboog, 2011.
MM	Georg Friedrich Meier, *Metaphysik*. 4 Vols., Halle: Justinus Gebauer, 1755–9.
MT	Alexander Gottlieb Baumgarten, *Metaphysik*. Translated from Latin to German by Georg Friedrich Meier, first edition (1766), with remarks by Johann August Eberhard, second edition (1783). Edited by Dagmar Mirbach, Jena: Dietrich Scheglmann Reprints, 2004.
VGG	Christian Wolff, *Vernünfftige Gedancken von Gott, der Welt und der Seele des Menschen, auch allen Dingen überhaupt*, new enlarged edition, Halle: Rengerischen Buchhandlung, 1747.
WC	Christian Wolff, *Cosmologia Generalis Methodo Scientifica Pertractata*, new edition, Verona: 1736.
WLL	Christian Wolff, *Philosophia Rationalis sive Logica Methodo Scientifica Pertractata*, third edition, Verona: 1735.
WO	Christian Wolff, *Philosophia Prima, sive Ontologia, Methodo Scientifica Pertractata, qua Omnis Cognitionis Humanae Principia continentur*, new edition, Frankfurt and Leipzig: 1736.
WPE	Christian Wolff, *Psychologica Empirica, Methodo Scientifica Pertractata*, new edition, Frankfurt and Leipzig: 1738.
WPR	Christian Wolff, *Psychologia Rationalis Methodo Scientifica Pertractata*, new edition, Frankfurt and Leipzig: 1740.
WTN1	Christian Wolff, *Theologia Naturalis Methodo Scientifica Pertractata*, first part, new edition, Frankfurt and Leipzig: 1739.
WTN2	Christian Wolff, *Theologia Naturalis Methodo Scientifica Pertractata*, second part, new edition, Frankfurt and Leipzig: 1737.

Part Two

The Translation

THE METAPHYSICS OF ALEXANDER
GOTTLIEB BAUMGARTEN[1]
PROFESSOR OF PHILOSOPHY

FOURTH EDITION
HALLE/MAGDEBURG
KARL HERMANN HEMMERDE
1757

Johann August Eberhard's Preface to the Second German Edition (1783)

The publisher of Baumgarten's *Metaphysics* has requested that I supervise this, the work's ninth edition. Of all the textbooks with which I have become acquainted, I consider this manual still to be the most perfect, an unmatched model of conceptual thoroughness, method, and determinacy. And so I found it wonderful news that the work still commands enough approval to require a new edition. I do not undertake this work in order to eulogize the contributions Baumgarten has made to philosophy in general or to metaphysics in particular. Experts know these well enough, and even those among them who hold the metaphysical sciences to be still so defective that they find themselves unable to locate the first grounds of certainty therein still revere Baumgarten's contributions. Even a philosopher as perceptive as Mr. Kant, who finds (as he expresses himself) nothing but analytical judgments in the present metaphysics,[a] and who wants to have several demands satisfied in regard to it before he will entrust it with instructing him with the same scientific rank as pure mathematics, recognizes A. G. Baumgarten as the foremost philosophical analyst. I cannot give here the reasons why I am convinced that with this the philosopher from Königsberg concedes to the one from Frankfurt a greater contribution to metaphysics than he himself appears to think. It must first be decided how well-founded the demands are that the former has made on metaphysics, how many of these were answered in the present stock of metaphysical knowledge, and how many of them can be answered. Without investigating this point now, the contribution itself that this competent and not easily satisfied judge conceded to his predecessor is of such great importance that it has certainly earned the heartfelt thanks of all who search after truth. This is also the judgment of another philosopher of whom German philosophy should be proud: "A textbook," he says "in which the original concepts that must serve as themes for any thinking person are explained with perfect strictness, and in which the marks that each term encloses are given correctly, and indicated through sharp outlines; a textbook of ontology that would serve us no further than to put us in a position, by means of the correct determination of these fundamental concepts, to exchange words

---

[a] The source of this comment is puzzling. Kant makes no such explicit claim until the *Prolegomena* (AA 4: 325n), which, however, seems not to have appeared before spring of 1783, and thus after the dating of this preface. If it is based upon Kant's announcement for his lectures in 1765–6, which seems unlikely, then this is a misunderstanding that turned out to be remarkably prescient. For at that time Kant held all metaphysics, including transcendental philosophy, to be analytical in method and had not yet developed the critical understanding of the distinction between the analytic and the synthetic.

for concepts as often as we find necessary in the progress our reflections—for the endeavoring researcher this would already be no *common* act of kindness."[a]

I initially wanted to insert a greater number of remarks in order to facilitate my audience's comparison of many concepts and the application of many truths. However, the acceleration of the printing and the more pressing work of my position have forced me to be content with very little in this respect. Should these remarks find some approval in the meantime, their number may be increased at a future opportunity. As for what remains, may the Almighty allow this treasury of distinct concepts of the understanding to flourish for the spread of true enlightenment in life and in the sciences, and particularly in that great science which should be the goal of all knowledge of the understanding, namely, in that of honoring God through all the actions of one's life.

Halle, 5 January 1783.
Johann August Eberhard

---

[a] See Moses Mendelssohn, *Anmerkungen zu Abbt's freundschaftlicher Correspondenz*, in Mendelssohn's *Gesammelte Schriften*, edited by G. B. Mendelssohn (Leipzig: F. A. Brockhaus, 1844), Vol. 5, 403–4. Mendelssohn is not speaking in this passage specifically about Baumgarten's textbook, but rather making the more general observation that some of the most serious errors, e.g. the error of Spinoza regarding substance and the error of Hobbes regarding potency, arise from a failure to delineate basic metaphysical concepts properly. Consequently, a textbook that delineation would achieve this delineation would provide no small service to philosophy. Baumgarten makes a similar point about the importance of precisely defined concepts in respect to Spinoza in his preface to the second edition.

Georg Friedrich Meier's Preface to the First German Translation (1766)

I have translated this metaphysical work into German merely to facilitate my own lectures on the subject. I have omitted nothing required for presenting beginners with an adequate and complete system of this science so that they, through their own efforts, can achieve full proficiency in it. I have, however, left out everything that is not necessary for this aim. And since I have often clarified the difficulties in the author's manner of writing, these are no longer present in the translation, and as a result I am able to conclude my lectures in half a year without doubling the lecture hours. At the same time, if I have delivered here no mere literal translation, I hope nevertheless that a fair judge will not suspect that I seek to erase the memory of Baumgarten's contribution to metaphysics; for indeed this book is nothing other than Baumgarten's own metaphysics. That blessed man desired to translate this work into German himself, but protracted illness and death hindered him from fulfilling this intention. The other changes that I have made, which are insignificant in themselves, merely allow me to be briefer in my lectures; for through them many things are gathered together in one paragraph that the author had presented in various separate paragraphs. I therefore have nothing further to say in offering this translation to my audience.

Georg Friedrich Meier

Preface of the Third Edition (1750)[1]

And so, on the chance that you find my words worthwhile, you have before you the third edition of my *Metaphysics*, which I wrote a decade ago and which I have not permitted to see daylight again without a new set of revisions. I have increased the number of sections, and have inserted more titles. I have changed some things, and I have added others. However, I will not repeat what I have already written in my previous prefaces, because any fair critic can read the preceding pages, and I certainly will not be able to compel any unfair critic to read them now. I have experienced critics of the latter kind in their examinations of whatever I have happened to write. And when I do not respond to such critics because of their lack of impartiality, others impute this, my very silence, to me as a fault. Let me note one example. In the first dissertation that I published, I had called a poem[2] "perfect sensitive speech." I still find this to be correctly said. However, one critic wrote that I called a poem "perfectly sensitive" speech, and then twisted the very well-known meaning of perfect, a meaning quite well-known even among schoolboys studying philosophy, into that popular sense in which "perfectly" can sometimes be substituted for "entirely" in vague discussions.[a] I myself had expressly fixed the meaning of "sensitive." Nevertheless, this gentleman also tediously attaches another meaning to this term, a meaning according to which the Germans of coarse or dull wit sometimes[3] indecently, or even obscenely, speak extremely "sensitive" words in jest. After a third such spiteful modification of both words and meanings, he coldly jests not at the expense of my words, which he will never understand, but at the expense of the specter that he himself conjures and unfairly declares to be my thought. I, to be sure, have remained silent. Now, I would not have written a word concerning this wretched little quarrel had it not seemed to others who do not know me that I, putting forth the pretext of more serious annoyances, am perhaps concealing a dearth of arms with which I would defend myself. Therefore, I am using this as my occasion to publically implore immortal God never to give me so much spare time that I could while it away, squander it, and waste it through quarrels about something so empty, when such things are stirred up against me. And consequently, I implore Him never to allow the idea of true honor to sink so low in my view that I, armed, would ever find it opportune to immediately attack whatever sort of things are spoken or written against me, waging a war that will never have a victory parade.[b] If bolder and wrongful attacks must at times be repelled, there will be no shortage of defenders, just as until now there has not been a shortage of

---

[a] Niggli (n. 75b, 115) and G/K (n. 130, 561) identify this as Theodor Johann Quistorp (1722–76).
[b] *bella ducam nullos triumphos habitura.* These words come practically verbatim from Lucan: *bella geri placuit nullos habitura triumphos* (*De Bello Civili vel Pharsaliae* I:12).

those who are to be commended with a public act of gratitude—those who, without having such a defense either asked or demanded of them, nevertheless consented, as befits gentlemen, to write on my behalf, or rather on the behalf of the truth that I have written.[a] In so doing they have been kind to a friend, spending indeed just a few hours refuting these things in a more useful manner than I[4] could have accomplished by writing, as it would seem, only for my own sake.

I think differently about quarrels in which no spirit of sophistry appears. If I could simply refer to what a student who formerly attended my lectures wrote against philosophers![b] I would say to him that I am not writing because he thought that some of my statements were incorrectly demonstrated, which is his philosophical liberty. However, one thing displeases me vehemently: violating his own conscience, if he cares to remember, he says that philosophers who are standing at the very threshold of their own science generally promise complete and supreme certitude beyond which something greater and more solid can indeed not be thought. The same, however, cannot be said about me, and I call as witnesses all those who have heard my introductions to philosophy either in Halle, or here in Frankfurt on the Oder. If assertions in this book, which I usually explain extemporaneously in my lectures, could be taken to that degree, not only do I avoid verbosely exaggerating or exalting them as if they were something else; in truth, I even interpret them, as one says, in an explicitly restrictive manner, and I do so very often and at many points while discussing them philosophically and in logical terms. Afterwards, I even warn that *supreme certitude* must not be confused with *complete certitude*; that such complete certitude must not be confused with those things that may seem complete under the cloak of so-called demonstration; that supreme certitude in no way belongs to humans; and indeed that complete certitude does not extend very broadly, even in the fields of science and philosophy themselves, as it would appear from those who, numbered among the wise, are unable to distinguish the true light sufficiently from the spurious light in stars of the first magnitude.

I would now like, however, to address something that specifically concerns this work we hold in our hands.[c] How swift is the circle of human affairs! How quickly things change! I have not yet reached the age of forty and yet I have already experienced an attack on a certain school of philosophy, I mean that of Leibniz and Wolff, by weapons that most people believed to be almost holy and inviolable, but which were soon judged to be ineffective <*imbellia*>. Thus, it seemed soon after as if the Leibnizian-Wolffian philosophy had triumphed. But now this philosophy is gradually being attacked by the same arguments, which nevertheless, precisely because they seem new to some, are once again being judged by these same people to be of great power. When I attended the summer lectures attacking Wolff that were held in Halle during the last few years, most people could scarcely stop themselves from laughing

---

[a] *Quod scripsi, scribentes*, certainly a play on Pilate's *quod scripsi, scripsi*. Cf. John 19.22.
[b] Niggli does not hazard a guess as to who this may be, and G/K claim ignorance.
[c] Here begins a passage translated by Moses Mendelssohn in letter 21 (1 March 1759) of *Briefe die Neueste Litteratur betreffend*. Reprint of the Berlin edition, 1759–60. Vol. 5.1 (Hildesheim/New York: Georg Olms Verlag: 1974), 135–40. See Niggli (n. 94, 124).

when an old gentleman[a] disputed the universality of the principle of sufficient ground and simple beings, even to the point of finding what he said to be frivolous. Yet behold! The same things are now being rehashed, even by a few of those who a couple of years earlier embraced, as it were, the philosophy in question. But this will not amaze anyone familiar with human nature. Whenever we are led by good fortune to an established doctrine, as if to a promontory, and are diligently seeking truth, then whatever we initially grasp onto, based upon some preconceived opinion, must be reforged[b] sooner or later, however true it may be, and, by means of this, it may in the end become suspicious and perhaps even dubious. But if indeed we are not hastening slowly enough,[c] arguments contrary to a doctrine at first approved become attractive through their charming novelty,[d] and when to this novelty is added the hope of becoming famous by embracing something unusual, these arguments precipitate our approval (an approval not much more careful than had been the first) in the direction of the contrary. And hence when I ponder such things, every day I welcome more and more the fate that befell my life. For having grown up surrounded by others hostile to this way of philosophizing, I first imbibed almost exclusively whatever could be objected to it, rather than its own doctrines. It so happened that I made some—no, on the contrary many—of these same teachings my own but only after an intense and careful investigation of the truth. Since I had to teach these things early in my career at a place where it was not yet actually permitted to appeal to the authority of such great men as were upholding the aforementioned philosophy, as some judge themselves permitted to do today, it was even more necessary for me to inspect and ponder anew the internal arguments of what I had to teach before publically agreeing with the doctrines of these men. Because of this, I now finally hold the advantage of no longer needing to hesitate or even to change my mind entirely, which I would gladly have done if compelled by the powers of the true. Let others doubt that first principle of knowing, which is considered as characteristic of the Leibnizian philosophy; let others doubt the first contingent principles of becoming that the same philosophy establishes, i.e. monads or simple beings. I used to deny both principles. I indeed doubted them both. But once I thought them over, I acknowledged both as true.[e] "I had long before worked through"[f] most of those arguments that are now being sold as new against the truth of both these principles. Let us turn to the first one.

Not the principle itself but rather its universality is said to be assailed, as if there were indeed ever a person so Epicurean as to have dreamed that everything were void

---

[a] Both Niggli (n. 83, 119) and G/K (n. 118, 563) identify this gentleman as Joachim Lange, who played an important role in the Pietists' fight against Wolff. Please see our introduction (p. 6) for more on Lange.

[b] *Revocanda sunt iterum sub incudem*, a Latin proverb; literally: "they must be called back to the anvil."

[c] *Lente festinemus*, according to Suetonius the motto of Augustus (*Aug*, 25): *festina lente* (literally: "hasten slowly"). To hasten slowly is to proceed at precisely at the right pace, neither too quickly nor too slowly.

[d] Cf. Quint. *Inst.* 1 6.39.

[e] Here ends the passage translated by Mendelssohn.

[f] Cf. Virgil, *Aen.* 6.105; cf. Niggli, n. 94, p. 124.

of ground.[a] It appears that what Leibniz has recently given to philosophy, and what is constantly under attack, is this very universality. That it is coextensive not only with everything that exists, but indeed also with everything that is possible, without exception, I judge to be correct. You demand a proof, or rather a demonstration. Which one? What if I counted the principle of ground among the indemonstrable propositions, i.e. those propositions of which you would become completely certain as soon as the mere terms are understood? Your denial of certitude will not refute me. For what if you have not yet understood the terms, e.g. what if you confuse the ground and sufficient ground, the positive and negative, the best and least good, the legitimate and illegitimate, what you do and do not know?[6] There is an old saying: "The half is greater than the whole."[b] Nevertheless, many people usually count this one among the indemonstrable propositions: "the whole is greater than any of its parts."[c] What if I said that "every possible thing has a ground" is an identical proposition?[7] If only these sorts of claims were never made about things that are less evident![8]

But let it be a demonstrative[d] proposition.[9] I should be able to provide a demonstration from what follows in the system alone, such as I show[e] in the final citations to §20. Moreover, a demonstration that does not beg what follows is naturally preferred, when it can be given. I think that the demonstration that I have put forth somewhat more fully in §20[f] is such. I have discovered some learned men calling this demonstration into doubt in two ways. First, some of them hold that a ground of everything possible is already presupposed in that very demonstration, although it is still in question. Very well, let's see what *presupposed*, which is ascribed to me, may mean

---

[a] The Leibnizian tradition has a complex relationship to the philosophy of Epicurus. On the one hand, the principle of sufficient ground requires a ground for composites, and thus agrees with atomism in general that there must be some most basic components of matter, whether spiritual or material. Nevertheless, Epicureanism, since it attributes the generation of complex bodies to pure chance or accident, it is also seen as denying any sufficient ground for the specific interactions of these bodies, and to this extent as also denying design (cf. §383 of this work). Another significant agreement between Leibniz and Epicurus is that once such bodies are given, no *further* activity on God's part (aside perhaps for conservation, in Leibniz's view) is required to explain the interactions of atoms or monads. However, Leibniz argues that the essence of every monad contains within itself the ground of all further interaction or harmonic change, whereas Epicureanism argues that interaction is thought to require no further reason at all. In this respect, Epicureanism can be said to violate the universal form of the principle of sufficient ground, although it maintains the principle in regard to the constitution of composite bodies. Notably, Kant discusses these aspects of Epicureanism very clearly in his early writings. See for example, AA 1: 222–8 and AA 2: 123–4.

[b] *Dimidium esse maius, quam totum*, from Hesiod: πλέον ἥμισυ παντόσ (*Works and Days*, line 41), translated by Gellius as *dimidium plus esse toto* (*Noctes Atticae* 18: 2, 13).

[c] *Totum esse maius qualibet sua parte*, from Euclid: καὶ τὸ ὅλον τοῦ μέρουσ μεῖζον ἐστιν (*Elements*, axiom 8).

[d] *Demonstrativa*. G/K (30) read *demonstrabilis*, "demonstrable." We have stayed with Baumgarten's *demonstrativa*, which survived every edition since it first appeared. In his *Acroasis Logica*, §168, Baumgarten writes: "An INDEMONSTRABLE PROPOSITION is that which becomes completely certain to us when the terms alone are understood; a DEMONSTRATIVE PROPOSITION is that concerning which more things are still required for us to become completely certain." Baumgarten holds that the system will supply that which is necessary to understand the mathematical certainty of the principle of sufficient ground.

[e] *Subinnui*. William Massey lists this non-classical and rare word in his *Corruptae latinitatis index: or, a collection of barbarous words and phrases* (London: 1775).

[f] Baumgarten re-wrote §20 in the second edition, expanding it in relation to the first. See our endnote 22 in that paragraph for the text of the first edition.

here. I think that I, sensibly, presuppose only those things that I judge to exist, or, at least, to be possible. Now, I ask you: Let us carefully read over the demonstration to see whether in it I ever judge[10] that the ground of something possible is possible before the apagogic demonstration[a] is completed, i.e. before I have shown that something without ground is contradictory. When I say this ground is either nothing or something, I certainly am not presupposing nor even judging to be possible what I explicitly state with a disjunction to be either impossible or possible. Thus I really considered the ground of every possible thing to be totally indeterminate throughout the demonstration, and I did not determine its possibility until the conclusion of the demonstration finally indicated that it must be necessary. Say, oh dear fellow, I ask you: Would you believe that I had already presupposed you[11] to be educated, if I were to say that your[12] education is either something or nothing?

A different path was taken by those who were not entirely satisfied by the demonstration in §20. They undermine this very demonstration through what logicians call comparison,[b] maintaining that through the same demonstration that I have employed one can in fact prove what I concede to be false. For their sake, I will now provide what in my view can be sufficiently recalled merely by citing what can be read in this short work itself. In my lectures I usually explain §20 quite clearly as follows: If nothing were the ground of some possible thing, then there would be nothing from which it could be known why that very thing would be possible (§14). That from which one is able to know why something is can itself be known; it is knowable and representable. Therefore if nothing were the ground of something, nothing would be representable and thus something (§8), which is absurd.[c] I will now fashion an example for comparison, one whose conclusion I admit is false, but through which I can confidently meet the force of the objection. Let us suppose: *Every possible thing has extension.* I deny the universality of the proposition. You deny this too, but apparently you maintain that this can be demonstrated in the same way as the ground of every possible thing; whence you infer that the ground of every possible thing is not duly demonstrated. You claim that the proof is similar like this: *Every possible thing either has extension or not* (§10). This I concede. *If it has extension, its extension is something* (§8). This I concede. *If it does not have extension, its extension is nothing* (§7). This I concede. *Therefore, the extension of every possible thing would either be nothing or something* (§10). This I concede. *If the extension of something possible were nothing, nothing would be something.* Now here is Rhodes; do not leap illegitimately.[d] It will be necessary, and your task, to prove the logical consequence of your major term with

---

[a] *Demonstratio apogogica.* An apagogic demonstration indirectly proves a proposition by showing its contrary to be contradictory or absurd. Baumgarten is quite fond of this approach; many of his arguments conclude simply q.a., "which is absurd." The apagogic argument in §20 is at stake here, but we also see such an argument a few sentences down in this paragraph, as well as in §23, 112, 271, 272, 361, and 742.
[b] Cf. §626f
[c] G/K render the final part of this sentence as "(§8 as foundation for the above)".
[d] *Hic iam est Rhodus, hic, ne saltum illegitimum committas.* Baumgarten is playing on "*Hic Rhodus, hic saltus* ["here is Rhodes, leap here]," the Latin translation of a saying from Aesop's "The Boastful Athlete." He must also have in mind Leibniz's "*natura non facit saltus* [nature does not make leaps]" (NE IV, 16).

the same clarity by which I—partly through citations from this booklet, partly through clearly-reasoned arguments—revealed the logical consequence of mine. I deny that you have done so and I think that the difference between my demonstration and whatever else to which it is compared should be located in this point. If I were to posit the extension of some possible thing to be nothing, impossible, not representable, i.e. if I were to posit the antecedent of your last hypothetical proposition, I nevertheless do not yet see why I am compelled to posit the consequent, which I concede is absurd, until you have proven with equal certitude that the extension of some possible thing ought to be impossible and nevertheless likewise representable, just as I proved that the ground of some possible thing (which you, negating the universal principle of ground, will be forced to call nothing due to your premises), precisely because it is called the ground, must be admitted to be likewise understandable, representable, and hence to be something and possible.

Since the topic requires it, permit me briefly to touch upon objections that certainly are not particular to my demonstration, but which nevertheless assail the truth demonstrated in it. You object: If the principle of ground were universal, (1) the first notes of things would have a ground, and there would be something prior to the first. I respond. Lest I lapse into the witticism of a comic,[13]

> *This man makes me laugh. He says that he is the first to know all, yet he alone is ignorant of all,*[a]

we must always distinguish the ground from the ground that we specifically know by proceeding through every single thing. The notes of things that are relatively first, or first with respect to human knowledge (also to clear human knowledge), certainly still have a ground, although we do not know this ground in respect to the rest of its predicates in a way that would allow us to separate it sufficiently from the others. And hence there is always something prior to the first in clear and distinct human knowledge, which can only ever be known somewhat obscurely by humans. The genealogical founders of all noble families always have ancestors prior to them. But the absolutely first being as such neither abstracts, nor reflects, and hence, since it knows all things most distinctly from everything else, it is never led back to absolutely first notes.

You object: If the principle of ground were universal, (2) then the false ascription of an attribute to a thing would have a sufficient ground. I respond: Let us avoid a new ambiguity. In normal speech, whatever is the best and legitimate in some genus usually claims for itself the name of the genus to which it pertains, just as those which are less good and less legitimate are then stripped of the name of the genus as unworthy, although the definition of the genus is still appropriate for these. Thus is it denied that someone of noble birth destitute of all virtue is noble, that a fearful and fleeing soldier is a soldier, and that a father who is cruel to his children is a father. Hence for something to arise from a sufficient ground, insofar as it arises less correctly, is a παράδοξον[b] for those who are accustomed to gracing only the best and legitimate sufficient ground with this name as if it were truly a title. Just because some

---

[a] Cf. Terence, *Adelphi*, IV: ii; Niggli n. 108.
[b] "paradox"

people hate without cause, you are not also going to deny that there is a cause of all contingent things, are you? Rather, let us inquire without verbal trifles: When I assign false attributes to a thing, is not my error here, which is a privation, something that can be understood from another privative sufficient ground? Yes, I answer: I discover the privative sufficient ground in my error, through which I ascribed the wrong essence to a thing. This error has a privative sufficient ground in turn, namely, the delusion of wit[a] that confuses the true essence of a thing with something spurious, and this delusion finally has a privative sufficient ground in a lack of acumen.[b] For the logician, let serve as an example the error of many logicians who thought it an attribute of the fourth [syllogistic] figure that it arises when the major term of the first figure is assumed. This was based upon a wrongly and confusedly perceived real definition of the fourth figure, according to which it is the inverse of the first.

You object: If the principle of ground were universal, (3) there would even be a sufficient ground for errors. I respond: There certainly is a sufficient ground for errors in the subject confusing the true with the false, although it is not in the true objects. The first sufficient ground of a chain of errors in a certain series of errors is the πρῶτον ψεῦδος,[c] long known by orthodox polemicists.

You object: If the principle of ground were universal, (4) the essences of things would also have had a sufficient ground. I respond: They have this in their essential determinations,[d] which constitute them, just as a whole has it in its parts. And again, these essential determinations, if they do not have their own internal sufficient ground in that of which they are the essential determinations, nevertheless certainly have a sufficient ground outside of the being in question—and certainly ultimately in the supreme intellect. For that reason, all of God's internal perfections are truly his essence, because every perfection for him lies in the reciprocal relation <ratione> of grounds <rationum> and arguments <ratiocinatorum>, insofar as every supreme perfection[e] can be conceived of as coming from every other supreme perfection.

You object: If the principle of ground were universal, (5) then the use of the powers of a spontaneous being would also have sufficient ground when they are turned to evil <malum>. This is the crux of the controversy that has wrongly <male> occupied even the most recent theodicy. All right then, let us suppose that there is a freedom that consists in the power of sometimes[14] deciding upon something without a sufficient ground. What will we gain? Your answer is: Since sins that do not have a sufficient ground in a preceding state are utterly unnecessary for the sinner, they can be more fairly imputed to their agent. However, I fail to see either proposition. If the necessary is of this sort, namely such that whatever has sufficient ground in a previous state is incapable of imputation, then, whether chosen through this dubious concept of freedom or through ours, the assumed necessity of sins remains the same, having no less a sufficient ground in a preceding state. For their proximate sufficient ground will then be that potency that we described, which already coexisted[15] in an antecedent

---

[a] Cf. §576 below
[b] Cf. §578 below
[c] "original falsehood"
[d] Cf. §39ff. below
[e] G/K: "the individual supreme perfections"

state, and which was at some point led to something without sufficient ground. Hence, this something could not fail to exist, and not without sufficient ground. Indeed, it has a sufficient ground in that potency that can decide upon something without sufficient ground, while nevertheless it still is a use of powers without a sufficient ground. In this case, the use of such powers will in fairness be imputed to us, if not the outcome which it produced.[16] "What?," my dissenting dearest[17] friends, "fairly?" Is the ground of condemning sin in us, or the evil use of powers, to have a ground, but a ground that is nevertheless conceded not to have been a ground? Am I not to be punished as the agent, i.e. as containing the ground of the deed or the abuse of powers, whose grounds are nevertheless denied in the same breath? If something happens by pure chance,[a] what does that have to do with me? Can I bring pure chance before a thoroughly impartial judge? Come lawyers one and all, however many you are, and decide now if the Gordian knot has been cut. Consider the penalty for the crime of treason for a sufficiently young son of treasonous parents. There are those who do not think that the usual punishment should fall to the son, because he would seem to be coerced into public hostility, and thus necessitated in a certain way. But the prosecutor presses hard and proves that the son, with full rights,[b] deserves the usual punishment on the grounds that this hostility came to pass by mere chance. This doctrine, however, seems more agreeable to me: The use of powers freely exercised for the sake of evil has a sufficient ground in the non-use of the powers that should have been exercised for the best. After all, every substance, every spirit, is always doing something. This non-use of powers that should have been exercised for the best had a sufficient ground in finite and limited choice and freedom, which could have been morally vigilant μετ᾽ εὐλάβειας,[c] and could have enjoyed the carefree sleep of the just, but rather, at the first moment of moral sleep, is instead bound to the opposite, namely, to sin, and liable to punishment due to a conquerable lack of righteousness.

However, the reader should not be kept waiting on the threshold any longer. So that I do not abandon my duty, allow me in a few words to pay the testimony of thankfulness I owe to those celebrated and famous men, some who ensured that this work emerged from the press much improved, and others who have followed whatever threads they have judged worthy in this trifling work in their own most learned lectures at various universities.

Written at Frankfurt on the Oder, 12 September 1749.

---

[a] Again, cf. §383.
[b] *optimo iure*. This is a technical term: in the Roman legal system, a *cives optimo iure* (citizen with full right) possessed full public and private rights. Cf. William Smith, *Dictionary of Greek and Roman Antiquities* (London: John Murray, 1870), 924.
[c] "with divine reverence"

Preface of the Second Edition (1743)[1]

I have had to prepare a second edition of this thin booklet yet again from afar. Although I could now hide behind the excuse that the errors were committed through the oversight of the printers, I hope nevertheless that neither my efforts to reduce these from here were in vain, nor was the diligent work of a friend currently living in Halle who did not shirk from correcting the page proofs while they were going to the press—a diligence that must be commemorated with a debt of gratitude. However I, for my own part, am not such a Suffenus[a] that I would pawn off on the staff of the press both the errors that were perhaps previously committed as well as those new ones that may have been introduced. I remember well the doubt, fear, and—should I say—almost depression with which I inked the closing stroke on this book when it was first sent out into the public. Should the goodwill of readers and judges once again surpass my slender hope, then I will again be delighted; for I do not deny that back then I was exceedingly happy to hear and read the opinions of the experts, which were indeed milder than my own. If only a few of these continue to cite and even praise me considerably, I would like at this moment to wish upon them every word that could possibly be said on behalf of one who must pay testimony to thankfulness and modesty, or, if I am silent, every word that could be gathered by those who are familiar with the way life goes. I am aware of at least one reader who has published in the *Supplements to the Leipzig Scholarly Chronicles*[b] (Latin Vol. IIII, sect. VI, p. 266 ff.) a fairly detailed account of this *Metaphysics* along with a judgment more honorific than deserved. Yet, he openly added several remarks at the same time indicating that he was less than pleased with some of what I had advanced. Who this may be has not yet been revealed. But based upon the reputation of the celebrated journal to which he contributes articles, I suspect nothing less than that he is a most distinguished gentleman.

However, I would have preferred if our most distinguished gentleman had not so interwoven his sentiments with mine as he has; for, whoever has not yet read mine cannot wholly distinguish the two. When he calls those who cast the charge of obscurity upon me "envious idiots"—it is not I who does so. "Those who repudiate[2] the principle of sufficient ground will teach that the world exists: they however deny an author in whom the ground of the production of the world exists"—these are his thoughts, not mine. "Because they do not permit simple elements, they dismiss the

---

[a] Catullus considered Suffenus an insufferably bad poet and as blind to his own errors out of excessive self-regard. Cf. Catullus, *Carmina* 22.

[b] *Supplementis ad acta eruditorum Lipsiensia*. A reprint of this review along with a German translation are included in G/K, 586–97.

most excellent argument through which[3] the world is understood to be created"—he himself says this, not I, etc.

There are cases in which, by changing my words, our distinguished gentleman at the same time so changed their sense that I seem to have said wholly different things. He says that I call "a being that would exist as the determination of another, or can be so, an accident," adding "therefore that which cannot exist as the determination of another, will be substance." Both of these manifestly contradict my §191. For me, substance is that which can exist even if it is not the determination (note, character, predicate) of another. What truly cannot exist unless it is a determination (note, character, predicate) of another, I call an accident. My pleasure in taking the opportunity to give an account of such definitions grows in proportion to the narrowness of the margin by which Aristotle departed from the truth in regard to them, along with the Scholastics, his so-called disciples, and Descartes. And this applies even to Spinoza, who, based upon an error that is supposed to be almost infinitely small, was nevertheless able to fabricate a fatal scheme for subverting religion itself, and thereby teaching by his illustrious example how true is the saying of Lucretius:

Small is the deviation of the elements.[a]

Aristotle had called substance "that which can neither be said about any subject, nor inheres in any subject."[b] *Sonerus*,[c] in his rare *Metaphysics*, says: "Substance is the ultimate subject of all predicates." Again: "substances are not said about other things, but all the rest are said about them."[d] Of the more recent writers who admire the philosophy that they have inherited from their fathers and grandfathers, the wise *Aepinus*[e] (I pass over others in silence) saw that it cannot be rightly denied that certain substances inhere in others, for instance in subjects; hence he calls "substance a being existing through itself, i.e. that which is either clearly not in another, or is indeed in another but such that it is a part or a copart of it, and such that it can be separated from it and exist separately without it."[f] I certainly would not wish to make this explanation my own; nevertheless, in consideration of his account, I did not call substance

---

[a] *Parvum est clinamen principiorum.* This is not a literal quotation. Lucretius writes: "*id facit exiguum clinamen principiorum* [a meager deviation of the elements causes this]," *De rerum natura*, II: 292. This is Lucretius' recipe for the will: small but free deviations of the mind's elements (atoms) constitute the will.

[b] Baumgarten's rendering of *Metaphysics* VII (1028b 36).

[c] I.e. Ernst Soner (1572–1612) was a professor of medicine and philosophy at Altdorf who composed a few hightly regarded commentaries on Aristotle including *Problemata miscellanea ex physicis et metaphysicis* (1610) and *Commentarium in libros XII Metaphysicae Aristotelis* (1657). Posthumously Soner became a famous voice of Socinianism, for which Leibniz criticized him in the *Theodicy* (§266). Prior to his discovery of Soner's Socinian beliefs, Leibniz describe him as having "contributed a great many things to the correct comprehension of Aristotle" (*Preface to an Edition of Nizolius*, G 4: 155).

[d] *Commentarium in libros XII Metaphysicae Aristotelis*, 302, as noted in G/K, 522.

[e] I.e. Franz Albrecht Aepinus (1673–1750), who was a professor of logic and theology at Rostock and the author of *Introductio in philosophiam* (1714).

[f] *Introductio in philosophiam*, P. 2, *Philosophia Transcendentalis sive Metaphysica*, P. 1, ch. 3, §. 2. The quotation given by Baumgarten differs slightly from that found in the 1714 edition, which reads: "A substance is either a being that clearly does not exist in another, or indeed does exist in another but such that it is a part or copart of that in which it exists, and such that it can be separated from it and also exist separately without it." See G/K, 533.

that which cannot exist as the determination or a predicate of another, as our distinguished gentleman imputes to me. I do not think that the concept of substance chiefly concerns whether something exists as a determination or predicate of another, nor whether it cannot exist as a predicate of another. Rather, I think that it chiefly concerns this: whether it could exist without being the determination or predicate of another. Along with wise Aepinus, I concede the first to be true of many substances and for that reason I cannot hold the second to be true of all. The third, however, is appropriate for all substances and for these alone. Hence for me the so-called defining characteristic is found in the well-worn expression "subsisting through itself." In order to capture the same thing clearly and distinctly Descartes adds in his *Fourth Set of Responses*: "that is, to be able to exist without the aid of any other substance,"[a] and in his *Principles of Philosophy*, Part 1, no. 15:[b] "By substance we can understand nothing other than that thing which exists in such a way that it requires nothing else to exist. And indeed we can think of only one substance that plainly would need nothing, namely, God. We perceive that other things, however, can only exist through the aid of God's concurrence. And moreover, for that reason the name of substance is not univocally appropriate for God and for these others, etc."[c] Based on his own definition, if he had wanted to say it openly, Descartes would have to admit that there are no substances aside from God. For I believe that nobody, based upon this concept [of substance], would concede to Antoine le Grand[d] that a stone is a substance when he says in his *Inst. Phil. Cart.* [*Teachings of Philosophy, According to the Principles of René Descartes*] (p. 28 of my copy) that "substance is a thing which needs no other substance to exist, like God, a stone, the sky." With descriptions of substance like these, everything that Spinoza had deduced from his own definition can be deduced through the right amount of interconnected syllogisms more inevitably than a river flowing downhill,[e] such as when, in his *Ethics*, definition III (from his rare *Posthumous Works*, 1) he called "substance that whose concept does not require the concept of something else from which it must be formed." If we could agree to uphold the greater part of Descartes' definition, then substance would be a thing requiring no other thing, for instance a subject, to exist. Created substances could then be introduced as well, and the entire construction of Spinoza would fall apart. However, I avoided the term "subject" lest it become a stumbling block and therefore expressed the matter like this: that which

---

[a] AT 7: 226. In the text, Baumgerten cites his own copy of *Renati des Cartes, Opera Philosophica* (Frankfurt, 1692), 107.

[b] Baumgarten incorrectly has 15 instead of 51. Cf. Niggli, 98.

[c] AT 8: 24.

[d] Antoine Le Grand (1629–99) was a Catholic theologian and an early proponent of the Cartesian philosophy. Because he lived much of his later life in London and engaged with the most important philosophers of the period, his writings are central to the reception of Descartes in England. The *Institutio Philosophiae, secundum principia Renati Descartes* (1672) mentioned here was translated into English by Richard Blome under the title *An Entire Body of Philosophy, According to the Principles of the Famous Renati Des Cartes* (1694). The lines quoted by Baumgarten are from P. 1, A. 2, No. 1; the translation is ours.

[e] *Prono potius alveo*; perhaps a reference to Quintilian, who compares good oratory to the power of a river, to which the riverbed offers no resistance: *Ceterum quanto vehementior fluminum cursus est prono alveo ac nullas moras obiiciente quam inter obstantia saxa fractis aquis ac reluctantibus, tanto, quae connexa est et totis viribus fluit, fragosa atque interrupta melior oratio.* See Prudence J. Jones, *Reading rivers in Roman literature and culture* (Lahnam: Lexington Books, 2005), 52.

can exist without being the determination of another.[a] In so doing, I concede that no created substance can exist without being determined by, or the consequence of, another. However, "determined" differs sufficiently enough from the concepts of "determination" or "predicate" that the philosopher need not worry about some of the syllables and the agreement of the long vowels. Every created substance can exist without being the determination or predicate of another, even of God himself. God exists without being the predicate of anything else. And therefore He can exist in this manner. We thus have a definition that is neither applicable solely to God, like the Cartesian definition, nor solely to created substances, as is the case when one calls substance something enduring and modifiable.

But let us return to our distinguished gentleman's review. In relating that I demonstrate the principle of indiscernibles in the strict sense, he presents a demonstration of the principle of the denial of total congruence, given in §270, when §271 should have been placed before the eyes of the reader, where the principle of the denial of total similitude is proven, which is said [by him] to have been proven in the cited passage. Perhaps rather less well-known principles were deserving of attention, such as those of consequence,[b] of the denial of total dissimilitude[c] and of the denial of total equality.[d] I call "place" the position of an actual being that is simultaneous with others outside of it (§281). He himself says I call "place the actual position of a being that is simultaneous with others outside of it." When I concede chance, I deny pure chance;[e] but our distinguished gentleman says I "overthrow chance". What I affirm concerning living powers in §413, he says that I affirm concerning powers in general, which, were it true, I would have been in error. Nowhere did I deduce the motion of all matter from the denial of an entirely homogeneous matter; nevertheless, I am said to have done so. In §773, I showed that the propagation [of the human soul] by means of transmission can occur in two ways <*duplici ratione*> without embracing origination through such transmission. The second of these is not what is usually understood by "creation" and, it seems to me, cannot correctly be termed propagation through transmission either. I have not described the hypothesis of concreation, in which souls are propagated by transmission, as involving their creation by God, but rather in such a way that the souls of the parents would concur significantly in this operation.

Let us now turn to that through which our distinguished gentleman

dashes a black mark
with a sideways quill.[f]

In the usual manner, I call "confusion" the diversity of conjunction.[g] He thinks that a diversity in conjunction appears in the conjunction of magnetic parts with one another, but nevertheless that these parts cannot for that reason be called confused.

---

[a] This is a covert reference to and rejection of Wolff's definition: "A subject that is enduring and modifiable is called *substance*" (WO, §768).
[b] I.e. §23.
[c] I.e. §268.
[d] I.e. §272.
[e] I.e. §383.
[f] I.e. "crosses off"; cf. Horace, *Ars Poetica*, 446.
[g] I.e. §79.

Our distinguished gentleman seems, however, to confuse the conjunction of things that are different, if indeed there be such, both with the diversity of conjunction and the diversity of order, things that ought to be distinguished properly. The different parts in a magnet are conjoined in an order, or orders, by nature, such that the flux penetrating them can affect iron, causing the poles of a freely suspended piece to turn north and south, like friends joining one another with a kiss, and enemies fleeing from each other. Suppose that a magnet undergoes calcination or is crushed to powder; then its many parts will still be conjoined, but in a different way. Now, in these same parts there is a diversity of conjunction, some confusion, the destruction of a hidden mechanism, and it is characteristic of a magnet brought too near to a flame to be something weak like a comet.[a] I will concede without hesitation that in those things that need to be explained concerning the phenomena of some given and particular confusion, it is usually correct to take into account the goal [i.e. the final cause]. But perhaps that which is necessary for illustration is, for that reason, not necessary for definition.

Once again, we find a common objection to the well-known definition of perfection: Sometimes various things agree in one, e.g. the agreement of the fluids of a human body at death, or the agreement of winds gathering themselves together to blow over a house, and yet there is no perfection in these. And I will not deny that when I first turned my attention to ontology with greater care, I likewise was very close to defining perfection as the agreement of realities in one reality,[b] in which case, unless I am completely mistaken, there would have been a better agreement between me and our distinguished gentleman. I should explain here why I have not, however, changed the definition of *the illustrious Wolff*.[c] Since, as with the above concept of confusion, I am once again being blamed for a definition that I did not invent but rather borrowed from Wolff (and not without gratitude), may I be permitted, in defense of both, to explain whether I should have defined some things differently just because of a desire to change and innovate, or rather whether I should have done so because of well-considered and deliberated grounds for preserving or altering a definition. Perhaps after such an explanation a fair judge may conclude that *Johann Jakob Moser*,[d] a man most skilled in public law,[4] erred not only when reporting my age

[a] *flammaeque nimis propinqui magnetis parvus aliquis cometa.* This is a very dark passage. Niggli (see her endnote 46) translates it thus: "*und die Flamme des zu nahen Magneten erhält eine Art kleinen Kometen*": "and the flames of the Magnet that is too close preserve a sort of small comet." Gawlick and Kreimendahl do not translate it in the body of their text; instead, they provide a provisional translation only in endnote 67 through the pen of a colleague, Armin Emmel: "[...] *und [die Kraft] eines dem Feuer zu nahegebrachten Magneten [schwindet wie] ein kleiner Komet [in der Nähe der Sonne]*": "and [the force] of a magnet that has been brought too close to the fire [disappears like] a small comet [near the sun]." Whatever its precise meaning, this comparison was likely suggested by Baumgarten's reading of Kepler's *De Cometis*. Kepler had earlier made extensive use of the analogy between gravitational force and magnetism, and in this work considers the effect of the sun's heat on the constitution of a comet passing near it.
[b] In §94, Baumgarten takes over Wolff's definition of perfection as the agreement of many things in one thing. The point here is whether he should have said "realities" instead of "thing."
[c] WO, §503: "*Perfection* is agreement in variety, i.e. the agreement of many things that are mutually different from one another in one thing. I call *agreement* the tendency of several things to obtain the same thing. Perfection was called *transcendental goodness* by the scholastics."
[d] Johann Jakob Moser (1701–85), a famous jurist and pioneer of German constitutional law, was professor of law at Tübingen and Frankfurt on the Oder and a government advisor.

when it pleased him to mention me in §6 of his *Gedancken von der Verbindung der Weltweisheit, besonders der Wolfischen, mit der Theologie,* [*Thoughts on the Connection of Philosophy, in particular Wolff's, with Theology*].[a] I prove that every being is real in §136[5] of my work, that realities can only agree with realities (§140)[6] and negations only with negations (§139).[7] Hence, the one being that is mentioned in the Wolffian definition of perfection, and that can be called the determining ground of perfection or its focus, is real, because it is a being, because it is one. Since this could be inferred (§141),[8] it was not necessary for it to be expressly pointed out in the definition. Since it is already obvious to any expert in ontology that it is not possible for anything except realities to agree with this reality, it indeed does not seem to me something that must be added in a definition (§94)[9] according to a rather well-worn rule of logic: "Any note which is sufficiently determined by another does not enter[10] into a definition."[11] All the things that God possesses in himself are real. Hence the agreement in him of many in one is the agreement of all of his predicates or determinations in one being, which is supreme. In finite beings there are always some realities and some negations. Insofar as the former cannot fail to agree in one, but the former cannot agree in one unless it is real, there is perfection in every finite being. Insofar as those things that I call negations[12] are not possible without realities and nevertheless must be in every finite thing, and indeed without agreeing with the realities, there is imperfection in every finite thing. Nothing need now be said in response to the examples of our distinguished gentleman until it is shown that in death and in the collapse of a house there is no reality and no perfection. As the logician would state: It is invalid to conclude from the denial of medical and architectural perfection to the denial of every perfection, including the cosmological and even more so the ontological. Whoever looks at a thing with metaphysical eyes ought to seek a broader horizon than the one whose

skyline opens no more than three forearms.[b]

That evil which I, along with the illustrious Leibniz, call metaphysical, our distinguished gentleman views as unsuitable to being called evil, although he soon furls his sails, providing the reason that "the nominal definitions of philosophers are arbitrary." Indeed, by all that is sacred to philosophy, I would ask all those who judge my *Metaphysics* not to think that I am one of those who, misunderstanding this rule of the logicians, unhesitatingly take it upon themselves to dare anything they want in fashioning definitions contrary to the received meaning. When we retain the well-established authority <*potestates*> of words, or invent them, or, as it were, fix ones that are fluid and vague, the choice ought to be prudent and circumspect. But I believed that through just such a choice, rather than through a blind one, whatever is opposed to metaphysical good, as the ground of such imperfection, is to be called metaphysical evil. Now the supreme perfection of God is truly a metaphysical good. To the extent that this perfection is

---

[a] Moser remarks that the foremost supporters of Wolff's philosophy feel it necessary, in accordance with fashion, to make innumerable and often arbitrary changes to his ideas, *even the twenty year-old Baumgarten*. Baumgrarten was in fact probably twenty-six when this was written. The point here is that Moser is also in error in suggesting that Baumgarten made changes to Wolff for other than philosophical reasons. The entire passage by Moser is reprinted in Niggli, 191–2.
[b] Cf. Virgil, *Eclogues* III: 105.

denied in finite things, even through their own essences, an imperfection is posited whose ground is correctly called metaphysical evil insofar as it is absolutely necessary.

In §389 I had said that if this world is a substance, then "the infinite substance is not unique <unicam>," because it had already been proven that the world must exist outside of the infinite substance. Our distinguished gentleman admits that he does not understand what this might mean, supposing it to be a typological blemish. To be sure, this is no error, neither by me nor by the printer. In §388–91 I refute metaphysical Spinozism, which asserts that infinite substance, or God, is the unique substance. I oppose this, saying in §389: "Infinite substance is not unique," i.e. it is a substance, just like we are accustomed to saying the Sun of our planetary system is not unique, i.e. it is a sun, or like the king of France is not the unique king, i.e. he is a king.[13] Thus, §390 ends with these very clear words: "The infinite substance is not the unique substance." And thus §391 begins: "Infinite power is not the unique power." Although I believe that I spoke perspicuously enough at the time for all those who do not hurriedly cast their eyes over only one <unicam> line, I have nevertheless still added the term "substance" to §389 in this edition.[a]

And when I added "kingdom of grace" in parenthesis as a metonym for the pneumatic world,[b] our distinguished gentleman admonishes me for calling the pneumatic world the kingdom of grace even though there are spirits estranged from the world of grace. Hence I need to clarify, first, that I used synonymous terms found in the writings of others next to those that are to be defined, and enclosed them in parenthesis so that the two may also be more easily distinguished from each another, and [secondly] that I certainly did not thoughtlessly appropriate the parenthetical metonyms that have been rejected, whose defects even now I usually enumerate in my lectures. Thus, I would never have called the essence of a thing its nature[c]—whence remarkable confusions would arise. Nevertheless, others have spoken in this manner. Enough of that. Now, it is well known that Leibniz called all the spirits the kingdom of grace.[d] Therefore I added that label.[e] I will certainly not concede to the objections of our distinguished gentleman, except in the theological sense. When the terms are philosophically understood, it is false to hold that the spirits estranged from the kingdom of grace cannot be considered as its members, and companions. After all, universal social law and especially philosophical civil law both teach that precisely because rebels do not remain submissive subjects (since they wish to escape from the power of supreme rulers and from association with them) they rightly and deservedly remain subjects, whether they want to or not. It is the same [in the kingdom of grace].

In regard to this new edition, I would have preferred to shorten it rather than to expand it as is usually the practice. Yet, there were no showy ornaments[f] that could be pruned back advantageously, unless perhaps a scythe could have been unsheathed

---

[a] Baumgarten inserts the word "substance" at the very end of §389 in the second edition. He also inserts "substance" in §390. The Latin *unicum* can mean both "only," as in "the only substance," and "one of a kind," as in "this painting is one of a kind." The reviewer incorrectly took Baumgarten to be saying that God is not one of a kind, when in fact he was saying that He is not the only substance. The insertion of "substance" in subsequent editions removes this ambiguity.

[b] I.e. §403.

[c] In §40 Baumgarten puts "nature" in a list of bracketed terms apposite "essence."

[d] *Monadology*, §87: "*le Regne Moral de la Grace*"

[e] In §404, 434, and 464, Baumgarten parenthetically adds "kingdom of grace." The reference in §464 was added in the second edition; the other two are there from the first.

[f] Cf. Horace, *Ars Poetica* 445f; cf. Niggli n. 60.

against the lists that have been put forth of degrees found in more powerful things.[a] Indeed, a summary of the primary themes of metaphysics does not demand these. But I was absolutely unwilling to erase any of the metaphysico-mathematical contributions I had made because I have read[14] that they have long been desired, and because I have been taught by my experience that through them a new sphere of meditation, as it were, is often opened up, and because in the end it will grant you, a thinker, an indisputably singular joy alongside a million other amusements if you were to conceive what is the greatest of that which is real and positive and thus discover God and the divine.[b] I wanted these to be set in different type, so that they would be that much more easily distinguished from the rest of the book, should someone wish either to inspect these alone or to skip them entirely.[c] I changed much, especially in the doctrine of the immortality of the mind.[d] I divided longer sections into shorter ones, perceiving in lectures that there is then a certain advantage if, as it were, smaller goals are reached more often, just as a discussion that seems to be about just one topic must be spread over many hours and not held all in one breath. I added some new definitions and proofs, such as those concerning the perfections of thinking,[e] thinking matter,[f] and pre-established harmony, which, in both its universal and psychological sense, I have changed from a hypothesis to a theorem. I have added no examples in this edition, since I have not yet changed my opinion found in the preface to the first edition. I have been asked to produce these separately, and I think this could be the more correct way to proceed. I have indeed already sketched out a sufficient number of pertinent things on paper, but I have never promised to publish any of these. Taken completely unaware, I was surprised that the catalogue of the Leipzig book fair has actually promised[15] examples of this sort, as if they were already about to appear at the fair.

Some friends have publically urged me to write about logic, the law of nature, or other chapters of practical philosophy in a manner similar to how I have touched upon metaphysics and ethics. Nevertheless, until there is a publisher who adds this one to his reasonable conditions—that my works reach my residence such that they may be submitted to the press after I have corrected what I largely judge as necessary for my own writing—then, the less leisure I find after [my] lectures, and the more certainly I am persuaded that the literary world can do without my trifles without any loss, that much more calmly will I altogether abstain from painstakingly writing such booklets.

Given at Frankfurt on the Oder, 14 September 1742

---

[a] Baumgarten is referring to his "mathematics of intensive quantities," whose principles we find in §165–90 (i.e. part I, chapter II, section VI, a section heading not inserted until the third edition), and whose application we find throughout the rest of the *Metaphysics*.

[b] Cf. St. Thomas (ST I, Q 1, Art. 5, ad 1), where he, referring to Aristotle's *De Animalibus* XI, says the slightest knowledge of the greatest things is more desirable than the greatest knowledge of slightest things.

[c] In the second edition, Baumgarten had these set in italics. This convention was removed in all subsequent editions.

[d] I.e. part II, chapter II, section IIII, "The immortality of the human soul" (§776–81; this section heading was inserted in the second edition). Three of the section's six paragraphs were entirely re-written.

[e] I.e. §515.

[f] I.e. §742. In the first edition, thinking matter is not mentioned.

To the Listener of Good Will
[Preface to the First Edition] (1739)[a]

Whom better should I address than YOU when custom dictates that I preface these pages, pages which I could almost have declared as having been written for you alone? There is no reason why I should apologize to YOU for once again offering a metaphysics after an infinite number of similarly titled works have been published. I have no greater idea as to how many such works have emerged from those most repeated words of Aristotle—μετὰ τὰ φυσικά[b]—than I do as to how many mortals have preceded me since the world began. May this *Metaphysics*, which has been delivered, devoted, and dedicated[c] chiefly for YOUR benefit, and YOURS alone, endeavor to declare itself the first. When I call upon YOU, I am invoking that circle of the most talented, those who are very excited by anything arduous, those fellow soldiers who struggle in the most friendly[1] rivalries with me through the gateway of the humanities and the fore-court of a more exact logic into the inner sancta[2] of the first principles of science. Anyone who considers the matter will easily see, first, why I had to refrain in this work from repeating in writing what I usually treat with care in my lectures on rational science;[d] and second, why I could not accomplish in a printed work what is expected of extemporaneous speakers when they lecture on a book, such that I also could have provided examples, doubts, anecdotes, and other illustrations in connecting the arguments. But without these, somebody might ask, what do YOU have other than a desiccated skeleton of metaphysics? Provided that the bones are strong enough and joined well enough together—believe me, I will be singularly thankful. Once YOU come [to the lectures], not only will you see but also hear: behold, the nerves grow, flesh is added, and it is covered by skin, and neither color nor life will be entirely wanting in the good lady, unless she should appear otherwise to YOU. Further, placing YOU right before my eyes like this, as the type of person I had briefly depicted above, DEAR READER, I ignore without difficulty the malevolent whispers of those who, establishing some pretext for obscure reasons that I know not, are poised to undermine YOUR favor with me, a favor for which I am solemnly grateful to YOU. Until now there has been no shortage of those who enjoy hearing me discuss philosophical themes, those who

---

[a] The preface of the first edition does not bear a title in any of the seven editions. They all, however, indicate it with a running head, "PRAEFATIO" (PREFACE) on all but the first page.

[b] Lit.: "after the physics."

[c] "delivered, devoted, and dedicated": it is impossible to carry over Baumgarten's beautifully cascading tricolon: *data, dicata, dedicata*. Please see Niggli, 89.

[d] Baumgarten also lectured on logic. His logic manual was published the year before his death as *Acroasis logica* (1761).

are proving (or will prove) through experience to the educated that they themselves have examined and distinctly grasped, in a sufficient manner, that which I have either discussed with them in public, or put on paper.[3] Inasmuch as it has been, and will be, permitted to cite living witnesses of this sort, there is no reason why I should regret[4] that very rule that I have resolved I must follow, since my task has been not solely to learn, but also to promote learning: *To regulate whatever I say so that a person of average intelligence is able to know clearly and perspicuously what I mean when mildly familiar with the doctrines that I offer and that must be taught, and when only mildly interested in that which I treat and that must be learned.* Weighing whatever I am about to expound to YOU according to this law, I will neither seize upon novelties because they are recent, nor spurn the old because it seems obsolete.

Whatever there is in my work that I have heard or read previously, I have since contemplated and made it my own, yet still in such a way that should be agreeable to all good persons. I now publically give back to everybody what is their own without laying any claim to it, reserving the legitimately transferred law of usufruct for YOU and me alone. I will never deny, in particular, that my knowledge of the truths shared with YOU in this booklet has been very much spurred on by the thoughts of Leibniz, Wolff, Bilfinger,[a] and Reusch[b], thoughts which Germany has graciously[5] welcomed from those illustrious and most celebrated reformers of metaphysics among us. What bubbling spring is so pure that it does not cause some small stone to roll around at the bottom? As distant as I am from blind agreements in philosophizing, that much, nay even more, am I happy to be a stranger to the hard heads of those men who not only conceal and stop up from others, as much as they can, the springs from which they greedily irrigate their own streams, but who even disturb these, and proclaim them to be poisoned or even inspired by heaven knows what bad star sign, and who do this so that it may more easily seem to the ignorant that they have invented[6] that which they offer, and so that others will accept as from them what they all nevertheless drink together from a common fountain. You have, READER OF GOOD WILL, those sources, which you may consult when I have not entirely satisfied YOU and through which you can correct me if I, unwitting, have committed errors.[7]

Concerning the writing style, I will say this. As much as the present style of my studies and the stiff precepts of the philosophical pen seem to tear me away from the delights of the purer richness of speech, both here on these pages and elsewhere, that much more do I keep them in mind, and that much more will I follow them, to the

---

[a] Georg Bernhard Bilfinger (1693–1750), a Leibnizian, was professor of mathematics and moral philosophy in Tübingen and a professor of philosophy at St. Petersburg. He is the author of *Dilucidationes de Deo, anima humana, mundo et generalioribus rerum affectibus* (1725). Kant discusses Bilfinger's *De viribus corpori moto isitis et illarum mensura* (1728) in *Thoughts on the True Estimation of Living Forces* (1746), §§71–91. In §20 of the same work, Kant adopts Bilfinger's rule that when two philosophers of good sense disagree on a point, one should seek the truth in a middle position wherein each are in part shown to be correct. Hinske, among others, sees this irenic view as characteristic of Kant's intellectual constitution and as presaging his treatment of the Antinomies as well as the critical synthesis of empiricism and rationalism. See his *Kants Weg*, 123–7.
[b] Johann Peter Reusch (1691–1758), a Wolffian, was professor of logic, metaphysics and theology in Jena and author of *Systema logicum* (1734) among other writings. Kant displays a familiarity with this work in his lectures on logic and in *On a Discovery* (AA 3:246).

extent that this is acceptable. And if I fail to achieve such effects, then I will pursue them all the more ardently. Nevertheless, to pursue the charms of speech; to seek various decorations; to use circumlocutions instead of traditionally accepted words, or at least those that are traditional within metaphysics; to refrain from explanations of things that Cicero did not express with his quite spotless voice—these I did not consider my task. Nor was it judged to be mine by those who are celebrated not only for their philosophical but also for their literary triumphs. However, if it was possible for something to be written less grating to the Latin ear, but[8] with the same brevity and in harmony with common modes of speech, then I beg your pardon for this as well. I also wish that[9] I did not have to ask forgiveness for the typographical errors. But since these pages were not printed where I currently live, the messenger, who was hastening to return, scarcely gave me as much leisure as I would have wished when I sat down to do the corrections; I was not permitted to correct the final page proofs entirely. Thus anything infelicitous, unwilled by me, should be avoided by consulting the list of the more serious errors that had to be attached, and by YOUR good will—you who are reading this.

If there perhaps are readers [of this work] who cannot attend [my] lectures,[10] but whose teachings might still be very useful to me, I will respect their fair judgment, accept however they wish to admonish me, and, above all, look forward to their refutations. However, I ask one thing from anyone who would differ in regard to matters they suppose are quite serious. May they not believe themselves to have been injured when I—compelled by the powers of the truth and duty, so much as I now indeed judge—speak or write something of which they do not approve. If they cannot tolerate what I offer, let them rise up with those arms permitted by religion: may they tolerate a man who shuns nothing more than those hostilities of which he would be accused, a man who grieves nothing more than being entangled in such rivalries through no treachery of his own. However, YOU, oh[11] friends and companions in my philosophical struggles, YOU MOST HONORED LISTENERS, enjoy these, my [words], gladly. Think over the modest powers of a fair and good man, and if I deserve it, continue to love me.

Halle, April 1739.

Synopsis[1]

I) Prolegomena to metaphysics (§1–3).
II) Treatise.
  1) Ontology (Part 1).
    A) Prolegomena to ontology (§4–6).
    B) Treatise on the predicates of beings
      (a) The internal predicates
        α. Universal (Chapter I).
          (א) The possible (Section I, §7–18).
          (ב) The connected (Section II, §19–33).
          (ג) The Being (Section III), whose determinations are:
            𝔄. Either realities or negations (§34–6).
            𝔅. Either external or internal (§37, 38) and these are:
              a. Either essential qualities, or affections (§39–66).
              b. Either quantities or qualities (§67–71).
          (ד) The one (Section IV, §72–7).
          (ה) The true, under which:
            𝔄. On order (Section V, §78–88).
            𝔅. On the true (Section VI, §89–93).
          (ו) The Perfect (Section VII, §94–100).
        β. Disjunctive (Chapter II)
          (א) The necessary and the contingent (Section I, §101–23).
          (ב) The alterable and the inalterable (Section II, §124–34).
          (ג) The real and the negative (Section III, §135–47).
          (ד) The singular and the universal (Section IV, §148–54)
          (ה) The whole and the part, under which:
            𝔄. On the whole and the part (Section V, §155–64)
            𝔅. The first principles of the mathematics of intensive quantities (Section VI, §165–90).
          (ו) Substance and accident, under which:
            𝔄. On substance and accident (Section VII, §191–204).
            𝔅. On state (Section VII, §191–204).
          (ז) The simple and composite,
            𝔄. Generally (Section IX, §224–9).
            𝔅. The monad specifically (Section X, §230–45).
          (ח) The finite and the infinite (Section XI, §246–64).
      (b) The external or relative predicates (Chapter III).
        α. The same and the different (Section I, §265–79).
        β. The simultaneous and the successive, under which:

            (א) On the simultaneous (Section II, §280–96).

            (ב) On the successive (Section III, §297–306).

          γ. The cause and the caused,

            (א) In general (Section IV, §307–18).

            (ב) In specific, under which:

                𝔄. On the efficient cause (Section V, §319–35).

                𝔅. On utility (Section VI, §336–40).

                ℭ. On the rest of the general causes (Section VII, §341–6).

         δ. The sign and the signified (Section VIII, §347–50).

   2) Cosmology (Part II).

     A) Prolegomena (§351–3).

     B) Treatise on the world.

        (a) On the concept of the world (Chapter I).

          α. The affirmative concept (Section I, §345–79).

          β. The negative concept (Section II, §380–91).

        (b) On the parts of the world (Chapter II).

          α. On the simple parts (Section I).

            (א) In general (§392–401).

            (ב) On spirits in specific (§402–5).

          β. On the composite parts

            (א) Their genesis from elements (Section II, §406–29)

            (ב) Their nature (Section III, §430–35).

        (c) On the perfection of the world (Chapter III), and

          α. On its subject, the best world, whose

            (א) Idea is observed (Section I, §436–47).

            (ב) Commerce of substances is observed, and the system for explaining it (Section II, §448–65).

          β. On the means of the world

            (א) On the natural means (Section III, §466–73).

            (ב) On the supernatural means

               𝔄. Generally (Section IV, §474–81).

               𝔅. On the hypothetical possibility of supernatural beings specifically (Section V, §482–500).

   3) Psychology (Part III).

     A) Prolegomena (§501–3).

     B) Treatise on psychology

        (a) Empirical psychology (Chapter I).

          α. On the existence of the soul (Section I, §504–18).

          β. On the faculties of the soul

            (א) The cognitive faculty

               𝔄. Inferior

                  𝔞. In general (section II, §519–33).

                  𝔟. In specific, on Sense (Section III, §534–56). Imagination (Section IV, §557–71).

Perspicaciousness (Section V, §572–8).

Memory (Section VI, §579–88).

The faculty of invention (Section VII, §589–94).

Foresight (Section VIII, §595–605).

Judgment (Section IX, §606–9).

Anticipation (Section X, §610–18).

The faculty of characterization (Section XI, §619–23).

𝕭. Superior

　　a. On the intellect generally (Section XII, §624–39).

　　b. On reason specifically (Section XIII, §640–50).

(ב) The appetitive faculty

𝕬. In general, under which:

　　a. On indifference (Section XIV, §651–55).

　　b. On pleasure and displeasure (Section XV, §656–62).

　　c. On desire and aversion (Section XVI, §663–75).

𝕭. In specific,

　　a. On the inferior appetitive faculty (Section XVII, §676–88).

　　b. On the superior appetitive faculty

　　　1) Willing and refusal (Section XVIII, §689–99).

　　　2) Freedom, and

　　　　A. That which is presupposed of it

　　　　　a) Spontaneity (Section XIX, §700–7).

　　　　　b) Choice (Section XX, §708–18).

　　　　B. Its nature (Section XXI, §719–32).

γ. On commerce with the body (Section XXII, §733–9).

(b) Rational psychology (Chapter II), under which:

α. On the nature of the soul (Section I, §740–60).

β. On the commerce of the soul with the body (Section II, §761–9).

γ. On the origin of the soul (Section III, §770–5).

δ. On the immortality of the soul (Section IV, §776–81).

ε. On the state of the soul after death (Section V, §782–91).

ζ. Compared with the non-human souls of:

　(א) Animals (Section VI, §792–5).

　(ב) Spirits (Section VII, §796–9).

4) Natural theology (Part IV).

A) Prolegomena (§800–2).

B) Treatise on God

(a) On the concept of God (Chapter I), in which is considered:

α. The existence of God (Section I), to which belongs:

Reality (§803–20).

Unity (§821).

Truth (§822).

Necessity (§823–7).

Sanctity (§828–9).

Substantiality (§830).
Omnipotence (§831–7).
Simplicity (§838).
Immutability (§839–42).
Infinitude (§843–5).
Uniqueness (§846–8).
Eternity (§849–50).
Impassivity (§851).
Nature (§852–60).
Immeasurability (§861).
Incomprehensibility (§862).
β. The intellect of God (Chapter II).
Existence (§863–5).
Object (§866–78).
Infallibility (§879).
Subjective certitude (§880–1).
Wisdom (§882–8).
Omniscience (§889).
γ. The will of God (Section III).
(א) Proportionality (§890–4).
(ב) Freedom (§895–9).
(ג) Inscrutability (§900).
(ד) Righteousness (§901–2).
(ה) Goodness
𝔄. Faithfulness (§903–5).
𝔅. Justice
a. Remuneratory (§906–7).
b. Punitive (§908–16).
(ו) Impartiality (§908–16).
(ז) Sincerity (§919–25).
(b) On the operations of God (Chapter II).
α. On creation (Section I).
(א) The object of creation (§926–41).
(ב) The end of creation (Section II, §942–9).
β. On providence (Section III).
(א) Which conserves (§950–3).
(ב) Which concurs (§954–62).
(ג) Which governs (§963).
(ד) Evil
𝔄. The providence which impedes it (§964–8).
𝔅. The providence which permits it (§969–70).
(ה) Which reigns (§971–5).
(ו) Which discerns (Section IV, §976–81).
(ז) Which reveals (Section V, §982–1000).

Prolegomena to Metaphysics[a]

§1

METAPHYSICS is the science of the first principles[b] in human knowledge.[c]

Eberhard's note: These first principles of knowledge contain the most general and abstract concepts, and therefore do not contain concepts from the *outer senses*. One can therefore call those concepts *non-sensible* (*unsinnliche*) that are contained in metaphysics. Of these some are non-sensible, because they are concepts of simple substances, others, because they apply to the simple and the composite. One can call the former *extrasensible* <*aussersinnliche*>, the latter *supersensible*[d] <*übersinnliche*>.

§2

To metaphysics belong ontology, cosmology, psychology, and natural theology.

§3

NATURAL METAPHYSICS[e] is the knowledge of the things falling within the purview of metaphysics that is acquired through their mere employment; it is useful to add to this the artificial metaphysics defined in §1 for the sake of (1) the development of concepts,[1] (2) the determination and conception of first propositions, (3) the consistency and certitude of proofs, etc.

conception] distinctness

---

[a] On the relation between this section and Kant's *Prolegomena to Any Future Metaphysics*, see Introduction, p. 29ff.
[b] Wolff: "That which contains the ground of something else in itself is called a principle" (WO §866).
[c] Wolff uses no such definition. "However, ontology, general cosmology and pneumatics are called by the common name 'metaphysics.' Metaphysics, therefore, is the science of being, of the world in general and of spirits" (PD §79). Baumgarten seems closer to Aristotle in *Metaphysics* (Bk. A, Ch. 2 and 3). For Kant's criticism of this definition see CPR A 843/B 871 ff., AA 29: 749, and AA 29: 946.
[d] According to Grimm, this term originated from the mysticism of Jacob Böhme, but only became popular after Kant's usage. However, before its appearance in Eberhard's *Vorbereitung zur natürlichen Theologie* in 1781 (and again in this work), Kant had used it only twice, both times in an unpublished sketch of the Appendix to the Transcendental Analytic.
[e] The distinction here between natural and artificial (not revealed) metaphysics again goes back to Aristotle (*Metaphysics*, Bk. A, Ch. 1), but also has roots in Wolff: "Commonplace and confused ontological notions constitute a particular species of natural ontology. Whence (WO §19) natural ontology can be defined as the collection of confused notions corresponding to the abstract terms with which we express general judgments about a being, acquired by the common use of the mind's faculties" (WO §21). Natural metaphysics is only mentioned once by Leibniz in passing (G 4: 380). Kant, however, modifies and makes extensive use of Baumgarten's version of the distinction.

PART I: ONTOLOGY

Prologomena

§4

ONTOLOGY (ontosophia, metaphysics (cf. §1), universal metaphysics, architectonics,[1] first philosophy) is the science of the more general predicates of a being.[a]

general predicates] general and more abstract predicates

§5

The more general predicates of a being are the first principles of human knowledge. Therefore, ontology rightly <*cum ratione*> belongs (§2) to metaphysics (§1, 4).

§6

Ontology contains the predicates of a being (§4): (I) the internal 1) universal predicates that are in each and every single thing,[2] and the internal 2) disjunctive predicates, of which only one of a pair is in each and every single thing;[3] and the (II) relative predicates.[4]

relative] external

Chapter I. The universal internal predicates of a being

Section I. The possible

§7

Nothing—which is negative (cf. §54), something that cannot be represented, something impossible, something inconsistent, (an absurdity cf. §13),[5] something involving or implying a contradiction, something contradictory—*is both A and not-A.*[b] Or, there is no subject of contradictory predicates, or, nothing both is and is not. 0=A + not-A. *This proposition* is called *the principle of contradiction,* and *it is absolutely primary.*[c]

---

[a] Wolff: "*Ontology or first philosophy* is the science of being in general, or insofar as it is being" (WO §1). Since in Latin the indeterminate comparative is sometimes used where English would prefer a superlative, one might be tempted to go still further and read the last part of Baumgarten's definition as "most general predicates of a being," which seems to make more sense. However, Meier renders it as "more general or more abstract predicates of a thing," which we have followed.

[b] Translators have had much difficulty with this sentence because of the large separation between the parts in italics, which form the main sentence, and have tended to take the subject to be "*Nihil negativum*" (i.e. "negative nothing") rather than simply "Nihil", which we believe is most correct. This is supported also by Meier's translation. Wolff: "We call *nothing* that to which no concept corresponds" (WO §57). "What neither is nor is possible is what one calls nothing" (VGG §28).

[c] Leibniz and Wolff also assert the primacy of the principle of contradiction. However, Baumgarten's treatment differs substantially from theirs. Leibniz rather inconsistently identifies the principle with the assertion that what involves a contradiction is false (*Monadology* no. 31; G 6: 612), that of two contradictory propositions one must be true and the other false (*Theodicy*, "Observations" no. 14, G 6: 413), that a proposition cannot be both true and false at the same moment (Correspondence

§8

That which is not nothing is SOMETHING:[a] the representable, whatever does not involve a contradiction, whatever is not both A and not-A, is POSSIBLE (§7).[b]

POSSIBLE] POSSIBLE, and a THING

§9

What is both A and not-A is not something (§8) and hence it is nothing and something contradictory (§7); or a subject implying something contradictory has no predicates; or, whatever both is and is not, is nothing. A + not-A=0.[6]

is not something ... and something contradictory] is not possible, consequently impossible

§10

Every possible thing is either A, or not-A, or neither (§8). Now, what is neither is nothing, because it would be both of these (§9). Therefore, *every possible thing is either A, or not-A*, or, for every subject, one out of each pair of contradictory predicates is suitable. *This proposition* is called *the principle of the excluded third or middle between two contradictories.*

§11

Every possible A is A, or, *a thing is whatever it is,*[c] or, every subject is its own predicate. If you deny this, then some possible A is not-A (§10), and hence both A and not-A, or nothing (§7), which is impossible (§9). *This proposition* is called *the principle of affirmation <positionis> or identity.*

§12[d]

When the impossible is posited, CONTRADICTION ARISES.[e] What not only appears to be, but also is, is called TRUE. What only appears to be, but is not, is called APPARENT.[f] Hence, any contradiction that arises is either true or apparent.

---

with Clarke, Second Letter no. 1, G 7: 355), that every proposition must be either true or false (Correspondence with Clarke, Fifth Letter no. 129, G 7: 420; also *New Essays* Bk. 2 Ch. 2, G 5: 343). Wolff's formulation is this: "It cannot happen that the same thing both is and is not, or what is the same, if A is B, it is false that the same A is not B" (WO §28). The originality of Baumgarten's definition lies in its formulation of the principle of contradiction as the very definition of nothing. See previous note.
[a] Wolff: "*Something* is that to which some concept corresponds" (WO §59).
[b] Same as Wolff (WO §85). Wolff goes on to prove in WO §102 and §103 that being possible and being something logically imply one another.
[c] Kant E3489, 1769–77: "expresses tautological propositions"
[d] Kant E3493, 1769–71? 1773–5?? (in the right-hand margin): "Apparent contradictions in the governance of the world. In the secrets. In the riddles. In the flashes of wit. That become resolved. A book would be shorter etc. etc. In the writing of a great man the contradictions are regarded as [merely] apparent."
[e] Kant E3490, 1776–89: "Boring pastime is a contradiction in terms. Amusing pastime is a tautology."
[f] Kant E3491, 1769–78: "visible darkness"
Kant E3492, 1770s: "a white lie <pia fraus>" ["Pius fraud" would be a more literal translation.]

§13

When A and not-A are posited, a contradiction[a] arises (§9, §12). When A and B are posited and by means of this not-A is also posited, something impossible is posited[b] (§9), and hence a contradiction arises (§12). The former is a PATENT[c] CONTRADICTION (direct, immediate, and explicit), while the latter is a LATENT[d] CONTRADICTION (indirect, hidden, mediated, and implicit). That in which a true contradiction is patent is ABSURD[e] (inconsistent).

§14[f]

A GROUND <*ratio*> (cf. §640, condition, hypothesis) is that from which it is knowable why something is.[g] What has a ground, or, that of which something is a ground, is said to be its CONSEQUENCE and DEPENDENT[7] on it.[8] The predicate by virtue of which something is either ground or consequence, or both, is the NEXUS.[9, h]

NEXUS] CONNECTION, combination and conjunction <*Der Zusammenhang, die Verbindung und Verknüpfung*>

§15[i]

Whatever is considered, but not in a nexus with those things that are posited

---

[a] Kant E3494, 1764–70: "explicit and implicit identity and contradiction"
[b] G/K: "Through the positing of A and B and at the same time of non-A something impossible is posited"
[c] Kant E3494, 1764–70: "not demonstrated"
    Kant E3496, 1776–89: "a white lie is a latent [contradiction]"
[d] Kant E3494, 1764–70: "demonstrated"
    Kant E3495, 1764–77: "a white lie"
[e] Kant E3497, 1776–89: "also tautology"
[f] Kant E3498, 1764–9 (at beginning of §14): "Ground is other than the grounded being./Nothing contains the ground in itself./Before, after. Antecedent and consequent."
    Kant E3500, 1770–8? (in right-hand margin beside §14, under E3499): "The real ground of actuality is the efficient cause."
    Kant E3499, 1764–78 (next to §14 at the beginning): "Logical, real opposition."
    Kant E3501, 1775–9 (above §14): "Those things are connected of which, when one is posited, the other is posited."
    Kant E3502, 1775–9 (in §14): "A condition is that which, when not posited, another is not posited."
    Kant E3503, 1775–9 (in §14): "When the grounded being is posited, the ground is not posited, but required."
    Kant E3504, 1775–9 (in §14): "Ground is either analytic (logical) or synthetic (real ground)."
    Kant E3505, 1775–9 (in §14): "A ground is that which, when posited, another is necessarily posited."
    Kant E3506, 1775–9 (in §14): "When a grounded being is not posited, the ground is not posited."
    Kant E3507, 1775–9 (in §14): "The ground is that which, when something is posited (when I posit it), another is posited (*added later*: determinately) according to a rule. / It is not valid to go from the grounded to the ground. / Condition: that which, when not posited, another is not posited."
[g] Wolff does not define ground as such in WO but in VGG writes that "the *ground* is that through which one can understand why something is" (§29). See the footnote to §20 below.
[h] This is already a significant departure from Wolff, who does not treat nexus or connection at all until the first pages of WC. Since ontology and general cosmology are strictly differentiated by the fact that the former provides the principles for the latter, Baumgarten's promotion of the concept of connection not only to an ontological term, but to one that must be treated under the very notion of possibility, deserves attention. This is particularly so, since for Kant transcendental connection or combination is so closely related to possibility.
    Kant E3508, 1764–75: "ideal and real."
    Kant E3509, 1764–75: "The nexus is also of coordinated things, not always subordinated things."
[i] Kant E3511, 1770–8 (in margin to left of §15): "On possibility. On something. On the thing."

externally to it, IS CONSIDERED IN ITSELF. Whatever is not even something representable when considered in itself is[10] IMPOSSIBLE IN ITSELF (intrinsically, simply, absolutely,[11] *per se*).[12, a] Whatever is possible when considered in itself is[13] POSSIBLE IN ITSELF (intrinsically, absolutely,[14] *per se*,[15] simply).[b, c]

§16

What is also possible in a nexus with some things that are posited outside of it is HYPOTHETICALLY POSSIBLE (respectively, relatively, extrinsically, through another,[16] qualifiedly).[d]

HYPOTHETICALLY] HYPOTHETICALLY and externally

§17

What is impossible only in some nexus with those things that are posited outside of it is HYPOTHETICALLY IMPOSSIBLE (respectively, relatively, extrinsically, through another,[17] qualifiedly).

HYPOTHETICALLY] HYPOTHETICALLY and externally

§18

Nothing absolutely impossible is hypothetically possible (§15, 16). Therefore, nothing hypothetically possible is absolutely impossible.[18] *Everything hypothetically impossible and possible is possible in itself* (§17, 15). Therefore, absolutely impossible things are neither hypothetically possible nor hypothetically impossible. Some things that are absolutely possible are hypothetically impossible.[19, e]

The last three occurrences of "hypothetically" are replaced by "externally" in Meier.[f]

---

[a] Kant E3510, 1769–78: "Something, nothing, no thing."
[b] From this paragraph onward Baumgarten makes heavy use of this distinction between a thing considered in itself or absolutely and a thing considered in a given nexus or hypothetically. This employment of the terms "absolute" and "hypothetical" might strike one as peculiar, as they later did Kant. For instance, according to this distinction, a thing that is hypothetically possible is possible in all relations, while what is absolutely possible may not be possible in all relations, since it is merely the internal possibility of the thing. For more on this distinction and Kant's criticisms of it, including some clarifying examples, see Introduction p. 30ff.
[c] Kant E3512, 1770–8 (attached to Baumgarten's gloss, not given here, clarifying the Latin term "*possibile in se*" in German as "*an und vor sich, innerlich, unbeding [sic] möglich*"): "in a certain, in every respect"
[d] The closest Wolff comes to hypothetical possibility and impossibility is again in WC §111, where he defines intrinsic possibility as what does not involve a contradiction when considered in itself, and extrinsic possibility as what does not produce a contraction when considered in this world. Baumgarten has clearly refined and generalized the same basic idea.
[e] These distinctions come from Leibniz (cf. inter alia, *Theodicy* §235). The absolutely possible contains no internal contradiction, considered only in itself (e.g. a talking dog). The hypothetically possible is possible only in a nexus with others; in other words, it is possible insofar as it does not contradict a given external state of affairs (e.g. a student who will one day be a doctor in this world). This pattern repeats for the impossible; the absolutely impossible contradicts itself internally (e.g. a square circle), and the hypothetically impossible contradicts a given external state of affairs (e.g. a talking dog in this world). What is absolutely possible may therefore be hypothetically impossible.
[f] Meier seems to use "externally" and "conditionally" as synonymous throughout his translation in a way different from Baumgarten.

Section II. The connected[20]

§19

Whatever is possible in a nexus, i.e. that in which there is a nexus, or that to which a nexus belongs, is CONNECTED[a] (rational) and whatever is impossible in a nexus is IRRATIONAL (unconnected, incoherent).[b, 21] Hence, irrational things are either impossible in themselves or hypothetically (§15, 17).

§20[22]

Everything possible either has a ground or does not (§10). If it has a ground, something is its ground (§8). If it does not have one, nothing is its ground (§7). Therefore, the ground of every possible thing is either nothing or something (§10). If nothing were the ground of some possible thing, it would be knowable from nothing why that thing is (§14), and hence the nothing itself would be representable and something (§8),[23] and nothing would be something (§14, 8). Hence something possible would be impossible (§7, 8), which is absurd (§9).[c] Therefore, something is the ground of every possible thing, which is to say everything possible is a consequence <*ratio-natum*>, which is to say that *nothing is without ground*, or when something is posited, something is posited as its ground. *This proposition* is called *the principle of ground*, which you may also gather from §265 and §279,[24] partially by abstraction, partially by avoiding a vicious circle.[d]

---

[a] Kant E3513, 1764–8: "(mutually) connected things, either through agreement or opposition"

[b] Wolff: "Those things are said to be *connected*, of which one contains the sufficient ground of the coexistence or succession of the other. While on the contrary, those things are *unconnected* of which one does not contain the sufficient ground of the coexistence or succession of the other" (WC §10).

[c] G/K have the last part of this sentence as: "(§7, 8 as presupposition for §9)"

[d] Wolff: "*If nothing is assumed to be, it must not for this reason admitted to be something.* Thus suppose that something is, because of the reason that nothing is. Then it would be admitted that either nothing is made into something or that nothing has brought about something. But both are absurd. Therefore, for this reason there is not something, because nothing is" (WO §69). "*The principle of sufficient ground is proven.* Nothing is without a sufficient ground why it is rather than is not; i.e. if something is posited as being, there will also be posited something from which it is understood why this thing is rather than is not. Indeed, either nothing is without sufficient ground why it is rather than is not, or something can be without sufficient ground why it is rather than is not. We suppose that A is without sufficient ground as to why it is rather than is not. Therefore, nothing will be posited from which it is understood why A is. Hence, it will be admitted that A is, because nothing has been assumed: Since this is absurd, nothing is without sufficient ground, or, if something is posited as being, it is also admitted that something is from which it is understood why it is" (WO §70). "Where something is at hand from which one can understand why a thing is, that thing has a sufficient ground. Therefore, where nothing of this sort is at hand, there is nothing from which one can understand why something is, namely, why it can become actual, and therefore it must arise from nothing. Accordingly, what cannot arise from nothing must have a sufficient ground why it is, since then it must be possible in itself and, if we are speaking of a thing that is not necessary, must have a cause that can bring it into actuality. Now, since it is impossible that something can come to be from nothing, everything that is must also have its sufficient ground why it is, i.e. there must always be something from which one can understand why it can become actual" (VGG §30). Dirk Effertz suggests that these two proofs differ in that in the former the ground is understood as an efficient cause (i.e. cause of existence), whereas in the latter it is understood to be a material cause (i.e. a cause out of which something comes to be). See his introduction to Christian Wolff, *Erste Philosophie oder Ontologie*, XXVII. It is notable that Baumgarten distinguishes the principle of ground from the principle of sufficient ground, which latter is found in §21 and 22 below.

§21

The ground of each and every thing[a] that is in something is its SUFFICIENT (complete,[25] total[26]) GROUND; the ground of only some of the things that are in it is its INSUFFICIENT (incomplete, partial) GROUND.

§22[b]

Nothing is without a sufficient ground, or, if something is posited, then some sufficient ground is posited for it as well. Each and every thing[c] in every possible thing has a ground (§20); hence, every possible thing has a sufficient ground (§21). *This proposition* is called *the principle of sufficient ground* (principle of appropriateness).

§23

Every possible thing is a ground, or *nothing lacks a consequence*; nothing is without corollary and recompense; nothing is completely sterile, useless, and unfruitful;[27] or, when something is posited, some consequence belonging to it is posited as well.[28] For every possible thing either has a consequence, or not (§10). If it has, then something is its consequence (§8). If it has not, then nothing is its consequence (§7). Therefore, the consequence of every possible thing is either nothing or something (§10). If nothing were the consequence of some possible thing, then it could be known from the latter (§14). Hence it would be something (§8), and thus something possible would be impossible (§7, 8), which is absurd (§9). *This proposition* is called *the principle of the consequence.*[d]

§24

Every possible thing is both a ground and a consequence (§20, 23) and hence connected and rational (§19)[29] in a double nexus[30] (§14), knowable both a priori and a posteriori.[31] *This proposition* may be called *the principle of things connected on both sides* (with regard to what precedes and what follows after).[32]

§25

The ground A of ground B is the ground of the consequence C. From the ground of B, it is possible to know why C is (§23); hence, A is the ground of C (§14).

The … C.] If A is the ground of B, then it is also the ground of C, which is grounded in B.

§26

The consequence C of the consequence B is a consequence of the ground A (§25, 14).

§27[33]

The ground A of some B upon which C depends is the MEDIATE GROUND of this C

---

[a] G/K: "of the individual things"
[b] Kant E3514, 1764–9 (at the beginning of §22): "In a series (of coordinated and) subordinated things."
[c] G/K: "The individual things"
[d] This principle is first found in Baumgarten, as is the next. Kant singles it out for criticism in his *Nova Dilucidatio* (AA 1: 408).

(a more distant, remote ground). A ground which is not mediate is the IMMEDIATE GROUND (a proximate ground).

§28[a]

A ground having a still further ground is called a QUALIFIED GROUND (an intermediate ground),[34] whereas one that does not is called an UNQUALIFIED GROUND (the ultimate ground).[35] The GROUNDS[b] and the CONSEQUENCES of something are also either considered as grounds and consequences SUBORDINATED to one another, or, if not, as COORDINATED.[36, c]

UNQUALIFIED] FIRST or last

§29

When a consequence is posited, some[37] ground of it is posited (§20, 14), and also a sufficient ground (§22); or, *it is valid to deduce a ground, and a sufficient one, from the consequence.*

§30

When a ground is posited, and hence a sufficient ground (§21), a consequence is posited (§23); or, *it is valid to deduce the consequence from a ground, and from a sufficient one.*

§31

When a ground, and a sufficient ground, is removed, some[38] *consequence is removed,* because if the latter were posited, the former would be too (§29).

§32

When a consequence is removed, then its ground, and its sufficient ground, is also removed, because if the latter were posited, the former would be too (§30).

§33

When A and B are connected to a third C, they are connected to one another. A is connected to C which is connected to B. Therefore, there is something in A which may be known through B why it is; hence, A and B are connected (§19).[39]

Therefore … connected] In the same way, there is a predicate in A that cannot be known except for if B, together with A, is combined with a third; therefore, there is just one predicate in B that can hence be, because it, together with A, is combined with a third. Therefore, A has a predicate that can be known from B and B has a predicate that can be known from A, and precisely for

---

[a] Kant E3515, 1769? 1764–6?? (at the beginning of §28): "The subaltern and primitive ground." Kant E3519, 1776–89 (above and in §28): "The ground is either sufficient for a grounded being or for itself; if the first, it is sufficient in the qualified sense, if the latter, it is simply sufficient."
[b] Kant E3516, 1771–7 (in margin, next to the lines ending in "still further" and "grounds"): "the primitive or subaltern ground."
[c] Kant E3517, 1776–89 (in margin, next to the lines ending in *rationes* and *coordinata*): "the ground, which is itself a grounded being."
Kant E3518, 1776–89 (under §28): "On condition in general—limiting."

the reason that they are both conjoined with a third. Therefore, all things are grounded in each other, and, themselves conjoined with each other, because of such a connection.

Section III. A being

§34[a]

What is either posited to be A, or posited not to be A, is DETERMINED.[b] What is however only posited to be either A or not-A, is UNDETERMINED. Or, if nothing is posited about the subject with respect to contradictory predicates except that one of these two belongs to it, then that subject is undetermined with respect to these predicates; however, it is determined if one of the two is posited in the subject.[c] That which can be determined is DETERMINABLE. Therefore, that about which it can be posited that it is either A, or that it is not-A, is determinable.[40]

§35[d]

The ground of what is to be determined is the DETERMINING GROUND. Therefore, every ground determines—the sufficient ground determines sufficiently, and the insufficient ground, insufficiently (§34, 21).[41] Hence, if the determining ground is posited, then the determined is posited (§30), and vice versa (§29). If the determined[42] is removed, then so too is the determining ground[43] (§32), and vice versa (§31).

§36[e]

Those things (notes and predicates)[44] that are posited in something by determining [it] are DETERMINATIONS. A determination is either positive and affirmative (§34, 10), and if true, REALITY, or it is negative (§34, 10), and if true, NEGATION.[f] Apparent negation is HIDDEN REALITY; apparent reality is VANITY.[45]

---

[a] Kant E3520, 1764–8 (at the beginning of §34): "logical predicate. Determines:"
[b] From here on, Baumgarten refines Wolff's notion of determination in a way that clearly influenced Kant. As Wolff writes: "If A is viewed as that of which B must be affirmed, or of which B, E and F, etc. must be affirmed, then A will be *determined*" (WO §112). Thus the generalized statement that determination regarding a predicate requires that either A or not-A be posited appears to be new with Baumgarten. This provides the basis for his definition of complete determination in §148, which Kant draws on in constructing the transcendental ideal (CPR A571/B600–A583/B661).
[c] Kant E3521, 1764–autumn 1771: "One who is human is determined in relation to scholarship, however, not as a human. I.e. not the logical subject human, but rather the real; namely, one who is thought through the concept of humanity."
[d] Kant E3522, 1764–autumn 1770: "that in which is the respect of the ground to the grounded is said to be determining./that which is undetermined in itself is determined by another."
[e] Kant E3523, 1766–71 (at the beginning of §36): "logical predicate or determination"
[f] Kant E3524, 1780–9 (next to "REALITY … NEGATION"): "in itself, not relative to another concept, which is logical, not metaphysical or transcendental."

§37[46, a]

The determinations of a possible thing are either representable in it even when it is not yet considered in a nexus, and these are ABSOLUTE DETERMINATIONS; or, if the determinations are only representable when it is considered in a nexus (§10), they are RESPECTIVE (assumptive) DETERMINATIONS. The respective determinations of possible things are RESPECTS (habituations, τὰ πρὸσ τι,[b] relations in a broad sense, either external or internal). The respects of possible things that are not representable in these things considered in themselves are RELATIONS (more strictly speaking, external). The relations of possible things are their EXTERNAL DETERMINATIONS (relative, external, extrinsic), and all the rest are INTERNAL DETERMINATIONS.

Meier translates respects <*respectus*> as "conditioned determinations <*bedingte Bestimmungen*>"

§38[c]

If those [determinations] that are in B are those that are in A, A and B are the SAME. Things that are not the same are DIFFERENT (others).

SAME] SAME and agree with one another || same] same or do not agree with one another

§39[d]

The internal determinations of a possible thing are either the unqualified grounds of the rest of the internal determinations among these, or not (§10). The former are the FIRST DETERMINATIONS (principles) or ESSENTIAL DETERMINATIONS <*ESSENTIALIA*>.

§40

The collection of the essential determinations in a possible thing, or its internal possibility, is ESSENCE[e] (the being <*esse*> of a thing, formal ground, nature, cf. §430, quiddity, form, formal aspect of the whole, οὐσία,[f] τινοτις,[g] substance, cf. §191, the first concept of a being).[47]

---

[a] Kant E3525, 1764–autumn 1770 (1772–5) (across from §37, by the conclusion of the first sentence): "Absolute and respective concepts./as that of the ground and the consequence are respective. Only the respective can be clarified."
Kant E3526, 1770–89 (across from §37, by the second and third sentence): "A book in the library/Lacking—negation: missing. What is not in its place. (Absent: what is not in its time)./ Defective—when lacking what should have been, i.e. the negation opposite to perfection: (lacking)./ Absent—when one knows otherwise where it is (it is not present)."
[b] Lit.: "things relative to something else," cf. Aristotle, *Categories*, 6a36–7.
[c] Kant E3527, 1764–autumn 1770? (1772–5?): "This is a logical respect. (*later addition*: Real)"
[d] Kant E3528, 1760s-1770s (in §39): "The being <*Wesen*> of a thing (used as an adjective)./A being <*Wesen*>: *ens*." [*Wesen* can mean either "being" or "essence."]
[e] Wolff: "Those things in a being that are neither mutually repugnant to each other, nor yet *per se* reciprocally determining, are called essential determinations and also constitute the essence of the being" (WO §143).
[f] "substance"
[g] "whatness, quiddity." Baumgarten coins this Greek word in parallel to the Latin *quidditas*.

§41

The internal determinations of a possible thing that are consequences of the essence are AFFECTIONS.

§42

An internal determination that is not an essential determination is a consequence of the essence (§39, 40), and hence an affection (§41).

§43

When essence is posited in a possible thing, affections are posited (§41, 30).

§44

When the affections are posited in a possible thing, some essence is posited (§41, 29).

§45

When the essence is removed, some affections are removed (§41, 31).

§46

When the affections are removed, the essence is removed (§41, 32).

§47

All internal determinations of a possible thing are connected to each other—every determination with every other determination. For, every affection is[a] connected with the essential determinations (§39), and these with essence (§40, 14), and hence, every determination with every other determination (§33).

§48

A UNIVERSAL NEXUS (harmony) is one that is among each and every thing.[b]

§49

There is a universal nexus among the internal determinations of something possible (§47, 48).

§50

Affections have their ground in essence (§41), and hence in a ground that is either sufficient, or not (§21, 10). The former are ATTRIBUTES, and the latter are MODES (predicable or logical accidents, cf. §191, incidentals, secondary predicates).

MODES] CONTINGENT QUALITIES

§51

Attributes have sufficient ground either in all the essential determinations, or only in

---

[a] G/K: "The affections <*Folgebestimmungen*> are namely individually"
[b] G/K: "exists between the individual things"

some (§50, 10). The former are CHARACTERISTIC ATTRIBUTES <*PROPRIA*>;[a] the latter, COMMON ATTRIBUTES.

§52

Every determination of a possible thing is either an essential determination (§39), or an attribute, or a mode (§42), or a relation (§37).

§53

Every possible thing is determined with regard to its possibility (§34, 8); hence what is possible in itself is determined with regard to internal possibility (§15). Since internal possibility is essence (§40), every possible thing has an essence, or is determined with regard to essence. Therefore, whatever is entirely undetermined is nothing (§7).[48]

or … essence] nothing is without essence, and it is impossible for something to be able to be undetermined in regard to its essence

§54

Aside from essence (§53), something possible is either determined with regard to all the affections that are also[49] compossible in it, or not (§34, 10). The former is an ACTUAL BEING, while the latter is called a PRIVATIVE (merely possible)[50] NON-BEING (nothing, cf. §7).[51]

PRIVATIVE NON-BEING] MERELY POSSIBLE THING

§55

EXISTENCE (act, cf. §210, actuality) is the collection of affections[52] that are compossible in something; i.e. the complement of essence or of internal[53] possibility,[54] insofar as essence is considered only as a collection of determinations (§40).

complement] fulfillment

§56

Every internal determination of something possible[55] pertains either to its essence, or to its existence.

§57

Everything actual is internally possible (§54); or, when its existence is posited, its internal possibility is posited (§55, 40). Or, it is valid to deduce possibility from being.[b]

§58

Nothing internally impossible is actual (§57); when the internal possibility is removed, actuality is removed (§55, 40).[56] Or, it is valid to deduce non-being from non-possibility.[c]

---

[a] Kant E3529, 1770–8 and 1775–8 (in the earlier part of the elucidation Kant glosses the Latin "*propria*" with the German "*eigentümliche*" (both mean "characteristic"), and then adds at a later date): "are such, whose concepts can be interchanged <*reciproceren*> with the subject."
[b] Kant E3530, 1780–9? 1776–9??: "From the assertorical to the problematic, but not vice versa."
[c] Kant E3531,1780–9 1776–9??: "From the negation of the assertorical (antecedent) not to the negation of the problematic."

§59

Some possible thing is not actual (§54), or, when some possibility is posited,[a] actuality can be removed. Or, it is not valid to deduce[57] being from something's[b] being possible.

§60

Some non-actual thing is possible (§59); when actuality is removed,[c] not all possibility is removed. Or, it is not valid to deduce complete impossibility from non-being.

§61

Something possible[d] that is determinable with regard to its existence is a BEING.[e]

Meier adds the following expansion that would fit just after "existence" *above:* or insofar as, on the one hand, it can be represented of it that it either is actual, or on the other, that it is not, but regardless of this could yet be actual

§62

A NON-BEING (negative, cf. §54)[58] would be something possible[f] but not determinable with regard to existence (§61). But this is impossible, and if it appears to be a being, it is a FICTIONAL BEING[g] (a being of reasoning reason,[59, h] cf. §647).

BEING] THING, or a thing of which one can merely say that the representation of it, considered as a representation, has possibility and actuality

Eberhard's note: The non-thing is namely that which appears to be a thing so far as one can make an image of it in one's imagination, but about which, however, one yet realizes as soon as one analyzes the object that it could not have external reality.

§63

Every being is possible (§61) and has a ground (§20) that is sufficient (§22) and a consequence (§23), and is hence doubly connected (§24). It has an essence (§53) and essential determinations (§40), and hence affections (§43), and is in a universal nexus (§49). All the determinations of a being are either essential determinations, or

---

[a] Kant E3533, 1780–9? 1776–9?? (above "some … posited"): "i.e. one cannot infer existence from a concept, neither of thorough determination nor of a reality."

[b] Kant E3532, 1780–9? 1776–9?? (above "something's"): "none". In the same reflection (between §59 and §60): "for if the major proposition is true, then absolutely nothing could follow from a particular proposition."

[c] Kant E3534, 1780–9 (above "actuality is removed"): "One cannot say 'when all [actuality] is removed, possibility is not removed'; what does not exist at all, must also not be possible in every respect."

[d] Kant E3535, 1780–9? 1776–9??: "what contains realities"

[e] Wolff: "What can exist, and consequently, that to which existence is not repugnant, is called a *being*" (WO §134). "Everything that can be, whether it is actual or not, we call a *thing*" (VGG §22).

[f] Kant E3536, 1776–89 (next to §62 "A NON-BEING … determinable"): "A thing and its predicates"

[g] Kant E3537, 1760s–70s: "Chimera, fantasy, ideal."

[h] *rationis ratiocinantis.* In scholastic philosophy, something is said to be "of reasoning reason" (a being, or distinction, etc.) to indicate that it is *merely* a product of reasoning, and therefore has no basis in external reality. See Suarez (DM 7.4–5). For Kant's usage cf. CPR A669/B697 and *Critique of the Power of Judgment* AA 5:468.

attributes, or modes, or relations (§52). When a being is posited, its essence is posited, and hence so too are all of its essential determinations.[60] If the essence is removed,[61] the being is removed.[62] If an essential determination is removed, then the essence is removed, and hence so too is the being itself (§53, 40).[63] Finally, every internal determination pertains either to its essence, or to its existence (§56).

§64

The attributes of a being are sufficiently determined through the essence (§35, 50). Hence, if the essence is posited, the attributes are posited (§35).[64] Therefore, if a being is posited, its attributes are posited (§63), and if the attributes are removed, then the essence and the being are removed (§35, 63).

§65

The modes of a being are not determined sufficiently through essence (§50, 35), and hence not determined with regard to existence (§55). Therefore, with regard to actual modes, a being is undetermined by its essence (§34, 54); i.e. *modes may be absent or present, while the essence of the thing remains unscathed.*[65]

§66

Existence does not conflict with essence, but is a reality (§36), and is compossible with it (§50, 55).

§67

The knowledge of diversity is DISTINCTION, and the ground of distinction in the thing that is to be distinguished[66] is a DISTINGUISHING MARK (difference, character, or distinctive character in a broad sense, cf. §350,[67] note, characteristic note). Now, every determination of a being is that from which it can be known that this being is neither undetermined, nor determined in some other manner (§36, 34). Therefore, every determination is a distinguishing mark of a being (§38, 14).

mark of a being] mark of a being, and there are as many types of marks of things as there are types of their determinations

§68

The distinguishing marks of a being are either external and relative, or internal (§67, 37). The latter are either the absolute or respective (§37)[68] essential determinations that pertain to essence, or the absolute or respective (§37)[69] accidental determinations that pertain to existence.

§69[a]

The internal distinguishing marks can be represented in a being considered in

[a] Kant E3538, 1773–89? 1769?? 1770–1?? (across from the beginning of §69 to the conclusion of §69): "the determination of a being is considered to the extent that it is posited, or as often as the posited is something."
Kant E3539, 1776–89: "The distinction of one thing from another through the plurality of the homogenous, which is contained in both, is size. The distinction of the non-homogenous is quality."

itself (§68, 37), and hence can be known in some way, or GIVEN. We can either CONCEIVE[70] of and understand (i.e. know distinctly) given things without assuming or relating them to anything else (without the presence of anything else),[71] or we cannot. The former are QUALITIES and the latter are QUANTITIES.[a]

After the first sentence Meier inserts: However, it does not follow from this that they can be entirely known with distinctness when they are represented in the thing merely considered in itself.

§70[b]

Things that are the same according to quality are SIMILAR ($\sim$); according to quantity, EQUAL (=); according to both, CONGRUENT ($\cong$). Things that are different according to quality are DISSIMILAR (Λ); according to quantity, UNEQUAL ($\neq$); according to both, INCONGRUENT ($\ncong$).[72]

Meier adds at the end: The quality of a thing can be an internal mark through which it is distinguished from things, the inequality of which one does not take into account; and similarly, quantity can be an internal mark through which one distinguishes it from things, the dissimilarity to which one does not take into account.

§71

Things that are merely similar are not congruent; hence, they differ in quantity (§70). Thus, quantity is the internal distinguishing mark of what is merely similar.

Section IIII. The one

§72

If some of the determinations of a being that are posited together are removed, then they ARE SEPARATED. Hence, they are INSEPARABLE if none of those posited together can be removed.

§73

When a being is posited, an essence is posited (§63), and therefore so too is a collection of essential determinations (§40). Hence, if a being is posited, then all the essential determinations are posited together, and indeed in such a way that none can be removed (§63, 40). Therefore, the essential determinations of a being are in themselves inseparable (§72, 15). The ONE is that whose determinations are inseparable, and indeed the TRANSCENDENTALLY ONE is that whose determinations as such are inseparable *per se.* *Therefore, every being is* transcendentally *one.*

---

[a] Kant E3541, 1790–1804? 1771–2?? 1776–89??: "better: 'amounts <*quanta*>'; that something is an amount <*quantum*> can be known absolutely; however, how big it is (quantity), can only be known relatively."
Kant E3540, 1776–89 (by the conclusion of §69): "what is possible through one thing posited a number of times is number."
[b] Kant E3542, 1776–89 (between §69 and 70): "amount and quantity"

TRANSCENDENTALLY ONE] AN UNCONDITIONED UNITY

§74

When A is one and B is one, and so forth, and they are partly the same and partly different, they are MANY. Whatever can be thought is either many or not (§10). The former determination is CATEGORICAL MULTITUDE (plurality),[73] whereas the latter is CATEGORICAL UNITY. [a]

§75

Each and every one of a being's determinations[b] is one, and each is partly the same [as the others], insofar as it is a determination of the same being, and partly different, and hence they are many. Therefore, there can be a multitude in a being considered in itself (§69), and this is an internal distinguishing mark belonging to it (§37) that we cannot understand without assuming some other thing (§74, 38). Hence, multitude is quantity (§69).

§76

Since the inseparability of determinations is the impossibility of separation (§72), it is either absolute or hypothetical (§15, 16). Hence, unity is either absolute or hypothetical (§73).

§77[c]

Whatever is, insofar as there are not many <*quod multa non sunt*>, is UNIQUE[d] (one, exclusively so).[74]

many is] many, or the one insofar as it is distinct from many, is

Section V. Order[75]

§78

If many things are posited mutually next to or after one another, they are CONJOINED. The conjunction of several things is either the same or diverse (§10, 38). If the first, it is COORDINATION and their identity is ORDER. The science of order used to be called MUSIC IN A BROAD SENSE.[76, e]

---

[a] Kant E3543, 1780–9? 1776–9?? (in the margin to the right of "categorical unity"): "Taken substantively./The adjective is hypothetical."; (in the margin to the right, probably also belonging to "categorical unity"): "quantitative and qualitative"

[b] G/K: "The individual determinations of a thing"

[c] Kant E3544, 1790–804? (1771–2?) 1776–89??: "That is singular, concerning which there are no more of the same sort."

[d] See Baumgarten's Second Preface, p. 89. Wolff: "*Unique* is said to be that to which there is nothing similar, or that which has nothing similar to it" (WO §283).

[e] Kant E3545, 1790–804? (1771–2?) 1776–89??: "Nonsense, wherein there is method."

§79

Diversity in the conjunction of many things is CONFUSION (disorder).[a] The conjunction of inseparable things is UNITEDNESS <*UNITIO*>.[77]

§80

Every DETERMINATION has a ground (§20, 36), and whatever can be known from some determined ground is said to be in CONFORMITY WITH THE GROUND (appropriate, agreeing).

§81

If, when A is posited, B is removed, then A and B are OPPOSITES.

§82

A determination that is opposite to that which is in conformity with a ground is contrary[78] to the ground (nonconforming, inappropriate) or a DEFECT.

§83

A proposition that expresses a determination in conformity with a ground is a NORM (rule, law) and indeed a NORM IN THE WIDER SENSE is the representation of a determination in conformity with a ground.[79]

§84

Wherever there are determinations, there are laws (§83, 80).

§85

The respect[80] of a being that is determined from this being's conjunction with others is POSITION. Therefore, where there is position, there are laws (§84, 37).

Therefore ... laws] Therefore, where its position is, there is a law

§86

Position is determined by conjunction. Hence, there are laws in conjunction (§85), and the same laws in the same conjunction (§38). Therefore,[81] in an order many things are conjoined in conformity with the same ground (§83, 78). What is in both A and B is COMMON to them. What is in A and not in B is, with respect to B, PROPER to A.[82] Therefore in order there are common rules.

§87

In a diverse <*diversa*> conjunction there are diverse <*diversae*> laws (§86, 38).[b] Therefore, in confusion there are no common laws (§79, 86).

---

[a] See Baumgarten's Second Preface, pp. 86–7.
[b] This sentence is inherently ambiguous. "*Diversa*" could be taken as meaning internally manifold (i.e. diverse) or as different from others. The first interpretation, which is suggested by the reference to §79, is what we have chosen. The other, supported by the references to §86 and 38, would be "In a different conjunction there are different laws."

This sentence is rendered by Meier as: In disorder, by contrast, there are no common laws, because things that are conjoined in different ways are conjoined according to different laws.

§88

If the rule of an order is unique, it is a SIMPLE ORDER; if there are several rules, it is called a COMPOSITE ORDER.

Section VI. The true[83]

§89

METAPHYSICAL (real,[84] objective,[85] material)[86] TRUTH is the order of many in one. TRANSCENDENTAL TRUTH is the order in a being's essential determinations and attributes.

TRANSCENCENTAL TRUTH] AN UNCONDITIONED METAPHYSICAL TRUTH

§90

Since the determinations of each being are conjoined—the essential determinations according to the principle of contradiction (§40, 7); the accidental determinations and attributes according to the principles of contradiction (§64, 7), ground (§20), and sufficient ground (§22, 50); the modes according to the principles of contradiction (§65, 7) and ground (§42, 20); the essential determinations and affections according to the principle of the consequence (§23, 41)[87]—they are hence conjoined according to common rules (§83, 86). Therefore, *every being is* transcendentally *true* (§89).

§91

The confusion opposed to transcendental truth would be a DREAM TAKEN AS OBJECTIVE (cf. §593).[88] An aggregate of dreams would be a FANTASY WORLD[a] (cf. §354).[89]

§92

CATHOLIC (universal)[90] PRINCIPLES (cf. §307, 311) are common to each and every[b] being.[91] Metaphysically true things (§90, 80) are determined in accordance with catholic principles (§7, 20, 22, 23),[92] and those things which are determined in conformity with

---

[a] Wolff: "Denial of the principle of sufficient ground changes the true world into a fantasy world <*mundus fabulosum*>, in which the human being's will takes the place of the ground of that which occurs" (WO §77). In "On Kant's Reply to Hume," Arthur O. Lovejoy claims that the "substance" of Kant's reply to Hume can be found in Wolff's thought that the principle of sufficient ground must be true, for otherwise the world would be a dream world. This essay is reprinted in *Kant: Disputed Questions*, edited by Molke S. Gram (Chicago: Quadrangle Books, 1967), 284–308. It should be noted, however, that Kant himself obliquely signals the difference between Wolff's argument and that of the Transcendental Deduction, explaining that without the synthesis of causality our representations would be entirely blind, "i.e. less than a dream" (A 112). See also *Prolegomena* AA 4: 376n, where Kant refers to this Wolffian doctrine.

[b] G/K: "to individual things"

these principles are metaphysically true (§89). Hence, METAPHYSICAL TRUTH can be defined as the accordance of a being with catholic principles.

§93

OBJECTIVE CERTAINTY (cf. §531)[93] is the apperceptibility[94] of truth in a being. Now, the truth of each being can be known clearly[95] (§90, 8). Therefore, *every being is objectively certain.*

OBJECTIVE CERTAINTY] CERTAINTY OF THINGS || objectively certain] certain considered in itself

Section VII. The perfect[96, a]

§94[b]

If several things taken together constitute the sufficient ground of a single thing, they AGREE.[c] The agreement itself is PERFECTION,[d] and the one thing in which there is agreement is the DETERMINING GROUND OF PERFECTION (the focus of the perfection).[97]

§95

In perfection, several things are determined in conformity to the same ground (§94, 80). Therefore, in perfection there is order (§78) and common rules of perfection (§86).

§96

If the determining ground of perfection is unique, it is SIMPLE PERFECTION; if there are several determining grounds, then it is COMPOSITE PERFECTION (§88, 95).

§97

Opposite RULES are said to COLLIDE and the defect arising from a collision of the rules of perfection is called an EXCEPTION, which is either true or only apparent depending on whether the norms truly or apparently (§12) collide in opposition (§81).[98]

§98

The agreement of essential determinations is TRANSCENDENTAL (essential)[99]

---

[a] Kant E3548, end of 1769–77? (1776–8?) 1778–9??: "perfection taken as adjective or substantive. Just like unity, truth, possibility."
[b] Kant E3546, 1764–6: "the perfection of a being in general is the sum total of reality."
[c] Kant E3547, 1764–9? (end of 1769–autumn 1770?): "they agree either logically, insofar as they do not contradict, or really, insofar as they are not really opposed to one another."
[d] Wolff: "*Perfection* is agreement in variety, or the agreement of many things that are mutually different from one another in one thing" (WO §503). Please see the preface to the second edition for Baumgarten's discussion of this paragraph.

PERFECTION, the agreement of affections is ACCIDENTAL PERFECTION, and both are INTERNAL PERFECTIONS. The agreement of relations is EXTERNAL PERFECTION.

§99

The essential determinations of each being agree with its essence (§63, 40) and its attributes (§50, 94). Therefore, *every being is* transcendentally *perfect*.

§100

Something is good if, when it is posited, a perfection is also posited. Therefore, *every being is* transcendentally *good* (§99).

Chapter II. The internal disjunctive predicates of a being

Section I. The necessary and the contingent

§101

The NECESSARY is that whose opposite is impossible, and what is not necessary is CONTINGENT.[a]

§102

That whose opposite is impossible in itself[100] is NECESSARY IN ITSELF[101] (metaphysically, intrinsically, absolutely, geometrically, logically). That whose opposite is only extrinsically impossible is HYPOTHETICALLY NECESSARY[102] (qualifiedly).[103] The determination of a being by virtue of which it is necessary is its necessity. Therefore necessity is either ABSOLUTE (of the consequent)[104] or HYPOTHETICAL[105] (of the consequence):[106, b] the former, insofar as something is necessary in itself and *per se*; the latter, insofar as something is only hypothetically necessary.[107]

Meier adds after "NECESSARY IN ITSELF": absolutely and unconditionally

§103

Possibility involves an opposite (§81, 7). Hence, the possibility of a being is its necessary determination (§101): intrinsic possibility is intrinsically necessary; extrinsic possibility, extrinsically necessary (§102).

---

[a] Kant E3549, 1760s–70s: "completely contingent"

[b] On the distinction between *necessitas consequentis* (necessity of the consequent) and *necessitas consequentiae* (necessity of the consequence), see Thomas Aquinas, *Summa contra gentiles* I.67, and *De veritate* I.23, ad 13.

§104[a]

That whose opposite is absolutely possible is CONTINGENT IN ITSELF (*per se*, intrinsically).[108] That whose opposite is hypothetically possible is EXTRINSICALLY CONTINGENT (hypothetically).[109] The determination of a being by virtue of which it is contingent is its CONTINGENCY.[110] Therefore, contingency is either ABSOLUTE,[111] in the case that something is at least contingent in itself and *per se*,[112] or HYPOTHETICAL,[113] in the case that something is hypothetically contingent.[114]

§105

Nothing absolutely necessary is contingent in any way (§102, 104). Therefore, whatever is contingent in any way is not absolutely necessary.[115] *Everything hypothetically necessary is contingent in itself and per se* (§18).[116] Therefore, something contingent in itself and *per se* is hypothetically necessary. Everything hypothetically contingent is also contingent in itself (§104).[117]

§106[b]

The essences of things are absolutely necessary in them (§40, 103).[118, c]

§107

If the essential determinations and attributes are removed, the essence is removed (§65, 81), and hence the internal impossibility of the being is posited (§81,[119] 40). Therefore, essential determinations and attributes are absolutely necessary determinations of a being (§103).[120]

Meier adds after "is removed": or if their opposite is posited in the thing

§108

The opposite of the modes in a being is absolutely possible (§65, 81), and hence modes are the determinations of a being that are contingent in themselves (§104). Therefore, they are not absolutely necessary (§105).[d] The opposite of the absolutely necessary determinations in a being is absolutely impossible in the same being (§102). Therefore, the latter are absolutely possible in a being (§81), and hence representable in the same

[a] Kant E3550, around 1769–71?: "Something is contingent either for a thing (i.e. it is not necessary for it), e.g. composition to the elements, or [breaks off]"
[b] Kant E3551, 1764–9: "There are contingent essences, namely the essences of all contingent things, e.g. motions."
[c] Wolff: "*The essences of things are necessary.* The essences of things are constituted by the non-repugnance of those things that are together in the same thing, but that yet are not determined by any others that are also in it. Now, since it is impossible for the same thing to be and also not to be, it is likewise not possible for those same things that taken together are not mutually repugnant to each other—although they are not reciprocally determined *per se*, nor determined through any other—to be mutually repugnant to each other. This non-repugnance is therefore necessary and consequently the essences of things are necessary" (WO §299). "*The essences of things are absolutely necessary.* They are indeed necessary when looked at absolutely, because the necessity in these is demonstrated assuming nothing except the definition. They are therefore absolutely necessary" (WO §303).
[d] Kant E3552, 1764–9? (next to second and third sentences): "The unconditionally necessary is as much in regard to the external as to the internal deter[minations] [breaks off]"

being considered in itself (§15). However, relations are not representable in a being considered in itself (§37). Therefore, no relations of a being are absolutely necessary; they are all contingent (§101).[121]

§109

Since in something the opposite of existence is possible (§54, 55), existence will either be absolutely necessary or contingent in itself (§102,[122] 10).[a] A being whose existence is absolutely necessary is a NECESSARY BEING,[b] whereas a being whose existence is intrinsically contingent is a CONTINGENT BEING.

in something] in some things

§110

All internal determinations of a necessary being are absolutely necessary. For they pertain either to essence or to existence (§56). The former and the latter are both absolutely necessary in a necessary being (§109, 106).

§111

There are no modes in a necessary being (§110, 108). Therefore, that which has modes is a contingent being (§109).

§112

Every contingent being has modes. For suppose that some contingent being had no modes, then all of its affections[123] would be absolutely necessary (§52,[124] 107), and hence its existence would be absolutely necessary (§55), which is absurd[125] (§109).

Meier adds after "affections": would be attributes, and thus

§113

The determinations of something that is one are inseparable (§73). Hence, the opposite of any one of these is impossible (§72, 81). Therefore, the determinations of something that is one are necessary (§101), and in fact the determinations of a being that is absolutely one are absolutely necessary, and those of a being that is hypothetically one are hypothetically necessary (§102, 176). United beings are necessarily conjoined (§79), either in themselves, or hypothetically (§102).[126]

§114

Necessary things are determinable only in a unique mode and in a unique ground.[c] For they are either A or not-A. A third mode and a third ground of determinability are impossible (§10). Now, suppose that something necessary is

---

[a] As Meier's translation suggests, the "something" here must be taken in its strictly logical sense, and thus not as implying that this is true of all things. Cf. G/K: "The opposite of the existence in regard to a thing is possible…"

[b] Kant E3553, 1760s–70s: "Necessary throughout."

[c] Kant E3554, 1780–9? 1776–9??: "Either in regard to a determination or to all: 1. the opposite is internally or absolutely unthinkable, i.e. there cannot be more necessary beings. i.e. under the condition under which something necessarily belongs to a thing, this thing cannot be determined

determinable by means of A. Then not-A is the opposite of this determination (§81), and hence impossible (§101). Therefore, there are no more modes and ways of determinability apart from the unique A (§77).[127] If something were determinable only in a unique mode and a unique ground A, then its opposite would be not-A, but this is impossible (§77). Were it not-A, its opposite would be A, but this is impossible (§77). There is no third option[a] (§10). Therefore, the opposite of something determinable only in a unique mode and in unique ground is impossible, to the extent that those are necessary (§102). Contingent things are not necessary, and hence they are not determinable only in a unique mode or in unique ground, nor by more than two (§10). Therefore, they are determinable in a two-fold mode. Things which are determinable in a two-fold mode and ground are not necessary, and hence they are contingent (§102). And thus these terms may be defined: (1) NECESSARY, as determinable only through a unique mode, (2) CONTINGENT, as determinable through a two-fold mode, (3) NECESSITY, through the uniqueness of determinability, (4) CONTINGENCY, through the doubleness of determinability.

§115

The hypothetically one as such has determinations that are separable in themselves (§76, 18), and hence its unity is intrinsically[128] contingent (§104).

§116

Transcendental unity is absolutely necessary (§73, 102); hence, it has no opposite (§102, 15).

§117

Since the opposite of order is confusion (§79, 78) and the absence of conjunction (§78, 81), order is absolutely necessary in things conjoined necessarily *per se*, and indeed in the same mode (§102). Therefore, wherever neither the conjunction nor the identity of the conjunction is absolutely necessary, the order is contingent in itself (§104).[129]

identity] agreement

§118

Transcendental truth is the order in the essential determinations and attributes (§89), and hence in things necessarily conjoined *per se* (§78, 107), and indeed in the same mode (§7, 22). Thus, transcendental truth is absolutely necessary (§117), and has no opposite (§102, 15).

Meier expands the first sentence as: Unconditioned truth is the order among all essential parts and attributes. These are not only together in all things in an absolutely necessary way, but also in the same way.

in another way; however, it can be subsumed under another condition. e.g. A bell cannot be other than internally empty and open; but the same metal can surely be cast into the form of a bar."
[a] *Tertium non datur:* lit. "a third is not given"

§119

The order of several things in one, whose non-conjunction or confusion is internally possible in a being, is the truth that is contingent in itself (§117, 89).

§120

A dream taken as objective and a fabulous world are non-beings (§118, 91), and if they seem to be beings, they are fictional beings (§62).

§121

The opposite of perfection is IMPERFECTION and in fact is (1) simple disagreement, which is imperfection IN THE PRIVATIVE SENSE, if among several things taken together some are not grounds of one thing; or (2) dissension, which is IMPERFECTION IN THE SENSE OF A CONTRARY, if among several things taken together, some agree with one thing and some with its opposite (§81, 94).[a]

if among several things taken together some are not grounds of one thing] if among several things posited at the same time, none of them contains a ground from among the determining grounds of perfection || IMPERFECTION IN THE SENSE OF A CONTRARY] IMPERFECTION THAT CONSISTS IN A FAULT

§122

Absolutely necessary perfection belongs to those things whose disagreement and hence dissension is impossible in itself (§121, 120), whereas perfection that is contingent in itself belongs to those things whose non-agreement or even dissent is possible in itself (§104, 121).

§123

Transcendental perfection is absolutely necessary (§122, 94), and hence has no opposite imperfection (§121, 102).

Section II. The alterable and the inalterable

§124

BEINGS FOLLOW ONE ANOTHER (succeed one another) when one of these exists after the other. The determination of beings by virtue of which they succeed one another is their succession.[130]

§125

When the determinations of a thing[b] succeed one another, it IS ALTERED: hence, if

---

[a] For this two-fold distinction of imperfection, especially for the English translation of this term, also see Kant's "Vienna Logic," *Lectures on Logic*, ed. and trans. by J. Michael Young (Cambridge: Cambridge University Press, 2004), 272.
[b] Kant E3555, 1764–autumn 1770 (inserted into the sentence): "capable of enduring"

the determinations of a thing are able to succeed one another, then it is ALTERABLE (variable);[131] if the determinations of a thing are not able to succeed one another, then it is INALTERABLE (fixed, invariable, constant).[132, a] However, the very succession of determinations in a being is its own ALTERATION, and, at the same time,[133] the alteration of its determinations.

§126

The alteration of a being is either the INTERNAL[134] ALTERATION of what is internal, or the EXTERNAL[135] ALTERATION, i.e. relative, alteration of relations (§125, 37).

§127

The ALTERABILITY of a thing, or the possibility of alterations in it,[136] is either absolute (§125, 15) or hypothetical (§125, 16). The INALTERABILITY of a thing, or the impossibility of alterations in it,[137] is either absolute (§125, 15) or hypothetical (§125, 17).

§128

No being that is inalterable *per se* is hypothetically alterable. Therefore, no hypothetically alterable being is absolutely inalterable.[138] *Everything hypothetically inalterable is alterable in itself.* Everything hypothetically alterable is alterable in itself.[139] Therefore, the absolutely inalterable is neither hypothetically alterable nor inalterable. Something absolutely alterable is hypothetically inalterable (§127, 18).[140]

Meier adds after "hypothetically inalterable": and alterable

§129

The determinations of alterable things can succeed one another (§125) and hence alterable things are determinable in many modes (§74, 34). Necessary things are not determinable in many modes (§114). Hence, necessary things are inalterable (§125).

§130

Absolutely necessary things are absolutely inalterable; hypothetically necessary things are hypothetically inalterable (§129, 127).

Meier adds after "absolutely inalterable": e.g. the essences of all things

§131

Nothing alterable is necessary (§129). Hence everything alterable is contingent (§101), and indeed, what is alterable in itself is contingent in itself, and what is hypothetically alterable is hypothetically contingent (§104, 127).

Meier reformulates this section, combining it with §133 below, as follows: The opposite of that which is alterable is possible. Thus everything, insofar as it is alterable, is also contingent. The unconditionally alterable is also unconditionally contingent, and the conditionally alterable is also in this regard contingent. Everything contingent has an opposite that is possible, and thus it

---

[a] Kant E3556, 1764–autumn 1770: "the subject is altered, the determinations are varied, the state [breaks off]"

can have a determination and can also not have it, not in the same way, but rather one after the other. And consequently everything contingent, insofar as it is contingent, is also alterable; the unconditioned in an unconditioned way, and the conditioned in a conditioned way.

§132

The essences (§106), essential determinations and attributes (§107) of things, the existence of a necessary being (§109), all its internal determinations (§110), transcendental unity (§116), truth (§118), and perfection (§123) are absolutely and internally inalterable (§130, 126)

§133

The modes of a being considered in itself can succeed one another in it (§125, 65), and hence both the modes themselves, and the being in which they are, are absolutely alterable (§125, 127). Now, every contingent being has modes (§112). Therefore every contingent being is absolutely and internally alterable (§126). The relations of a being are intrinsically contingent (§108). Therefore, they are able to succeed one another in that being considered in itself (§124, 104). Hence, they are absolutely alterable in every being (§127). Every being, with regard to all its relations, is alterable (§125).[141]

§134

Essence is not alterable (§132). Hence, every contingent being is alterable with regard to its existence (§133, 56). Hence, the existence of a contingent being is alterable (§125), and is thus neither an essential quality nor attribute, although it is still an internal determination (§55) and therefore a mode (§52). If the existence of a thing is a mode, then its existence is absolutely alterable (§133) and hence intrinsically[142] contingent (§131). Therefore, if the existence of a being is a mode, then it is a CONTINGENT BEING[143] (§109). Hence, a CONTINGENT BEING can be defined as a being whose existence is a mode.

Section III. The real and the negative

§135

If a negation is posited, then a reality is removed (§36,[144] 10). Hence, negations and realities are mutually opposite to each other (§81). We call realities, and the beings in which they are, REAL BEINGS, or positive beings. Negations, however, are called NEGATIVE BEINGS.[a]

§136

A purely negative being would be that in which there is no reality, and hence no

---

[a] Kant E3557, 1771–8 (next to and between §135 and 136): "Whether matter, motion are realities./ Whether vice is a reality or a negation./Negations in respect to objects are limits./Reality is affected by negations./Plurality of reality and degree./Space and time have no degree./Extensive, protensive and intensive magnitude."

realities (§36), no possibility (§8), no connectedness[a] (§19), no actuality (§55), no unity (§73), no truth (§89), no perfection (§94). Therefore, a purely negative being is not a being, and if it seems to be a being, it is[145] a fictional being (§62). Therefore, since there is some reality in every being, every being is real (§135).

§137

Since every being is real (§136), either no negation will inhere in it, or a specific one will inhere in it along with its realities (§10), and this [negation] is indeed either absolutely necessary or contingent in itself (§102, 104). The former is a negation in the strict sense (in the strict sense, a negative being). The latter is a privation or a privative being. Negative essential determinations and attributes are NEGATIONS IN THE STRICT SENSE (§106, 107), and negative modes are PRIVATIONS (§108).[146]

a specific one] some || *Meier adds after* "absolutely necessary": as is the negated essential quality or attribute || *Meier adds after* "in itself": e.g. negated modes

§138

No privations are absolutely necessary in a being (§137, 105) and hence internal privations are neither essential determinations nor attributes (§107). Therefore, internal privations are modes (§52). And thus a necessary being does not have internal privations[147] (§111), and whatever has them is a contingent being (§111).[148]

§139

A negative being, as such, is not positive (§135). But, if it, insofar as it is a negation, were to agree with a reality, it would be a reality (§94, 36). Hence, a negative being, as such, does not agree with a reality in the real being to which it belongs (§137).

Meier adds after "negation,": were the ground of a reality or

§140

Realities, as such, agree only with realities. For, to be the consequence of pure realities is a reality (§36, 14).

agree ... realities.] can only be the ground of a reality or only agree with a reality.

§141

Every being is perfect (§99) and real (§137), and hence its perfection, as such, is the agreement of realities in one reality (§94, 140).[b]

as such] insofar as it is a true thing

§142

When negations are posited in a being, lack of agreement is posited (§141, 139), and

---

[a] Kant E3558, 1764–75 (next to §136 "connectedness—perfection"): "by the opposite of the real <*opposito realis*>"
[b] Kant E3559, 1780–9? (1776–9?) (under §141, no clear relation): "limitation <*limitatio*>."

hence imperfection (§121). Hence, when negations in the strict sense are posited in a being, absolutely necessary imperfection is posited (§137).

§143

The absolutely necessary imperfection of a being is either its attribute or essential quality (§107, 108). However, because there is no sufficient ground of negations in realities (§139), there is no imperfection in the attributes of the being if there is not also one in its essential determinations (§50); nor is there imperfection in the essential determinations of a being if there is not also one in its affections (§23).

Meier adds after "(§139),": or of realities in negations

§144

When privations are posited in a being, imperfection is posited (§142), but imperfection that is contingent in itself (§138).

§145

There is no essential perfection without accidental perfection (§98, 140), nor is there accidental perfection without essential perfection (§98). There is no essential imperfection without accidental imperfection, nor is there accidental imperfection without essential imperfection (§143, 98); nor are essential perfection and imperfection opposites (§81, 142).

Meier adds before the first sentence: Every reality of every thing must have grounds and consequences that are realities. || nor are … §142).] thus a thing can be essentially perfect and essentially imperfect at the same time, though from different points of view; and not every essential perfection is opposed to every essential imperfection.

§146

If when a thing is posited, imperfection is also posited, then it is an EVIL. Hence, negations are an evil (§142). When these are negations in a strict sense, it is METAPHYSICAL EVIL, which when it is posited, absolutely necessary imperfection is also posited (§142). Or if they are privations, it is CONTINGENT EVIL (a physical evil, in the broad sense,[149] cf. §788),[150] which when it is posited, imperfection that is contingent in itself is also posited (§144).

§147

When the realities of a being are posited, its perfection is posited (§141). Hence, realities are good (§100), and indeed absolutely necessary realities are a METAPHYSICAL GOOD, and realities contingent in themselves are a CONTINGENT GOOD (a physical good, understood broadly,[151] cf. §787).[152]

Meier inserts after "METAPHYSICAL GOOD": or the metaphysical goodness of a thing

Section IIII. The singular and the universal

§148

The collection of all determinations compossible in a being is its COMPLETE DETERMINATION. Hence, a being is either completely determined or not (§10). The former is SINGULAR (an individual),[153] and the latter is UNIVERSAL. Either of these is called MORE INFERIOR with respect to all the universal things that it contains within itself, while the latter [i.e. the things not determined] are called superior with respect to former [i.e. the more inferior].[154]

§149[155, a]

A universal being considered in its inferior being, and a singular being considered in terms of the other predicates belonging to it beyond a certain universal, is CONSIDERED <*SPECTATUR*> CONCRETELY, and is then called CONCRETE. However, the universal being that is indeed considered <*attenditur*>, but not in its inferior, and the singular being in which, however, only a certain superior predicate belonging to it is CONSIDERED <*attenditur*>, is considered <*SPECTATUR*> ABSTRACTLY and is then called ABSTRACT. The universal in the concrete is called the PHYSICAL UNIVERSAL (in many, in the thing), and the universal in the abstract is the LOGICAL UNIVERSAL (after many, after the thing).[b]

being considered in its inferior] thing considered as a determination of its inferior

§150

The universal that can only be represented concretely in individuals, or, that which contains only individuals under itself, is a SPECIES. That which can only be represented concretely in universals, or, that which also contains universals under it, is a GENUS, and the LOWEST of these is that which is in no [further lower][c] genus, which is to say, that which contains no genus under it. The SUPREME of these is that in which there is no genus, which is to say, that which is contained under no genus. And finally, the SUBORDINATE genera are those that are not the supreme.

§151

The determinations of an inferior being that are not determined in its superior[156] are its DIFFERENCE. Hence, the GENERIC DIFFERENCE is the collection of determinations that are determined in the genus and not determined in its superior. SPECIFIC DIFFERENCE is the collection of the determinations of the species[157] that are not determined in its lowest genus. NUMERICAL DIFFERENCE (thisness, the principle of individuation) is the collection of determinations of an individual that are not determined in the species (§148).[158]

individual …are] individual that are determined in the individual, but are

---

[a] Kant E3561, 1780–9? (1776–9?) (beginning): "nominalists and realists."
[b] Kant E3560, 1765–6: "Occamists (Thomists) are nominalists. Scotists are realists <*Occamistae (Thomistae) nominalistae. Scotistae realistae*>"
[c] Here we follow Mirbach's interpolation "*weiteren unteren*" (2: 1060).

§152

Singular beings are internally entirely determined (§148), and hence are actual (§54).

Meier adds after "actual": or nothing can be represented as an individual thing, if it is not thought of as an actual thing

§153

Since the superior is in the inferior[159] (§149, 148),[160] the species, the lowest genus, the subordinate genera, and the supreme genus are in the individual; the genera are in the species; the superior genera are in the lowest and subordinate genera, and the supreme genus is in all the lower genera (§150).[161]

§154

The determinations of the supreme genus are in its inferiors (§148),[162] i.e. in the subordinate genera and in the lowest genus, in the species and in individuals; the determinations of the subordinate genus are in its[163] inferior genera,[164] species, and individuals; the determinations of the lowest genus are in the species and individuals; the determinations of the species are in individuals (§153, 35), *i.e. the determinations of the superior are in its inferiors, whether they be positive or negative (§36). This proposition* is called *the maxim of all and none <dictum de 0[mni] et N[ullo]>*.[165]

maxim of all or none] conclusion from the universal to the particular

Section V. The whole and the part

§155

The one that is entirely identical with many taken together is a WHOLE, and the many taken together that are identical to the whole are its PARTS. Those parts that must be taken together with a given part[166] so that [together] they are entirely identical with the whole are its coparts, or COMPLEMENTS TO THE WHOLE (supplements).

§156

Any part taken together with its fellow parts that are complementary to the whole is an ACTUAL PART, and a POTENTIAL PART is any given part taken together with others.[a]

§157

The whole is entirely identical with its actual parts[b] (cf. §155, cf. §156), and hence also *equal, similar, and congruent* (cf. §70).

its … parts] all its actual parts taken together

---

[a] Kant E3562, 1770–8: "not 2/3 + 3/4 = 1. Concerning the 21 quarters of the city of Paris."
[b] Kant E3563, 1776–89 (changes the definition to read): "A composite entirely identical with its parts is a whole < *Compositum prorsus idem cum suis partibus est totum>*."

§158

A being whose essence is part of another is an INCOMPLETE BEING[a] and a being whose essence is not part of another is a COMPLETE BEING.[b]

§159

A multitude of parts is MAGNITUDE (absolute, cf. §161)[167] or continuous quantity (§75).[c] A multitude of wholes is NUMBER (absolute, cf. §161)[168] or discrete quantity (§75). If the wholes of which a number consists are looked upon again as parts, it is a BROKEN NUMBER (fraction)[d]; if not, it is a WHOLE NUMBER.[169]

Meier adds after "of parts": or determinations of a thing

§160

That whose part is equal to a whole is GREATER (>); that whose whole is equal to a part is LESS[170] (<).

a whole] another whole; a part] a part of another

§161

The MINIMUM is only[171] greater than nothing, or the minimum is that than which a smaller being is impossible;[e] the MAXIMUM is only[172] less than nothing, or, the maximum is that than which a greater is impossible.[f] A greater multitude is a COMPARATIVE MULTITUDE (cf. §74); a smaller multitude is FEWNESS. A greater magnitude is a COMPARATIVE MAGNITUDE (cf. §159); a smaller magnitude is

---

[a] Kant E3564, 1776–89: "That which cannot exist unless either as a part or as a consequence or as an accident <*Quod non existere potest nisi vel ut pars vel ut rationatum vel ut accidens>.*"

[b] Kant E3565, 1776–89 (between §158 and 159): "totality of either a quantum or a composite as such. A part of a whole, either a part of a quantum or of a composite <*totalitas vel quanti vel compositi qua talis. Pars totius vel quanti vel composite>.*"

[c] Kant E3566, 1771–2? (1769–71?): "The quantum of a quantity—indeterminate <*quantum quantitates—indeterminatae>*/a quantity is determined <*determinata est quantitas>*/(*deleted*: parts are assignable <*partes assignabiles sunt>*)/A giveable quantum is that (*crossed out*: whole) which can be actual as something complete. Assignable parts are those which can be clearly known in themselves. (*deleted*: the parts of that) That in which the multitude of the assigned parts is indeterminate (whose parts can only be completely given through a whole) is a continuum <*quantum dabile est, quod [totum] ut completum potest esse actuale. partes assignabiles sunt, quae in se possunt clare cognosci [cuius partes] in quo partium assignabilium multitudo est indeterminata (cuius partes nisi per totum omnimode dari non possunt), est continuum>.*" [Note: The editor of AA states that there are two underscores under Baumgarten's "parts," and that this probably means this word should be added at this point in Kant's note, and either "is MAGNITUDE" or "is continuous quantity" taken as the predicate.]

[d] In his parenthetical metonym Baumgarten uses both *fractio* and *minutia*, which both translate as "fraction". See R.E. Latham, *The Revised Medieval Latin Word List* (Oxford: Oxford University Press, 1965), 300.

[e] Kant E3567, 1762–3: "False; for that is greater than nothing whose part is equal to nothing; therefore nothing is a part of something, which is repugnant <*Falsum est; nam quod est nihilo majus, illius pars nihilo aequale; ergo nihilum est pars alicujus, quod repugnat>.*"

[f] No such term or definition is found in Wolff. Nicholas of Cusa, however, defines the maximum in a similar way as "that than which nothing can be greater," and the minimum as "that than which nothing can be lesser" (*De Docta Ignorantia* 1: 2–3).

SMALLNESS (cf. §159). A greater number is COMPARATIVE (cf. §159); a smaller number is RARITY.[173]

Meier reformulates the first line to read: It is impossible for the SMALLEST to be still smaller than it is, and it is impossible for the GREATEST to be still greater than it is.

§162

To be altered into less is to BE DIMINISHED, whereas to be altered into more is to BE INCREASED. Therefore, whatever may be increased or diminished is alterable (§125), indeed with respect to quantity (§160, 70), and hence internally (§126, 69).

§163

The essences of things, the essential determinations and attributes, every internal determination of a necessary being, and the transcendental unity, truth, and perfection in beings cannot be intrinsically increased or diminished (§162, 132).

§164

The internal determination of a being that can be increased or diminished is a mode (§163, 52), and that in which such an internal[174] determination, which may be increased or diminished in it,[175] occurs is a contingent being (§111).

Section VI. The first principles of the mathematics of intensive quantities[176, a]

§165[177]

The smallest possibility is the non-repugnance of the smallest and fewest[178] beings (§161, 8). Therefore, the more and greater compossible beings there are, the greater is the possibility (§160), until it is the greatest possibility, which is when there are the most and largest compossible beings (§161). Hence, every hypothetical possibility of a being is greater than its intrinsic possibility (§16,[179] 15).

§166[b]

The smallest ground is that which has only one smallest consequence (§161). Therefore, the more and greater consequences it has, the greater it is (§160) until it is the greatest ground having the greatest number of consequences (§161).[180] The magnitude of a ground stemming from the number of consequences is FECUNDITY, and from the magnitude of these, is WEIGHT (gravity, dignity, nobility).

---

[a] From his handwritten notes it is clear that this section influenced Kant's understanding of quantity, particularly the quantity of reality in sensation. He refers specifically to it in this role as the "second application of mathematics to natural science" in *Prolegomena* §24, AA 4: 306–7.

[b] Kant E3568, 1764–8 1769? (1770–1?) 1773–5?? (1762–3??) (across from the beginning of §166, perhaps next to the conclusion of §165): "Absolutely possible (this is in some respect) <*Absolute (h.e. respectu quodam) possibile>./*Also possible in a certain respect <*in certo respectu etiam possibile>*."

§167[181]

The smallest nexus belongs to only one smallest ground (§166, 14). Therefore, the more and greater grounds there are, the greater is the nexus (§160) until it becomes the greatest nexus of the most and greatest grounds (§161), i.e. of the most fecund and grave grounds (§166). A greater nexus is HARMONY.[182]

§168[183]

The smallest hypothetical possibility is that through which only one smallest being enjoys the smallest nexus (§16,[184] 161). Therefore, the more and greater beings that are possible in a greater nexus, the greater is the hypothetical possibility (§160) until it is the greatest hypothetical possibility, which is when the most and greatest beings are possible in the greatest nexus (§161), i.e. the most fecund and grave consequences of the most fecund and grave grounds (§167).[185]

§169[186]

The sufficient ground is the most fecund ground (§166, 21). The smallest among the sufficient grounds, however, is that which is sufficient for only one smallest consequence (§166, 161). Therefore, the more and greater consequences for which it suffices, the greater is the ground (§160) until it is the greatest ground sufficient for the most and greatest consequences (§161), and likewise the most fecund and noble ground (§166).[187]

§170[188]

The more distant ground is greater than the closer (§166, 27), and hence an unqualified sufficient ground is greater than all qualified sufficient grounds (§169, 28).

§171[189]

The smallest essence is the collection of the fewest[190] and smallest essential determinations (§40, 161). The more and greater essential determinations there are, the greater it is (§160), until it is the greatest essence, which is the collection of the most and greatest essential determinations (§161).

§172[191]

The smallest universal nexus is where everything[a] is either a smallest ground or a consequence of such (cf. §48, 167). Therefore, where everything[b] is a greater ground, or the consequence of a greater ground, or both, the universal nexus is greater (§160) until it is the greatest nexus, which is where all the individual things[c] are the greatest grounds (§161), i.e. the most fecund and grave (§166).

§173[192]

The smallest unity is when the fewest and smallest determinations of only one <*unici*>

---

[a] G/K: "the individual"
[b] G/K: "the individual"
[c] G/K: "the individual"

smallest being are inseparable[193] (§73, 161). Therefore, the more and greater determinations of more and greater beings that are inseparable, the greater is the unity (§160), until it is the greatest, which is when the most and greatest determinations of the most and greatest beings[194] are inseparable (§161). The smallest uniqueness is when one <*unum*> smallest being differs from the fewest and smallest beings through only one smallest difference (§77, 161). Therefore, the greater is the being that is distinguished from more and greater beings through more and greater differences, the greater is the uniqueness (§160) until it is the greatest uniqueness, which is when the greatest being is distinguished from all the beings that are also the greatest in their own genus through the most and greatest differences (§161).[195]

§174[196]

The smallest identity is when only one smallest determination is common among the fewest and smallest[197] beings (§38, 161). Hence, the more and greater determinations that are common in more and greater[198] beings, the greater is the identity (§160) until it is the greatest identity, which is the communion of the most and greatest determinations in the most and greatest beings (§161).

§175[199]

The smallest order is the smallest identity in a conjunction[200] (§78, 161).[201] Therefore, the greater the identity of a conjunction, the greater is the order (§160, 174), until it is the greatest, which is when there is the greatest identity of conjunction (§161), i.e. when the most and greatest things are conjoined as often and as much in the same way, as often and as much as they can be (§174). The smallest unity is the necessary conjunction of the fewest and smallest things (§79, 113, 161). Therefore, the more things that are conjoined, the extensively greater is the unity; the greater the things joined with greater necessity, the intensively greater is the unity, until it is the necessary conjunction of the most things, which is the extensively greatest unity, or until it is the conjunction of only two or three of these, provided that they are the greatest things and the conjunction is the most necessary conjunction that can exist between them, which is the intensively greatest unity.

§176

Since the knowability of DETERMINATIONS from the ground is CONFORMITY WITH its GROUND (§80), this conformity will be the smallest if the determination can be known only from the smallest ground (§161, 166) with the smallest possibility of knowledge[202] (§165). The greater is the ground from which the determination is to be known and the more possible this knowledge is,[203] the greater is the conformity of the determination with the ground[204] (§160) until it is the greatest conformity, which is maximally knowable from the greatest grounds (§161).[205]

§177[206]

The determination conforming to the sufficient, more fecund, and graver ground (§166, 169), and hence the more remote and unqualified ground (§170), has greater conformity (§176) than the determination only conforming to the insufficient, less fecund, less grave (§166, 169), or closer ground, or only with the qualified sufficient ground (§170).

§178[207]

The smallest defect is opposed to the determination of the smallest conformity with the ground (§82, 161). Hence, the greater is the defect, the greater is its conformity in the opposite (§160, 176), until it is the greatest defect, which is opposed to the determination in which the conformity is the greatest (§176, 161).

§179[208]

The defect contrary to the sufficient, more fecund, graver, more remote, and unqualified ground is greater than the defect contrary only to the insufficient, less fecund, less grave, closer, and qualified sufficient ground (§178, 177).

§180[209]

The magnitude of the conformity with the ground in a determination, which a law expresses, is the STRENGTH OF THE LAW. The law expressing a determination of comparatively greater conformity with the ground is STRONG, of comparatively poorer conformity, WEAK.[210, a] Hence, a law is maximally weak or minimally strong that expresses a determination of the smallest conformity with the ground (§161, 176). The greater the conformity with the ground[211] expressed by the law, the stronger is the law (§160), until it is the strongest law, which expresses a determination in which there is the greatest conformity (§161).[212]

of the conformity … determination] of the agreement of a determination with its ground

§181[213]

A law expressing a determination conforming to a ground that is sufficient, more fecund, graver, more distant (among whose consequences it belongs, or[214] a ground to which may be subordinated a comparatively closer ground),[215] and unqualified is stronger than a weaker law expressing a determination only conforming to a ground that is insufficient, less fecund, less grave, closer (which is subordinated to that more distant ground with which it is being compared),[216] and only qualifiedly sufficient (§180, 177).

§182[217, b]

A law[c] expressing a determination conforming to the sufficient and more distant ground is called a SUPERIOR LAW, and the law expressing a determination conforming to the

---

[a] Kant E3569, 1780–9: "Strictly determined, broadly <*stricte determinat, late*>./One who admits exceptions is more latitudinous <*latitudinarius, qui admittit exceptiones*>."
[b] Kant E3571, 1776–89: "The intensive magnitude of laws rests on the necessity, i.e. the lack of exceptions. There is no rule without exception, but law is without exception <*Nulla regula sine exceptione, sed lex est absque exceptione*>."
[c] Kant E3570, 1780–9? (1762–3?) (next to "A law … SUPERIOR"): "the more it approaches universality and lacks restrictions <*quo magis ad universalitatem accedit et caret restrictionibus*>."

closer is called an INFERIOR LAW. *Therefore, superior laws are stronger than inferior laws, and the supreme law is the strongest* (§181).[218]

§183[219]

The greatest order has the most common rules (§175, 86), and hence is maximally composite (§88), and thus simple order, however great it be, is still not the greatest (§175, 88).

§184[220]

The smallest metaphysical truth is the smallest order of many in one (§175, 89), or the smallest conformity with universal principles (§176, 92). The more and greater are the things joined together in a being in accordance with more and stronger rules, the greater is the truth in that being (§175, 180) until it is the greatest truth, which is when the most and greatest beings are discerned to be most appropriate to the strongest rules (of the universal principles, §182) (§160, 161).

§185[221]

The smallest perfection is only one smallest agreement of the fewest and smallest beings[222] in one smallest being (§94,[223] 161). Hence, the more and greater beings, the more beings in which they agree and the greater they are, the more often[224] and the more closely they agree, the greater is the perfection (§160), until it is the greatest perfection, which is the greatest agreement of the most and the greatest beings in one (§161, 169).[225] Moreover, since the supreme perfection is thus maximally composite (§183,[226] 96), simple perfection, however great it may be, is nevertheless not the greatest (§96).

§186[227]

The smallest exception is made from the weakest rule of perfection on account of the strongest (§178, 97). Therefore, the stronger the rule of perfection from which the exception departs, and the weaker the rule is on account of which it departs, the greater is the exception (§160), until it is the greatest exception, which is the exception departing from the strongest and hence the supreme rule of perfection (§182) on account of the weakest law (§161). If the sufficient and insufficient grounds of perfection collide, the exception from the sufficient is greater and the exception from the insufficient is less. If the more fecund and the less fecund collide, the exception from the more fecund is greater, and the exception from the less fecund is less. If the grounds of the graver and less grave perfection collide, the exception from the graver is greater, and the exception from the less grave is less. If the more distant and closer grounds subordinated to it are brought into conflict, the exception from the more distant is greater, and the exception from the closer is less. If the unqualifiedly sufficient ground and the qualified sufficient ground are brought into conflict, the exception from the unqualified is greater, and the exception from the qualified ground is less (§181). If the superior and inferior rules of perfection collide, the exception from the superior is greater and the exception from the inferior is less (§182). Hence, the exception contrary to the supreme law of perfection, i.e.

the exception which is made to the supreme rule of perfection because of the least rule of perfection, i.e. the exception conforming to the least rule of perfection, is the greatest (§187,[228] 182).

§187

The smallest good is that which, when posited, the smallest perfection is posited (§100, 161). The greater the perfection that must be posited when a good is posited, the greater is this good (§160), until it is the BEST,[229] which, when posited, the supreme perfection is posited (§161).

§188

The smallest contingent being is that whose opposite is minimally possible (§104, 161). Therefore, the greater the possibility of one of its opposites, the greater is the contingency of the other (§160). The greatest contingency is the contingency of that whose opposite has the greatest possibility (§161).[230]

§189

The greater is the separability of the determinations of something that is hypothetically one, the greater is the contingency of its unity (§115, 188). The more that non-conjunction and confusion are possible, the more contingent is the opposed order (§117, 188). The more that non-conjunction or confusion of the various determinations[231] <*variorum*> of some being is possible, the more contingent is its opposite truth (§119, 188). The more that imperfection is possible, the more contingent is the opposite perfection (§122, 188).

§190[232]

The smallest alteration is the succession of only one smallest being in only one smallest being (§161, 125). Therefore, the more and greater beings that succeed one another in more and greater beings, the greater is the alteration (§160) until it is the greatest, which is the succession of the most and greatest beings in the most and greatest beings. The smallest possibility of the smallest change in a being is its smallest alterability (§161, 127). Therefore, the more possible and the greater the alteration is in a being, the greater is its alterability, until it is the greatest,[233] which would be the greatest possibility of the greatest alteration (§161). The smallest reality in a being is the greatest paucity and insignificance of its truly positive determinations (§135, 161). The more and the greater are its truly positive determinations, the more real it is. Therefore, the MOST REAL BEING is that in which there are the most and greatest realities (§161, 36). These absolutely necessary realities are the SUPREME GOOD, or the METAPHYSICAL BEST (§187, 147), while realities that are contingent in themselves are the CONTINGENT SUPREME GOOD (physical,[234] understood broadly).[235]

Section VII.[236] **Substance and accident**

§191

A being either cannot exist except as a determination of another (in something else),[237] or it can (§10). The former is an accident (a predicable or physical thing, cf. §50, whose being <*esse*> is belonging <*inesse*>, συμβεβηκός [a]),[238] and the latter is a SUBSTANCE[239, b] (a being subsisting *per se*, form,[c] ἐντελέχεια, οὐσία, ὑπόστασις, ἐνέργεια),[d] because it can exist, although it is neither in something else, nor the determination of something else.[240, e]

§192

The existence of an accident as such is INHERENCE, whereas the existence of substance as such is SUBSISTENCE.

§193

If accidents seem to subsist *per se*, then they are SUBSTANTIATED PHENOMENA.[f]

SUBSTANTIATED PHENOMENA] APPARENT SUBSTANCES

§194

Accidents[241] cannot exist except in something else. Now, there is nothing else apart from substances and accidents (§191). Therefore, accidents cannot exist except in substances, or, *accidents do not exist outside of their own substances*[242] (§58).

§195

Essential determinations, attributes, modes, accidents, and relations (§191, 52) cannot exist except in substances (§194).

§196

That in a substance in which accidents are able to inhere, or substance to the extent that it is a subject (cf. §344) in which accidents are able to inhere, is called SUBSTANTIAL,[243] and accidents do not exist outside of what is substantial (§194).

---

[a] Lit., "standing together," or "being in agreement."

[b] Kant E3573, 1764–autumn 1770: "Substance is a real subject <*Subiectum reale est substantia*>"
Kant E3574, 1764–9 (under E3573): "an accident can be a logical subject <*accidens potest esse subiectum logicum*>."

[c] Kant E3572, 1764–78 (over "subsisting *per se*, form"): "substrate, stable <*substratum, stabile*>"

[d] This clutch of familiar Aristotelian terms can be translated as "full reality, substance, that which lies underneath, activity."

[e] Wolff: "An enduring and modifiable subject is called *substance*. A being, however, that is not modifiable is called an *accident*" (WO §768).

[f] Wolff: "A *substantiated phenomenon* is that which appears in the form of a substance <*instar substantiae*>" (WC §299). Although this precise term is not found in Leibniz, the underlying idea clearly has roots in his work, and is indeed ascribed to him by Kant. Kant adopts the term as his own in his explanations of matter in the first *Critique*, particularly in the Schematism and Amphiboly.

§197

If accidents inhere in a substance, then there is some ground of inherence (§20), or POWER, IN THE BROADER SENSE (efficacy, energy, activity, §216), and a sufficient ground (§22). This [latter] is POWER[244] IN THE STRICTER SENSE (and sometimes called simply POWER for the sake of brevity).

If … inherence] If accidents are actual in a substance, then this actuality must have a ground

§198

Power in the stricter sense[245] is either a substance or an accident (§191). Now, it is not an accident, since it is the sufficient ground of all accidents (§197). Therefore, it is a substance, and to the extent that accidents can inhere in it as in a subject, it is substantial (§196).

§199

Every substance is endowed with something substantial (§191, 196) and hence with power (§198).[246] Every substance is substantial (§196, 191), and hence is power in both the broader and the stricter sense (§198, 197).

§200[247]

If substances appear to be accidents, then they would be PREDICATED SUBSTANCES; singular substances are SUPPOSITS[a] <SUPPOSITA>.[b]

PREDICATED SUBSTANCES] APPARENT ACCIDENTS

§201

Power is attributed to substantiated phenomena (§199, 193),[248] and, moreover, substantiated phenomena are powers in the broader sense, or are endowed with powers in the broader sense (§197, 23). And if power in the stricter sense is attributed to accidents, then they are substantiated phenomena (§198, 193).

§202

Every substance absolutely and necessarily has essential determinations and attributes (§107). Hence, every substance has accidents (§191, 195). But either it has modes, or it does not (§10). If a substance has modes, it is a contingent being and if it has none, it is a necessary being (§111). Therefore, substance is either necessary or contingent. The subsistence of a contingent substance is a mode (§134, 192).[249]

§203[250]

The smallest power is the ground of only one smallest inherent accident (§197, 166). Therefore, the more and greater the inherent accidents of which it is the ground, the

[a] Kant 3575, 1775–89? (1769–75?): "Substantiated phenomenon <*Phaenomenon substantiatum*>"
[b] Baumgarten glosses *SUPPOSITA* with "*einzle vor sich bestehende Dinge.*" Leibniz kept alive the mediaeval concept of the *suppositum,* which he glosses as "substantial individual" in his essay on transubstantiation (cf. Leibniz, "On Transubstantiation," in Leibniz's *Philosophical Papers and Letters,* translated by Leroy E. Loemker (Chicago: University of Chicago Press, 1956), Vol. 1, 178–85). See also MM 1: 261.

greater it is, until it is the greatest ground, which would be the ground of the most and greatest inherent accidents (§197, 166).

§204

The science of powers is philosophical DYNAMICS and mathematical DYNAMOMETRICS. [251]

Section VIII. State[252, a]

§205

A contingent supposit[253] is determined[254] by means of modes[255] and relations (§184,[256] 200). Hence, fixed or intrinsically inalterable parts (§107, 133) coexist in it along with alterable parts (§133).[b] This manner of coexistence is STATE. Therefore, a contingent supposit[257] has a state. The state of united things is UNION.[258]

§206

The coexistence of modes with the fixed parts is the INTERNAL STATE. Hence, a contingent supposit[259] has an internal state (§205).

§207

The relations of a substance are internally alterable in it (§133).[260] Therefore, relations co-existing with fixed parts produce what is called AN EXTERNAL STATE (§205).

§208

When a mode is altered, the internal state is altered (§125, 206) and when a relation is altered, the external state is altered (§125, 207). Now, modes and relations are alterable (§133, 207). Therefore, alterations of state are possible in a contingent substance (§206, 207).

§209

The alteration of a mode is a MODIFICATION.[c] Therefore, a modification is an alteration of an internal state (§208), and a contingent substance is modifiable (§128). The alteration of a relation is VARIATION.[d, 261]

§210

The alterations of a state are accidents (§191) and hence they can only exist in substances (§194) and indeed only when a power, also in a stricter sense,[262] is posited

---

[a] Kant E3577, 1776–89: "Whether it is the same to say: a thing has altered, or: its state (inner, at best) has altered."
[b] Kant E3576, 1766–78? before 1764?: "If these things were true, the state of no being would be immutable <*Si haec vera essent, status nullius entis esset immutabilis*>."
[c] Kant E3578, 1770–8? 1769??: "It is in fact the case that a mode is not altered, but rather a substance. For that which is altered remains; the alteration is only the exchange of its determinations."
[d] *VARIATIO.* Baumgarten's German gloss supplies "an external variation <*eine äussre Veränderung*>."

(§197, 22). This power of alteration, or, in general, the sufficient ground of an inherent accident (§197), is either something substantial that alters, i.e. in general, that in which an accident inheres, or it is a power different from it. If it is the former, then the substance whose state is changed, or, in general, that in which the accident inheres, is said to ACT (§10, 38). If it is the latter, then the substance whose state is changed, or, in general, that in which the accident inheres, is said to SUFFER. Hence, ACTION (act, operation) is an alteration of state and in general the actualization of an accident in a substance through its own power, whereas SUFFERING is an alteration of state and, in general, the actualization of an accident in substance through the power of another.[a]

§211[b]

A substance that acts upon a substance outside of itself INFLUENCES the latter, and indeed INFLUENCE (transeunt action) is the action of a substance upon a substance outside of it. An action that does not influence is IMMANENT.

§212[c]

If the suffering of a substance that is influenced by another is at the same time the action of the very substance that suffers, then the SUFFERING and INFLUENCE are called IDEAL. But if the suffering is not the action of the suffering substance, then the SUFFERING and INFLUENCE are called REAL.

§213

The action of a suffering substance upon an active substance is REACTION, and their mutual action and reaction is CONFLICT.

§214[263]

The smallest action, suffering, and reaction are those through which only one smallest accident is actualized (§161, 210). Therefore, the more and greater the accidents that are actualized, the greater are the action, suffering, and reaction (§160,[264] 213), until they are the greatest, which is when the most and the greatest accidents are actualized (§161, 210).

§215

ACTION and SUFFERING are called SIMPLE if they are not wholes of other actions

---

[a] Kant E3579, 1769–78 (next to the last two sentences): "The (*crossed out*: human) body (*later addition*: the lifeless) effects; the living (makes) acts (*later addition: operatur*); the free does (*later addition: facit*)."

[b] Kant E3580, 1764–8? (1771–2?): "a substance that actualizes (produces) a substance creates.* <*substantia substantiam actuans (producens) creat**>/(conserves for the sake of duration <*durationis causa conservat*>)/a substance that adds a complement to the acting substance concurs <*substantia substantiae actrici complementum addens concurrit*>./* (*added later*: creates for the sake of the origination of the substance <*causa ortus substantiae creat*>)"

[c] Kant E3581, 1769–77? 1778–9??: "If all suffering of substance is really a determination of the activity of the suffering subject, then no substance can itself be internally determined through God to other and greater accidents than are possible on the basis of its nature; otherwise, another fundamental power and substantiality would be produced in it, and therefore transform it, and not be the identity of the subject."

and sufferings, while those which are such wholes are called COMPOSITE. And the more partial actions and sufferings they consist of, the more composite they are (§160). Hence, the greatest action and the greatest suffering is maximally composite (§214, 161).

§216[a]

Every existing substance acts (§210, 199) and hence each has the possibility or FACULTY of acting (active potency, power, cf. §197)[265] (§57). If it suffers, it has the possibility of suffering, i.e. RECEPTIVITY (passive power, capacity) (§57).[b]

§217

The FACULTY and RECEPTIVITY of real influences are REAL, of ideal influences, IDEAL, of simple actions, SIMPLE, and of composite actions, COMPOSITE.

§218

Faculties and receptivities are either absolute (§216, 15) or hypothetical (§16). The latter are always greater than the former (§165, 216).

§219[266]

A hypothetical faculty would be the smallest through which only one action of a substance would be possible in the smallest nexus (§216, 161). The more and greater actions of a substance that are possible in a greater nexus, the greater is the hypothetical faculty (§168, 160). A greater hypothetical faculty is PROFICIENCY (readiness, dexterity).

---

[a] Kant E3582, 1766–77: "The internal possibility of a power (*later addition:* of action) is the faculty. e.g. Someone can have a great faculty for science, but still have no power of acumen etc. etc."
Kant 3583, 1776–9? (1780–9?) (next to §215 and E3582): "The internal sufficient ground for this is power; if it is also externally sufficient then it is a living power; if it is externally insufficient, then it is a dead power. Dead power because of a hindrance is endeavor <*conatus*>."
Kant E3584, 1776–9? (1780–9?): "Faculty and power,/potency—act./Power acts, the faculty does not."
Kant E3585, 1780–9 (next to §216ff.): "The internal principle of the possibility of action is faculty*, e.g. a machine**./*(The internal determining ground of the faculty to act is endeavor <*conatus*>. Faculty with an endeavor to act is power. Power, in as much as it is internally sufficient for the actuality of action, but without effect, is dead power; this always proves a hindrance. (*later addition:* Internally and externally sufficient power is living.)/**(*later addition:* Faculty together with its determining ground (e.g. an applied lever) is power. Power (therefore faculty together with its determining ground) (*crossed out:* is brings) is by itself sufficient for the actuality of the action. Therefore when a power is posited (*per se*), an action is posited. The determining ground (*crossed out:* of) in the power alone can oppose another. (*crossed out:* this) The state of a power in such opposition is endeavor <*conatus*> and that which contains the ground of the fact that the action does not arise is the hindrance. Every endeavor is an action, against which something however works. For this reason it is dead power. Living power is not greater than the endeavor, but it produces a desired effect./N.B. A time is required for an endeavor to become a living power. For if the support were taken away from a weight and gravitation were to work no further, then the single impulse would give it no motion.)"
[b] Wolff: "The possibility of acting is called *potency* without qualification <*simpliciter*>, and then immediately with addition *active potency*; the possibility of suffering is called a passive potency. Potency is certainly attributed to a being insofar as a possible action is conceived through that potency belonging to that being; however, a potency for suffering is attributed to a being insofar as it can suffer through that potency belonging to it. An active potency is also called a *Faculty*" (WO §716).

§220[a]

Although positing a faculty and receptivity does not posit action or suffering (§216, 59), nevertheless such is posited when a power in the stricter sense[267] is posited (§210, 30). This[268] will be the complement of the faculty to act, i.e. that which is added to the faculty for the action to come to exist. Hence, a given specific POWER, IN THE STRICTER SENSE,[269] is either sufficient for a given specific action, or not (§21, 210); the former is called a living power, and the latter, a DEAD POWER or solicitation.[b]

§221[c]

An IMPEDIMENT (obstacle) is that which is opposed to the inherence of an accident. Hence an impediment is also opposed to an alteration (§210).

§222

RESISTANCE is an impediment to an action. And since what is opposed to the inherence of accidents and alterations (§191, 81) is an accident, the impediments and resistances have sufficient ground in a power (§197, 27). When an impediment is posited, an impeding power is posited; when resistance is posited, a resisting power is posited (§22).

§223

A substance that more closely influences a substance is PRESENT to it and those substances present most closely to each other TOUCH EACH OTHER[270] or are

---

[a] Kant E3586, 1769–75 (next to §220–2): "Action means: to contain the sufficient ground of the accidents./The possibility of action is faculty./The internal sufficient ground of action is power./It is dead if (*crossed out:* externally) there is present a ground of the opposite./The opposed ground is impediment; if it is another substance: resistance."
Kant E3588, 1776–8? (1773–5?) 1766–9??: "Substance, in as much as it contains the sufficient ground of a determinate accident, acts; in as much as it contains the ground of accidents in general, has a power. This is either internally sufficient or insufficient; in the latter case it is a mere faculty, in the former it is either externally insufficient, i.e. an endeavor or externally sufficient: living force./Along with every dead power there is also another opposed power that is dead."
Kant E3589, 1776–89: "Where there is power there is also action (in lifeless beings), but not for this reason also effect, because an internal or external obstacle (*crossed out:* a) is the reaction of a power that cancels the effect of the former. In living beings faculty and power are distinguished; in lifeless e.g. a rope has so much faculty for bearing a load held by it as the actual power of connection that it exercises."
Kant E3590, 1780–9: "The real relation of a substance as cause to (*crossed out:* its) the (crossed out: there) effect that is possible through it is called power. Prior to the effect this is called endeavor; without the effect, because an opposition occurs, dead power."

[b] "DEAD POWER or solicitation". Baumgarten's Latin reads "*MORTUA* sollicitatio," and he glosses "*MORTUA*" with "a dead power <*eine todte Kraft*>." Solicitation is an infinitesimal impetus, and is related to dead power in Leibniz: "And the impetus of the living power relates to the naked solicitation of the dead power as the infinite relates to the finite, or the lines in our differential calculus relate to their elements." Cf. Leibniz, G 2: 154–6; G 6: 238. Today this would simply be referred to as the force on a body at a given point in space.

[c] Kant, E3587, 1773–5? (next to §221–2): "Agreeing powers: Here one adds to the other something of the same kind, e.g. the sun's attraction to [that of] the moon. not allied <*verbundene*>: there the result is 0. Opposed: -a; take so much away, so that the difference of the addition from the subtraction is double of the amount of the extra. For this reason the danger of decrease is always greater than the profit of the addition <*accessorii*>."

contiguous,[271] such that, moreover, a closer influence is PRESENCE, and mutually immediate presence, or immediate conflict, is CONTACT.[272] Insofar as something neither influences another, more closely, nor suffers from it[273] more closely, it is said to be ABSENT from it.[274]

Section VIIII.[275] The simple and the composite

§224

A COMPOSITE BEING (in the strict[276] and simple sense) is a whole of parts outside of parts, whereas a non-composite BEING IS SIMPLE (in the simple and rigorous sense). A COMPOSITE BEING, IN THE BROAD SENSE, is whatever has parts, and a less composite being is COMPARATIVELY SIMPLE.[277]

§225[a]

Either all the parts of composite beings are accidents when taken both singly and together, or some of their parts are substances (§10, 191). In the former case, the composite being is an accident (§224, 155). In the latter, it is a COMPOSITE BEING, IN THE STRICTER[278] SENSE (real).

§226

Suppose that things mutually posited outside of each other can in no way constitute a whole, or be COMPOSED, then it would be intrinsically impossible for anything to be composed (§224, 15). In those things that are composite, therefore, the mode of composition is the opposite of internal impossibility (§81), i.e. it is the internal possibility and the essence of composite beings (§40).

§227[b]

ORIGINATION is the alteration from non-existence[279] to existence. The alteration from existence to non-existence[280] is PERISHING. Hence, the origination and perishing of a necessary being and a necessary substance is absolutely impossible (§132, 202).

§228

ORIGINATION FROM NOTHING is the origination of something, none of whose parts pre-exists it, and ANNIHILATION is the perishing of something, none of whose parts remains in existence afterwards. The origination from nothing and the annihilation of a necessary being and a necessary substance are absolutely impossible (§227).

---

[a] Kant E3591, 1764–9 (top of the page on which §225–7 and the first half of the line of 228 are printed): "Because every nexus is logical or real. So is [breaks off]"
[b] Kant E3592, 1780–9? 1762–3?? (beginning): "origination is the existence that follows non-existence *<ortus est existentia, quae sequitur non-existentiam>*."
Kant E3593, 1769–autumn 1770? (1776–8? 1773–5? 1776–8?) (§227–8): "Arising and passing away, beginning and ending. The latter regards accidents."

§229

Because they are accidental (§210), origination and origination from nothing, perishing and annihilation can only exist in substances (§227, 228), but not in necessary substances, (§227, 228). Therefore, they can only exist in contingent substances (§202).

Section X. The monad[281]

§ 230

Substance is either simple or composite (§224). The former is called a MONAD (an atom, perfect unity).

§ 231

Every part of a composite substance is either something substantial, or an accident. Accidents are not outside of what is substantial (§196). Therefore, those things that are substantial in a composite substance are posited apart from each other (§224).

Meier combines and supplements this and the next paragraph as follows: Every part of a composite is either something substantial, or an accident. Now since accidents are not actual apart from substances, the parts of a composite substance that are not accidents do not belong among the parts of it that occur apart from one another. Now a composite substance must, however, have such parts. Consequently, the parts of a composite substance that are found apart from one another are substantial things, substances and powers in the stricter sense, and thus a composite substance is a composite thing in the stricter sense.

§ 232

A composite substance has powers, and hence has substances that are posited apart from each other as its parts (§231, 198). Hence, it is a composite being, in the stricter[282] sense (§225).

§ 233[a]

A composite substance can exist only as a collection of other substances posited mutually outside of one another (§232, 155) and composed in a certain way (§226). Therefore, it can only exist as a determination of others (§36, 38). Therefore, it is an accident (§191), and, if it seems to subsist by itself and if a power is attributed to it, then this is a substantiated[b] phenomenon (§193, 201).

§ 234

Every substance is a monad (§233, 230). A composite being in the stricter[283] sense is not a monad (§225). Therefore, it is a substantiated phenomenon (§193, 201).

---

[a] Kant E3594, 1773–9? (1771–2?): "Substance is a phenomenon capable of enduring <*Substantia phaenomenon est perdurabile*>."
[b] Kant E3595, 1780–9: "Composite, quantitatively [and] qualitatively speaking <*Compositum quantitative, qualitative dictum*>."

§ 235

A composite being, in the stricter[284] sense, consists of monads (§225, 234).

§ 236

A monad can only originate from nothing. For, its parts are the substantial and the accidents inhering in the substantial (§196). The substantial does not exist prior to substance; for when it exists, power exists and hence substance exists (§198). No accident exists prior to its substance (§194). Therefore, no part exists prior to the monad that is to originate. Hence, the monad cannot originate other than from nothing (§228).

§ 237

If the substantial survives, the substance has not yet perished (§198). Indeed, no accident survives its substance (§194). Therefore, a monad can only perish through annihilation (§228, 196).

§ 238

When posited next to one another, conjoined beings are SIMULTANEOUS; when they are posited after each other, they are SUCCESSIVE. A whole composed of simultaneous beings is a SIMULTANEOUS BEING, and that of successive beings, is a SUCCESSIVE BEING.

§ 239

The order of simultaneous beings that are posited mutually outside of each other is SPACE, and that of successive beings is TIME.

§ 240

When simultaneous beings are posited outside of each other, space is posited. When space is posited, simultaneous beings mutually outside of one another are posited. When successive beings are posited, time is posited, and when time is posited, different beings[285] (§74) that follow <*succedentia*> one other are posited (§239, 78).

§ 241

That in which there is space is EXTENDED and is said to fill up space or place (to be in space or place, which is to say, to be filling).[286] Now there is space in every composite being in the strict sense (§240,[287] 224).[288] Therefore, every composite being in the strict sense is extended and fills up space. Every extended being has simultaneous parts outside of parts (§240),[289] and hence is composite (§224).

§ 242

A monad is[290] not extended, nor does it fill up space (§241, 230). But a whole of monads (§235) is extended (§241).

§ 243

Every composite being has a magnitude (§159, 224). The magnitude of a composite being in the strict and the stricter sense is QUANTITATIVE MAGNITUDE. Hence, a monad does not have quantitative magnitude (§230).

§ 244[291]

PHYSICAL DIVISION is the decrease of quantitative magnitude. Just as the individual is that whose logical division is impossible (§148), the INDIVISIBLE is that whose physical division is impossible. Therefore, indivisibility is either absolute or hypothetical (§15, 17). Nothing that is absolutely indivisible is hypothetically divisible. Something absolutely divisible is hypothetically indivisible (§18). Hence a monad is indivisible (§243) and indeed *per se* (§15).

§ 245

Composite beings can only exist as determinations of others (§225, 233). Now, aside from composite beings, there is nothing else except simple beings (§224, 38). Therefore, if a composite being exists, then monads exist (§230, 233).

Section XI. The finite and the infinite[292]

§ 246

The quantity of a quality is DEGREE (the quantity of strength). Hence, we can only understand a degree by assuming another (§69).

§ 247[a]

The lowest or smallest degree is that than which less is impossible; the greatest degree is that than which a greater is impossible (§246, 161). The greater degrees are wholes of many of the smallest degrees (§155, 160). Hence, *when a greater degree is affirmed, it follows that the smaller is to be affirmed, and when a smaller degree is negated, it follows that the greater degree is to be negated* (§157). In any greater degree whatsoever, there is a multitude of degrees, which is called INTENSITY (§159). If this is enlarged, the QUALITY,[293] to which the degree belongs, is INCREASED;[b] if it is diminished, the quality, to which the degree belongs, is DECREASED.

§ 248

To be a real being is a quality (§69) belonging to every being (§136). And since there is a certain number of realities in every being (§136, 159), every being has a certain degree of reality (§246, 159). Hence, this will either be the greatest, or not (§10, 247). And since that degree of reality in comparison with which a greater is possible, or

---

[a] Kant E3597, 1776–89 (replaces Baumgerten's German gloss, not given here, for the Latin "*INTENSIO,*" namely, "*angestrengt*" with a near synonym "*angespannt*"): "strained."
[b] Kant E3596, 1764–9 (next to "INCREASED … DECREASED"): "simile of the bow."

that which is not the greatest (§247), is called a LIMIT (a boundary <*terminus*>,[a] cf. §350,[294] end, cf. §341),[295] that which has a limit will be FINITE (cf. §341,[296] limited), while that which does not have a limit will be INFINITE (real, unlimited). Therefore, a being having the maximum degree of reality, or that which is the most real being (§190),[297] is infinite, whereas every other being is finite. A finite being whose limits we either cannot determine, or do not wish to determine, is INDEFINITE (the imaginary infinite, mathematically infinite).[298]

§ 249

Finite beings have a limit, hence a degree (§248), and therefore a quantity (§246). Hence philosophical and mathematical knowledge of all finite beings is[299] possible (§93, 22). The ESSENTIAL LIMIT of a given finite being is that limit beyond which it is impossible for there to be anything more in this being due to its own essence. The mathematics of non-extended things is the MATHEMATICS OF INTENSIVE QUANTITIES (§247).[300]

§ 250

In every finite being, some reality is denied (§248, 247). Therefore, some negation must be posited (§135, 81), and indeed also an imperfection (§142) that is essential and accidental (§143), and hence absolutely necessary (§107) negation (§36) in the strict sense (§137), i.e. metaphysical evil (§146).

§ 251

The greatest degree of reality belonging to the infinite being is absolutely necessary (§248, 102), and hence absolutely inalterable (§130).

§ 252

If an infinite being were internally alterable, then the determinations, which would then succeed one another, would alter its degree of reality (§246, 125). But this degree is internally inalterable (§251).[301] Therefore, an infinite being is internally inalterable.

§ 253

With respect to its internal determinations, the internally inalterable is actually everything it can be (§125). Therefore, with respect to its internal determinations, an infinite being is actually everything it can be (§125).

§ 254

With respect to its internal determinations, that which is not actually everything it can be is a finite being (§253, 248).

---

[a] Kant E3598, 1770–8: "Space and time have boundaries <*Spatium et tempus habent terminos*>." Kant sometimes distinguishes *limes* from *terminus* in the same way he distinguishes limit <*Schranke*> from boundary <*Grenze*>. See, for instance, AA 28: 644 and *Prolegomena* AA 5: 352ff.

§ 255

What is internally alterable is a finite being (§252, 126). Therefore, every contingent being is finite (§133), although it can be indefinite and mathematically infinite in many ways <*multis rationibus*> (§248).[302]

§ 256

An infinite being is a necessary being (§255, 109).

§ 257

If a being has a degree of reality in comparison with which a greater is possible (§247, 69),[303] then some quality belonging to it (§248), and hence an internal determination, can be intensified[304] and hence altered (§247, 162). Therefore, a finite being is internally alterable (§248, 126) and hence it is not a necessary being (§132); its existence is a mode (§134) and the being itself is contingent (§109).

§ 258

A necessary being is infinite (§257, 248).

§ 259

With respect to its internal determinations, that which is actually everything that it can be is a necessary being (§132), and therefore infinite (§258).[305] Hence, an infinite being can be defined[306] as a being that, with respect to its internal determinations, is actually everything that it can be (§253).

§ 260[307]

With respect to its internal determinations, a contingent being is not actually everything that it can be (§133). A finite being is a contingent being (§257). Hence, a finite being can be defined as a being that is not actually everything that it can be with respect to its internal determinations (§254). This is also evident because when one of two contradictorily opposed things is defined affirmatively, the other can be defined, though negatively, through the same notes (§81, 248).

§ 261

Infinitude is a reality (§36) whose ground is the greatest degree of reality (§248, 14). Finitude or limitation is a negation (§36) whose ground is a limit (§248, 14).

§ 262

The modes and relations of a being are either realities or negations (§36) and hence when these are altered in a finite being, its limit is altered (§248). Now, all alteration of a finite being is an alteration of a mode or relation (§52, 132). Therefore, all alteration of a finite being is the alteration[308] of its limits, and hence of its limitation (§261, 30).

§ 263

A finite being has modes (§257, 112). These are either realities or negations (§36).

The opposite of either is absolutely possible in a finite being (§108). Hence, privations are absolutely possible in every finite being (§137). And hence so too are both imperfection and contingent evil (§144, 146) (physical, in the broad sense).[309]

§ 264

Every finite being is[310] partly evil, partly good (§147, 137), and in every finite being contingent good and evil are intrinsically possible (§147, 263).

Chapter III. The relative predicates of a being

Section I. The same and the different

§ 265[a]

The smallest similitude is between two things in which there is common one smallest quality (§174, 70). Now indeed, some qualities are common to every being (§8–§100).[311] Therefore, all beings are similar to each other to some degree (§246). And hence, there is a similitude, and indeed a universal identity, in beings (§70). The more and greater qualities that are common to more beings, the greater is the similitude (§174, 70). The smallest equality is found in two things in which there is one smallest common quantity. Therefore, the more and greater quantities that are common to more beings, the greater is the equality (§174, 70).[312]

§ 266

The smallest congruence is the smallest similitude and equality, and the greater both of these are, the greater is the congruence (§265, 70).[313] The IDENTITY, SIMILITUDE, EQUALITY, and CONGRUENCE of essential determinations are called essential; of essential determinations and attributes, NECESSARY; of modes, CONTINGENT;[314] of affections, ACCIDENTAL.

§ 267

IDENTITY and DIFFERENCE with respect to every predicate[b] is TOTAL, and with respect to some predicates, PARTIAL. Therefore similitude, equality, and congruence are either total, or partial (§70).

§ 268

Since there is a partial similitude of all beings (§265), beings are not totally different (§267). We may call this proposition *the principle of denied total dissimilitude and difference*.[315]

---

[a] Kant E3599, 1764–75 (next to §265ff.): "Sameness and difference belong to the relation of comparison."
[b] G/K: "with respect to individual predicates"

§ 269

The total identity of singular beings is NUMERICAL IDENTITY.[a] *It is impossible for two singular beings outside of one another to be utterly or*[316] *totally the same.* For, since two beings would be posited, many beings would also be posited. Hence they would be partially the same and partially different (§74). Therefore, they would not be totally the same (§267). Those singular beings that are totally the same are the same in number, and are not partially the same and partially different (§267). Hence, they are neither many, nor are they two (§74). *This proposition* is called *the principle* (of identity)[317] *of indiscernibles in the broad sense, or of denied total identity.*[318]

§ 270

It is impossible for many actual beings outside of one another to be totally congruent. For, if they exist mutually outside one another, then any given one will possess its own proper <*sua et propria*> existence (§86),[319] which will be different from the existence of any other (§38).[320] Hence, there would be at least either one unique attribute or mode (§77),[321] and in fact either a quality or a quantity (§69), which was in one being but not in another (§38, 55). Hence the two beings would not[b] be totally congruent (§70, 267). Totally congruent beings are the same with respect to all internal distinguishing marks (§267, 70). Hence the existence of one is not different from the existence of the other (§70), and therefore they do not exist mutually outside of one another. *This proposition* shall be *the principle of denied total congruence.*[322]

§ 271

It is impossible for many actual things mutually outside of one another to be totally similar. For, either they would be totally equal, or not. If the first, they would be totally congruent (§70, 267), which is absurd (§270).[c] If they were not totally equal, then there would be a quantity in one that was not in the other (§70, 38). This would have a sufficient ground (§22). Hence, there would be a quality in one of the totally similar beings that was not in the other (§69, 14), which is absurd (§70,

---

[a] Kant E3600, 1773–89: "identical generically, specifically, and numerically <*Generice, specifice et numerice identica*>"

[b] Kant R3601, 1766–9? (1764–6?) 1773–5?) (across from §270 "not … from the existence"):

"totally the same <*totaliter adem*>	–	same in number <*numero idem*>
congruent <*congruentia*> with respect to the internal <*quoad interna*>	–	in different relations <*in diversis relationibus*>
with respect to quantity <*quoad quantitatem*>	–	they are also with respect to quality, because only the homogenous can be equal <*sunt etiam quoad qualitatem, quia non nisi homogenea possunt esse aequalia*>
with respect to quality <*quoad qualitatem*>	–	they can also be with respect to quantity, and then would have been congruent <*possunt esse etiam quoad quantitatem, et tum forent congruentia*>"

[c] G/K: "(§70, 267 as a presupposition for §270)"

267).[a] *This proposition* is the *principle* (of identity)[323] *of indiscernibles in the strict sense, or, of denied total similitude.*

§ 272

It is impossible for many actual things mutually outside of one another to be totally equal. Either they will be totally similar, or only partially (§265). If the first, they would be totally congruent (§70, 267), which is absurd (§270).[b] If they were only partially similar, there would be a quality in one that would not be in the other (§267, 70), and hence there would not be totally the same degree of reality in both (§248), and in fact there would be some quantity of one that would not be the quantity of the other (§246). Therefore, they would not be totally equal (§267, 70). *This proposition* shall be *the principle of denied total equality.*[324]

§ 273

All actual beings mutually outside of one another are partially different (§268), incongruous (§270, 70), dissimilar (§271) and unequal (§272).[325]

§ 274

If A and C are both the same as a third, B, they are the same among themselves. For, those things in B are in A (§38). Those things in C are in B (§38). Therefore, those things in C are in A. Hence, A and C are the same (§38).

§ 275

Beings that are congruent, similar, and equal to the same third thing are congruent, similar, and equal to one another (§70, 274).

§ 276

When the same congruent, similar, and equal sufficient ground is posited, the same congruent, similar, and equal consequence is posited, and vice versa (§38, 70).

§ 277

When the same essence is posited, the same attributes are posited, and vice versa (§276, 50).

§ 278

When a different, incongruent, dissimilar, and unequal sufficient ground is posited, a different, incongruent, dissimilar,[c] and unequal consequence is posited, and vice versa. Hence, when a different essence is posited, different attributes are posited, and vice versa (§277, 276).

§ 279

The identity and diversity (§38), congruence and incongruence, similitude and

---

[a] G/K: "(§69, 14 as a presupposition for §70, 267)"
[b] G/K: "(§70, 267 as a presupposition for §270)"
[c] Baumgarten puts these parallel terms out of order, writing: "a different, dissimilar, incongruent, and unequal …"

dissimilitude, and equality and inequality (§70) of actual beings mutually outside of one another are only representable in any one of these beings if[326] the being is considered in a nexus with those posited outside of it (§14). Hence, they are relations (§37). Those beings between which a nexus exists <*intercedit*> are connected (§14, 19). Now, a nexus exists among all[a] actual beings mutually outside of one another (§265–73). Therefore, all actual beings are connected (§47). Hence, there is a nexus between all actual beings, or more correctly, there is a universal harmony (§48, 167).

Section II. Simultaneous beings[327]

§ 280[b]

Since extension is the quality of a composite being insofar as it fills up space (§69, 241), and space can be greater and smaller (§239, 175), a degree of extension is possible in something extended (§246), i.e. FIGURE. Hence, a monad does not admit of a figure, but a whole of monads does (§242).[c] A composite being of greater extension is SPACIOUS; of less extension, NARROW.[328]

§ 281

The position of an actual being that is simultaneous with others outside of it is its PLACE, whereas the position of an actual being that is successive to others outside of it is AGE.

§ 282

The place of every simultaneous being is determined from its conjunction with different actual beings outside of it (§85, 281). Hence, coexisting beings differ in place (§38). Therefore, things that are simultaneous and are posited mutually outside of one another are not in the same place[329] (§281). The age of every successive being is determined from its conjunction with actual things posited before and after it (§85, 78). Hence, these differ in age. Hence, beings that are mutually successive to each other cannot be the same in age.[330]

§ 283

MOTION is the alteration of place. Hence all motion is an alteration of relation (§281, 85) and the smallest motion would be if only one position of one smallest being was

---

[a] G/K: "the individual"

[b] Kant E3602, 1766–autumn 1770? (1764–8) 1773–5?? (beginning): "the boundary of space is distinguished from the limits <*terminus spatii distinguitur a limitibus*>/A spherical surface is not properly bounded anywhere. but it is bounding <*Superficies sphaerica proprie non est alicubi terminata. sed est terminans*>."
Kant E3604, 1773–7? (1776–9?) (beginning): "The quality of the boundary of what is extended is the figure."

[c] Kant E3603, 1771–2 (1773–9?) 1769–autumn 1770?? (across from this and the next sentence): "Because the boundary is a ground of the limit, it is not a part, in that it adds nothing to the magnitude, but much rather cuts it off; the cutting-off, however, belongs to both things that are cut off; therefore the boundary is common."

altered in relation to one smallest actual being outside of itself (§161). Hence, this motion is greater the more positions of more and greater beings are altered in relation to more and greater mobile and external beings.[331] Those beings which do not move ARE RESTING, and the absence of motion is REST.

§ 284[a]

Coordinated beings touching <*contingentia*> one another are CONTIGUOUS, and the non-contiguous are distant. The place of beings that are distant from one another is SITUATION <*SITUS*>. An *action*, or immediate and proximate influence, *at a distance is impossible* in itself and[332] *per se* (§223, 15).

§ 285

A simultaneous and successive being[333] of contiguous parts is CONTINUOUS, but a simultaneous and successive being[334] of mutually distant parts is DISCONTINUOUS.

§ 286

The parts of an extended being that are posited outside of one another are either simple or composite (§224). The former, insofar as they are not extended (§242),[335] are called POINTS. A continuous series of points interposed between distant points[336] is a LINE.

§ 287

The extension of a line is determined by the number of points out of which it is composed (§241, 286), and if the fewest points are interposed between given distant points, then it is the SHORTEST line between them. The shortest line between given points is a STRAIGHT LINE, and if it is not straight, then it is CURVED.[337]

§ 288

A straight line between distant points is their DISTANCE and the greater this line is, the greater is the distance between them (§287, 284). And if the distance is greater, the distant points are MORE REMOTE, whereas when it is less, they are CLOSER.

§ 289[b]

A continuous series of lines interposed between distant lines[338] is a SURFACE. The extension of a surface is determined by the number of lines out of which it is

---

[a] Kant E3605, 1780–9: "The community of boundaries. Two points do not touch, therefore distant."
[b] Kant E3606, 1764–8? 1769? (end of 1769–autumn 1770?) 1773–5??: "Two points always lie in a line, three points (*crossed out:* in a surface and four in a corporeal space.), through which no common straight line can be drawn, lie in a surface, and four points, through three of which no straight line can go, lie in a corporeal space. Still from these data two bodies are possible, namely according to two opposite directions./This is just to say. If a point is given, then from a given distance another point can be given in infinitely many places (i.e. it lies in the surface of a sphere). If two points are given, then the third point lies in a circle*. If three points are given, then the fourth point lies in two positions on opposite sides**. All positions of the points can be geometrically determined from certain data, the final position of the fourth point, however, only in regard to our body./*(the third point is determined, but not its place.)/**(for then no rotation is possible.)"

composed (§241, 175), and the shortest extension between given distant lines is a FLAT SURFACE, whereas a non-flat surface is CURVED (a hump).[339] A continuous series of surfaces interposed between distance surfaces[340] is a MATHEMATICAL SOLID (a mathematical body, cf. §296).[341]

§ 290

The only extension possible in a line is LENGTH. That which is added to length in a surface is WIDTH. That which is added to the extension of surfaces in mathematical solids is (height or) DEPTH.

§ 291[a]

If by taking a quantity as a unit, we understand another homogenous or similar quantity, then we MEASURE <*METIMUR*> the MEASURED <*MENSURATAM*> extension based on that MEASURE <*MENSURA*>, and this action is called MEASURING <*DIMENSIO*>.

§ 292[b]

A line only admits of one dimension of extension (§291, 287); a surface, two (§291, 289); and a mathematical solid, three (§280, 246).

§ 293

Since the parts of space are in beings posited simultaneously outside of one another (§239,[342] 155), they are simultaneous, and, what is more, space is a simultaneous being (§238).

§ 294

Since motion is an accident (§283), it can only exist in substances and indeed only when a power is posited (§210), which is called MOTIVE POWER.[343] And since rest

---

[a] Kant E3607, 1764–autumn 1770: "*Continua* not only have limits, but also boundaries."
Kant E3608, 1765–6? 1769? (across from §290): "The mathematical concepts are unity, plurality, number, infinity, (proportions) (*crossed out:* equality, inequality), composition of a magnitude from another one or a few or from its parts, or also from many magnitudes by synthesis, either positive or negative; hence the idea of equality, inequality and proportions. The objects of mathematics are space, time, motion or every other ground estimated either as a totality or as a ground, the former through the plurality that is in it, the latter through that which is posited from it."
Kant E3609, 1764–autumn 1770? (1773–5?) (next to §291–2): "If (*crossed out:* magnitudes of) the quality of a magnitude is of such a kind that the raising of the action (*crossed out:* the coordination) (which is one with a certain extensive magnitude) intensively to the second degree is an instance of multiplication, then there are not more than three dimensions. Wherever, however, the magnitude does not grow intensively by multiplication but rather extensively by addition, there is only one dimension. Of things that are simultaneous, one can represent the generation of the collection from unity, as with flow."
[b] Kant E3610, 1764–8? (1773–5?) 1776–8?? (across from §292–3): "It is remarkable that in regard to point, line and surface, if they move (perpendicularly), the motion of the elements do not overlap one another, but that this does happen in the case of body. It also need not occur perpendicularly, if only it is not in the direction coinciding with the motion of the previous elements. The question is: why do they coincide, then, in the case of the fourth dimension, namely that after the generation of a body. Is the ground of this not something located in the combination in general?"

is an impediment to motion (§221, 283), when rest is posited, a power that resists[a] motion is posited (§222), which is called the POWER OF INERTIA (*impenetrability,[b] laziness, inherent power*).

power is] power in the narrow sense is

§ 295

An extended being to which the power of inertia is attributed is MATTER (cf. §344),[344] and it is a substantiated phenomenon (§234, 201). The matter to which this power alone is attributed is PRIME (merely passive) MATTER (cf. §423).[345]

§ 296

The matter to which motive power is attributed is a physical BODY (cf. §289, secondary matter, cf. §295),[346] and it is a substantiated phenomenon (§295, 201).

Section III. Successive beings[347]

§ 297

The time that is simultaneous to the thought[348] of that very time itself[349] is PRESENT TIME; the time that the present follows is PAST TIME; and the time that follows the present is FUTURE TIME.

§ 298

Actual beings of the present time are EXISTING BEINGS[350] (in the present time, actual beings). Actual beings of a past time, if they are not[c] at the same time actual beings, which is to say, if they no longer exist,[351] are PAST BEINGS (matters of fact). Actual beings of a future time are FUTURE BEINGS, and if they are not at the same time actual beings, then they are POTENTIAL BEINGS <*ENTIA IN POTENTIA*>.

§ 299

The continuation of existence[352, d] is DURATION. That in which duration is possible is called something CAPABLE OF ENDURING. An actual being that is not in fact capable of enduring is called INSTANTANEOUS (momentary). A being capable of

---

[a] Kant E3611, 1780–9? (1776–9?): "as if rest were an accident <*quasi quies esset accidens*>."

[b] *Antitypia.* Although this term is used throughout ancient and early modern philosophy to name the integrity or indestructability of a body, the equation of it here with a power of impenetrability and its association with inertia clearly find their source in Leibniz (G 1: 17–18; G 6: 236–7).

[c] Kant E3612, 1780–9 (across from §298 "are not … longer"): "Only in the phenomena <*in phaenomenis*>."

[d] Kant E3613, 1776–89 (in §. 299 Kant changed "*Exsistentiae*" into "*Exsistentia*" and added): "as quantity <*ut quantitas*>". According to AA, he forgot to cross out the second word "*continuatio*," which the editor perhaps too hastily believed must be excised in the new definition. It is possible, however, that Kant was simply modifying the sentence to read "continuation, existence as quantity, is duration", in which case the "*continuatio*" would be preserved and an interesting change would result.

enduring that is of a greater duration is PERMANENT (stabile, constant, perpetual, eternal), whereas one of lesser duration is something BRIEF (fluctuating, transitory, inconstant).[353]

§ 300

The time simultaneous to the momentary is called an INSTANT (a moment). The time which follows other instants is called LATER. The time that the other instants have followed is called earlier. That which is prior to all is called the FIRST and that which is later than all is called the LAST.

§ 301[354]

The alteration of a being into something present is called the BEGINNING; into something past, the END. Unification is the beginning of the union (§79, 205) and the beginning of contact is IMPACT.[355]

§ 302

ETERNITY (in the rigorous sense, cf. §299) is duration without BEGINNING and end.[356] Duration only without end is PERPETUITY <*AEVITERNITAS*> and duration simultaneous with all time[357, a] is SEMPITERNITY.

§ 303[358]

An existence that continues without beginning is simultaneous with all past and present time (§301, 297) and an existence that will continue without end is simultaneous with all future time (§301, 297). Therefore, everything eternal is sempiternal (§302).

§ 304

A potential being either has a proximal sufficient ground of existence in actual beings, or not (§27, 10). The first is a PROXIMALLY POTENTIAL BEING, and the latter is a REMOTELY POTENTIAL BEING.

§ 305

An actual being, as long as it endures, cannot fail to endure (§9, 7), and hence it necessarily exists (§299, 101),[359] or, *whatever is, as long as it is, necessarily is.*[360]

§ 306

Those beings that mutually determine the place and age of each other are connected (§281, 85). Hence, things that are simultaneous are connected with respect to space, and those that are successive are connected with respect to time (§238, 239). Now, all actual beings posited mutually outside of one another are either simultaneous

---

[a] Kant E3614, 1776–8? (1778–89?): "with every part of time <*omnibus partibus temporis*>."

or successive (§238, 298). Therefore, there is a connection and universal harmony between all actual beings (§48, 167).[361]

Section IIII.[362] **Cause and caused**

§ 307

That which contains the ground of another is its PRINCIPLE. That which depends on a principle is something FOUNDED. The principle of existence is a CAUSE and the thing founded by a cause is the CAUSED. That which is not able to exist except as caused by another being posited outside of it is a BEING FROM ANOTHER <*ENS AB ALIO*> (dependent). However, that which is able to exist even if it is not caused by another being posited outside of it is a BEING FROM ITSELF <*ENS A SE*> (independent).

§ 308[a]

The existence of a contingent and hence finite being is a mode (§134, 257). Hence, existence is sufficiently determined neither through the essence of a contingent and finite being (§65), nor, therefore, through its attributes (§64, 25). Therefore, the sufficient ground of a contingent and finite being's existence is not found in its internal determinations (§52). But nevertheless a sufficient ground is necessary for the contingent and finite being to exist (§22, 101). Therefore, it is necessary that the sufficient ground of its existence be outside the contingent and finite being, and since those things that contain this [the sufficient ground of existence][363] are causes (§307), the finite and contingent being can only exist as a being caused by something posited outside of it, i.e. it is a being from another (§307).

§ 309

A being from itself is neither contingent nor finite (§308, 307) and hence it is necessary (§109) and infinite (§258).

§ 310[b]

A necessary and infinite[364] being (§258) can exist even though it is not caused by

---

[a] Kant E3615, 1764–72? (1765–6? 1773–5?) (across from the beginning): "A being from itself does not change <*Ens a se, non mutatur*>. For in no determination it is through another, therefore not to something other."

[b] In the argument stretching from §307–10, we see the sketch of a cosmological argument; cf. Wolff in his WTN1: "A necessary being exists. The human soul exists (WPE, §21), or we exist (WPE, §14). Because nothing is without a sufficient ground for why it is rather than is not, it is necessary that a sufficient ground be given for why our soul exists, or why we exist. And indeed, this reason is contained in ourselves or in some other being different from us. But if you maintain that we have the ground of our existence in a being which, in turn, has the ground of its existence in another, the sufficient ground will only be reached if you come to a halt at some being that does have the sufficient ground of its own existence in itself. Therefore, either we ourselves are the necessary being, or a necessary being is given that is other and different from us (WO, §309). Consequently, a necessary being exists" (WTN1, §21).

something posited apart from it (§109, 102). Therefore, it is a being from itself and independent (§307).

§ 311

The principle of possibility is called the PRINCIPLE OF BEING (of composition).[365] The cause is called the PRINCIPLE OF BECOMING (of generation).[366] The principle of knowledge is called the PRINCIPLE OF KNOWING and if from [this principle] neither more nor less than a given founded thing can be known, it is called ADEQUATE to that founded thing.[a] Essence is both the principle of being and the principle of knowing with respect to modes (§65, 50).

§ 312[b]

Of related things, the principle is called the TERM OF THE RELATION,[c] whereas the dependent thing is called the SUBJECT OF THE RELATION. If either one of these can become the term of relation for the other, these are CORRELATES.

TERM] SOURCE[d]

§ 313

Between the cause and what is caused there is a NEXUS (§307, 14), which is called CAUSAL, and insofar as it is attributed to a cause, it is called CAUSALITY, whereas insofar as it is attributed to what is caused, it is called DEPENDENCY.[367]

§ 314

When there are many causes of one and the same caused being <*causati*>, they are CO-CAUSES, and they are said to CONCUR in the caused being. A cause that does not have a co-cause is a SOLITARY CAUSE. The one co-cause among the remaining ones that contains the greatest ground of the caused beings is the PRINCIPAL CAUSE (the primary cause). The co-causes of the primary cause are SECONDARY (non-principal causes).[368] All co-causes are mutually connected (§313, 33).

§ 315

One of the co-causes is either the cause of the others, or not (§10). In the former case,[369] the co-causes are SUBORDINATED CO-CAUSES, whereas in the latter case,

---

[a] Wolff: "If a principle contains in itself the ground of the possibility of another, it is called the *principle of being*; if rather it contains the ground of the actuality of another, it is named the *principle of becoming*" (WO §874). And again: "A proposition through which the truth of another proposition can be understood is a *principle of knowing*" (WO §876).

[b] Kant E3616, 1771–8: "Respect and relation; the former: of comparison, the latter: of influence."

[c] Also possible is "END OF THE RELATION," in the sense of the terminal thing to which the relation is directed. Baumgarten, however, suggests as a German translation for this term "*der Grund*" or the "ground" of the relation, contrasting it with "*der Gegenstand der Verhältniss*" or the "object of the relation", which is his suggested translation of "*subiectum relationis*." Wolff: "Of related things, the one that refers to the other is called the subject of the relation; the one, however, to which the other refers, is called the term [or end] of the relation" (WO §864).

[d] Meier employs "source" <*die Quelle*> as a translation for *principium* or principle.

they are COORDINATED. There is a FIRST CAUSE of all subordinated causes, and the rest are SECONDARY.

§ 316

Among the subordinated co-causes, either the same thing in the closer cause, upon which the caused thing more closely depends, depends on a more remote cause, or something else in the closer cause does (§315, 27). If the former is the case, the CO-CAUSES ARE ESSENTIALLY SUBORDINATED; if the latter, ACCIDENTALLY.

Meier formulates the first sentence to read: If the co-causes of a thing are subordinated to one another, then that which is in the nearer cause depends either on the remote cause as to why and how the nearer cause causes the thing, or on something else.

§ 317

The cause of a cause essentially subordinated to it is also the cause of what is caused (§316, 25).

§ 318

A cause is either sufficient or insufficient (§307, 21), and is either qualified or unqualified (§28). A cause is either mediate, in which case a given caused being depends upon it through another, or it is immediate, in which case a given caused being depends upon it, but not through another (§27).[370]

Section V. The efficient cause[371]

§ 319[a]

The cause of a reality through an action is an EFFICIENT CAUSE; that of a negation, however, is a DEFICIENT CAUSE. The efficient cause, just like the deficient cause, acts; hence, they are substances (§210). And indeed, if accidents are viewed as efficient causes, then they are substantiated phenomena (§201, 200). The beings caused by efficient or deficient causes are EFFECTS.

as efficient causes] as efficient or deficient causes

§ 320

An efficient and deficient[372] cause is either mediate, which actualizes an effect through another efficient or deficient[373] cause, or immediate, which actualizes an effect but

---

[a] Kant E3617, 1765–6 (beginning): "An accident, insofar as it is a cause, is not called efficient <*Accidens, quatenus est causa, non dicitur efficiens*>/Substance, insofar as its accident is a cause, is similarly not efficient <*Substantia, quatenus ipsius accidens est causa, itidem non est efficiens*>."
Kant E3618, 1760s–70s (beginning): "either an efficient or an indispensable condition <*vel efficiens vel conditio sine qua non*>"
Kant E3619, 1776–9? 1770–7?? 1780–9?? (beginning): "Buffon seeks the nexus of effective causes, others that of final causes. Epicurus the first in the organization."

not through another efficient or deficient[374] cause.[375] An efficient and deficient cause coordinated with another efficient and deficient[376] cause is called the ASSOCIATE CAUSE of the latter and if the other, i.e. associated, cause is insufficient for a given effect, this other[377] associate cause is called an AUXILIARY CAUSE.

§ 321

The complement to the effect of an insufficient associated cause is AID <*AUXILIUM*>. To be an auxiliary cause is TO AID <*IUVARE*>. Therefore, an aiding cause is not a solitary cause (§320) and a solitary cause does not aid (§314).

§ 322

A non-principal efficient or deficient[378] cause subordinated to an efficient or deficient cause[379] is an INSTRUMENTAL (assisting, ministering) CAUSE.

§ 323

A single action with its own effect is called an EVENT. A relation belonging to an event is a CIRCUMSTANCE. The collection of relations concurring in an event is an occasion and its cause is an OCCASIONAL CAUSE. The smallest agreement of the fewest and smallest circumstances in a given event is the smallest occasion (§161). The more and greater are the circumstances, and the more they agree in an event, the greater is the occasion (§160), until it is the greatest occasion, which would be the greatest agreement of the most and greatest circumstances in a given event. The greater occasion with respect to place is OPPORTUNE and its opposite is INOPPORTUNE, whereas the greater occasion with respect to time is TIMELY and its opposite is UNTIMELY.[380]

§ 324

If [even] the smallest circumstance is in event A which is not in event B, events A and B are not completely the same (§267, 323), and hence they are partially different (§267). That is, *the smallest circumstance changes a thing externally.*

§ 325

If events A and B are to some degree internally equal and are considered in very different circumstances, then the diversity depending on this is only in the relations (§323), and hence it is external (§36).[381] Therefore, the internal identity of events in different circumstances, places, times (§281,[382] 85), and so on, can neither be increased, nor diminished (§162). That is, *place and time do not change a thing internally.*

§ 326

When a principle is posited, something founded is posited (§307, 30). When a cause is posited, something caused is posited (§311). When an efficient and deficient cause is posited, an effect is posited (§319). When an occasional cause is posited, an occasion is posited (§323) and vice versa (§29).

§ 327

When the same, similar, equal and congruent principle is posited, and hence when the efficient, deficient (§319), and occasional (§323) causes (§307) are posited, the same, similar, equal, and congruent founded beings (§276, 307), caused beings, effects, and occasions are posited and vice versa.

§ 328

When the principle is denied, and hence when the efficient, deficient (§319) and occasional (§223)[383] *cause (§307) is denied, the founded being, the caused being, the effect, and the occasion is denied (§307, 31) and vice versa (§32).*

§ 329

Every effect is similar to the efficient or deficient cause (§265), i.e. *as is the cause, so is the effect* (§70). The effect is either similar to the efficient cause with respect to the specific difference of both, or not (§10). The former is called a UNIVOCAL EFFECT and the latter an EQUIVOCAL EFFECT.

§ 330

An effect having a proximal ground of existence in a given action is this action's IMMEDIATE (proximate and continuous, cf. §285) EFFECT.[384] MEDIATE (remote) EFFECTS are those that have merely a more remote ground of their own existence in a given action. All the effects of an action, taken in every intensity, form the COMPLETE EFFECT. An INCOMPLETE EFFECT is either only a certain effect or an effect considered in a lesser degree.

§ 331

The complete effect is as great as the action through which it is actualized (§330, 214), and hence it is equal to the action (§70). Now the action is as great as the living power through which it is actualized (§220, 166), and hence the action is equal to the living powers by which it is actualized (§70). Therefore, the action of the efficient cause is equal to its living powers (§319). Hence, *the complete effect is equal* (proportional) *to the living powers of the efficient cause* (§275).

§ 332

The nobility or dignity of some effect that must be subordinated essentially to some efficient cause pertains to its complete effect (§330, 317, 166).[385] Therefore, *the effect is not more noble than its efficient cause, to which it is essentially subordinated* (§331, 160).[a]

---

[a] Kant E3620, 1764–autumn 1770? 1773–5?: "The causality in the cause is not more noble than the effect."

§ 333

The qualities (§329) and quantities (§331), and hence the determinations, of a cause can be known from an effect (§70, 67). Therefore, the effect is the principle of knowing with respect to the cause (§311), i.e. *the effect attests to the cause.*

§ 334

Every contingent and finite being is a being from another (§308). Therefore, the existence of an existing being does not inhere through its own power (§307), and hence a foreign power posited apart from the finite and contingent real being is the sufficient ground of the existence inhering in it (§210). Therefore, a substance posited apart from it brings about its existence by influencing that being (§211). Hence, every real contingent and finite being is an effect (§319) and has an efficient cause (§326).

does not inhere] does not exist

§ 335

A causal nexus between the efficient and deficient cause and the effect is called an EFFECTIVE NEXUS. Hence, the associated causes are connected by an effective nexus (§320, 314).

Section VI. Utility[386]

§ 336

What is good for another is USEFUL, whereas what is not good for another is USELESS, and what is bad for another is HARMFUL. Hence, UTILITY is a respective goodness (§37), which is called PASSIVE if it is attributed to a thing for which another can be useful, and ACTIVE if it is attributed to that which can be useful.[387]

§ 337[a]

The smallest utility is that through which one smallest being posits one smallest perfection in another single smallest being (§336, 161). Hence it is increased to the extent that more and greater beings posit more and greater perfections in more and greater beings (§187).[388] The degree of utility is called its WORTH, and the judgment of the worth is called its PRICE (valuation).[389, b] Hence the valuation of the price is either true or apparent (i.e. imaginary) (§12).

---

[a] Kant E3621, 1776–89 (to Baumgarten's gloss, not given here, of *"VALOR"* with *"Wert"* and *"PRETIUM"* with *"Preis, Achtung, Schätzung, Würdigung"*): "Estimable (worthy of estimation)/ Inestimable (incapable of estimation),/just as incorrigible has a double meaning."

[b] Although "value" would perhaps be a more natural translation for *valor* (translated here as "worth"), we have sought to keep evident the connection with the distinction Kant draws between worth <*Wert*> and price <*Preis*>. Cf. AA 4: 435, AA 6: 286–9 and AA 6: 434.

§ 338

USE is the actualization of utility. ABUSE is either apparent use or use in which what is useful perishes. Since one can know from the useful the perfection of that for which it is useful (§336, 100), the useful and that for which it can be useful[390] are connected, and their nexus can be called the NEXUS OF UTILITY.

§ 339

If someone uses something useful, then through this, the perfection of another is actualized (§338, 100), and the useful, through use, becomes the cause of the perfection of that for which it is useful (§307).[391] And this causal nexus can be called the NEXUS OF USE. When someone uses something, that thing is useful (§336, 57) and nobody uses what is entirely useless (§338, 58). However, some useful things are in want of use (§59) and hence something that nobody uses is useful nonetheless (§60).[392]

§ 340

Things useful for one and the same thing are connected with it (§339). Therefore, all things useful for one thing are connected among themselves (§314).[a] If A is useful to the useful thing B that is essentially subordinated to it, it is also useful for that C for which B is useful (§317).

Section VII. The remaining types of causes[393]

§ 341

When one uses or abuses something for the sake of actualizing what seems good to oneself, then this very thing, which seems good to the agent, is called the END <FINIS>[b] (cf. §248). The causes of the end, or those things that the agent can use or abuse for the sake of the end, are called the MEANS[394] (destined, limited[c] (cf. §248), remedies),[395] and the representation of the end is called the INTENTION. Now, the end is the principle of use or abuse (§338, 307),[396] and hence is the final cause[d] (§338, 307).

§ 342

The grounds of an intention in the one intending[397] are called the IMPELLING CAUSES. The end is the effect of the action and the means[398] that the agent uses or abuses (§341, 319). Hence, the complete end is equal to the action and the means.[399] The means and the action are equal (proportional) to the complete end

---

[a] G/K render this sentence differently as: "Therefore, all useful things are connected among themselves to one."

[b] Kant E3622, 1760s–70s: "objective"

[c] *finita*. Finite has always been used in this translation, but to preserve the obvious connection between an "means" and the "goal," "limited" has been used in this one instance.

[d] It is notable that, unlike Leibniz and Wolff, Baumgarten says almost nothing about final causes throughout the *Metaphysics*. Wolff: "That for the sake of which the efficient cause acts is called the *end* and likewise the *final cause*. One says, however, that the efficient cause acts for the sake of something, if it acts in order for this thing to be or to happen" (WO §932).

(§331). Seizing the occasion (§323) and removing the impediments (§221) are means[400] (§341).

§ 343

The causal nexus of means and ends is the FINAL NEXUS, and all the co-ends[401] are mutually connected (§314, 341). The end of the ends essentially subordinated to it is also the end of the means[402] (§317, 341). The first end, or that to which all co-ends are subordinated, is called the ULTIMATE END, or the GOAL, and this is either simply ultimate, or qualifiedly such in a given subordination of ends (§28). The rest are INTERMEDIATE ENDS.[403]

§ 344

If a being is conceived of as determinable, then it is called the MATTER FROM WHICH (cf. §295, 296).[404] If it is conceived of as in the very act of determination, then it is called the MATTER CONCERNING WHICH (an object, a subject of occupation). If it is conceived of after the determination has occurred, then it is called the MATTER IN WHICH, and this, along with the matter from which, is called the SUBJECT.[405, a]

§ 345

Since matter and form contain the ground of an actual determination (§344, 40),[406] they are causes (§307). The former is a material cause, and the latter a formal cause.[407] The material and formal co-causes are connected among one another (§314), and the nexus of these co-causes along with the beings they found (§307), and among one another (§314), can be called a SUBJECTIVE NEXUS for the former, and a FORMAL NEXUS (essential) for the latter.[408]

form] form or the essence of the thing

§ 346[b]

An EXEMPLAR is that to which the similar is intended [to be similar], and since it is an impelling cause (§342), it is a cause (§307), which is called exemplary, and what is caused by this is called the replica (ectype, copy).[409] An EXEMPLAR which does not have another exemplar is an ARCHETYPE (original).[410] The exemplar, replica, and co-examplars are connected in a causal nexus (§313), which is an EXEMPLARY (typical)[411] NEXUS.

---

[a] Cf. C.S. Peirce, "Notes on Metaphysics," *Collected Papers* VI (Cambridge, MA: Harvard University Press, 1974), 249. "Matter being taken relatively, the same thing can have this or that as its matter in different respects; and so matter is distinguished into *materia ex qua* [matter from which], *in qua* [matter in which] and *circa quam* [matter concerning which]. *Materia ex qua* is the material; silver is the *materia ex qua* of a dime. *Materia in qua* is the subject in which the form inheres; *materia circa quam* is the object."
[b] Kant E3623, 1764–75: "Idea. Archetype. Model. Example. Similarity, analogy are different."

Section VIII.[412] The sign and the signified

§ 347

A SIGN is the means for knowing the existence of another thing and the end of the sign is the SIGNIFIED. Hence, the sign is the principle of knowing the signified (§311), and the nexus between the sign and the signified is the nexus of SIGNIFICATION, which is called MEANING (power, potency) when attributed to the sign.

§ 348

The actually signified thing (§347) is either present, in which case the sign is called a DEMONSTRATIVE SIGN, or it is in the past, in which case the sign is called a MNEUMONIC SIGN (a memory aid, a *μνημόσυνον*[a]),[413] or it is in the future (§298), in which case the sign is called a FORETOKEN.

Meier renders the first part of this sentence as: The signified is something actual, and it is therefore either that which is present or past or future

§ 349

The science of signs (semiotics, philosophical semiology, symbolics)[414] is CHARACTERISTICS, and this science is (I) HEURISTICS, if it concerns the invention of PRIMITIVE signs, which are not composed of signs,[415] as well as DERIVATIVE signs, which are composed of signs. If the mode of their composition is similar to the essence of the signified, then they are ESSENTIAL SIGNS. The heuristics of derivative signs is[416] COMBINATORIAL.[417] The science of signs is (II) HERMENEUTICS if it concerns the knowledge of the things signified by signs. This is UNIVERSAL HERMENEUTICS. The characteristics of foretokens is called the MANTIC ART.

is similar] is to a high degree similar ‖ HERMENEUTICS if it concerns the signified knowledge of signs] THE UNIVERSAL ART OF INTERPRETATION or the science that knows the signified from the sign

§ 350[418]

The sign of a representation is a TERM (cf. §248, a symbol). The terms more commonly used by the human voice are WORDS. SPEECH (in the broader sense) is a series of words signifying connected representations. A collection of words more commonly used in a larger specific region is a PARTICULAR LANGUAGE. A language more commonly used in a smaller specific region, which is different from that more commonly used in other smaller regions, is an IDIOM. A more perfect idiom is a DIALECT. Terms that are depicted and must be observed by the eyes are CHARACTERS IN THE STRICTER SENSE (cf. §67). These characters are either of words, and are NOMINAL, or they are the immediate characters of the things to be signified by words, and then they are REAL. If these signify something else than that to which they are most similar, then they are HIEROGLYPHS, or if they are of societies,

---

[a] "remembrance" or "memorial"

they are INSIGNIA. And if they can be read in every particular language, then the collection of them is a UNIVERSAL LANGUAGE.

The terms … WORDS.] The terms, which usually consist of human voices, are WORDS (*vocabula*).

Eberhard adds the remark: The collection of the rules of a language is its GRAMMAR, just as the collection of the rules that are common to all languages is UNIVERSAL GRAMMAR. Every grammar, if it is treated scientifically, is A PHILOSOPHICAL GRAMMAR.

PART II: COSMOLOGY

Prologomena

§351

GENERAL COSMOLOGY is the science of the general predicates of the world, and this science is either based upon experience that is nearest to hand, in which case it is EMPIRICAL COSMOLOGY, or it is based upon the concept of the world, in which case it is RATIONAL COSMOLOGY.[a]

general predicates] genera || concept of] abstract concepts of

§352

Since it contains the first principles of psychology, physics, theology, teleology, and practical philosophy, cosmology rightly belongs (§2) to metaphysics (§1).

§353

Cosmology teaches the (1)[1] concept, (2)[2] parts, and (3)[3] perfection of the world.

concept] the abstract concepts[b]

Chapter I. The concept of the world

Section I. The affirmative concept

§354[c]

A world (cf. §91, 403, 434, the universe, πᾶν[d])[4] is a series (multitude, whole) of actual and finite beings that is not part of another.[e]

---

[a] "*General cosmology* is the science of the world or universe, insofar as, to be sure, it is a composite and modifiable being" (WC §1). Wolff identifies two sorts of general cosmology: "one of these is scientific, and the other experimental. *Scientific general cosmology* demonstrates a general theory concerning the world from the principles of Ontology; on the other hand, on the basis of observations *experimental general cosmology* elicits a theory established in scientific cosmology, or one which is to be so established" (WC §4). And again: "Because those theories that are demonstrated in scientific cosmology are elicited in experimental Cosmology on the basis of observations, experimental cosmology presupposes scientific cosmology. To the extent, however, that it is not repugnant that these theories bequeathed in scientific cosmology are elicited on the basis of observations or phenomena (WC §3, 4), *the other, experimental cosmology* can, to a certain degree, be developed ahead of scientific cosmology, and can be joined with scientific cosmology" (WC §5).

[b] Meier uses the plural throughout the following titles.

[c] Kant E3624, before 1764? 1765–6? (1766–autumn 1770? 1771–2?): "absolute universality of the concept <*universalitas absoluta conceptus*>/absolute universality of the whole, that is, the metaphysical universe of things. this universality should have proven that there is only one world and supreme cause <*universalitas absoluta totius, h.e. rerum universitas metaphysica. haec probaret, unicum tantum esse mundum, causam esse summam*>."

[d] "all"

[e] Wolff: "A series of finite beings that are simultaneous as well as successive and connected among themselves is called a WORLD, or also a UNIVERSE" (WC §48).

§355

This world exists. Therefore, the world is possible in itself (§57, 18).

§356

In this world, actual beings are posited apart from one another. Hence, there is a universal and actual nexus (§279, 306).

§357

In every world there are actual parts (§354, 155), each of which is connected with the whole (§14, 157), and hence each part is connected with every other[a] (§33). Therefore, in every world there is a nexus of parts and a universal harmony (§48);[5] i.e. *a world admits of no islands*. Said otherwise: The parts of a world are either actual beings posited mutually outside of one another, and hence each is connected with every other (§279, 306), or they are internal determinations of a world, not posited mutually outside of one another (§10, 37), and hence each is connected with every other (§49). Οὐκ ἐστίν ἐπεισοδιώδης, ἐστίν ὥσπερ στράτευμα.[b, 6]

§358

In this world there exists an effective nexus (the kingdom of power)[7] (§335), a nexus of utility (§338) and of use (§339), a final nexus (the kingdom of wisdom)[8] (§343),[9] a subjective nexus and a formal nexus (§345), an exemplary nexus (§346) and a nexus of signification (§347). Hence, these sorts of nexus are possible in a world (§57).

subjective nexus and a formal nexus] nexus of essence and of material with their consequences

§359

Since each world is a being (§355, 62), it will be one (§73 [354, 155]) and true (§90 [357, 355, 354, 92]). Hence, in every world there is order (§89) and common rules (§86). A dream world is not a world (§120).

§360

Every world is perfect (§90, 359) and good (§100).

§361

All the parts[c] of every world are contingent beings (§354, 257). Hence, their existence is a mode (§134). Now, the existence of all the parts[d] of a world, taken together, is the existence of a world (§155). Therefore, the existence of a world is a mode, and every world is a contingent being (§111). Said otherwise: Suppose that a given world is a necessary being. Then all of its internal determinations would be absolutely necessary, and hence no part of that world would have modes (§108, 157) nor be a contingent

---

[a] G/K: "the individual is connected reciprocally with the individual"
[b] "They are not incoherent; they are, so to speak, like an army". This is an allusion to Aristotle, *Metaphysics* XII (1075a11–a13).
[c] G/K: "The individual parts"
[d] G/K: "of the individual parts"

being (§134), but rather every part of this world would be a necessary being (§109), and hence infinite (§258), which is absurd (§354).[a]

§362

Every world is one (§359) and yet has modes (§361, 112), and hence determinations separable in themselves (§72, 65), and hence a hypothetical (§76) and intrinsically contingent (§115) unity.

is one] is an unconditioned unity

§363

In no world is the conjunction of the parts absolutely necessary (§362, 102), and yet there is a coordination (§78). Therefore in every world there is an order that is contingent in itself (§117), and hence also an intrinsically contingent truth (§119).

§364

Since all the real parts of a world (§136) agree[10] in the degree of reality that must be attributed to their world (§354, 257), yet also such that, inasmuch as they are contingent beings (§354, 257), they are also in themselves capable of not agreeing or of not agreeing as fully: in every world there is a perfection that is contingent in itself (§122).

§365

Every world is absolutely and internally alterable (§361, 133).

§366

In every world, there are absolutely necessary realities (§359, 360), hence a metaphysical good (§147), and realities contingent in themselves (§362–4), hence, a physical good in the broad sense (§147).

§367

This world is one (§359), contingently in itself (§362). In this world, there is an intrinsically contingent order (§359) and truth (§363). In it there is also an intrinsically contingent perfection and goodness (§364), a metaphysical good and a physical good in the broad sense (§366), and this world is both absolutely and[11] internally alterable (§365, 154).

§368[12]

The smallest world would be the whole[13] of the smallest and fewest actualities (§161, 354). Hence, the more and greater finite beings it has for parts, the greater it would be (§160) until it is the greatest world, which would be the aggregate of the greatest and the most parts among the finite beings (§161).

---

[a] G/K again render the last part of this sentence as "(§258 as a presupposition for §345)".

§369

The STATE OF A WORLD is the whole of all the simultaneous states in its parts. Now, this world has parts, among which fixed ones coexist alongside alterable ones (§367).[14] Therefore this world has a state (§205).[15]

§370

The existence of every world, including this world, is a mode (§361, 134). Hence, it can be absent or present while the essence of the world remains unscathed (§65). And since the actuality of every world, including this world (§133), is absolutely alterable, the beginning and end[16] of every world is absolutely possible (§301, 65).

§371

A world can only originate from nothing. For, suppose that some world were to originate such that some part of it existed beforehand: because, and as long as, this part of the world existed, the world was something existing in part, just as it will always be something not truly non-existing, should it come to exist <*si existi-terit*>. Hence, a world which appears to originate after a pre-existing part does not originate[17] (§227): although such a world would not yet have originated, it would, however, no longer be merely possible as long as the whole of the existing part was indeed already determined with regard to existence (§54). Therefore, the world that does not originate from nothing does not originate (§228).[18] And thus a world that is not annihilated does not perish as long as it remains partially existing in the remaining part, just as it always was, when it existed. Hence it does not alter into something non-existing[19] (§227). Therefore, a world cannot perish except by annihilation (§228).

Meier's reformulation is enlightening: The world cannot arise except from nothing. Suppose that a world arose such that one of its parts was already actual apart from it: then prior to its beginning it would be a whole having a part that was actual. And since it also would already be determined in regard to its actuality, it would not be a merely possible thing. For because and as long as this part is actual prior to the world's beginning, the latter would in part be actual, and it can never be actual in another way, as long as it endures, and hence such a world would not be a thing that is not actual. Consequently, if it appears that a world arises and that a part of it is actual prior to this: then it is a false representation, and if a world should arise, then it cannot arise except from nothing. In just the same way, a world does not perish if it is not annihilated. For as long as a part of it still remains left over, the world remains a thing that is in part actual; and if it was actual, then it could never have been actual in any other way. Thus, as long as a part of it is still there, it cannot be converted into a thing that is not actual. If, therefore, a world should perish, it must be annihilated.

§372

Every world, including this world, is a finite being (§255, 361), and hence philosophical and mathematical cognition of it is possible (§249). Every world, including this one, is partially good and partially evil (§264), and contains metaphysical (§250) and contingent or[20] physical evil in the broad sense, an imperfection that is contingent in itself and absolutely possible (§263).

§373

Every world is partially similar to the infinite being, to every other world, and to each of its own parts. But it is impossible for there to be many actual worlds mutually apart from one another that are totally the same (§269),[21] different (§268),[22] congruent (§270), similar (§271), or equal (§272).

§374

Since the parts of a world are either simultaneous or successive (§238, 354),[23] if they are posited mutually apart from one another, then they are connected in a world through time, or space, or both (§239, 306).

§375

Every world is a being from another (§361), i.e. dependent (§308), and this world has an efficient cause posited apart from it, of which it is an effect (§334) that attests to its cause (§333).

§376

The parts of every world are actual (§354), and hence all the parts[a] possess truth (§90) and certainty (§93) as internally determined (§54) determinations (§37, 93) in their own world, as indeed do the parts of this world in this world.

§377

Finite beings that are not only absolutely possible and not merely hypothetically possible in any given nexus, but are also such in the universal nexus of SOME WORLD, are called the POSSIBLE BEINGS of that world. Hence, the possible beings of this world are those that, when considered in its universal nexus, are still hypothetically possible, and hence have a greater degree of possibility (§165, 246).

§378

If even one part of this world were different from what it is, then this world would not be wholly the same thing that it is (§155, 267). Now, all the parts of this universe could be different from what they are (§354, 260). Therefore, worlds are possible that are partly different from this world (§38), and partly the same as it (§265); i.e. there are many (§74).

§379

This world is uniquely singular (§77). For suppose that there are many, then together with this world, they would constitute a multitude or a series (§74). Hence this world would not be a world (§354), or all of these worlds would be parts of this, the only unique world (§354, 77).

uniquely singular] singular and alone actual

---

[a] G/K: "the individual parts"

Section II. The negative concept of the world

§380

A PROGRESSION (regression) TO INFINITY would be a series of contingent beings mutually posited apart from one another, one of which is the qualified cause of another, without there being an unqualified cause. If in this progression to infinity the caused being is presumed to be the cause of itself, then it is CURVILINEAR (circular). If the caused being is not presumed to be the cause of itself, then it is RECTILINEAR.

without ... unqualified cause] however, such that there would be at hand a first cause neither for the whole series, nor for a single one of its parts

§381

A progression to infinity, posited to however great an extent, would be a contingent being (§380, 155), and hence would have an efficient cause posited apart from it (§334). This could not be a contingent being; for, insofar as it would again be a being from another (§308),[24] it would not be the cause of a progression to infinity, except as a qualified cause (§28).[25] Therefore, it would not be posited apart from the progression, but would be a part of it (§155,[26] 380). Therefore, the efficient cause of a progression to infinity must be a necessary (§109) and independent (§310) being. This being exists in whatever manner it can exist (§259). But it can exist although it is not caused by another being posited apart from it (§310). Therefore, it is not caused by another being posited apart from it, but rather is the unqualified cause of its own effects (§28).[27] Hence, a progression to infinity, which must be without an unqualified cause (§380) and yet still must have one, is impossible (§7), and is not to be posited in this or in any world.

§382[a]

FATE is the necessity of events in a world. Fate based on the absolute necessity of the world would be[28] SPINOSISTIC FATE, and a non-being (§361, 105), which must not be posited in this or in any world (§354, 58).

§383[b]

An event in a world whose sufficient ground is unknown is CHANCE. CHANCE whose sufficient ground does not exist would be PURE CHANCE, which is impossible (§22) and must not be posited in this or in any world (§354, 58).

§384

An ORDINARY event is one whose existence is determined according to the rules[29] of some certain order. An EXTRAORDINARY event is not ordinary. An ABSOLUTELY EXTRAORDINARY event would be that whose existence was determined according

---

[a] Kant E3625, 1769–75 (next to §382): "Nature and Freedom."
[b] Kant E3626, 1776–8 (over §383 "not ... PURE"): "respective chance. absolute *<casus respectivus. absolutus>*."

to no rules of any order, whereas a RELATIVELY EXTRAORDINARY event would be that which does not come about through rules of some certain given order. An event that is extraordinary because of confusion is INORDINATE.

Meier reformulates the last sentence to read: The extraordinary is called the DISORDERLY, because of the disorder that belongs to it.

§385

The absolutely extraordinary would not be true (§384, 89), and hence would be impossible (§90, 62) and must not be posited in this or in any world (§354, 58).

be true] have metaphysical truth

§386

An event without any proximate sufficient ground would be an ABSOLUTE LEAP. An event without an ordinary proximate sufficient ground is a RESPECTIVE LEAP.

Meier expands the second sentence to read: An event, however, that although it indeed has a proximate sufficient ground, does not have an orderly one, would happen through a leap in a certain respect.

§387

That which would exist without any proximate sufficient ground (§27) would exist through pure chance[30] (§22, 383), and hence an absolute leap is impossible (§386, 284), and must not be posited in this or in any world (§354, 58). Furthermore, every relative leap, if it is not inordinate, is nevertheless something extraordinary (§384).[31]

§388

The world is neither an infinite substance (§372, 248) nor an internal determination of an infinite substance (§365, 252), and hence, the world is not the essence (§40), attribute, mode (§50), or modification (§209) of an infinite being. Hence, every world is to be posited apart from the infinite substance, and so this world also exists apart from the infinite being, which for this reason is called an EXTRAMUNDANE BEING, a being that is actual apart from this world.

§389

Every world, and hence this one, is either a substance or an accident (§191). If this world were a substance, then it would subsist apart from the infinite substance (§388) precisely such that the infinite substance would not be the unique substance[32] (§77).

§390

If this world is an accident, it is nevertheless not an accident of an infinite substance; otherwise, it would not exist outside of its substantial being (§196,[33] 388), and it cannot exist except in a substance or in substances (§194). Therefore, if this world is an accident, then the infinite substance is not the unique substance[34] (§77, 389).[35] Now, one of these two cases is necessary (§191, 10). Therefore, the infinite substance is not the unique substance.

otherwise ... substances] otherwise it could not exist separate from it. However, also in this case the world could not be actual other than in one or several finite substances

§391

Infinite power is not the unique power (§390, 198); there are many finite powers in every world and hence in this world (§390, 388).

Chapter II. The parts of the universe

Section I. The simple parts of the universe

§392

Every world is either a simple or a composite being (§224).[36] This world is a composite being. One who holds this world to be a simple being, and holds it to be oneself, is an EGOIST.

§393

All the parts of a composite world, each taken individually <*singulae*> and together, cannot be accidents. For, since such a world could only exist in substances (§155, 191), and yet could inhere neither in an infinite substance (§388) nor in only one finite substance (§224, 194), it would require many finite substances in which to inhere (§77). But these substances would constitute a series of finite actualities, and this series, if it would not be part of a world composed of mere accidents, would still constitute together with that world a series of finite actualities greater than this world (§160), and hence this world would not be a world (§354). If, however, this series, which these finite substances would constitute, were part of its world, then that world would not be composed of mere accidents (§155). Hence a world composed of mere accidents is impossible (§61, 62). Every composite world is composite in the stricter sense (§225). Every world is either a substance (§389, 392) or composite in the stricter[37] sense.

§394

The parts of a composite world are either substantial or accidental (§393), and the former are indeed monads (§235). Hence every composite world, and this world, consists of monads (§392). Whence, once again, it should be clear that no world is able to originate except from nothing, nor perish except through annihilation (§237, 393).

§395

This world, which is composite in the stricter[38] sense (§393), consists of monads, and there is nothing substantial in it whatsoever aside from monads (§394). Whoever denies the existence of monads is a UNIVERSAL[39] MATERIALIST.[40] Whoever denies the existence of the monads, or the parts, of a universe (e.g. of this universe) is a COSMOLOGICAL MATERIALIST (cf. §757).[41]

, or … universe)] of the world or whoever maintains that monads are not parts of the composite world, that is of ours,

§396

The monads of every composite world, and hence of this one, are possible (§8), rational (§24), one (§73), true (§90), objectively certain (§93), perfect (§99), good (§100), contingent (§257), alterable (§133), real (§136),[42] and universally connected (§357) beings (§63). They are endowed with power, or indeed are powers, also in the stricter sense (§199). They have an internal (§206) and an external state (§207), and are modifiable (§209). They are neither extended nor does any single one fill up space, but rather aggregates do (§242). They have no quantitative magnitude (§243), are indivisible (§244) and finite (§354). Hence, they have a certain limit to their powers (§249),[43] which is a metaphysical evil (§250). They are partially similar to one another (§265, 268), but are nevertheless partially dissimilar and unequal (§273). No single monad admits of figure, and yet they are such that a whole of them does (§280).

quantitative magnitude] extended magnitude

§397

Since they are actual beings posited mutually apart from another (§354, 224), the monads of every and hence this composite world are either simultaneous or successive, or both (§238). Hence, single monads have a position (§148), which is either place in simultaneous monads or age in successive monads, or both (§281),[44] although no single monad fills up space (§396).

single monads] each monad || *Meier adds after* "position": in relation to one another

§398

If any given finite monad of every universe, and hence this universe (§354), is posited as subsisting, it will subsist (§192) apart from the rest, and cannot be in wholly the same place as any other (§282).[45] A substance, in whose place another substance apart from it cannot be posited, is IMPENETRABLE (a solid).[46] Therefore, every substance and hence all the monads of every composite world, and of this one, are impenetrable (§230).

Meier reformulates the first sentence as follows: No monad of this world, because it is actual apart from the rest that make up the world, can be in one and exactly the same place as another.

Eberhard adds the note: Our very first concept of impenetrability is obtained through feeling. We feel, namely, the opposition of substance to the alteration of its place, which could not be the case, if two substances could take up the same place.

§399

The monads of this and of every composite and hence extended world (§241, 393) are POINTS[47] (§286), but by no means MATHEMATICAL[48] POINTS, in which nothing aside from absence of extension is posited (§396–8). They are neither congruent nor do they coincide when posited next to one another (§70, 396). But rather if the coexistence of many is posited, then, since each one is impenetrable (§398), they are posited as simultaneous and mutually outside of one another in some certain order (§396, 78), and hence there is space in their aggregate (§239). Therefore, every aggregate of monads of this and of every composite world is extended (§241). The mathematical point, i.e. an abstract or possible point (§149), if one were to imagine it to exist, would be a ZENONICAL POINT, a fictional being (§62). If by PHYSICAL POINT you mean a being that is actual and completely determined in addition to simplicity, then some monads of this universe are physical points, namely, those from the aggregate of which an extended being arises.[49]

fictional being] non-being; is actual … simplicity] in addition to its simplicity, yet has all the remaining determinations without which it could not be actual

§400

All monads of a composite and hence of this world are in a universal nexus (§357). Hence, each and every monad is either the ground or consequence, or both, of every other single monad[a] (§14, 48). The ground can be known from the consequence (§29). Therefore, from any given monad of every composite world, and hence of this composite world, one can know the parts of the world to which this monad belongs (§14), i.e. every *monad*[b] of every composite world, and hence of this composite *world*, is a power (§199)[50] for representing *its own universe* (*they are active mirrors* of their universe (§210), *indivisible* (§244), *microcosms, abbreviated worlds, and concentrations of their own worlds,*[51] or they have a power, they are endowed with a power for representing their own universe).[52]

§401

Monads that represent their own worlds (§400) either represent it to themselves while at least partially conscious of their perceptions, or not (§10). And hence the monads of this universe represent this world either only[53] obscurely, or at least partially clearly. The former are BARE MONADS (slumbering monads).[54]

§402

Monads that clearly represent the world either represent it to themselves distinctly, at least in part, or not. The former UNDERSTAND (§69).[55] Therefore, they have the faculty of knowing distinctly (§216), i.e. THE INTELLECT (in a strict sense, cf. §519).[56] An INTELLECTUAL substance, i.e. a substance endowed with intellect,

[a] G/K: "hence the individuals are grounds or consequences of one another, or both"
[b] G/K: "the individual monads"

is a SPIRIT (an intelligence, a person).[57] Therefore, the intellectual monads of this universe are spirits[58] (§230). Whoever admits only spirits in this world is an IDEALIST.

§403

The NEXUS of the spirits of any world among one another is PNEUMATIC. Now in every world, and this world, to which spirits belong, every spirit is connected with every other spirit. Therefore, in this and in every world to which spirits belong, there is a universal pneumatic nexus (§357)[59] (cf. §354,[60] a pneumatic, intellectual, and moral[61] world, cf. §723,[62] a kingdom of grace).

§404

Every substance is a monad (§234). Every spirit is a substance (§402). Therefore, a spirit is a monad and also a simple being (§230).

§405

All the spirits of every world, and of this world, to which spirits belong are monads (§404), powers for representing their own world at least partially distinctly (§402). Neither extended nor individually space-filling, they have no quantitative magnitude. Indivisible and finite, they are only endowed with a certain degree of powers, and are subject to metaphysical evil. All spirits are partially the same as each other, but also both partially dissimilar and unequal, and no single spirit admits of figure (§396), and one is the most perfect of all (§77, 185).[63]

Section II. The first generation of bodies[64]

§406

A whole of monads is called a MONADATUM <*MONADATUM*>. Therefore this and every composite world is a monadatum (§394).

§407

Moreover, the monads in a composite world either have the parts of the composite world as their own monadata, or not (§10, 406). In either case,[65] a monadatum of this sort will be an extension (§396) of impenetrable and partially dissimilar parts (§398), i.e. PARTIALLY HETEROGENEOUS EXTENSION (non-uniform, dissimilar), and hence it will not be a TOTALLY HOMOGENEOUS EXTENSION (uniform, similar), i.e. the extension of wholly similar parts (§271).

§408

The simultaneous monads of this world mutually determine each other's place, while the successive monads determine each other's age (§281, 85); hence, they mutually influence each other (§211) and are posited as in conflict (§213). Therefore, in this world influence and conflict are universal (§48, 306) (*a war of all against all*,[a] *discordant harmony, harmonious discord*, §364).[66]

§409

Some monads in this world mutually influence one another more remotely (§408, 27); some, being present to one another, mutually influence one another more closely, (§223), and because an absolute leap is impossible in the world (§387), some, touching one another, mutually influence one another most proximally (§223).[67]

§410

Because all the monads of this world mutually influence each other (§408), *there is no* transeunt *action* or influence of one of these *without a reaction* (§213).[68]

§411

A transeunt action, or the influence of the parts of the world upon others that are outside of them, is either simple or composite (§215). A simple action is the smallest (§247, 214). To this corresponds either the smallest reaction or a larger one (§160, 161). If it is the smallest, it is equal to the influence (§70). If a larger reaction were posited, the degree to which the reaction exceeds the influence posits a reaction of the influencing monad (§410), and hence its influence will not be simple (§215), which is contrary to the hypothesis. Therefore an equal reaction responds to a simple influence (§70).

§412

A composite influence of the parts of the world upon others outside of these very parts is a whole of many simple influences (§215, 214). An equal reaction corresponds to any one of these (§411). Now, if you add equals to equals, the sums are equals (§70). Therefore, an equal reaction corresponds to every composite influence of the parts of the world. Hence, every *reaction* of the parts of the world to others outside of these very parts *is equal* to the influence or transeunt *action* (§411).[69]

§413

The living powers of the monads in the world, which conflict among one another through mutual contact, are equal (§412, 331), and because these same powers cannot be the most proximate grounds of contradictories (§140, 36), they, mutually determining most proximally the place (§408, 409), and hence conjunction, among one another (§281, 85), do not contain the most proximate ground of mutual separation (§72). Hence, unless a third power supervenes, the monads touch each other inseparably (§386) united (§79),[70] and constitute one (§73)[71] being.

---

[a] "*Bellum omnium contra omnia*"; compare with Hobbes' celebrated characterization of nature as "*bellum istud omnium contra omnes*," in *De Cive* I: 13; "*istud*" adds intensity to "*bellum*," almost "that damn war." Hobbes had used the near equivalent "*bellum omnium in omnes*" earlier in *De Cive* I: 12. See *Elementa Philosophica de Cive* (Amsterdam, 1742). *Leviathan* (1651) repeats this in English, which was eventually Latinized slightly differently into "*bellum omnium contra omnes*." See *Opera philosophica quae latine scripsit omnia*, edited by William Molesworth (London, 1841), Vol. 3, 100.

§414

Thus beings COHERE that mutually touch each other such that they can only be separated by a third power. Therefore, the monads of a world that mutually touch one another cohere (§413). *There is no contact without cohesion.*[72] Therefore some monads of this world cohere (§409), constituting one (§413) extended (§407) being.

§415[73]

There can be no alteration in a composite world without motion. For instance, let there be an A that is to be altered from B into not-B. Previously it coexisted as B with those things simultaneous to itself posited outside of it, and now it coexists as not-B; hence it will enter into a different relation (§37, 38) with these things, a different position (§85), and a different place (§281), and there will be motion (§283, 125). Whenever such alteration, or such motion, arises in a composite world, the state of the altered being, and of the universe of which it is a part, is partly the same as the states preceding it (§265), and partly different (§125). Hence, just as there was some certain motion insofar as a new state differs from a former state, so, insofar as the state remains the same, this endurance of state is,[74] in a composite world, likewise the endurance of place (§299), an absence of a specific motion, or rest (§283), and there is an impediment (§221) and resistance (§222) to a specific motion.

§416[75]

The monads in the universe that constitute an extended being (§414) are always acting (§216, 285) through their own power (§400), representing every single state of their universe, as well as their own and even future states (§298). Insofar as these states are the same, enduring with previous states, this power impedes a specific motion, or resists a specific motion (§415, 210); however, insofar as these states are different from previous states (§415), this power effects another specific motion, or moves (§415, 210). The aggregate of the predicates appropriate to every part is attributed to the whole (§155). Hence, some monads of this universe constitute an extended being to which the power of inertia may be attributed (§294), and hence matter (§295). The matter of neither this nor any other universe can be wholly homogeneous (§407).

§417

The monads of this universe that constitute matter do not produce it in the sense of prime (§295) or merely passive matter, but as matter to which a motive power is attributed (§416), i.e. second matter and a physical body (§296).[76] If one part of this world is moved, its relation to every other simultaneous part of the world is altered (§283, 281). Hence, there is no PARTICULAR MOTION in the world, i.e. of some part of the world, without universal motion (§283). Hence, in this world, all matter is in motion (§415), and there is no REST for this, unless it is RELATIVE,[77] i.e. the absence of some determinate motion (§283), which, if it becomes so great that no motion of a being at rest can be observed, is an EVANESCENT MOTION. *There is no ABSOLUTE REST in the world, no absence of all motion.*

§418[78]

An extended being, or an aggregate of monads each of which is impenetrable, for this reason presently resists the motion of those beings posited outside of it that would occupy its place (§398, 222); hence it presently exerts the power of inertia (§294). An extended being or an aggregate of monads, no power of which is wholly equal to any other power posited outside of it, and no whole of which is wholly equal, in terms of powers, to any other monadatum previously posited outside of it (§272, 406), is never in a complete EQUILIBRIUM or equality of powers among those that conflict, and hence it now exerts a motive power (§294). However, every monadatum in this world is such an extended being (§414, 396). Therefore, due to one and the same power of representing that belongs to their own monads (§400) and inasmuch as this power contains the ground of remaining in place, rest, and a certain absence of motion in the impenetrable monads, the monadata in this world produce the power of inertia. And inasmuch as the same power of representing contains the ground of the alteration of place and a certain motion in monads that are never wholly in equilibrium, the monadata in the world produce a motive power (§417), matter (§416), and physical bodies (§417). Thus, it is far from the case that these two powers [i.e. inertia and motive power] are mutually opposed to one another such that when one power is posited with respect to a different motion (§87), the other power may not likewise be posited in the same subject; rather it is the case that in any extended being of this world they are simultaneous with respect to different motions (§417), and the same power, when attributed to a given extended being, is a motive power with respect to a given motion, and with respect to the motion opposite to this, it is the power of inertia, and vice versa (§415).

§419

Since powers are attributed to bodies (§296), bodies are composite beings in the strict sense (§225, 198). Hence, the mode of composition is their essence (§226);[79] they consist of monads (§235), and have a quantitative magnitude (§243).

Meier reformulates this section to read: All bodies are composed of monads and substances as from their own parts, and they have powers in the narrower sense; hence they are composite things in the narrower sense, and apparent substances. The kind of composition in them is their essence, and they have an extended magnitude.

§420

Bodies have parts outside of parts (§296, 224). The primary actual parts mutually outside of one another that belong to bodies are called ELEMENTS.

§421

The elements are either the absolutely primary parts of bodies, i.e. those which themselves do not again have parts outside of parts, or they are relatively such, whose further composition one chooses to ignore (§420). The former are simple beings, or monads (§419, 224).

i.e... . parts] which themselves consist of no further parts

§422

What is not matter is called IMMATERIAL, whereas what is matter is called MATERIAL. The absolute elements of bodies *<elementa corporum absolute talia>* are immaterial (§421, 295). The INCORPOREAL is that which is not a body, whereas that which is a body is CORPOREAL. Now, every corporeal being is material (§296). Therefore, the absolute elements of bodies are incorporeal. Hence, no single element is a body (§296).

§423

A philosophy that takes the relatively first for the absolutely first is called a PHILOSOPHY OF THE LAZY.[a] Since it is false, such relative elements (§421), which are material and corporeal (§422), must not be taken as elements in the absolute sense, i.e. as immaterial and incorporeal (§422). Hence, the former are more appropriately called ELEMENTS simply as such, while the latter are called PRIME MATTER (cf. §295).[80]

§424

A being indivisible *per se* is called an ATOM. Every monad is indivisible *per se*[81] (§244). Hence, every monad is an atom. Therefore, elements are atoms (§423), and hence they are called the atoms of nature.[82]

§425

We call OBSERVABLE (phenomena) that which we are able to know (confusedly)[83] through the senses. Bodies that are too small to be observed by us are called CORPUSCLES. A philosophy that explains the phenomena of bodies by means of corpuscles is CORPUSCULAR PHILOSOPHY.

OBSERVABLE] AN APPEARANCE

§426

Corpuscles either have other corpuscles again as parts, or not (§10, 155). The latter are called PRIMATIVE CORPUSCLES; the former, DERIVATIVE CORPUSCLES.

§427

All matter of the kind found in this world consists of elements (§418, 419). Hence, the quantitative magnitude that is to be attributed to it (§419, 423) is the multitude of the elements united in order to constitute a certain matter (§159, 413). Hence the elements, or the parts of a certain matter, are in the same place as this matter, just as they are in the same place as their monadatum (§155, 406). Therefore, if the place of these elements were to alter such that they were no longer in the same place as the matter that they had earlier constituted, then they would not remain parts of this matter (§155). Now, however, all alteration of relation is possible in a being considered

---

[a] See Kant's *De mundi*, AA 2:406; to be distinguished from "*ignava ratio*," or "lazy reason." See, e.g. Leibniz, *Theodicy*, Part 1 §55 and Kant A689/B717 and A772/B801.

in itself (§133).[84] Therefore, all alteration of location is possible in all elements considered in themselves (§281, 85). Therefore, that motion is also possible through which the parts of matter cease to be the parts of that which they formerly were (§283). If they are thus moved, matter is divided (§244, 162). Therefore, *all matter* of the kind found in the world is *divisible*, at least in itself and *per se* (§18).

§428

If the *matter in the world* is said to be *infinitely divisible*, then this is understood either absolutely, as saying that there are no indivisible parts in it, and is false (§424, 419), or it is understood respectively,[85] as saying that in dividing this matter no parts can be observed by us except those that are further divisible (§248),[86] and it is then true that matter is indefinitely divisible (§425).[87]

§429

A MATERIAL ATOM would be an intrinsically indivisible corpuscle, which is nothing (§427, 425). Therefore, ATOMISTIC PHILOSOPHY, which explains the phenomena of bodies by means of material atoms, is mistaken.

Section III. The nature of bodies[88]

§430[a]

The NATURE (cf. §431, 466)[89] of a being is the collection of those of its internal determinations that are the principles of its alterations, or, in general, of the accidents inherent to it. Hence, to the nature of a being pertains its (1) essential determinations (§39), (2) essence (§39), (3) faculties, (4) receptivities (§216), and (5) all the powers with which it is equipped (§197). The beginning of a nature is its ORIGIN; its duration, LIFE; and its end, DEATH (cf. §556).[90]

principles of its alterations] ground of the actuality of its alterations

§431

The nature of bodies is their mode of composition (§419), along with every faculty, receptivity, and inertial and motive power that they exert (§296, 430). Furthermore, sometimes it is simply called nature (cf. §430, 466).[91]

§432

Since there is universal truth in the world (§363, 90), all of its alterations have common norms (§86, 89) according to which the nature of its parts is determined (§431), and hence also the motion of bodies in the world (§283). The superior norms are called the LAWS OF MOTION, and the inferior, the RULES OF MOTION.

RULES OF MOTION] PARTICULAR LAWS OF MOTION

---

[a] Kant E3627, 1773–8 (beginning): "Nature is here taken only as an adjective."

§433

A MACHINE is a composite being in the strict sense that is moveable according to the laws of motion. Therefore, *every body <omne corpus>* in the world is a *machine* (§419, 432).[92] Every machine in the world is a contingent being (§361). The nature of a machine determined by the laws of motion is MECHANISM. On the other hand, whatever is not composite is not a machine; hence, no monad is a machine (§230).

§434

A nexus of machines is a MECHANICAL NEXUS, and hence the nexus of the bodies in the world is mechanical (§433) (the corporeal or material world, cf. §354,[93] the kingdom of nature). However, in a world in which there are spirits and bodies, bodies are connected with spirits (§357). Hence, in a world in which there are spirits and bodies, there is a nexus (1) of bodies among one another, (2) of spirits among one another (§403), and (3) of bodies and spirits mutually, thus a pneumatico-mechanical and a mechanico-pneumatic nexus[94] (a harmony of the kingdom of nature and the kingdom of grace).

§435

A MECHANICAL PHILOSOPHY explains the phenomena of bodies by means of their mechanism. There is a PHYSICO-MECHANICAL FATE (simply physical or mechanical)[95] based on the mechanism of bodies. However, if any event is determined by this, it is contingent in itself (§361, 354),[96] and only hypothetically necessary (§382, 105).

There … bodies] The necessity of the alterations of bodies that is grounded in their mechanism is MECHANICAL FATE

Chapter III. The perfection of the universe

Section I. The best world[a]

§436

The most perfect world is that in which the greatest of the most parts and the most of the greatest parts that are compossible in a world agree in as great a *<unum>* being as is possible in a world. Hence, the most perfect world has the greatest composite perfection, and if only a simple perfection is appropriate for a world, then it is not the most perfect (§185).

Meier simplifies the first sentence to read: The most perfect world is that in which there is as many and as great parts as are possible together in a world, and in which there is as great of agreement as is possible in a world.

---

[a] Kant E3628, 1780–9: "The world as the highest derived good."

§437

If the most perfect world is posited, the supreme perfection that is possible in a world is posited (§436).[97] Hence, *the most perfect world* is also the *best* of all possible worlds (§187). Now, the parts of the world are actual (§354), and these are either simultaneous or successive (§306). Therefore, the *most perfect world*[98] embraces as many (1) simultaneous, (2) successive, and (3) as great beings as are compossible in the best[99] world;[100] i.e. it is (1) *extensively*, (2) *protensively*, and (3) *intensively* the best and[101] greatest of the worlds (§436, 368).[102]

§438[103]

Even if only two contingent beings that are posited outside of each other in a world are compossible, either as simultaneous or as successive, one of whose perfection either subtracts nothing from the perfection of the other, or does not subtract from the perfection of the other so much as it adds to the perfection of the whole, then the EGOTISTICAL WORLD, such as an egoist posits, is not the most perfect. And even if there is only one non-intellectual monad possible in itself that is compossible with spirits in the world, whose perfection either subtracts nothing from the perfection of the spirits, or does not subtract from the perfection of the spirits so much as it adds to the perfection of the whole, then the IDEALISTIC WORLD, such as is posited by the idealist, is not the most perfect (§437).

§439

The materialist denies that there are monads in this world (§395). Hence, he fashions for himself a world that is impossible (§394). Therefore, the MATERIALISTIC WORLD, such as the materialist imagines, is neither any nor the most perfect world[104] (§436).

§440[105]

Furthermore, the *most perfect world is finite* (§372), as are likewise all of its parts, even its most perfect ones (§354, 257). Therefore, neither the most perfect world itself nor any being within it whatsoever is really infinite (§248). Nevertheless, it is not only possible that both the most perfect world and many of its parts are in many ways mathematically *infinite*, but furthermore that the most perfect world itself is of just such *infinite* mathematical *extension, protension, and intension* for all who either cannot or do not wish to determine the limits of the greatest contingent being. That is to say, it is intensively, extensively, and protensively indefinite (§248, 437).

§441

In the most perfect world there is the greatest universal nexus (§437,[106] 94),[107] harmony, and agreement (§436, 357)[108] that is possible in a world.

§442

Since every world is perfect (§360), the most imperfect world is that in which there is the smallest perfection that is possible in a world: i.e. the smallest agreement of the fewest[109] and smallest beings in one <*unum*> smallest being (§354, 185) and hence simple perfection (§96)[110] without exceptions (§97).[111] The most imperfect world is the smallest (§368).[112]

§443[113]

Even when the most perfect world is posited to be the best of the worlds (§437), nevertheless it is still not posited to be the supreme good, i.e. the metaphysically best. Even when the greatest and most realities that are compossible in any world are posited in it, nevertheless they are not absolutely the most and greatest realities (§190), and even less are they absolutely necessary, since the existence of every reality[a] is a mode (§361). And even when the greatest degree of reality to be reached in a certain universe is attributed to the most perfect world, nevertheless in contingent beings it will only be a limit (§248, 250), which is properly different (§38) from the absolutely greatest, necessary, and inalterable (§251) degree of reality of a really infinite being.

reality is a mode] one of its realities is contingent

§444

There is order in every perfection (§95). Hence, in the most perfect world there is the greatest order that is possible in a world (§437, 175).[114] Therefore, there are the most general rules of perfection, e.g. *the more, the greater, the more spacious* (§280),[115] and *the longer lasting* (§299), *all else being equal, the better (§437, 187).*[116] There is also a maximally composite order (§183), yet such that all the inferior and superior rules can in the end be known together from one and the same supreme and strongest rule of perfection (§182, 185).

general rules of perfection] rules of order

§445

Since there are the most rules of perfection in the most perfect world (§444), there can also be very many exceptions (§97, 372), provided that they do not destroy <*tollant*> the greatest agreement (§440), and hence those exceptions that are possible would be, all else being equal, the fewest (§161) and the smallest (§186).[117]

§446

If a sufficient and insufficient ground of perfection collide in the most perfect world, the exception would be to the insufficient. If the more fecund and the less fecund collide, the exception would be to the less fecund. If the more serious and the less serious collide, the exception would be to the less serious. If the more distant and the closer subordinated to the more distant collide, the exception would be to the closer. If the qualifiedly sufficient and the unqualifiedly sufficient collide, the exception would be to the qualifiedly sufficient. If the inferior and the superior collide, the exception would be to the inferior. Finally, if any rule of perfection in the most perfect world collides with the supreme rule, then the exception is to the former (§186, 445).

---

[a] G/K: "individual realities"

§447

Not only are §361–76, 354, and 436 valid concerning the most perfect world, but those beings that §380–8, 247, and 354[118] teach to be absent from every world are also most absent from it. For example, Spinosistic fate is so absent from it (§382) that, rather, indefinite and even hypothetical (§104, 127) contingency and alterability must be extensively, intensively, and protensively attributed to it (§440, 437).[119]

Section II. The interaction of mundane substances[120]

§448

Since there is universal harmony in this world (§356), there is universal influence (§408), and this will either be real everywhere, or ideal everywhere, or sometimes real, sometimes ideal (§212). The harmony of the world's monads mutually influencing each other is the INTERACTION OF MUNDANE SUBSTANCES. Therefore the substances of every world, and of this world, are in universal interaction (§357). The doctrines that seem able to explain this are called the SYSTEMS FOR EXPLAINING THE INTERACTION OF THE WORLD'S SUBSTANCES, and if these are employed to explain all interaction of all substances, these are UNIVERSAL (general), cf. §761. If the parts of the world are posited as being in interaction such that the occurrence of their alterations in one part of it can be known from the power of another part of the interaction, then they are HARMONIC ALTERATIONS.[121] The ideal mutual influence of all the world's substances is UNIVERSAL PRE-ESTABLISHED HARMONY (cf. §462),[122] and someone positing it in this world is a UNIVERSAL HARMONIST, whose system[123] is called the SYSTEM OF UNIVERSAL PRE-ESTABLISHED HARMONY.

If … HARMONIC ALTERATIONS] HARMONIOUS ALTERATIONS are the alterations of the substances of the world which, due to their community among one another, have a sufficient ground in the power of other substances of the world.

§449

The system of universal pre-established harmony does not deny <*tollit*> the mutual influence of substances upon one another, but rather maintains it (§448). This system does not deny that one substance of the world suffers from another (§448, 212), but instead maintains that any alterations that a substance suffers from another substance in this world are produced through its own power (§210). This system does not deny the mutual conflict of the parts of the world (§213), nor a faculty and receptivity for transeunt actions (§217), much less the influence of the infinite substance and the receptivity for such influence in finite substances (§448). Not only does it not deny that spirits can act upon bodies, and bodies upon spirits, but it even maintains that bodies and spirits mutually influence each other in this world (§408, 434), and that they can mutually touch one another (§223, 409).[124]

§450[125]

PHYSICAL INFLUENCE is the real influence of a substance that is part of a world upon another part of the world. Hence, UNIVERSAL PHYSICAL INFLUENCE is the universal harmony of substances in a world, whereby one really influences another, and someone supposing it in this world is a UNIVERSAL INFLUXIONIST. The system of the universal influxionist is the SYSTEM OF UNIVERSAL PHYSICAL INFLUENCE.

§451

The system of the universal physical influence does not deny <*tollit*> the mutual and universal (§450, 48) harmony of the world's substances, but rather pre-established (§448) harmony. Not everyone is a universal influxionist who maintains that the substances of this world mutually influence one another, that they collide with one another, that they mutually suffer from each other, and that both bodies with respect to spirits, and spirits with respect to bodies, can mutually touch one another (§449, 450). The universal influxionist (1) denies <*negat*> that any substance of this world acts when it suffers from another substance of this world, and that it produces its own sufferings through its own power (§450, 212); (2) supposes that the sufferings of one substance of this world are really produced by the influence of another substance upon it (§450).[126] Hence, according to the system of universal physical influence, no substance, or part of the world, acts through its own power in any of its harmonic alterations (§448). Now however, all the alterations of a mundane substance can be sufficiently known from the power of any other given monad belonging to the same world (§354, 400). Therefore, according to the system of universal physical influence, all alterations are harmonic (§448) and hence no mundane substance acts in any of its alterations, but rather in all alterations it really suffers from other mundane substances, which nevertheless, for the same reason, would not be acting at all (§210), and hence they would not be powers (§197), which contradicts §199.

Meier adds after "(§354, 400)": to the extent that it is not produced by the infinite substance

§452

Whoever supposes that the infinite substance alone really influences all the substances of this world that seem to suffer[127] from another substance of this world, and indeed, according to this doctrine,[128] that they are really suffering, is a UNIVERSAL OCCASIONALIST (an assistantist), and this system is the UNIVERSAL SYSTEM OF OCCASIONAL CAUSES[129] (the Cartesian, or better, the Malebranchian system, the system of assistance).[130] This contradicts §400 and 408, and is hence false. The same is obvious from the fact that, according to occasionalism, no harmonic alteration in any mundane substance belongs to that very substance, but is only the action of an infinite substance (§448). Hence, this system likewise denies all power and energy in finite beings (§451).[131]

§453

Even if it does not deny universal harmony (§448), the system of occasional causes certainly still denies the universal mutual influence of this world's substances (§452, 448), that the latter is a physical (§450) and ideal (§212) influence (unless perhaps you would speak of an apparent, imaginary influence (§12)),[132] and that the former is pre-established.[133] Not everyone is a universal occasionalist who supposes that the infinite substance really influences all the sufferings of finite substances, nor is everyone who supposes that the infinite substance alone really influences these, but rather he who maintains that (1) all[134] the sufferings of finite substances are real, and (2) that they proceed from the influence of the infinite substance alone (§452).

§454

The systems of universal pre-established harmony and universal physical influence[135] are thus alike (§70), in that they (1)[136] do not deny the universal mutual influence of substances of this world, nor universal harmony, nor the real universal influence of the infinite substance upon these (§448, 450),[137, 138] and (2)[139] they suppose that sufferings of the substances of this world are actions of some finite substance. They are dissimilar in that the latter excludes the suffering substance from action and the former does not (§449, 451).

§455

The universal system of pre-established harmony and occasional causes[140] are similar in that they deny the real influence of a substance of this world upon another part of the same world (§70). They are dissimilar (§70) in that the former posits certain ideal sufferings of these, while the latter posits real sufferings (§449, 453).

§456

The universal systems of physical influence and occasional causes are similar in that both suppose that the real sufferings of one substance in this world depend on another part of the same world. They are dissimilar (§70) in that the former denies that the infinite substance alone influences these, while the latter maintains this (§451, 452).

§457

UNIVERSAL[141] SYSTEMS FOR EXPLAINING THE INTERACTION OF MUNDANE SUBSTANCES,[142] if they explain all interaction of every mundane substance in a similar manner, are called SIMPLE. Therefore, the universal systems of pre-established harmony, physical influence, and occasional causes[143] are simple systems (§448, 456).[144] COMPOSITE UNIVERSAL[145] SYSTEMS are those that explain some instances of interaction of some mundane substances in a manner different from others.

§458

Aside from the universal systems of pre-established harmony, physical influence, and occasional causes,[146] no fourth simple universal[147] system (§457) is possible (§448,

452).[148] There can be infinitely, or better, indefinitely many composite systems (§457, 248).[149]

§459

Through pre-established harmony, or the mutual ideal influence of the many substances of the world posited in interaction, a greater nexus is actualized than is through their physical influence (§167). For, in physical influence, the suffering of the substance that really suffers does not have a sufficient ground in its own powers (§450, 212). In pre-established harmony, the suffering of the suffering substance has a sufficient ground (1) in its own powers and (2) in the substance ideally influencing [it] (§449). Hence, in pre-established harmony, the influencing substance is equally as fecund as in physical influence, while the suffering substance is however more fecund than in physical influence (§166).

§460

Through the influence attributed to infinite substance alone[150] upon really suffering substances posited in interaction, whatever they suffer,[151] the suffering substance is not more fecund than through physical influence (§453). However, the other finite part of the interaction[152] is still less fecund (§453, 166). Therefore, a greater nexus among substances posited in interaction is actualized through pre-established harmony joined with the concurrence of the infinite substance than through the influence attributed to infinite substance alone[153] (§167).

§461

In the most perfect world, there is the greatest nexus of things which are possible in a world (§441). Therefore the substances that are possible in it, and as many as are possible in it, are connected through pre-established harmony joined with the concurrence of the infinite substance (§460, 459).

§462

If universal pre-established harmony joined with the concurrence of infinite substance is possible in the most perfect world, then this world is such as the universal harmonist supposes it to be (§448, 461), and it is not such as someone who adopts any other system may conceive of some composite world (§451). On the contrary, each PARTICULAR PRE-ESTABLISHED HARMONY, i.e. of certain parts of the world, must be admitted in the most perfect world (§154).

§463

Since the necessary condition <*conditio, sine qua non*> of universal pre-established harmony is its possibility in the most perfect world, this possibility must be demonstrated by one who will demonstrate pre-established harmony according to[154] §462.[155] It is thus otherwise obvious: From any given monad of any given world, every part[a] of the world to which it belongs can be known (§400), and therefore every mundane

---

[a] G/K: "the individual parts"

alteration[a] as well (§354, 155). However, of just such a kind are all the sufferings of any given mundane monad that[b] it suffers from another monad of its own world (§210). Now, a suffering monad is a power (§199). Therefore, this very monad that suffers from another mundane monad is itself the ground of this, its own suffering, and of all of its parts (§354, 155), and is hence the sufficient ground of its own suffering (§14, 21); and thus a given[156] suffering belonging to it is simultaneously the action of the suffering monad (§210). Therefore, all the sufferings of the monads of any given world, which they suffer from other mundane monads, are, to this extent, ideal (§212). Therefore, the influence of a mundane monad upon another is indeed always of this sort, and never real or physical (§450). Hence, in this world too, all of its substances are in universal interaction (§448) through pre-established harmony alone, and none ever through physical influence. The system of universal pre-established harmony is a true doctrine, and therefore every particular pre-established harmony is true (§462); and every universal and particular physical influence, as well as its system (§450), and the system of occasional causes[157] (§452), are false.

§464

In the most perfect world, there is the greatest nexus that is possible in a world (§441). Therefore, if there are bodies and spirits in the most perfect world (§438), in that same world there is the greatest mechanical, pneumatic, and pneumatico-mechanical nexus (§441) (the greatest pre-established (§463) harmony of the kingdom of nature and the kingdom of grace (§434, 403)).[158]

§465

A DUALIST is someone who supposes that this world consists of spirits and bodies apart from one another. Hence, the most perfect world (§439)[159] is neither egotistical nor idealistic (§438); it is as the dualist conceives it.[160]

Section III.[161] The natural

§466

The collection of the natures in all the parts of the world, each taken individually *<singulis>* and together, is UNIVERSAL NATURE (natured nature, cf. §859).[162] Hence, the nature of this and of the most perfect universe is an aggregate or collection of all essential determinations, essences, faculties, receptivities, and powers with which all of its parts, monads, elements, spirits, matter, and bodies are equipped. Hence every mode of composition of all the bodies in it, every inertial power, every motive power, and every mechanism is a part of universal nature (§431, 433).

---

[a] G/K: "individual alterations"
[b] Reading *quas* for *quam*.

§467

The essence of the composite world and the mode of its composition (§226), along with the essences of each of its parts, is only a fairly small (§161) part of universal nature (§466, 155).

§468

Universal nature has alterable internal parts (§466), and the universal nature of the most perfect world has the most of these (§437). Hence, the universal nature of any world whatsoever is a contingent (§131) and finite (§255) being, and indeed the universal nature of the most perfect world has, mathematically, a threefold infinite contingency[163] (§447).[164]

infinite] mathematically infinite

§469

An EVENT that is to be actualized[165] by the nature of any contingent being is NATURAL,[166] CONTRADISTINGUISHED FROM A SUPERNATURAL EVENT (cf. §474).[167] Whereas an event that is to be actualized[168] by the determined nature of a determined contingent being is NATURAL,[169] CONTRADISTINGUISHED FROM THE PRAETERNATURAL (cf. §474).[170] Whatever can be actualized by a certain nature is PHYSICALLY POSSIBLE for that very nature, and whatever cannot be is PHYSICALLY IMPOSSIBLE for it. There are beings possible in themselves that nevertheless cannot be actualized by any nature whatsoever (§15, 430); therefore, they can be physically impossible for many natures. Not everything physically impossible for some beings is absolutely such. Those things that are physically impossible for some contingent being are either such in any state in which its nature is considered, and are NATURALLY IMPOSSIBLE IN THE UNQUALIFIED SENSE (merely, entirely, utterly),[171] or rather only when its nature is considered exclusively in a certain state, and they are NATURALLY IMPOSSIBLE IN A QUALIFIED SENSE (now and in this manner).[172] The unqualified natural impossibility of realities is MERELY NATURAL IMPOTENCE. Not every natural impossibility is merely natural impotence or absolute impossibility (§467). The opposite of the physically impossible is the PHYSICALLY NECESSARY, and of the physically possible, the PHYSICALLY CONTINGENT. Not everything physically necessary is absolutely necessary (§102). Some things that are contingent in themselves can be physically necessary for many things (§104). Physically necessary things are either unqualifiedly or qualifiedly such.

§470[173]

SOMETHING NATURAL FOR A CERTAIN BODY is to be actualized by the latter's determinate nature. SOMETHING NATURAL FOR A CERTAIN CORPOREAL WORLD is that which is to be actualized through the universal nature of the bodies of a certain world (§466). SOMETHING NATURAL FOR A SPECIFIC CONTINGENT SPIRIT is that which is to be actualized through this spirit's determinate nature. SOMETHING NATURAL FOR A SPECIFIC PNEUMATIC WORLD is that which is to be actualized by the universal nature of the spirits of a certain world (§469).

§471

The succession of natural beings in a world is the COURSE OF NATURE.[174] Hence, the course of nature is opposed to the succession of either supernatural or preternatural beings (§469), and is considered in some body <*aliquo corpore*>, or in some whole corporeal world, or in some spirit, or in some whole pneumatic world, or in universal nature (§470, 466).

NATURE] NATURE, and it is either a succession of absolutely or of relatively natural events

§472

The order of natural things in the world is the ORDER OF NATURE, and it is opposed to the conjunction of supernatural or preternatural beings. It is only considered in a specific body, corporeal world, spirit, or pneumatic world (§469, 470), or in universal nature (§466).[175] All of these orders[a] have their own common norms (§86). Therefore, in this world there are the norms of natural order, common laws and rules (§432), which are different (§38),[176] but yet similar (§70). The collection of similar laws is RIGHT <*IUS*>, cf. §971 (in the broader sense). The collection of the laws of the order of nature is the RIGHT OF NATURE, IN THE BROADEST SENSE, whose parts are the laws and rules of motion (§432), and the laws of the nature of spirits.

and it is … beings] and it is either of absolutely or relatively natural events ‖ similar laws] similar rules

§473

When something natural follows something natural, it OCCURS ACCORDING TO THE COURSE OF NATURE, and[177] according to the course of the nature of a certain body, or a certain nexus in a certain material world, or a certain spirit, or even[178] a certain nexus in a certain pneumatic world, (§471), or, in any case, according to the course of universal nature (§466).[179] If it succeeds or coexists with something natural, it OCCURS ACCORDING TO THE ORDER OF NATURE, and according to the order of nature of a certain body, or a certain nexus in a certain material world, or a certain spirit, or even[180] a certain nexus in a certain pneumatic world (§472), or, in any case, according to the order of universal nature (§466).[181] Therefore, something natural that succeeds and coexists with natural things is actualized according to the laws of nature (§472).[182] Something natural for a certain body or for a certain nexus in the material world[183] is actualized according to the laws and rules of motion through the mechanism of bodies (§433)[184] and hence it can be mechanically explained (§435, 433).

Section IIII.[185] The supernatural

§474

A SUPERNATURAL EVENT is an event in the world not actualized by the nature of any contingent being. An event not actualized by the determinate nature of the certain

[a] G/K: "These individual orders"

contingent being in which it occurs is, with respect to this being, PRETERNATURAL. Hence, with respect to universal nature, the supernatural is preternatural, and the preternatural is supernatural (§466). A supernatural event, insofar as it is considered extraordinary, is a MIRACLE. Hence a miracle is preternatural with respect to universal nature. Every miracle is supernatural, but not everything supernatural is a miracle.[186]

Eberhard adds the note: This distinction of the SUPERNATURAL and the MIRACLE is not grounded in the concepts themselves, but rather is made because of a certain manner of speaking in the churches. Because of this, Wolff and others have also dispensed with it in cosmology.

§475

The supernatural and[187] miracles are the opposite of the natural and the naturally ordinary (§81, 474). Now, the natural and naturally ordinary are contingent in every world (§354, 257). Therefore, the supernatural and miracles are possible (§101).

possible] possible in themselves

§476

Whatever is actualized through the nature of a contingent being in the world is neither[188] supernatural, nor is it[189] a miracle (§474). Hence, whatever is actualized through the nature of a spirit that is part of the world is neither supernatural, nor a miracle (§354, 257).

§477

The actions of finite spirits upon other parts of the world that are not actualized by the determinate[190] nature of the suffering beings, and that are hence preternatural (§474) and extraordinary (§472, 384)[191] with respect to the suffering beings, are nevertheless not supernatural, nor are they miracles (§474). Hence, if they are called COMPARATIVE MIRACLES, then comparative miracles are not miracles, which are called STRICT MIRACLES to contradistinguish them from the former. If such actions are posited above <*supra*> nature, then these can be conceded only concerning the specific nature of a specific body or of a corporeal world (§470).[192]

COMPARATIVE MIRACLES … former.] such miracles are not true miracles, and one calls the latter, in order to distinguish it from the former, MIRACLES IN THE NARROW SENSE.

§478[193]

An extraordinary event whose natural cause we were not aware of is a PRODIGY (a sign, cf. §347, a revelation or portent). Prodigies are either strict miracles (§474, 477), or natural events, i.e. MIRACLES FOR US.

MIRACLES FOR US] MIRACLES TO THE COMPREHENSION OF THE ONE WHO PERCIEVES

§479

Since the supernatural and[194] miracles are not actualized through universal nature (§474, 466) and are nevertheless contingent beings (§474, 354) and hence effects

(§334), when they exist, they have an extramundane being as an efficient cause (§388), to which they testify (§333).

§480

A non-natural event that follows natural events occurs CONTRARY TO THE COURSE OF NATURE (§471, 473). Now, something that is supernatural and[195] a miracle is not a natural event (§474, 469). Therefore, something that is supernatural and[196] a miracle and that follows natural events comes about contrary to the course of nature, and indeed contrary to the course of universal nature (§471). What is preternatural for a specific body, or a specific corporeal world, or a specific spirit, or a specific pneumatic world, comes about only contrary to some course of nature (§474, 471).[197] Hence, not everything that occurs contrary to some specific course of nature is supernatural, or[198] a miracle (§474).

§481

The supernatural and[199] miracles are not absolutely extraordinary (§475, 385); they are neither contrary to every order of the world (§359, 7) nor, nevertheless, are they naturally ordinary (§472, 474). And since a non-natural event coexisting with, or succeeding, natural events OCCURS CONTRARY TO THE ORDER OF NATURE, things that are supernatural and[200] miracles are contrary to every order of universal nature. Therefore, they do not occur according to the common norms of a specific order of nature (§472).[201] Therefore, they are extraordinary relative to the order of nature (§384). The supernatural and[202] miracles are extraordinary with respect to the order of universal[203] nature (§472). The preternatural is extraordinary with respect to a certain body or corporeal world, to a certain spirit or pneumatic nexus, and with respect to a determinate order of nature in these (§474, 472), such that it occurs contrary to this determinate order (§384).[204] Therefore, neither[205] every being that is extraordinary with respect to some specific order of nature, nor every being that is contrary to some given natural order,[206] is supernatural, much less a miracle[207] (§474).

Section V. The hypothetical possibility of the supernatural[208]

§482

This is the law of order in the most perfect world (§84), and it is one of the superior laws (§182): *The best of all compossibles in the most perfect world is joined together with the best* (§444). *This law* is called *the law of the best*[209] in the world (cf. 822),[210] to which is subordinated *the law of the best in nature: the best of all natural things in the most perfect world is joined together with the best* (§469, 444).

§483

Suppose there is a natural event in the most perfect world, and hence an event according to the order of events of nature (§473), compossible with the rest. Suppose there is a supernatural event under the same circumstances, hence an event contrary to the order of events of nature[211] (§481), compossible with the rest, but better than the natural event. Since opposite events, i.e. a natural and supernatural, e.g. miraculous,[212] event, cannot exist together (§81),[213] in such a case the rules of order of universal[214] nature and a superior rule of perfection (§482)[215] are brought into collision (§97).

brought into collision] result in a contradiction

§484

Since in the most perfect world, the rules of the order of both particular and universal[216] nature are inferior and subordinate to the law of the best in the world[217] (§182, 482), an exception to the laws of the order of nature (§446) would be made in the case of §483, and something supernatural, or more correctly,[218] a miracle (§483), would come about that is most appropriate for the supreme order of the most perfect world (§444).

§485

The supernatural and[219] miracles by means of an absolute leap would be impossible (§387); hence no supernatural things,[220] no miracles, come about by means of an absolute leap (§475). Since, nevertheless, the most proximate natural and ordinary sufficient ground of events in a world is the nature of a specific contingent being (§472, 469), when the supernatural and[221] miracles occur, they occur through a relative leap (§474, 386).

§486

The supernatural and[222] miracles occurring in the corporeal world cannot be explained mechanically (§435, 433), and even less can the PNEUMATIC ones that occur in the pneumatic world (in the realm of grace) (§433, 403).

§487

If a supernatural and[223] miraculous event is posited in the world instead of a natural event, the world is not totally the same as it would have been if a natural event had been part of it (§267, 155). Therefore, when a supernatural event, and[224] miracle, is posited in the world instead of a natural effect, the state of the world coexisting with the given supernatural event, or[225] miracle, is posited as partially different than it would have been had the supernatural event, or[226] miracle, not been accomplished (§378,[227] 369).

§488

Nothing is utterly sterile (§23); hence nothing supernatural,[228] no miracle, is without a correlate, or consequence <*rationato*>. When it is posited, something else is posited in turn (§14), and hence again a consequence (§23), and so on. Therefore, the logical consequences <*consectaria*> of every supernatural thing,[229] every miracle, are posited indefinitely (§248)[230] throughout the successive states of the world after the supernatural event or[231] miracle (§30,[232] 369).

§489

If, in the case recounted in §487 and §488, a natural event would have been posited in the world instead of a supernatural event, or[233] a miracle, this would have had its consequences indefinitely throughout every state of the world following it (§23, 369). But the consequences of a natural and supernatural, or[234] miraculous, effect cannot be wholly the same (§267, 38). Therefore, when a supernatural effect,[235] or a miracle, is posited in the world instead of a natural effect, all the states of the world following the supernatural effect, or[236] the miracle, are partially different from what they would have been had the given supernatural effect, or[237] miracle, not been accomplished.

§490

In the system of occasionalism every suffering of a finite substance is supernatural (§474, 453), although some suffering could be conceived that would not be a miracle insofar as it is considered as ordinary (§384).[238]

§491

Since the supernatural, and[239] a miracle, is an action (§474, 323), it will be either simple or composite (§215), and this indeed will either be simultaneous or successive, or both (§238). A simultaneous being, whether simple or composite, emerges in an instant, devoid of earlier and later parts (§300).

§492

The more fecund and the more noble something supernatural, and[240] a miracle, is, the greater it is (§491, 214) (§166); hence, the greatest would be the most fecund, most noble, and most composite (§214, 215).

§493

A NATURALIST, IN THE BROADER SENSE[241] (cf. §999),[242] is someone who denies every supernatural event in this world. Therefore, the naturalist denies the existence of miracles in this world (§474); and if he does this because he denies their possibility, he errs (§475).

their possibility] their internal possibility

§494[243]

When the nature of this world is posited as it is, i.e. as of mathematically infinite extension, intension, and protension (§440, 466), then it is also in the same way of infinite contingency (§468, 361), and can only exist as the effect of an extramundane cause, to which it attests (§375), just as does the supernatural, and do miracles, when they exist (§479). Hence, one who does not confuse the limits of one's own theory of the universal nature of this world with the limits of said nature itself and thereupon does not carelessly conclude merely from one's own ignorance of natural causes that such causes must be entirely denied, is, in that case, neither unjust to a cause common to universal nature, the supernatural, and miracles (§375, 479), nor is that person a naturalist.

§495

Suppose that a natural event and a supernatural event in the most perfect world were, under the same circumstances, compossible with all of the world's other parts, but, with regard to logical consequences, equally good. The natural event will satisfy the law of the best in the world[244] as well as the supernatural does (§482), and likewise it will also satisfy the law of perfection that[245] the order of nature prescribes (§472); hence it will satisfy more than the supernatural (§481). In this case, therefore, the supernatural, or[246] a miracle, would not come about in the most perfect world (§482, 445).[247]

§496

Since the universal nature of even the most perfect world is finite (§468), it is not the sufficient principle of all the accidents that can inhere in the best world (§430, 259). Therefore, suppose the best event that is compossible with all the other best events in the best world,[248] but one, however, that is not to be actualized naturally and ordinarily, and suppose that the same event can be actualized supernaturally and extraordinarily; in this case, like in §484, the supernatural, or more correctly[249] a miracle, would also come about most appropriately in the order of the most perfect world (§482, 444).

§497

As many and as great of the best things as can occur naturally and ordinarily in the best world do come about in it naturally (§495). As many and as great of the best things[250] as either absolutely cannot occur naturally and ordinarily in it, or as cannot do so equally well, do come about in the best world supernaturally and[251] miraculously (§484, 496). The former miracles[252] can be called SUPPLEMENTARY MIRACLES, and the latter, CORRECTIVE MIRACLES. There is equal ground for the supernatural.[253]

§498

The number of supernatural events and[254] of miracles in the most perfect world is only as great as the number of the possible events that belong to it that cannot be actualized naturally and equally well according to the order of nature[255] (§159,[256] 497)—no more, no less (§160).

§499

If any supernatural event in the best world is ever better than a natural event, even[257] with regard to its logical consequences <*consectaria*>; if any possible event of the best world is ever naturally impossible through universal nature: then, the most perfect world is not such as the naturalist, in the more general sense,[258] thinks it to be (§498, 493).

event in] event possible in

§500

Not everyone is a naturalist in the more general sense[259] (§493) who denies that some preternatural beings (§474),[260] extraordinary effects of finite spirits (§476), comparative miracles (§477), prodigies, and[261] things that are miracles for us (§478) that occur contrary to the course of nature (§480) and some[262] order (§481) are miracles in this world (§474).

PART III: PSYCHOLOGY

Prolegomena

§501

PSYCHOLOGY is the science of the general predicates of the soul.

general] more abstract

§502

Since it contains the first principles of theological systems, aesthetics, logic, and the practical sciences, psychology rightly (§501) belongs (§2) to metaphysics (§1).

§503

Psychology (1)[1] deduces its assertions based upon experience that is nearest to hand, in which case it is EMPIRICAL PSYCHOLOGY,[a] and (2)[2] deduces its assertions based upon the concept of the soul through a longer series of arguments, in which case it is RATIONAL PSYCHOLOGY.

Chapter I. Empirical psychology

Section I. The existence of the soul

§504

If there is something in a being that can be conscious of something, that is a SOUL. Something exists in me (§55) that can be conscious of something (§57). Therefore a soul exists in me (I, a soul, exist).

§505

I think; my soul is altered (§125, 504). Therefore, thoughts are accidents of my soul (§210), at least some of which have a sufficient ground in my soul (§21). Therefore, my soul is a power (§197).

§506

Thoughts are representations. Therefore my soul is a power for representing (§505).

---

[a] Wolff: "*Empirical psychology supplies principles to rational psychology.* Indeed, the ground for what happens in our souls is given in rational psychology. However, principles are established in empirical psychology, from which is given the ground of those things that happen in the human soul. Therefore, empirical psychology supplies principles to rational psychology" (WPE §4).

§507

My soul, at the very least, thinks about some parts of this universe (§354). Therefore, my soul is a power for representing this universe, at least partially (§155).

§508

I think about some bodies of this universe and their alterations. I think less about alterations belonging to this body, more about alterations belonging to that body, and the most about alterations belonging to one body, and this last body is indeed a part of me (§155). Hence, MY BODY is the one whose changes I think more about than I do those of any other body.

MY BODY] MY BODY or my living flesh

§509

My body has a determinate position (§85), place, age (§281), and situation (§284) in this world.

§510

I think about some things distinctly, and some confusedly. One who is thinking about something confusedly does not distinguish its notes, although one nevertheless represents or perceives them. For, if one distinguished the notes of something confusedly represented, then one would have thought distinctly what one confusedly represented. If one did not at all perceive the notes of something confusedly thought, then through these one would not be able to distinguish the thing confusedly perceived from others. Therefore, one who is confusedly thinking something represents some things obscurely.

represents some things] represents some notes of it

§511

There are obscure perceptions in the soul (§510). The collection of these perceptions is called the FOUNDATION OF THE SOUL.

§512

Based on the position of my body in this universe, it can be known why I would perceive this thing more obscurely, that thing more clearly, and something else more distinctly (§306, 509), i.e. I REPRESENT ACCORDING TO THE POSITION OF MY BODY[3, a] in this universe.

THE POSITION] THE MEASURE OF THE POSITION

---

[a] Kant E111, 1764–8 1769–72? 1766–78??: "(*added later:* of the soul in the body or (of the body) through a body in the universe) according to either the internal or the external state of a body, <(*animae in corpore vel (corporis) per corpus in universo) pro statu corporis vel interno vel externo)*>; (*added later:* and constitution <*et constitutione*>)"

§513

My soul is a power (§505) for representing (§506) the universe (§507) according to the position of its body (§512).

§514

The whole of the representations in the soul is a TOTAL PERCEPTION,[4] and its parts are PARTIAL PERCEPTIONS.[a] The collection of the obscure representations among these is the FIELD OF OBSCURITY (field of darkness), which is the foundation of the soul (§511), whereas the collection of clear representations is the FIELD OF CLARITY (field of light), which includes the FIELDS OF CONFUSION, OF DISTINCNESS, OF ADEQUACY, and so on.

§515[5]

True knowledge is a reality (§12, 36), the opposite of which—namely (§81, 36) no knowledge, i.e. the lack of knowledge or IGNORANCE, and apparent knowledge, i.e. ERROR—are negations. The smallest knowledge is the minimally true knowledge of the one smallest being (§161). Therefore, the truer the knowledge is of more and greater beings, the greater it is (§160) until it is the greatest, which would be the truest knowledge of the most and greatest beings.[6] The degree of KNOWLEDGE in which it knows more things is its RICHNESS (abundance, extension, riches, vastness);[7] the degree in which it knows fewer things is its NARROWNESS; the degree in which it knows greater things is its DIGNITY (nobility, magnitude, gravity, majesty);[8] the degree in which it knows smaller things is its WORTHLESSNESS (meagerness, shallowness). The truer the things that knowledge joins together in a greater order, the more true it is (§184), and hence the greater it is. Knowledge conveying truer things is EXACT KNOWLEDGE (properly prepared), and knowledge exhibiting the less true is CRUDE. A greater order in knowledge, or METHOD, is the METHODICALNESS of knowledge (acroamatic, disciplined *<disciplinale>*), and less order in knowledge is the TUMULTUOUSNESS of knowledge. Knowledge and its representations in my soul are either smaller or greater (§214), and insofar as they are grounds, they are ARGUMENTS IN THE BROAD SENSE, and power or efficacy is attributed (§197) to them. No knowledge is wholly sterile (§23); nevertheless knowledge of greater efficacy or STRENGTH is STRONGER, and knowledge of less strength, which is FEEBLENESS, is WEAKER (unengaged, inert). The weaker representations that arise alter the state of the soul less, and the stronger ones more (§208, 214).

§516

Perceptions that, along with some partial perception, are[9] parts of the same whole

---

[a] Wolff: "I call a *total perception* that which embraces all those perceptions that we have together in some given moment" (WPE §43). In the note to the same paragraph, Wolff continues: "For example, if I behold fresh troops in a field, in one gaze I likewise behold the field beyond them, a forest viewed from a distance, the boundary of heaven and earth, and other objects. And indeed at the same moment, I also represent objects that are absent to me, as for instance the church in which I often see the military commander. Various thoughts also arise in my mind according to the diversity of objects that I represent to myself. All these perceptions likewise complete the total perception" (WPE §43).

of perception, are called ASSOCIATED PERCEPTIONS, and the strongest of the associated perceptions PREDOMINATES (it rules over the soul).[10]

§517

The more notes a perception embraces, the stronger it is (§23,[11] 515). Hence, an obscure perception comprehending more notes than a clear one is stronger than the latter, and a confused perception comprehending more notes than a distinct one is stronger than the latter. Perceptions containing many perceptions in themselves are called PREGNANT PERCEPTIONS. Therefore, pregnant perceptions[a] are stronger. Hence ideas[b] have great strength (§148).[12] Terms having a pregnant meaning[c] are EMPHATIC (emphases). The science of these is EMPHASEOLOGY. The power of proper names is not small.

ideas] representations of singular things

§518

The state of the soul in which the ruling perceptions are obscure[d] is the KINGDOM OF DARKNESS, whereas the state of the soul in which the ruling perceptions are clear is the KINGDOM OF LIGHT.

Section II. The inferior cognitive faculty

§519

My soul knows some things (§506). Therefore, it has a COGNITIVE FACULTY, i.e. a faculty[e] of knowing some things (§57, 216) (the intellect in the broad sense, cf. §402).[13]

§520

My soul knows some things obscurely and some confusedly (§510). Now, all else being equal, the soul that perceives a thing and perceives that it is different from other things perceives more than the soul that perceives but does not distinguish (§67).

---

[a] Kant E112, 1765–6: "*Bismilla. Adanilla.*" [As noted in AA 15: 7–8, in the Parow transcript of Kant's Anthropology lectures of winter 1772/1773, we read that Kant thought these to be Arabic for "Allah bless this" and "May Allah be praised."]

[b] Baumgarten and Meier reserve the term "idea" to refer to representations of singular or completely determined individuals, much as Kant later does. This is why proper names have great power, as Baumgarten remarks below; for they refer to ideas, and thus to representations with a multitude, indeed indefinitely many, notes. Wolff: "The representation of a thing <*rei*> is called an IDEA, insofar as it refers to a certain thing, or to the extent that it is considered objectively" (WPE §49). On the other hand: "We call a NOTION a representation of things universally or in general, and a species" (WPE §49).

[c] Kant E112 (see above): "through rousing perceptions <*perceptionibus commoventibus*>"

[d] Kant E113, 1776–89? 1770–2??: "on obscure representations and the state of the soul in these <*de repraesentationibus obscuris et statu animae in iis*>."

[e] Wolff: "Just as the active potency is usually called a *Faculty* in general (WO §776), so are the active potencies of the soul called its *Faculties*" (WPE §29). WO §716 and not §776 seems to be the correct reference. We provide the key text from WO §716 above in a footnote to §216.

Therefore, all else being equal, clear knowledge is greater than obscure knowledge (§515). Hence, obscurity is a lesser degree of knowledge, and clarity a greater degree of knowledge (§160, 246). And on the same grounds, confusion is lesser or inferior, and distinction greater or superior. Hence the faculty of knowing something obscurely and confusedly, or indistinctly, is the INFERIOR COGNITIVE FACULTY.[14] Therefore, my soul has an inferior cognitive faculty (§57, 216).

§521

A representation that is not distinct is called a SENSITIVE REPRESENTATION. Therefore, the power of my soul represents sensitive perceptions through the inferior faculty (§520, 513).

§522

I represent things to myself such that some of their notes are clear, and others are obscure. Perception of this sort is distinct with regard to the clear notes, and it is sensitive perception with regard to the obscure notes (§521).[15] Hence, there is distinct perception that is mixed with something of the confused and obscure, and sensitive perception to which belongs something of the distinct. The latter, on account of the lower <*sequiori*> part, is formed through the inferior cognitive faculty (§520).[a]

Meier formulates the second sentence to read: Such a representation is distinct to the extent that it has clear notes, and at the same time sensible, to the extent that it has obscure notes. || distinct perception] distinct knowledge || lower] sensitive

§523

The notes of a representation are either mediated or immediate (§67, 27). Only the latter are considered in judging the clarity in a given perception.

§524

The notes of a perception are either sufficient, or insufficient (§21, 67), or absolutely necessary (§106, 107), or contingent in themselves (§108), or absolutely inalterable and constant (§132), or variable, i.e. alterable, in themselves (§133). Sometimes only the former of these are called notes eminently <*per eminentiam*>.

Meier reduces this paragraph to the following: There are as many kinds of notes of representations as there are kinds of grounds and determinations.

§525

The notes of a representation are either negative or real (§135). Perception that has the former kind of notes is called a NEGATIVE PERCEPTION, whereas perception that has the latter kind of notes is called a POSITIVE PERCEPTION. The former would either be WHOLLY NEGATIVE PERCEPTIONS, if all their notes were negative, thus

---

[a] Wolff: "What we learn in addition by experience, we are said *to know a posteriori*; what becomes conspicuous to us through reasoning, we are said *to know a priori*. That *cognition* is *mixed* which is acquired partly *a posteriori*, and partly *a priori*" (WPE §434). "*When reason is not pure, experience concurs with it in knowing*" (WPE §496). "The concurrence of reason and experience in knowing is usually called *the marriage of reason and experience*" (WPE §497).

through which nothing would be perceived (§136), or PARTIALLY NEGATIVE, if their notes were either[16] truly or[17] apparently negative (§12).

§526

Some notes are more fecund and serious than others (§166), and sufficient notes are both in comparison with the insufficient (§169, 524).

§527

Something is EASY when slight powers are necessary to actualize it, whereas when greater powers are required, it is DIFFICULT. Hence something is EASY FOR A CERTAIN SUBJECT when a small part of the powers at this subject's command is necessary to bring it about; and a thing is DIFFICULT FOR A CERTAIN SUBJECT when the greater part of the powers at this subject's command is required. Therefore, ease and difficulty admit of degrees (§246).

§528[18]

The perception whose notes are only sufficient for distinguishing it with the greatest difficulty from the one most different thing is minimally clear (§161). Therefore, the more easily I am able to distinguish a perception from more things that are more similar, the clearer it is to me (§160) until it is the clearest perception for me, which would be that which I am capable of distinguishing most easily from the maximally similar (§161). The representation whose notes are merely insufficient for distinguishing it most easily from one maximally similar thing is minimally obscure. Therefore, the more things, and the greater their difference, from which a perception can nevertheless not be distinguished, and the greater the power employed, the more obscure the perception is until it is the most obscure perception for me, which is that which can be distinguished from nothing, even the maximally different, with all of my power being employed (§161).

§529

I AM ATTENTIVE to that which I perceive more clearly than other things. I ABSTRACT away that which I perceive more obscurely than other things. Therefore, I have a faculty of being attentive and one of abstracting (§216), but both of these are finite (§354) and hence they are only in a certain degree and not the supreme degree (§248). The more that is taken away from a finite quantity, the less is left over. Therefore, the more I am attentive to one thing, the less I am able to be attentive to others. Therefore, a stronger perception[19] that greatly occupies [my] attention obscures a weaker perception, or causes [me] to abstract from a weaker perception (§528, 515).[a]

ABSTRACT away] WITHDRAW MY THOUGHTS from

---

[a] Kant E114, 1770–1? 1775–8? (between §529 and 530, next to 530): "Distinction of the objective and subjective."

§530[a]

A perception that, in addition to those notes to which I am most attentive, contains other less clear notes is a COLLECTIVE PERCEPTION.[b] That collection of notes in a COLLECTIVE thought to which I am most attentive is called the PRIMARY PERCEPTION,[c] whereas the collection of less clear notes is called the ANCILLARY (secondary) PERCEPTION. Hence, a collective perception is the whole of primary and ancillary perception (§155).

§531

Suppose that there are two clear thoughts of three notes each, but such that the notes that are clear in the one thought are obscure in the other: the first will be clearer (§528). Therefore, clarity of perception is increased by the clarity of the notes due to distinction, adequation, etc. Suppose that there are two clear thoughts of equally clear notes, where one thought contains three notes and the other contains six: the later will be clearer (§528). Therefore, clarity is increased by a multitude of notes (§162). Greater clarity due to the clarity of notes can be called INTENSIVELY GREATER CLARITY, while greater clarity due to the multitude of notes can be called EXTENSIVELY GREATER CLARITY. An extensively clearer PERCEPTION is LIVELY.[20] The liveliness of THOUGHTS and of SPEECH is BRILLIANCE (splendor), and its opposite is called DRYNESS (a difficult type of thinking and speaking). Either type of clarity is PERSPICUITY.[d] Hence, perspicuity is either lively, or intellectual, or both. A PERCEPTION whose power manifests itself in knowing the truth of another perception, and ITS POWER, is PROBATIVE. A perception whose power renders another perception clear, and ITS POWER, is EXPLANTORY (revealing). A perception whose power renders another perception lively, and ITS POWER, is ILLUSTRATIVE (depictive). A perception that renders another perception distinct, and ITS POWER, is RESOLVING[e] (explicative). Consciousness of truth is CERTITUDE (subjectively considered, cf. §93). Sense certitude is PERSUASION, whereas intellectual certitude is CONVICTION.[21] Someone who thinks a being and its truth, all else being equal, thinks more than someone who thinks the being alone. Hence, a THOUGHT and

---

[a] Kant E117, 1775–89: "A secondary concept that adheres to an expression."
Kant E118, 1776–8? 1790–1804?: "To develop the obscure adhering [representation]."
Kant E119, 1776–8? 1790–1804?: "Not principal and accessory (where there is the same kind of object), but rather primary and secondary (adhering), where they are of different kind.—Parerga. e.g. Golden frame, Arabesque./(should be vehicles of the primary perception.)/The melody is something adhering to the song and can create a disruption or advantage for the content.—Secondary concept of popular songs, vaudeville.—To a large man adheres the representation of a tall man.—flat—comical expressions. Bad mannered."
[b] Kant E115. 1775–89: "accompanying representation."
[c] Kant E116, 1770–1? 1775–8? (near "PRIMARY PERCEPTION ... ANCILLARY PERCEPTION"): "Subjectively or objectively primary or ancillary <*Subiective vel objective primaria aut adhaerens*>. (*later addition:* The former is commonly understood). What is objectively the primary representation (how the object should be represented), is subjectively only the secondary representation, and vice versa."
[d] Kant E120, 1775–89: "Lucidness, enlightening."
Kant E121, 1776–8? 1790–1804?: "Lucid concepts, enlightening."
[e] Kant E122, 1775–89: "conjoining, valid < *conjungens, bündig*>."

KNOWLEDGE that is certain, all else being equal, is greater than an UNCERTAIN thought, which is not certain (§515). Knowledge that is more uncertain than justified is SUPERFICIAL KNOWLEDGE; knowledge that is certain to the required degree is truly SOLID KNOWLEDGE.[22] The clearer, livelier, more distinct and more certain is knowledge, the greater it is. A PERCEPTION having the certitude of another as a corollary, and ITS POWER, is either PERSUASIVE or CONVINCING. Certain perspicuity is EVIDENCE.

lively, or intellectual] lively, or distinct || having ... corollary] in which the certainty of another is grounded || EVICENCE] INCONTROVERTIBILITY

§532

Both the intensively and the extensively[23] clearer perception can be sensitive perceptions (§522, 531), and thus a more lively perception is more perfect than a less lively one (§531, 185). A more lively perception can be stronger than a perception that is intensively clearer and even distinct (§517, 531).

§533

The science of knowing and presenting <*proponendi*> with regard to the senses is AESTHETICS (the logic of the inferior cognitive faculty, the philosophy of graces and muses, inferior gnoseology, the art of thinking beautifully, the art of the analogue of reason).[24]

Meier reformulates this paragraph to read: The science of the rules of the perfection of sense knowledge and of the meaning of it is THE SCIENCE OF THE BEAUTIFUL, and it deals with the improvement of all the lower powers of knowledge.

Section III. The senses

§534

I think about my present state. Therefore, I represent my present state, i.e. I SENSE it. The representations of my present state, or SENSATIONS (appearances),[25] are representations of the present state of the world (§369). Therefore, my sensation is actualized by the soul's power for representing according to the position of my body (§513).

§535

I have a faculty of sensing (§534, 216), i.e. SENSE. SENSE either represents the state of my soul, which is then INTERNAL SENSE, or the state of my body, which is then EXTERNAL SENSE (§508). Hence sensation is either INTERNAL SENSATION, and actualized through an internal sense (consciousness, more strictly considered),[26] or EXTERNAL SENSATION, and actualized through an external sense (§534).

§536

The parts of the body with whose appropriate motion an external sensation coexists are the INSTRUMENTS OF THE SENSES (sense organs). Through these I have the faculty of sensing (1) any body whatsoever touching mine, i.e. TOUCH, (2) light, i.e. SIGHT, (3) sound, i.e. HEARING, (4) currents of bodies rising up into my nose, i.e. SMELL, (5) salts, which are dissolved by the internal parts of the mouth, i.e. TASTE.

§537

The more a sense organ is appropriately moved, the stronger and clearer is the sensation, whereas the less a sense organ is appropriately moved, the weaker and more obscure is the external sensation (§513, 512). The place in which bodies so disposed can still appropriately move a sense organ such that they are clearly sensed is the SPHERE OF SENSATION. The most appropriate place in the sphere of sensation is the POINT OF SENSATION.[27]

the less … moved] the weaker this movement is

§538

The smaller and more remote from the point of sensation[28] are the things that are to be sensed, the weaker and more obscure is the sensation of these; while the sensation of these is stronger and clearer the greater and closer to the point of sensation[29] they are (§537, 288).

§539[30]

The smallest sense would be that which represents the one greatest being that is most closely and most appropriately present with the smallest degree of truth, light, and certitude[31] (§531, 538).[32] Hence, the more, the smaller, and the more remote are the bodies less appropriately moving the organ, and the more truly and certainly it represents these, the greater the sense is (§219, 535).

§540

The greater SENSE is called ACUTE; the lesser, DULL. The more apt the sense organs either are, or are rendered, for an appropriate motion, the more acute is the external sense, or the more acute it becomes. The more inept the sensory organs are, or are rendered, the duller is the external sense, or the duller it becomes (§537, 539).[33]

§541

The law of sensation is: *Just as the states of the world and my states follow one another, so too should the representations of their present states mutually follow one another* (§534). Hence, the rule of internal sensation is: *Just as the states of my soul follow one another, so too should the representations of the present states of the same mutually follow one another.* And the rule of external sensation is: *Just as the states of my body follow one another, so too should the representations of the present states of the same mutually follow one another.*

§542

The strength of sensations is great compared to all other perceptions[a] (§512, 517). Hence, sensations obscure all other perceptions[b] (§529). Nevertheless, many other sensations, when taken together, can become stronger than this or that sensation, especially a weaker one, and can in turn obscure it; and even more can one sensation be obscured through another stronger sensation, or through many other individually weaker sensations that, when taken together, are stronger (§529, 517).

§543

External sensation is facilitated when (1) it belongs to a well-prepared organ (§536); (2) when the body that is brought near to excite motion appropriately in the organ is most suited to the sphere of sensation, or more specifically (3) as suited as possible to the point of sensation (§537), both in terms of (4) quality (§536) and (5) quantity (§538); and not only if (6) stronger heterogeneous sensations are impeded, but also indeed if (7) all the somewhat weaker yet more numerous sensations are impeded, or rather (8) when other completely heterogeneous perceptions are impeded as well (§542).[34] External sensation is impeded (1) by impeding the sense organ such that it is not moved appropriately; (2) or at least by presenting it in such a way that it is less moved (§537); (3) by moving the sensible object further away, (4) or by reducing it, (5) or by absolutely impeding it so that it does not become present; (6) by arousing stronger sensations; (7) by distracting one's attention by means of many other sensations or (8) perceptions, each one of which is weaker, but which taken together nevertheless obscure the sensation that is to be impeded (§542, 221).

quality] its composition or quality ‖ (8) perceptions] (8) perceptions of an entirely different kind

§544

Since the senses represent the singular beings of this world, and hence represent wholly determined beings as such (§535, 148), and hence in a universal nexus (§357), and since a nexus, however, especially of something relative, cannot be represented without both sides of the connection (§14, 37), in every sensation, everything connected with something sensed, or with that which is sensed, is represented, but not clearly, and hence for the greater and most part obscurely. Therefore, there is something obscure in every sensation, and hence to some extent there is always an admixture of confusion in a sensation, even a distinct one. Whence it follows that every sensation is a sensitive perception that must be formed through the inferior cognitive faculty (§522). And since EXPERIENCE is clear knowledge by means of sense, the AESTHETICS of gathering and presenting experience is EMPIRICAL.[35]

beings as such] beings, and indeed insofar as they are such ‖ connection] connection being represented at the same time

---

[a] G/K: "other individual representations"
[b] G/K: "other individual perceptions"

§545

DECEPTIONS OF THE SENSES are false representations that depend on the senses, and these are either sensations themselves, or they are the reasoning for which sensation is a premise, or they are perceptions held to be sensations through the fault of subreption <*vitium subreptionis*>[a] (§30, 35).

§546

Since the sensations themselves represent the present state of the body, or of the soul, or of both (§535), they perceive actual internal and external states (§205, 298), and hence possible states (§57), and indeed possible states of this world (§377). Therefore, they are the most true sensations of the whole world[36] (§184), and none of these is a deception of the senses (§545). But if a deception of the senses is found in reasoning, its fault lurks either in its form or in one of the premises. If a perception of another sort is held to be a sensation through the error of subreption, a double error has arisen by rushing headlong into judgment, and is nevertheless easily reducible to the second case (§545).

hence possible states] hence states possible in themselves; premises] premises, which is not a sensation

§547

ILLUSIONS are artifices for deceiving the senses.[b] If sense deceptions arise from these, they are EFFICACIOUS, if not, they are INEFFICACIOUS. Therefore, the more a person is troubled by many prejudices having a common term with the sensations,

---

[a] This term has a long history of juridical and philosophical use. In Roman law *subreptionis* describes a fraud perpetrated through the concealment of key facts and is contrasted with one that is *obreptionis*, which does so through the presentation of false information. In his *Logica*, Wolff defines subreption: "We call the fault <*vitium*> of subreption the error <*error*> committed in the act of experiencing when we seem to experience for ourselves what we experience least of all. Those who seem to experience for themselves the physical influence of the soul on the body, the attractive force of a magnet, and love and hate belonging to inanimate things commit this fault. The very same fault introduced many chimeras into scholastic physics" (WLL §668). In his *Ethica*, he explicitly connects subreption to erroneous intuitive judgments that are not guided by the intellect but instead are hasty generalizations based on insufficient experience: "To be sure, although experience is of single things (WLL §665), when we indeed express in words those same things that we experience, we use signs that denote universal beings, unless either there is some proper noun, or some appellative is turned into a proper noun when a demonstrative pronoun is added, and intuitive judgments are formed based on those things that we experience (WLL §55). And in the act of experiencing, the fault or error of subreption is easily committed when we seem to experience for ourselves what we experience least of all (WLL §668); however, universal notions cannot be formed apart from a second and third mental operation (WLL §55). Intuitive judgments are formed through the intellect, which guards against the error of subreption (WLL §669 ff.); the interior faculties must be guided in experience by the correct use of the intellect" (*Ethica* §133). Kant first employs the term in his *On the Form and Principles of the Sensible and the Intelligible World* of 1770, and afterwards throughout the critical works, where he describes transcendental, moral and even aesthetic errors of subreption (see, for instance, AA 2: 412, A 643/B 671, AA 5:116, and AA 5: 116). For the history of this term and its relation to Kant, see Hanno Birken-Bertsch, *Subreption und Dialektik bei Kant*.
[b] *PRAESTIGIAE sunt artificia fallendorum sensuum.* G/K: "*BLENDWERK DER SINNE ist ein Kunstgriff der trügerischen Sinne* [illusion of the senses is an artifice of the deceiving senses]." We take *fallendorum sensuum* to be a gerundive of design, and not a participial phrase.

and the less they guard against the error of subreption, the more illusions can be efficacious in regard to them (§545). Before a person free from all prejudices and errors of
subreption, every illusion will be inefficacious (§546).

§548[a]

Propositions such as (1) *Whatever I do not experience or sense clearly* (§544)[37] *does not
exist*, i.e. the PREJUDICE OF THOMAS,[b, 38] or *is impossible*; (2) *whatever is* (partially)
the same as another representation is that very same perception; (3) *one of those things
that coexist or mutually succeed each other really influences the other* (*i.e. the sophism:
after this, therefore because of this*[c])[39] are all major premises apt for deceptions of the
senses (§546) and hence for efficacious illusions (§547).

all ... illusions] apt to provide the major premise to arguments through which the senses are
deceived, thus also to fool the senses through a powerful illusion

§549

For the same reason that a different stronger perception obscures a weaker perception
(§529), different weaker perceptions clarify a stronger perception (§531).[40] Hence a
different and stronger clear perception succeeding a weaker perception of some object,
by the very fact that it is new in the field of clear perceptions, is perceived more (§529).
Therefore, the very novelty of a stronger clear sensation succeeding a different weaker
perception clarifies it (§542,[41] 534). Hence, weaker opposites clarify a thing (§81, 531).
Opposites juxtaposed to one another shine forth more brightly.[42]

§550

If the very same sensation, to the extent that it is observed, is contained in many total
perceptions immediately following one another, the light of novelty is found in the
first perception (§549). This light is partly absent in the second, more so in the third,
and so forth. Hence, unless the sensation is illuminated from a different source, it
will be less clear in the second total perception, and still less clear in the third, always
succeeding a similar perception that obscures it more (§529). Therefore sensations,
insofar as[d] they can be observed to be the same for long, are obscured by time (§539).

Meier has the last sentence as: Therefore, if, as far as one can perceive, sensations are not altered
for a long time, then they are obscured by the length of time, and they do not endure in the
same strength.

§551

Sensations do not remain the same in strength (§550). Therefore, once they are the
strongest that they can be, they remit (§247).

---

[a] Kant E123, 1775–89 (probably to the page heading "SENSUS"): "Of inner sense"
[b] Cf. Jn 20:24–9. According to the Bible, Thomas the Apostle refused to believe in the resurrection of
Jesus until he had direct sensible evidence.
[c] *post hoc, ergo propter hoc*
[d] Kant E124, 1769–89 (added to "insofar as"): "with respect to quality <*qvoad qvalitatem*>"

§552[a]

I AM AWAKE while I am sensing an external being clearly; thus, while I am starting to sense, I AM AWAKENING. If all sensations have a degree of clarity that is usual in a sound person, someone is then said to be IN CONTROL of ONESELF.[b] If certain of these sensations become so lively in someone that they noticeably obscure the rest, one is BESIDE ONESELF[c] (one forgets oneself; one is not present to oneself).[43] The state of being beside oneself due to internal sensations is ECSTASY[d] (a vision, rapture, a leaving of one's mind).[44]

§553[e]

The natural ecstasy of a soul will be actualized through its own nature (§552, 470), and the ecstasy of a soul that is not actualized through its own nature will be preternatural (§474),[45] which, if it is not actualized through universal nature, will be supernatural (§474). Miraculous ecstasy is possible (§475, 552), even hypothetically (§482–500).[46]

universal … supernatural] through the nature of any contingent things, will be supernatural and a miracle || possible] possible in itself

§554

If the degree of clarity in waking sensations is notably diminished on account of vapours rising from drink into the brain, one is DRUNK or INEBRIATED; and if this happens due to sickness, one's state is called VERTIGO, which is either simple or dark, i.e. scotoma.[f, 47]

§555

If clear external sensations cease, either the vital motions of the body, insofar as it is

[a] Kant E125, 1776–8? 1769?? 1770–1?? (beginning): "Sleep (*later addition:* internal) and drunkenness (*latter addition:* external cause) in a healthy state./Fainting and death in sickness. In the latter [breaks off]"
Afterwards, perhaps 1775–9 (inserted above this reflection): "The cause is in the body or in the soul (through affect or reflection)."
[b] Kant E126, 1764–8? 1769? end of 1769–autumn 1770? 1776–8?: "Not subordinated to the will."
[c] Kant E127, 1776–8? 1780–9??: "Stunned./put into involuntary and vigorous motion, beside oneself, the former is impotence, the latter (*crossed out:* is) rage."
Kant E128. 1770–1? 1776–8? (1769?): "Out of one's mind (distracted) (in regard to the sensations). one's [sic] not powerful (in regard to the affects). (*later addition:* Anger makes one impotent, often unruly.)"
Kant E129, 1770–1? 1775–89?: "tramontana (*later addition:* Sirocco) means: Put out of one's composure. Beside oneself. Out of one's mind. Stunned. (*crossed out:* delighted) ecstatic. (*later addition:* dazed) (*later addition:* perplexed) (*later addition:* baffled)"
[d] Kant E130, end of 1769–8: "A degree of lifelessness."
Kant E131, 1776–8? 1780–9?: "stunned through pleasant sensations, through unpleasant ones."
[e] Kant E132, end of 1769–78: "One must seek to arouse no delight."
[f] *Scotomia*, which Thomas suggests correcting to *scotoma*. In *The New World of Words: or, Universal English Dictionary*, seventh edition, compiled by Edward Phillips and John Kersey (1720), which is contemporaneous with Baumgarten's *Metaphysics*, we read that scotoma is "a Dizziness or Giddiness, causing a dimness in the Sight, so that on a sudden the Patient is as it were in the dark, and thinks every thing goes round."

observed, remain generally[48] the same and I GO TO SLEEP (I fall asleep), or these are even more noticeably diminished, and I FAINT.

§556[a]

The state of obscured external sensations in which the vital motions of the body, insofar as it is observed, remain generally[49] the same as when they are in a state of wakefulness is SLEEP, and one who is in this state SLEEPS; and the state in which these are noticeably diminished is a FAINT[b] (a syncope, lypothymia, lipopsychia,[50] and ecthlipsis); and the state in which they absolutely cease is DEATH. Therefore sleep, a syncope, and death are quite similar to each other (§265).

Meier combines the first sentence of this paragraph and the whole of the previous one to read: If the clear external sensations cease, then either: the motions of the body without which life is impossible remain (as much as one can perceive) and are almost exactly the same as when awake, and then I SLEEP, and the state arising in this case is SLEEP; or these motions also markedly diminish, and I FAINT, and the state arising in this case is FAINTNESS; or these motions entirely cease, and I die, and the state arising from this is DEATH.

Section IIII. Imagination[51]

§557

I am conscious of my past state, and hence of a past state of the world (§369). The representation of a past state of the world, and hence of my past state (§369), is an IMAGE (imagination, a sight, a vision). Therefore I form images, or imagine, through the power of the soul for representing the universe according to the position of my body (§513).[c]

§558

I have a faculty of imagining, or the FACULTY OF IMAGINATION[52, d] (§557, 216). And since my imaginations are perceptions of things that were formerly present (§557, 298), they are perceptions of the senses that, while I imagine, are absent (§223).

faculty … IMAGINATION] POWER OF IMAGINATION, or the faculty of images

§559

A PERCEPTION that becomes less obscure in the soul IS PRODUCED (it is

---

[a] Kant E133, end of 1769–78:

"life	much or
waking	long
death	
sleep"	

[b] Kant E134, end of 1769–78: "Women: fainting, men: dizziness."
[c] Wolff: "The faculty for producing perceptions of sensible things that are absent is called the *faculty of imagining* or *imagination*" (WPE §92).
[d] Kant E135, end of 1769–78: "Unchosen <*Unwillkührlich*>"

explicated), whereas a perception that becomes more obscure IS COVERED UP <*INVOLVITUR*>. And when a perception that was once covered up is produced, it IS REPRODUCED (it recurs). Now, things that were sensed are produced (i.e. developed) by imaginations (§558), and hence they were once produced (§542) and afterwards covered up (§551). Therefore, perceptions are reproduced through the faculty of imagination, and nothing is in the faculty of imagination that is not first in the senses[a] (§558, 534).

§560

The motions of the brain that coexist with the successive representations of the soul[53] are called MATERIAL IDEAS. Hence in the body there are material ideas belonging to the sensing or imagining soul (§503).[b]

§561

Imagination and sensation are of singular beings (§559,[54] 534), and hence of beings located in a universal nexus (§257).[55] Whence the law of the imagination:[c] *When a partial idea is perceived, its total idea recurs* (§306, 514). This proposition is also called the *association of ideas*.

singular beings] singular beings of this world || *When ... recurs*] *If one represents a singular concept that was formerly a part of a past whole, then through this the whole representation again comes into the mind* || ideas] singular concepts

§562

Since I represent, and hence imagine (§557), according to the position of my body (§512), and yet the beings I sense externally are closer to my body than those that I imagine (§535, 558),[56] it is clear why the former can be clearer and stronger than the latter (§538).[57] For, as long as the sensations that coexist with imaginations still obscure the latter (§542), I imagine nothing as clearly as I have sensed, but rather such that the degree of clarity in imagination depends on the degree of clarity in sensation (§561).

sensation] sensation that is to be repeated in the imagination

§563

Those things that I have sensed and reproduced more often are parts of more total ideas than those that I have sensed or reproduced more rarely (§514). Therefore, the images of the former[58] are perceived in a greater nexus (§561) with many more ancillary notes than the images of the latter[59] (§530), and hence they are extensively

---

[a] *Nihil est in phantasia, quod non ante fuerit in sensu.* This explicitly echoes the famous Scholastic formula: "there is nothing in the intellect that is not first in the senses," which Leibniz, in controverting Locke, states as *nihil est in intellectu quod non fuerit in sensu* (*New Essays* Bk 2, Ch. 1).

[b] G/K silently change this reference to §508, which seems more logical.

[c] Wolff: "*This proposition is the law of the imagination or images: if we ever perceive in any way, and a perception of one of these is produced anew: imagination also produces a perception of another*" (WPE §117).

clearer, or much more lively, than the latter. For the opposite reason (§81), those beings that I have more rarely sensed and reproduced have the greater light of novelty if they are sensed than do those that I have sensed more often (§549). Therefore, the sensations of those beings more rarely sensed and reproduced are, all else being equal, more lively than those of beings more often sensed and reproduced (§531).[60]

§564

Just as sensation obscures imaginations, so for the same reason the stronger imagination of something more recent obscures the weaker imagination of something older (§562). Hence, of those beings sensed equally clearly, I imagine the more recent one more clearly, unless I am impeded from elsewhere.

§565[61]

The smallest faculty of the imagination would be that which represents most obscurely one most strongly sensed thing[62] (§562) that has also been reproduced the most often (§563) and most recently (§564), along with, however, the weakest, most antecedent, and most heterogeneous associated perceptions (§529). The more truly,[63] clearly, and certainly[64] the imagination can reproduce more beings that are sensed more weakly[65] and reproduced more rarely after a longer time with stronger associated and antecedent perceptions, the greater it is (§219).

§566

The more dull or acute is the sense from which I imagine the thing that has been sensed, the more obscure[66] or clear[67] can its imagination of the thing be (§562, 540).

sense ... sensed] sense, the object of which has been sensed by it in time past and which I now imagine

§567

I distinguish imaginations from sensations (1) by their degree of clarity (§562), and (2) by the impossible coexistence of the state of the past, which imaginations convey, with the state of the present, which sensations convey (§298). And hence if stronger imaginations and weaker sensations, to the extent they are observed, are equal in clarity, nevertheless another difference remains, namely the difference in their circumstances (§323). As soon as it is clear from this that not both perceptions are sensations, I hold the sensation to be the one in which I clearly perceive the greatest compossibility and nexus with associated sensations and imaginations, especially those just past, and with perceptions of future and especially of impending things (§544). Therefore I clearly know that the other one is not a sensation (§38, 67).[68]

§568[a]

The imagination is facilitated (§527) when: (1) that which is to be imagined is sensed more clearly (§562); (2) it is reproduced more often (§563), (3) through intervals of weaker representations so that it always has the light of novelty (§549), (4) and thus not very long ago (§564); (5) it follows and (6) accompanies weaker heterogeneous perceptions (§516, 549) and hence heterogeneous perceptions that are either not clear, or not very clear (§562); and moreover (7) it follows or accompanies representations that were more often associated with that which is to be imagined (§561).

§569

The imagination is impeded (1) by partially or entirely impeding, according to §543, the sensation and (2) reproduction of that which is not to be imagined [i.e. of what would be imagined, if the imagination of it were not impeded in this way], and especially (3) by impeding a reproduction interrupted by weaker perceptions, because a non-interrupted continuation itself obscures (§550). It is also impeded (4) by the very delay of its reproduction while many things are meanwhile considered more vividly (§564). It is impeded (5) if it follows or (6) is accompanied by stronger heterogeneous perceptions, and hence sensations, imaginations, or perceptions that are such when each are taken individually, or together (§542), and which (7) were never, or more rarely, associated with that which is not to be partially or entirely[69] imagined [i.e. of what would be fully imagined, if the imagination of it were not impeded in these ways] (§561, 221).

(3) ... obscures] (3) if one interrupts it by means of weaker representations, because an uninterrupted continuation itself weakens it[b]

§570

Since there is something of the obscure in every sensation (§544), and since an imagination is always less clear than the sensation of the same thing (§562), a great deal of confusion is involved even in a distinct imagination. Every imagination is sensitive (§522), and must be formed by the inferior cognitive faculty (§520). The science of thinking by imagining and presenting what is thus thought is the AESTHETICS OF THE IMAGINATION.[70]

than ... thing] than the previously occurring sensation that it reproduces

§571

If the faculty of the imagination wholly represents the same things that I have sensed, then the imaginations are true (§546, 38) and are not EMPTY IMAGES or

---

[a] Kant E136, end of 1769–78 (beginning): "Through signs or description of what one saw."
[b] Meier's translation thus differs from Baumgarten in a way parallel to §603 below. In his commentary, Meier explains that one hinders the imagination if one "interrupts its business by means of other representations, even if these should also be weaker than the imagination that one would like to drive from the senses and to hinder; for through the very length of time, through which an imagination continues, it is weakened" (MM 3: §564).

false imaginations, even if they are not perceived with wholly equal clarity (§558,[71] 562). Proficiency in forming empty images is an UNBRIDLED IMAGINATION; on the other hand, proficiency in imagining truly is a DISCIPLINED IMAGINATION.

Section V. Perspicasiousness[72, a]

§572[b]

I perceive the correspondences[c] and differences of things. Therefore, I have a faculty of perceiving the correspondences and differences of things (§216). The prior faculty would be the smallest if it were sufficient for representing most weakly[73] the one smallest correspondence of only two of the most strongly[74] perceived and most similar things among the weakest associated and antecedent heterogeneous perceptions. Therefore, the more clearly it perceives more and greater correspondences between more things that are less well-known and more different, hence the congruities, equalities (and therefore the equalities of relations <*rationum*>, or PROPORTIONS),[75] and similarities among stronger associated and antecedent heterogeneous perceptions, the greater it is (§219).[76] Proficiency in observing the correspondences of things is WIT, IN THE STRICT SENSE.

§573

The faculty of perceiving the differences of things would be the smallest that least intensely[77] perceives the one smallest difference of only two of the most strongly[78] perceived maximally different things among the weakest preceding and associated heterogeneous perceptions. Therefore the more strongly[79] it represents more and greater differences of more things that are less well-known and more similar, hence the incongruities, inequalities, and therefore the inequalities of relations or DISPROPORTIONS[80] and dissimilarities among stronger associated and antecedent heterogeneous perceptions, the greater it is (§219). Proficiency in observing the differences of things is ACUMEN. Acute wit is PERSPICACIOUSNESS.[d, 81]

Acute wit] Acute wit or witty acumen

§574

This is the law of the faculty of perceiving perspicaciously <*perspiciendi*> the correspondences of things, and hence of wit (§572): *If a characteristic of A is represented as a characteristic of B, A and B are represented as the same* (§38). This is the law of the faculty of representing the differences of things, and hence of acumen (§573): *If a*

[a] Kant E137, 1776–8? (1775–6?) 1770–1?? (to the heading "Perspicaciousness"): "Towards knowledge of manifoldness: distinction; towards (*crossed out*: knowledge) of unity: agreement [or, harmony]."
[b] Kant E138, 1776–8? 1770–1?? (beginning, on the right side next to the third sentence): "Unity of comparison and that of connection. The latter is either logical or real."
[c] *Identitates*, lit. "identities." We have followed both Meier and G/K, who use *Übereinstimmungen*, since this seems more natural.
[d] Cf. Kant, *Anthropology*, AA 7:21.

characteristic of A is represented as repugnant to B, A and B are perceived as different (§38).

§575

I perceive the correspondences and differences of things either distinctly, or sensitively (§521). Hence the faculties of perceiving correspondences and differences, and, indeed, wit, acumen, and perspicaciousness[82] (§572, 573), are either sensitive or intellectual (§402). The AESTHETICS OF PERSPICACIOUSNESS is the part of aesthetics concerned with thinking and presenting with wit and acumen.[83]

perceive] know

§576

Since all the beings in this world are partly the same and partly different (§265, 269), the representations of the correspondences and differences in these beings, and hence the PLAY (or fruit) OF WIT, i.e. the thoughts depending on wit, and SUBTLETIES, i.e. the thoughts depending on acumen,[a] are actualized through the power of the soul for representing the universe (§513). False plays of WIT are called its DELUSIONS, and false subtleties are called INANE QUIBBLES.

universe] world according to the position of the body

§577

Since the higher degrees of the soul's faculties are proficiencies (§219), and since the frequent repetition of homogeneous actions—or of actions that are the same in terms of a specific difference—is EXERCISE, the proficiencies of the soul are augmented by exercise (§162). The PROFICIENCIES of the soul that do not depend on exercise, but that are instead natural, are called INBORN (natural dispositions). Those that depend upon exercise are called ACQUIRED. Those which are supernatural are called INFUSED, and the proficiencies of the cognitive faculties are called THEORETICAL.

the proficiencies ... exercise] through exercise the faculties of the soul become proficiencies, and greater proficiencies || INFUSED] DIVINE

§578

Acumen and wit, taken more strictly, and hence perspicaciousness[84] (§572, 573), are theoretical proficiencies (§577, 519). The greater are the inborn proficiencies, the more easily are they augmented by exercise (§577, 527). The same goes for the proficiencies of sensing and imagining (§535, 558).[85] Whoever quite noticeably lacks wit is STUPID (a dullard).[86] Whoever quite noticeably lacks acumen is OBTUSE. Whoever quite noticeably lacks both is TASTELESS.[87] Since every error takes the false and the true to be the same thing (§515),[88] each is a delusion belonging to the faculty for perceiving the correspondences of things (§576, 572), and it is to be impeded by acumen (§573,

---

[a] Wolff: "The acumen through which we perceive universals in singulars, especially in the higher scale of genera or abstract things, we call the acumen of discerning the abstract in the concrete" (WPE §335).

221). Hence, errors are an occasion for subtleties [i.e. a chance to use one's acumen] (§576, 323).

subtleties] acute thoughts

Section VI. Memory[89]

§579

I perceive a reproduced representation to be the same as one I had formerly produced (§572, 559); i.e. I RECOGNIZE (I recall) it. Therefore, I have a faculty of recognizing reproduced perceptions, or MEMORY (§216), and it is either sensitive or intellectual (§575).[a]

produced] produced, i.e. I know it to be again the representation that I had previously, or I remember it

§580

The law of memory is: *When many successive perceptions up until the present are represented as having something partially in common, something partially common is represented as contained in the antecedent and in the subsequent* (§572), and indeed a memory is actualized through the power of the soul for representing the universe (§557, 576).[b]

universe] world according to the position of its body

§581

Those things that are perceived in such a way that they can be more easily recognized in the future, I COMMIT TO MEMORY. Hence those things that are more often and more clearly reproduced by being attentive to the correspondences and differences of singular perceptions (§580), according to §537,[90] 538,[91] 549, and 568, are profoundly committed to memory (§527).

recognized] remembered[c]

§582

If a perception recurs, either I am able to recognize it clearly and then I am said to HOLD its object in MEMORY, or I am not (§10), and I HAVE FORGOTTEN its object. Hence the inability to recognize reproduced perceptions is FORGETTING. That through which I remember something that I have forgotten CALLS SOMETHING BACK TO MEMORY for me. I call something back to memory through associated ideas, i.e. I RECOLLECT. Therefore, I have a faculty of recollecting, or RECOLLECTION (§216).

---

[a] Wolff: "We call the faculty of recognizing reproduced ideas (and consequently the things represented through these) *Memory*. Seeing that therefore we are able to recognize reproduced ideas (note to WPE §173), *we have memory*."
[b] There is no law of memory in Wolff.
[c] Since this change is consistent throughout, this fact will not be noted further.

§583

Recollection is memory (§582, 579), and it follows this rule: *I remember reproduced perceptions by means of associated ideas* (§580, 516).[92] Recollection recalled through associated ideas of place *<loci>* is LOCAL MEMORY, and that through associated ideas of time *<aetatis>* is SYNCHRONIC MEMORY.

§584[93]

The smallest memory would be that which would least intensely[94] recognize the one smallest thing reproduced the most intensely,[95] often, and recently among maximally weak previous and associated heterogeneous perceptions. Therefore, the more intensely[96] it knows more and greater things that have been reproduced less intensely[97] and more rarely after a longer time has passed among the strongest heterogeneous perceptions (§564), and among stronger preceding and associated heterogeneous perceptions, the greater it is (§219).

§585

A greater memory is called GOOD and HAPPY, and insofar as it can recognize many great things, it is called EXTENSIVE[98] (rich, vast).[99] Insofar as it can also recognize something reproduced less intensely[100] among adequately strong, associated, preceding, and heterogeneous representations, it is called FIRM. Insofar as it can recognize something after a longer interval of time occupied by sufficiently strong and heterogeneous perceptions, it is called TENACIOUS. Insofar as it can recognize something reproduced more rarely, it is called CAPABLE. Insofar as it can recognize something more intensely,[101] it is called VIGOROUS. Insofar as very little is necessary for it to remember, it is called READY.

§586

A conspicuous lack of a good memory is FORGETFULNESS, and an error depending on memory is called a LAPSE OF MEMORY. Now, memory can convey that a previous perception agrees with a later one to a degree that, in fact, it does not. Therefore, memory is FALLIBLE *<LABILIS>*; i.e. lapses *<lapsus>* of memory are possible for it. Memory that is not especially faulty is FAITHFUL. The memory of one who is witty is not especially faithful (§576), but its fidelity is augmented by acumen (§573).

that is ... faulty] that has a proficiency for not erring

§587

The collection of rules for perfecting memory is called the MNEMONIC ART. The mnemonics of sensitive memory (§579) is the part of aesthetics (§533) that prescribes[102] the rules for extending, confirming, conserving, exciting and restoring a larger and more faithful memory (§586, 585).

§588

If an antecedent image is held to be in agreement with a following sensation or image to such a degree as it is not, then an empty image arises (§571) through a lapse of memory (§586) based on the source of errors (§578). And if it is held to be a sensation (§548) from the same source (§586, 578), then sense deception arises (§546).

Section VII. The faculty of invention[103]

§589

By SEPARATING and combining images, i.e. by only being attentive to a part of some perception, I INVENT. Therefore, I have the POETIC[104] faculty of invention (§216).[a] Since a combination is a representation of many things as one, and hence is actualized through the faculty of perceiving the correspondences of things (§572, 155), the faculty of invention is actualized through the power of the soul for representing the universe (§557, 576).

universe] world according to the position of the body

§590

This is the rule of the faculty of invention: *Parts of images are perceived as one whole* (§589).[b] Hence the perceptions that have arisen are called FICTIONS (figments), and those which are false are called CHIMERAS, or empty images (§571).[105]

of images] of different images

§591

Suppose that, in invention, things that cannot be associated are combined (§589), or that things are separated such that if they are removed, then that which is to be imagined is removed as well (such as the essential determinations, essence (§63), and attributes (§64)); or suppose that in invention, either every mode and every relation, or some modes and some relations, are removed that are necessary for constituting something actual and individual without others being substituted, and that nevertheless something is invented that is represented as if it were individual and actual (§54, 148): then in every one of these cases chimeras (§590) arise through the delusion of the faculty of perceiving the correspondences of things (§576, 578), or better, empty images (§590) arise that are greatly reinforced by a lapse of memory through false recognition (§588, 515).

§592[106]

The smallest faculty of inventing would be that which would only combine the two smallest and strongest[107] images the least intensely,[108] or separate the one smallest part of the one greatest image the most slightly (§530, 589). Therefore, the more, the

---

[a] Wolff: "The faculty of producing images of things that have never been perceived by a sense through the division and composition of images is called *the faculty of invention*" (WPE §144).
[b] No such law is found in Wolff.

greater, and the less strong[109] are the images that it will combine, the more it separates[a] more and greater parts of more and smaller images, and the more, and likewise the more strongly,[110] it does both of these, the greater it is (§219, 590). A greater faculty of invention can be called FERTILE (fecund); one inclined to chimeras can be called EXORBITANT[b] (extravagant, rhapsodic); one which avoids these can be called ARCHITECTONIC. The AESTHETICS OF THE MYTHICAL is the part of aesthetics that devises and presents fictions.

ARCHITECTONIC] WELL-ORDERED

§593

If I imagine clearly while sleeping, I DREAM. The imaginations of dreaming are DREAMS, TAKEN SUBJECTIVELY (cf. §91), which are either true (§571) or false (§588, 591), either natural dreams (§470) actualized through the nature of the soul according to §561, 574,[111] 580, 583, 590, or not natural to the soul and preternatural to it. If the latter are not actualized by universal nature, they will be supernatural (§474).

§594[112]

The imagination of someone sleeping is more unbridled (§571), and the faculty of invention more exorbitant, than of someone wide awake (§592). Those asleep produce more lively imaginations and fictions not obscured by stronger sensations (§549). SLEEP WALKERS[c] are those whose dreams are usually accompanied by such more observable[113] motions of an external body as accompany the same sensations among those who are awake. FANTASISTS[d] (visionaries, fanatics) are, however, those who, while awake, customarily take certain imaginations for sensations, while those who absolutely confuse them with sensations are DELIRIOUS, such that DELIRIUM is precisely the waking state of habitually[114] taking imaginations for sensations and sensations for imaginations.

fictions ... stronger sensations] fictions, because there are present no stronger sensations through which they could be obscured

Eberhard adds the note: If the sensation, which the visionary holds an imagination to be, is an external one, then one calls it a vision <*visio*> or apparition <*apparitio*>. One calls it the former if it happens in an ecstasy, and the latter if it does not happen in an ecstasy.

---

[a] Kant E139, 1770–1? 1776–8? (in the right margin next to "separates—greater"): "Eloquence. Being well-spoken. Style".

[b] Kant E140, 1776–8? 1790–804??: "in regard to the thoughts magnitude. Confused/in regard to understandability mere sounds" [Note: "Confused" could belong to the next line of the reflection (AA).]

[c] See Meier's *Essay on the Explanation of Sleepwalking* (*Versuch der Erklärung des Nachtwandelns*, 1758).

[d] Meier: "*Schwärmer*." Usually translated as "enthusiast," and related to "*Schwärmerei*," or "enthusiasm," a state of mind which Kant characteristically warns against and describes often as consisting in the belief that one can know, sense or feel supersensible objects (see, e.g. AA 5:75).

Section VIII.[115] Foresight

§595

I am conscious of my future state, and hence of the future state of the world (§369). The representation of the future state of the world, and hence mine, is FORESIGHT. I foresee, and hence I have a faculty of foreseeing (§216), which must be actualized by the power of the soul for representing the universe according to the position of my body (§513).

§596

The law of foresight is: *If a sensation and an imagination having a common partial perception are perceived, a total perception of a future state emerges in which the different parts of the sensation and imagination are joined together: i.e. the future is born from the present impregnated by the past.*[a]

§597

Since I represent, hence also foresee (§595), according to the position of my body (§512), the things that I sense externally are truly closer to the body than those that I foresee, and which I am only going to sense in the future (§535, 595); it is obvious from this why the former can be clearer and stronger than the latter (§529). And hence because sensations that coexist with foresights still obscure these (§542), I foresee nothing as clearly as that which I am about to sense, but indeed such that the degree of clarity in my foresight will, however, depend on the degree of clarity in the future sensation (§596).

§598

That which I have sensed and imagined more often I foresee more clearly than that which I have sensed and imagined more rarely (§563, 596). Now, imaginations convey objects that have been sensed, that is, things that have been perceived the most strongly (§542, 558). Hence imaginations are stronger than foresights, which convey objects not yet most strongly perceived (§597), and together with sensations, they also wholly obscure foresights (§529). And since the foresight of a moment closer in time can be clearer than the foresight of a more distant moment (§597), in this case the foresight of the closer moment will also obscure the foresight of the more distant moment, and the obscurity of the more distant moment will clarify the foresight of the closer moment (§549). Therefore, of things that are to be sensed equally clearly, I foresee the closer moment more clearly than the more distant moment (§549).

§599[116]

The smallest faculty of foresight would be that which would nevertheless represent least intensely[117] one most strongly[118] and closely sensed thing (§597) that has been sensed and reproduced by the imagination very often among maximally weak associated and previous heterogeneous perceptions. Therefore, the more strongly[119] it

---

[a] Cf. Leibniz, *Monadology* §22.

represents those that are sensed least intensely,[120] the more distant they are, the more rarely they are sensed or reproduced by the imagination among stronger previous and associated perceptions, the greater is the faculty of foresight (§219).

§600

The duller or acuter is the sense by which I now partially foresee a sensed being, and the lesser or greater is the faculty of the imagination of I who am going to foresee (§565), the obscurer or clearer the foresight will be (§596).

§601

I distinguish foresights from sensations and imaginations (1) by the degree of clarity which they concede to both sensations and imaginations (§597, 598) and (2) by the impossibility of their coexistence with past and present states. But if a stronger foresight and a weaker imagination or a weaker sensation are of equal clarity, as far as can be observed, they can nevertheless be distinguished by the second characteristic (§67). For if I know from the circumstances what are not sensations according to §567, then I also clearly know (§38, 67) that something is not an imagination if it is discovered to be unconnected with previous and subsequent associated imaginations and sensations (§557, 357), and if likewise it could not have been sensed (§377).[121]

their coexistence] the coexistence of their object

§602

Foresight is facilitated (§527) when that which is to be foreseen (1) is to be sensed more clearly (§597);[122] (2) when it has for the greater part already been sensed (3) and reproduced by the imagination (§598); (4) when it has already been foreseen more often (§563), and (5) through intervals of weaker perceptions so that it always has the greater light of novelty (§549) and (6) such that it is to be sensed not long afterwards (§598); (7) when it has weaker previous and associated heterogeneous perceptions, and hence when it does not follow and accompany such clear, or at least not very clear, sensations and imaginations (§697,[123] 598); but rather (8) when it follows and accompanies stronger imaginations and sensations sharing partial perceptions in common with that which is to be foreseen (§596, 597).

(7) when it] (7) when, through the collection of the mind, it

§603

Foresight is impeded (1) when a future sensation of something to be foreseen is impeded according to §543; (2) when a present sensation and (3) imagination that are largely of things corresponding to that which is to be foreseen are impeded; (4) when the initial foresights are impeded, especially (5) when these are not[a]

---

[a] G/K interpolate *non* here, so that the phrase reads "not interrupted." Every Latin edition reads "interrupted." As we have seen above, since the first member a continuous stream of perceptions (etc.) is illuminated by novelty, the stream becomes less novel as it progresses, and hence darker or more obscure. When this stream is interrupted, it can begin again, with the fresh light of novelty. So the interpolation seems correct; if the stream is not interrupted, it becomes impeded, or obscure.

interrupted by weaker perceptions, because the very continuation itself obscures foresights (§550); (6) when that which is to be foreseen is postponed (§598);[124] (7) when it has stronger previous and associated heterogeneous imaginations and sensations, or moreover (8) weaker ones sharing a perception in common with that which is to be foreseen.

(7) … sensations] if the mind is distracted among stronger representations, in particular sensations and images of another kind that precede the foresight and are associated with it || weaker] weakened

§604

Since there is something of the obscure in every sensation (§544) and imagination (§570), and since a foresight of something is less clear than a sensation and imagination of the same thing (§597, 598), even in a distinct foresight there is a large admixture of confusion and obscurity. Moreover, all of my foresight is sensitive (§522), and is to be actualized by the inferior cognitive faculty (§520). The mantic art (§350)[125] that directs the knowledge and presentation of this faculty is thus also part of aesthetics (§533).[126]

§605

If the things that are foreseen are completely the same as those which are to be sensed, the foresights are true or are PRESENTIMENTS, although they are not perceived in the same way or as equally clearly as sensations (§597). If a presentiment is sensed, the FORESIGHT IS FULFILLED. A foresight that is not to be fulfilled is FALSE, and is a source of practical errors (§578).

Section VIIII. Judgment[127]

§606

I perceive the perfection and imperfection of things, i.e. I JUDGE. Therefore, I have a faculty of judging (§216). The smallest faculty of judging would be the one representing the least intensely[128] the one smallest perfection or imperfection of the one smallest thing that is most strongly[129] perceived among the weakest previous and associated heterogeneous perceptions. Therefore, the more strongly[130] the faculty of judging represents more perfections and imperfections of more and greater things perceived less intensely[131] among stronger associated and previous heterogeneous perceptions, the greater it is (§219). Proficiency in judging a thing is JUDGMENT, and

However, Meier does not add the "not" in his later translation. Indeed, in his commentary, Meier provides a rather straightforward interpretation. He says that the foresight is hindered "If one interrupts a foresight, and busies one's attention with representations of another kind. Should these also be weaker than the foresight that one wants to suppress, then one does still at least succeed in weakening it. Thus one can at the very least weaken a vivid concern, if one busies one's thoughts with other representations, with considerations of the goodness of God, with studying, and so forth" (MM 3: §606). See the parallel case with regard to the weakening of imagination in §569 above. Nevertheless, Meier's gloss does not seem to fit with Baumgarten's next clause, which clearly stresses that continuation (i.e. non-interruption) obscures foresights.

it is called PRACTICAL if it concerns things that are foreseen, and THEORETICAL if it concerns others. Insofar as it uncovers many perfections and imperfections of things, despite their being even more obscurely perceived, it is PENETRATING

a faculty of judging] a faculty of judging, which is actualized through the power of the soul for representing the world according to the position of its body, because everything in the world is in part perfect and in part imperfect

§607

The law of the faculty of judging is: *When various aspects of a thing are perceived as either harmonizing or disharmonizing, either perfection or imperfection is perceived* (§94, 121). Since this occurs either distinctly or indistinctly, the faculty of judging, and hence judgment (§606), is either sensitive or intellectual (§402, 521).[132] Sensitive judgment is TASTE IN THE BROADER SENSE (flavour, palate, smell). CRITICISM IN THE BROADEST SENSE is the art of judging. Hence the art of forming taste, or the art concerning judging sensitively and presenting its judgment, is AESHETIC CRITICISM (§533).[133] One who delights in intellectual judgment is a CRITIC IN THE BROADER SENSE, whence CRITICISM IN THE MORE GENERAL SENSE is the science of the rules of distinctly judging perfection or imperfection.

indistinctly] sensibly || *When … is perceived*] *When the manifold of something is known either as harmonizing or as not harmonizing, then its perfection or imperfection is known* || Sensitive judgment] The proficiency to judge sensitively || delights … judgment] has the proficiency for judging perfections and imperfections distinctly

§608

Taste, in the broader sense, concerning SENSIBLE THINGS, i.e. those things which are sensed, is the JUDGMENT OF THE SENSES, and it is attributed to the sense organ through which the object that is to be judged is sensed. Hence, there is a judgment of the eyes, of the ears, and so on. This faculty of judging, like every faculty of judging, is actualized through the power of the soul for representing the universe (§513), since all the things in this world are partially perfect and partially imperfect (§250, 354). False judgments are LAPSES OF JUDGMENT. The faculty of judging that is inclined to lapses is called PRECIPITOUS JUDGMENT.[134] Such a precipitous TASTE is CORRUPTED. The proficiency of JUDGMENT for avoiding lapses is its MATURITY. Such a mature taste is an UNCOMMON TASTE (purer, learned), and when smaller similarities and dissimilarities are also uncovered in judging, this perspicaciousness is called DELICATE TASTE.[135] The lapses of sense judgment are deceptions of the same (§545).

Taste] The proficiency to sensitively judge || The faculty of judging] The proficiency for judging

§609

The greater is the inborn memory (§579), recollection (§582), faculty of invention (§589), proficiency of foresight (§595), and judgment, the more easily are they increased by exercises (§577,[136] 606).

Section X. Anticipation[137]

§610

When someone represents a foreseen perception as being the same as something that they will perceive in the future, they ANTICIPATE, and therefore have a faculty of anticipating, or ANTICIPATION IN A BROADER SENSE. Perceptions actualized through anticipation of this sort are ANTICIPATORY PERCEPTIONS IN A BROAD SENSE and are either sensitive or intellectual (§402, 521).[138] ANTICIPATORY PERCEPTIONS MORE STRICTLY CONSIDERED and ANTICIPATION are only sensitive. Sensitive anticipations are the object of the aesthetic mantic art (§604).[139]

§611

The law of anticipation is this: *If some of the perceptions following a present perception are represented that share something partially in common with antecedent perceptions, then this partial commonality is represented as contained in the antecedent and the subsequent perceptions* (§572). Therefore, just as memory is related to imagination, so too is anticipation related to foresight (§579, 610).

§612

Sensitive anticipation is the EXPECTATION OF SIMILAR CASES, and this is its rule: *I sense or imagine or foresee A, which shares much in common with another foreseen B; hence, I represent that B will be the same as A* (§611). When a mind anticipates, by means of ideas that are associated with something foreseen, that which it previously did not, it PRESUMES, and hence has a faculty of presumption (§216), which will be related to anticipation just as recollection is related to memory (§582, 610).

hence ... A] and for this reason represent that B will be the same as A

§613

The faculty of presuming is an anticipation that follows this rule: *The mind anticipates a perception that is foreseen through associated mediating ideas.*

The mind ... ideas] I anticipate a foreseen thing by means of representations that are associated with it

Eberhard adds the note: We perceive in the sensible faculty of anticipation only degrees. The more often, namely, I have noticed that A has much in common with B, the more probable it is to me that B will be the same as A. This degree of the sensible faculty of anticipation, of anticipating something future according to the rule of probability, can be called the anticipation of similar cases in the narrow sense.

§614[140]

The smallest anticipation would be that which would nevertheless perceive the least intensely[141] one, smallest, and most imminent thing that is foreseen most often and most strongly[142] among maximally weak previous and related heterogeneous perceptions (§610, 611).

§615[143]

The more strongly anticipation perceives more and greater things that are to be foreseen more rarely and less intensely[144] among stronger[145] previous and related hetereogeneous perceptions prior to a longer time that is to be spent with other very strong perceptions (§564), the greater it is (§219), and the less it needs presumptions (§613).

§616

A remarkable proficiency for anticipating is the FACULTY OF DIVINING, and it is natural (i.e. inborn), acquired, or infused (§577). The last of these is the GIFT OF PROPHECY. An anticipatory perception coming from the faculty of divining is DIVINATION, and when it comes from the prophetic gift, it is an ORACLE (a prophecy).[146]

infused] supernatural

§617

Errors stemming from anticipation are EMPTY ANTICIPATORY PERCEPTIONS, which are deceptive foresights confused with true foresights through a delusion of the faculty of perceiving the correspondences of things (§578, 605). If I have any antici-patory perceptions, or expectations of similar cases (§612), or presumptions (§613), these are actualized by the power of the soul for representing the universe (§595, 576).

universe] world according to the position of the body

§618

If something foreseen is incorrectly held to be the same to some degree as some antecedent sensed object, or image, or something else foreseen, a false foresight arises (§605) through an empty anticipatory perception (§617, 576).[147]

Section XI. The faculty of characterization[148]

§619

I perceive signs together with the signified, and therefore I have a faculty of joining signs together in a representation with the signified, which can be called the FACULTY OF CHARACTERIZATION[149] (§216). And since there is a nexus of signi-fication in this world (§358), the perceptions of the faculty of characterization[150] are actualized through the power of the soul for representing the universe (§513). The nexus of signification is known either distinctly or indistinctly, and hence the faculty of characterization[151] will be either sensitive (§521) or intellectual (§402).

joining ... signified] combining signs and signified things with one another in my understanding || universe] world according to the position of its body

§620

If the sign is joined together in perception with the signified, and the perception of the sign is greater than the perception of the signified, this is called SYMBOLIC KNOWLEDGE.[a] If the perception of the signified is greater than the perception of the sign, the[152] KNOWLEDGE will be INTUITIVE (intuited).[b] In either kind of knowledge, the law of the faculty of characterization[153] is this: *One of the associated perceptions becomes the means of knowing the existence of the other* (§347).

§621

Suppose that, through a delusion of the faculty of knowing the correspondences of things, something is taken to be a sign, which is not, and something is taken to be signified, which is not (§576): false symbolic and intuitive knowledge will arise (§620). Suppose in the same manner something is taken to be a prognostication, which is not; in this case, false foresights will be produced that will be greatly strengthened by apparent anticipatory perceptions and presumptions (§605, 515).

§622

The smallest faculty of characterization[154] would least intensely[155] join the one smallest sign together with the one smallest signified thing among the weakest previous associated and heterogeneous[c] perceptions. Therefore, the more strongly the faculty of characterization[156] joins more and greater signs together with more and greater signified things among stronger associated and previous heterogeneous perceptions, the greater it is (§219).[157] The science of sensitive knowledge that is concerned with signs, and the science of this sort of presentation <*propositionis*>, is the AESTHETICS OF CHARACTERIZATION,[d] and it is both heuristics and hermeneutics (§349).[158, e] The characterization of speech is PHILOLOGY (grammar, in the broad sense), and the philology that teaches the things common to many particular languages is

---

[a] Wolff: "But even if our knowledge terminates <*terminatur*> in the act by which we enunciate with words those things that are contained in ideas, or by which we represent that knowledge with other signs, we surely do not intuit these very ideas indicated with words or other signs; it is *symbolic knowledge*" (WPE §289). From the note to this paragraph: "Thus, I have symbolic cognition of the triangle if I think it to be a figure bounded by three lines; surely I intuit no idea of the triangle, much less of the ideas by which it is bounded, or even of the number three concerning these. Similarly, I have symbolic cognition of the chiliogon if I indicate in words, as if silently speaking to myself, that the chiliogon is a figure bounded by a thousand sides; surely, I intuit no idea of every single side, or of the number one thousand, or even of the very chiliogon itself" (WPE §289).

[b] Wolff: "*Knowledge*, which is completed in the very intuition of ideas, is called *intuitive*, or we are said *to know a thing intuitively* insofar as we are conscious of the idea that we have of it." (WPE §286) The note to the same paragraph reads: "For example: while I intuit a present tree, and I am conscious of those things that are in the same gaze, I have intuitive cognition of the tree. If a triangle is traced out on a slate for me, so to speak, or if I represent a triangular rafter and moreover am conscious of this shape, I know a triangle intuitively" (WPE §286).

[c] Kant E141, 1769–804 (right margin): "Mama and Mumum."

[d] Kant E142, 1769–804 (above): "Desire to speak oneself."

[e] Kant E143, 1770–1? 1776–8? (right side next to sentences three and four): "On speaking and on people with a *passion for speaking. On doing nothing of the sort. One that can make good his words. Society./*(*later addition:* talkative, garrulous.)"

UNIVERSAL.[a] The philology that teaches (I) the general rules that must be observed in all speech with regard to: (1) words and their parts is ORTHOGRAPHY, BROADLY CONSIDERED; (2) their modification is ETYMOLOGY (similarity <*analogia*>); (3) their nexus or construction is SYNTAX; and (4) their quantity is PROSODY. The collection of these disciplines[159] is GRAMMAR (in the stricter sense). The philology that teaches the general rules that must be observed in all speech with regard to (5) the meaning of words is LEXICAL (lexicography), and with regard to (6) their script is ORTHOGRAPHY <*GRAPHICE*>. The philology that teaches (II) the special rules that must be observed in sensitive speech (e.g. ELOQUENCE, or the rules of perfection), is (1) ORATORY, in the general sense; (2) or in particular, RHETORIC, when it concerns free oratory, or POETICS, when it concerns rule-bound oratory. These disciplines, along with all of their branches,[b] are UNIVERSAL insofar as they demonstrate rules that are common in many particular languages.

§623[c]

Since the external sensations of someone sleeping are not clear (§556), even sleep consisting of weaker images will be more suitable for sensitive foresight than the state of someone awake (§598, 539). The collection of rules for anticipating based on the foresights of dreams <*insomniorum*> is the ART OF INTERPRETATING DREAMS.

foresight] representation

Section XII. The intellect[160]

§624

My soul knows some things distinctly (§522). The faculty of knowing something distinctly is the SUPERIOR COGNITIVE FACULTY (the mind),[161] the intellect[d] (§402), and it belongs to me (§216).

§625

Since I have a faculty of being attentive, or ATTENTION,[e] a faculty of abstracting, or ABSTRACTION[f] (§529), and a faculty of separating or abstracting the part from the whole (§589), and since these reveal themselves in sensations, imaginations, and

---

[a] That is, Leibniz's *characteristica universalis*.
[b] G/K: "their individual branches"
[c] Kant E144, 1770–8? 1790–1804?? (beginning): "On sleeping and waking. Dream. Interpretation. Madness. Premonition."
[d] Wolff: "The faculty for distinctly representing a thing is called the *intellect*" (WPE §275).
[e] Wolff: "The faculty of effecting such that one of the perceptions in a composite perception has greater clarity than the rest is called *Attention*" (WPE §237).
[f] Kant E145, before 1764 1764–8 1766–78??: "I know by abstracting very little from many things, and by concretely thinking much about a few. <*Abstrahendo de multis parum, concrete cogitando de paucis multum cognosco.*>"
   Wolff: "If we regard those things that are distinguished in perception such that those that have been perceived are separated from the thing, we are said *to abstract them*. Therefore, we attribute a *faculty of abstracting* to the mind as far as we consider those things that belong to the perceived thing such that they are separated from it" (WPE §281).

foresights, etc., exactly as their objects are related to my body (§538, 600),[162] they are actualized through the power of the soul for representing the universe according to the position of my body (§513).[163]

§626[a]

Attention successively directed at the parts of a total perception is REFLECTION. Attention toward a total perception after reflection is COMPARISON.[b] I reflect. I compare. Therefore I have a faculty of reflecting and a faculty of comparing (§216), which are actualized through the power of the soul for representing the universe according to the position of my body (§625).

§627

The law of attention is: *That of which I perceive more and fewer obscure notes than I do of other things, I perceive more clearly than these* (§528). Hence, the rule of reflection is: *If in the perception of the whole, I perceive more, and less obscure, notes of this part, I am more attentive to it than to the rest* (§626). And this is the rule of comparison: *By reflecting on the parts of a total perception I perceive more and clearer notes belonging to it, and afterwards I am more attentive to it* (§529).

§628

The smallest attention would be that which would make the one smallest perception only one degree clearer than the remaining most obscure ones. Hence, the more and greater perceptions it makes clearer than ones that are very clear, the greater is the attention (§219).[164] Proficiency in apperceiving more things is the SPAN <*EXTENSIO*> OF ATTENTION; likewise, proficiency in apperceiving certain things much more clearly than ones that are very clear is the INTENSITY <*intentio*> OF ATTENTION. Proficiency in being attentive longer to the same thing is the STEADFASTNESS <*PROTENSIO*> OF ATTENTION.[165]

§629

This is the law of abstraction: *When I perceive fewer, and less clear, notes belonging some things than I do of others, then these are represented more obscurely than the others* (§528). And hence this is rule of separating: *If in the perception of the whole, there are fewer, and less clear, notes belonging to this part than to the others, then this part is perceived more obscurely than the others* (§625).

---

[a] Kant E146, 1770–9 (to Baumgarten's gloss, not given here, of the German "*Überlegung*" for the Latin "*REFLEXIO*"): "Not investigation."

[b] Wolff: "The successive direction of attention to those things perceived in a thing is called *Reflection*. Whence likewise it is proven what the *faculty of reflection* is, that is to say, that it is the faculty of successively directing one's own attention, according to choice, at those things which belong in a perceived thing. Wherefore, since it is evident that we are continually capable of shifting our attention successively towards other parts of a total perception, just as with whatever will be seen by us (§256), *the soul has a faculty of reflection beyond things that are perceived*" (WPE §257).

§630[166]

The smallest abstraction would be that which would make one smallest perception only one degree obscurer than the remaining very clear perceptions. Hence the more and greater perceptions that abstraction makes more obscure than ones that are very obscure, the greater it is (§219).

§631

This is the law of my intellect: *If in comparing I abstract away those things that are not compared, what is left over is distinctly perceived* (§627). Since my intellect is finite (§248), this law is the law of a finite intellect,[a] which, in being attentive, reflecting, comparing, abstracting, and separating is actualized through the power of the soul for representing the universe (§625, 626).

If ... perceived] If, while I compare something, I withdraw my thoughts from all other things, then this thing is distinct || universe] world according to the position of its body

§632

The representation of a thing through the intellect is its CONCEPTION.[b] Hence, the CONCEIVABLE is that whose distinct perception can be formed, and the CONCEIVABLE IN ITSELF is that which, considered in itself, can be conceived. Now, in every possible thing, there are essences and affections (§53, 43) that are not totally the same (§267, 41) and that, to such a degree, can be mutually distinguished from one another (§67). Therefore, there are notes (§67) in every possible thing that can be understood clearly, and hence every possible thing is conceivable[167] in itself.

thing through] thing, and particularly of its essence, through || whose distinct] which, and particularly of the essence of which, distinct || essences and affections] essences, essential determinations and affections || thing that] thing, as well as in the essence of every thing, that

§633

INCONCEIVABLE IN ITSELF (the absolutely inconceivable) would be something, considered in itself, whose distinct perception is hidden.[c] This is merely nothing (§632, 7). By contrast, something is RELATIVELY CONCEIVABLE if the powers of some given intellect are sufficient to know it distinctly, whereas something is RELATIVELY INCONCEIVABLE (something posited beyond a given intellect), if the powers of some given spirit are insufficient to know it distinctly. Hence many things properly conceivable in themselves (§632) can be posited beyond my intellect (§631).

---

[a] Wolff: *"Our intellect is limited not only in respect to objects, but also with respect to the mode of representing objects"* (WPE §279).

[b] *Conceptio*, which Baumgarten glosses as *"das Verstehn oder Verständniss einer Sache."*

[c] G/K: "The (absolutely) inconceivable in itself would be that whose distinct representation, when it is considered in itself, contains a contradiction." Baumgarten's text makes no mention of a contradiction here. His reasoning seems clearly to be that for a perception that is distinct, and thus distinct in itself, to be indistinct (i.e. hidden) when considered in itself, is contradictory. So it is not that what is inconceivable in itself is merely something that contains a contradiction, but rather that the very notion of something inconceivable in itself is contradictory.

§634

Since distinctness is the clarity of a thing and its notes, it can be enlarged through both the intensive and the extensive multitude and clarity of notes (§531). An EXTENSIVELY MORE DISTINCT PERCEPTION will be that which has more, and more lively, notes than other distinct perceptions, and that perception which has notes that are intensively clearer than other distinct perceptions will be PURER (intensively more distinct).[a]

§635

The more I, while reflecting and comparing, am attentive to a thing, the more extensively distinct [my] understanding <*intellectio*> of it becomes (§634, 631). And the more again I am attentive to the notes of that which has been understood while reflecting and comparing, and likewise, the more I abstract away from those things that have not been compared, the purer is the understanding <*intellectio*> that is produced (§634, 559).

Meier reformulates this paragraph as follows: The more I am attentive to something and at the same time reflect upon it and compare it more, the more distinct is the representation in regard to extension. The more I am attentive to the notes of a distinctly known thing, however, and during this reflect upon and compare these notes, while at the same time abstracting from all others, the purer is the distinct representation of this thing.

§636

The less I am attentive to a thing, or the less I reflect even while nevertheless being sufficiently attentive, or the less I compare even while nevertheless reflecting sufficiently, the less extensively distinct my understanding <*intellectio*> of it becomes. The less I repeat these same acts with regard to the notes of what has already been understood, and the less I abstract away those that have not been compared, the more impure does [my] distinct perception remain (§634, 631).

§637

The smallest intellect would be that which would only distinguish[168] the fewest and least clear notes of the one smallest thing among maximally weak previous, related and heterogeneous perceptions. Therefore, the more and the clearer the notes of more and greater things that an intellect distinguishes[169] among stronger previous and related heterogeneous perceptions, the greater it is (§219).[170] The perfection of the intellect in forming intensively distinct notes is the DEPTH OF THE INTELLECT, and greater depth is the PURITY OF THE INTELLECT.[b] The perfection of the same in forming extensively distinct notes is the BEAUTY OF THE INTELLECT.[171]

---

[a] Wolff: "Because we are accustomed to terminating the analysis of our notions in those things which, through the wealth of the senses, we indeed perceive clearly but yet confusedly, the *intellect* is never free from the senses and the imagination, and consequently is never entirely pure (WPE §314)" (WPE §315).

[b] Kant E147, 1776–8 (to the last two sentences): "A brighter, more correct, wider, more founded understanding (distinction from the brooding [understanding])."

§638

If [my] attention to a certain object diminishes while I am being attentive to many associated and heterogeneous perceptions, I AM DISTRACTED. Hence the sensations themselves are obscured by distraction (§543), and all attention for a certain object is impeded by distraction (§221). The COLLECTION OF ONE'S MIND is the abstraction of a mind distracted by many heterogeneous perceptions, by means of which attention to a certain object is increased. And hence the collection of one's mind, as well as abstraction, are impediments to distraction (§221). Now, the impediment of an impediment is a means to an end (§342). Hence, the collection of one's mind will promote attention, as will abstraction, which is clear from §549. Attention will promote abstraction, and hence also the collection of one's mind (§529).

§639

Whoever brings about distinct perceptions through the intellect uses (§338) the intellect. Proficiency in using the intellect is called the USE OF THE INTELLECT, which in me is an acquired proficiency (§577). Whoever has not yet acquired the use of the intellect to the extent that is required for speaking[172] is an INFANT. Whoever has not yet acquired as much use of the intellect as is usually required for the more serious affairs of community life is NATURALLY[173] a MINOR, just as someone is NATURALLY[174] an ADULT who has acquired as much use of the intellect as is usually required for the more serious affairs of community life. Whoever enjoys notably less intellect than is usual in most others of the same age is SIMPLE, IN A BAD SENSE. Those in whom no or almost no use of the intellect is observed at that age when it properly should be observable are INSANE <*MENTE CAPTI*>.[a]

Section XIII.[175] Reason[b]

§640[c]

I perceive the nexus of some things confusedly, and the nexus of some things distinctly. Therefore, I have an intellect that perceives a nexus of things perspicaciously (§402, 216), i.e. I have REASON.[d] I also have faculties that know a nexus more confusedly, and these include (1) the inferior faculty for knowing the correspondences of things (§572, 279), to which pertains a sensitive wit (§575); (2) the inferior faculty for knowing the differences of things (§572, 279), to which pertains sensitive acumen (§575); (3) sensitive memory (§579, 306); (4) the faculty of invention (§589); (5) the

---

[a] Kant E148, 1765–6? 1764–8 1769? (across from the conclusion): "The regiment of the understanding."
[b] The English translation of "*ratio*" (reason, ground) must here be decided by context. Whenever it has been helpful, we have indicated the word with a gloss.
[c] Kant E149, 1775–89: "Analogue of the intellect <*Analogon intellectus*>: Connection of ideas without consciousness./Analogue of reason <*Analogon rationis*>: Connection of ideas without consciousness of their ground."
[d] Wolff: "*Reason* is the faculty of intuiting or perceiving the nexus of universal truths" (WPE §483). Wolff refers here to Leibniz, *Theodicy*, Preliminary Dissertation, §23, where he says that reason is "the inviolable linking together of truths."

faculty of judging (§606, 94), thus sensitive judgment (§607) and that of the senses (§608); (6) the expectation of similar cases (§610, 612); and (7) the sensitive faculty of characterization[176] (§619, 347). All of these, insofar as they are similar to reason in representing the nexus of things, constitute the ANALOGUE OF REASON (§70),[a] or the collection of the soul's faculties for representing a nexus confusedly.

perceive] know

§641

Reason (§640) is the faculty for perspicuously perceiving the correspondences and differences of things distinctly (§572, 579), and hence it is intellectual wit and acumen (§575), intellectual memory or PERSONALITY (§579, 306), the faculty of judging distinctly (§606, 94) to which intellectual judgment pertains (§607), intellectual anticipation or PROVIDENCE (forethought) (§610), and the intellectual faculty of characterization[177] (§619).

§642

Since everything in this world is in a universal nexus (§356–8), reason is actualized through the power of the soul to represent the universe according to the situation[b] of the body (§631), and indeed according to this law: *If in A I clearly[178] know a C,[179] and this is something from which I will clearly[180] know why something must be clearly[181] known in B, I conceive of A and B as connected* (§14, 632).

conceive of] distinctly know

§643

That which can be known through some ground *<ratione>* is called REASONABLE *<RATIONABILE>*, and that which can be known through none is called UNREASONABLE *<IRRATIONABILE>* (contrary to reason *<rationem>*). Now, every possible being is doubly rational *<rationale>* and connected[182] (§24). Both its ground *<ratio>* and its consequence *<rationatum>*, along with the nexus between these two, are conceivable in themselves (§632, 14). Therefore, everything possible is reasonable. Everything unreasonable, or whatever is contrary to reason, is impossible (§7, 8).

§644

When the powers of some given faculty of reason are not sufficient for cognizing the nexus of something,[c] this thing is posited OUTSIDE THE SPHERE OF A GIVEN FACULTY OF REASON[183] (it is either beneath or beyond a given faculty of reason, or neither beneath nor beyond a given faculty of reason and nevertheless outside of

---

[a] Wolff: "Therefore, since there is also something similar to reason (WPE §492 and WO §195) in this expectation of similar cases [i.e. WPE §505], the expectation of similar cases is that which ought to be called the analogue of reason" (WPE §506).

[b] Thomas suggests this may be a mistake, and thus should be "position" *<positu>* instead of "situation" *<situ>* (see §85, 284, 509), clearly because Baumgarten uses "position" in all previous similar formulations. However, it is possible that this change from "position" to "situation" derives from the fact that reason, which perceives the wider nexus, is under consideration.

[c] G/K: "a determinate nexus"

its horizon).[184] Therefore, many reasonable things can be posited outside the sphere of the reason[185] (§643) of the person whose reason, like mine (§631, 640),[186] is limited.

Eberhard adds the note: The distinction between things that are *contrary* to reason and those that are *above* human reason is therefore grounded and may be employed. If, therefore, something is contrary to reason, it must be contradictory. From the fact that human reason does not see the ground, it follows only that it is *above* such reason.

§645

The smallest reason would be the smallest intellect that perceives the smallest nexus of only one thing. Therefore, the greater the intellect that perceives a greater nexus of more things, the greater is reason (§219).[187] Proficiency in perceiving a greater nexus of things is the SOLIDITY OF REASON, while proficiency in perceiving a nexus of more things is the SAGACITY OF REASON.[a] And hence reason is either purer, or more impure (§637).

§646

The perceptions of reason are reasonings,[b] and, if true, then REASON is said to be SOUND,[c] whereas if false, it is said to be CORRUPTED. The collection of true reasonings is called REASON TAKEN OBJECTIVELY, in contradistinction to reason, taken as subjectively defined (§640). The USE OF REASON is proficiency in using reason, which I have acquired (§577). Its intensity is the CULTIVATION OF REASON. Hence, all philosophical knowledge of truth cultivates reason (§577).[d] A false syllogistic rule corrupts it greatly.

perceptions of reason] representations brought about through reason ‖ SOUND] HEALTHY

§647

Someone who attributes the errors of the analogue of reason (§640, 646) to corrupt reason is deluded, due to a lack of acumen, by the faculty for knowing the correspondences of things (§576). Nevertheless, errors of this sort can corrupt reason if they become premises (§646).

if they become premises] if reason makes them into premises of its reasonings

§648

Since each cognitive faculty within me is limited, and hence has a certain and determinable limit (§248, 354),[188] the cognitive faculties of the soul, when compared to another, admit of some determined relation <*rationem*> and proportion to one another

---

[a] Cf. Kant, *Anthropology*, §56; AA 7:223–4.
[b] Wolff: "A third operation of the mind (and which is called *reasoning*) is the formation of judgments from other previous ones" (WPE §366).
"The general principle of reasoning, or the general principle of the rules of reasoning, is called the law of reasoning" (WPE §372).
[c] "Those rules that can explain reasoning, or those that the soul observes while reasoning legitimately, are called the rules of reasoning or of syllogisms. However, it is called reasoning legitimately if the proposition which has been introduced was true" (WPE §372).
[d] Wolff: "Philosophical knowledge is knowledge of reason" (WPE §499).

($572),[189] according to which one is either greater or less than the other (§160). The determined proportion of someone's cognitive faculties to one another is their WIT, IN THE BROADER SENSE. Wit that has many proficiencies is QUICK, whereas wit with few or none is SLOW. The wit that alters from slow to quick IS EXCITED, and the wit that alters from vigorous to slow GROWS NUMB.[190] The faculty that is greater than the rest in wit, taken in the broader sense, gives the name to the subject whose wit, in the broad sense, is under consideration. Hence, it is clear who are MORE EMINENTLY WITTY [IN THE STRICT SENSE], ACUTE, OF GOOD MEMORY, PROVIDENT, JUDICIOUS, INTELLIGENT,[191] REASONABLE, etc.

greater or less than] greater than, less than or equal to || many proficiencies] many theoretical proficiencies

§649

Because the cognitive faculties that mutually relate to one another in a specific proportion are themselves more apt for knowing a certain genus of things than for knowing others (§648), the wit taken in the broader sense that is more apt for knowing a certain genus than it is for knowing others receives its name from that genus of knowledge. Hence it is clear that there are, for example, EMPIRICAL,[192] HISTORICAL, POETIC, PROPHETIC, CRITICAL, PHILOSOPHICAL, MATHEMATICAL, MECHANICAL, and MUSICAL WITS. Wits taken more broadly that are remarkably more apt than many others for knowing all genera of things are UNIVERSAL WITS, and insofar as they exceed many others in the degree of most of their cognitive faculties, they are called SUPERIOR WITS.

than for knowing others] than if they stood in another relation

§650

HABIT is the proficiency that reduces the necessity of attention in certain actions. Now any acquired theoretical proficiency alters the wit taken more broadly (§577, 648). Hence, this wit can be altered greatly and very often by exercises and habit, and in this way the wit can either be excited or numbed[193] (§648).[194] Whence it is clear how a witty person [in the strict sense] can become judicious, etc., and how someone with poetic wit can become philosophical (§649).

the proficiency that reduces] a proficiency large enough to reduce

Section XIIII. Indifference[195]

§651

Through the faculty of judging, I either perceive something's perfection, or its imperfection (§606). I know perfection or imperfection either symbolically or intuitively (§620). Hence, either I intuit the perfection of something and am PLEASED, or I intuit its imperfections, and am DISPLEASED, or I intuit neither its perfection nor its imperfection and I am neither pleased nor displeased, and it is INDIFFERENT to me

(I am indifferent towards it). What pleases me I intuit as good, under the aspect of the good (§100), and what displeases me I intuit as evil, under the aspect of evil (§146).[a] That which is indifferent to me I intuit as neither good nor evil, neither under the aspect of the good, nor under the aspect of evil (§100, 146).

under the aspect of the good] insofar as it appears to be good because of some ground ‖ under the aspect of evil] insofar as it is evil because of some ground, or appears evil to me ‖ neither under … evil] neither insofar as it is good because of some ground, nor insofar as it is evil because of some ground

§652

In that which is indifferent to me I intuit either no perfection or imperfection at all, and it is COMPLETELY INDIFFERENT TO ME, or I do not intuit in it a certain and determined perfection alone, or its opposite, and it is thus RESPECTIVELY[196] INDIFFERENT TO ME with respect to this perfection. That which I do not represent is UNKNOWN TO ME. Whence it follows that I intuit no perfection or imperfection at all of that which is unknown (§651). Therefore, that which is unknown to me is completely indifferent, and it neither pleases nor displeases me. That which is partially unknown to me is indifferent to me relative to the perfections of the unknown parts. That which I only symbolically apperceive,[197] even if I am most conscious of it[198] as good[b] or evil[c] symbolically, I nevertheless do not intuit clearly[199] as such (§620), and hence it neither pleases nor displeases me, but rather is indifferent to me (§651) to the extent that it is observed.[200]

§653

A WHOLLY INDIFFERENT MIND[d] would be one whose total perception contains nothing at all pleasing or displeasing. A PARTIALLY INDIFFERENT MIND is one that has partial perceptions that are fully or respectively[201] indifferent to itself. Therefore, a mind for which at least one thing is either minimally pleasing or displeasing is not totally indifferent. A mind that is not pleased or displeased by all of its partial perceptions with respect to all possible perfections is partially indifferent.

[a] In the *Critique of Practical Reason* (AA 5: 60n.), Kant comments on this scholastic formula, writing: "Moreover, the expression 'under the aspect of the good' <*sub ratione boni*> is also ambiguous. For it can as much mean that we represent something to ourselves as good, when and *because we desire* (will) *it*, as that we desire something *for the reason that we represent it to ourselves as good*, so that the desire is the determining ground of the concept of the object as something good, or the concept of the good is the determining ground of the desiring (of the will). For in the first case 'under the aspect of the good' would mean that we will something *under the idea of the good*, while in the second that we do so *as a consequence of this idea*, which must then precede the willing as its determining ground." Presumably Kant would have the same to say about the kind of relation described here between pleasure and the good.
[b] Wolff: "*The good* is whatever perfects us and our state, or likewise, whatever renders us, and our internal and external states, more perfect" (WPE §554).
[c] Wolff: "Whatever renders us and our state, either internal or external, more imperfect, is evil" (WPE §656).
[d] Kant E150 1776–8? 1764–77??: "that [mind] which has no choice at all nevertheless cannot be entirely insensible. But only it cannot judge."

§654

That which a certain and determined power of representation intuits as neither good nor evil is called SUBJECTIVELY (indifferent)[202] NEUTRAL. Such are the things that are unknown to me, and those things that are clearly[203] known only symbolically (§652). The OBJECTIVELY NEUTRAL is that which is neither good nor evil, and this again would either be the ABSOLUTELY INDIFFERENT, which would posit no perfection and imperfection at all, and is not a being (§100). Or it would be the RESPECTIVELY[204] INDIFFERENT, which contributes nothing to a certain perfection or its opposite. No such thing is found in the best world (§441). Therefore, someone who intuits things as they are is absolutely indifferent toward no thing <*nullam rem*> (§651).

Section XV. Pleasure and displeasure[205]

§655

The state of the soul that originates from the intuition of perfection is PLEASURE[a] (satisfaction), and the state of the soul that originates from the intuition of imperfection is DISPLEASURE[b] (dissatisfaction). Hence, the STATE OF INDIFFERENCE is the state of the soul in which it senses neither displeasure nor pleasure. Pleasure and displeasure originating from a true intuition are called TRUE, and those originating from a false intuition are called APPARENT. Hence the intuition of perfection and things that are good as such produces pleasure; the intuition of truly good things produces true pleasure; and the intuition of apparently good things produces apparent pleasure; the intuition of imperfection and things that are evil as such produces displeasure; the intuition of true evils produces true displeasure; and the intuition of apparent evils produces apparent displeasure (§12).

intuition of perfection] what pleases ‖ intuition of imperfection] what displeases ‖ false intuition] apparent intuition

§656

PLEASURE or DISPLEASURE that originate from the intuition of simple perfection and imperfection is SIMPLE, and those originating from the intuition of composite perfection and imperfection are COMPOSITE; those from sensitive intuition, SENSITIVE; those from something sensual, the PLEASURE OR DISPLEASURE of the SENSES; those from something distinct, RATIONAL (intellectual)[206] (§521,[207] 640). In a total perception of something not wholly indifferent, either those things that are pleasing are stronger than the non-pleasing,[208] and that state is the PREDOMINANCE

---

[a] Wolff: "*Pleasure* is the intuition or intuitive knowledge of the perfection of anything, whether true or apparent" (WPE §511). Note this is different from the above, which identifies pleasure with a state of the soul that accompanies the intuition of perfection, rather than with this intuition itself.

[b] Wolff: "Displeasure is the intuition or intuitive knowledge of the perfection of anything, whether true or apparent." (WPE §518).

OF PLEASURE, or the displeasing are stronger than the non-displeasing,[209] and that state is the PREDOMINANCE[a] OF DISPLEASURE, or the non-pleasing[210] are equal in strength to the pleasing, and the non-displeasing[211] are equal in strength to the displeasing, and this is the STATE OF TOTAL EQUILIBRIUM (§516, cf. §661).[212]

§657

A stronger pleasure obscures[b] previous and associated weaker heterogeneous pleasures and displeasures. A stronger displeasure obscures previous weaker heterogeneous displeasures that are associated with pleasures of this same sort (§529). Hence, in the predominance of pleasure, preceding and related displeasures are obscured, whereas in the predominance of displeasure, preceding and related pleasures are obscured (§656). A weaker pleasure clarifies stronger preceding pleasures that are also associated with displeasures of this same sort. A weaker displeasure clarifies a stronger preceding heterogeneous displeasure that is also associated with pleasures of this same sort (§549).

§658

The smallest pleasure and displeasure are states that originate from the smallest[213] intuition, i.e. the least true, clear, and certain (§531, 620)[214] intuition that is possible of the one smallest perfection and imperfection among much stronger preceding and associated heterogeneous pleasures or displeasures (§651, 161). Therefore, that much greater are the pleasures and displeasures that originate from a greater,[215] i.e. more true, lively, distinct, clear, or certain (§531)[216] intuition of more and greater perfections or imperfections among weaker previous and associated heterogeneous pleasures and displeasures of this same sort (§160, 657).[217] The cause of a pleasure DELIGHTS. Whatever increases pleasure is AGREEABLE (favorable); whatever decreases it is DISAGREABLE (non-gratifying). Whatever increases displeasure is BURDENSOME; whatever reduces it is GRATIFYING[c] <GRATUM>.

§659

Since the intuition of things which are present is clearer[218] (§542), truer, more certain (§546), and hence greater (§531),[219] the pleasures and displeasures originating from what is present can be greater than those originating from what is past and future (§658).[d] However, if one of these is represented as containing much greater, and more, perfections and imperfections, or if the mind is distracted by many past and future pleasing and displeasing things, the pleasure and displeasure originating from these can become stronger than that from present things (§658, 543). Pleasure or displeasure,

---

[a] Kant E151, 1776–89 (above on the side of the Latin page that starts approximately here): "fooling around, but not playing the fool."
[b] Kant E152, 1776–8? 1790–804?: "Hence the moderate are the best, for the strong stun or befuddle and leave behind weakness. (Finally a rich person must live as a poor one. Enjoyed amusements make the quiet gloomy.) A rare pleasure. A good meal. They engage in foretaste, but in enjoyment they can be deceived. Unexpected."
[c] Kant E153, 1776–89: "vitalizing." To the right: "sweet and spicy <dolce piquante>"
[d] Kant E154, 1765–6: "That I do not have something good that I could have possessed does not pain me for as long as it does when I no longer possess something that I previously had."

without which the mind is almost indifferent or is in complete equilibrium, is sensed very clearly.

§660

GOOD FOR ME are those things which, when posited in me, a reality is also posited, and EVIL FOR ME are those things which, when posited in me, a negation, taken more broadly, is also posited. And since I am more conscious, i.e. more truly, clearly, and certainly (§531)[220] conscious, of my state, or the state of my body, or of both, than of many other things (§508), it is obvious why those things that I intuit as good for me or evil for me produce greater pleasures and displeasures than many other things, although I may judge these to be better or worse (§658). Among the things that are good and evil for me, some exist outside of me and some do not. The latter are for me PERSONAL (internal) goods and evils, while the former are ADVENTITIOUS (external), [and they are] useful [and harmful] for me (§336).[a] Personal things can please or displease me more than adventitious things (§658).

reality] perfections; negation] imperfections

§661

If I intuit something as only good, then PURE <*PURA*> PLEASURE[b] originates. If, however, I intuit something as only evil, then SHEER <*MERUM*> DISPLEASURE originates. If I intuit something as equally good and evil at the same time, then, with respect to its object, the STATE OF PARTIAL EQUILIBRIUM originates (cf. §656).[221] If something is intuited as good and evil at the same time, but unequally, either the intuition of the object as good will be greater, and SWEET DISPLEASURE[c] originates, or the intuition of the object as evil will be greater, and BITTER PLEASURE originates. Now every finite being is partly good and partly evil (§264). Therefore, if I intuit a finite object as it is, there will be no sheer pleasure or sheer displeasure from it, but rather all finite things partially please and partially displease (§651, 654).[d]

§662

The perfection that is a phenomenon <*perfectio phaenomenon*>, or the perfection

---

[a] Baumgarten ends this complex sentence with the ambiguous "useful for me <*mihi utilia*>." This can only refer to the personal and adventitious things that are good for me, since their respective evils, being useless (cf. §336), cannot be useful. AA suggests appending "and/or useless" or "harmful", or "useful and harmful" (AA 15: 9). We have indicated this as above. Notably, Meier has this part of the sentence also as "which are useful or harmful for me."

[b] Kant E155, 1771? 1772? 1776-8?: "A pure pleasure, to which one entirely gives over oneself (in regard to which one reproaches oneself for nothing). One affected or weighted down, which is combined with a reservation. To be joyful without worry."

[c] Kant E156, 1770-1? 1776-8? (in the left margin extending downward from "SWEET DISPLEASURE"): "From different grounds, of which the one is indeed the foil of the other. However, they must not be (*crossed out:* equal) contradictorily opposed, e.g. vice and virtue. It is an inhibited and overwhelming power."

[d] Kant E157, 1776-8? 1770-1?? (under Baumgarten's glosses, not given here, of "*DULCE TAEDIUM*" with "*ein süsses Missvergnügen*" and of "*AMARA VOLUPTAS*" with "*eine bittre Lust*"): "subtle mischief. Execution."

observable by taste in the broader sense, is BEAUTY,[a] whereas the imperfection that is a phenomenon <*imperfectio phaenomenon*>, or the imperfection observable by taste in the broader sense, is UGLINESS. Hence beauty as such delights the one who intuits it (§658), and ugliness as such is burdensome to the one who intuits it (§618).[222] When intuitions alter, pleasure and displeasure alter (§326, 328). Now, every intuition of mine is alterable in itself (§257). Therefore, every pleasure and displeasure of mine is alterable in itself. Nevertheless, those that are altered with more difficulty than most others are called CONSTANT (durable) PLEASURES and DISPLEASURES, while those that are altered more easily than those that are constant are TRANSITORY (brief, fluctuating).[223]

The perfection that is a phenomenon] Perfection, insofar as it is an appearance ‖ imperfection that is a phenomenon] imperfection, insofar as it is an appearance

Section XVI. The faculty of desire[224]

§663[b]

If I endeavor or make an effort to produce some perception, i.e. if I determine the power of my soul, or myself, to produce some perception, I DESIRE. The opposite of what I desire, I AVERT. Therefore I have a faculty of desiring and averting (§216), that is, a FACULTY OF DESIRE (will, more broadly speaking, cf. §690).[225] My very endeavors, or efforts, or determinations of my powers, are the DESIRES (appetites)[c] of my desiring, and the AVERSIONS of my averting.

§664

What I desire (1) I foresee to be contained in future successions of my total perception, (2) I anticipate will exist as determined through my power for actualizing it, and (3) it is pleasing. I do not desire those things that I utterly do not foresee, and hence which are unknown (§652, 595), those things which I utterly do not anticipate will exist through any power of mine,[226] and those things that are utterly not pleasing and which hence are completely indifferent to me (§652). I avert those things that (1) I foresee, and that (2) I anticipate to be impeded through some effort[227] of mine, and that (3) are displeasing. I do not avert those things that I utterly do not foresee and hence are unknown, those things that I anticipate to be impeded through no effort[228] of mine, and those things that are utterly not displeasing. Hence I do not avert those things which are completely indifferent to me (§652).

---

[a] Wolff: "Whatever pleases is called *beautiful*, whereas whatever displeases is called *ugly <deforme>*" (WPE §543). "*Beauty consists in the perfection of a thing, insofar as the very power of this thing is apt for producing pleasure in us*" (WPE §544). "Hence *beauty* can be defined as that which is the aptitude of a thing for producing pleasure in us, or, that which is observable of perfection: for it is in this observability that this aptitude consists" (WPE §545).

[b] Kant E158, 1769–71? 1772? 1772–7?? 1764–8?? (beginning): "There is an involuntary endeavor to alter or to prolong one's representations."

[c] Wolff: "*Desire* in general is the inclination of the soul toward an object because of the good that is perceived in it" (WPE §579).

§665

This is the law of the faculty of desire: *I make an effort to produce those things that I foresee as pleasing and I anticipate will exist through my effort* (§664, 663).[a] *I desire the opposite of those things that I foresee as displeasing and I anticipate to be impeded through my effort.* Hence I can desire many good things and many evil things under the aspect of the good. I can avert many evil things and many good things under the aspect of evil (§651).

I make ... effort] I strive to bring forth what pleases me, what I at the same time foresee, and what I expect will become actual through my striving || I desire ... effort] I desire to hinder what displeases me, what I at the same time foresee, and what I expect can be hindered through my striving

§666

There are many good things that I cannot desire: those (1) that are unknown, (2) that are indifferent to me, (3) that are erroneously displeasing, (4) that are perhaps pleasing but utterly unforeseen, and (5) that are perhaps foreseen, but which I utterly do not anticipate will exist through any effort[229] of mine. There are many evil things that I cannot avert: those (1) that are unknown, (2) that are completely indifferent to me, (3) that are erroneously pleasing, (4) that are perhaps displeasing but utterly unforeseen, (5) that are perhaps foreseen, but which I do not anticipate to be impeded through any effort[230] of mine (§664, 665).

§667

Since intuition (§619),[231] judgments (§608), and hence pleasure and displeasure (§655), foresights (§595) and anticipations (§610) are actualized through the power of the soul for representing the universe according to the position of my body and, through these, desire and aversion are actualized, these[232] will also be actualized through the power of the soul for representing the universe according to the position of my body (§513, 317).

§668

The smaller and greater are the cognitive faculties required for desiring and averting (§667),[233] the smaller or greater is the faculty of desiring or averting that follows from these, or that is determined by these (§331).

§669

Whoever desires or averts intends the production of some perception (§341, 663). Hence, the perceptions containing the ground of this sort of intention are the impelling causes of desire and aversion, and thus they are called the INCENTIVES OF THE MIND <*ELATERES ANIMI*> (§342). KNOWLEDGE, insofar as it contains the incentives of the mind, is MOVING (affecting, touching, burning, pragmatic,

[a] Wolff: "the general principle of the rules of the appetite is called the *law of the appetite*. Whence *the ground of the rules of the appetite is rendered from the law of the appetite*" (WPE §903). "*This proposition is the law of the appetite: whatever we represent to ourselves as good for ourselves, we desire* <appetimus> *it*" (WPE §904).

practical, and, more broadly, living), and insofar as it does not contain these incentives, it is INERT (theoretical and, more broadly, dead) and when this knowledge is otherwise perfect enough (§515, 531), it is called SPECULATION (speculative, empty, hollow).[234] Hence, symbolic knowledge, as such, is notably inert (§652), and only intuitive knowledge is moving (§652). Hence, in the state of total indifference, the total perception would be inert[235] (§653), but on the contrary, in the state of pure pleasure and sheer displeasure, or in the state in which either predominates, the total perception is moving[236] (§656, 661). The knowledge that has a motive power, all else being equal, is greater than inert knowledge, and it is also greater than speculation (§515). Therefore the vaster, nobler, truer, clearer, hence more lively or distinct, more certain, and more brilliant knowledge is, the greater it is (§515, 531).[237]

§670

The state of equilibrium with respect to a certain object is a state in which that object pleases and displeases equally (§661). Hence, in such a state of equilibrium, equal incentives are perceived for desiring and averting something (§669). If, in the state of equilibrium, the knowledge moving someone to desire a certain object is wholly equal to the knowledge moving them to avert the same object,[238] then the state that would then arise would be the STATE OF PERFECT EQUILIBRIUM. In the state of equilibrium,[239] I desire what is foreseen, insofar as it is good <*pro ratione boni*> (§331), to the extent that it pleases, and I avert what is foreseen, insofar as it is evil <*pro ratione mali*> (§667), to the extent that it displeases, and indeed not only to the extent that it is pleasing or displeasing in itself now, but also inasmuch as it remains pleasing or displeasing in the circumstances in which the future is foreseen (§664) under an intuition of the powers (§669) that the mind anticipates will be required for producing or impeding it (§665).[240] It is now equally pleasing and displeasing. Therefore, I desire and avert the same thing equally at the same time.[241]

§671

Since one perception is produced more easily than another (§527), not just any perception is actualized by just any desire, but for any given perception, a certain degree of the powers of the soul is required (§331).[242] If there is as much DESIRE or AVERSION as the production of its object, or its opposite, requires, they are EFFECTIVE. If they are not such, then they are INEFFECTIVE. If there is as much desire or aversion as the desiring or averting person anticipates to be required for the production of their object, or its opposite, then they are COMPLETE, whereas if there is less, they are INCOMPLETE.[243] The KNOWLEDGE THAT MOVES effective desires or aversions, and ITS MOTIVE power (§222),[244] is LIVING (more strictly, cf. §669, rousing or sufficient for what is to be done). The KNOWLEDGE, and ITS MOTIVE power (§222),[245] of ineffective desires or aversions is DEAD (more strictly, cf. §669, insufficient for whatever must be done, solicitation). The KNOWLEDGE that moves complete desires or aversions, and ITS POWER, is COMPLETELY MOVING, and the knowledge that only moves incomplete desires and aversions is IMCOMPLETELY MOVING. Living knowledge, all else being equal, is greater than dead knowledge, and incompletely moving knowledge is less than completely moving knowledge (§669).

produced more easily] produced or hindered more easily || DEAD] DEAD and consists at most in mere stimulation

§672

Since in an empty anticipation I can take a certain degree of desire or aversion to be sufficient for producing an object, or its opposite, which is in fact insufficient (§617), my complete desires and[246] aversions can nevertheless be ineffective. For this same reason, provided that I expect that greater desires and aversions are required than those which are in fact sufficient, incomplete ones can be effective (§671).

complete] decisive || incomplete ones] ones that are not decisive

§673

In the state of equilibrium following foresight and anticipation,[247] desire is equal to aversion (§670). Therefore, there would be complete aversion and complete desire for the same thing (§671), and likewise there would be incomplete desire while there would be complete aversion to the same thing, and there would be incomplete aversion[248] while there would be complete desire for the same thing (§81, 671). Therefore, if I desired or averted completely in the state of equilibrium,[249] I would have desired or averted the same thing incompletely, which is impossible (§7). Therefore I neither desire nor avert completely in the state of total, or partial (§656, 661), or perfect, or imperfect (§670) equilibrium following foresight and anticipation.[250] And if[251] I thus desire or avert completely,[252] I am not in a state of equilibrium following the foresight and anticipation[253] of an object that is to be actualized, and its opposite (§671).

Meier simplifies this paragraph as follows: In the state of equilibrium I desire and avert the object in equal degree. If, therefore, the desire for the same were decisive, then so must also be the aversion of it, but that is impossible. For if I decisively desire something, then I avert it either not at all or at least not decisively. If I therefore, in regard to an object, stand in the state of equilibrium, whether it be a complete equilibrium or not, a full one or not: then I desire it neither decisively nor do I avert it decisively. Whenever I therefore decide upon something I am not in a state of equilibrium.

§674

If I, anticipating that something foreseen is about to exist or must be impeded[254] by my determined effort,[255] simultaneously intuit that thing as good and evil, but such that either pleasure or displeasure predominates, then the state of my mind thence arising is called the STATE OF PREPONDERANCE. In the state of preponderance, unequal incentives for desiring or averting are perceived (§669). Therefore,[256] the stronger desire is than aversion in the state of preponderance, or the stronger aversion is than desire, the more pleasure predominates over displeasure, or the more displeasure predominates over pleasure (§331, 665). This pleasure or displeasure is obtained not only from the object considered in itself but also from the object considered in future circumstances, and indeed under an intuition of the powers that must be expended for it to be produce or impeded (§670).[257]

Meier reformulates the first sentence above to read: If I desire and avert a certain object at the same time, but such that I either desire it more than I avert it or vice versa, then in regard to it I am in a state of preponderance.

§675

EFFICACIOUS DESIRES and AVERSIONS are called (1)[258] serious, i.e. they are not simulated, while INEFFICACIOUS DESIRES AND AVERSIONS are simulated; (2)[259] they are called serious and not simulated insofar as they are grounds, have consequences, and something depends on them (§197). Accordingly, none are entirely[260] INEFFICACIOUS, since these would be completely sterile (§23). However, incomplete and ineffective desires and aversions are of (a) lesser efficacy (§671); (b) the complete ones are of greater efficacy, even if they are ineffective (§672); with respect to these, the incomplete ones are sometimes called comparatively inefficacious, just as these, if they are ineffective, are called inefficacious with respect to the effective; (c) the effective desires and aversions are of the greatest efficacy; with respect to these, both the incomplete and the ineffective ones are sometimes called comparatively inefficacious (§671).[261] In a state of indifference, I absolutely do not desire, nor do I avert (§664, 665), and therefore not efficaciously in any sense. In a state of equilibrium remaining after the foresight and anticipation[262] of an object and its opposite, I neither efficaciously desire nor avert to that degree that we have considered a means[263] (§673). This degree of efficacy in desires and aversions either requires pure pleasure or sheer displeasure, or a state of preponderance (§661, 674).[264]

Section XVII.[265] The inferior faculty of desire

§676

Since the FACULTY OF DESIRE follows the cognitive faculty (§665, 668), either it follows the inferior cognitive faculty and is INFERIOR, (§520) or it follows the superior cognitive faculty (§624). I desire and avert something that is sensitively represented (§521). Therefore, I have an inferior faculty of desire (§216). The DESIRES AND AVERSIONS that are actualized through it are SENSITIVE, and they are produced through the soul's power for representing the universe according to the position of the body (§667). The faculty of sensitive desires is the CONCU-PISCIBLE FACULTY, and the faculty of sensitive aversions is the IRASCIBLE FACULTY, and together with the inferior cognitive faculty, they are sometimes called the FLESH.[266]

§677

Sensitive desires and aversions arise either from obscure representations or from confused ones (§676, 520). And, insofar as they are the impelling causes of desiring and averting, both are stimuli (§669). A stronger desire that originates from an obscure stimulus is INSTINCT (sympathy, love),[267] and aversion of this same sort is FLIGHT (natural antipathy, natural hate).[268]

INSTINCT] BLIND DRIVE || FLIGHT] BLIND AVERSION

§678

The (stronger)[269] desires and aversions originating from confused knowledge are AFFECTS (sufferings, affections, perturbations of the mind), and their science is (1) PSYCHOLOGICAL PATHOLOGY, which explains the theory of these; (2) AESTHETIC PATHOLOGY, which contains the rules[a] as to how they are to be excited, restrained, and signified, and to this pertains oratorical, rhetorical, or poetic pathology (§622);[270] and (3) PRACTICAL PATHOLOGY, which exhibits the obligations of the human being with respect to their affects.

restrained, and signified] decreased, suppressed and signified

§679

Since those affects that are stronger desires arise from stronger sensitive pleasure (§678, 665), this pleasure will increase an associated pleasure (§162), whence these sorts of AFFECTS are called AGREEABLE (§658), and insofar as the pleasure from which they originate obscures an associated displeasure (§529), they are called GRATIFYING (§658).[b] Since those affects that are stronger aversions arise from stronger sensitive dissatisfaction (§678,[271] 665), this dissatisfaction will increase an associated dissatisfaction (§162), whence these sorts of AFFECTS are called BURDENSOME, and insofar as the displeasure from which they originate obscures some associated pleasure, they are called NON-GRATIFING (§658). Affects that are composed out of both the gratifying and the non-gratifying are MIXED.

§680

As internal sensations (§678, 535), affects remit once they have become the strongest that they can be (§551); time is their cure (§550). Since stronger affects arise from a stronger intuition (§655, 679), this intuition will obscure the symbolic knowledge of pleasing or displeasing things (§9,[272] 620). Hence, stronger affects are ineffable, and if they somehow break out into words, they often remit for this very reason (§529).

§681

Whatever increases the stronger sensitive pleasures and displeasures increases the affects (§678). Hence the more composite, the more noble (§515), the truer, the livelier, the more certain, and the more brilliant are the pleasure or displeasure from which affects arise (§658, 669), the greater are these affects (§656).[273] If one were only

---

[a] Wolff: "those rules that the soul observes in desiring <*appetendo*> are called the rules of the appetite" (WPE §903).
[b] See Cicero's distinction between the agreeable <*iucundus*> and the gratifying <*gratus*>: "I am still grateful for this truth, even if it is not agreeable to me <*nam ista veritas, etiam si iucunda non est, mihi tamen grata est*>" (Ep. ad Att. 52). As well, see M.J.B. Gardin Dumesnil, *Latin Synonyms, with their different significations and examples taken from the best Latin authors.* Trans. J. M. Gosset (London: Richard Taylor and Co., 1809), 327.

to sense the cause of an affect as evil or good, and another were at the same time to imagine it to themselves and foresee it, then the affect of the latter, all else being equal,[274] will be greater than that of the former (§595, 557).

§682

An agreeable affect is JOY.[275] Joy based on the present (on account of future consequences) is GLADNESS <*LAETITIA*>.[276] Joy based on the past (on account of future consequences) is SATISFACTION. The satisfaction based on what the joyful person has done is SELF REPOSE. Joy based on something evil that is no longer imminent is CHEERFULNESS.

§683

Joy based on an uncertain future is HOPE, and the joy based on a more certain future is CONFIDENCE, and insofar as one desires its presence, it is EAGERNESS. Eager confidence in a difficult good is COURAGE, and greater courage is AUDACITY.

§684

Joy based on honor is GLORY[a] (cf. §942),[277] and the joy based on the imperfection of another is MALEVOLENCE. The malevolence that delights in something disgraceful for another person is MOCKERY.[278] Joy based on the perfection of another person is LOVE. Love for a benefactor is GRATITUDE (gratefulness); for the miserable, COMPASSION; for the comparatively perfect, FAVOR; for the inferior, BENEVOLENCE; and for someone who is not at all useful to the one who is benevolent, CLEMENCY.

§685

A burdensome affect is SADNESS.[279] Sadness based on the past (on account of future consequences) is MOURNING. Sadness based on the present (on account of future consequences) is[280] SORROW[281] (grief),[282] and[283] mourning[284] based on what the mourning person has done is CONTRITION.

§686

Sadness based on something rather uncertain in the future is DREAD, and sadness based on something imminent, FEAR. Fear based on something greater is HORROR; horror based on something certain is DESPERATION, and horror based on something unexpected is TERROR. Sadness based on uncertain hope is TIMIDITY; on the delay of desire, YEARNING; and on something previously represented as good, DISGUST.

§687

Sadness based on contempt is SHAME; on the imperfection of another,

---

[a] Wolff: "*Glory* is the joy that is felt based on the kind judgment of others about us or our own. ... However, the *judgment* of others about us or our own is called *kind* if they judge that those things that we have done have been well and correctly done by us, and if they judge those things that belong to us are good" (WPE §765). "*Glory* is the affect that originates if we suppose that those things that we have done, or those which belong to us, are considered as good by others" (WPE §769).

COMMISERATION; and on the perfection of another, HATE. Hate based on the desire of the good of another is ENVY, and terror based on injury is WRATH.

§688

The intuition of something as not reproduced is AMAZEMENT. The drive *<instinctus>* to know that which we do not yet know is CURIOSITY, and according to the diversity of wits, more broadly considered, it is HISTORICAL, concerning historical knowledge, or PHILOSOPHICAL, concerning philosophical knowledge, or MATHEMATICAL, concerning mathematical knowledge.[a] The insane, in whose soul only burdensome affects reign, are MELANCHOLIC, and those in whom anger reigns are[285] FURIOUS.

Meier formulates the first sentence as follows: Amazement is the intuitive cognition of a thing insofar as it is new, or insofar as we have not previously had the representation of it.

Section XVIII.[286] The superior faculty of desire

§689

THE FACULTY OF DESIRE, insofar as it follows the superior cognitive faculty (§665, 668), is called SUPERIOR (mind).[287] I desire and avert some things distinctly represented by the intellectual faculty of judging (§607).[288] Therefore, I have a superior faculty of desire (§216). The DESIRES AND AVERSIONS to be actualized through that faculty are RATIONAL (§941),[289] and are produced through the power of the soul for representing the universe according to the position of the body (§667, 642).

§690

Rational desire is VOLITION *<VOLITIO>*.[b] I will *<volo>*. Therefore I have a faculty of willing, the WILL (§216). Rational aversion is NOLITION. I refuse *<nolo>*. Therefore, I have a faculty of refusing *<nolendi>*, REFUSAL *<NOLUNTATEM>* (§216). The superior faculty of desire is either will or refusal (§689). Representations that are the impelling causes of volitions and nolitions are MOTIVES. The incentives of the mind (§669) are either stimuli or motives (§677, 521).

Representations ... nolitions] The rational incentives of the mind

§691

To will or refuse without motives is to determine one's own power according to something distinctly represented, or its opposite (§663), which, however would not be distinctly represented (§690). Since this is impossible (§7), I neither will nor refuse without motives. Now in a state of total and complete indifference, I would will or

---

[a] This follows Wolff's division of human knowledge into three types: the philosophical (the knowledge of the reasons of things); the historical (the mere knowledge of things); and the mathematical (the knowledge of the quantity of things). Cf. DP, Ch. 1.
[b] Wolff: "*Rational desire* is sad to be that which originates from distinct representation of the good. [...] Rational desire is moreover called *volition <Voluntas>*" (WPE §880).

refuse without motives (§690, 655). Therefore in such a state, I neither will nor refuse. Motives are either true or apparent (§12).

§692

Since volitions and nolitions follow the intellect (§690), they either follow the pure intellect, in which there is utterly no admixture of confusion, and these are PURE VOLITIONS AND NOLITIONS, or they follow that intellect in which there is some admixture of confusion, and these are volitions and nolitions in which there is some sensitive admixture. Pure volitions and nolitions are only[290] produced from pure foresight and anticipation (§641), as well as purely intellectual judgment (§665). Hence all of my volitions and nolitions are such that in them there is a sensitive admixture (§604).

§693

There are always stimuli (§692, 677) among the motives that determine my willing or refusing (§690). And if certain associated stimuli among the motives impel me to the opposite of what the motives determine, then a CONFLICT BETWEEN THE INFERIOR AND SUPERIOR FACULTIES OF DESIRE (dissension) arises (a conflict between sensitive and rational desire, between flesh and reason).[291] If on the contrary, no stimuli impel me to the opposite of what the motives determine, then a HARMONY OF THE INFERIOR AND SUPERIOR FACULTIES OF DESIRE (agreement) arises. That faculty of desire is VICTORIOUS through which I completely desire or avert after a conflict.

§694

An agreement of the faculties of desire (§661, 693) originates in me from pure intellectual pleasure and sheer intellectual[292] displeasure (§656)[293] In the state of indifference, the faculties are neither[294] in agreement nor dissension (§693, 691). In the state of equilibrium that still remains following the foresight and anticipation of an object and its opposite,[295] the impelling causes to which the motives belong would be equally as strong as the opposite stimuli (§670). Therefore, neither of the faculties of desires would be victorious in that state (§693, 673). Therefore, I am then[296] in a state of preponderance when the inferior faculty of desire is victorious and when the superior faculty of desire is victorious (§674).

§695

The IMPELLING CAUSES[297] of desires or aversions that are sufficient for complete desires or aversions are COMPLETE, and those that are insufficient are INCOMPLETE. Hence complete stimuli are sufficient for complete sensitive desire or aversion (§677). Complete motives are sufficient for complete volitions and nolitions (§671).[298] Complete motives with associated stimuli are sufficient for the complete volitions and nolitions in which there is some sensitive admixture (§690, 692). However, a VOLITION OR NOLITION based on incomplete motives alone, or based on incomplete motives along with associated stimuli, is ANTECEDENT (previous, inclination, or excitation). Hence an antecedent volition is incomplete (§671), and nevertheless, it is efficacious in the first and[299] second sense of §675, although not in the same manner and degree as the complete volition.[300] A VOLITION OR NOLITION based on complete motives alone, or on complete motives with associated stimuli, is CONSEQUENT[a] (final, decisive, a decree).[b] And a CONSEQUENT volition or nolition is a DECISION (a proposition, or deliberate choice in the broad sense).[301] A decision is a complete volition or nolition (§671), and hence efficacious to the degree that we have called a means, although not always to the third degree that we have observed in §675.[302, c]

COMPLETE] DECISIVE

§696

The collection of the acts of the cognitive faculty concerning the motives and stimuli of that which is to be decided is DELIBERATION. Therefore, these questions arise in deliberation concerning any decision that must be made: (1) Is this thing itself and its opposite possible? (2) Is either one physically possible for me? That is, can either be actualized through my powers (§665), not just unqualifiedly, but also qualifiedly (§469)?[303] (3) How much power is necessary for actualizing it, and how much for its opposite (§671)? (4) How much good can come from one of these opposites? (5) How much from the other? (6) How much evil can come about from one of these opposites? (7) How much from the other? (8) How great will the good be from one of these opposites? (9) How great from the other? (10) How great will the evil be from one of these opposites? (11) How great from the other? (12) Which is better (§665)?

§697

SOMEONE DELIBERATING, insofar as they direct their mind to mathematical knowledge, ESTIMATES REASONS (calculates). By considering how much good or evil is to be hoped for from either side, they COUNT THE IMPELLING CAUSES, which they WEIGH. By judging[304] how great are the goods or evils that are to be hoped for, and by weighing carefully which is better, they PREFER one or the other. If they decide which is preferred, they CHOOSE. If someone deliberating were to decide[d] on something to find out whether their powers, and the extent of their powers, would be sufficient for actualizing it, they ATTEMPT it. And if someone deliberating were to consider all the impelling causes that seem bigger than the others in weighing to be as many smallest causes as they know there to be degrees of magnitude belonging to each and every impelling cause,[e] and thus compares them all,[f] they would SUM UP the impelling causes.

direct their mind to] seek to achieve || And if … all] And if they hold all motive causes that

---

[a] Wolff: "The rational appetite that originates from incomplete motives is called *antecedent will*: however, that which originates from complete motives is named *consequent will*. The same must be held concerning aversion" (WPE §920).
[b] Wolff: "A *decree* is a determination of the will to do something, or not to do so" (WTN1, §497).
[c] Compare with §675 (c): They are efficacious, but not always the most efficacious.
[d] Following a suggestion by Thomas, and in agreement with G/K, we have read *decernit* as *decernat*.
[e] G/K: "degrees of magnitude in the individuals"
[f] G/K: "compares the individuals"

appear greater to them when they are weighed to be so many smaller ones as is required for them to be equal to those that they hold to be smaller, and if in such a way they compare them with one another

§698

Anyone whose mind is conspicuously lacking in incentives is SLUGGISH, and anyone who is conspicuously equipped with these is ACTIVE. Anyone in whom pleasure usually predominates is ALWAYS CHEERFUL (a joyful person).[305] Anyone in whom displeasure usually predominates is ALWAYS SAD. Anyone for whom a preponderance toward the opposite is easy is FLEXIBLE; whereas, anyone for whom this is difficult is FIRM.

§699

Anyone who has a strong proficiency in deliberation is CIRCUMSPECT (considerate),[306] and anyone who is used to desiring and averting without deliberation is INCONSIDERATE. Anyone circumspect who decides with difficulty is INDECISIVE (not determined), while anyone circumspect who easily decides is READY (determined). Anyone circumspect who often changes their major propositions in practical syllogisms, or MAXIMS,[307] is VARIABLE (inconstant, changing). Anyone circumspect who very rarely alters good maxims is CONSTANT, whereas anyone circumspect who very rarely alters evil maxims is INCORRIGIBLE. Anyone who, in attempting something, employs the correct degree of powers is STRENUOUS, while anyone who is faulty in excess is VIOLENT, and anyone who is faulty in defect is WEAK (exceedingly impotent).[308]

READY] OF QUICK RESOLUTION || MAXIMS] THEIR CUSTOMARY DISPOSITIONS <*GEWÖHNLICHEN GESINNUNGEN*>

Section XVIIII. Spontaneity[309]

§700

I am altered (§505–699) internally (§126). Therefore, I am a finite (§254) and contingent (§257) being. Therefore, my existence is a mode (§134), and all of my states are also contingent in themselves (§205, 108). Therefore, the alterations of all of these are contingent as well (§124, 125). Therefore, all of my actions and all of my sufferings are contingent in themselves (§210). And hence all of my future actions are as well (§298). Hence, none of my actions and none of my sufferings are absolutely or intrinsically necessary (§105).

§701

NECESSATION[a] (constraint) is the alteration of something from contingent to necessary, and hence this is either ACTIVE, if it belongs to that which neces-

---

[a] "Necessitation" <*necessitatio*> is Baumgarten's own neologism, as noted by Clemens Schwaiger in "The Theory of Obligation in Wolff, Baumgarten, and the Early Kant," in *Kant's Moral and Legal Philosophy*, edited by Karl Ameriks and Oterfried Höffe (Cambridge: Cambridge University Press, 2009), 69–70.

sitates, which properly is nothing but a substance (§198), or it is PASSIVE, if it belongs to that which is necessitated. Passive necessitation is sometimes attributed to accidents that alter from contingent to necessary either through action or suffering, and sometimes to the substance in which these sorts of necessitated accidents exist.

§702

ABSOLUTE NECESSITATION (constraint) would be the necessitation through which something contingent in itself would alter into something absolutely necessary. Now, nothing can be altered into something absolutely necessary (§130). Therefore, neither can any action, nor therefore any action of mine. Hence the absolute necessitation of any action of mine is impossible (§7). All my actions are and always remain contingent in themselves, in the very act and after it, and hence their opposite is also possible in itself (§700, 104).

§703

There is a very large hypothetical possibility for the opposite of many of my actions (§168). Hence, the contingency, and also hypothetical contingency, of many of my actions is very large (§188, 700). And hence future actions are very contingent future things (§298).

§704

An action depending on a sufficient principle that is inside the agent is a SPONTANEOUS ACTION.[a] Whence spontaneity is attributed to (1) an action that depends on a sufficient principle that is inside the agent, and to (2) the substance accomplishing actions of this sort. Now every action properly as such depends on a principle that is inside the agent (§210, 37). Therefore, every action is properly spontaneous as such. Nevertheless, whereas alterations composed from actions and sufferings are sometimes called actions because of the more effective <*potiori*> part, insofar as they are sufferings, they are conceived of as not being spontaneous (§210).

§705

Many of my actions, or better, all of them properly speaking, and hence all the actions of my soul, are spontaneous, and therefore spontaneity is attributed to these as much as to my soul (§704). If something that alters itself is called an AUTOMATON, then the soul will be an automaton.

§706[310]

The smallest spontaneity is when a principle intrinsic to an agent suffices for only one smallest action (§704, 161). Therefore, the more and greater are the actions for which a

---

[a] Wolff: "*Spontaneity* is the intrinsic principle of determining oneself in acting. *And actions* are called *spontaneous* insofar as the agent determines these through a principle intrinsic to oneself without an extrinsic determining principle" (WPE §933).

principle intrinsic to an agent suffices, the greater is that agent's spontaneity, until it is the greatest, which would be in that agent in whom it suffices for the most and greatest actions. My soul possesses very great spontaneity (§705).

§707

EXTERNAL NECESSITATION (constraint from without) depends on a power existing outside of the necessitated substance, and it is either ideal or real (§701, 212). An action that is really and externally necessitated would be neither spontaneous, nor properly action (§704), but rather a real suffering (§210). Real external necessitation is UNQUALIFIEDLY EXTERNAL NECESSITATION (constraint). Therefore, actions constrained by unqualified external necessitation would be real sufferings. SUBSTANCES and ACTIONS that are not absolutely necessitated are FREE (cf. §719)[311] FROM ABSOLUTE COSTRAINT. SUBSTANCES and ACTIONS that are not necessitated by unqualifiedly external constraint are FREE from UNQUALFIEDLY EXTERNAL CONSTRAINT. Therefore, all my spontaneous alterations are free from[312] absolute constraint (§702), and all my actions, all of my soul's spontaneous actions, i.e. all actions properly speaking (§704), and my soul itself, insofar as it acts spontaneously, are free from unqualifiedly external constraint.

Section XX. Choice[313]

§708[314]

ACTIONS that are physically possible for me are POSITED AS WITHIN MY COMMAND, whereas realities that are physically impossible for me are POSITED AS OUTSIDE OF MY COMMAND. Therefore, a given action is either only unqualifiedly, or also qualifiedly posited as within my command, or a given action is either also unqualifiedly, or only qualifiedly outside of my command (§469). The opposite of the actions posited as within the command of some agent is either posited as within the command of the same agent, or as outside[315] of it (§9), and both, once again, either unqualifiedly or qualifiedly (§469). Those very actions, along with their opposites, that are at least posited unqualifiedly in the command of a given person are FREE AS TO THEIR EXECUTION by that person (cf. §719); and those actions whose opposite is posited as unqualifiedly outside of the command of a given person are MERELY NATURAL for that person. An ACTION that is free as to its execution and whose opposite is an equal physical possibility for a certain agent is PHYSICALLY[316] INDIFFERENT to the agent (indifferent in terms of the exercise of the act).

realities] real actions

§709

Merely natural actions are naturally necessary.[317] Hence in contradistinction to these, actions that are free as to their execution are physically contingent (§708, 469).[318] Hence, future actions are sometimes simply called FUTURE CONTINGENCIES.

§710

INTERNAL NECESSITATION (constraint) is that which depends on the internal determination of a necessitated substance. This is attributed to substances and their actions: (1) Because the actions of substances are considered to be necessitated by their own essence alone, which would then be ABSOLUTE (essential).[319] Necessitation of this sort, since it would alter actions into absolutely necessary actions (§702, 107), is wholly impossible (§702). (2) Because some actions are altered through the nature of a substance from being otherwise physically contingent for it to being physically necessary for it, either unqualifiedly or qualifiedly[320] (§469),[321] and this necessitation is PHYSICAL (natural).[322] Hence merely natural actions can be said to be necessitated through internal physical constraint (§709, 708).[323] Actions and substances internally constrained in neither sense by these are FREE (cf. §719)[324] FROM EITHER ABSOLUTE OR PHYSICAL INTERNAL NECESSITATION. Now, actions that are free as to their execution, and substances, insofar as these also accomplish actions of this sort, are constrained in neither sense (§709, 708), and therefore they are free from both absolute and physical internal constraint.

§711[a]

Many of my actions, and many of the spontaneous actions of my soul, are free as to their execution (§708). And therefore, these actions possess freedom[325] from unqualifiedly external constraint (§707) and freedom from both absolute and physical internal constraint (§710). These also belong to the soul insofar as it accomplishes such actions.

§712[b]

PREFERENCE is the knowledge that a substance has at its command from which can be known according to the laws of desires and aversions why it determines itself thusly and not otherwise concerning actions that are free as to their execution. But this can be known from foresight, anticipation, pleasure or displeasure (§665), stimuli, and motives (§677, 690). Therefore, the foresight, anticipation, pleasure or displeasure, stimuli, and motives that are known by a certain substance constitute its preference. If a SUBSTANCE thus[326] determines its own power concerning actions that are free as to their execution in the same way as can be known from its preference, IT DESIRES OR AVERTS ACCORDING TO PREFERENCE. Therefore, one who desires or averts something one does not foresee, and that one does not at all expect would arise through any effort[327] of their own, and that is neither pleasing nor displeasing, and who lacks all stimuli or motives, neither desires nor[328] averts according to preference. I desire and avert many things at my own preference. Therefore, I have a faculty of desiring and averting according to my own preference, i.e. CHOICE <*ARBITRIUM*>.

---

[a] Kant E3629, 1765–6 (across from §711): "(*crossed out:* All compulsion is either a) All necessitation (is either a necessitation) contrary to will (or with will,) either aesthetic or physical, a necessitation of the will itself [breaks off]"

[b] Kant E3630, 1762–3? 1764–8? (1769?) (beginning): "Action, in as much as it arises from the faculty of desire in such a way that I can be conscious of myself, I am not determined to it [breaks off]."

Those actions whose determination is posited as within the command <*potestate*> of a given substance are, for it, CHOSEN <*ARBITRARIAE*>. Many of my actions are chosen.

laws ... aversions] laws of the faculty of desire

§713

I DESIRE OR AVERT PREFERENTIALY (1) whatever I desire or avert according to preference, and then I desire nothing, or avert nothing, without preference, or RELUCTANTLY (§712, 665); or (2) if a preference contains sheer displeasure, or pure pleasure, or some remarkable preponderance. I desire or avert RELUCTANTLY (without preference, against preference)[329] when the preponderance is not very great towards preference, or when many and likewise great things seem to impel me to the opposite of that which I desire or avert. In this last sense[330] of reluctant, nevertheless, I desire or avert according to preference, and in that sense the reluctant action is still chosen (§712).

and then ... RELUCANTLY] According to this definition I desire or avert nothing RELUCTANTLY <*ungern*> that is free for me with regard to its execution

§714

Since CONSTRAINT IN THE STRICT SENSE (cf. §701)[331] is the production of a reluctant action, a CONSTRAINED ACTION, or an ACTION THAT IS RELUCTANT DUE TO AN UNQUALFIEDLY EXTERNAL CONSTRAINT,[332] would be an action that I accomplish with no preference, or against all preference, due to an unqualifiedly external constraint. But this would not then be an action, properly considered (§707). If I do something reluctantly according to preference as described in §713, then the preponderance of that which I desire or avert is either considered to be produced by me, and I am said to HAVE FORCED MYSELF, or, it is considered to be produced by something else outside of me (§22), and the ACTION is said to be RELUCTANT or CONSTRAINED DUE TO[333] QUALIFIEDLY EXTERNAL CONSTRAINT (which is to say, a mixed action resulting from a chosen action and a reluctant action due to unqualifiedly external constraint).[334]

§715

Reluctant actions, those to which I am said to force myself or to be qualifiedly externally forced by other things, come about according to my own preference (§714), and hence they are chosen (§712). They are called necessitated insofar as they are conceived as not being necessary if I myself, or other things, had not produced the preponderance that produced them (§701, 188).

§716

ACTIONS THAT ARE RELUCTANT DUE TO IGNORANCE OR ERROR are those actions that I would not carry out according to preference unless I were ignorant or in error about something. Since these actions nevertheless come about according to preference, they are also chosen (§712).

§717[335]

The smallest choice would be that which determines only one action according to the smallest preference (§161). Therefore, the more and greater are the actions it determines according to the greater preference, the greater is the choice (§160) until it is the greatest choice, which would be that which determines the greatest and most actions according to the greatest preference (§161, 712).

§718

Since choice is the faculty for desiring or averting according to one's own preference (§712), a substance endowed with choice will either have only a faculty of sensitively desiring or averting according to its own preference, or only a faculty of willing or refusing according to its own preference, or both a faculty of willing or refusing according to its own preference and a faculty of sensitively desiring or averting according to its own preference (§676, 689).

Section XXI. Freedom[336]

§719

The faculty of sensitively desiring and averting according to one's own preference is SENSITIVE CHOICE. The faculty of willing or refusing according to one's own preference is FREEDOM (free choice),[a, 337] cf. §707, 708, 710 (moral freedom, freedom in the unqualified sense).[338] The freedom of purely willing or refusing is PURE FREEDOM. Therefore a substance endowed with choice will only have sensitive choice, or only pure freedom, or freedom mixed with sensitive choice (§718). Those ACTIONS are FREE concerning which it is posited as within the command of some substance to determine itself to them through freedom, and this very SUBSTANCE, insofar as it is also able to perform free actions, is FREE.

§720

I sensitively desire and avert many things according to my own preference. Therefore, I have sensitive choice (§216, 719). I will and refuse many things according to my own preference. Therefore I have freedom (§216, 719). Many actions of mine, many actions of my soul, and the soul in many of its own actions are free. Something of the sensitive is mixed with all of my volitions and nolitions (§692).[339] Hence pure freedom does not belong to me;[340] for in my freest actions, my freedom is mixed[341] with sensitive choice (§719).[342] Both sensitive and free choice are actualized through the power of the soul for representing the universe according to the position of my body in it (§712, 667).

---

[a] Wolff: "The freedom of the soul is the faculty of spontaneously choosing that which pleases it from among many possible things, when it is not determined by essence toward any of these" (WPE §941).

§721

VOLUNTARY ACTIONS are (1) whatever actions are determined through the superior faculty of desire; in that case, INVOLUNTARY ACTIONS are those which are not determined by the superior faculty of desire. And in this sense, all voluntary actions are free,[343] but not all free actions are voluntary (§719).[344] For instance, suppose that I determined myself through sensitive choice when it was posited as within my command to determine myself through freedom, then an action of this sort will be involuntary, and yet free (§719).

are those … desire] are those that are brought about by another faculty ‖ are free] are free, if I am at the same time free in regard to their execution

§722

VOLUNTARY ACTIONS are (2) whatever actions are in no way reluctantly determined through the superior faculty of desire. In that case, INVOLUNTARY ACTIONS are those that I reluctantly will. In this sense, all my voluntary and involuntary actions are free (§719). But not all free actions are either voluntary or involuntary in this sense (§721).

reluctantly will] rationally desire or avert contrary to choice

§723

That which is more closely connected with freedom is MORAL IN THE BROAD SENSE (cf. §787).[345] Hence FREE DETERMINATIONS are MORAL DETERMINATIONS, PROFICIENCY in free actions is MORAL PROFICIENCY, and the LAWS of moral determinations are MORAL LAWS. MORAL PHILOSOPHY and MORAL THEOLOGY teach these, and the STATE resulting from them is a MORAL STATE.[346] Hence the MORALLY POSSIBLE is, (1) IN THE BROADER SENSE, that which can only be done through freedom, or in a free substance as such; (2) IN THE STRICTER, i.e. MORALLY PERMISSIBLE SENSE, it is that which can only be done through freedom determined in conformity with moral laws.[347] The MORALLY IMPOSSIBLE is, (1) IN THE BROADER SENSE, that which cannot be done solely on account of the freedom in a free substance;[348] (2) IN THE STRICTER or MORALLY IMPERMISSIBLE SENSE, it is that which is impossible through the freedom that must be determined in conformity with moral laws. Therefore, the MORALLY NECESSARY is that whose opposite is morally impossible; (1) IN THE BROADER SENSE, it is that whose opposite is only impossible through freedom, or in a substance insofar as it is free, and (2) IN THE STRICTER SENSE, it is that whose opposite is impermissible. Moral necessitation is OBLIGATION. Obligation to a reluctant action will be MORAL CONSTRAINT.

on account of] purely as a result of ‖ must be determined in conformity with moral laws] that is determined in conformity with one of the moral laws

§724

There can be no moral necessity in either sense where there is no freedom (§723).

Therefore, moral necessity does not destroy freedom and is not its opposite (§81), but is rather its consequence or logical conclusion <*consectarium*> (§14). Hence, not only can actions that are morally necessary, necessitated, and constrained be free, but they are such necessarily (§723).[349] Indeed, if THE MOST UNIVERSAL MORAL LAW is posited, i.e. the law determining all the free actions of every free substance (cf. §822),[350] then all free actions are either morally necessary or impermissible (§723).

§725[351]

The smallest freedom is that which only actualizes one volition or nolition according to the smallest preference. Therefore, the more and greater are the volitions or nolitions that it actualizes according to greater preference, the greater is the freedom, until it is the greatest freedom, which would be the freedom actualizing the greatest and most volitions or nolitions according to supreme preference (§719). Therefore, the more distinct is the preference according to which I will or refuse something, the more freely do I will or refuse it. Therefore, the more conscious I am of my motives, the more freely do I will (§712). It is morally necessary that one who wills or refuses most freely perceives the motives of willing and refusing most distinctly whenever they will or refuse (§723).[352]

§726

The law of choice is this: *From among those things that are free as to their execution, I desire whatever I prefer and I avert whatever I prefer.* And hence this is the rule of freedom: *From among those things that are free as to their execution,*[353] *I will and refuse whatever I prefer.* My free actions, as long as they are determined according to preference, are not necessitated through their impelling causes, stimuli, or motives by physical, non-external constraint (§707); for, the stimuli and motives are my representations (§677, 690). Hence they are my internal determinations (§37). My free actions are not necessitated through their impelling causes by internal physical constraint, as long as they are and remain actions that are free as to their execution when the motives are posited (§711, 710). On the contrary, speaking accurately, motives and stimuli indeed do not act upon the soul, and hence do not compel it (§714),[354] nor do they necessitate it morally (§723, 701), since they are only accidents of my soul (§505).

§727

If I am said to compel myself, it is posited as within my command to determine myself through freedom to that to which I compel myself; hence, I compel myself freely (§714, 719). If I am externally compelled in a qualified sense by something, I am determined according to a preference that is conceived as produced by something posited outside of me (§714). But if, in that case, it was posited as in my command to determine myself through freedom to that to which I was externally compelled in a qualified sense, then action of this sort is nevertheless free (§719).[355] Many of my actions to which I compel myself, or to which I am externally compelled in a qualified manner, are free.

Meier formulates the second and third sentences as follows: If I am constrained to something in a certain way from outside, and it is in my command for me to determine myself to it through freedom, then such an action is nevertheless free.

§728

Qualifiedly external constraints will be (1) productions of stimuli based on pleasing things, i.e. ENTICEMENTS, (2) productions of stimuli based on displeasing things, i.e. THREATS, (3) productions of motives based on pleasing things, i.e. PERSUASIONS, (4) productions of motives based on displeasing things, i.e. DISSUASIONS, (5) the continual actualization itself of displeasing things until the one compelling can be certain that the preponderance to reluctant action is followed, i.e. EXTORTION (§714). Many of my actions, even if I am compelled to these through threats and entice-ments, persuasions and dissuasions, and even extortions, are nevertheless free (§727).

§729

Through the system of pre-established harmony are denied <*tolluntur*> all the reluctant actions of the soul that would be produced by any finite thing through external constraint,[356] understood unqualifiedly (§714, 449). And in actions that are constrained through a qualifiedly external power,[357] that very preference from which they would originate, and which would really be produced by another finite being outside of the soul, is denied <*tollitur*> (§727, 449). Moreover, since according to this system the soul never really suffers from anything finite, and thus never does so in any of its free actions, in this sense, total independence from everything and from the whole world is ascribed to the soul (§354, 307).

And in … denied] And if it is in a certain way externally constrained, then through the same [system] it is maintained that the preponderance in the constrained preference is brought about through the soul's own power

§730

My free volitions and nolitions are called ELICITED ACTS OF THE SOUL, whereas the free actions of the rest of the faculties are called MASTERED ACTS, and insofar as they depend on the freedom of the soul, MASTERY is ascribed to the soul over these. Hence the mastery of the SOUL OVER ITSELF[358] is the faculty that produces the actions of one faculty, and then of another faculty, and then that once again produces their opposite, all according to a distinct preference. Therefore, the greater is the freedom, the greater is the mastery of the free soul over itself (§725). A significant lack of mastery over oneself is MORAL SLAVERY, IN THE BROAD SENSE. Whatever functions to promote mastery over oneself is LIBERAL (noble),[359] and whatever promotes slavery is SERVILE.

My … these.] The free rational desires and aversions of my soul are the actions of freedom itself, or the IMMEDIATELY FREE ACTIONS, whereas the free actions of the other faculties of the soul, however, depend upon freedom only as mediated by many intervening alterations, and are called ACTIONS THAT FOLLOW THE COMMAND OF FREEDOM, or which are mediately free.

§731

The actions of the soul that do not depend on freedom, except through many intermediate acts, are INDIRECTLY (mediately)[360] SUBJECTED to it; however, DIRECTLY (immediately) SUBJECTED to it[361] are those that I do or disregard through freedom without many other observable intermediate actions. Actions that are subjected to FREEDOM,[362] even through an indirect act, are nevertheless[363] free (§719).

§732

The determined proportion of the faculties of desire among one another in a certain subject is that subject's INNATE CHARACTER, and this is either UPRIGHT, when someone is habitually dominated by the superior faculty of desire, or ABJECT, when someone is habitually dominated by the inferior faculty of desire, whose greatest degree is called ADDICTION.[a, 364] And since a certain proportion of these faculties would more easily be directed to a certain type of desirable or loathsome thing, in this way are constituted the various types of TEMPERAMENTS OF THE SOUL. Therefore the temperament of a soul can be altered greatly and very often through exercises and habituation <*consuetudine*> (§650, 577).

Section XXII.[365] The interaction of the soul and the body

§733

Many of the motions of my body depend on my choice (§14). Those depending on a choice of which I am conscious are called the CHOSEN MOTIONS OF THE BODY (§712), and the chosen motions depending on the superior faculty are VOLUNTARY (§721). THE SOUL'S CONTROL OVER THE BODY is the dependency of the motions of the body on the choice of the soul. Hence my soul has control over my body.

depending on] depending more closely on; choice of] freedom of

§734

In the chosen and voluntary motions of my body, it can be sufficiently known from the soul why an event comes to pass in the body at this time and place and not another (§733). Therefore, the soul acts upon the body (§210), and influences it (§211).

§735

In the affects of the soul, there coexists a motion in the body that conforms to them. Since this motion can be sufficiently known from these same affects, this provides a new proof for the influence of the soul upon the body (§734).

---

[a] *PASSIO DOMINANS.* Baumgarten and Meier equate this with the German *Hang*, which is a technical term in Kant usually translated as "propensity," since Kant associates *Hang* with the Latin "*propensio*" and not "*passio dominans*." He thus defines it very differently than does Baumgarten here. Cf. *Religion*, AA 6:28.

§736

In external sensations, it is possible to sufficiently know from the power of the body why a certain alteration occurs in the soul. Therefore, the body acts upon the soul (§710),[366] and influences it (§211). Therefore, there is mutual influence (§734, 735), mutual harmony (§14), and interaction (§448) between my soul and my body.

§737

I do not experience that the chosen motions of the body are sufficiently determined through a power proper to the body or that sensations are sufficiently determined by a power proper to the soul. Therefore, one who assumes this major premise: "Whatever I do not experience, does not exist," thence concludes: "Therefore, the chosen motions of the body are not sufficiently determined through a power proper to the body, and external sensations are not sufficiently determined through a power proper to the soul. Hence, the body really influences the soul, and the soul really influences the body (§212) through physical influence (§450) ([arrived at] through experience)." If one takes this conclusion to be a sensation [i.e. something empirical], then the error of subreption (§546) is giving rise to fallacies of one's senses, because a false major premise has been assumed (§548).[a]

§738

The alterations of the body that depend on the soul, and the alterations of the soul that depend on the body, are harmonic[367] (§448).[368] In the harmonic alterations of the soul and body, an alteration of the soul coexists with an alteration of the body, or follows it, and the alteration of the body coexists with the alteration of the soul, or follows it (§733–6). Therefore, one who assumes this major premise: "Of those beings that coexist with or succeed one another, one really influences the other," thence concludes: "therefore, in harmonic alterations, the body really influences the soul, and the soul really influences the body ([arrived at] through experience)." If one takes this conclusion to be a sensation [i.e. something empirical], then the error of subreption (§546) is giving rise to fallacies of one's senses (§548).

Of those … other] Things whose alterations accompany one another or follow after one another affect each other in a real way || *Meier adds at the end:* Therefore, physical influence of the soul and the body on each other can be just as little proven or disproven through experience, as can pre-established harmony and occasional causes.

§739

My soul and my body constitute me, and I am one. Therefore, they are united with one another (§73, 79).[369] Their interaction, insofar as by means of it one human being

---

[a] G/K: "If he holds this conclusion to be a sensation, then the fallacies of his senses arise from the acceptance of a false major premise through the error of subreption." Cf. Meier: "Now if he holds this conclusion to be a sensation, then it is a fallacy of his senses, which arises through the error of subreption from a false major premise." We take the present active indicative form of the verb "*oriuntur*" as suggesting Meier's interpretation.

endures,[370] is a union (§205),[371] which is the closest, insofar as it very great (§734–6), and there is no union as great as this between my soul and any other body (§508).

Chapter II. Rational psychology

Section I. The nature of the human[372] soul

§740

A HUMAN SOUL is a soul in the closest interaction with a human body. And since a soul along with the body with which it is in the closest interaction constitutes an ANIMAL, a human soul along with the body with which it is in the closest interaction constitutes the animal that we call the HUMAN BEING.

§741

The human soul represents its own body to itself according to choice (§740). Therefore it acts (§210), and also moves its own body (§740, 734).[373] Therefore, it desires and averts (§712). Therefore, it acts and is a power for representing its own body (§210).[374] The human body is material (§296) and hence divisible (§427) as well as internally alterable (§244), and is thus a finite being (§255).[375] It is actual and it is a part of the world (§354). It can be known from the position of the human body in the universe why the human soul represents this, and not something else, obscurely, clearly, or distinctly[376] (§740, 736). Therefore, THE HUMAN SOUL is the power for representing the universe according to the position of the human body in it (§513,[377] 155).[a]

to itself according] and moves itself according

§742[378, b]

The following are required for thought: (1) the perception of a thing, (2) the perception of the notes sufficient for distinguishing the thing (§524), and (3) this thing's distinction itself (§67). Thought, however, is an accident (§191). Therefore, it can only exist in a substance or in an aggregate of substances (§194). An aggregate of substances would be THINKING MATTER[c] if the alterations of its parts or the collection of its accidents, by themselves and as a whole, resulted in a thought, [although] none of these was a thought prior to this.[379] This would be an aggregate of finite substances in the world (§354), one substance of which would confer more to

---

[a] G/K note that this reference is wrong, and suggest §515 in its place. However, §512 seems more likely.

[b] See the preface to the second edition for an explanation of why this paragraph was completely rewritten.

[c] *MATERIA COGITANS.* Locke planted the seeds of thinking matter in his *Essay Concerning Human Understanding* (Bk. IV, Ch. 3, Sec. 6), a possibility which he nevertheless downplays. The concept is rather closely associated with the French materialists Paul-Henri Thiry Baron D'Holbach (1723–89), Julien Offray de La Mettrie (1709–51) and Claude Adrien Helvetius (1715–71). See John Yolton, *Thinking Matter: Materialism in Eighteenth Century Britain* (Minnesota: University of Minnesota Press, 1983), 14ff.; Nicholas M. J. Churchich, *Critical Essays: Philosophical, Theological, and Scientific* (New York: Vantage Press, 2005), 231.

thinking than the rest (§272), and would suffer aid <*auxilia*> from them (§210, 321). But this substance will only suffer ideally (§451, 463). Therefore, in every [aggregated] thinking matter in the world, all the things required for thought that are to be furnished by what is finite would have a sufficient ground (§210, 212) in the unique power of one substance, and nevertheless: (1) this substance dominating a given aggregate would never possess thought by itself, which contradicts §30 and §220; (2) all the things required for thought that must furnished by what is finite would have a sufficient ground in the given dominating substance, according to what has been demonstrated, while at the same time, only once they[380] have been actualized through the aggregate of substances, i.e. only if they have a sufficient ground in the power of many finite substances (§210), which is absurd (§7).[a] Thinking matter is impossible in the world. Whatever can think is either a substance, i.e. a monad (§234), or a whole of which a part would be a substance capable of thought. Therefore, every soul is a substance, i.e. a monad (§504). Whatever can understand, can think (§69). Therefore, whatever can understand is either a substance, i.e. a monad, a spirit (§402), or a whole of which a part is a spirit. A whole of spirits is a MYSTICAL BODY[b] (a moral person). The intellectual soul is a spirit (§504, cf. §402, 296[c]). The human soul is a substance (§740). Therefore it is a monad, i.e. a spirit (§741).

§743

The human soul subsists *per se* (§742, 192). Therefore it is not a substantiated phenomenon (§193). However, since it represents according to the position of the human body in the universe, which is in perpetual motion (§417, 296) and which hence always alters its position (§283, 281), the soul's representations are always being altered (§512). And since these are the internal determinations of the human soul (§37, 741), the human soul is an internally alterable and hence a contingent (§202) and finite (§255) substance. That every human soul is a finite and contingent substance is likewise obvious from the following: The human soul represents according to the position of the body (§741). Therefore, it perceives some things distinctly, and others indistinctly (§512). However, to conceive something distinctly is a reality (§515, 531). Therefore, the human soul does not have the greatest degree of reality (§161), and hence has a limit (§248). Therefore it is a finite and contingent (§257) substance (§742).

---

[a] G/K: "(§210, the presupposition of which is §7)"
[b] This phrase originally referred to the unity of all Christians in one body as described in *Epistle to Romans*, Ch. 12, 4 and 5. See, for instance, Thomas Aquinas, *Summa Theologica*, Part 3, q. 8, a. 1. Kant uses it to describe the systematic unity of the moral world in the *Critique of Pure Reason* (A 809/B 837) and in the *Metaphysics of Morals* (AA 6:367). See also the Herder lecture notes from Kant's metaphsyics course (AA 28:144) and Reflection 5401. It occurs also in Achenwall's *Juris naturalis pars posterior*, Book 2, §15, from which Kant also lectured.
[c] G/K consider this to be a problematic reference, since §296 concerns matter as a physical body. However, since the reference is found in all the editions containing this re-written paragraph, perhaps Baumgarten's point is contradistinction.

§744[381]

The human soul knows, desires, and averts (§741). These are partially different actions (§267). Therefore, the human soul has partially different faculties (§216), which are not powers strictly[382] speaking (§197, 59); much rather, these are conceived through the one power of the soul for representing, in the strict sense (§521–[383]720);[384] nor are they mutually posited outside of one another, since accidents (§191) do not exist outside of their substance (§194); nor can they be accurately said to act mutually upon one another, since action is only proper to substance (§210), and even less can they be said to mutually influence one another (§211).

§745

The human soul, which is a monad (§742)[385] and contingent (§743), can only originate from nothing[386] (§236); it can only perish through annihilation (§237);[387] it is not extended, nor does it fill up space (§241), i.e. it does not completely fill a place <*non est in loco repletive*> (§241). Nevertheless, since it coexists with those monads that are simultaneous and posited outside of itself, it is in space (§239) and thus in a place (§281) such that some of those monads that are posited outside of it are closer, and others are more remote (§288, 282). If the collection of those that are simultaneous and closer to the HUMAN SOUL is called its SEAT, then the human body is the seat of the soul pre-eminently over all other bodies, and some of its parts pre-eminently over its other members are seats of the soul (§409).[388]

§746

The human soul does not have a quantitative magnitude (§744, 243), and is indivisible (§244). Perishing through division is PHYSICAL CORRUPTION. Therefore physical corruption of the human soul is impossible in itself (§15,[389] 745),[390] i.e. the human soul is absolutely PHYSICALLY INCORRUPTIBLE.

quantitative magnitude] extended magnitude ‖ indivisible] absolutely indivisible

§747

Indeed, the human soul does not admit of the three dimensions belonging to extended beings (§290, 745). Nevertheless, philosophical and mathematical knowledge of it is still possible, just as of the human body (§743,[391] 249). The human being consists of a finite soul and a finite body (§741, 743), and hence is internally alterable as well as being a finite and contingent being (§202, 257). Therefore, philosophical and mathematical knowledge of the human being is possible (§249), i.e. philosophical ANTHROPOLOGY and mathematical anthropology, or ANTHROPOMETRY, just as is empirical anthropology through experience. The collection of rules that are to be observed in knowing the human being is ANTHROPOGNOSTICS.

does not … to] cannot be measured as can ‖ as of the human body] just as it is of the human being, because it consists of two parts

§748

If a finite being were altered into an infinite being, the infinite would originate (§125,

227) and not be eternal (§302), which is absolutely impossible (§252).[392] The alteration of a human being into an infinite being is APOTHEOSIS. Therefore, apotheosis is absolutely impossible.

§749

The total similitude and equality of human souls, or even of only two, is impossible (§271, 272). Therefore, the total agreement or identity of the sensations, imaginations, foresights, judgments, tastes, displeasures, pleasures, stimuli, motives, errors, desires, aversions, volitions, nolitions—either in many or in very few humans—is a chimera (§590).

§750

The human soul moves its body (§740, 734).[393] Therefore, it has a FACULTY of moving that which is posited outside of it, i.e. a LOCOMOTIVE FACULTY (§216),[394] which, just as the rest of the soul's faculties (§744), is actualized through its power of representing the universe according to the position of the body (§741, 417).[395]

§751

The human soul represents some parts of this universe to itself as singular parts (§740, 736), therefore as thoroughly determined (§148). To the thorough determination of the parts of this world pertains a nexus of these same parts with the all the rest (§357).[396] Therefore, the human soul represents some parts to itself as connected with all the parts of the world. However, a thing can only be known as connected with another if the other is somehow known (§14). Therefore, the human soul perceives all the parts of this universe, and therefore it also perceives all the states of this universe (§369).[397, a]

§752

According to the position of its body, the human soul represents to itself (i) a present state of the world, i.e. it senses (§534,[398] 751); (ii) a past state, i.e. it imagines (§557); and (iii) a future state, i.e. it foresees (§595). The sensations of the human soul are representations of all the parts of the world[b] that are simultaneous with it, which are more or less distinct, confused, or obscure, corresponding to how the objects of the sensations are in relation to the human body (§751). The imaginations of the human soul are the representations of all past parts of the world[c] that precede the sensing soul, i.e.[399] those which existed before a specific act of sensation. Likewise, these imaginations are more or less distinct, confused, or obscure, corresponding to how their objects were in relation to the human body (§751).[400] The foresights of the human soul are representations of all the future parts[d] of the world that are to exist after the act of the sensing soul, and these are less or more distinct, confused, or obscure corresponding to how their objects will be in relation to the human body (§751).

---

[a] G/K: "the individual parts of this universe, therefore also the individual states of this universe"
[b] G/K: "the individual parts of the world"
[c] G/K: "the past individual parts of the world"
[d] G/K: "the future individual parts of the world"

imaginations of the human soul … sensation] imaginations of the human soul, in each of its present states, are representations of the past parts of the world that precede the said present state || foresights of the human soul … soul] foresights of the human soul, in each of its present states, are representations of all future parts of this world that follow this state

§753

Just as §752 proved that sensation, etc., is in every human soul, the same can be shown regarding the rest of the actions of the soul that are to be discovered in it through experience, and specified through empirical psychology (§576 ff.).

§754

The human soul distinctly represents according to the position of its body (§741). Therefore, it understands (§402) and is a spirit (§742, 216).[401] Hence it is again obvious that all human souls are unequal and that one is the most perfect of all (§405). The human soul is a finite spirit (§743) and part of this world (§355).

distinctly represents] can in part distinctly represent

§755

Every spirit is a substance (§402). Therefore it is a power (§199),[402] and hence the sufficient ground for the inherence of some accidents (§197), and to this extent an agent (§210). And since it is an intellectual substance (§402), it has the faculty of actualizing some distinct representations (§216). Therefore, it has a faculty of determining its power towards these (§210) and hence of desiring (§663). Since it averts the opposite of whatever it desires, a spirit has the faculty of averting (§663). The desires and aversions of a spirit are its internal determinations (§37). Therefore, they are in a universal nexus with the rest of its internal determinations (§49). Therefore, they are also in a universal nexus with the rest of its knowledge, which is an internal determination (§37), and for this reason they come about according to the preference of a spirit. Therefore, a spirit has choice (§712), and since its preference can be distinct (§402), it is free or has freedom (§719).

Every spirit] Every finite spirit || power] power in the narrow sense || internal determinations] internal and contingent determinations || Therefore, they are in a universal nexus] Therefore, at least some of these are free as to their execution, and are in a universal nexus

§756

The human soul is a spirit (§754). Therefore, it has freedom (§755). And since spirituality,[403] intellectuality, personality (§641, 754),[404] freedom, absolute simplicity (§744), and incorruptibility absolutely and necessarily belong to it (§746), they are not its modes[405] (§108). Hence they are either essential determinations or attributes, because they are internal determinations (§37, 52). If one of these is denied, then the human soul would be denied (§63).[406] Hence a human soul that is entirely unable to conceive of something distinctly or to determine itself distinctly according to preference, that loses all its personality and freedom,[407] that is composed of many powers as parts mutually posited outside of one another[408] or that is to be corrupted physically, is a chimera (§590).

§757

The human soul is immaterial and incorporeal (§744, 422). Those who deny that the human soul is an immaterial substance are MATERIALISTS IN THE PSYCHOLOGICAL SENSE (cf. §395),[409] and are in error, since they take the human soul to be a mere accident of the body (§742), or to be a material atom (§429), or to be some other very subtle corpuscle (§426). The universal materialist is also a materialist in the psychological sense (§395), but not everyone holding that the human soul is a material substance is necessarily a universal materialist (§395).

§758

The power for representing the universe according to the position of the human body in it, hence including this power's dependent modes, is the collection of the internal determinations of the soul, which are the principles of its alterations and inherent accidents (§751–5). Therefore, this same power, including those of its determinations that depend on the position of the body, is the nature of the human soul (§430). Hence, whatever is actualized in the human soul through this power determined according to the laws and rules of every faculty[a] is natural[410] to the human soul (§470), insofar as it is contradistinguished from the supernatural (§469).[411] In this sense, free and moral actions are also natural for the soul (§756, 755), although these are not merely natural (§709).[412] Aside from this proper sense of nature in the human soul, and hence of what is natural for it, there are other improper and synecdochic senses. Sometimes these senses wrongly originate from the confusion of the parts with the whole. And sometimes they wrongly originate because a particular name stuck to what can be conceived in the human soul through a particular mode, modification or state of nature, and then after this, when the rest of the natural properties <*naturalibus*> that lacked a particular name had to be contradistinguished, they were given the name of the genus in the strict sense, because then only this was available. Thus, for example, those that are inborn are always called natural in contradistinction to those that are acquired; and those which are natural are always contradistinguished from those which are artificial, related, chosen, or, in the end, obtained through habit, etc. (cf. §710).

The power ... modes] The collection of the faculties of the power of representing the world insofar as it is determined through the position of the human body

§759

Those properties that are natural to the human soul according to the laws prescribed by its power, and which succeed one another in the human soul, come about following the course of nature with respect to the human soul (§758, 471), and along with that which coexists in the human soul according to the same laws, they follow the order of nature with respect to the human soul (§473). The preternatural, or those things that[413] are not actualized through the power of the soul to represent the universe according

---

[a] *singularum facultatum.* This is ambiguous; it could mean "of the individual faculties," or "of every faculty." G/K opt for "*der einzelnen Vermögen,*" i.e. of the individual or singular faculties.

to the position of its own body following the laws and rules of its faculties, are super-natural if they are not actualized through universal nature (§474).

§760

The human soul belonging to the best world is in the greatest universal pneumatic and pneumatico-mechanical nexus (§464, 754). Therefore, it is connected with the all the spirits and bodies[a] belonging to the best world (§48), but unequally (§272). Therefore, the human soul is most particularly <*maxime*> connected with one body and one spirit (§161).

Section II. Psychological systems

§761

PSYCHOLOGICAL SYSTEMS are doctrines that seem well-suited[414] for explaining the interaction of the soul and the body in the human being. Therefore, psychological systems are particular systems (§462), and they are either simple or composite (§457). None are possible aside from the psychological systems of pre-established harmony, physical influence, and perhaps occasional causes[415] (§458).

§762

If one of the simple general systems[416] is maintained, then one of the simple psychological systems is also maintained (§761, 457). Therefore, if universal pre-established harmony is demonstrated (§463), then psychological pre-established harmony is likewise demonstrated.[417] However, if one of the simple psychological systems[b] is maintained, then one of the general systems need not necessarily be maintained, not even the most similar (§761, 457). If the human soul and the human body can be in the closest interaction through pre-established harmony, they are also connected in the best world through pre-established harmony (§461), such that physical influence or the system of occasional causes[418] must not be admitted except when the interaction is impossible through pre-established harmony (§462).

not even ... similar] nor need one generally accept precisely the same one in cosmology, as one accepts in psychology, if one wishes to explain in the particular case how the community of the soul with the body is constituted

§763

Because it is simple, the psychological system of physical influence posits that all harmonic alterations of every human soul and body occur through physical influence (§457). Therefore, if one harmonic alteration of either one human soul or one human body can be proven possible through pre-established harmony in the best world, then the place of the system of physical influence in the best world can no longer be

---

[a] G/K: "with the individual spirits and bodies"
[b] Reading *systematibus* for *systematis*. No edition makes this correction. Please see endnote 416 above.

defended (§762). Because it is simple, the psychological system of pre-established harmony posits that all harmonic alterations of every human soul and body happen through a pre-established harmony; on the same ground, the psychological system of occasional causes[419] posits that the same things happen through infinite power alone[420] (§457). Therefore, if one alteration of either one human soul or one human body were[421] impossible in the best world according to pre-established harmony, the place of its psychological system in the best world could no[422] longer be defended. Therefore, if one harmonic alteration of either one human soul or one human body is possible in the best world through pre-established harmony or physical influence, then the place of the system of occasional causes[423] in the best world (§762, 460) can no longer be defended. The psychological system of physical influence is no more obvious through experience than are the systems of pre-established harmony and occasional causes[424] (§737, 738).

§764

The psychological system of physical influence maintains that in harmonic alterations the human soul really influences its body and that the human body really influences its soul (§761, 450). Hence according to the psychological system of physical influence, (1) in none of the harmonic alterations occurring in the human body does the body act through its own power (§212).[425] However, all the alterations of the human body, as parts of the world that the soul represents, can be known sufficiently from the power of the soul (§354, 751).[426] Therefore, they are all harmonic (§448), and, according to the psychological system of physical influence, in none of its own alterations does the body act through its own power; in every alteration, rather, it really suffers from the soul. If the body never acts, it does not react (§213). Therefore, according to the system of physical influence, in the world there is transeunt action of the soul upon the human body without reaction whenever the soul acts upon its body,[427] which, if it occurred even once, would go against §410.

influences its body] influences its body, and brings about all the harmonious alterations in it || its soul] its soul, and brings about all the harmonious alterations in it || own power] own power, hence none of its own natural alterations at all

§765

The psychological system of physical influence maintains that (2) the human body really influences its soul whenever an alteration occurs in the human soul that can be known sufficiently from the power of the body (§764, 448).[428] Therefore, according to the psychological system of physical influence, the body really influences the harmonic alterations encountered in the soul, although the body nevertheless—as must be maintained according to the same system (§764)—never acts in its own alterations. According to the system of physical influence, the soul does not act at all in sensing (§212), while it nevertheless represents the present state of the world, no less than rest of the world's states, to itself through its own proper power (§751).

Meier reduces this paragraph to the following: The body must affect the soul in a real way, and therefore act at some time, and yet it never acts, so consequently this system contradicts itself, and is impossible. The human soul must behave purely passively in regard to all its natural alterations and therefore must bring about neither its sensations nor any of its other natural representations, which is false.

§766

The human body consists of elements (§420), or monads, that represent its own world, and every single one of the world's parts can be known from every single one of these elements,[a] (§400), and hence so can all the alterations of the soul,[b] which are parts of the world (§354). Therefore, every action of the soul is a harmonic alteration (§448,[429] 22). Now, every volition and nolition of the soul is its own[430] action (§210,[431] 690). Therefore, every volition and nolition of the human soul is a harmonic alteration belonging to it. Now, according to the psychological system of physical influence, the human soul does not act by its own power in its own harmonic alterations, but really suffers from the body. Therefore, according to the system of physical influence, the soul, while not acting on anything whatsoever in any of its own volitions and nolitions, suffers from the body, which goes against freedom (§755).

Meier reduces this paragraph to the following: All rational desires and aversions of the soul would be mere passions [if the system of physical influence were true], and they would have no spontaneity, thus also there would be no freedom of the will, which is absurd.

§767

According to the psychological system of occasional causes[432] (1) the human body does not act in any of its harmonic alterations, but an infinite being does (§761, 452); whence, in the same manner as was shown in §764, it is obvious that, according the system of assistance, the body does not act in any of its alterations, but only an infinite being does. (2) According to this same system, the human soul does not act in its own harmonic alterations, but only an infinite being does (§761, 452); whence in the same manner as was shown in §766, it is obvious that, according to the psychological system of assistance, the human soul does not act in any of its volitions and nolitions on anything whatsoever, and in these only really suffers from an infinite being, which would likewise go against freedom (§755).

Meier reformulates this paragraph as follows: According to the psychological system of occasional causes, only the infinite substance brings about all harmonic alterations of the human soul and the human body: consequently 1) [only it brings about] all alterations of the body, and the body itself loses through this all its own activity, and cannot be composed of true substances, which is false; and 2) [only it brings about] all alterations of the human soul, through which it in the same way loses all of its activity and freedom.

---

[a] G/K: "from these as individuals can be known the individual parts of the world"
[b] G/K: "the individual alterations of the soul"

§768

According to the psychological system of pre-established harmony, each part of the interaction actualizes the harmonic alterations occurring within itself through its own power, and ideally suffers from the other part (§761, 448). Hence the psychological system of pre-established harmony maintains that (1) the chosen motions of a body, no less than its merely natural and vital motions, are sufficiently determined through its own mechanism and through that of the bodies around it; and that (2) the sensations of the soul, no less than any of its freest thoughts, are sufficiently determined through its own representative power (§758, 433).

thoughts] thoughts, desires and aversions

§769

Suppose that psychological harmonists want to give the reason for some harmonic alteration in a human being, seeking it (1) in the power of that very part of the interaction in which the harmonic alteration is observed; (2) in the other part of the interaction that they maintain it ideally influences; and (3) in the infinite power that they maintain as concurring with these. And suppose I say that they are deceived; they most certainly gave the true reason (§448, 450), although they added a false one through their hypothesis. Suppose in the same case an influentialist or an occasionalist fails; not only do they disregard a large part of the true reason, but they also deny it (§450, 452).

Section III. The origin of the human soul[433]

§770

When a human being is conceived, the soul that will then be in the closest interaction with its body (which is of the kind human beings have on this earth) either pre-exists conception, or begins to exist at conception itself, or, finally, somewhat afterward.[434] Whoever posits the first is called a PREEXISTENTIST.

§771

Those who maintain that the existence of the human soul begins at conception itself, or somewhat afterward,[435] either prefer its origination from the parents, and are called TRADUCIANS, or else they claim the soul first[436] originates from nothing, and are called INDUCIANS (infusians, coexistentists).

§772

Whoever maintains that the human soul is actualized[437] from nothing is called a CREATIONIST. Hence the inducian is a creationist (§771). A preexistentist can be creationist (§770). The traducian is not a creationist, and vice versa (§771). Whether the traducians derive the originating soul from the soul of the parents, like a small flame from another small flame, or from the body, they must admit either that the new soul originates from a simple part of the parents, or from a composite part (§224).

If it is the first, then the soul does not originate, but rather pre-exists (§227); if the second, then the new soul will not be a monad but a composite being in the strict sense (§225), which goes against §756, 757. The soul can originate only from nothing (§745). Therefore, it does not originate from the parents (§228).

§773

If the PROPAGATION OF HUMAN SOULS THROUGH TRANSMISSION <*TRADUCEM*> is taken to be the unity of continually different human souls with a body (such as human beings have on this earth) through a continuous succession of parents and progeny in the world by which the human race (such as it is on this earth) is propagated in such a manner that the souls of the offspring, as well as their bodies, pass over and are transmitted from the bodies of the parents to their own proper place where they dwell quite apart,[438] then this propagation can be conceived of (1) as likewise involving the origin of the soul. It is thus claimed that the soul that is about to come into the closest interaction with a body (such as the body is for a human being on this earth) simultaneously originates through the intervening act of conception, and this again either from the parents (which was treated in §772), or through the parents. In the second case, it must be assumed that God can introduce a determinate power into the human soul through which it could produce only specific <*aliqua*> individuals of its own species from nothing, and that this is accompanied by God's own concurrent creative power for producing most of the realities in the soul that is about to originate, since only some very limited realities proceed from the soul of the parents. Whoever maintains this opinion can be called a CONCREATIONIST.[439]

§774

The propagation of human souls through transmission can be conceived (2) such that it does not involve the origin of the soul. Rather, it is claimed that the pre-existing soul already existed[440] in the closest interaction with a part of the semen, or, more accurately, with a semen-like microscopic organism, back through many generations prior to the intervening act of conception, and thus that the representative power of that very soul was slowly increased and unfolded, just as the body of the selected semen-like microscopic organism, which was to enter upon a greater stage, was also gradually brought closer and closer to its own great transformation and developments (§773).

§775

The origin of the soul and the propagation of the soul through transmission can be distinguished (§773, 771). Those who also maintain the origin of the soul through transmission from the parents can be distinguished from those who maintain that it must be derived from the parents (§773,[441] 772). Therefore, not everyone who admits transmission, however understood, is guilty of psychological materialism (§772, 757).

Section IIII. The immortality of the human soul[442]

§776[443]

As long as either one smallest alteration that is natural to a being inheres in it, or in general, one smallest accident naturally inheres in it, its nature endures (§469, 29), and the being is alive (§430). If all the alterations that are natural to a being are finished or cease, or, in general, all the inherent accidents end or cease in it, its nature ends (§469, 23), and the being dies (§430). Therefore, the LIFE OF THE HUMAN BODY, or the duration of the nature that it possesses as a human body, is continued as long as there remains one smallest vital or chosen motion that is natural for it insofar as it is a human body (§733, 740). The DEATH OF THE HUMAN BODY, or the end of the nature that it possesses as a human body, is the complete cessation of vital and chosen motion. Therefore, death as defined in §556 is the death of the human body.

§777

Since an animal is composed of a soul and the body with which it is in the closest interaction (§740), its nature is composed of the nature of the body and of the soul, both posited in the closest interaction (§430). Hence, as long as there are some harmonic alterations of the soul and the body that are posited in the closest interaction, an ANIMAL IS ALIVE. The cessation of all harmonic actions of the body and soul posited in the closest interaction is THE DEATH OF THE ANIMAL. Now, all harmonic alterations of the soul and the dying body posited in the closest interaction cease through the death of the body (§776, 448).[444] Therefore, the death of the body is also the death of the animal, and the death of the human body is the death of the human being (§740). Therefore, death as defined in §556 is the death of the human being (§776).

§778

THE DEATH OF THE ANIMAL is either ABSOLUTE, i.e. the cessation of all harmonic alterations of the soul with every animal body, or it is only RESPECTIVE (a transformation and metamorphosis of the animal),[445] i.e. the cessation of the harmonic alterations of a soul with only some certain body with which it was in the closest interaction. The death of the human being is either absolute or only respective; i.e. when a body dies, of the kind we as humans experience there to be on this earth, either all closest interaction of a human soul with any *<aliquo>* body ceases, or it enters into a new interaction of the same sort with another body (§776, 777).[446]

§779

Since every day some parts of the human body cease to be in the closest interaction with the soul, and some parts enter into this interaction, it is clear in what sense it can be said that the human being dies and is revived daily (§777).[447] The doctrine according to which it is maintained that the death of the human being is only animal transformation is called the BANISHMENT OF (absolute) DEATH.[a]

§780[448]

THE LIFE OF THE HUMAN SOUL, or the duration of its nature, continues as long as there is one smallest surviving accident that is natural for it insofar as it is a human soul[449] (§776). Now, as long as the human soul endures, there is perception or representation of the past, present, and future states of the world (§742, 400), which, according to the position of a certain body, can be distinct (§741),[450] i.e. an accident (§741) that is natural (§758) for it. Therefore, the human soul, as long as it exists, is alive. THE DEATH OF THE HUMAN SOUL, or the end of its nature, is likewise the end of its existence. Now the existence, nature, or life of every human soul is contingent in itself (§743, 430). Therefore, the death of the human soul is possible in itself (§81, 104).

§781[451]

A MORTAL BEING is a being that can die, and the possibility of dying is MORTALITY. That which cannot die is IMMORTAL, and the impossibility of dying is IMMORTALITY. Mortality and immortality are either absolute or hypothetical (§15, 16). The human body and the human being not only possesses a fairly great absolute mortality, but also a fairly great hypothetical mortality (§777, 168), and the soul that is to be annihilated possesses not only absolute mortality, but also hypothetical mortality (§745, 780). Absolute immortality indeed cannot be attributed to the soul (§780); however, since what is indestructible cannot die in the innumerable ways in which the body can die (§746), the soul possesses a very great hypothetical immortality. No substance of this world (§354, 358)[452] is annihilated (§227, 228).[453] Therefore, when the body (such as humans have on this earth) dies, the surviving human soul lives immortally (§780, 742). THNETOPSYCHISTS err in holding that the human soul dies along with the body.

No substance ... immortally] If it can be proven that the human soul will never be annihilated, then it remains when the human being dies and when the body of the kind that human beings have on this earth also dies, and the soul lives immortal in eternity

Section V. The state after death[454]

§782[455, b]

The human soul preserves its spirituality, freedom, and personality after death (the death of the body and human being, such as we experience on this earth) (§781, 756). If the preservation of its own intellectual memory is called immortality, then in this

---

[a] The seminal text here is Leibniz's "A New System of Nature," published in the *Journal des savants*, 27 June 1695 (G 4: 481), where he announces the natural impossibility of death "in a strict metaphysical sense."

[b] Kant E3631, 1780–9 (above): "Separation of the soul from the body."

sense also the human soul is immortal (§781, 641). In terms of exercise, either its total perceptions over a very long time are only sensitive, or they soon light upon the intellectual. Those who maintain the first are HYPNOPSYCHISTS, and if they deny that the soul ever understands after the death of this body, they are PSYCHOPANNYCHISTS. Before its death, the human soul had clearly or distinctly known something (§754). This reality (§520), which is never completely sterile (§517) insofar as it is a reality, has nothing but realities indefinitely as logical consequences <*consectaria*> (§140), and it is indefinitely in a universal nexus with the spirituality, intellect, and reason <*ratione*> of the soul, which again are realities (§531, 49), and which as such have nothing but realities indefinitely as logical consequences (§23, 140). Hence the nexus among clear or distinct knowledge of this life and the spirituality, intellect, and reason <*rationem*> of the soul is again a reality that has real logical consequences (§140) indefinitely. However, the real and natural logical consequences of all of these cannot be increased indefinitely (§23, 162) without distinct perceptions (§631), conclusions (§642),[a] and volitions or nolitions (§665, 690). Hence the human soul, which naturally preserves its nature after death (§780, 781), at least eventually shows an intellectual life in spiritual actions (§639), and the psychopannychists are in error.

HYPNOPSYCHISTS] ADVOCATES OF THE SLUMBER OF THE SOUL ‖ PSYCHOPANNYCHISTS] ADVOCATES OF THE ETERNAL NIGHT

§783[456]

After death, the understanding <*intelligens*> human soul either exercises its personality in order to call to mind distinctly its own state in this life, or it does not (§782). Those who hold the latter can be called THE FRIENDS OF THE CUP OF FORGETFULLNESS.[b] The former is more natural (§583, 561).

§784

The state of the human soul after death can be considered (1) when the absolute death of the human being is maintained (§778).[457] In that case, it is maintained that the human soul after death is destitute of all body, or that there is no body with which it will again come to be in the closest interaction (§742, 740). Its status can also be considered (2) when the respective death of the human is maintained, such that the soul is again sent[458] into the closest interaction[c] with a new body (§778). The commencement[d] of a new closest interaction with a new body is called PALINGENESIS (regeneration, metensomatosis, and metempsychosis, taken more broadly). Those who maintain palingenesis either defend the cup of forgetfulness and likewise posit a new body (of

---

[a] §646 seems to be a more likely reference.

[b] *PATRONI LETHAEI POCULI.* According to post-Homeric legend, the Lethe <Λήθη> was one of the five rivers of Hades, and the dead drank from it to forget their past lives before being reborn. Cf., inter alia, Plato (*Republic* 10.620c) and Virgil (*Aenid* 6:703–51). Λήθη also means oblivion or forgetfulness in ancient Greek.

[c] Kant E3632, 1765–6? (1769?) (across from "closest interaction"): "removal of either a virtual or a local nexus <*remotio nexus vel virtualis vel localis* >."

[d] Kant E3633, 1764–9? (1771–2?) 1773–5?? (next to "commencement … PALINGENESIS"): "The separation of the soul from the body is either local or virtual <*Separatio animae a corpore est vel localis vel virtualis*>."

the kind known on this earth) or they maintain it without either of these additions.[a] The former improbably[459] defend METEMPSYCHOSIS in the strict sense, as well as CRASS METEMPSYCHOSIS (§783).[460]

§785

The human soul that endures after the death of the body that it had on this earth (§781)[461] still represents all the parts of this universe[b] (§752, 780),[462] and therefore the bodies of this universe (§155). The bodies that are simultaneous to the soul act on it, and they suffer from it. The soul suffers from the bodies that are simultaneous with it, and influences them (§408), but the soul does not influence two of these equally, neither does it suffer from two of these equally (§272). Therefore, there is one body with which the human soul that endures after the death of the body comes into the closest interaction (§448,[463] 739). And hence if the soul of this sort is called separate, then it must be understood in respect of the body such as we experience there to be for humans on this earth,[464] and the death of the human being is only an animal transformation (§779)[465] and palingenesis, which, however, may have been wrongly confused with crass metempsychosis (§784).[466]

animal transformation] an exchange of one body for another || metempsychosis] metempsychosis, through a lack of acumen

§786

The human soul that endures after the death of this body is in the closest interaction with another one (§785).[467] In its different states, this new body will sometimes be more congruent with the former body, and sometime less so (§270, 265). Therefore, it will have some state in which it will be the most congruent with the body that, in this life, was in the closest interaction with the soul (§161), and hence it will be the same[468] (§70).

different states] different successive states

§787[469]

Just as the perfection of a finite spirit (1) is either absolutely necessary, or contingent (§147), (2) either natural or supernatural (§496), (3) either internal or external (§98), (4) either moral in the broad sense or not (§723): so also those things that are good for a spirit, or which, when they are posited, perfection is also posited (§100), are: (1) either metaphysical or contingent (§147), (2) either natural or supernatural (§469), (3) either personal or adventitious (§660), (4) either moral in the broad sense, or not (§723). Those things that are morally good in the broad sense in a given spirit are more closely connected with its freedom either *a priori* (§24) as grounds (§14) and as antecedents of a certain one of its states, or *a posteriori* (§24) as consequences (§14)

---

[a] Kant E3634, 1780–9 (next to the last two sentences): "Metempsychosis of Michelangelo, Galilei and Newton. (of Nelli in Florence)." [Note: As noted by Lehmann and following him by Ameriks and Nargon in their translation of Kant's *Lectures on Metaphysics* (Cambridge: Cambridge University Press, 1997), 594, note 233, Kant speaks in his anthropology lectures of one Nelli of Florence, who remarked on the metempsychosis of genius, specifically mentioning the three above.]

[b] G/K: "the individual parts of the universe"

and as logical consequences of a certain one of its states (§596), or both (§24). Those that more closely depend on a given [faculty of] freedom are called MORAL IN THE STRICT SENSE, and sometimes unqualifiedly. Hence, those things which are GOOD for a spirit and that depend more closely on its freedom are MORAL, STRICTLY SPEAKING, and the perfection that is posited when such things are posited is BLESSEDNESS. The collection of perfections that belong to a spirit is HAPPINESS. The complement of its blessedness with respect to happiness, [i.e. what must be added to blessedness in order for a finite spirit to be happy] is PROSPERITY, and those goods that, when posited, prosperity is posited, are PROSPEROUS (the physical good, in the strict sense). The happiness of a finite spirit is the collection of prosperity and blessedness.

§788[470]

The EVILS of a spirit that more closely depend on its freedom are MORAL, STRICTLY SPEAKING (§787) (the evils of fault, sins), whereas the MORAL EVILS IN THE BROAD SENSE of a spirit are more closely connected with its freedom. Imperfection based on the latter is MORAL CORRUPTION IN THE BROAD SENSE, whereas an imperfection based on the former is MORAL CORRUPTION IN THE STRICT SENSE. The collection of imperfections that belongs to a spirit is UNHAPPINESS. The complement of its moral corruption in the strict sense with respect to unhappiness [i.e. what must be added to moral corruption in order for a finite spirit to be unhappy] is MISERY, and the evils that, when posited, the misery of the soul is posited, are INJURIES <*DAMNA*> IN THE BROAD SENSE (physical evils in the strict sense). Unhappiness is the collection of misery and moral corruption.

§789

The human soul in THIS LIFE, i.e. as long as it lives in the closest interaction with a body of the kind we experience there to be for humans on this earth, continually alters (§418, 754).[471] None of these alterations is absolutely objectively indifferent (§654). Therefore, they are all either good or bad, or both. Those alterations of the soul that are good and evil at the same time (as indeed all things are (§264)),[472] are either equally, or unequally good and bad (§70). The more good alterations there are than evil ones, the more they posit happiness than unhappiness, whereas the more evil alterations there are than good, the more they posit unhappiness than happiness. Based on the better part, the former alterations must be termed good, and the latter evil (§787, 788).

§790

Suppose a thing that is just as evil as it is good. It would not have the supreme degree of reality (§246, 248). Therefore, it would be a finite being (§248) and hence contingent (§257), and its opposite would also be possible (§101). Since its existence would be contingent (§109), the existence of its opposite would be possible (§101). But the opposite of a thing of this kind could only exist outside of it (§81, 7).[473] Moreover, the good and the evil of this opposite would be wholly equal to that of the thing already supposed (§81,[474] 267). Therefore, two totally equal actual things outside of one another would be possible, which goes against §272. Therefore, a thing that would be just as good as evil cannot exist. Therefore, there are no alterations of the human soul, unless they are either good or evil. Therefore, every human soul in this life is either happy, or unhappy (§789).

this life] this life, in every moment of its duration,

§791

The human soul that endures after the death of the body continues to alter (§781, 782). Therefore, its happiness or unhappiness is increased in any given moment of its endurance (§790, 162). Therefore, either the human soul that endures after the death of the body will enjoy greater happiness than in this life, and is a BLESSED SOUL,[475] or it will be troubled by greater unhappiness, and is a DAMNED SOUL.[476] The blessedness into which the soul is supposed to enter at once after this life either coexists with the soul as long as the latter endures, or is at length followed by damnation. The damnation into which the soul is supposed to fall at once after this life either coexists with the soul as long as the latter endures, or it is at length followed by blessedness (§790, 789). In either case, the former is more natural (§739, 740).

Section VI.[477] The souls of brutes[478]

§792

Since each soul is that which in a being can be conscious of something (§504), it has a cognitive faculty (§519), and this faculty is either inferior or superior (§520, 524[a]). The first would be a MERELY SENSITIVE SOUL. An animal that has only a sensitive soul is a BRUTE, whereas an animal whose soul is a spirit is a RATIONAL ANIMAL <*ANIMAL RATIONALE*>.[b] Therefore, the human being is a rational animal (§754, 740).

§793

The souls of the brutes are in the closest interaction with an animal body (§740),[479] and hence clearly and obscurely represent their own body (§792, 736). Therefore, the souls of brutes are powers for representing the universe according to the position of their body in it (§741).[480] Hence, they are substances (§198), monads (§234), and simple beings (§230) without parts outside of parts[c] (§224). They are finite (§202, 792), indivisible (§244) and hence physically incorruptible (§746), immaterial and incorporeal (§422). They are equipped with sensation, imagination, foresight, and the rest of the faculties that must be actualized without distinct knowledge through the power for representing the universe according to the position of the body (§792), and hence

---

[a] G/K correct §524 to §624.
[b] Here, and throughout this section, *rationale* in its various declensions is consistently translated as "rational" and not "ground."
[c] G/K: "indivisible"

they must be impelled by sensitive desire and aversion (§667), choice (§718), instincts, flights, and stimuli (§677), and even by affects (§678).

§794[481]

With the easier questions: *Whether brutes have a soul, and whether it is a rational soul* (§792, 793), the following must not be confused: (1) whether all the bodies appearing[482] on this earth, aside from the human, are destitute of a soul (§504); (2) whether some of these are[483] seats of a rational soul (§745); and (3) whether all those that are[484] animal bodies either already enjoy some use of reason, or eventually will (§782, 639).[485]

§795

The souls of brutes are destitute of an intellect (§792). Therefore, they are not spirits (§402). They lack personality (§641), reason (§640), will, refusal (§690), and freedom (§719). They are not immortal as human souls are (§781–4). They are capable of neither happiness nor unhappiness, neither now nor ever (§787, 738).

Section VII.[486] The finite spirits aside from human beings

§796

The SPIRITS endowed with a higher essential degree of intellect than human beings are SUPERIOR, whereas those that have a lower grade are INFERIOR. They are both finite,[487] and either happy or unhappy (§790). The former are GOOD SPIRITS (beautiful spirits), and the latter, EVIL SPIRITS.

§797

Every finite spirit, whether it be superior or inferior to the human being, has an actual body that it is in the closest interaction with (§785, 796),[488, 489] one that either constantly gravitates towards a certain centre outside of itself, or not. The former is an inhabitant of a certain total body in the universe, i.e. of either a fixed one [i.e. a star] or a wandering one [i.e. a planet], etc.

§798

Whatever degree of intellect a superior finite spirit may have, it nevertheless does not have the greatest degree (§248), and hence it does not represent everything most distinctly (§637), but rather such that it can[490] be known from its body why it represents these and not other things more purely, more deeply, more distinctly, confusedly, or obscurely (§797, 512). Therefore, every finite spirit has an inferior cognitive faculty (§520).

§799

There will be no finite spirit, either superior or inferior to the human being, that can be physically[491] corrupted (§746); and hence even if one of its bodies is destroyed, it will nevertheless survive unless it is annihilated (§745). As long as it endures, it preserves personality by increasing rather than decreasing, or entirely ceasing, the use of the intellect, reason, and freedom (§782), and it is more natural for it to remember its previous states distinctly than is the cup of forgetfulness[492] (§783). Therefore, just like the human soul (§781, 783), every finite spirit is immortal according to its own nature, i.e. according to its power for representing the universe (§782),[493] and, as long as it endures, it is more natural for it to remain in the blessedness or damnation into which it once entered, than it is for a spirit at some point markedly blessed to then become damned, or vice versa (§791).

PART IIII: NATURAL THEOLOGY

Prolegomena

§800

NATURAL THEOLOGY is the science of God, insofar as he can be known without faith.[a]

§801

Natural theology contains the first principles of practical philosophy, teleology, and revealed theology. Therefore, it rightly belongs (§2) to metaphysics (§1).

§802

Natural theology considers (1) the concept of God,[1] and (2) his operations.[2]

Chapter I. The concept of God

Section I. The essence of God

§803

THE MOST PERFECT BEING is that to which belongs the highest perfection among beings, i.e. that being in which as many and as great things agree as greatly with as

---

[a] This definition differs greatly from Wolff in his *Preliminary Discourse*: "That part of philosophy which deals with God is called Natural Theology. For that reason, natural theology can be defined as the science of those things that can be understood to be possible through God. And indeed philosophy is the science of possible things, insofar as they are possible" (DP §57). In the *Natural Theology*, Wolff echoes his previous definition: "Natural theology is the science of those things that are possible through God; that is to say, it is the science of those things that belong to him, and those things which are understood as able to be done <*fieri*> through those things that belong to him" (WTN1 §1). In the addition to §1, Wolff explains why he does not define natural theology traditionally, as Baumgarten will do: "Theology is popularly defined as the science of God and divine things acquired through the principles of reason. This is not because, as one might think, this definition holds something different than does ours. For, the divine things are those which are therefore conceived of as possible because God is granted [to exist] and because such attributes belong to him. And although we did not add to our definition 'that very science with the support of the principles of reason,' or, as others love to say, 'the science to be acquired only through the natural light without doubt according to the correct use of the faculties of the soul that belong to it by nature,' this is nevertheless understood *per se*. We treat natural theology as a part of philosophy. However, it is proper to all philosophy that knowledge of possible things is acquired only by seeking it through the light of nature, that is, by the correct use of the faculties of the soul that naturally belong to it" (WTN1 §1). Still, Baumgarten's definition seems more to the point. According to Wolff's definition it is not immediately clear that truths drawn from articles of faith by means of natural reason would not belong to natural theology (although Wolff would indeed have denied this). Baumgarten clarifies this by defining natural theology as what can be known philosophically in the absence of faith. Notably, the same formula is found in Baumgarten's definition of philosophy itself: "Philosophy is the science of the qualities in things that are to be known without faith" (*Acroasis logica* §35). See our Introduction, p. 21 above.

many and as great things as can agree with the most and the greatest of the things possible in any one being (§185). Therefore, some plurality is absolutely necessary[3] in the most perfect being (§74).[4]

Meier renders the first sentence as: THE MOST PERFECT THING is that to which absolutely the very greatest perfection belongs among all things: i.e. in which as many and as great of manifold parts agree as much with as many and as great of determining grounds, as all of this is possible in one thing.

§804

The predicates of the most perfect being are called its perfections.[5] In the most perfect being, there are as many of the most highly agreeing perfections as there can be in one being simultaneously, or as are compossible (§803).

§805

Every perfection of the most perfect being is as great as it can be in any one being (§803, 804).

§806

The most perfect being is a real being (§803, 135). Therefore, as much reality belongs to it as there can be in a being. The most perfect being is the most real being (§805, 804),[6] i.e. the being in which there are the most and greatest realities. It is the supreme good and metaphysically the best (§190).

§807

All realities are truly positive, and no negation is a reality (§36). Therefore, if all realities are indeed maximally joined together in a being, no contradiction would ever arise from them (§13). Therefore, all the realities in a being are compossible. Now, the most perfect being is the most real of beings (§806). Therefore, the totality of realities <omnitudo realitatum> belongs to the most perfect being, and indeed the greatest realities that are possible in any being (§805, 190).[7]

is the most real of beings] has all realities that are compossible

§808

When a reality is posited, a negation is denied (§36). Now, all realities must be posited in the most perfect being (§807). Therefore, all negations must be denied.

all negations … denied] it does not at all have a negation among its internal determinations

§809

In every impossible thing, something must be posited and denied at the same time (§7). It is either a negation, or a reality (§36, 90). No reality is to be denied in the most perfect being (§807). No negation is to be posited in the most perfect being (§808). Therefore, nothing in the most perfect being is to be denied and posited at the same time. The most perfect being is possible (§8).

§810

Existence is a reality compossible with the essence and the rest of the realities (§66, 807). Therefore, the most perfect being has existence (§807).[a]

§811

GOD is the most perfect being. Therefore God is actual (§810, 55).

§812

The predicates of God are perfections (§811, 804); they are all the greatest realities (§807).[8] His very possibility is the greatest (1) internal and absolute possibility (§165), since the most and the greatest things are compossible in him (§805, 807); and it is the greatest (2) external and hypothetical possibility, since the most fecund and serious grounds in him have the most fecund and serious consequences in every nexus of all the possible worlds that there can be outside of God (§168).

§813

There are no negations in God (§808), therefore no negations in the strict sense, no privations (§137), no metaphysical, contingent (§146), physical, or moral evil in any sense[9] (§788).

sense, no] sense, neither absolutely necessary nor contingent negations, no ‖ any sense] any sense, and consequently there is no imperfection in him

§814

In the concept of God, not only are wholly negative notes impossible (§525), but indeed so too are those partially such (§813, 808), although many maximally real things in him seem negative to us (§12),[10] partly because we express negations with affirmative terms, and partly because we do not sufficiently remember to affirm the negation of a negation (§36, 81).

§815

The PERFECTIONS of God are either absolute or respective in him, and among the latter there are some relative perfections (§37):[11] either[12] they can be represented by us without a note of action and are INACTIVE, or[13] they cannot be and are OPERATIVE.

---

[a] This is essentially a Leibnizian version of Descartes' *a priori* or ontological argument. Compare this with Wolff's treatment, which begins the second volume of his natural theology: "*God necessarily exists.* For God contains all compossible realities in the absolutely highest degree (WTN2 §15). This being [i.e, the most perfect being] is truly possible (WTN2 §19). Wherefore, since the possible can exist (WO §133), existence can belong to the same; consequently, since it is a reality (WTN2 §20), and since the realities are compossible that can belong to one being (WTN2 §1), it is included in the number of compossible realities. Now, necessary existence belongs to the absolutely highest degree (WTN2 §20). Therefore necessary existence coincides with God, or, which is the same, God necessarily exists." (WTN2 §21).

§816[a, 14]

The first concept of God is the internal perfection of God from which all the remaining internal perfections can thus be eventually deduced such that this very perfection cannot be afterwards deduced from another internal perfection of God by those desiring to avoid circular logic (§40, 39). Now, such a deduction of the remaining internal perfections is possible from the infinite perfections of God (§24, 49), since any given ground is the greatest (§812, 166), most sufficient (§169), and hence the unqualifiedly final (§170) and greatest essence (§171).[15] Therefore, the first concepts of God are infinite, and any of these, when chosen to be the essence, is nevertheless the unique essence of: God (§40, 77).

first concept] essence || logic] logic, and the representation of it is the first concept that one forms in a systematic theology concerning God || Therefore .... essence of God] Accordingly, every perfection of God can be regarded as his greatest essence; and, if any of these perfections were to be taken as the essence of God, then none of the remaining ones can be regarded as being his essence at the same time. Thus regardless of this fact, God has only one essence and there are therefore also possible infinitely many first concepts of God in a systematic theology

§817

Although there is in God the greatest (§808, 167) and maximally universal nexus (§172), and thus everything in God in the truest sense originates from everything else (§876),[16] nevertheless it is easier for us to know the rest of his perfections from one perfection of God than it is from another (§527). Therefore, it is preferable to[17] choose as the essence that perfection from which we hope to deduce the rest most easily (§816). It is so far from the case that all plurality in God is impossible that, rather, it is absolutely necessary that some plurality be posited in and through his very essence (§812, 816).[18]

§818

Aside from any essence that you may choose (§817), God is also determined in regard to the rest of his internal perfections (§816) as much as anything whatsoever can be determined in regard to an internal perfection (§812). Therefore, God is actual (§54).

§819

God is determined in regard to existence (§818, 811). Therefore, God is a being (§61, 57), and neither a negative nor privative non-being (§7, 54).

---

[a] Kant R3635, 1762–3? (1764–8?):
"Internal predicate of God <*Dei praedicatum internum*>

External <*externum*> { independence <*independentia*>
dependence of all on him <*dependentia omnium ab illo*>"

§820

From God's possibility, it is valid to draw the conclusion that he exists, i.e. his existence is sufficiently determined by his very essence (§809–11),[19] and his existence is indeed the greatest (§805) collection of the most and greatest affections compossible in any one being, or the eternal (§320)[20] complement (§55) of the greatest essence (§816), regardless of which you choose (§817).[a]

§821

The greatest (§812) unity belongs to God (§819, 73), i.e. the inseparability of the most and greatest realities (§173). Hence, it is clear (1)[21] in what sense he could eminently be said to be the perfect unity, for instance, how even those perfections of God that seem to be maximally sterile are nevertheless part of his[b] essence (§816); (2) when the supreme unity of God is posited, not only is it not the case that a certain plurality of inseparable perfections is denied, but rather that they are posited in that unity (§74).[22]

unity, for instance:] unity, and also

§822

The greatest (§812) transcendental truth belongs to God (§819, 90), i.e. supreme order of his own perfections (§175, 89), supreme possibility (§812), the supreme nexus (§817),[23] and supreme agreement <*convenientia*> with the strongest rules (§179,[24] 184) such as *the law of the best, in general:*[25] *that the best be joined together with the best* (§482, 187); and such as *the law of the best in beings: that in the most perfect being, the best of the compossibilities be joined together with the best* (§803).[26]

transcendental] unconditional metaphysical ‖ *Meier adds at the end:* Consequently, God is the most certain thing, because he has the greatest metaphysical truth, which can be proven from his essence and from all other possible things, just as can his actuality.

§823

A non-actual God would be a being enjoying all realities, and yet missing some reality (§66, 812). In regard to all internal perfections, he would be determined as greatly as a being can be internally determined (§818), and yet, in regard to some of these perfections, he would not be so determined (§54). Therefore, the opposite of divine existence is impossible in itself (§15). The existence of God is absolutely necessary (§102). God is the necessary being (§109),[27] whose supreme existence (§820) is also his essence (§819), with §817, however, being preserved.[28]

whose ... preserved] and has no contingent qualities, and because of this no internal state

---

[a] This is an expansion of §810–11. Once again, compare with Wolff: "*God exists through his own essence. For God is a being from himself* (WTN1 §67). And to be sure, a being from itself has the sufficient ground of its own existence in its own essence (WTN1 §31). And for the reason that God has the sufficient ground of his own existence in the same, consequently when the divine essence is posited, at the same time its existence also is (WO §118). Therefore he exists through his own essence" (WTN1 §72).

[b] Kant E3636, 1776–8: "logical perfection (sufficient) or practical."

§824[29]

If God were not actual, then the principle of contradiction (§823, 7), which is the first principle of both the form and the matter in all our proofs, would be false.[a] Therefore, even though many sciences could be completely proven without any theological premise (§1–800), nevertheless, unless God were actual, there would be neither these sciences themselves nor their objects (e.g. §61, 354, 504); indeed, on the contrary, they would not be possible (§8).

§825

God is the necessary being (§823, 824). There are no modes in a necessary being (§111). Therefore, there are no modes, or predicable accidents, in God.

§826

If we discern something IN A NECESSARY BEING that is partially the same and partially different from those things represented in a contingent being, and nevertheless we do not understand the differences well enough and have not found a particular name for it, then we call it an ANALOGUE OF THAT WHICH we have noticed AS SIMILAR IN A CONTINGENT BEING. It is ATTRIBUTED TO GOD BY ANALOGY EMINENTLY (excellence) if the realities in its concept seem to prevail, or REDUCTIVELY[b] (by way of negation)[30] if negations seem to reign.[31]

§827

If we discern some things in a necessary being concerning which it is absolutely necessary that they be hypothetically necessary, then, insofar as they are similar to modes in regard to their hypothetical necessity (§108), they are[c] called ANALOGUES OF MODES (§826), and insofar as it is absolutely necessary that they exist with hypothetical necessity in God through [his] essence (§823, 54),[32] they are attributes[33] (§107).[34] Hence the divine attributes can be divided into the attributes that are more similar to the attributes of finite beings, and those that are more similar to the modes of finite beings. However, these last are nevertheless attributes, since, in the essence of God, there is the sufficient ground (1) of their existence, insofar as they are contradistinguished from the indeterminate (§54). A contingent being can be undetermined (§34, 134) in regard to many attributes. A necessary being can be undetermined in regard to no attributes, also by means of its essence (§820). In the essence of God, there is the sufficient ground (2) of the endurance, eternity, and immutability of those attributes that are in God at any moment.[d] The essential limit of contingent beings is

---

[a] As Allen Wood has noted, Kant treats the ontological argument in the *Lectures on Philosophical Theology* as an analytical argument (e.g. AA 28: 1027). See his *Kant's Rational Theology*, 102–3. Wood, however, does not note that in this Kant is following Baumgarten.
[b] *Per reductionem.* Baumgarten himself glosses this as *"in geläuterter Bedeutung"* [in a refined sense].
[c] Kant E3637, 1760s–70s (next to "are ... hypothetical"): "nexus with the contingent <*nexus cum contingentibus*>."
[d] Wolff: *"A being from itself has the ground of existence in its own essence. And indeed, a being from*

the sufficient ground of why they must change internally and continually as long as they exist. In the necessary being, essential infinitude is the sufficient ground of the opposite: (3) it is the ground of why other attributes instead of these could have existed in God forever and ever <*ab aeterno in aeternum*>,[a] and hence (4) why the existence of these and not others is determined thusly and not otherwise, i.e. only through hypothetical necessity (§102).

§828

HOLINESS is the reality of a being that truly[35] denies many of its true imperfections;[b] hence, the MOST HOLY is that whose reality denies all of its imperfections. Now, through the totality of all the greatest realities in God is denied all imperfections in the same (§142,[36] 808). Therefore, God is the most holy.

§829

In God there is no imperfection (§828). Therefore, there is no essential, no accidental, no internal, and no external imperfection (§121,[37] 88).[38] The same is clear from §813.

§830

In God there is a sufficient ground for why his perfections exist in him (§822,[39] 823). Therefore, there is a power, in the strict sense[40] (§197). Hence, God is a substance (§199).

a substance] the necessary substance

§831

God has the greatest (§812) power (§830), and therefore he has the power sufficient for actualizing the most and greatest accidents (§203).

§832

Accidents do not exist outside of their substances (§194).[41] Therefore, the power sufficient for actualizing the most and greatest accidents suffices for actualizing the most substances. Therefore, it suffices for actualizing everything (§191, 247). The power sufficient for actualizing something is POTENCY. Hence OMNIPOTENCE is the power sufficient for actualizing everything. God is omnipotent (§831).

---

itself is independent from every other being (WTN1 §30), and consequently it does not have the ground of its own existence in another (WO §851). Thus it has this in itself (WO §70). Wherefore, since the sufficient ground of why something does or can belong to it or be actual (WO §168), the ground of existence of the being by itself ought to be contained in its very essence" (WTN1 §31).

[a] Cf. 1 Chr. 29: 10.

[b] Wolff: "*Holiness* is the consistent and perpetual will only to do what is right" (WTN1 §1063).

§833

Whatever is absolutely impossible is nothing (§7).[42] Therefore, whatever would be capable of the absolutely[43] impossible would be capable of nothing (§469).[44] God is capable of everything (§832). Therefore, the omnipotence of God does not extend to the absolutely impossible. That which is impossible for something is[45] that for which its powers to actualize are not sufficient (§469).[46] In this sense nothing <*nulla res*> is impossible for God. Therefore, everything <*omnis res*> that is impossible for us and for all finite beings is possible for God (§832).[a]

whatever ... nothing] whatever can make this actual, can do nothing

§834

Miracles are possible (§475). The power of God is sufficient for actualizing everything possible (§832). Therefore, God can accomplish miracles in the strict sense <*rigorosa*> (§477, 833).

§835

God can actualize all possible worlds (§832). Therefore, he can actualize the best (§436) and the most imperfect world, without exception (§442).

§836

God is substance (§830), and has no modes (§825).[47] Therefore, he is a necessary substance (§202), and neither has an internal state (§206)[48] nor is he modifiable (§209). Whence, it is once again obvious that the world cannot be a modification of God (§388).

§837

In a necessary substance, all origination and perishing, as well as origination from nothing and annihilation, are absolutely impossible. God is a necessary substance (§836). Therefore, in God all origination and perishing are absolutely impossible (§227, 228).

§838

Every substance is a monad (§234). God is a substance (§830). Therefore, he is a monad, and a simple being (§230).[49] When the supreme simplicity of God is posited, it is indeed denied that he is composed in any fashion <*ulla ratione*> from parts outside of parts (§224). And yet, the most real (§807) difference of many things in God is not denied (§807), for it is false even in finite [substances] that all really different things are posited mutually outside of one another (§755).[b]

---

[a] G/K: "All that is impossible for us and for every finite thing is possible for God." In this and the last sentence, the use of "thing" <*res*> is essential; for while much is impossible for us and for God (namely whatever is contradictory), many *things*, i.e. non-contradictory possibles, are impossible for us but possible for God.

[b] Problematic reference. §756 seems to be the more logical reference, wherein Baumgarten calls the human soul that would be composed of parts outside of parts "a chimera."

§839

God is a necessary being (§823, 824). The determinations of every necessary being are absolutely and internally inalterable (§132).[a] Therefore, God is absolutely and internally inalterable (§126, 127).[b] The same thing is clear in this manner: If God were absolutely and internally alterable, at least one of his internal perfections could exist after another (§124). Hence, the existence of the perfection that would precede it could be denied. This is an internal reality of God (§37). Therefore, one of God's realities could be separated from the others (§72),[50] which goes against the supreme unity of God (§821).

§840

If God were composite, he would be extended (§241), and the power of inertia would have to be attributed to him (§832, 294). Hence, he would be material (§295). Therefore, he would be divisible (§427), and so also internally alterable (§244, 126), which goes against §839. Therefore, God is a simple being (§224). And since he is a substance (§830), he is a monad (§230). It is once again obvious that universal materialists err (§395).[51]

§841

In God there are no simultaneous things posited mutually outside one another, no parts (§840), hence no space (§239). Therefore, God is neither extended, nor does he fill up space in the sense that extended things are said to fill it up (§241).

§842

God does not have a quantitative magnitude (§838, 243), although he is the greatest being (§161), possessing the most and greatest realities (§807, 812). It is once again obvious that God is indivisible, and indeed absolutely (§244).

quantitative magnitude] extended magnitude

§843

The totality of the greatest realities that there can be is the greatest degree of reality (§247, 248). This belongs to God, the most real being (§807, 812). Therefore, God is a real and infinite being (§248). The same is obvious from the fact that God is a necessary being (§823, 258).

Meier adds at the end: Consequently, in regard to all of his internal determinations God is actually everything at once that he can be.

[a] G/K: "All determinations of a necessary thing are absolutely and internally inalterable." However, "*omnis entis necessarii*" means "of every necessary being."
[b] Wolff: "*The will of God is unalterable.* If it can become <*fieri*>, then we would suppose that the will of God is alterable. Since something actual alters insofar as it no longer remains the same (WTN1 §290) that which God previously wished he will not wish, but something else different than it, and what he now wishes he will not wish later, but something rather different from this. Therefore, because in turn the eternal is not that which it is, since it previously was not, or it is not something that will be, since it now is not (WTN1 §39), God does not wish eternally; whereas, since this is absurd, it is impossible for the divine will to alter" (WTN1 §368).

§844

All the perfections of God have the greatest degree of their own reality that they can have in a being (§812). Hence all of these perfections are themselves also infinite (§248). Agreement in the most perfect being pertains to the supreme reality of any one of these perfections (§139, 140). Therefore, in a being in which there is [at least] one infinite reality, there are all, and a being in which there are all realities, these realties are supreme (§843).[52] Therefore, that in which there is [at least] one infinite reality is God (§811).[53] From this one can gather on what ground many perfections of God—first these, then those—could have been chosen as first concepts (§816)—and why there may not be admitted an equally potent author of evil aside from God. MANICHAEISM is the doctrine maintaining that an author of evil exists who is equally as potent as God, and this doctrine is an error.

§845

In regard to his internal perfections, God is actually whatever he can be (§843, 259). It is once again obvious that God is internally inalterable, (§252)[54] and a necessary being, but only if the [vicious] circle is avoided (§843, 256).

§846[55]

Many gods are impossible. For as long as there were many, they would be partly different (§74), and hence something in one god would not be in the other (§38). This would either be a reality or a negation (§36). If it were a reality, then that which lacks it would not be God (§807). If it were a negation, then that which contains it would not be God (§808). If one reality were posited in one god but another of equal value in another god, in neither case would there be the totality of realities; hence, neither would be God (§807). Now, the God whom we have been contemplating up to this point (§811–45) is thus supremely one <*unum*>, composed of all the greatest and absolutely inseparable realities (§821). Consequently, any being different from him neither is nor can be what God, the necessary being, is according to what we have seen to this point (§811–45). For this reason, the God whom we have contemplated thus far is the unique <*unicum*> God (§77). POLYTHEISM is the doctrine that maintains the existence of many gods, and it is an error. We more truly venerate the supreme uniqueness in God (§842) in so far as he, the greatest being, is distinguished (§173) through the most and greatest differences (§844) from all things, even those things that are the greatest of their kind, e.g. the universal nature of the best world, and the greatest spirit among finite things. This very great difference thus extends to the relations themselves, so that a relation as excellent and great as that between God and a given third being cannot exist between a thing that has not, up to this point, been considered to be God, and the [same] third thing (§812, 817). Indeed, the supreme uniqueness of God denies the equality of anything that is not God with him, even if it is otherwise the greatest, and it denies not only nearly total similitude, but also any similitude that itself would deny the infinite dissimilitude that must be maintained between God and all other things (§844). However, the supreme uniqueness of God does not deny the plurality of the greatest things within God, nor the supremely infinite respective difference of these very same things (§37, 174). Indeed, it much rather posits in his infinite characteristics something that distinguishes God from all things (§67).

§847

Once again the simplicity of God is obvious as follows: If God were composite, his parts would be substances posited outside of one another (§225, 282). Only one <*unicum*> of these would be an infinite substance (§846). Therefore, the rest would be finite (§77, 248). Hence, some absolutely necessary imperfections would have to be posited in God (§250, 155), which goes against §828.

§848

God does not have a figure (§280, 847). CRASSER ANTHROPOMORPHISM is the error that attributes a figure to God, e.g. a human figure. SUBTLER ANTHROPOMORPHISM is the error that attributes to God the imperfections of finite things, e.g. those of humans (§828).

§849[a]

There is nothing successive in God (§839, 124). Nor, therefore, is there time in God (§239).[56] Thus[57] he is not in time such that he would form a part of successive things (§124, 837). And while origination and perishing are absolutely impossible for him (§837), he has the greatest (§812) and only really infinite (§844, 846) duration (§299). Hence, he is eternal (§302), coexists with all time, and is sempiternal (§303). He was, is, and will be (§298). God exists.

such ... things] in such a way that he either follows other things, or after him other things follow

§850

If an eternal contingent being is posited, its eternity differs greatly from the eternity of God[58] (§67).[59] (1)[60] Its duration is subject to a continuous successions of modifications (§209,836).[61] (2)[62] Although its eternity does not indeed have the limits of protension, it cannot for that reason really be said to be infinite (§259, 849). (3)[63] Its eternity would be time without beginning and end, whence it could be called infinite, but only mathematically and therefore not really so (§248, 849), because, in regard to its internal determinations, a successive being (§238) is never actually whatever it can be (§259).[64]

never actually] never at one time actually

---

[a] Kant E3638, 1776–8? (1766–8? 1769? 1773–5?): "He is not alterable./His existence is not alterable; persistent."

§851

God is a necessary (§823, 824) and infinite (§843) being. Hence, he is from himself <*a se*> and an independent being (§310). He thus exists (§849) such that he is not caused by another being posited outside of himself, and he is the unqualified cause of his own effects (§318).[65] All perfections of God are really infinite[66] (§844).[67] Hence, no perfection of God is caused by a being posited outside of God, nor can it be (§381, 248, 310).[68] Now, if suffering were a predicate of God, then this predicate would be caused by some being posited outside of God (§210). Therefore, God is entirely without suffering <*omnino impassibilis*>;[69] he does not suffer from any being that is posited outside of him, neither ideally nor really (§212), nor does anything posited outside of him whatsoever act upon him (§210). And therefore he does not react (§213). Every action of God in the universe is without a reaction, whether ideal or real in kind (§212).

§852

IMAGES are (1) signs of the figure of something else. Now, God does not have a figure (§848). Therefore, images of God are impossible in this sense (§347). Images are (2) signs similar to something else to a notable degree. Since every being is like God to some degree (§265), every more perfect being will be an image of God (§70, 811). Likewise, the more perfect it is, the more similar it is to God, and therefore the greater an image of God it is (§265, 160).

§853

The world is the totality of finite actualities (§354). God is not a totality of finite actualities (§844). Therefore, God is not the world, and neither this nor any world is God. The same is clear from §361, 823, from §365, 839, from §370, 837, and from §388, 843.

§854

This world has an extramundane efficient cause (§375, 388), and this cause is a necessary substance (§381, 319). Therefore, a necessary substance is possible (§333, 69). If a necessary substance is possible, it is actual (§109), and sempiternal (§302). Therefore, a necessary substance exists. God is a necessary substance (§836). Therefore, God exists.

§855

God is an extramundane being (§843, 388), and the world is not an essential determination, essence, attribute, mode, modification, or accident of God (§843). Hence God is not the unique substance (§391).[a] THEOLOGICAL SPINOZISM is the doctrine denying that God is an extramundane being, and it is an error.[70]

§856

Just as §811 proves the existence of God *a priori*, so does §854 establish it as

---

[a] Kant E3639, 1776–9? (1780–9?): "Because things subsist through God, it appears as if they subsist in him./He is not the soul of the world <*Non est anima mundi*>."

exhaustively proven *a posteriori*, and both do so independently of the propositions denied by egoism (§392), idealism (§402), and materialism (§395). Therefore, they can be employed to convince egoists, idealists, materialists, and the like, of the existence of God.

Meier renders the last sentence as: It follows that these can be convinced of the existence of God without them abandoning their particular philosophies.

§857

God is not material (§295, 841); therefore he is immaterial (§422). God is not a body (§296); therefore he is incorporeal (§422). Therefore, he is physically incorruptible (§746).[71] The same is clear from §837.

§858[a]

Among finite beings, the greatest image of God is the most perfect world (§436, 852); in the world, it is substances (§400, 857); among the substances, it is the spirits (§402, 531); among the spirits,[72] it is those enjoying the greatest intellect (§637); among those enjoying the greatest intellect, it is those that are the happiest (§787); among those most remote from any and especially[73] moral evil (§788, 813), it is the most holy (§828).

§859[b]

The (naturing <*naturans*>, cf. §466)[74] nature of God is the collection of his internal perfections (§430) through which he is the unqualified cause of his own effects without in any way suffering.[75] Therefore, whatever is absolutely possible is physically possible for God (§833),[76] and nothing is physically impossible for God that would not be impossible in itself (§469, 833).[77] Whence there would be nothing physically necessary for God that was not at the same time absolutely necessary, and absolutely contingent things are also physically contingent for God (§469, 104), thus not only all the preternatural, but also the supernatural events of the world (§474, 475).

cause … suffering] and independent effective cause of all his effects

§860

If naturalists in a more general sense deny all supernatural events in this world because they deny their hypothetical possibility, then they err. For, since miracles are also possible (§834) in a nexus with God, who must be posited external to them (§855, 474), they also have an extrinsic possibility (§16, 859).[78]

§861

It is impossible for there to be a degree of reality that is homogenous with that of God and all of his perfections (§843, 844), since uniqueness belongs to God and all of his perfections (§846, 844). And therefore the manifest degree of reality in God and all of his perfections cannot be understood based upon a homogenous quantity assumed

[a] Kant E3640, 1776–9? (1780–9?) (beginning): "The greatest caused thing. The highest created good."
[b] Kant E3641, 1776–9? (1780–9?) (beginning): "as an active being he has nature."

as a unit <*una*>. Therefore, we cannot measure God, nor any of his perfections (§291). What we cannot measure is IMMEASURABLE. Therefore, God and all of his perfections are immeasurable. Hence we also understand this immeasurability[79] from the fact that someone who measures must have as many clear perceptions as there are parts, degrees, or various things in that which they genuinely measure. Hence someone who genuinely measures God or anything internal to God must have really infinite and clear perceptions, but such is not to be found in any finite intellect (§844).

uniqueness ... perfections] God and each of his perfections is the single one of its kind and in the highest degree

§862

God is conceivable in himself (§632, 809), even for the human being (§804–1000), and can be provided with a correct definition, or much rather, with a real one, in very many ways (§816).[80] Something is called COMPREHENSIBLE, if FULL KNOWLEDGE OF IT[81] is possible,[82] i.e. knowledge excluding all ignorance, and hence complete historical, philosophical, and mathematical knowledge. Something is INCOMPREHENSIBLE TO SOMEONE whose powers are not sufficient for acquiring complete knowledge of it, and it is more incomprehensible to one, the more distant one necessarily is from such complete knowledge. The greater something is, the more difficult or impossible is its comprehension for the finite knower (§160, 527). Hence the greatest being is maximally incomprehensible for all finite beings (§261). DEISM is the doctrine maintaining that almost nothing is conceivable about God, except perhaps his existence, and it is an error, although[83] God and all the things in him are maximally incomprehensible to us, and to all finite beings[84] (§861, 806).[85]

Section II. The intellect of God

§863

Distinct knowledge is a reality (§531).[86] All realities are in God (§807). Therefore, God knows distinctly. Therefore, he has an intellect. He is an intellectual substance (§830) and a spirit (§402).

§864

All the greatest realities are in God (§812). The more things that are known more distinctly, the greater is the distinct knowledge (§634).[87] Therefore, the most distinct will be the distinct knowledge of all things (§161). Now, the distinct knowledge of all things is possible (§632). Therefore, the distinct knowledge of all things belongs to God, and this is the most distinct knowledge.

§865

The intellect of God is supreme (§863, 812), and inalterable (§839). Therefore, there are no previous and subsequent thoughts in the intellect of God (§125). His intellect is supreme since it represents the most and clearest notes of the most and greatest beings within the strongest and most different associated thoughts. Therefore, the intellect of God is the deepest, most extensive <*patentissimus*>, and purest (§637).[a]

§866

God knows himself as completely as possible (§865). Knowledge concerning God[88] is THEOLOGY[b] IN THE BROADER SENSE. That theology in which God understands himself is EXEMPLARY *ἀρχέτυπος*[89] THEOLOGY, insofar as the theologies of finite beings must strive to be like it (§346).

§867

God, representing all things, represents all possible worlds to himself (§864). This is an internal perfection of God (§37), and his essence (§816)

worlds to] worlds most distinctly to

§868

God knows the essences of all finite beings most distinctly (§864). Therefore, insofar as the essences of things are represented in the intellect of God, they depend (§14) on it and are eternal in it (§849).

§869

God represents all possible worlds to himself most distinctly (§867). Therefore, he represents the best world (§436), the most imperfect world (§442), and this world. The WORLD, insofar as it is sensitively represented, is SENSIBLE (observable), whereas insofar as it is distinctly known, it is INTELLIGIBLE. God knows this intelligible world most distinctly. Therefore, he knows most distinctly all the monads, and all the souls, of this world (§864)[90] One who is rich in <*pollens*> the most distinct knowledge of the human soul is a SCRUTINIZER OF HEARTS. Therefore, God is a scrutinizer of hearts (§740), and he perceives perspicuously <*perspicit*> every soul's, or every monad's, representation of the sensible world (§400, 741),[91] and indeed much more perfectly than a given monad or soul knows itself and its own representation of the world (§864).

After the first sentence Meier inserts: This representation is an internal perfection of God, and therefore his essence. || represented, is] represented, or the world considered as a spectacle of sensibility, is || known ... INTELLIGIBLE] represented, it is the world CONSIDERED AS AN OBJECT OF THE UNDERSTANDING

§870

In God there is no sensitive knowledge (§864, 521). Therefore, he does not have the inferior cognitive faculties (§520). Nothing is obscure or confused to him, and hence

---

[a] Wolff: "*The divine intellect is most perfect.* The most perfect intellect is that which represents every possible thing the most distinctly (WPR §647). And thus seeing that everything possible is distinctly represented by the divine intellect, it is also the most perfect" (WTN1 §168).

[b] Kant E3642, 1770–8 (according to AA, next to the underlined word "THEOLOGY"; however, AA does not indicate which instance is meant): "ectypal: based on mundane properties. applied through reduction <*ectypa: e mundanis affectionibus. per reductionem accomodata*>: analogical."

he understands nothing more clearly than anything else (§528). He does not pay attention, abstract (§529), reflect, or compare (§626).

§871

Since God knows all signified things most distinctly, he has an intuition of all things (§620, 864). He also knows all signs, and all the symbolic knowledge of the souls in the world (§864, 869). However, in him the perception of signs is never greater or less than the perception of the signified (§870); both are always the greatest (§864).[92]

§872

God represents every nexus most distinctly to himself (§864). Therefore, he has supreme reason <*rationem*> (§640). His reason <*ratio*> is supreme, since his intellect is supreme, and hence it is inalterable, and perspicuously perceives the greatest nexus of the most things (§645) without any chain of reasoning (§865).

§873[93]

God's knowledge is of supreme extension and majesty, the most exact (§864), and the most ordered (§822). It lacks all ignorance and errors, all narrowness and triviality, while in it, nothing is tumultuous (§515). It is the most clear and distinct knowledge of all truth, and hence it is the most certain, containing nothing of the obscure, confused, inadequate, incomplete, impure, superficial, probable, dubious, or improbable, and nothing of the dead, inert, or speculative (§669, 671).[94] He knows all certain principles most distinctly, all things founded by them <*principiata*>, and the entire nexus of the principles and of what they found (§864, 872). Therefore, his knowledge is supreme science <*summa scientia*>. God understands most distinctly all the ignorance of souls and all their errors, all the triviality and narrowness of their knowledge; he understands whatever in such knowledge is crass, tumultuous, dark, confusing, inadequate, incomplete, impure; he understands all the moral certitudes, probabilities, doubts, improbabilities,[95] opinions, arguments, and scruples of souls, as well as all their inert and dead speculations[96] (§869).

§874

God knows (§873)[97] (I)[98] all determinations of all things,[99] insofar as these are considered as merely possible. This is the KNOWLEDGE <*SCIENTIA*> OF SIMPLE INTELLIGENCE.[a]

§875

God knows (§873) (II)[100] all the determinations of the actual beings (1) of this world, which is FREE KNOWLEDGE[b] (of vision). This is (α)[101] knowledge of past things through DIVINE RECOLLECTION, (β) knowledge of present things

---

[a] The distinctions between the Medieval concepts of knowledge of simple intelligence and knowledge of vision (§875), and between these and concept of middle knowledge (§876), which was first articulated by Luis de Molina (1535–1600), are discussed by Leibniz in *Theodicy*, Part 2, §39–43.

[b] *SCIENTIA LIBERA*. Although "free science" would be more consistent with our translation of §873, we have used the traditional term of "free knowledge." We have used this approach also for

through the KNOWLEDGE OF VISION, and (γ) knowledge of future things through FOREKNOWLEDGE. PHILOSOPICAL SOCINIANISM is the doctrine that denies the divine knowledge of future contingencies, and it is an error.[102]

§876

God knows all the determinations of the actual beings (2) of a world other than this one, which is MIDDLE KNOWLEDGE. For any event of this world, another could exist (§363, 324).[103] However, any such event would have its own partially different logical consequences indefinitely throughout all of the states of the world that are yet to follow (§488). Therefore, if indeed another event had existed instead of only one event of this world, then this world would be partially different than it is throughout all successive states, and indeed even throughout all antecedent states (§357, 278). Therefore, God knows through middle knowledge (§378) whatever could have existed instead of any event in this world along with all its logical consequences.

all its logical consequences] all their grounds and consequences

§877

God is always most distinctly conscious of the world's[104] present state (§875).[105] Therefore, he never sleeps (§556). This is also obvious from §870. He does not sense as we do (§870, 544), but is wide awake (§552,[106] 826), through his eminent knowledge of vision (§875).

§878

God has eternally represented a future thing to himself, as much as he can (§875, 843). Therefore, when that thing takes place in the present world, nothing is added to God's knowledge (§161), although it alters from an object of foreknowledge to an object of vision (§125). God will eternally represent a past thing to himself, as much as he can (§875, 843). Therefore, when the present becomes the past, it will indeed change from an object of vision into an object of recollection, although nothing will be subtracted from God's knowledge (§161). God eternally intuits all the successive states of this world (§875), whence the internal inalterability of divine knowledge can be thought (§839).

§879[107]

One who cannot err is INFALLIBLE. Therefore, God is infallible (§873). The smallest infallibility is when it is least impossible for someone to confuse one minimal truth with a falsehood. Therefore, one who is unable to confuse more and greater truths with falsehoods, and the greater is the impossibility of such confusion,[108] the more infallible one is.[109] Therefore, when we attribute the greatest infallibility to God (§812), we venerate the one who is absolutely unable to confuse the most and greatest truths with any falsehood.

unable to confuse] unable—due to his knowing constantly and inalterably all that is possible and also the greatest truths in the most perfect way—to confuse

---

"knowledge of vision," "foreknowledge," and "middle knowledge." The technical difference between knowledge and science is explained in the vocabulary note in our introduction above.

§880[110]

The smallest certitude is the least clear knowledge of one smallest truth (§161). The clearer, the more, and the greater are the truths known, the greater the certitude will be[111] (§160). Therefore, when we attribute supreme subjective certitude[a] to God (§873, 812), we venerate the one who knows the most and greatest truths the most distinctly. This same God is objectively the most certain (§93, 812), since his truth is supreme (§822), and his existence is demonstrable through his essence, and through the existence of any finite being whatsoever (§856).

since … whatsoever] since he has the greatest metaphysical truth, which can be proven from his essence and from all other possible things, just as can his actuality

§881

God's free knowledge is his respective perfection (§875, 815). And since it is absolutely necessary that God's free knowledge is the most true (§879),[112] it conveys to God that this world exists contingently in and through itself (§361). Hence it is absolutely necessary that God's free knowledge is hypothetically necessary (§102). Therefore, God's free knowledge is an analogue of a mode (§827).

§882[b]

WISDOM IN GENERAL is the perspicuous perception of a final nexus, whereas

---

[a] This paragraph began with a preamble concerning subjective certitude in the first edition, which was removed as of the second edition. Please see the endnote attached to the paragraph number.

[b] Kant E3643, 1769? (end of 1769–autumn 1770?) (1764–8?) 1773–5??: "Wisdom is the knowledge of the good (of that which is good in its entirety (in all actual relations)) from the idea of the whole as a ground of choice./Whatever is to be good in all respects must be derived from the idea of the most perfect whole./(Prudence is the knowledge of the means to ends that are not fully in our command. Therefore, in view of the opinion and freedom of other people.)/The wisdom of man consists in that he dispenses with ends that are not in his command."
Kant E3644, 1770–8: "Wisdom is related to the good./Prudence to the useful."
Kant E3645, 1770–8: "The faculty of knowing the relation of all things* to the highest good** is wisdom; to (good in the appearance) particulars: prudence (not of God)./(*later addition*: The adequacy of knowledge to the highest good and to its possibility is either purely theoretical—science, or moral: wisdom.)/*(*later addition*: The faculty of the knowledge of the (*crossed out*: means) best means to the same is a wisdom of skill; the faculty of the knowledge of the end together with the willing of it: moral wisdom.)/**(*later addition*: either to it itself or to the highest derived good. The former is the ground of the latter, but only in the divine understanding.)"
Kant E3646, 1771–2? (1776–8?): "Wisdom in general is the perfection of knowledge to the extent that it is adequate to the whole of all ends (either the physical or moral whole)."
Kant E3647, 1776–8: "Wisdom is the (subjective) principle of the unity of all ends (*crossed out*: a pr) according to reason, therefore happiness unified with morality."
Kant E3648, 1776–8: "The highest good has two parts. Which is the condition, which is the conditioned. Morality or happiness?"
Kant E3649, 1776–8: "Whether we can fathom the ends of the divine wisdom in nature and whether that is physico-theology?—He alone is holy—blessed—wise."
Kant E3650, 1776–9? (1780–9?): "The divine understanding derives all knowledge of the particular from the whole of all possibility and every particular end from the whole of all ends. Everything from himself."
Kant E3651, 1776–9? (1780–9?): "Skillfulness is the faculty of reason in regard to the means to preferred ends, prudence in regard to the sum of all subjective ends./Wisdom: the faculty to determine every particular end through the whole of all objective ends./Hence 'a man' and 'wise' is a contradiction, except in morality as a model."

WISDOM IN PARTICULAR is the perspicuous perception of ends, and PRUDENCE is the perspicuous perception of means.[113] Hence, God is the wisest of all <*omnisa-pientissimus*> (§872), and when we say this, we venerate the one who perspicuously perceives (1) all ends, (2) all means, (3) all of their possible nexuses (§343) (4) in regard to all their qualities (5) and quantities (6) in the greatest possible nexus, (7) the most certainly and most ardently[114] (§880, 873).

certainly] perfectly, thus most certainly

§883

God knows <*scit*> all ends. Hence, he knows the best as well as the worst ends. He knows which of these can be a means[115] for another, and hence all possible subordination and also coordination of all ends (§315). He knows all the qualified goals, and those that are unqualifiedly last (§343) according to all their goodness and the degree of their goodness. He knows every possible nexus along with their means, and indeed such that none ever seems to him to be other than it is (§879), whereby nevertheless he likewise understands how any end whatsoever seems to each and every soul that knows it (§869). Therefore, concerning the best ends, God knows best that they are the best (§882).

§884

God knows <*novit*> all the means, and hence the best as well (§882),[116] i.e. the means in which, when posited, supreme perfection is posited (§187). Now, when the means are posited, the end is posited (§326, 341). Therefore the best means are subordinated to the best end. And God knows, insofar as they are subordinated to the best end, how and to what extent they are subordinated (§883).

§885

A CERTAIN MEANS is that which is really such, and is as great, as it is recognized <*cognoscitur*> to be. Hence it is opposed to an apparent means, which only seems to be such and is utterly not, or is not as great as it seems. It is also opposed to an uncertain means, whose true goodness, or degree of goodness, is not established.[117] The best means are the most certain, both insofar as they are not apparent means, and insofar as God is the most certain both of their goodness and of their degree of goodness (§882). And yet he nevertheless perspicuously perceives all the possible doubts of souls concerning these same means (§869, 873).[118]

§886

The more fecund a means is, the greater is the perfection posited by it (§166, 341). Therefore, the most fecund means are the best means, and vice versa (§187). God knows the most fecund means (§884), and whatever amount of fecundity they possess (§882),[119] as well as the amount of fecundity ascribed to any one of these by given souls (§873).[120]

more fecund] more fecund and profound || greater] more manifold and greater || most fecund means are] most fecund and most noble are || knows the most fecund] knows the most fecund and noble || fecundity they] fecundity and profundity they|| fecundity ascribed] fecundity and profundity ascribed

§887

The best means are complete[a] (§886) in relation to the best end (§884). Therefore, they are not incomplete (§81). If they were excessive, then they would contain some things contributing nothing to the end. And these, therefore, would not actualize a good (§341), and yet they also would not be utterly sterile (§23). Hence, they would be evil (§146). Therefore, the best means are equal to <*adaequata*> to the best end. God knows the means that are equal to the best end (§884). Means certain and equal to their end are those that WHOLLY ACHIEVE THE END.[b] God knows the means that wholly achieve the best ends (§885).[c]

§888[d]

The actualization of an end through the fewest means that wholly achieve it is the SHORTEST WAY. The use of the best means is always the shortest way. For then the end is indeed actualized through means wholly achieving it (§887), all of which[e] are the most fecund (§886), and none of which are excessive (§887).[f] Hence these will be the fewest that they can be (§161).[121] God knows every shortest way (§887).

§889[g]

OMNISCIENCE is the science of all things. God is the most omniscient (§873). When we call him such, we venerate the being exhibited in §863–88.

the science] the most perfect knowledge

---

[a] G/K: "fully effective"
[b] Kant E3654, 1766–78 (next to Baumgarten's gloss, not given here, of the Latin "*FINEM EX ASSE CONSEQUENTIA*" with the German "*den Zweck völlig erreichen*"): "The adequacy in regard to means."
[c] Kant E3655, end of 1769–75? (1776–8?) (between §887 and 888): "Not everything is end or means, at least not everything good in the consequences of certain causes."
Kant E3656, 1780–9 (across from the conclusion): "The divine wisdom is the ground of the agreement of his choice with himself, without exception or collision, based on a plan."
[d] Kant E3653, 1766–9: "As a means in and by itself (in the execution), there can indeed be nothing more than in the end, i.e. there is not more in the cause than in the effect. But as a means in the intention there can be more than what is required for the end, due to an error. However, there can exist much more aside from what fulfills the entire end, and the law of parsimony is not for God."
Kant E3657, 1780–9 (across from the beginning): "The parsimony of the divine decree in the choice of that which alone is needed as a means to the highest represented good is not an attribute of the divine wisdom. It is the attribute of one without might, who, when he does more in one case than what is conducive to some need, neglects other needs."
[e] G/K: "of which the individual"
[f] Kant E3652, 1765–6 (across from the third and fourth sentences): "It is the same whether many or few means lead to the end, if only the end is achieved; superfluous means are only reproachable in regard to the human being because they hinder his other ends. Yet because the sufficient ground of the means is only in the end, there can be nothing more in the former than what is required for the latter."
[g] Kant E3657a, 1766–78 (beginning): "Freedom of the divine will."

Section III. The will of God

§890

God most distinctly intuits all the perfections or imperfections of everything (§889, 871). Whatever is in God is the greatest ground (§23, 812). Hence in him, the intuition of perfections or imperfections is the most alive (§669, 873).[122] Therefore, the greatest (§812) satisfaction and dissatisfaction (§655) belongs to God.

§891

There is no satisfaction and dissatisfaction of God that is not the truest (§880), most distinct (§870), and the most rational (§822). He is never totally indifferent (§653), nor ever partially so towards anything (§654). He has neither sensitive pleasure nor displeasure (§656), neither desire nor aversion, neither instincts nor fears (§677), no affects (§678), and neither apparent satisfaction nor dissatisfaction (§655).

rational] conjoined

§892

Since God only intuits himself most distinctly as good, as the best and as the most holy being (§866, 828), he derives the purest pleasure from himself (§661). This is the supreme repose of God within himself (§682). Exemplary[123] theology is the most delightful (§866). God does not receive sheer dissatisfaction from anything (§891, 661). All of his dissatisfaction and satisfaction is inalterable (§839). Hence, he does not know transitory pleasures and displeasures (§662); nothing is burdensome to him (§658). His supreme dissatisfaction does not obscure his supreme pleasure in any way (§870), and nothing outside of him can actualize any pleasure or displeasure in him (§851).

§893

In God there exists the free knowledge of this world, although, notwithstanding this, it is possible for this knowledge to be both of no world and of another world (§881). However, free knowledge of this world does not exist in God unless through the power of God (§851, 197). Therefore, God has determined his own power to actualize the free knowledge not of no world, not of another world, but of this world. Therefore, God desires and averts (§663). Now, he neither desires nor averts sensitively (§891). Rather, his desire and aversion follows knowledge (§668, 822).Therefore, he wills and refuses, and he has supreme (§812) volition and nolition (§689), i.e. which most perfectly follows supreme omniscience (§668, 889).

this knowledge ... of another world] there to be no free science at all or for there to exist one of another world || in God] in God, together with its object apart from God, || to actualize ... this world] not to actualize no free science or the free science of another world, but rather of this world itself, and precisely this and no other world apart from it did he determine his power to produce || *After the sentence ending* "(§891)." *Meier inserts:* Thus, should he desire or avert, then indeed his entire omniscience is eternally actual in him, while he eternally desires.

§894

VOLITION OR NOLITION is PROPORTIONAL TO THE INTELLECT[124] when it follows the intellect's mathematical knowledge, i.e. when it desires according to the distinctly[125] known degree of goodness in the beings that are to be desired, or when it averts according to the distinctly[126] known degree of imperfection in the beings that are to be averted. If a will establishes that a being is good or evil to the same degree as it in fact is, then this VOLITION OR NOLITION is PROPORTIONAL TO OBJECTS.[127] Therefore, supreme (§812) proportionality belongs to divine volition and nolition (§893), since it supremely follows the most distinct and infallible knowledge of the degrees of perfection and imperfection (§879, 883).

Therefore ... imperfection] To the divine will belongs this double proportion in the supreme degree while his understanding, which knows most distinctly and infallibly all perfections and imperfections of all things, constantly determines his will most perfectly

§895

God acts (§210) as long as he wills (§893). All the actions of God can (§833) and do (§851) depend on an internal sufficient principle for acting, which is in God. Therefore, spontaneity, and indeed supreme spontaneity (§872), belongs to divine actions and to God himself (§704), while it is sufficient for the most and greatest actions (§706,[128] 832). The maximally spontaneous actions of God are either immanent, or transeunt (§211).

immanent ... transeunt] those through which he actualizes within himself his own infinite accidents, or those though which he actualizes [something] in the world apart from himself

§896

God is free from absolute internal (§710, 702) and physical (§710, 859) constraint, as well as from external constraint (ideal as much as real) (§707, 851), and even from the qualifiedly external moral constraint (§723) of motives (§726) that bring about reluctant actions through violence in a qualified sense (§714). God is free from enticements, threats, persuasions, dissuasions, and extortions (§728).

§897

All actions are posited as in God's command (§708, 859).[129] Therefore, if both a given action and some action opposed to it are possible in themselves (§15), i.e. if a given action is contingent in itself (§104), and hence has an opposed action that is contingent in itself (§104), then both are in God's command. Therefore, all actions contingent in themselves are free as to their execution for God, and, in regard to the performance of the act, they are indifferent (§708) to God, because with respect to God the physical possibility of both is supreme (§844).[130] Hence, the actualization of this universe, or of none, or of another, was free as to its execution for God (§835). God was, is, and will be as indifferent concerning the performance of an act toward the best world, as concerning the performance of an act toward the most imperfect world (§849).

All actions] All real actions || given action] given real action

§898

Since God determines himself by acting according to preference (§893, 712), and indeed distinct preference (§893), he has freedom (§719) and, moreover, the greatest freedom (§812); i.e. he actualizes the greatest and most actions according to the most distinct preference (§725). FATALISM, the doctrine that denies divine freedom, is an error.[131]

§899

God wills most freely (§898). Therefore, he wills the good (§719, 665). God averts most freely (§898). Therefore, he averts evil (§719, 665). Volition, or love[132] of the good, and hate, or the nolition of evil, are infinite in God (§844): (1) they are extensively infinite since God loves every good, and hates every evil (§898, 889); (2) they are protensively infinite since they are eternal (§849); and 3) they are intensively infinite, since they are the most proportionate (§894). Because dead and merely speculative knowledge is not possible in God (§873), extensively infinite divine volition or nolition tends towards (1) the universal[133] objects of simple intelligence, which furnish concepts for us, and whatever in these same objects is good or evil, concerning which God cannot be totally indifferent (§891); towards (2) the objects of middle knowledge, the actual objects of another universe; and towards (3)[134] the objects of free knowledge (§874–6).[135] THE WILL OF GOD, insofar as it desires the objects of free knowledge, i.e. the actual beings of this universe, is reductively[a] (§826) called CONSEQUENT; and insofar as it tends towards the universal and actual beings of another universe, it is reductively (§826) called ANTECENDENT (§695). The former is effective (§671), while both are efficacious, even the antecedent, not only because it is serious, but also because it belongs to the motives of a decree (§675).[b]

---

[a] See the footnote to §826.
[b] Cf. Leibniz, *Theodicy*, passim, but especially his answer to objection two in his "Summary of the controversy reduced to formal arguments." Through his antecedent will, God loves all the goods of every possible world, and hates all evils. Through his consequent will, God decrees, or selects, the best possible combination of goods and evils to constitute the best of all possible worlds.
Kant E3658, 1769–autumn 1770? (1765–6?): "Objectively antecedent will is that whose motive (*crossed out*: object) is that which is universal in objects <*Voluntas obiective antecedens est, cuius [obiect] motivum est, quod in obiectis est universale*>. Objectively consequent will is that whose motive is that which is individual in objects <*Voluntas obiective consequens est, cuius motivum est, quod in obiectis est individuale*>."
Kant E3659, 1769–71? (1764–8): "The best will determines particular (*crossed out*: perfection) volition in totality, that is, as one usually says: in the universal, insofar as it is constrained by particular conditions <*Voluntas optima determinat [perfectionem] volitionem particularem in omnitudine, h.e. secundum morem loquendi humanum: in universali, quatenus restringitur per conditiones particulares*>."
Kant E3660, 1773–8? (1770–1?) 1766–9?? (under E3659): "The divine will, insofar as it relates to what is common to objects and to others that he does not will, is called antecedent; insofar as it relates to that through which it distinguishes itself from all others, it is called consequent."
Kant E3661, 1780–9: "antecedent will is that which relates to a universal concept of an object (as undetermined)./consequent: to the determinate concept of the object."
Kant E3662, 1780–9: "The object of the highest intelligence is the highest good according to knowledge and, as author, according to the will./The highest good in the whole and also the relation of every particular to it:/0. the relation to universal concepts of the good. antecedent will./1. to the completely determined knowledge of this world. consequent will."

§900

A WILL whose impelling causes are incomprehensible is INSCRUTABLE. Now, the impelling causes of the divine will are its own most distinct preference (§898) and hence an internal perfection in God (§37), which is incomprehensible to us (§862). One who conceives of specific motives of God with some degree of distinction has still not comprehended the divine will (§862). Hence one who strives for some understanding <*intellectio*> of the divine motives does not suppose that they can comprehend the will of God (§664). The greater are the number of the impelling causes of a certain will, and the less completely they can be known, the more incomprehensible is the will (§160).[136] Hence, since the will of God is said to be maximally incomprehensible to us (§812), we understand that (1) most of his motives are not to be understood; and (2) for the most part, we fail to comprehend any one of them (§862, 898).

impelling causes of … preference] complete motive of the divine will is his omniscience, and his most perfect preference || *Meier clarifies the fourth sentence:* Therefore, whoever has the aim of discovering some motive grounds of God cannot be blamed for also holding the will of God to be inscrutable.

§901

The conformity of a free ACTION with its own ground, hence with the moral (§723) law (§83), is its RIGHTEOUSNESS. Therefore, insofar as all of God's actions, which are most free (§898, 725), are in conformity with the moral (§723) law of the best (§822)—*the best is freely joined with the best*[137]—they are the most righteous actions. Supreme righteousness (§899) or moral (§723) holiness (§828) belongs to the divine will.

§902

The actions of God, which are most free, are not absolutely necessary, since the opposite of these is possible in itself (§102). All of God's transeunt actions in the world (§854, 211) have an opposite action that is possible in itself (§361).[138] Hence none of these is absolutely necessary. And since the opposite of all the actions of God, which are most free, can be actualized through the omnipotence of God (§897), none of these is physically necessary for him, and, what is more, neither is any action of God in the world (§470,[a] 859). Moreover, none is even morally necessary in that sense, as if through freedom, the opposite of any of these would be rendered physically impossible for God (§723). Since, however, God's supreme freedom always determines itself most righteously (§901), all of his actions are also morally necessary while they are morally the holiest (§723, 724).

§903

GOODNESS (kindness) is the determination of the will to do something good <*bene*> for another.[139] A BENEFIT is an action done out of goodness that is very useful to

[a] G/K plausibly suggest the proper reference is to §469.

someone else.[140] The smallest goodness would be the smallest propensity or disposition of the will[141] conferring the smallest good on one smallest being, i.e. a minimally
worthy being[142] (§161). Therefore, the more and greater are the benefits that goodness
desires to confer to the greater extent on more and worthier[143] beings, the greater it is
(§160). A benefit is a greater good (§336, 187).

do ... another] make another more perfect to a higher degree

§904

God wills that benefits be conferred on others (§903, 899). Therefore, he is supremely
(§812) kind (§903). When we call God the most kind, we venerate the being who
infinitely, eternally (§899), and immutably (§839) loves conferring the most and
greatest benefits on the most and worthiest beings (§903).

§905

The love of human beings is PHILANTHROPY. The love that wills the proportionate
reciprocated love of the loved one is JEALOUS LOVE. And this, along with mercy,
favor, goodwill, and compassion, is universal and the greatest in God (§684, 904). And
since an intense constant love is FAITHFULNESS, God, eternally and infinitely loving,
is supremely faithful (§904, 812).

§906

Proportional goodness towards persons, or spirits, is JUSTICE (cf. *Ethics* §317).[a, 144]
The smallest justice would be the smallest goodness following the smallest, minimally
clear, minimally certain, minimally living mathematical knowledge (§903, 161).
Therefore, the (1) more intensely one loves to confer (2) more and (3) greater benefits
upon more persons according to the known degree of perfection or imperfection in
the spirit (5) and the more clearly (6) certainly (7) and ardently this degree is known,
that much greater is the justice (§903, 160).[145] God is supremely (§812)[146] just (§904,
894). When we call God the most just, we venerate his supreme goodness (§904),
which is the most proportional (§894) and the most ready to confer the most and
greatest benefits upon the most persons according to the most distinct, infallible, and
maximally living knowledge of the degrees of evident perfection or imperfection in
every spirit.

---

[a] Baumgarten's *Ethica Philosophica* (1751), §317: "If proficiency in attributing to each his own
is called JUSTICE, it will either it will be the virtue towards someone of observing the duties
owed to that very person, and it will be the UNIVERSAL proficiency of conforming to
JURISPRUDENCE <*IURI*> itself, i.e. to the collection of laws that one must observe, which
is a virtue to which the whole of ethics obliges (e.g. *Ethica* §1); or, it will be particular, the
proficiency of attributing to each his own of the rest of humanity, and it is ready to attribute
either one's own according the law of nature, and is EXTERNAL JUSTICE, virtue, honesty
(*Ethica* §300), or one's own according to ethics, and is internal justice, the proportional goodness
towards men (*Metaphysics* §906)."

§907[a]

A REWARD (remuneration) is a contingent[147] good conferred on a person on account of a moral good. JUSTICE in conferring rewards is REMUNERATORY, the supreme instance of which we venerate in God (§906, 812) when we admire the justice most prepared to confer the most proportional rewards according to all, and even the smallest, moral goods of all spirits.

§908[b]

A PUNISHMENT is a contingent evil inflicted on a person due to a moral evil. Some PUNISHMENTS and REWARDS can be sufficiently conceived based on the essence of the sin and the nature of the one who sins, or based on the essence of moral good and the nature of the one who acts well, and they are then NATURAL. Some rewards can only be sufficiently conceived based on the choice of another conferring them, and they are CHOSEN REWARDS. Some punishments can only be sufficiently conceived based on the choice of another inflicting them, and they are CHOSEN PUNISHMENTS.

sins] sins through freedom || acts well] acts well through freedom

§909

A SINNER is someone in whom there are moral evils. Someone in whom some moral evils are lacking is, in respect of these, called INNOCENT IN THE BROADER SENSE (guiltless, cf. *Ethics* §319).[c] The sinner, everything else being equal, is not as good as someone who is innocent (§187). Therefore, the sinner is not loved as much from the most proportional goodness (§906). Therefore, God wills to confer some benefits on the innocent that he does not will to confer on the sinner (§904). God is not indifferent (§891) with respect to these benefits that are not to be conferred on the sinner. Hence, according to his most distinct preference, he averts conferring[148] them on the sinner (§898, 669). Therefore, he wills the opposite of these sorts of benefits (§663, 690). Evils are opposite to benefits (§81, 903), and are contingent[149] (§146). Therefore, God wills that certain contingent[150] evils, i.e. punishments (§908), are to be inflicted on the sinner on account of moral evils.

---

[a] Kant E3663, 1766–71? (1773–5? 1776–8?): "One could still ask whether the reward is a matter of justice or beneficence."
Kant E3664, 1776–8 (Kant underlined the words "moral good" and inserted a symbol after these words and then the same symbol before the world "merit" in the right margin, then inserted these words): "For if the moral good in general is merely (*crossed out:* wisdo) wise goodness."
[b] Kant R3665, 1773–5? (1766–71?):
"Rewards are either gifts <*Praemia vel sunt munera*>: gratuitous rewards <*praemia gratuita*>
— — — payments <*mercedes*>: — — — owed <*debita*> [rewards].
morals <*moralia*>: of wisdom <*sapientiae*>,
Pragmatics <*pragmatic*>: of prudence <*prudentiae*>"
[c] Baumgarten's *Ethica Philosophica* (1751), §319: "The proficiency of harming nobody, either internally or externally, is innocence. The former is internal and the latter external innocence in the stricter sense, since taken in the broader sense, it is a virtue free from accusation."

§910[a]

JUSTICE[b] in inflicting punishments is PUNITIVE (vindictive, the avengeress, the vindicatress, Nemesis),[151] and it belongs to God (§909). This is supreme justice (§812), since it is most prepared to punish most proportionally all sins of all sinners (§906). PHILOSOPHICAL DIPPELIANISM[c] is the doctrine that denies the punitive justice of God, and it is an error.[152]

§911

The opposite of a natural reward is a natural punishment, while the opposite of a chosen reward is a chosen punishment (§908). Therefore, while the remunerative justice of God dispenses chosen rewards, his vindictive justice imposes chosen punishments. These natural punishments themselves are chosen with respect to the one without whose choice[153] the nature of the one sinning would not have a sufficient ground (§908). The same is true of natural rewards.

§912

The collection of causes that are posited outside a spirit, and that concur in its prosperity or misery, is either GOOD or EVIL FORTUNE. What is actualized through fortune is FORTUITOUS, and is contingent[154] (§146,[d] 787). The goods of this sort that are conferred on a spirit due to goodness are rewards (§907), and, since they can only be sufficiently known as coming from the choice of God (§854), they are chosen (§908). Evil fortuitous events inflicted on a spirit are UNFORTUNATE. Unfortunate events inflicted on a spirit due to moral evils are punishments, and since they can

---

[a] Kant E3666, 1766–71? (1773–8?): "Punitive justice is distinguished from vengeful justice; the former exercises the justice of the one whose right has been injured, and the latter that of the one whose person has been injured."
Kant E3667, 1766–78: "God does not punish the offense to his person (offence to [his] majesty), but rather, because the human being knows God only according to the analogy with human beings, he punishes the malice that the human being expresses to his person that the human being (*crossed out:* they) would be capable of in relation to other human beings. (*crossed out:* Hence) Otherwise we would entangle ourselves in the infinity of the crime."
Kant E3668, 1770–8? (1766–9?) (beginning): "Punative justice belongs to wisdom."
Kant E3670, 1780–9: "distributive justice is not instrumental, but final <*iustitia distributiva non est instrumentalis, sed finalis*>."
Kant E3671, 1790–1804? (1776–8?) 1771–2?? (changes this first sentence to read): "The justice of God is not remuneratorial, but punitive; it is either pragmatic <*Iustitia dei non est remuneratoria, sed punitiva; est vel pragmatic*>: of the regent, or moral: of the judge, because it is a sin <*quia peccatum est*>."
Kant E3672, 1790–1804? (1776–8?) 1771–2??: "Whether there is a crime of offending divine majesty."
[b] Kant E3669, 1770–8? (1766–9?): "distributive or vindictive <*distributiva vel vindicativa*>."
[c] After Johann Conrad Dippel (1673–1734), a physician, alchemist and radical Pietistic theologian. Dippel was extremely unorthodox and sensational in his writings. His theology centered on the conception of God as love (thus Baumgarten's definition), and human freedom, which he held to be a consequence of this love. Perhaps his most representative work in this regard is *Fatum Fatuum* (1710). Often said to have been a possible model for the fictional character Dr. Frankenstein, Dippel lived most his life at Castle Frankenstein and died at Castle Wittgenstein. For more on him, see F. Earnest Stoeffler, *German Pietism During the Eighteenth Century*, in the series Studies in the History of Religions, Supplements to Numen, 24 (Leiden: Brill, 1973), 182–91.
[d] G/K prefer §147, which clearly discusses contingent good. §146, on the other hand, discusses contingent evil.

only be sufficiently (§854)[a] known as coming from the choice of God, punishments are chosen (§908).

§913

Miraculous and supernatural rewards and punishments are in themselves (§475) and hypothetically (§860) possible for divine omnipotence (§833, 834), and these, but not these alone (§911, 912), are chosen (§908, 898).

§914

Whatever is real and positive in an EVENT is called its REMOTE MATERIAL, and its complete determination is called its PROXIMATE MATERIAL. In finite beings, whatever is negative for the same event *<eidem>* is called its FORMAL ASPECT *<FORMALE>*. Hence evils and punishments (§908) are either considered materially and formally at the same time, and they are partly good, and partly evil, like all finite beings taken precisely or formally (§264). They are then loved infinitely by God insofar as they are good, and hated infinitely by him insofar as they are evil (§899). Or they are considered only materially, in terms of the remote material, and they are positive and real, and only the objects of divine love (§899).[155] Or they are considered only formally, in terms of the proximate material and the formal aspect, and they are only negations strictly considered, or privations (§137), and they are only the objects of divine hatred (§899).

whatever … event] the collection of its negations

§915

God wills punitive justice (§910), the remote material of the punishment, and whatever reality is in the proximate material, but not the formal aspect (§914). Now, it is a reality that such punishments truly befall this sinner and not another but the one to whom they are most proportional (§36, 909).[156] Therefore, God wills this reality (§899). Hence the distinction of contingent[157] evils (§146), and indeed that of punishments (§908) and of sinners (§788), must be further distinguished into the privative and the positive (§525).

§916[b]

FORBEARANCE (judicious patience) is the justice that only punishes at what seems to be the best occasion. Because God infallibly knows the best opportunities for all punishments (§889, 879), he also wills most proportionally (§894, 914) this

---

[a] G/K plausibly suggest that this is a problematic reference.
[b] Kant E3673, 1775–8 (ff.): "All these attributes are the moral ones (*crossed out:* which), most of all on the ground that God wants the internal part of the human heart to agree with him (*crossed out:* in accordance with) and his presence."
Kant E3674, 1775–8: "In punishment he wants forbearance among men./The beneficence that puts off the punishment of the offender for his betterment."
Kant E3675, 1780–9: "He punishes according to the order of nature as a whole only after an extended time./He punishes only in accordance with the infinite progression."

proximate material of any punishment whatsoever, since it is a reality (§36). Hence he is supremely forbearing.

§917ᵃ

IMPARTIALITY is aversion to deciding based on apparent stimuli. Indeed, no stimuli (§898), and even less appearances (§889, 12), are possible in God, and since his most holy will averts these as much as it averts what would be determined from them (§902), he is the most impartial.

§918ᵇ

FAIRNESS is impartial justice. God, who is the most just (§906) and most impartial (§917), is the most fair.

§919ᶜ

SINCERITY is goodness in signifying one's own mind and this is supreme (§812) in God (§904)[158] since he is the most prepared to signify as much of his mind in all things as his supreme wisdom recommends, with the most proper signs (§884, 888).[159]

§920ᵈ

VERACITY is sincerity in speech. Since divine wisdom judges that it is best to signify the divine mind through speech, God is the most veracious (§919).

§921[160]

The smallest duration of the smallest nature would be the smallest life. The greater is the duration of a greater nature, the greater is the life, until the greatest life, which would be the supreme duration of the most perfect nature (§430, 161). Supreme life must be attributed to God (§859, 850).

§922[161]

Since the greatest life is absolutely necessary for God (§921), because it is his very

---

ᵃ Kant E3676, 1775–8: "He (*crossed out:* wants) loves impartiality in the judgment of men./He does not have favorites, e.g. the Jewish people."
 Kant E3677, 1780–9: "The human being cannot always derive the particular good, which God distributes, from the universal provision; hence one is authorized to view it as a particular provision and to thank God for it, yet also to believe that in a manner unknown to one this is nevertheless universal."
ᵇ Kant E3678, 1775–8: "He administers equity, i.e. before his court a violation of equity is an offense of strict right."
 Kant E3679, 1780–9: "He directs from the standpoint of a human being, which is a limited being. The human being can view many things as a preference that God bestows on him over others."
ᶜ Kant E3680, 1775–8: "He wants sincerity, which is commonly very much missing in regard to God when one affects praise and devotions that one does not feel, pretends to believe much out of fear and goes out of one's way to flatter./(*later addition:* God is open in those of his revelations that are necessary for us, not hidden, not mysterious and equivocal. He does not lead us into temptation.)"
ᵈ Kant E3681, 1775–8: "He wants honesty among human beings./(*later addition:* One must not say of God whatever is fully identical with the predicates through which we think his moral perfections.)"

essence (§816) and existence (§823, 780ª), God is not only immortal but *he alone has* absolute *immortality* (§781).

because ... existence; one may consider it to be either his essence or his actuality

§923

In God, supreme moral perfection is joined together with supreme metaphysical and physical perfection (§806,[162] 859) through his supreme righteousness (§901). He is thus most distinctly conscious of these perfections (§866), whence he enjoys these with supreme pleasure (§892) and is the most blessed (§787).

righteousness] moral holiness

§924

God is supremely (§812) happyᵇ (§923, 787) since (1) not only is every moral corruption and misery absent from him (§813),[163] but these are indeed neither physically (§859) nor morally (§902) possible in him; and since (2) he is the happiest independently and from himself <*a se*> (§851), (3) without any alteration to his own goods, or any alteration to his intuition of these (§839).

§925ᶜ

A being that is more perfect than another is SUPERIOR to it. God, the supreme spirit (§889, 796), is a SUPERMUNDANE BEING insofar as he has greater perfection than any whole world, even if it is the best (§361, 843). And since it is impossible for several most perfect beings to be posited outside of one another (§846), God is the absolutely supreme being.

greater] an infinitely many times greater; impossible] absolutely impossible

Chapter II. The operations of God

Section I. The creation of the world

§926

An efficient cause actualizes an effect (§319, 210). God is the efficient cause of this universe (§854). Therefore, God actualized this universe either from eternity <*ab aeterno*>, i.e. such that this world would not have a beginning,[164] or he did so in time <*in tempore*>, which is to say, not from eternity (§10).[165] In neither case does a part of the world pre-exist the world (§371, 394). Therefore, in either case the world was actualized from nothing (§228), and it is God who actualized these from nothing

---

ª G/K suggest that the reference to §780 is a relic of the first edition, which refers to the annihilation of the soul in both §780 and §922. There certainly seems to be no reason to refer to §780 as of the second edition. Please see our translations of §780 and §922 from the first edition in the endnotes.

ᵇ Kant E3682, 1771–8: "blessedness. Self-sufficiency in well-being."

ᶜ Kant E3683, 1775–8 (beginning): "He is above (*crossed out:* nature) the world as the creator (nature) and as lawgiver (freedom)."

(§854). To actualize something from nothing is TO CREATE. Therefore, God is the creator of this universe.[a]

§927

CREATION BY EMANATION would be the actualization of the universe from the essence of God, in such a way that: (1) the world would not have been actualized from nothing (§926), since necessary being is the essence of God (§109, 816),[166] which however goes against §926; (2) either the entire essence of God, or a part of it, could be altered into the universe (§870),[167] which goes against §839; (3) a part of God would be posited outside of God (§388), and God would be composite (§225), which goes against §838. It is clear in many ways that creation by emanation is impossible (§7).

§928

All the monads of this universe are finite beings (§396), and hence they are all beings from another <*entia ab alio*> (§308). They can all only be actualized from nothing (§229,[168] 236). Therefore, all the monads of this universe are created (§926). A being that can only exist through creation is a CREATURE. Therefore, all the monads of this universe are creatures, and indeed creatures of God (§381, 854). Whatever is substantial in this universe is a creature of God (§396).

§929

All the spirits of this universe (§404), all the human souls (§744, 741), and all the elements of this world are creatures of God (§928, 423), each one having been actualized in a simultaneous (§238) and instantaneous (§299, 228) creation. Now, the bodies of this world are aggregates of elements (§155, 420), and hence whatever is substantial in bodies, no matter how many subsistent parts *per se* they have, is a creature of God (§928).

§930

That which can only exist as caused by another can only endure as caused by another (§299). Hence, the world and all of its parts can only endure as beings from another (§928, 375). Therefore, a creation actualizing an independent duration in creatures is impossible, and is not an object of divine omnipotence (§833). The creation of this universe is possible (§926, 57). Therefore, no duration independent in itself has been actualized through the creation of this universe.

---

[a] Wolff insists that creation is a miracle: "*The creation of the world and the constitution of the order of nature is the original miracle.* The creation of the world (WTN1 §768) and constitution of the order of nature (WTN1 §770) is a miracle. And indeed, no less the world than the order of nature derives its origin from a miracle. Truly, those things that in turn come about contain a sufficient ground in the essence and nature of bodies, to the extent that they are experienced, and which everyone who enquires into the grounds of natural things spontaneously grants, for indeed they come about naturally (WC §509). And accordingly, because there is an original miracle from whence something in the universe derives its origin, a miracle upon which in turn the rest naturally depend (WTN1 §772), the creation of the world and constitution of the order of nature is the original miracle" (WTN1 §773).

parts] substantial parts ‖ no … universe] this world has not received an independent duration through its creation by God

§931

Whatever does not pertain to the existence of the world and its substantial parts is not created (§926). Now, the essences of creatures, and hence their metaphysical evil (§146), do not pertain to their existence (§132, 134). And hence neither the essences nor the metaphysical evils of creatures are created, unless you wish to say that all the determinations of an actualized creature have been created, which goes against the notion <*contra notionem*> of §926.

§932

The non-existence of this universe, or of any universe, is possible in itself (§370, 361). All things possible in themselves are also possible for God (§859).[169] Hence, by means of his omnipotence, God could have not created the universe, or he could have created another one. If another had existed, then this one would not have existed (§379, 926). Nevertheless, without suffering (§851),[170] he created this universe through supreme spontaneity (§895) in an act of creation that was free as to its execution (§897), and therefore he did so most freely (§898).

§933

God created this world most freely (§932). Therefore, he willed to create it (§893). He willed it efficiently (§671) and hence completely, because he is infallible (§879), and consequently from complete motives. Therefore, God decided to create this world (§695), and indeed efficaciously in every sense (§675).[171]

motives] motives, through his consequent will, and he has therefore decided for the creation of this world and for the actuality of this world

§934

In his most proportional will (§894), God decided the creation of this world (§933). Hence, he decided on the existence of this world according to a recognized degree of goodness in it (§926). In his most proportional will (§379), he did not decide on the existence of another world. Therefore, God did not recognize goodness in the existence of any other world as much as he recognized it in the existence of this world (§70). Now, the knowledge of God is the most distinct and maximally infallible (§879). Therefore, the existence of this preferred world, which was chosen above all the rest (§697), is the best existence of a world that there can be (§187).

§935

When the existence of this world is posited, the supreme perfection that there can be in a world is posited (§187, 934). The most perfect world is that world in which the supreme perfection that is possible in a world is posited (§185). Therefore, this world is the most perfect of all possible worlds.

§936

In this world there are the most of the greatest parts, and the greatest of the most parts, that there can be in a world, and the agreement in it is as great as there can be in a world (§436, 935). This world is extensively, protensively, and intensively the greatest of the worlds (§437). It is indeed really finite, although it can be called infinite in many ways (§440). It is the best world (§443), and in it there is the greatest universal nexus (§441), order (§444), and harmony (§462) that there can be.

§937

Suppose a world that is totally equal in perfection to this world. It would need to be posited outside of this world, since otherwise it would be another part of this world (§354, 155). The perfection of this world cannot be outside of this world, nor can the perfection of an absolutely equally perfect world be posited outside of this one world (§194).[172] Therefore, if such a world were possible, two totally equal perfections would be possible mutually outside of each other, which goes against §272. Therefore, the most perfect world is unique (§77).

§938

We can be certain that this world is the best (§935, 936). Therefore, this doctrine is not a philosophical hypothesis. Those who demand an *a posteriori* demonstration of this either understand by "*a posteriori* demonstration" one having an intuitive judgment among its premises, which they can find in §933, among whose premises the intuitive judgment *this world exists*[173] is included, or they are asking to experience the difference between this and an inferior world, and hence to be set outside of this world (§548), an amazing ecstasy[174] (§552).[175]

§939

Whatever God created, he willed to create (§932). However, he did not at all will the formal aspect of contingent[176] and specifically moral evils (§914). Therefore, he did not will to create them[177] (§926). God is not the creator of any contingent[178] evil, and hence not of any moral evil,[179] formally considered.

§940

An AUTHOR is the cause of a free action, and both the action as well as what it caused are the effects, or the DEEDS <*FACTA*>, of the author. Now, God created the world most freely (§932). Therefore, God is the author of creation and of this world. God is only the author of those things he wills (§719, 891). Now, God does not will the formal aspect of any contingent[180] evil, or of any sin (§914). Therefore, God is not the author of any contingent[181] evil, or of any sin, formally considered. A MORAL CAUSE IN THE STRICT SENSE is an author through the free determination of another, as for example through enticement, threat, persuasion, dissuasion, extortion, etc. (§728). Now, the moral cause is the author, strictly speaking. Therefore, God is not the moral cause, strictly speaking, of any sin or contingent[182] evil, formally considered.

§941

One who actualizes the impelling causes for moral evil, formally considered, is a TEMPTER TO EVIL. If God actualized the impelling causes for moral evil, formally considered, then he would become the moral cause of the same in the strict sense. Therefore, God is never a tempter to evil (§940).

Section II. The end of creation[183]

§942

The acknowledgment[184] of a greater perfection in someone is HONOR. Greater honor is GLORY[a] (cf. §684).[185] Therefore, the glory of God is the greater knowledge of his supreme perfections. The more [creatures] who recognize more greatly, and therefore more clearly, certainly, zealously, and truly, more and greater perfections of someone, the greater is the glory (§160).[b] Hence, the supreme glory of God is the clearest, truest, most certain, and most zealous knowledge of the most and greatest of his perfections in the most [creatures] (§161). The glory of God is a good (§866).

§943

The supreme perfections of God can be known very clearly, truly, certainly, and zealously through this world (§333, 375). Therefore, those who are capable of recognizing his glory from the world are useful for the glory of God (§336). This utility has been actualized through the creation of the world and all the spirits in it (§926). Therefore, the creator of this universe uses it for bringing about his own glory, which he most distinctly knows as good (§889, 942). Therefore, God had an end in creating (§341).[c]

§944

God created the world according to his supreme knowledge of the final nexus (§943), and hence most wisely (§882). Hence, in creating all the best ends of the best world, which are in it in the most perfect[186] subordination and coordination (§883), he knew and brought about their best (§884), most certain (§885), and most fecund (§886) means <*remedia*> that wholly achieve their ends (§887) in the shortest way (§888). It is again obvious that God did not create any contingent[187] evil, formally considered (§146, 914).

---

[a] Wolff: "The collection of divine attributes, insofar as they are recognized by rational creatures, is called the *Glory of God*. Whence God is said to manifest *his glory* insofar as he reveals his absolutely supreme perfection, or if you prefer, his attributes, to human beings. And humankind is said *to promote the divine glory* insofar as it bears witness in words and deeds that it recognizes the absolute supreme perfection of God, and rejoices in its certainty of the same" (WTN1 610).
[b] Kant E3684, 1764–9 (across from the third sentence): "end without motives <*finis absque motivis*>."
[c] Wolff: "*God chooses the means by which the end that he intends through the existence of this world is obtained.* And indeed the end that God intended through the existence of this world is the disclosure of his own absolutely supreme perfection (WTN1 §608), and the perfection of this very world (WTN1 §607)" (WTN1 §624).

§945

In creating the world, the end of God was not any specific internal perfection of his own. Indeed, it is impossible for any of these to be actualized or increased through the world (§851), and God does not will the impossible (§891, 893). Now, with the exception of God, whatever is, is the world or part of the world (§846, 354).[188] Therefore, the end of God in creating the world was the perfection of creatures (§928).

§946

The end of God in creating the universe was the creation of as much perfection of creatures as is possible in the best world (§945, 944). Therefore, the ends of God (§944) are all of the things that are useful for creatures (§336), and everything used by them (§338). The science of the divine ends in creatures is TELEOLOGY, and it is PHYSICAL insofar as it exhibits the ends of bodies, and PNEUMATIC insofar as it exhibits the ends of spirits.[189]

divine ends ... TELEOLOGY] divine ends, of why he has created the creatures, is TELEOLOGY

§947

A good determination of a spirit based on the motives of divine glory is the CELEBRATION OF DIVINE GLORY (the worship of God).[190] The glory of God and its celebration is RELIGION. Now the glory of God is[191] useful for his worship (§336, 712),[a] and both glory and worship are useful for religion (§336). Therefore, the ends of creation were the worship of God and religion (§942, 946).

§948

The prosperity and blessedness, or happiness, of spirits is useful for the glory of God (§787, 942), for his celebration, and for religion (§947,[192] 336). Therefore, the prosperity and blessedness, or happiness, of spirits, to the degree possible in the best world, were the ends of creation (§946, 942).

§949

All creatures, whether viewed as means or as ends, are useful for the glory of God, which[193] is useful for the celebration of divine glory (§943, 947). Hence, all the co-ends of religion in creation are subordinated to religion (§315, 947). Therefore, religion is the final end of creation (§343).

end of creation] end of creation, and for its sake he has created the world

---

[a] GK consider §712 to be a problematic reference, which it clearly is.

Section III. Providence

§950[a]

This world endures (§299), but at no moment independently (§930). Therefore, it cannot endure for even one moment unless it is caused by something posited outside of it (§307). Therefore, a power outside of the world produces <*operatur*> its endurance in any given moment of this endurance (§210).[b] This is God (§855, 839). Therefore, God produces <*operatur*> the endurance of the universe at any given moment.[c] The actualization of this endurance is CONSERVATION. Therefore, God is the conserver of this universe.

§951

Conservation is a continual influence[d] of God (§950, 895), and it is real (§212), because no finite thing can effect its own existence (§308). Creation is the same (§926). Hence, it is not wrong to call conservation "continued creation."[e]

§952

Those things that were not created are not conserved (§950, 926). Therefore, God does not conserve the essence of things, the metaphysical evil of finite things (§931),[194] the formal aspect of contingent[195] evil, or moral evil formally considered (§939).

§953

Whatever can exist only through creation can endure only through conservation (§950, 926). Now, all of the monads of this world, and whatever else is substantial in it, are the creatures of God. Therefore, all the monads of the world, and whatever else is substantial in it,[196] are conserved by God at any given moment of their endurance (§928).

§954[197]

Since the efficient causes, with the exception of God, and all the substances of this world (§319, 846) are subordinated to God, he is simply the first efficient cause, and all of the rest are secondary (§315, 28). Now, all the actions of finite substances are, at the same time, sufferings caused by the other finite substances that influence them (§451). Therefore, in a mediated way, God concurs with all the actions of finite substances as an efficient cause (§314, 320). However, seeing that all the sufferings of finite substances caused by other finite substances are at the same time their very own actions (§463), not only when they are chiefly conceived of as acting, but also when

---

[a] Kant E3685, 1776–89 (perhaps also to the heading): "actualizing and directing the world <*actuatio mundi et regimen*>"

[b] G/K consider §210 to be a problematic reference, but it could also refer to the action of God in producing endurance.

[c] Kant E3686, 1771–8 (next to the last two sentences): "The preservation in time of the form that is adequate to the final end is called gubernation: management."

[d] Kant E3687, 1771–8: "not influence, which is (*crossed out:* an action) a modification, not the actualization of substance <*non influxus, qui est [actio] modificatio, non actuatio substantiae*>."

[e] Kant E3688, 1776–89: "A continued beginning is a contradiction."

they are observed to be suffering, God, who actualizes the sufficient ground of this alteration and thus their power through conservation (§953) at the very moment in which they are altered, concurs immediately with the actions of all finite substance as an efficient cause (§320). For, his action pertains to the present existence of a finite substance (§210, 55).

Now, all the actions] Now, all the natural actions ‖ with all the actions] with all the natural actions ‖ *Meier adds a final sentence:* Thus, God concurs immediately not only when the creatures are represented as active, but rather also and most of all when they are represented as naturally passive.

§955

The immediate concurrence of God is his presence (§223). Therefore, God is most closely present to all the substances of the world (§954). That which is most closely present to every substance, as well as to each substantial part of every one of them, is called INTIMATELY PRESENT to these very things. Now, God is most closely present to all the substantial parts of the bodies in this universe (§421). Therefore, God is intimately present to all the bodies in this universe.

§956

God is closest to every monad of this world, intimately present to each body (§955) at any given moment, and is such with regard to all the actions of creatures (§954). Therefore, God is most omnipresent.

§957

Wherever God is, he is complete and indivisible (§842), thus also with regard to substance and essence (§830, 816).[198] Therefore, God is present to all the monads and bodies of this world with regard to substance and essence (§955).

§958[a]

The conservation of all the powers of this universe in their very activity is the PHYSICAL CONCURRENCE OF GOD, and it, because and insofar as[199] it also extends to all the actions of all substances,[b] is called GENERAL (universal).

§959

The entire concurrence of God is most free (§932). Therefore, if he were to concur with the formal aspect of an evil action, God would be its author (§940). Therefore, he concurs with all physically and morally evil actions materially (§958), but certainly not formally (§940).

---

[a] Kant E3689, 1771–2? (1773–5?) (end of 1769–autumn 1770?): "Concurrence with nature or freedom./Providence with respect to laws (determining them) is general; providence with respect to events is special <*Providentia respectu legum (illas determinans) est generalis, eventuum est specialis*>."

[b] G/K: "the individual actions of individual substances"

§960[a]

The CONCURRENCE of a moral cause in the strict sense is MORAL. God actualizes the motives of his own worship (§947). Therefore, he concurs morally with certain actions in this universe (§940).[200] The moral concurrence of God that is additional to the general concurrence is SPECIAL. Therefore, God concurs specially with certain actions in this universe.

§961

God does not tempt toward evil (§941). Therefore, he does not concur morally with the formal aspect of any morally evil action (§940). Therefore, neither does he do so specially (§960).

§962

The supernatural CONCURRENCE OF GOD that is additional to special concurrence is the MOST SPECIAL, and is possible both in itself (§475) and hypothetically (§860). It is actual in this world whenever some action in the latter could not be actualized equally well through the special concurrence of God (§498, 935).

hypothetically] hypothetically, in view of the omnipotence of God || It ... God] Such is actual in the world whenever it is the case that the degree of goodness required by the law of the best world cannot be brought about in an action of creatures through the special concurrence of God

§963

GOVERNING is the action by which many means are successively actualized for some further end. Therefore, the better the means, and the more of the best means (and hence[201] the means obtaining the end in the shortest way (§888)), that are actualized for better and more final ends, the more perfect is the governing (§185).[202] What ends God had in creating, he has and actualizes by conserving (§951, 944). Therefore, when we are venerating him as the supreme governor of the universe, we are honoring the one who at any given moment actualizes the best and most means proceeding in the shortest ways to the best ends that, in the end, lead to the final aim of this universe.[203] If, when governing, God (1) institutes a certain limit to the powers (and hence the actions, §331) of a creature <*rei creatae*>, this is called DETERMINING IN THE STRICTER SENSE; (2) when he subordinates to his own ends a creature's <*rei creatae*> action that the creature had not undertaken towards these ends, this is called DIRECTING IN THE STRICTER SENSE.

§964

The first sin is called the FALL, and the potential for falling is called FALLIBILITY, and this is either absolute or hypothetical (§15, 16). The opposite of hypothetical fallibility is CONFIRMATION IN THE GOOD.

---

[a] Kant E3690, before 1766? (1764–9?) (beginning): "He does not concur with the formal aspect of actions. He is not the author of evil according to ordinary direction <*Non concurrit ad formale actionum. Non est auctor mali secundum directionem ordinariam*>."

§965

Absolute fallibility pertains to the essence of the finite spirit (§40, 964) and hence is absolutely necessarily in a finite spirit (§106), thus a metaphysical evil (§146). Absolute fallibility is not co-created for any spirit (§931), and its opposite could not be co-created for any creature <*creaturae*> (§833). A falling spirit acts (§964, 788). Therefore, God concurs with the material aspect of the fall (§918),[a] but indeed not with the formal aspect either physically or morally (§909, 911).[b] Therefore, he is neither the author of the fall formally considered, nor the moral cause in a strict sense (§940).

A ... acts] The fall into sin is a free action

§966

The fall is contingent in itself (§964), insofar as it is an alteration of a finite being (§361). Therefore, the opposite of the fall is also possible in itself (§104). Therefore, an impediment to the fall is also possible in itself (§221). Therefore, God could have impeded every fall (§833).

The fall ... itself] Every sin and every fall into sin is a free action || every fall] every fall into sin, and consequently all sin in this world

§967

MORAL IMPEDITION is the actualization of motives to the opposite of a given alteration. God actualizes very many motives for the happiness of spirits (§948). The happiness of spirits is the opposite of their fall (§81, 787). Therefore, God morally impedes every fall.[c]

given alteration] of a free act || their fall] sin and fall into sin || every fall] all sin and every fall into sin

§968

When an impedition is not moral, it is called PHYSICAL IMPEDITION. The fall is a sin (§964), and therefore a moral action (§788). Therefore, it is free as to its execution (§719, 722), and hence physically contingent (§709). Therefore, apart from the freedom of the one who falls and this person's own motives (§967), many other motives were possible that, if they had been posited, then the fall, which in fact followed (§378), would not have followed. These are physical impediments to the fall (§81, 221). Therefore, God could have impeded the fall physically (§833).[204]

The ... sin] Sin and the fall into sin is a free action || then the fall] then the sin and the fall into sin || Therefore, God ... physically] Therefore, through his omnipotence, God could have prevented all sins that actually occur in the world

§969

God morally impedes every sin, and through omnipotence he can impede them

[a] G/K consider this to be a problematic reference, which it clearly is.
[b] G/K helpfully correct this reference to §939, 914.
[c] Kant E3691, 1775–8 (between §967 and 968): "Permission. Allowance is not permission."

physically (§968).[205] However, he does not impede every sin physically. Not to impede is PERMISSION. Therefore, this is either physical (§968)[206] or moral (§967).

§970

God does not morally permit any fall (§967) or sin (§969).[207] However, he physically permits some sins in this world. Suppose that these are physically impeded: then it would not be this world in which they were impeded, but another (§378) and less good world (§937). Therefore, God physically permits certain sins in this world, because the world in which they are physically permitted is the best means for religion (§949, 935).

§971

RIGHT IN THE BROADER SENSE is a moral faculty (taken as a quality of a person), and one who has the right to decide whatever they please in regard to something is COMPLETE LORD over it. Complete lordship over persons is COMPLETE COMMAND.

§972

God has right over his own most righteous actions (§901,[208] 971). In these, he decides over the world and every creature (§934). Therefore, God is[209] the complete lord of the world and all the creatures in it. Therefore, he has complete command over the spirits of this world (§971).

God ... actions] God has a right to all his free actions, because they are in the highest degree regular || Therefore, God ... it] To this belongs God's decree regarding the world and all its parts, together with the actions through which he brings them about

§973

Whoever has complete command over a spirit has the right of obliging that very spirit in whatever way may be pleasing. Whoever has the right of obliging a given spirit in whatever way may be pleasing has the right of making laws for it. For, the author of the obligation that the law expresses is said TO MAKE LAW. Whoever holds the right to make laws is a LEGISLATOR.[210] Therefore, God is the legislator for all the spirits of this world (§971, 972).

§974[211, a]

Whoever alone has supreme potency and command over several spirits is their MONARCH,[b] whereas whoever has complete potency and command over them is a DESPOT.[c] Now God alone has supreme potency (§832) and command over all created

---

[a] Kant E3692, 1773–8? (1769?): "Lawgiver in the beginning,/Ruler in the duration,/Judge in the end. really in the infinity of the progression."

[b] Kant E3693, 1776–8: "which is not subjected to the command of another."

[c] Kant E3694, 1776–8: "Is the one who binds the creature in accordance with an absolute will, without* taking into consideration needs in regard to the laws. Therefore there are despotic and patriotic laws./*(to take into consideration the agreement of its own will which is governed through reason, i.e. as machines.)"

spirits, and indeed complete control (§971). Therefore, his very monarchy is supremely and maximally despotic, to which all created spirits are subordinated (§844).[a]

§975

The PROVIDENCE OF GOD is the action through which he bestows the greatest goods on as many creatures as his supreme goodness can. Therefore, by conserving (§950), concurring (§954), and governing (§963); by morally impeding evil (§967), and only permitting it physically if impeding it would detract from his ends (§970); and by making the best laws for his state (§973, 974), God exercises PROVIDENCE[212] (§903–20)[213] through the impelling cause <causa impulsiva> toward happiness, thus as THE REFORMER OF HEARTS,[b] through fortune, thus by HOLY FORTUNE, and through the innate good of any given nature, thus by a FOSTERING NATURE.[214] EPICUREANISM denies the providence of God, and is an error (§515).

PROVIDENCE] universal PROVIDENCE ‖ through the impelling … fostering nature] This providence, while it is concerned in particular with: 1) the incentives of finite spirits to their happiness, has a power connected to the heart; 2) concerning fortune and misfortune, it is the divine aspect of what one calls fortune; 3) and concerning the good which was placed in the nature of every creation, it is called the divine aspect in nature

Section IIII. Divine decrees[215]

§976[c]

God's decree concerning the existence of the world is supremely free (§933),[216] and hence inalterably (§839),[d] eternally (§849), and irresistibly (§844, 222)[217] follows the most distinct and accurate knowledge of every part of this world and of all the goods

---

[a] Kant explicitly rejects the idea of God as an unlimited despot in several texts. See e.g. *Religion within the Bounds of Mere Reason* AA 6: 141, where he expresses his disagreement with many of the properties Baumgarten ascribes to God. Kant's point is that we must represent God through the role he is to play as author of the moral law who at the same time seeks to assure not only that we follow it, but also that we do so for the sake of the law itself.

[b] *Verticordiam*, an epithet for Venus, who was said to restrain maidens from unchastity. See Adam Ferguson, *The History of the Progress and Termination of the Roman Republic*. London: 1783. p. 368. Baumgarten glosses it as "[*die*] *hertzenlenckende Kraft*," "the power for directing or turning the heart," a direct transliteration from the Latin.

[c] Kant E3695, 1770–8 (beginning): "The will that is determined in regard to universal grounds (*crossed out:* of it) of the will to certain action is antecedent. That which is determined in regard to the individual: consequent."
Kant E3696, 1776–89 (ff.): "Here God is represented as if he decreed over everything possible, which part to select for his choice."

[d] Wolff: "*God is the most holy, such that it is not permitted to conceive of greater holiness than that of the divine.* And indeed all free actions of God are right (WNT1 §1059), and there are certainly none in which any defect is to be noticed. For the reason that it can in no way be doubted that God always wills what is right, and since his will is inalterable (WTN1 §368), it also cannot happen that he could be diverted from what is right in any way, or in any small detail. And thus since to him belongs the consistent and perpetual will only to do what is right, and since to the truly holy one belongs a consistent and perpetual will only to do what is right, it is understood that God is holy" (WNT1 §1065).

and evils in it[218] (§889).[219] This can be conceived by humans in this manner: The major premise is the divine purpose (πρόθεσις): Let there exist the collection of the best things outside of God (§822, 901). The minor premise is divine foresight or providence (πρόγνωσις): This best world is the collection of the best things compossible outside of God (§935). The conclusion is divine foreordination (προορισμός): Let there exist this best world.[a]

divine foreordination] the decree itself

§977

There are no more worlds than this one, nor more finite beings than those that are part of this world (§379). God did not decree anything more in regard to contingent beings than was included in the decree concerning the existence of this world (§976). Therefore, this decree is called universal insofar as it is extended to all realities of this universe, and it is called unique insofar as there are not many decrees (§77).

§978

PARTICULAR DECREES OF GOD are either parts of a universal and unique decree (§977) or they are PRIMITIVE DEGREES OF GOD, which then would be either opposed to the universal decree, or at least not included under it. There are no decrees of the latter kind in God (§976).

§979

The decrees of God are all acts of a will that is most proportional to its objects[220] (§894) and that most perfectly follows its knowledge of the degree of perfection or imperfection in the object that is to be desired or averted[221] (§976). And the same is obvious in this way: If it is supposed that, in some decree of God, the object's foreseen perfection or imperfection was not in any way the motive: then God was ignorant of it, which goes against §875, or he abstracted from it, which goes against §870, or his knowledge was most distinct, but dead, which goes against §890.

---

[a] Kant E3697, 1776–89 (next to the last line of §976 and the first of 977): "A decree is a subsequent will, therefore with respect to the individual. An antecedent will is that whose impelling cause is only something general that is common to every object of choice. (*crossed out:* No decree) A decree concerning the founding of this world is a decree of an individual; therefore it is not universal. No universal decree is given. but a universal or total decree, a decree not different from the particular, but from the partial. <*Decretum est voluntas consequens, ergo respectu individui. Voluntas antecedens est, cuius caussa impulsiva est tantum generale aliquod, quod omnibus obiectis arbitrii commune est. Decretum [nullum] de condendo hoc mundo est decretum individui, ergo non est universale. Non datur decretum universale. sed decretum universum sive totale, diversum non a [partial] particulari, sed partiali>.*"

§980[a]

If a DECREE[b] OF GOD is called ABSOLUTE when its motive[c] is not an object's foreseen perfection or imperfection, and, on the contrary, HYPOTHETICAL when it does follow an object's foreseen perfection or imperfection, then none of God's decrees concerning contingent beings are absolute; they are all hypothetical (§979). THEOLOGICAL ABSOLUTISM[d] is the doctrine maintaining that God's decrees concerning contingent things are absolute, and it is an error (§515).[222]

§981

A decree concerning the eternal[223] happiness of some spirit is PREDESTINATION IN THE STRICT SENSE, whereas PREDESTINATION IN THE BROAD SENSE is a decree about the future.[224, e] A decree concerning the eternal[225] unhappiness of some spirit is REPROBATION. Both are hypothetical (§980). PREDESTINATIONISM, or absolutism in the conception of predestination in the strict sense, is an error (§515).[226]

Section V. Revelation[227]

§982

REVELATION IN THE BROAD SENSE (cf. §986, 989)[228] is when God signifies the divine mind to his creatures. Therefore, creatures are taught about divine knowledge and will by divine revelation. However, they are never taught everything (§862), but always only as much as is pleasing to providence (§975).[f]

§983

God is the author of universal nature (§940, 466). Therefore, whatever a creature understands through its own nature about the mind of God according to universal

---

[a] Kant E3700, 1776–89 (beginning): "Whether the divine will is determined in itself through motives, or is merely thought by us according to this analogy?"

[b] Kant E3699, 1776–89 (beginning, next to "DECREE … imperfection"): "At no point is the divine choice absolutely unconditioned, although perhaps unconditioned in regard to the moral quality of the person as despotism; for God's intention could indeed be directed to the best of the world as a whole and this be the condition.* God cannot (rationally) sacrifice a creature to the world-whole, although he can well allow it to sacrifice itself./*(Here it is assumed that God uses the rational creature merely as a means to perfection of the whole. But there is no moral worth in the world in which the rational being is merely used as a means.)"

[c] Kant E3698, 1776–89: "there is a highest good of the world, insofar as it is opposed to the highest good of the individual <*est summum bonum mundi, quatenus opponitur summo bono individui*>."

[d] Kant E3701, 1770s–80s: "Doom."

[e] Kant E3702, 1776–89: "just as with the end of will <*tanquam fine voluntatis*>"

[f] Wolff: "*In divine revelation, everything ought to be conveyed in those words, or presented in those signs, through which the one for whom revelation is made wholly understands the speaking or revealing mind of God*" (WTN1 §491). And again: "*In divine revelation, neither more nor fewer words occur than those which suffice for understanding the mind of the revealing God* (WTN1 §492), and those words are selected whose benefit is certainly granted so that the one for whom the revelation is made obtains those things" (WTN1 §492).

nature, it knows through divine revelation (§982), which is natural (§469). Such is natural theology (§800).

§984

All finite beings are means for knowing the divine mind (§858, 880), and all the powers for representing this universe signify their creator (§929) as the best and wisest (§933). The soul itself is a power for representing its own God (§741, 744).

§985

The divine mind is revealed[229] naturally to the soul through the soul[230] itself, through every monad[a] to which it is present, and hence through every body[b] and sense (§984). The ends of God[231] are revealed through the use of every thing[c] (§946), and his[232] will is revealed through knowledge of what is best (§894).

§986

REVELATION IN THE STRICT SENSE (cf. §982, 989)[233] is divine supernatural revelation given to humans through speech. It is a most special concurrence with religion, and is possible in itself and hypothetically. It is actual in this world whenever religion cannot be actualized equally well through natural revelation alone[234] (§962, 949).[d]

hypothetically] hypothetically through the omnipotence of God

§987

Suppose that a merely natural revelation is made for certain individuals in this world, e.g. humans. Suppose further that under these same circumstances a revelation is made supernaturally to these same individuals, a revelation which is more fecund,[235] noble,[236] clear, true, certain, and brilliant than the merely natural revelation (§669): then a revelation in the strict sense that is most appropriate for the order of this world (§484) can come to pass in it, and exists in it (§986).

§988

Suppose that there is some indication of the divine mind in this world that would be very good for religion (§947) but that cannot be actualized naturally, whereas it nevertheless can be actualized supernaturally: then revelation in the strict sense will occur in this world (§496, 987).

§989

Revelation in the strict sense that cannot be naturally known by creatures is REVELATION IN THE STRICTEST SENSE (cf. §982, 986).[237] Therefore, any knowledge of the divine mind that would be very good for religion, but which is

---

[a] G/K: "individual monads"
[b] G/K: "individual bodies"
[c] G/K: "individual things"
[d] G/K change §949 to §494, which makes sense.

naturally unknowable for certain creatures, is in fact actualized in those creatures through revelation in the strictest sense (§988).

Revelation … SENSE] Revelation in the strict sense, which makes known to creatures things that they cannot know at all in a natural way, is REVELATION IN THE STRICTEST SENSE

§990

If that which is taken to be the revelation of God in the strict sense nevertheless does not promote the greater glory of God and religion, nor supply[238] more fecund,[239] noble,[240] clear, true, certain or brilliant knowledge of God than does natural revelation, then it is not the revelation of God in the strict sense (§986, 495).

§991

In the mind of God there is no contradiction (§822). Therefore, whatever truly contradicts natural revelation is not the revelation of God in the strict sense (§983, 989),[241] nor in the strictest sense (§989).[242]

§992

The revelation of God in both the strict and the strictest sense does not contradict natural revelation (§991), and hence neither does it contradict reason taken as objective, insofar as it is known by sound human reason taken as subjective (§646, 984).

sound] healthy

§993

HOLY[243] FAITH TAKEN OBJECTIVELY is the collection of those things that must be believed regarding revelation in the strict sense, just as the faith held in revelation in the strict sense is HOLY FAITH TAKEN SUBJECTIVELY.[244] Therefore, not only those things that are naturally and absolutely unknowable to creatures belong to the holy faith (§989, 986).[245]

HOLY FAITH TAKEN OBJECTIVELY] THE CONTENT OF HOLY FAITH[a]

§994

Holy faith taken objectively, insofar as it is believed by a person through faith taken subjectively,[246] does not contradict reason taken objectively, to the extent that it is known by sound human reason taken subjectively (§992, 993).

Holy faith taken objectively] The content of holy faith || sound] healthy

§995

Revelation in the strict sense signifies supremely possible things (§986, 822). Now, those things which go against reason are impossible (§643). Therefore, neither revelation (either in the strict or the strictest sense[b] (§989)) nor holy[247] faith taken objectively,[248] go against reason. Indeed, those things that go against reason are not

---

[a] As Meier consistently substitutes this locution in the following, the fact has not been further noted.
[b] Reading *strictissime* for *strictissima* (AA).

the revelation of God either in the strict or the strictest sense, nor are they holy[249] faith taken objectively.

§996

The HOLY[250] MYSTERIES are those things posited as beyond the reason of creatures in holy[251] faith taken objectively. There are mysteries in every revelation in the strictest sense (§989, 644). Therefore, they are not repugnant to revelation in the strict sense (§989), nor do they go against reason (§643).

§997

God is maximally sincere in all of his revelations (§919). Hence, if his wisdom judges speech, and indeed supernaturally actualized speech, to be the most apt sign for indicating the divine mind to humans, then he is most truthful in revelation in the strict sense (§920).

§998

In revelation in the strict and strictest sense, God is a supremely sincere and most capable (§997, 889), and hence most trustworthy <*fide dignissimus*>, witness (§986, 946). His revelation in the strict sense gives supreme certainty to faith.

§999

A NATURALIST IN THE STRICTER SENSE (cf. §493)[252] denies the revelation of God in the strict sense in this world. The (theoretical)[253] ATHEIST denies the existence of God, and errs[254] (§811, 854). In neither sense[a] does naturalism necessarily maintain atheism (§493).

§1000

If naturalists in the stricter sense deny that revelation in the strict sense exists in this world because (1) it is a supernatural event (§986) and hence seems impossible (§860); because (2) they believe holy[255] faith to be against reason and hence impossible; or (3) because they deny divine providence over the human race (§975), then they err through their own fault (§982, 986), and are ignorant of the most benign God (§903),

Whose honor, name and praise shall always remain.[256]

---

[a] *sensu neutro*: §493 discusses naturalism in the broad sense, and here Baumgarten is concerned with naturalism in the stricter sense.

Index to the Paragraphs of the *Metaphysics*

of desire, superior §689, 690
of desire, victorious §693, 694
of divination §616
of foresight §595, 599
ideal §217
irascible §676
of invention, or poetic §589, 590, 592, 594, 609, 640
of judging §606, 608, 640, 641
of judging, precipitous §608
locomotive §750
of perceiving the correspondences and differences of things §572, 640, 641
of presuming §612, 613
of reflection §626
real §217
simple §217
faint §566
fainting §555
fairness §918
faith, theological, taken objectively §993, 998
faithfulness §905
fall §964, 966
fallibility §964, 965
falling asleep §555
fantasists §594
fatalism §898
fate §382
physico-mechanical or physical §435
Spinosistic §382
favor §684
favorable §658
fear §686
fecundity, of reason §166
feebleness of knowledge §515
fictions §590
field of adequation §514
of clarity §514
of confusion §514
of distinction §514
of obscurity §514
figure §280
finite §248, 249, 250, 264, 661, 833, 984
finitude §261
firm §698
first, the §300
flesh §676
flexible §698

flight §677
focus of perfection §94
forbearance §916
forcing oneself §714, 727
foreknowledge §875
foresight §595–8, 600–4, 609, 712, 752
false §605, 618, 621
fulfilled §605
forethought §641
foretoken §348
forgetfulness §582
forgetting §582
forgetting oneself §552
forgetting something §582
form §40, 345
formal aspect, of the whole §40
of physical evil §952
of the event §914
fortuitous §912
fortune, good §912
bad §912
foundation of the soul §511
founded §307, 326, 328
freedom §719, 720, 725, 730, 756, 902
pure §719, 720
its rule §726
furious §688
future beings §298
contingencies §709

genus §150, 153
highest §150
lowest §150
subordinate §150
gift, of prophecy §616
glory §684, 942
glory of god §942, 947, 949
goal §343
God §811–14, 818–25, 828–57, 859, 861–80, 882–99, 904–6, 909, 914–26, 932–4, 939–41, 943, 944, 945, 950, 952–7, 959–63, 965–7, 969, 970, 972–5, 977, 978, 983, 985, 997, 998
good §100, 187, 665, 666
adventitious or external to me §660
contingent §147
for me §660
metaphysical §147

reprobation §981
resistance §222
respects §37
rest §283
 absolute §417
 relative §417
resting §283
revelation §982
 more strictly speaking §986–8, 990–2,
  995, 998
 most strictly speaking §989, 991, 992,
  995, 998
reward §907
 chosen §908, 911, 912
 natural §908, 911
rhetoric §622
richness of knowledge §515
right of nature, most broadly §472
 more broadly §971
righteousness, of action §901
rule §83
rule, of comparison §627
 of the expectation of similar cases
  §612
 of external sensation §541
 of the faculty of invention §590
 of the faculty of presuming §613
 of freedom §726
 of internal sensation §541
 of recollection §583
 of reflection §627
 of separating §629
rules of motion §432

sadness §685
sagacity, of reason §645
same, the §38, 269, 274
satisfaction <*complacentia*> §655, 891, 892;
 <*satisfactio*> §682
scrutinizer of hearts §869
seat of the human soul §745
self repose §682
semiotics or semiology §349
sempiternal §302
sensation §529, 534, 537, 538, 541, 542,
 544, 546, 549–51, 562, 578, 638,
 736, 737, 752, 768
 external §535, 537, 538, 541, 543
 internal §535, 541

senses §535, 539
 acute §540
 dull §540
 external §535, 540
 internal §535
sensing §534
sensual, the §608
separated, to be §72
separating §589, 629
servile §730
shame §687
sharp, more eminently §648
sign §347
 demonstrative §348
 essential §349
 mnemonic or a memory aid §348
 primitive, foretoken, derivative §348,
  349
signification §347
signified, the §347
similar, the §70, 271, 275
similitude §265, 267, 749
 accidental §266
 essential §266
simple, in the bad sense §639
simultaneous, the §238, 240, 282, 306
sincerity §919
singular, the §148, 152, 561
sinner §909
sins §788, 915, 969
situation §284
slavery, moral, in the bad sense §730
sleep <*dormitare*> §555
sleep <*somnus*> §556, 623
sleep walkers §594
sleeping §556
sluggish §698
smallness §161
smell §536
socinianism, philosophical §875
solidity §645
something §8
sorrow §685
soul §504–7, 511, 513, 519, 520, 534,
 705, 707, 720, 729, 733, 734, 739,
 756, 765, 792, 793, 795
 blessed, human §791
 damned, human §791
 human §740, 747, 750, 754, 756, 757,

760, 762, 766, 767, 772, 780, 786,
789, 791, 929, 984
  merely sensitive §792
  separate §742ᵃ
space §239, 240, 293
  filling up §241
spacious §280
species §150, 153
speculation §669
speech §350
sphere of sensation §537
spinozism, theological §855
spirit §402, 404, 405, 476, 477, 755, 796,
797, 799, 858, 929, 974
  inferior §796
  superior §796, 798
spirits, good §796
  evil §796
splendor of speech and thought §531
spontaneity, smallest §706
state §205
  external §207
  of indifference §655, 675, 691, 694
  internal §206
  moral §723
  of partial equilibrium §661, 670, 673,
675, 694
  of perfect equilibrium §670, 673
  of preponderance §674, 675
  of total equilibrium §656, 673, 675, 694
  of the world §369
stimuli §677, 695, 712, 726
strength, of knowledge §515
  of laws §180
strenuous §699
  less §699
struggle of the inferior and superior
faculty of desire §693
stupidity §578
subject, the §344
  of occupation §344
  of relation §312
subsistence §192
substance §40, 191, 199, 200, 202, 205,
208, 209, 227, 228, 231, 234, 389,
390, 398, 710, 718, 719, 838, 854
  averting, according to preference §712
  capable of something §832

desiring, according to preference §712
free §719
free from either absolute or physical
internal constraint §710
free from external constraint
unqualifiedly §707
free from internal and absolute
constraint §707
impenetrable §398
predicated §200
substantial, the §196, 928, 929
subtleties §576, 578
succeeding, being §124
succession §124
successive, the §238, 240, 282, 306
suffer, to §210
suffering §210, 214, 215, 678, 700
  and addiction §732
  ideal §212
  real §212
superior, the §148
supposit, the §200
surface, curved, flat §289, 292
symbol §350
syncope §556
syntax §622
system, psychological, of assistance §763,
767
  psychological, of pre-established
harmony §763, 768
  psychological, of physical influence
§763, 764, 766
  universal, of assistance, more broadly
Cartesian and of occasional causes
§452, 457, 490
  universal, of physical influence §450,
451, 454, 456, 457
  universal, of pre-established
harmony §448, 449, 454, 455, 457,
459, 460
systems, general, of explaining the
commerce of mundane substances
§448
  composite §457, 458
  simple §457, 458, 761
  psychological §761

taste §536

ᵃ The reference to the separate soul refers only to the first edition.

acquired §577
in the broader sense §607
corrupt §608
inborn §577
infused §577
moral §723
Proficiency §219
theoretical §577
taste, uncommon, delicate §608
tasteless §578
teleology §946
physical §946
pneumatic §946
temperament of the soul §732
tempter to evil §941
term *see terminus*
terminus (boundary, term) §248, 350
term of relation §312
terror §686
theology, archetypal §866, 892
in the broader sense §866
moral §723
natural §800, 802, 983
thisness §151
thnetopsychites §781
threats §728
time §240, 325
future §297
past §297
present §297
timeliness §323
timidity §686
touch §536
touching one another §223
traducians §771, 772
transformation, animal §779
true, the §12
truth, metaphysical §89, 92, 119, 184, 189
transcendental §89, 118, 132, 163
tumultuousness of knowledge §515

ugliness §662
understand, to §69
undetermined §34
unequal §70
unfavorable §658
unfortunate §912
unhappiness §788
union §205, 739

closest §739
unique, the §77
unitedness §79
unity §76, 132, 163, 173, 189
categorical §74
perfect §230
universal, the §148, 149
unknown, to me §652, 654
partially, to me §652
unlimited §248
unreasonable §643
untimeliness §323
use §338, 888
of reason §646
of the intellect §639
useful, the §336, 337, 340
utility §336
active §336
passive §336

valuation §337
vanity §36
variable §699
variation §209
vastness of knowledge §515
veracity §920
vertigo §554
violent §699
vision <*visio*> §552, 557
vision <*visus*> §536
visionaries §594
volition §690, 692, 720, 766
analogue of both [volition and
non-volition] in God §899
antecedent, excitation, inclination,
previous §695
pure §692
subsequent, decisive, decree, final §695

way, shortest §888
weak §699
weight, of the ground §166
whole, the §155, 157
width §290
will §690, 691
inscrutable §900
proportional §894
wisdom §882
wise, more eminently §648

Part Three

Ancillary Materials

Glossary

With some exceptions, Latin adjectives are put in masculine singular, and verbs in the infinitive alone. Latin nouns are only given in the nomitive singular (e.g. *mens*), unless part of an idiomatic expression (e.g. *mente capti*). English verbs are in the infinitive, with (to) appended. The glossary is drawn largely but not exclusively from the head words in the index.

Latin–English

A se	From itself
Ab alio	From another
Ab extra	From without
Abiectus	Abject
Absens	Absence
Absolute primum	Absolutely first
Absolutus	Absolute
Absonus	Inconsistent
Abstractio	Abstraction
Abstractus	Abstract
Abstrahere	Abstracting (to) abstract
Absurdus	Absurd
Abusus	Abuse
Accidens	Accident
Accidentalis	Accidental
Accidentia praedicabilia	Accidents, predicable
Acquiescentia in se ipso	Self repose
Acquisitus	Acquired
Actio	Action
Activus	Active
Actualis	Actual
Acumen	Acumen

Acuminis	Acumen
Acutus	Acute
Adaequatus	Adequate
Adiaphoron	Neutral
Adiunctus	Incidental
Administrus	Assisting
Admiratio	Amazement
Adspectabilis	Observable
Adventicius	Adventitious
Aequalis	Equal
Aequalitas	Equality
Aequilibrium	Equilibrium
Aequitas	Fairness
Aequivocus	Equivocal
Aestheteria	Instruments of the senses
Aesthetica	Aesthetics
Aestimatio	Valuation
Aetas	Age
Aeternitas	Eternity
Aeviternitas	Perpetuity
Affectiones	Affections
Affectus	Affects
Agathodaemones	Good spirits
Agere	Acting (to) act
Aliquid	Something
Almus	Fostering
Amarus	Bitter
Amor	Love
Analogon	Analogue
Anceps	Indecisive
Angustia	Narrowness
Angustum	Confined
Anima	Soul
Animal	Animal
Animositas	Courage

Animus	Mind
Annihilatio	Annihilation
Anthropognosia	Anthropognostics
Anthropologia	Anthropology
Anthropomorphismus	Anthropomorphism
Antipathia	Antipathy
Antitypia	Impenetrability
Apotheosis	Apotheosis
Apparens	Apparent
Appetere	Desiring (to) desire
Appetitio	Desire
Appetitus	Appetite
Arbitrarius	Chosen
Arbitrium	Choice
Archetypon	Archetype
Archetypus	Archetypal
Architectonica	Architectonics
Ars mnemonica	Mnemonic art
Artissimus	Closest
Assistentianus	Assistantist
Associatio	Association
Atheus	Atheist
Atomus	Atom
Attendere	Attending
Attentio	Attention
Attributa	Attribute
Auctor	Author
Audacia	Daring
Auditus	Hearing
Augere	Increasing
Automaton	Automaton
Auxiliaris	Helping
Auxilium	Help
Aversari	Avert (to)
Aversatio	Aversion

Beatitudo	Blessedness
Beatus	Blessed
Beneficium	Benefit
Benevolentia	Benevolence
Benignitas	Kindness
Bliteus	Tasteless
Bonitas	Goodness
Bonus	Good
Brevis	Brief
Brutum	Brute
Cacodaemones	Evil spirits
Campus	Field
Capacitas	Capacity
Capax	Capable
Caput obtusum	Obtuseness
Caput stupidum	Stupidity
Caro	Flesh
Cartesianum	Cartesian
Casus	Chance
Categoricus	Categorical
Catholicum	Catholic
Causa	Cause
Causalis	Causal
Causalitas	Causality
Causatus	Caused
Certitudo	Certitude
Certus	Certain
Character	Character
Characteristica	Characteristics
Chimaera	Chimera
Circa quam	Concerning which
Circularis	Circular
Circumspectus	Circumspection
Circumstantia	Circumstance
Civitas dei	City of god

Claritas	Clarity
Clarus	Clear
Clementia	Clemency
Coactio	Constraint
Coactus	Constrained
Coexsistentiani	Coexistentists
Cogere semet ipsum	Forcing oneself
Cogito	Think (to)
Cognitio	Knowledge
Cohaerentia	Coherence
Collectio animi	Collecting one's mind
Collisio	Collision
Combinatorius	Combinatorial
Commercium	Interaction
Commiseratio	Commiseration
Commodus	Favorable
Communis	Common
Comparatio	Comparison
Comparativus	Comparative
Complacentia	Satisfaction
Complementum	Complement
Completus	Complete
Complexus	Collective
Compos	Control
Compositus	Composite
Comprehensibilis	Comprehensible
Concausa	Co-cause
Conceptibilis	Conceivable
Conceptio	Conception
Concreatianus	Concreationist
Concretum	Concrete
Concursus	Concurrence
Conditio	Condition
Confirmatio	Confirmation
Conflictus	Conflict

Confusio	Confusion
Confusis	Confused
Congruentia	Congruence
Coniunctio	Conjunction
Coniungus	Conjoined
Connatus	Inborn
Connexus	Connected
Connumerare	Sum up (to)
Conscientia	Consciousness
Consectaria	Logical consequences
Consensus	Harmony
Consentire	Agree (to)
Conservatio	Conservation
Constans	Constancy, constant
Consuetudo	Habit
Contactus	Contact
Contiguus	Contiguous
Contingens	Contingent
Contingentia	Contingency
Contingere	Touch (to)
Continuus	Continuous
Contra ordinem naturae eveniens	Event occurring against the order of nature
Contra rationem	Contrary to reason
Contradictio	Contradiction
Convenientia	Appropriateness
Convictio	Conviction
Convincens	Convincing
Coordinatio	Coordination
Coordinatus	Coordinated
Corporeum	Corporeal
Corpus	Body
Corpuscularis	Corpuscular
Corpusculum	Corpuscle
Correlatum	Correlate
Corruptio	Corruption

Corruptus	Corrupt
Cosmologia	Cosmology
Cosmologicus	Cosmological
Creare	Create (to)
Creatiani	Creationists
Creatio	Creation
Creatura	Creatures
Criticus	Critic, criticism, critical
Cultura rationis	Cultivation of reason
Cupiditas	Eagerness
Curiositas	Curiosity
Cursus naturae	Course of nature
Curvilineus	Curvilinear
Curvus	Curved
Damnatus	Damned
Damnum	Injury
Datus	Given
Debilis	Weak
Decretum	Decree
Defectus	Defect
Deficiens	Deficient
Deformitas	Ugliness
Deismus	Deism
Delectans	Delighting
Deliberans	Deliberating
Deliberatio	Deliberation
Delicatus	Delicate
Deliquium animi	Faint
Delirium	Delirium
Delirus	Delirious
Demonstrativus	Demonstrative
Dependens	Dependent
Derivativus	Derivative
Desiderium	Yearning
Desperatio	Desperation

Despotes	Despot
Destinatus	Destined
Determinabilis	Determinable
Determinans	Determining
Determinatio	Determination
Determinatus	Determined
Deus	God
Dexteritas	Dexterity
Dialectus	Dialect
Dictum	Maxim
Differentia	Difference
Difficilis	Difficult
Dignitas	Dignity
Diiudicare	Judge (to)
Dimensio	Measuring
Dippelianismus	Dippelianism
Dirigere	Directing (to) direct
Discongruentia	Incongruent
Discretus	Discrete
Discrimen	Distinguishing mark
Displicentia	Displeasure
Displicere	Displeasing
Disproportio	Disproportion
Dissensus	Conflict
Dissimilia	Dissimilar
Dissuasio	Dissuasion
Distantia	Distance
Distinctio	Distinction
Distinctivus	Distinctive
Distinctus	Distinct
Distrahi	Distracted (to be)
Diuturnus	Permanent
Diversus	Different
Divinatio	Divination
Divisio	Division

Domesticum	Personal
Dominare	Rule (to)
Dominus	Lord complete
Donum propheticum	Gift of prophecy
Dormiens	Sleeping
Dormitare	Sleep (to)
Dualista	Dualist
Dulcis	Sweet
Duratio	Duration
Dynamica	Dynamics
Ebrius	Inebriated
Eclipses iudicii	Lapses of judgment
Ecstasis	Ecstasy
Ecthlipsis	Ecthlipsis
Ectypon	Ectype
Effectus	Effect
Efficaces	Efficacious
Efficacia	Efficacy
Efficiens	Effective, efficient
Effrenis	Unbridled
Egoista	Egoist
Elateres	Incentives
Elementum	Element
Elicitus	Elicited
Eligere	Choose (to)
Eloquentia	Eloquence
Emendans	Corrective
Emphaseologia	Emphaseology
Emphasis	Emphasis
Empiricus	Empirical
Energia	Energy
Ens	Being, a
Epicureismus	Epicureanism
Erecta	Upright
Error	Error

Essentia	Essence
Essentialia	Essential determinations
Essentialis	Essential
Etymologia	Etymology
Evanescens	Evanescent
Eveniens	Occurring
Eventus	Event
Evidentia	Evidence
Evigilare	Awaken (to)
Evolvere	Develop (to); explicate (to)
Ex nihilo	From nothing
Exceptio	Exception
Exemplar	Exemplar
Exemplaris	Exemplary
Exemplatum	Replica
Exercitium	Exercise
Experientia	Experience
Explicans	Explanatory
Exsilium mortis	Banishment of death
Exsistentia	Existence
Exspectatio	Expectation
Extensio	Extension
Extensus	Extended
Externus	External
Extorsio	Extortion
Extra se rapi	Beside oneself
Extramundanus	Extramundane
Extraordinarius	Extraordinary
Extrinsecus	Extrinsic
Fabulosus	Fantasy
Facilis	Easy
Factum	Fact
Facultas appetitiva	Faculty of desire
Facultas characteristica	Faculty of characterization
Facultas cognoscitiva	Cognitive faculty

Facultas comparandi	Faculty of comparison
Facultas concupiscibilis	Concupiscible faculty
Facultas diiudicandi	Faculty of judging
Facultas divinatrix	Faculty of divining
Facultas fingendi s poetica	Faculty of invention or the poetic faculty
Facultas identitates diversitatesque rerum percipiendi	Faculty of perceiving the correspondences and differences of things
Facultas irascibilis	Irascible faculty
Facultas locomotiva	Locomotive faculty
Facultas praesumendi	Faculty of presuming
Facultas praevidendi	Faculty of foresight
Facultas reflectendi	Faculty of reflection
Fallaciae sensuum	Deceptions of the senses
Fallax	False
Fanatici	Fantasists
Fastidium	Disgust
Fatalismus	Fatalism
Fatum	Fate
Favor	Favor
Fecunditas	Fecundity
Felicitas	Happiness
Felix	Happy
Feri	Become (to)
Fetus	Fruit
Fictio	Fiction
Fictus	Fictional
Fidelitas	Faithfulness
Fides	Faith
Fiducia	Confidence
Fidus	Faithful
Figura	Figure
Finalis	Final
Fingere	Invent (to)
Finis	End
Finitudo	Finitude

Finitus	Finite, ended
Firmus	Firm
Flexilis	Flexible
Forma	Form
Formalis	Formal
Fortis	Strong
Fortuita	Fortuitous
Fortuna	Fortune
Fuga	Flight
Fundus	Foundation
Futurus	Future
Gaudium	Joy
Generalis	General
Genericus	Generic
Gloria	Glory
Gradus	Degree
Grammatica	Grammar
Graphice	Handwriting
Gratitudo	Gratitude
Gratus	Gratifying
Gravitas	Gravity
Gubernatio	Governing
Gustus	Taste
Habitus	Proficiency
Haecceitas	Thisness
Harmonia praestabilita	Pre-established harmony
Harmonicus	Harmonic
Harmonista	Harmonist
Hebes	Dull
Hermeneutica	Hermeneutics
Heuristica	Heuristics
Hilaritas	Cheerfulness
Historicus	Historical
Homo	Human being
Honor	Honor

Horror	Horror
Hypnopsychitae	Hypnopsychites
Hypothesis	Hypothesis
Ictus	Impact
Idea	Idea
Idealis	Ideal
Idealista	Idealist
Identitas	Identity
Idioma	Idiom
Ignorantia	Ignorance
Ignotum	Unknown
Illecebra	Enticement
Illicitus	Impermissible
Illimitatus	Unlimited
Illubenter	Without preference
Illustrans	Illustrative
Illustratio	Celebration
Illusio	Delusion
Imaginatio	Imagination
Imago	Image
Imbecillitas	Feebleness
Immanens	Immanent
Immaterialis	Immaterial
Immediatus	Immediate
Immensus	Immeasurable
Immortalitas	Immortality
Immutabilis	Inalterable
Immutabilitas	Inalterability
Impartialitas	Impartiality
Impassibilis	Without suffering
Impedimentum	Impediment
Impeditio	Impedition
Impenetrabilis	Impenetrable
Imperatus	Mastered
Imperfectio	Imperfection

Imperium	Mastery
Imperscrutabilis	Inscrutable
Impletur	Fulfill (to)
Implicans	Implying
Impossibilis	Impossible
Impotentia	Impotence
Impulsivus	Impelling causes
In actu	Actual
In concreto	Concretely
In genere	In general
In potentia	Potential
In potentia remota	Remotely potential
In qua	In which
In se	In itself
Inaequalis	Unequal
Incerta	Uncertain
Incommodus	Unfavorable
Incompletus	Incomplete
Incomprehensibilis	Incomprehensible
Inconceptibilis	Inconceivable
Inconsideratus	Inconsiderate
Inconstans	Inconstant
Incorporeus	Incorporeal
Incorruptibilis	Incorruptible
Indefinitus	Indefinite
Independens	Independent
Indeterminatus	Undetermined, inderterminate
Indifferens	Indifferent
Indifferentia	Indifference
Indiscernibilis	Indiscernible
Individuatio	Individuation
Individuum	Individual
Indivisibilis	Indivisible
Indoles	Innate character
Induciani	Inducians

Inebriari	Drunk (to be)
Inefficaces	Inefficacious
Inefficiens	Ineffective
Iners	Innert
Inertia	Inertia
Infallibilis	Infallible
Infans	Infant
Infelicitas	Unhappiness
Inferior	Inferior
Infimus	Lowest
Infinitudo	Infinitude
Infinitus	Infinite
Influxionista	Influentialist
Influxus	Influence
Influxus physicus	Physical influence
Infortunium	Unfortunate
Infusiani	Infusians
Infusus	Infused
Ingeniosus	Witty
Ingenium	Wit
Ingratus	Non-gratifying
Inhaerentia	Inherence
Inire	Inhere (to)
Initium	Beginning
Innocens	Innocent
Inopportunitas	Inopportune
Inordinatio	Disorder
Inordinatus	Inordinate
Inseparabilitas	Inseparability
Insignia	Insignia
Instans	Instant
Instantaneus	Instantaneous
Instinctus	Instinct
Instrumentalis	Instrumental
Insufficiens	Insufficient

Intellectualis	Intellectual
Intellectus	Intellect
Intelligere	Understand (to)
Intelligibilis	Intelligible
Intempestivitas	Untimeliness
Intendi	Increased (to be)
Intensio	Intensity
Intensive	Intensively
Interitus	Perishing
Internus	Internal
Interruptus	Discontinuous
Intime	Intimately
Intuitiva	Intuitive
Intuitus	Intuited
Invidia	Envy
Invitum	Reluctant
Involuntaria	Involuntary
Involvi	Cover up (to)
Ira	Anger
Irrationabilis	Unreasonable
Irrationalis	Irrational
Irrepraesentabilis	Cannot be represented
Irrisio	Mockery
Iucundus	Agreeable
Iudiciosus	Good judgment (to be of)
Iudicium	Judgment
Ius	Right
Iustitia	Justice
Iuvans	Helping
Iuvare	Help (to)
Labilis	Fallible
Labilitas	Fallibility
Laetitia	Joy
Languidus	Weak
Lapsus	Fall

Late dictum	Broadly speaking
Latitudo	Width
Latius dictus	More broadly speaking
Legislator	Legislator
Lethaei poculi patroni	Friends of the cup of forgetfulness
Lex	Law
Lexica	Lexical
Liber	Free
Libera a coactione	Free from constraint
Libera ratione exsecutionis	Free in terms of execution, freely executed
Liberalis	Liberal
Libertas	Freedom
Licitus	Permissible
Limes	Limit
Limitatus	Limited
Linea	Line
Linearum	Linear
Lingua	Language
Lipopsychia	Lipopsychia
Lipothymia	Lipothymia
Localis	Local
Locus	Place
Longanimitas	Forebearance
Longitudo	Depth
Lubenter	Preferentialy
Lubitus	Preference
Lucta	Struggle
Luctus	Mourning
Lusus	Play
Machina	Machine
Maeror	Grief
Maestitia	Sorrow
Magnitudo	Magnitude
Maius	Greater
Malevolentia	Malevolence

Malum	Evil
Manichaeismus	Manichaeism
Mantica	Mantic art, the
Manticus	Mantic
Materia	Matter
Materia prima	Prime matter
Materialis	Material
Materialista	Materialist
Mathematice solidum	Mathematical solid
Mathematicus	Mathematical
Mathesis intensorum	Mathematics of intensive quantities
Maturitas	Maturity
Maxima	Maxims
Maximum	Maximum, greatest
Mechanicus	Mechanical
Mechanismus	Mechanism
Mediatus	Mediate
Medium (as a substantive)	Means
Medius	Middle
Melancholicus	Melancholic
Mens	Mind
Memoria	Memory
Mens mota	Rapture
Mensura	Measure
Mensuratus	Measured
Mente capti	Insane
Mentis excessus	Leaving one's mind
Merus	Sheer, mere
Metaphysica	Metaphysics
Metaphysicus	Metaphysical
Metempsychosis	Metempsychosis
Methodicus	Methodicalness
Methodus	Method
Metiri	Measure (to)
Metus	Dread

Mina	Threat
Minimum	Minimum, smallest
Ministerialis	Ministering
Minorennis	Minor
Minui	Diminished (to be)
Minus	Less, fewer
Minus plenus	Incomplete
Miraculum	Miracle
Miseria	Misery
Misericordia	Mercy
Mixtus	Mixed
Mnemonicus	Mnemonic
Modificatio	Modification
Modus	Modes
Molestus	Burdensome
Momentaneus	Momentary
Momentum	Moment
Monadatum	Monadatum
Monarcha	Monarch
Monas	Monad
Moralis	Moral
Moraliter	Morally
Morbus caducus, morbus comitialis, morbus herculeus	Epilepsy
Mori	Die (to)
Mors	Death
Mortalis	Mortal
Mortalitas	Mortality
Mortuus	Dead
Motivum	Motive
Motrix	Motive
Motus	Motion
Movens	Moving
Multitudo	Multitude
Multus	Much, many
Mundus	World

Musica	Music
Musicus	Musical
Mutabilis	Alterable
Mutabilitas	Alterability
Mutari	Altered (to be)
Mutatio	Alteration
Mysterium	Mystery
Mysticus	Mystical
Mythicus	Mythic
Natura	Nature
Naturalis	Natural
Naturalista	Naturalist
Naturaliter	Naturally
Necessarium	Necessary
Necessitas	Necessity
Necessitatio	Necessitation
Negare	Deny (to)
Negatio	Negation
Negativus	Negative
Nexus	Nexus
Nihil	Nothing
Nobilitas	Nobility
Noctambulus	Sleep walker
Nolitio	Nolition
Noluntas	Refusal
Non actuale	Non-actual
Non ens	Non-being
Non publicus	Uncommon
Norma	Norms
Nota	Note
Nudus	Bare
Numericus	Numerical
Numerus	Number
Obdormire	Sleep (to go to)
Subjective sumptus	Taken subjectively

Obiective sumptus	Taken objectively
Obiectum	Object
Obligatio	Obligation
Oblivio	Forgetting
Obliviositas	Forgetfulness
Oblivisci	Forget (to)
Obscurus	Obscure
Observabilia	Observable the
Obstaculum	Impediment
Occasio	Occasion
Occasionalis	Occasional
Occasionalista	Occasionalist
Occupatio	Occupation
Odium	Hate
Olfactus	Smell
Omnimoda determinatio	Complete determination
Omnipotentia	Omnipotence
Omniscientia	Omniscience
Onirocritica	Interpretation of dreams
Ontologia	Ontology
Ontosophia	Ontosophia
Opportunitas	Opportunity
Oppositum	Opposite
Oratio	Speech
Oratoria	Oratory
Ordinarius	Ordinary
Ordo	Order
Organa sensuum	Sense organs
Origo	Origin
Orthographia	Orthography
Ortus	Origination
Paenitentia	Contrition
Palingenesia	Palingenesis
Pars	Part
Partialis	Partial

Particularius	Particular
Parvitas	Smallness
Passio	Suffering
Passio dominans	Addiction
Passivus	Passive
Patens	Clear, obvious
Pathologia	Pathology
Pati	Suffer (to)
Patientia	Patience
Paucitas	Smallness
Peccator	Sinner
Peccatum	Sin
Penetrans	Penetrating
Per emanationem	Eminently
Per se subsistens	Subsisting by itself
Perceptio adhaerens	Ancillary perception
Perdurabilis	Capable of enduring
Perfectio	Perfection
Perfectissimus	Most perfect
Perfectus	Perfect
Permissio	Permission
Personalitas	Personality
Perspicacia	Perspicaciousness
Perspicuitas	Perspicuity
Persuasio	Persuasion
Pertinax	Obstinate
Perturbatio	Perturbation
Phaenomena	Phenomena, appearance
Phantasia	Imagination
Phantasma	Image
Phantastae	Fantasists
Philanthropia	Philanthropy
Philologia	Philology
Philosophia	Philosophy
Philosophicus	Philosophical

Physice	Physically
Physicomechanicum	Physicomechanical
Physicus	Physical
Piger	Lazy
Placere	Please (to)
Planus	Flat
Plena	Complete
Pneumaticus	Pneumatic
Poena	Punishment
Poetica	Poetics
Poeticus	Poetic
Polytheismus	Polytheism
Ponderare	Weigh (to)
Pondus	Weight
Positio	Affirmation
Positivus	Positive
Positus	Position, posited, held
Possibilis	Possible
Possibilitas	Possibility
Posterius	Later
Postremum	Last
Potentia	Potency
Potentialis	Potential
Potestas	Command
Practicus	Practical
Praeceps	Precipitous
Praedestinatio	Predestination
Praedicatus	Predicate, predicated
Praedominium	Predominance
Praeexsistentianus	Preexsistentist
Praeferre	Prefer (to)
Praegnans	Pregnant
Praeiudicium thomisticum	Prejudice of thomas
Praemium	Reward
Praesagia	Anticipatory perceptions

Praesagiens	Anticipating
Praesagitio	Anticipation
Praescientia	Foreknowledge
Praescindere	Separate (to)
Praesens	Praesent
Praesensio	Presentiment
Praesentia	Present
Praestabilitus	Pre-established
Praestigia	Illusion
Praesumens	Presuming
Praeteritus	Past
Praeternaturalis	Praeternatural
Praevisio	Foresight
Pretium	Price
Primarius	Primary
Primus	Prime
Primus	First
Principalis	Principal
Principiatus	Founded
Principium	Principle
Prius	Earlier
Privatio	Privation
Privativus	Privative
Pro lubitu	According to preference
Pro positu corporis	According to the position of the body
Probans	Probative
Prodigium	Marvel
Producere	Produce (to)
Profunditas	Depth
Prognosticon	Foretoken
Progressus in infinitum	Progression to infinity
Promptitudo	Readiness
Promptus	Ready
Propagatio animae humanae per traducem	Propagation of the human soul through transmission
Propiora	Closer

Proportio	Proportion
Proportionalis	Proportional
Proprium	Proper, characteristic
Prosodia	Prosody
Prosperitas	Prosperity
Prospicientia	Forethought
Providentia	Providence
Providus	Provident
Proximus	Proximate
Prudentia	Prudence
Psychologia	Psychology
Psychologice maiorennis	Psychologically adult
Psychologicus	Psychological
Psychopannychitae	Pyschopannychists
Pudor	Shame
Pulcritudo	Beauty
Punctum	Point
Punitivus	Punitive
Puritas	Purity
Purus	Pure
Pusillanimitas	Timidity
Q.a. <quod [est] absurdum>	Which is absurd
Qualitas	Quality
Quantitas	Quantity
Quantitativus	Quantitative
Quidditas	Quiddity
Quies	Rest
Quiescere	Rest (to)
Quotidie	Daily
Rapi extra se	Beside oneself being
Raritas	Rarity
Ratio	Reason, ground, relation
Ratio sufficiens	Sufficient ground
Ratiocinium	Reasoning
Rationabilis	Reasonable

Rationalis	Rational
Rationatum	Consequence
Reactio	Reaction
Realis	Real
Realissimum	Most real
Realitas	Reality
Receptivitas	Receptivity
Recognoscere	Recognize (to)
Recordari	Recall (to)
Recordatio divina	Divine recall
Rectilineus	Rectilinear
Rectitudo	Righteousness
Recurrere	Recur (to)
Reflexio	Reflection
Regimen	Control
Regnare	Predominate (to)
Regnum	Kingdom
Regressus in infinitum	Regression to infinity
Regula	Rule
Relatio	Relation
Relative	Relatively
Relativus	Relative
Religio	Religion
Remedium	Means
Rememorativum	Memory aid
Reminiscentiae	Recollection
Reminisci	Recollect (to)
Remittere	Decrease (to)
Remotiorus	Remote more
Remotus	Remote
Remuneratio	Remuneration
Remuneratorius	Remuneratory
Replens	Filling up
Repraesentatio	Repraesentation
Reprobatio	Reprobation

Reproducere	Reproduce (to)
Res facti	Matters of fact
Resistentia	Resistance
Resolvens	Resolving
Respectivus	Respective
Respectu	With respect to
Respectus	Respect
Revelatio	Revelation
Reviviscere	Revived (to be)
Revocare aliquid in memoriam	Call something back to memory
Rhetorica	Rhetoric
Rigorosus	Strict
Robur	Strength
Sagacitas	Sagacity
Saltus	Leap
Sanctissimus	Most holy
Sanctitas	Holiness
Sanus	Sound
Sapientia	Wisdom
Sapor	Taste
Satisfactio	Satisfaction
Scientia	Science, knowledge
Scientia libera	Free knowledge
Scopus	Goal
Scrutator cordium	Scrutinizer of hearts
Secundarius	Secondary
Secundum quid	Qualified, qualifiedly
Secundus	Second
Sedes	Seat
Semiologia	Semiology
Semiotica	Semiotics
Semperhilaris	Always cheerful
Sempertristis	Always sad
Sempiternitas	Sempiternal
Sensatio	Sensation

Sensibilis	Sensible
Sensitivus	Sensitive
Sensus	Sense
Sentire	Sense (to)
Separare	Separate (to)
Separatus	Separate
Servilis	Servile
Servitus	Slavery
Siccitas	Dryness
Signatum	Signified, the
Significatu latiori	In the broader sense
Significatu psychologico	In the psychological sense
Significatu stricto	In the strict sense
Significatus	Signification
Signum	Sign
Similitudo	Similitude
Similis	Similar, the
Simplex	Simple
Simpliciter talis	Unqualified, unqualifiedly
Simultaneus	Simultaneous
Sinceritas	Sincerity
Singularis	Singular
Singulum	Every, every single
Situs	Situation
Socinianismus	Socinianism
Socius	Associate
Socors	Sluggish
Soliditas	Solidity
Solitarius	Solitary
Somniare	Dream (to)
Somnus	Sleep
Spatiosum	Spacious
Spatium	Space
Specialis	Special
Specialissimus	Most special

Species	Species
Specificus	Specific
Spectatum	Considered
Speculatio	Speculation
Spes	Hope
Sphaera sensationis	Sphere of sensation
Spinosisticus	Spinosistic
Spinozismus	Spinozism
Spiritus	Spirit
Splendor	Splendor
Spontaneitas	Spontaneity
Status	State
Stimuli	Stimuli
Strenuus	Strenuous
Stricte dicta	Strictly speaking
Suasio	Persuasion
Subactus	Disciplined
Subalternus	Subordinate
Subiectivus	Subjective
Subiectum	Subject
Subsistentia	Subsistence
Substantia	Substance
Substantialis	Substantial
Substantiatus	Substantiated
Subsum	Subjected (to be)
Subtilior	Subtler
Subtilitas	Subtlety
Succedentia	Succeeding beings
Successio	Succession
Successivus	Successive
Sufficiens	Sufficient
Summum bonum	Highest good
Summus	Highest, supreme
Superficies	Surface
Superius	Superior

Supernaturalis	Supernatural
Superpondii	Preponderance
Supplens	Supplementary
Suppositum	Supposit
Supra	Beyond
Symbolicus	Symbolic
Symbolum	Symbol
Syncope	Syncope
Syntaxis	Syntax
Systema	System
Tactus	Touch
Taedium	Displeasure
Tardus	Slow
Teleologia	Teleology
Temperamentum	Temperment
Tempestivitas	Timeliness
Tempus	Time
Tenebras	Darkness
Tenere	Hold (to)
Tentare	Test (to)
Tentator ad malum	Tempter to evil
Terminus	Term, boundary
Terror	Terror
Theologia	Theology
Theologica	Theological
Theoreticus	Theoretical
Thnetopsychitae	Thnetopsychites
Timor	Fear
Tollere	Remove (to); deny (to)
Torpescere	Grow numb (to)
Torpesceus	Numbed
Totalis	Total
Totus	Whole
Traduciani	Traducians
Transcendentalis	Transcendental

Transcendentaliter	Transcendentally
Transformatio	Transformation
Transiens	Transeunt
Transitorius	Transitory
Tristitia	Sadness
Tumultuarium	Tumultuosness
Typicus	Typical
Ubertas	Richness
Ulterior	More distant
Ultimus	Ultimate
Ultrix	Avengeress
Unicum	Unique, one
Unio	Union
Unitas	Unity
Unitio	Unitedness
Universalis	Universal
Unus	One
Usus	Use
Utilis	Useful
Utilitas	Utility
V.c. [valet consequentia]	It is valid to deduce
Valor	Worth
Vanitas	Vanity
Vanus	Empty
Variabilis	Variable
Variatio	Variation
Varius	Changing
Vastitas	Vastness
Vastus	Vast
Vaticinium	Oracle
Vegetus	Vigorous
Vehemens	Violent
Veracitas	Veracity
Veritas	Truth
Vertigo	Vertigo

Verum	True, the
Verus	True
Via	Way
Vigilare	Awake (to be)
Vilitas	Worthlessness
Vindicativus	Vindictive
Vindicatrix	Vindicatress
Vis	Power
Visio	Vision
Visionarii	Visionaries
Visus	Vision
Vita	Life
Vivere	Alive (to be)
Vividus	Lively
Vivus	Living
Vocabulum	Word
Volitio	Volition
Voluntarius	Voluntary
Voluntas	Will
Voluptas	Pleasure
Zelotypia	Jealous love
Zenonicus	Zenonical

English–Latin

Abject	**Abiectus**
Absence	**Absens**
Absolute	**Absolutus**
Absolutely first	**Absolute primum**
Abstract	**Abstractum**
Abstract (to)	**Abstrahere**
Abstraction	**Abstractio**
Absurd	**Absurdum**
Abuse	**Abusus**
Accident	**Accidens**

Accidental	**Accidentalis**
According to preference	**Pro lubitu**
According to the position of the body	**Pro positu corporis**
Acquired	**Acquisitus**
Act (to)	**Agere**
Action	**Actio**
Active	**Activus**
Actual	**Actualis, in actu**
Acumen	**Acuminis**
Acumen	**Acumen**
Acute	**Acutus**
Addiction	**Passio dominans**
Adequate	**Adaequatum**
Adventitious	**Adventicium**
Aesthetics	**Aesthetica**
Affections	**Affectiones**
Affects	**Affectus**
Affirmation	**Positio**
Age	**Aetas**
Agree (to)	**Consentire**
Agreeable	**Iucundus**
Alive (to be)	**Vivere**
Alterability	**Mutabilitas**
Alterable	**Mutabilis**
Alteration	**Mutatio**
Altered (to be)	**Mutari**
Always cheerful	**Semperhilaris**
Always sad	**Sempertristis**
Amazement	**Admiratio**
Analogue	**Analogon**
Ancillary perception	**Perceptio adhaerens**
Anger	**Ira**
Animal	**Animal**
Annihilation	**Annihilatio**
Anthropognostics	**Anthropognosia**

Anthropology	**Anthropologia**
Anthropomorphism	**Anthropomorphismus**
Anticipating	**Praesagiens**
Anticipation	**Praesagitio**
Anticipatory perceptions	**Praesagia**
Antipathy	**Antipathia**
Apotheosis	**Apotheosis**
Apparent	**Apparens**
Appearance	**Phaenomena**
Appetite	**Appetitus**
Appropriateness	**Convenientia**
Archetypal	**Archetypus**
Archetype	**Archetypon**
Architectonics	**Architectonica**
Assistantist	**Assistentianus**
Assisting	**Administrus**
Associate	**Socius**
Association	**Associatio**
Atheist	**Atheus**
Atom	**Atomus**
Attending	**Attendere**
Attention	**Attentio**
Attribute	**Attributa**
Author	**Auctor**
Automaton	**Automaton**
Avengeress	**Ultrix**
Aversion	**Aversatio**
Avert (to)	**Aversari**
Awake (to be)	**Vigilare**
Awaken (to)	**Evigilare**
Banishment of death	**Exsilium mortis**
Bare	**Nudus**
Beauty	**Pulcritudo**
Become (to)	**Feri**
Beginning	**Initium**

Being, a	**Ens**
Benefit	**Beneficium**
Benevolence	**Benevolentia**
Beside oneself	**Extra se rapi, rapti extra se**
Beyond	**Supra**
Bitter	**Amarus**
Blessed	**Beatus**
Blessedness	**Beatitudo**
Body	**Corpus**
Boundary	**Terminus**
Brief	**Brevis**
Broadly speaking	**Late dictum**
Brute	**Brutum**
Burdensome	**Molestus**
Eminently	**Per emanationem**
Call something back to memory	**Revocare aliquid in memoriam**
Cannot be represented	**Irrepraesentabilis**
Capable	**Capax**
Capable of enduring	**Perdurabilis**
Capacity	**Capacitas**
Cartesian	**Cartesianum**
Categorical	**Categoricus**
Catholic	**Catholicum**
Causal	**Causalis**
Causality	**Causalitas**
Cause	**Causa**
Caused	**Causatus**
Celebration	**Illustratio**
Certain	**Certus**
Certitude	**Certitudo**
Chance	**Casus**
Changing	**Varius**
Character	**Character**
Characteristic	**Proprium**
Characteristics	**Characteristica**

Cheerfulness	**Hilaritas**
Chimera	**Chimaera**
Choice	**Arbitrium**
Choose (to)	**Eligere**
Chosen	**Arbitrarius**
Circular	**Circularis**
Circumspection	**Circumspectus**
Circumstance	**Circumstantia**
City of God	**Civitas Dei**
Clarity	**Claritas**
Clear	**Patens**
Clear	**Clarus**
Clemency	**Clementia**
Closer	**Propiora**
Closest	**Artissimus**
Co-cause	**Concausa**
Coexistentists	**Coexsistentiani**
Cognitive faculty	**Facultas cognoscitiva**
Coherence	**Cohaerentia**
Collecting one's mind	**Collectio animi**
Collective	**Complexus**
Collision	**Collisio**
Combinatorial	**Combinatorius**
Command	**Potestas**
Commiseration	**Commiseratio**
Common	**Communis**
Comparative	**Comparativus**
Comparison	**Comparatio**
Complement	**Complementum**
Complete	**Completus, plena**
Complete determination	**Omnimoda determinatio**
Complete lord	**Dominus**
Composite	**Compositus**
Comprehensible	**Comprehensibilis**
Conceivable	**Conceptibilis**

Conception	**Conceptio**
Concerning which	**Circa quam**
Reasoning	**Ratiocinium**
Concreationist	**Concreatianus**
Concrete	**Concretum**
Concretely	**In concreto**
Concupiscible faculty	**Facultas concupiscibilis**
Concurrence	**Concursus**
Condition	**Conditio**
Confidence	**Fiducia**
Confined	**Angustum**
Confirmation	**Confirmatio**
Conflict	**Conflictus, dissensus**
Confused	**Confusis**
Confusion	**Confusio**
Congruence	**Congruentia**
Conjoined	**Coniungus**
Conjunction	**Coniunctio**
Connected	**Connexus**
Consciousness	**Conscientia**
Consequence	**Rationatum**
Conservation	**Conservatio**
Considered	**Spectatum**
Constancy, constant	**Constans**
Constrained	**Coactus**
Constraint	**Coactio**
Contact	**Contactus**
Contiguous	**Contiguus**
Contingency	**Contingentia**
Contingent	**Contingens**
Continuous	**Continuus**
Contradiction	**Contradictio**
Contrary to reason	**Contra rationem**
Contrition	**Paenitentia**
Control	**Compos, regimen**

Conviction	**Convictio**
Convincing	**Convincens**
Coordinated	**Coordinatus**
Coordination	**Coordinatio**
Corporeal	**Corporeum**
Corpuscle	**Corpusculum**
Corpuscular	**Corpuscularis**
Corrective	**Emendans**
Correlate	**Correlatum**
Corrupt	**Corruptus**
Corruption	**Corruptio**
Cosmological	**Cosmologicus**
Cosmology	**Cosmologia**
Courage	**Animositas**
Course of nature	**Cursus naturae**
Cover up (to)	**Involvi**
Create (to)	**Creare**
Creation	**Creatio**
Creationists	**Creatiani**
Creatures	**Creatura**
Critic, criticism, critical	**Criticus**
Cultivation of reason	**Cultura rationis**
Curiosity	**Curiositas**
Curved	**Curvus**
Curvilinear	**Curvilineus**
Daily	**Quotidie**
Damned	**Damnatus**
Daring	**Audacia**
Darkness	**Tenebras**
Dead	**Mortuus**
Death	**Mors**
Deceptions of the senses	**Fallaciae sensuum**
Decrease (to)	**Remittere**
Decree	**Decretum**
Defect	**Defectus**

Deficient	**Deficiens**
Degree	**Gradus**
Deism	**Deismus**
Deliberating	**Deliberans**
Deliberation	**Deliberatio**
Delicate	**Delicatus**
Delighting	**Delectans**
Delirious	**Delirus**
Delirium	**Delirium**
Delusion	**Illusio**
Demonstrative	**Demonstrativus**
Deny (to)	**Negare, tollere**
Dependent	**Dependens**
Depth	**Longitudo, profunditas**
Derivative	**Derivativus**
Desire	**Appetitio**
Desire (to)	**Appetere**
Desperation	**Desperatio**
Despot	**Despotes**
Destined	**Destinatus**
Determinable	**Determinabilis**
Determination	**Determinatio**
Determined	**Determinatus**
Determining	**Determinans**
Develop (to)	**Evolvere**
Dexterity	**Dexteritas**
Dialect	**Dialectus**
Die (to)	**Mori**
Difference	**Differentia**
Different	**Diversus**
Difficult	**Difficilis**
Dignity	**Dignitas**
Diminished (to be)	**Minui**
Dippelianism	**Dippelianismus**
Direct (to)	**Dirigere**

Disciplined	**Subactus**
Discontinuous	**Interruptus**
Discrete	**Discretus**
Disgust	**Fastidium**
Disorder	**Inordinatio**
Displeasing	**Displicere**
Displeasure	**Displicentia, taedium**
Disproportion	**Disproportio**
Dissimilar	**Dissimilia**
Dissuasion	**Dissuasio**
Distance	**Distantia**
Distinct	**Distinctus**
Distinction	**Distinctio**
Distinctive	**Distinctivus**
Distinguishing mark	**Discrimen**
Distracted (to be)	**Distrahi**
Diverse	**Diversum**
Divination	**Divinatio**
Divine recall	**Recordatio divina**
Division	**Divisio**
Dread	**Metus**
Dream (to)	**Somniare**
Drunk (to be)	**Inebriari**
Dryness	**Siccitas**
Dualist	**Dualista**
Dull	**Hebes**
Duration	**Duratio**
Dynamics	**Dynamica**
Eagerness	**Cupiditas**
Earlier	**Prius**
Easy	**Facilis**
Ecstasy	**Ecstasis**
Ecthlipsis	**Ecthlipsis**
Ectype	**Ectypon**
Effect	**Effectus**

Effective	**Efficiens**
Efficacious	**Efficaces**
Efficacy	**Efficacia**
Efficient	**Efficiens**
Egoist	**Egoista**
Element	**Elementum**
Elicited	**Elicitus**
Eloquence	**Eloquentia**
Emphaseology	**Emphaseologia**
Emphasis	**Emphasis**
Empirical	**Empiricus**
Empty	**Vanus**
End	**Finis**
Ended	**Finitus**
Energy	**Energia**
Enticement	**Illecebra**
Envy	**Invidia**
Epicureanism	**Epicureismus**
Epilepsy	**Morbus caducus, morbus comitialis, morbus herculeus**
Equal	**Aequalia**
Equality	**Aequalitas**
Equilibrium	**Aequilibrium**
Equivocal	**Aequivocus**
Error	**Error**
Essence	**Essentia**
Essential	**Essentialis**
Essential determinations	**Essentialia**
Eternity	**Aeternitas**
Etymology	**Etymologia**
Evanescent	**Evanescens**
Event	**Eventus**
Event occurring against the order of nature	**Contra ordinem naturae eveniens**
Every, every single	**Singulum**
Evidence	**Evidentia**

Evil	**Malum**
Evil spirits	**Cacodaemones**
Exception	**Exceptio**
Exemplar	**Exemplar**
Exemplary	**Exemplaris**
Exercise	**Exercitium**
Existence	**Exsistentia**
Expectation	**Exspectatio**
Experience	**Experientia**
Explanatory	**Explicans**
Explicate (to)	**Evolvere**
Extended	**Extensus**
Extension	**Extensio**
External	**Externus**
Extortion	**Extorsio**
Extramundane	**Extramundanus**
Extraordinary	**Extraordinarius**
Extrinsic	**Extrinsecus**
Fact	**Factum**
Faculty of characterization	**Facultas characteristica**
Faculty of comparison	**Facultas comparandi**
Faculty of desire	**Facultas appetitiva**
Faculty of divining	**Facultas divinatrix**
Faculty of foresight	**Facultas praevidendi**
Faculty of invention or the poetic faculty	**Facultas fingendi s poetica**
Faculty of judging	**Facultas diiudicandi**
Faculty of perceiving the correspondences and differences of things	**Facultas identitates diversitatesque rerum percipiendi**
Faculty of presuming	**Facultas praesumendi**
Faculty of reflection	**Facultas reflectendi**
Faint	**Deliquium animi**
Fairness	**Aequitas**
Faith	**Fides**
Faithful	**Fidus**

Faithfulness	**Fidelitas**
Fall	**Lapsus**
Fallibility	**Labilitas**
Fallible	**Labilis**
False	**Fallax**
Fantasists	**Fanatici, Phantastae**
Fantasy	**Fabulosus**
Fatalism	**Fatalismus**
Fate	**Fatum**
Favor	**Favor**
Favorable	**Commodus**
Fear	**Timor**
Fecundity	**Fecunditas**
Feebleness	**Imbecillitas**
Fewer	**Minus**
Fiction	**Fictio**
Fictional	**Fictus**
Field	**Campus**
Figure	**Figura**
Filling up	**Replens**
Final	**Finalis**
Finite	**Finitus**
Finitude	**Finitudo**
Firm	**Firmus**
First	**Primus**
Flat	**Planus**
Flesh	**Caro**
Flexible	**Flexilis**
Flight	**Fuga**
Forcing oneself	**Cogere semet ipsum**
Forebearance	**Longanimitas**
Foreknowledge	**Praescientia**
Foresight	**Praevisio**
Forethought	**Prospicientia**
Foretoken	**Prognosticon**

Forget (to)	**Oblivisci**
Forgetfulness	**Obliviositas**
Forgetting	**Oblivio**
Form	**Forma**
Formal	**Formalis**
Fortuitous	**Fortuita**
Fortune	**Fortuna**
Fostering	**Almus**
Foundation	**Fundus**
Founded	**Principiatus**
Free	**Liber**
Free from constraint	**Libera a coactione**
Free in terms of execution, freely executed	**Libera ratione exsecutionis**
Free knowledge	**Scientia libera**
Freedom	**Libertas**
Friends of the cup of forgetfulness	**Lethaei poculi patroni**
From another	**Ab alio**
From itself	**A se**
From nothing	**Ex nihilo**
From without	**Ab extra**
Fruit	**Fetus**
Fulfill (to)	**Impletur**
Future	**Futurus**
General	**Generalis**
Generic	**Genericus**
Gift of prophecy	**Donum propheticum**
Given	**Datus**
Glory	**Gloria**
Goal	**Scopus**
God	**Deus**
Good	**Bonus**
Good judgment (to be of)	**Iudiciosus**
Good spirits	**Agathodaemones**
Goodness	**Bonitas**

Governing	**Gubernatio**
Grammar	**Grammatica**
Gratifying	**Gratus**
Gratitude	**Gratitudo**
Gravity	**Gravitas**
Greater	**Maius**
Greatest	**Maximum**
Grief	**Maeror**
Ground	**Ratio**
Grow numb (to)	**Torpescere**
Habit	**Consuetudo**
Handwriting	**Graphice**
Happiness	**Felicitas**
Happy	**Felix**
Harmonic	**Harmonicus**
Harmonist	**Harmonista**
Harmony	**Consensus**
Hate	**Odium**
Hearing	**Auditus**
Help	**Auxilium**
Help (to)	**Iuvare**
Helping	**Auxiliaris, iuvans**
Hermeneutics	**Hermeneutica**
Heuristics	**Heuristica**
Highest	**Summus**
Highest good	**Summum bonum**
Historical	**Historicus**
Hold (to)	**Tenere**
Holiness	**Sanctitas**
Honor	**Honor**
Hope	**Spes**
Horror	**Horror**
Human being	**Homo**
Hypnopsychites	**Hypnopsychitae**
Hypothesis	**Hypothesis**

Idea	**Idea**
Ideal	**Idealis**
Idealist	**Idealista**
Identity	**Identitas**
Idiom	**Idioma**
Ignorance	**Ignorantia**
Illusion	**Praestigia**
Illustrative	**Illustrans**
Image	**Imago**
Image	**Phantasma**
Imagination	**Phantasia, imaginatio**
Immanent	**Immanens**
Immaterial	**Immaterialis**
Immeasurable	**Immensus**
Immediate	**Immediatus**
Immortality	**Immortalitas**
Impact	**Ictus**
Impartiality	**Impartialitas**
Impediment	**Impedimentum, obstaculum**
Impedition	**Impeditio**
Impelling causes	**Impulsivus**
Impenetrability	**Antitypia**
Impenetrable	**Impenetrabilis**
Imperfection	**Imperfectio**
Impermissible	**Illicitus**
Implying	**Implicans**
Impossible	**Impossibilis**
Impotence	**Impotentia**
In general	**In genere**
In itself	**In se**
In the broader sense	**Significatu latiori**
In the psychological sense	**Significatu psychologico**
In the strict sense	**Significatu stricto**
In which	**In qua**
Inalterability	**Immutabilitas**

Inalterable	**Immutabilis**
Inborn	**Connatus**
Incentives	**Elateres**
Incidental	**Adiunctus**
Incomplete	**Incompletus, minus plenus**
Incomprehensible	**Incomprehensibilis**
Inconceivable	**Inconceptibilis**
Incongruent	**Discongruentia**
Inconsiderate	**Inconsideratus**
Inconsistent	**Absonum**
Inconstant	**Inconstans**
Incorporeal	**Incorporeus**
Incorruptible	**Incorruptibilis**
Increased (to be)	**Intendi**
Increasing	**Augere**
Indecisive	**Anceps**
Indefinite	**Indefinitus**
Independent	**Independens**
Indifference	**Indifferentia**
Indifferent	**Indifferens**
Indiscernible	**Indiscernibilis**
Individual	**Individuum**
Individuation	**Individuatio**
Indivisible	**Indivisibilis**
Inducians	**Induciani**
Inebriated	**Ebrius**
Ineffective	**Inefficiens**
Inefficacious	**Inefficaces**
Inertia	**Inertia**
Infallible	**Infallibilis**
Infant	**Infans**
Inferior	**Inferior**
Infinite	**Infinitus**
Infinitude	**Infinitudo**
Influence	**Influxus**

Influentialist	**Influxionista**
Infused	**Infusus**
Infusians	**Infusiani**
Inhere (to)	**Inire**
Inherence	**Inhaerentia**
Injury	**Damnum**
Innate character	**Indoles**
Innert	**Iners**
Innocent	**Innocens**
Inordinate	**Inordinatus**
Inopportune	**Inopportunitas**
Insane	**Mente capti**
Inscrutable	**Imperscrutabilis**
Inseparability	**Inseparabilitas**
Insignia	**Insignia**
Instant	**Instans**
Instantaneous	**Instantaneus**
Instinct	**Instinctus**
Instrumental	**Instrumentalis**
Instruments of the senses	**Aestheteria**
Insufficient	**Insufficiens**
Intellect	**Intellectus**
Intellectual	**Intellectualis**
Intelligible	**Intelligibilis**
Intensity	**Intensio**
Intensively	**Intensive**
Interaction	**Commercium**
Internal	**Internus**
Interpretation of dreams	**Onirocritica**
Intimately	**Intime**
Intuited	**Intuitus**
Intuitive	**Intuitiva**
Invent (to)	**Fingere**
Involuntary	**Involuntaria**
Irascible faculty	**Facultas irascibilis**

Irrational	**Irrationalis**
It is valid to deduce	**V.c. <valet consequentia>**
Jealous love	**Zelotypia**
Joy	**Gaudium, laetitia**
Judge (to)	**Diiudicare**
Judgment	**Iudicium**
Justice	**Iustitia**
Kindness	**Benignitas**
Kingdom	**Regnum**
Knowledge	**Cognitio, scientia**
Language	**Lingua**
Lapses of judgment	**Eclipses iudicii**
Last	**Postremum**
Later	**Posterius**
Law	**Lex**
Lazy	**Piger**
Leap	**Saltus**
Leaving one's mind	**Mentis excessus**
Legislator	**Legislator**
Less	**Minus**
Lexical	**Lexica**
Liberal	**Liberalis**
Life	**Vita**
Limit	**Limes**
Limited	**Limitatus**
Line	**Linea**
Linear	**Linearum**
Lipopsychia	**Lipopsychia**
Lipothymia	**Lipothymia**
Lively	**Vividus**
Living	**Vivus**
Local	**Localis**
Locomotive faculty	**Facultas locomotiva**
Logical consequences	**Consectaria**
Love	**Amor**

Lowest	**Infimus**
Machine	**Machina**
Magnitude	**Magnitudo**
Malevolence	**Malevolentia**
Manichaeism	**Manichaeismus**
Mantic	**Manticus**
Mantic art, the	**Mantica**
Many, much	**Multus**
Marvel	**Prodigium**
Mastered	**Imperatus**
Mastery	**Imperium**
Material	**Materialis**
Materialist	**Materialista**
Mathematical	**Mathematicus**
Mathematical solid	**Mathematice solidum**
Mathematics of intensive quantities	**Mathesis intensorum**
Matter	**Materia**
Matters of fact	**Res facti**
Maturity	**Maturitas**
Maxim	**Dictum, maxima (pl.)**
Maximum	**Maximum**
Means	**Medium (as a substantive), remedium**
Measure	**Mensura**
Measure (to)	**Metiri**
Measured	**Mensuratus**
Measuring	**Dimensio**
Mechanical	**Mechanicus**
Mechanism	**Mechanismus**
Mediate	**Mediatus**
Melancholic	**Melancholicus**
Memory	**Memoria**
Memory aid	**Rememorativum**
Mercy	**Misericordia**
Mere	**Merus**
Metaphysical	**Metaphysicus**

Metaphysics	**Metaphysica**
Metempsychosis	**Metempsychosis**
Method	**Methodus**
Methodicalness	**Methodicus**
Middle	**Medius**
Mind	**Mens, animus**
Minimum	**Minimum**
Ministering	**Ministerialis**
Minor	**Minorennis**
Miracle	**Miraculum**
Misery	**Miseria**
Mixed	**Mixtus**
Mnemonic	**Mnemonicus**
Mnemonic art	**Ars mnemonica**
Mockery	**Irrisio**
Modes	**Modus**
Modification	**Modificatio**
Moment	**Momentum**
Momentary	**Momentaneus**
Monad	**Monas**
Monadatum	**Monadatum**
Monarch	**Monarcha**
Moral	**Moralis**
Morally	**Moraliter**
More broadly speaking	**Latius dictus**
More distant	**Ulterior**
Mortal	**Mortalis**
Mortality	**Mortalitas**
Most holy	**Sanctissimus**
Most perfect	**Perfectissimus**
Most real	**Realissimum**
Most special	**Specialissimus**
Motion	**Motus**
Motive	**Motive, motrix**
Mourning	**Luctus**

Moving	**Movens**
Multitude	**Multitudo**
Music	**Musica**
Musical	**Musicus**
Mystery	**Mysterium**
Mystical	**Mysticus**
Mythic	**Mythicus**
Narrowness	**Angustia**
Natural	**Naturalis**
Naturalist	**Naturalista**
Naturally	**Naturaliter**
Nature	**Natura**
Necessary	**Necessarium**
Necessitation	**Necessitatio**
Necessity	**Necessitas**
Negation	**Negatio**
Negative	**Negativus**
Neutral	**Adiaphoron**
Nexus	**Nexus**
Nobility	**Nobilitas**
Nolition	**Nolitio**
Non-actual	**Non actuale**
Non-being	**Non ens**
Non-gratifying	**Ingratus**
Norms	**Norma**
Note	**Nota**
Nothing	**Nihil**
Numbed	**Torpesceus**
Number	**Numerus**
Numerical	**Numericus**
Object	**Obiectum**
Obligation	**Obligatio**
Obscure	**Obscurus**
Observable	**Adspectabilis, observabilia**
Obstinate	**Pertinax**

Obtuseness	**Caput obtusum**
Obvious	**Patens**
Occasion	**Occasio**
Occasional	**Occasionalis**
Occasionalist	**Occasionalista**
Occupation	**Occupatio**
Occurring	**Eveniens**
Omnipotence	**Omnipotentia**
Omniscience	**Omniscientia**
One	**Unus, unicum**
Ontology	**Ontologia**
Ontosophia	**Ontosophia**
Opportunity	**Opportunitas**
Opposite	**Oppositum**
Oracle	**Vaticinium**
Oratory	**Oratoria**
Order	**Ordo**
Ordinary	**Ordinarius**
Origin	**Origo**
Origination	**Ortus**
Orthography	**Orthographia**
Palingenesis	**Palingenesia**
Part	**Pars**
Partial	**Partialis**
Particular	**Particularis**
Passive	**Passivus**
Past	**Praeteritus**
Pathology	**Pathologia**
Patience	**Patientia**
Penetrating	**Penetrans**
Perfect	**Perfectus**
Perfection	**Perfectio**
Perishing	**Interitus**
Permanent	**Diuturnus**
Permissible	**Licitus**

Permission	**Permissio**
Perpetuity	**Aeviternitas**
Personal	**Domesticum**
Personality	**Personalitas**
Perspicaciousness	**Perspicacia**
Perspicuity	**Perspicuitas**
Persuasion	**Suasio, Persuasio**
Perturbation	**Perturbatio**
Phenomena	**Phaenomena**
Philanthropy	**Philanthropia**
Philology	**Philologia**
Philosophical	**Philosophicus**
Philosophy	**Philosophia**
Physical	**Physicus**
Physical influence	**Influxus physicus**
Physically	**Physice**
Physicomechanical	**Physicomechanicum**
Place	**Locus**
Play	**Lusus**
Please (to)	**Placere**
Pleasure	**Voluptas**
Pneumatic	**Pneumaticus**
Poetic	**Poeticus**
Poetics	**Poetica**
Point	**Punctum**
Polytheism	**Polytheismus**
Position, posited	**Positus**
Positive	**Positivus**
Possibility	**Possibilitas**
Possible	**Possibilis**
Potency	**Potentia**
Potential	**In potentia, potentialis**
Power	**Vis**
Practical	**Practicus**
Praesent	**Praesens**

Praeternatural	**Praeternaturalis**
Precipitous	**Praeceps**
Predestination	**Praedestinatio**
Predicable accidents	**Accidentia praedicabilia**
Predicate, predicated	**Praedicatus**
Predominance	**Praedominium**
Pre-established	**Praestabilitus**
Pre-established harmony	**Harmonia praestabilita**
Preesxistentist	**Praeexsistentianus**
Prefer (to)	**Praeferre**
Preference	**Lubitus**
Preferentialy	**Lubenter**
Pregnant	**Praegnans**
Prejudice of Thomas	**Praeiudicium Thomisticum**
Preponderance	**Superpondii**
Present	**Praesentia**
Presentiment	**Praesensio**
Presuming	**Praesumens**
Price	**Pretium**
Primary	**Primarius**
Prime	**Primus**
Prime matter	**Materia prima**
Principal	**Principalis**
Principle	**Principium**
Privation	**Privatio**
Privative	**Privativus**
Probative	**Probans**
Produce (to)	**Producere**
Proficiency	**Habitus**
Progression to infinity	**Progressus in infinitum**
Propagation of the human soul through transmission	**Propagatio animae humanae per traducem**
Proper	**Proprium**
Proportion	**Proportio**
Proportional	**Proportionalis**
Prosody	**Prosodia**

Prosperity	**Prosperitas**
Providence	**Providentia**
Provident	**Providus**
Proximate	**Proximus**
Prudence	**Prudentia**
Psychological	**Psychologicus**
Psychologically adult	**Psychologice maiorennis**
Psychology	**Psychologia**
Punishment	**Poena**
Punitive	**Punitivus**
Pure	**Purus**
Purity	**Puritas**
Pyschopannychists	**Psychopannychitae**
Qualified, qualifiedly	**Secundum quid**
Quality	**Qualitas**
Quantitative	**Quantitativus**
Quantity	**Quantitas**
Quiddity	**Quidditas**
Rapture	**Mens mota**
Rarity	**Raritas**
Rational	**Rationalis**
Reaction	**Reactio**
Readiness	**Promptitudo**
Ready	**Promptus**
Real	**Realis**
Reality	**Realitas**
Reason	**Ratio**
Reasonable	**Rationabilis**
Reasoning	**Ratiocinia**
Recall (to)	**Recordari**
Receptivity	**Receptivitas**
Recognize (to)	**Recognoscere**
Recollect (to)	**Reminisci**
Recollection	**Reminiscentiae**
Rectilinear	**Rectilineus**

Recur (to)	**Recurrere**
Reflection	**Reflexio**
Refusal	**Noluntas**
Regression to infinity	**Regressus in infinitum**
Predominate (to)	**Regnare**
Relation	**Relatio, ration**
Relative	**Relativus**
Relatively	**Relative**
Religion	**Religio**
Reluctant	**Invitum**
Remote	**Remotus**
Remote more	**Remotiorus**
Remotely potential	**In potentia remota**
Remove (to); to deny	**Tollere**
Remuneration	**Remuneratio**
Remuneratory	**Remuneratorius**
Replica	**Exemplatum**
Repraesentation	**Repraesentatio**
Reprobation	**Reprobatio**
Reproduce (to)	**Reproducere**
Resistance	**Resistentia**
Resolving	**Resolvens**
Respect	**Respectus**
Respective	**Respectivus**
Rest	**Quies**
Rest (to)	**Quiescere**
Revelation	**Revelatio**
Revived (to be)	**Reviviscere**
Reward	**Praemium**
Rhetoric	**Rhetorica**
Richness	**Ubertas**
Right	**Ius**
Righteousness	**Rectitudo**
Rule	**Regula**
Rule (to)	**Dominare**

Sadness	**Tristitia**
Sagacity	**Sagacitas**
Satisfaction	**Satisfactio, Complacentia**
Science	**Scientia**
Scrutinizer of hearts	**Scrutator cordium**
Seat	**Sedes**
Second	**Secundus**
Secondary	**Secundarius**
Self repose	**Acquiescentia in se ipso**
Semiology	**Semiologia**
Semiotics	**Semiotica**
Sempiternal	**Sempiternitas**
Sensation	**Sensatio**
Sense	**Sensus**
Sense (to)	**Sentire**
Sense organs	**Organa sensuum**
Sensible	**Sensibilis**
Sensitive	**Sensitivus**
Separate	**Separatus**
Separate (to)	**Praescindere, separare**
Servile	**Servilis**
Shame	**Pudor**
Sheer	**Merus**
Sign	**Signum**
Signification	**Significatus**
Signified	**Signatus**
Similar	**Similis**
Similitude	**Similitudo**
Simple	**Simplex**
Simultaneous	**Simultaneus**
Sin	**Peccatum**
Sincerity	**Sinceritas**
Singular	**Singularis**
Sinner	**Peccator**
Situation	**Situs**

Slavery	**Servitus**
Sleep	**Somnus**
Sleep (to go to)	**Obdormire**
Sleep (to)	**Dormitare**
Sleep walker	**Noctambulus**
Sleeping	**Dormiens**
Slow	**Tardus**
Sluggish	**Socors**
Smallest	**Minimum**
Smallness	**Parvitas**
Smallness	**Paucitas**
Smell	**Olfactus**
Socinianism	**Socinianismus**
Solidity	**Soliditas**
Solitary	**Solitarius**
Something	**Aliquid**
Sorrow	**Maestitia**
Soul	**Anima**
Sound	**Sanus**
Space	**Spatium**
Spacious	**Spatiosum**
Special	**Specialis**
Species	**Species**
Specific	**Specificus**
Speculation	**Speculatio**
Speech	**Oratio**
Sphere of sensation	**Sphaera sensationis**
Spinosistic	**Spinosisticus**
Spinozism	**Spinozismus**
Spirit	**Spiritus**
Splendor	**Splendor**
Spontaneity	**Spontaneitas**
State	**Status**
Stimuli	**Stimuli**
Strength	**Robur**

Strenuous	**Strenuus**
Strict	**Rigorosus**
Strictly speaking	**Stricte dicta**
Strong	**Fortis**
Struggle	**Lucta**
Stupidity	**Caput stupidum**
Subject	**Subiectum**
Subjected (to be)	**Subsum**
Subjective	**Subiectivus**
Subordinate	**Subalternus**
Subsistence	**Subsistentia**
Subsisting by itself	**Per se subsistens**
Substance	**Substantia**
Substantial	**Substantialis**
Substantiated	**Substantiatus**
Subtlety	**Subtilitas**
Succeeding beings	**Succedentia**
Succession	**Successio**
Successive	**Successivus**
Suffer (to)	**Pati**
Suffering	**Passio**
Sufficient	**Sufficiens**
Sufficient ground	**Ratio sufficiens**
Sum up (to)	**Connumerare**
Superior	**Superius**
Supernatural	**Supernaturalis**
Supplementary	**Supplens**
Supposit	**Suppositum**
Supreme	**Summus**
Surface	**Superficies**
Sweet	**Dulcis**
Symbol	**Symbolum**
Symbolic	**Symbolicus**
Syncope	**Syncope**
Syntax	**Syntaxis**

System	**Systema**
Taken objectively	**Obiective sumptus**
Taken subjectively	**Subjective sumptus**
Taste	**Sapor, gustus**
Tasteless	**Bliteus**
Teleology	**Teleologia**
Temperment	**Temperamentum**
Tempter to evil	**Tentator ad malum**
Term	**Terminus**
Terror	**Terror**
Test (to)	**Tentare**
Theological	**Theologica**
Theology	**Theologia**
Theoretical	**Theoreticus**
Think (to)	**Cogito**
Thisness	**Haecceitas**
Thnetopsychites	**Thnetopsychitae**
Threat	**Mina**
Time	**Tempus**
Timeliness	**Tempestivitas**
Timidity	**Pusillanimitas**
Total	**Totalis**
Touch	**Tactus**
Touch (to)	**Contingere**
Traducians	**Traduciani**
Transcendental	**Transcendentalis**
Transcendentally	**Transcendentaliter**
Transeunt	**Transiens**
Transformation	**Transformatio**
Transitory	**Transitorius**
True	**Verus**
Truth	**Veritas**
Tumultuosness	**Tumultuarium**
Typical	**Typicus**
Ugliness	**Deformitas**

Ultimate	**Ultimus**
Unbridled	**Effrenis**
Uncertain	**Incerta**
Uncommon	**Non publicus**
Understand (to)	**Intelligere**
Undetermined, inderterminate	**Indeterminatus**
Unequal	**Inaequalis**
Unfavorable	**Incommodus**
Unfortunate	**Infortunium**
Unhappiness	**Infelicitas**
Union	**Unio**
Unique	**Unicum**
Unitedness	**Unitio**
Unity	**Unitas**
Universal	**Universalis**
Unknown	**Ignotum**
Unlimited	**Illimitatus**
Unqualified, unqualifiedly	**Simpliciter talis**
Unreasonable	**Irrationabilis**
Untimeliness	**Intempestivitas**
Upright	**Erecta**
Use	**Usus**
Useful	**Utilis**
Utility	**Utilitas**
Valuation	**Aestimatio**
Vanity	**Vanitas**
Variable	**Variabilis**
Variation	**Variatio**
Vast	**Vastus**
Vastness	**Vastitas**
Veracity	**Veracitas**
Vertigo	**Vertigo**
Vigorous	**Vegetus**
Vindicatress	**Vindicatrix**
Vindictive	**Vindicativus**

Violent	**Vehemens**
Vision	**Visio, visus**
Visionaries	**Visionarii**
Volition	**Volitio**
Voluntary	**Voluntarius**
Way	**Via**
Weak	**Debilis, languidus**
Weigh (to)	**Ponderare**
Weight	**Pondus**
Which is absurd	**Q.a. <quod [est] absurdum>**
Whole	**Totus**
Width	**Latitudo**
Will	**Voluntas**
Wisdom	**Sapientia**
Wit	**Ingenium**
With respect to	**Respectu**
Without preference	**Illubenter**
Without suffering	**Impassibilis**
Witty	**Ingeniosus**
Word	**Vocabulum**
World	**Mundus**
Worth	**Valor**
Worthlessness	**Vilitas**
Yearning	**Desiderium**
Zenonical	**Zenonicus**

Selected Bibliography

The following is a list of some of the more recent works in English that make substantial use of Baumgarten's philosophy. A few less recent but influential ones have also been included. It is not intended by any means to be exhaustive. Those desiring a fuller bibliography should see the following: Clemens Schwaiger, *Alexander Gottlieb Baumgarten—Ein Intellekuelles Porträt* (Stuttgart-Bad Canstatt: frommann-holzboog, 2011), 179–99; Alexander Gottlieb Baumgarten, *Metaphysica/Metaphysik: Historisch-kritische Ausgabe*, translated, introduced and edited by Günter Gawlick and Lothar Kreimendahl (Stuttgart-Bad Canstattt: frommann-holzboog, 2011), 627–34; Alexander Gottlieb Baumgarten, *Ästhetik*, Latin-German, translated and edited by Dagmar Mirbach, 2 Vols. (Hamburg: Felix Meiner Verlag, 2007), Vol. 2, 1253–305.

Allison, Henry. *The Kant-Eberhard Controversy.* Baltimore: Johns Hopkins University Press, 1973.

Ameriks, Karl. "The critique of metaphysics: Kant and traditional ontology," in *The Cambridge Companion to Kant,* edited by Paul Guyer. Cambridge: Cambridge University Press, 1992. 249–79.

—*Kant's Theory of Mind: An Analysis of the Paralogisms of Pure Reason*, 2nd edition. Oxford: Oxford University Press, 2000.

Beck, Lewis White. *Early German Philosophy: Kant and His Predecessors.* Bristol: Thoemmes Press, 1996.

Davey, Nicholas. "Baumgarten's Aesthetics: A Post-Gadamerian Reflection," *British Journal of Aesthetics*, 26 (1989), 101–15.

Dyck, Corey W. "The Divorce of Reason and Experience: Kant's Paralogisms of Pure Reason in Context," *Journal of the History of Philosophy*, 47 (2009), 249–75.

Gregor, Mary J. "Baumgarten's *Aesthetica*," *Review of Metaphysics*, 37 (1983), 357–85.

Guyer, Paul. "The Origins of Modern Aesthetics: 1711–35," in *The Blackwell Guide to Aesthetics*, edited by Peter Kivy. Oxford: Blackwell, 2004. 15–44.

Henrich, Dieter. *The Unity of Reason.* Edited by Richard L. Velkley, translated by Jeffery Edwards, Louis Hunt, Manfred Kuehn and Guenter Zoeller. Cambridge: Harvard University Press, 1994.

Longuenesse, Béatrice. *Kant and the Capacity to Judge,* translated by Charles T. Wolfe. Princeton: Princeton University Press, 1998.

Makkreel, Rudolf A. "The Confluence of Aesthetics and Hermeneutics in Baumgarten, Meier, and Kant," *Journal of Aesthetics and Art Criticism*, 54 (1996), 65–75.

Mirbach, Dagmar. "*Magnitudo aesthetica*, Aesthetic Greatness: Ethical aspects of Alexander Gottlieb Baumgarten's Fragmentary Aesthetica (1750/1758)," *Nordic Journal of Aesthetics*, 36–7 (2008/2009), 102–28.

Nuzzo, Angelica. "Kant and Herder on Baumgarten's *Aesthetica*," *Journal of the History of Philosophy*, 44 (2006), 577–97.

Polonoff, Irving I. *Force, Cosmos, Monads and Other Themes of Kant's Early Thougt* (sic). Kantstudien Ergänzungshefte, 107, Bonn: H. Bouvier Verlag, 1973.

Schönfeld, Martin. *The Philosophy of the Young Kant: The Precritical Project*. Oxford: Oxford University Press, 2000.

Tonelli, Giorgio. *Kant's "Critique of pure reason" within the tradition of modern logic: A commentary on its History*. ed. David H. Chandler Zürich: Georg Olms, 1994.

Watkins, Eric. *Kant and the Metaphysics of Causality*, Cambridge: Cambridge University Press, 2005.

Wessell Jr., Leonard P. "Alexander Baumgarten's Contribution to the Development of Aesthetics," *Journal of Aesthetics and Art Criticism*, 30 (1972), 333–42.

Wood, Allen W. *Kant's Rational Theology*. Ithaca: Cornell University Press, 1978.

Textual Variants

A key to our notes is found below. If text is only found in one edition, then only the number of that edition is used. If text is introduced and used in subsequent editions, then the first edition in which the text appears is used, followed by a range of numbers, or with f (and following edition), or ff (and all following editions). If a latter edition replaces the text of a previous edition, then the original text is indicated, followed by an abbreviated indication of the replacement text; in both cases, the edition is marked according to the procedure above. In cases where Baumgarten alters the Latin but the translation remains the same, the Latin variants are both indicated. If references to paragraphs are changed or inserted, they are indicated without quotation marks. Baumgarten divides the text into newer sections in the second and third editions, which we indicate with "section heading inserted." Our other remarks should require no explanation, such as "sentence inserted," "reference inserted," and "rest of paragraph inserted". AA is mentioned only if it differs from 4.

1: "text" – **text only found in that edition, and included at that point**

2ff: "text" inserted – **text found as of that edition**

1: "text"; 2ff: "other ... text" – **text in the first edition replaced in subsequent edition(s)**

1: different paragraph. "Text." – **the text in the quotation marks is found only in that edition; replaced in subsequent edition(s)**

1: different sentence. "Text." – **the sentence in quotations marks is found only in that edition; replaced in subsequent edition(s)**

1: §56 – **reference is different**

3ff: section heading inserted – **section heading found as of that edition**

1: *Latin text*; 2: *different Latin text* – **Latin is changed but translation remains the same**

Alexander Baumgarten's *Metaphysics*. The translation.

1   1f: "The Metaphysics by Alexander Gottlieb Baumgarten"; 3ff: "The Metaphysics of Alexander Gottlieb Baumgarten"

Preface of the third edition (1750)

1 3: "NEW PREFACE"
2 3, 6f.: *poëma*; 4, 5: *poema*
3 3–6 *non numquam*; 7: *nonnumquam*
4 1–5: *ago*; 6f, AA: *ego.*
5 3–6: *Quod si*; 7: *Quodsi*
6 3, 4, 5, 6: period; AA, 7: question mark.
7 3: period; 4ff.: question mark
8 3: period; 4ff.: exclamation mark
9 3–4: period; 5ff.: comma; 4 begins next sentence without a capital
10 3, 4 *iudidicem*; AA, 5: *iudicem*; 6f.: *indicem*
11 3: *in loco*; 4ff.: *in te*
12 3: *eius*; 4ff.: *tuam*;
13 3: period; 4ff.: full colon
14 3–6: *non numquam*; 7: *nonnumquam*
15 3–6 : *coexsistens*; 7: *coëxsistens*
16 3: "if not the outcome, its effects will in fairness be imputed to us"; 4ff.: "the use ... produced."
17 7: exclamation mark inserted

Preface of the second edition (1743)

1 2: "NEW PREFACE"; 3ff.: "PREFACE OF THE SECOND EDITION"
2 2f, 5ff: *inficiantur*; 4: *infitiantur*
3 2–6: *quo*; 7: *qua*
4 2–3: "an old man of good judgment"; 4ff.: "a man ... law"
5 3ff.: reference inserted
6 3ff.: reference inserted
7 3ff.: reference inserted
8 3ff.: reference inserted
9 3ff.: reference inserted
10 2–5: *ingrediuntor*; 6f.: *ingrediuntur*
11 3ff.: italics added (not reproduced in the translation)
12 3ff.: "that I call negations" inserted
13 3ff.: "or ... king," inserted.
14 2: *legerem*; 3ff.: *legeram*
15 2: *vere pollicitum*; 3ff.: *vere esse pollicitum*

To the listener of good will [Preface to the first edition] (1739)

1 1: *amicisſimis*; 2ff.: *amiciſſimis*. Such typographical changes will no longer be indicated in this edition. Also, the seemingly random use of an ampersand for "*et* [and]," especially in 6 and 7, will not be indicated.

2	1: *intimiora*; 2ff.: *interiora*
3	1: *in papyrum*; 2ff.: *in cartam*
4	1–7: *poeniteat*; AA: *paeniteat*
5	1–3: "conspicuously"; 4–7: "graciously"
6	1–7: *promsisse*; AA: *prompsisse*
7	1–3: continues "and these authors have been cited lest you think that I have robbed the chest of blind Crispinus, nor indeed need you be questioned in anything." The reference to Crispinus is from Horace (*Satire*, I, 1, 120–121).
8	1: "with the same precision,"
9	1–4 *utinam!* 5, AA: *utinam*
10	1: *aestumatissimus auditoribus*; 2ff.: *auditoribus*
11	1–7: "*oh!*"; AA: "*oh*"

Synopsis

1	1: no synopsis: 2ff.: synopsis inserted after preface to the second edition; 3ff.: synopsis follows the preface to the third edition

Prolegomena to Metaphysics

1	1–3, 5–7, AA: *conceptuum*; 4: *conceptum*

Part I: Ontology

1	2ff.: "metaphysics … architectonics" inserted
2	1: "(C[hapter] I),"
3	1: "(C[hapter] II);"
4	1: "(C[hapter] III)."
5	3ff.: puts "an absurdity" in brackets and inserts reference
6	4ff.: "A + not-A=0" inserted
7	1: no capitals
8	1f.: "in truth, both are CONNECTED or in a NEXUS"
9	1: difference sentence. "The ground is something as much as is the consequence."
10	1: "ABSOLUTELY"
11	2ff.: "absolutely" set in lower case and inserted inside bracket
12	2ff.: "*per se*" inserted
13	1: "ABSOLUTELY"
14	3ff.: "absolutely," set in lower case and inserted inside bracket
15	2ff.: "*per se*" inserted
16	2ff.: "through another" inserted
17	2ff.: "through another" inserted
18	2ff.: sentence inserted
19	2ff.: sentence inserted
20	1f.: different section title "The rational"

21   1f.: different sentence. "What is possible in a nexus is RATIONAL; what is impossible in a nexus is IRRATIONAL."

22   1: different paragraph. "Every possible thing is a consequence, or nothing is without a ground. If you deny this, then some possible thing, e.g. A, is not a consequence, or it does not have a ground, or the ground of A is posited to be nothing. Therefore, nothing is something (§14). Hence, something is nothing and not nothing (§8), which is absurd (§7). *This proposition* is called *the principle of ground.*"

23   4ff.: "it … (§8)" inserted

24   2, 3, 4: §279; 5ff.: §297

25   3ff.: "complete" inserted

26   2ff.: "total" inserted

27   2ff.: "nothing … unfruitful" inserted

28   1: rest of paragraph different. "If you deny this, then some possible thing does not have a consequence, or nothing is posited as the consequence of the same possible thing: hence it can be known from something, why nothing comes into existence (§14); hence the nothing is representable, and nothing is something (§8), which is absurd (§7)."

29   1: §18

30   1f.: *dupliciter connexum* (§14) *et rationale*; 3ff.: *nexu duplici* (§14) *connexum et rationale*

31   2ff.: "knowable … a posteriori" inserted

32   4ff.: "*This proposition* … after)" inserted

33   1: different paragraph. "If A becomes the ground of B and the consequences of A are not the grounds of B, A is called the CLOSEST GROUND of B; if A in truth becomes the ground of B, and the consequences of A are however the grounds of B, A is a MORE DISTANT GROUND of B (remote, mediate), and its consequences are the INTERMEDIATE GROUNDS of B."

34   2ff.: "an intermediate ground" inserted

35   2ff.: "the ultimate ground" inserted

36   4ff.: sentence inserted

37   3ff.: "some" inserted

38   3ff.: "some" inserted

39   1f.: §14.

40   2ff.: previous two sentences inserted

41   4ff.: sentence inserted

42   1f.: "determining ground"; 3ff.: "the determined"

43   1f.: "the determined"; 3ff.: "determining ground"

44   2ff.: "(notes and predicates)" inserted

45   3ff.: sentence inserted

46   1f.: different paragraph. "The determinations of something are either representable in it, considered in itself, or not (§10). The former are INTERNAL (intrinsic) determinations, the latter are RELATIONS, or EXTERNAL determinations (extrinsic, relative, respective, τὰ πρὸσ τι)."

47   2ff.: "οὐσία ... being)" inserted

48   2ff.: "or … (§7)" inserted

49   1: "the rest of the internal determinations"; 2ff.: "all … also"

50   4ff.: "(merely possible)" inserted

51   2ff.: "cf. §7" inserted

52   1: "the complex of internal determinations beyond the essence"; 2ff.: "collection of affections"

53	3ff.: "internal" inserted
54	1: §46
55	1: "of a being"; 2ff.: "of something possible"
56	2ff.: reference inserted
57	1: *non valet C*; 2ff.: *N.V.C*, "it is … deduce"
58	2ff.: reference inserted
59	1: "of reason"; 2ff "of reasoning reason"
60	1f.: §53, 40; 3ff.: reference moved further down in paragraph
61	1-5,7: comma; 6: semicolon
62	1: this and the following sentence are joined as one sentence; 2ff. split them
63	3ff.: reference inserted
64	1: §38, corrected to §39 in errata; 2ff.: §35
65	2ff.: italics used
66	3ff.: "in the thing … distinguished" inserted
67	2ff.: "in a … §350" inserted
68	3ff.: "absolute … (§37)" inserted
69	3ff.: "absolute … (§37)" inserted
70	1: no capitals
71	3ff.: "(without the presence of anything else)" inserted
72	3ff.: symbols for congruent, dissimilar, unequal, and incongruent inserted
73	3ff.: "plurality" inserted
74	2ff.: "(one, exclusively so)" inserted
75	1f.: "THE TRUE"; 2ff.: "ORDER"
76	2ff.: sentence inserted
77	3ff.: sentence inserted
78	1: word capitalized
79	3ff.: "and indeed … ground" inserted
80	1f.: "relation"; 3ff.: "respect"
81	1: *E.*; 2ff.: expanded to *Ergo*
82	2ff.: sentence inserted
83	3ff.: section heading inserted
84	3ff.: "real" inserted
85	4ff.: "objective" inserted
86	3ff.: "material" inserted
87	3ff.: "the essential … (§23, 41)" inserted
88	2ff.: reference inserted; 3ff encloses reference in parentheses
89	2ff.: reference inserted
90	2: *Catholica s. universalia*; 3ff.: *Catholica (universalia)*
91	2ff.: sentence inserted
92	3ff.: §23 inserted
93	2ff.: reference inserted
94	1: "knowability"; 2ff.: "apperceptibility"
95	2ff.: "clearly" inserted
96	1f.: "Section VI"; 3ff.: "Section VII"
97	3ff.: "the focus of the perfection" inserted
98	3ff.: "which is … in opposition" inserted
99	1,2,6f.: no parentheses around "essential"; 5: only opening parenthesis
100	3ff.: "in itself" inserted
101	1f.: "ABSOLUTELY"; 3ff.: "IN ITSELF"

102   1: "and" follows "necessary"; deleted in 2ff
103   2ff.: parentheses around "qualified"
104   3ff.: "of the consequent" inserted
105   2ff.: "The determination of a being ... hypothetical" inserted (excepting material indicated as inserted in 3ff)
106   3ff.: "of the consequence" inserted
107   3ff.: "the former ... necessary" inserted
108   2ff.: "intrinsically" inserted
109   2ff.: "(hypothetically)" inserted
110   2ff.: sentence inserted
111   3ff.: capitalized
112   3ff.: "in the case ... *per se*" inserted
113   3ff.: capitalized
114   2ff.: sentence inserted; 3ff. "in ... contingent" inserted at end (see other modifications in the above endnotes concerning this sentence)
115   2ff.: sentence inserted
116   1: "Nothing contingent in itself is absolutely necessary (§104, 102)"
117   2ff.: this and the previous sentence inserted
118   1: §102; 2ff.: §103
119   1: §51; 2ff.: §81
120   1: §102; 2ff.: §103
121   2ff.: this and the previous three sentences inserted
122   5ff.: §103
123   1: "the internal determinations that are to be admitted beyond its essence"; 2ff.: "its affections"
124   1: §82
125   1f.: Q.A.; 3ff.: *q.a.*
126   3ff.: sentence inserted
127   3ff.: rest of paragraph inserted
128   2ff.: "intrinsically" inserted
129   1: §154
130   2ff.: sentence inserted
131   2ff.: "(variable)" inserted
132   2ff.: "(fixed, invariable, constant)" inserted
133   2ff.: "at the same time" inserted
134   1: lower case
135   1: lower case
136   2ff.: "or the possibility of alterations in it" inserted
137   2ff.: "or the impossibility of alterations in it" inserted
138   2ff.: sentence inserted
139   1: "(§127,18)"; 2ff.: moved down two sentences
140   2ff.: this and the previous sentence inserted
141   2ff.: this and the previous three sentences inserted
142   1: *intrinsece*; 2ff.: *intrinsecus*
143   1f.: lower case
144   1: §26
145   1: "a [being] of reason, or"
146   3ff.: sentence inserted
147   1: "And thus, there are no internal privations in a necessary being"; 2ff.: "And ... privations"

148   1: §109; 2ff.: §111
149   1f.: "A PHYSICAL EVIL, in the broad sense"; 3ff.: "A CONTINGENT EVIL (a physical evil, in the broad sense)"
150   2ff.: "cf. §788" inserted
151   1f: "A PHYSICAL GOOD, in the broad sense"; 3ff.: "A CONTINGENT GOOD (a physical good, in the broad sense)"
152   2ff.: "cf. §787" inserted
153   1: "or," inserted before "an individual"
154   3ff.: sentence inserted
155   1f.: different paragraph. "A universal being is either seen in a more determined being, which is to say an inferior being, i.e. a being in which more determinations are posited than in itself, or it is not (§10). In the prior case, it is seen CONCRETELY, in the latter, ABSTRACTLY. The former is the PHYSICAL UNIVERSAL (in many, in a fact); the latter is the LOGICAL UNIVERSAL (after many, after the fact)."
156   1: "The determinations of a more determined, or inferior, being that are indeterminate in the superior, or less determined, or more universal being"; 2: the same text, with "INFERIOR" and "SUPERIOR" in capitals; 3ff.: "The determinations … superior"
157   1–3, 6f, AA.: *speciei*; 4f.: *in speciei*
158   3ff.: reference inserted
159   1: "Since the less determined or the superior is in the inferior or more determined"; 2ff.: "Since … inferior"
160   2: §151 inserted; 3ff.: changed to §148
161   3ff.: "and the supreme … genera" inserted
162   3ff.: reference inserted
163   3ff.: "its" inserted
164   3ff.: "genera" inserted
165   1: no italics
166   1: "each and every part"; 2ff.: "a given part"
167   2ff.: "(absolute, cf. §161)" inserted
168   2ff.: "(absolute, cf. §161)" inserted
169   2ff.: sentence inserted
170   1f.: lower case
171   1: *soli*; 2ff.: *solo*
172   1: *soli*; 2ff.: *solo*
173   2ff.: this and the previous sentence inserted
174   2ff.: "internal" inserted
175   1: "in a being"; 2ff.: "in it"
176   3ff.: section heading inserted
177   2: paragraph italicized
178   1: "of the two smallest"; 2ff.: "of the smallest and fewest"
179   1: §17
180   2: this and the previous sentence italicized
181   2: paragraph italicized
182   3ff.: sentence inserted
183   2: paragraph italicized
184   1: §17
185   1: §161
186   2: paragraph italicized

187   1: §161
188   2: paragraph italicized
189   2: paragraph italicized
190   1: "of the two smallest"; 2ff.: "of the fewest and smallest"
191   2: paragraph italicized
192   2: paragraph italicized
193   1: "The smallest unity of a being is if two of its smallest determinations are inseparable"; 2ff.: "The smallest … inseparable"
194   2ff.: "of the most and greatest beings" inserted
195   3ff.: this and the previous sentence inserted
196   2: paragraph italicized
197   1: "among two"; 2ff.: "among the fewest and smallest"
198   2ff.: "and greater" inserted
199   2: paragraph italicized
200   1: "in a conjunction of three things'
201   1: rest of paragraph different. "Therefore, the more things that are coordinated, and the greater the identity of coordination, so much greater is the order (§160, 174) until it is the greatest, which would be when the most are thus coordinated such that there would be the greatest identity of coordination that is possible (§161)."
202   2ff.: "with the smallest possibility of knowledge" inserted
203   2ff.: "and the more possible this knowledge is' inserted
204   2ff.: "of the determination with the ground" inserted
205   2: "this conformity will be the smallest … from the greatest grounds (§161)" italicized
206   2: paragraph italicized
207   2: paragraph italicized
208   2: paragraph italicized
209   2: paragraph italicized
210   2ff.: sentence inserted
211   2ff.: "with the ground" inserted
212   2: this and previous sentence italicized
213   2: paragraph italicized
214   2: *s.*; 3ff.: *seu*
215   2ff.: "or … ground" inserted
216   2ff.: "with which … compared" inserted
217   2: paragraph italicized
218   1: sentence not italicized
219   2: paragraph italicized
220   2: paragraph italicized
221   2: paragraph italicized
222   1: "of the three smallest beings"; 2ff.: "of the fewest and smallest beings"
223   1: §84; 2, 3, 6, AA: §94; 4, 5, 7: §93
224   2ff.: "the more often" inserted
225   2ff.: "§169" inserted
226   1: §184
227   1: different paragraph. "An exception contrary to a sufficient, more fecund, more serious, more distant, and unqualified ground of perfection, i.e. an exception which is made from a stronger law (§181, 97), is greater than an exception contrary to the

insufficient, less fecund, less serious, closer, and only qualifiedly sufficient ground of perfection (§187, 177)." 2: paragraph italicized

228   1–3: §178
229   1: no capitals
230   2ff.: sentence inserted
231   3ff.: "of the various determinations" inserted
232   1: different paragraph. "The greater is the possibility of succession in some being, the greater is its changeability." 2: paragraph italicized
233   6: "greatest" missing
234   2: capitalized
235   3ff.: "physical, understood broadly" set in parentheses
236   1f.: "Section VI"
237   2ff.: "(in something else)" inserted
238   2ff.: "(a ... συμβεβηκόσ)" inserted
239   1: "or a BEING SUBSISTING PER SE"
240   2ff.: "(a being subsisting ... something else" inserted
241   1: no italics
242   1: no italics
243   1: "is called SUBSTANTIAL, and is the subject of these"; 2ff.: "or substance ... is called substantial"
244   1: rest of paragraph different. "Therefore power is the sufficient ground of accidents inhering in substances."
245   2ff.: "in the stricter sense" inserted
246   2ff.: rest of paragraph inserted
247   1: different paragraph. "Everything endowed with force possesses something substantial (§198). Hence it is a substance (§196). Therefore substance can be defined as a being endowed with force (§199)."
248   1: rest of paragraph different. "and the accidents to which force is attributed are substantiated phenomena."
249   3ff.: sentence inserted
250   1: different paragraph. "The smallest force is sufficient for only one, smallest, hardly inherent accident is sufficient (§197, 169). Therefore, the more and greater accidents for which the force is sufficient to actualize, to this extent is it greater, until it is the greatest force, which would be sufficient for actualizing the most and greatest accidents (§197, 169)." 2: paragraph italicized
251   1f.: "philosophical and mathematical dynamics" 3ff.: "philosophical DYNAMEOMETRICS"
252   3ff.: section heading inserted
253   1: "A singular contingent substance"; 2ff.: "A contingent supposit"
254   1: *determinata*; 2ff.: *determinatum*
255   1: "(§202)"
256   1–3: §148 [§148 seems to have been the correct reference, but §184 remains in 4ff]
257   1: "a singular contingent substance"; 2ff.: "a contingent supposit"
258   3ff.: sentence inserted
259   1: "a singular contingent substance"; 2ff.: "a contingent supposit"
260   1: different sentence: "The relations of a substance are not fitting considered in themselves (§37), hence nor are they internally inalterable in it."
261   3ff.: sentence inserted
262   2ff.: "also in a stricter sense" inserted

263　2: paragraph italicized

264　1: §260

265　2ff.: "and active potency, force, cf. §197" inserted; 3ff.: deletes "and" and moves the opening parenthesis forward

266　2: all but the last sentence italicized

267　2: "in the stricter sense" inserted

268　1: "The power"; 2ff.: "This"

269　1–3: no capitals; 2ff.: "in the stricter sense" inserted

270　1f.: "and that which is most closely present to another touches the other"; 3ff.: "and … other"

271　4ff.: "or are contiguous" inserted

272　1: "and immediate presence is CONTACT"; 2ff.: "and … CONTACT"

273　3ff.: "nor suffers from it" inserted

274　2ff.: sentence inserted (excepting material indicated as inserted in 3ff)

275　1f.: "Section VII"

276　2: "stricter"; 3ff.: "strict"

277　2ff.: "(in the simple and … COMPARATIVELY SIMPLE" inserted

278　1f.: "strict"; 3ff.: "stricter"

279　1–3: "from the merely possibile"; 4ff.: "from non-existence"

280　1–3: "to mere possibility"; 4ff.: "to non-existence"

281　3ff.: section heading inserted

282　1f.: "strict"; 3ff.: "stricter"

283　1f.: "strict"; 3ff.: "stricter"

284　1f.: "strict"; 3ff.: "stricter"

285　1–3: "things which are posited outside of it"; 4ff.: "different beings"

286　1: "and FILLS UP SPACE"; 2ff.: "and is said … be filling)"

287　1: §239

288　1f.: §225

289　1: §239

290　2ff.: "is" inserted

291　1: different paragraph. "Division is the decrease of quantitative magnitude. Hence a monad is indivisible."

292　1f.: Section VIII

293　1: no capitals

294　2ff.: "cf. §350" inserted

295　2ff.: "cf. §341" inserted

296　2ff.: "cf. §341" inserted

297　3ff.: "or that which is the most real being (§190)" inserted

298　2ff.: sentence inserted

299　3ff.: "is" inserted

300　3ff.: this and the previous sentence inserted

301　1: §257

302　3ff.: "although … (§248)" inserted

303　6f.: §109

304　1: "its internal determinations can be intensified"; 2ff.: "some … intensified"

305　1: different sentence. "In terms of its internal determinations, an infinite being is actually whatever it can be (§256, 132)."

306　1: "Hence, [it] can be defined"; 2ff.: "Hence, an infinite being can be defined"

307　1: different paragraph. "A finite being can be defined as a being that, in terms of its internal determinations, is not actually whatever it can be (§254, 257)."

308 1–3: "variation"; 4ff.: "alteration"

309 1f.: different sentence. "And hence so too are both contingent imperfection in itself, and physical evil in the broad sense (§146)."

310 3ff.: "is" inserted

311 1–5: "(§8–100)"; 6f.: "(§8, 100)"; 2: sentence in italics

312 2: this and the previous two sentences in italics

313 2: sentence in italics

314 4ff.: "of essential determinations and attributes, necessary; of modes, contingent" inserted; 5–7: "(CONTINGENT)." The various editions differ widely in comma use in this paragraph.

315 3ff.: sentence inserted

316 1f.: *s.*; 3ff.: *seu*

317 2ff.: "(of identity)" inserted

318 2ff.: " or of denied total identity" inserted

319 2ff.: reference inserted

320 2ff.: reference inserted

321 2ff.: reference inserted

322 2ff.: sentence inserted

323 2ff.: "(of identity)" inserted

324 2ff.: sentence inserted

325 1: §272

326 1: *si*; 2ff.: *nisi*

327 1f.: "The simultaneous and the successive"

328 2ff.: sentence inserted

329 1: "nor [are] successive beings [posited] mutually outside of one another in the same age"

330 2ff.: this and the previous sentence inserted

331 2: "and the smallest motion would be…and external beings" italics

332 3ff.: "in itself and" inserted

333 1: "An extension"; 2ff.: "A … being"

334 1: "an extension"; 2ff.: "a … being"

335 1: §241

336 1: "two distant points"; 2ff.: "distant points"

337 2ff.: sentence inserted

338 1: "two distant lines"; 2ff.: "distant lines"

339 2ff.: sentence inserted

340 1: "two distant surfaces"; 2ff.: "distant surfaces"

341 2ff.: "(a mathematical body, cf. §296)" inserted

342 6f.: §139

343 2ff.: "POWER" inserted

344 2ff.: reference inserted

345 2ff.: sentence inserted

346 2ff.: "(cf. §289, second matter, cf. §295)" inserted

347 3ff.: section heading inserted

348 1–4: "thought"; 5–7: "change"

349 3ff.: "that very time itself" inserted

350 1f.: "or in the PRESENT time," inserted after "EXISTING BEINGS"; 3ff.: moved inside bracket, "or" deleted

351 2ff.: "if they are … if they no longer exist" inserted

352   1: "The existence of an existing being that is neither originating nor perishing"; 2ff.: "The continuation of existence"
353   2ff.: sentence inserted
354   1: different paragraph. "The time simultaneous to the origin of something is called its BEGINNING, and to the perishing, its END."
355   3ff.: sentence inserted
356   1: different sentences. "The duration of a being without origin and perishing is ETERNITY. Hence eternity is duration without <*sive*> beginning and end (§301)," reading *sine* for *sive*.
357   1–4,7: *tempori*; 5, 6: *tempore*
358   1: different paragraph. "In a necessary being and substance, hence in an infinite being (§256), origin and perishing are absolutely impossible (§227); hence a necessary being and substance, an infinite being, is eternal (§302, 299), and hence the same being, absolutely necessarily (§102), is sempiternal (§302)."
359   6f.: §201
360   2ff.: "or, whatever is, as long as it is, necessarily is" inserted
361   3ff.: §167 inserted
362   1f.: Section III
363   1: *quamquae*; 2ff.: *quam quae*
364   1–5: "infinite"; 6f.: "finite"
365   2ff.: "(of composition)" inserted
366   2ff.: "(of generation)" inserted
367   2ff.: "insofar … dependency" inserted
368   3ff.: brackets inserted around "non-principle causes"
369   1–5: *casu* 6: *causa*; 7: *caussa*
370   2ff.: sentence inserted
371   3ff.: section heading inserted
372   3ff.: "and deficient" inserted
373   3ff.: "or deficient" inserted
374   3ff.: "or deficient" inserted
375   2ff.: sentence inserted
376   3ff.: "and deficient" inserted
377   4: "other" inserted
378   3ff.: "or deficient" inserted
379   1f.: "to a principle efficient cause"; 3ff.: "to an efficient or deficient cause"
380   3ff.: this and the previous two sentences inserted
381   AA: §37
382   1: §287
383   1f.: §323
384   1: "is its effect (continuous, IMMEDIATE) and proximal"; 2ff.: "is … EFFECT"
385   2ff.: §166 inserted
386   3ff.: section heading inserted
387   1–3: "is useful"; 4ff.: "can be useful" in both instances in this sentence
388   2: this and the previous sentence in italics
389   1: "PRICE and VALUATION; 2ff.: "PRICE (valuation)"
390   1–3: "is useful"; 4ff.: "can be useful" (in both instances in this sentence)
391   6f.: §207
392   3ff.: sentence inserted
393   3ff.: section heading inserted

394   1f.: REMEDIA; 3ff.: MEDIA
395   2: "cf. §248, *media*" inserted; 3ff.: *media* changed to *remedia*
396   6f.: §207
397   3ff.: "in the one intending" inserted
398   1f.: *remediorum*; 3ff.: *mediorum*
399   1f.: *remediis*; 3ff.: *mediis*
400   1f.: *remedia*; 3ff.: *media*
401   1–7: *confines*; AA: *cofines*
402   1f.: *remediorum*; 3ff.: *mediorum*
403   4: "The rest are INTERMEDIATE ENDS" inserted
404   2ff.: reference inserted
405   1: "However, essential determinations are FORM."
406   1: §39
407   1: "Hence, essence is a formal cause."
408   1: "and their NEXUS can be called SUBJECTIVE and FORMAL"; 2ff.: "and the nexus of these ... latter"
409   1: "or ectype"; 2ff.: "(ectype, copy)"
410   2ff.: "(original)" inserted
411   1: "or typical"; 2ff.: "(typical)"
412   1f.: "Section IIII"
413   3ff.: "μνημόσυνον " inserted
414   2ff.: "(semiotics, philosophical semiology, symbolics)" inserted
415   3ff.: "which are not composed of signs" inserted
416   3ff.: "which are composed .... derivative signs is" inserted
417   1: different beginning to paragraph. "The science of signs is semiotics or semiology or CHARACTERISTICS, and this science is COMBINATORIAL HEURISTICS, if it concerns primitive as well as derivative signs"
418   1: different paragraph. "The complex of terms mostly used in a certain region is a PARTICULAR LANGUAGE; the complex of terms readable in all particular languages is a UNIVERSAL LANGUAGE; the science of the rules of a language is called GRAMMAR, and the science of the rules common to [all particular] languages is UNIVERSAL GRAMMAR. The science of speech is UNIVERSAL PHILOLOGY."

Part II: Cosmology

1   1: "(C[hapter]) 1,"
2   1: "(C[hapter] 2),"
3   1: "(C[hapter] 3)"
4   2ff.: "cf. §91... πᾶν)" inserted
5   6f.: §4
6   3ff.: sentence inserted
7   2ff.: "(kingdom of power)" inserted
8   2ff.: "(kingdom of wisdom)" inserted
9   1: §342
10   1–5: *consentiant*; 6f.: *consentiunt*
11   1–6: *est*; 7: *et*

12	2: paragraph in italics
13	1: "3" inserted between "whole" and "of the smallest"
14	2ff.: reference inserted
15	1: §202
16	1: *ortus et interitus*; 2ff.: *initium et finis*
17	4ff.: "because… originate" inserted
18	1–3: §227
19	1–3: "as long as it, with a surviving part, does not change into something merely possible"; 4: "as long as it … non-existing"
20	4ff.: "contingent or" inserted
21	1: §268
22	1: §269
23	2ff.: §354 inserted
24	6f.: §108
25	1: §27
26	2ff.: reference inserted
27	1: §27
28	1: "is"; 2ff.: "would be"
29	1: "common rules"; 2ff.: "rules"
30	1: different text. "That which would exist without a most proximate sufficient ground would either have intermediate and more distant grounds, or not (§27, 10). If the latter, it would exist without a ground, and would be impossible (§20). If the former, it would exist through pure chance"; 2ff.: "That … chance"
31	3ff.: sentence inserted
32	2ff.: "substance" inserted
33	6f.: §19
34	2ff.: "substance" inserted
35	1: §399
36	1: §257
37	1f.: "strict"; 3ff.: "stricter"
38	1f.: "strict"; 3ff.: "stricter"
39	2ff.: "UNIVERSAL" inserted
40	2: "(cf. §757)"
41	3ff.: sentence inserted
42	1: "singular (§148)"
43	1: "(§200), and with an internal (§206) and external (§207) state; they are modifiable (§209) and non-extended, nor does any single one fill up space, but rather each aggregate does (§242); nor do they, indivisible (§244) and finite (§354) have quantitative magnitude (§243); hence, they have a specific grade of force (§249)"; 2ff.: "or indeed … (§249)"
44	1: §287
45	1f.: different sentence. "It is not possible for several monads to be in the same place in any, and hence this, universe (§282)."
46	2ff.: "(a solid)" inserted
47	3ff.: capitals used
48	1f.: "(Zenonical)"
49	3ff.: this and the previous sentence inserted
50	1: §198
51	2ff.: italics in this sentence added

52 3ff.: brackets inserted
53 2ff.: "only" inserted
54 2ff.: "or at least … monads)" inserted
55 1: "cognize distinctly"; 2ff.: "(§69)"
56 2ff.: "(in a strict sense, cf. §519)" inserted
57 2ff.: "(an intelligence, a person)" inserted
58 1: "(intelligences)"
59 6f.: §257
60 2ff.: reference inserted
61 2ff.: "intellectual, and moral" inserted
62 2ff.: "cf. §723" inserted
63 2ff.: "and one is the most perfect of all (§77, 185)" inserted
64 1f.: different title: "The composite parts of the world"
65 1: "If the former"; 2ff.: "In either case"
66 2ff.: "(*a war* … §364)" inserted
67 1: §228
68 2ff.: italics added
69 2ff.: italics added
70 1f.: §73
71 3ff.: reference inserted
72 2ff.: sentence inserted
73 1f: different text. "Every impenetrable monad that is part of an extended being contains within itself the ground of why the place of another monad may not alter into that place which is its own, or that which it itself occupies (§398). Therefore it contains the ground of an opposite motion (§283, 81), and resists it (§221, 222). Therefore certain monads of this universe constitute an extended being (§414), to which the power of inertia (§294), and hence matter (§295), is attributed."
74 3: *et*; 4ff.: *est*
75 1f.: different text. "Neither in this nor in any world is matter totally homogeneous (§407, 415)."
76 3ff.: sentence inserted
77 1f.: no capitals
78 1f.: different text. "In this world *all matter is in motion* (§417) since that which posits a motive force (§294) will either be in that moved matter, or outside of it (§10); i.e. the moved matter either moves itself, or is moved (§210, 283). If it is the former, it is a body; if the latter, something determining (§306) the place of the simultaneously moved parts of the world (§417) reacts through a force attributed to itself (§410). And hence in this case there is matter to which a motive force is attributed (§294), i.e. a body. Therefore the monads of this world constituting matter constitute a body (§415)."
79 1: §235
80 2ff.: reference inserted
81 1: "(§230, 15)"
82 1: "ATOMS OF NATURE"
83 3ff.: parenthesis placed around "confusedly"
84 1: §207
85 1f.: "relatively"; 3ff.: "respectively"
86 2ff.: reference inserted
87 2ff.: "that matter … (§425)" inserted

88   3ff.: section heading inserted
89   2ff.: references inserted; 3ff.: parentheses inserted around references
90   2ff.: sentence inserted
91   2ff.: references inserted
92   2ff.: italics added
93   2ff.: reference inserted
94   2ff.: "a pneumatico-mechanical … nexus" inserted
95   1: "(§431 or simply physical)"; 2ff.: "(simply … mechanical)"
96   1: §355
97   1f.: different sentence. "The *most perfect world* is the *greatest* of the possible worlds (§436, 368)."
98   2ff.: italics added
99   3ff.: "best" inserted
100   1: "embraces as many simultaneous and successive beings as there are compossible in a world"; 2ff.: "embraces … world"
101   3ff.: "best and" inserted
102   3ff.: reference inserted
103   1: different text. "If many parts of the world posited outside of one another are compossible in a world, the world such as the egoist thinks this to be is not the most perfect (§437, 392). If non-intellectual monads are compossible with spirits in a world, the world such as the idealist thinks this to be is not the most perfect (§402, 437). On the contrary, in both cases the prior is true (§57). Therefore the most perfect world is neither such as the egoist, nor such as the idealist thinks it to be."
104   1: "the most perfect world is not such as the materialist considers it to be"; 2ff.: "the MATERIALISTIC … world"
105   1: different text. "The most perfect world consists of the greatest parts that are possible in a world (§436), and hence it consists of the greatest monads that are possible in a world (§394). Now, monads representing their own world at least in part clearly to themselves are greater than those representing it utterly obscurely (§230, 402). But yet, both are possible in a world (§57). Therefore, in the most perfect world, there are monads representing the world clearly and distinctly. Therefore, there are spirits (§402)."
106   1: §440
107   2ff.: reference inserted
108   2ff.: reference inserted
109   2ff.: "fewest" inserted
110   2ff.: reference inserted
111   1: §197
112   2ff.: sentence inserted
113   1f.: different text. "When the most perfect world is posited, the supreme perfection that is possible in a world is posited (§436). Hence, *the most perfect world* is also the best *of all possible worlds*."
114   2ff.: reference inserted
115   6f.: §281
116   2ff.: "e.g. … (§473, 187)" inserted
117   2ff.: "and hence … smallest (§186)" inserted
118   1–4: §380–8, 247, and 354; 5ff.: §380–8, 247–354
119   1f.: "the supreme or greatest contingency (§188) and mutability (§190) that is possible in a world (§437) must also be attributed to it. Hence, that which §380–8,

247, and 354 teach are absent from every world are the most distant from the best world"; 3ff.: "but those beings ... to it (§440, 437)."

120 3ff.: section heading inserted

121 2ff.: this and the previous two sentences inserted

122 2ff.: reference inserted

123 1: *sententia*; 2ff.: *systema*

124 1: §419

125 1: begins with "If any part of the world thus suffers from another part of the world such that this very suffering is not likewise the action of the suffering part itself, there is a real influence upon the suffering part (§212). But a really influencing part will either be infinite substance alone, or that part of the world which influences, such that a phenomenon likewise really influences (§10, 248)."

126 2ff.: rest of paragraph inserted

127 1: "substances of this world that suffer"; 2ff.: "substances ... suffer"

128 4ff.: "according to this doctrine" inserted

129 1f.: "SYSTEM OF UNIVERSAL ASSISTENCE"; 3ff.: "UNIVERSAL ... CAUSES"

130 1: "(the Cartesian system, and, more broadly, the system of occasional causes)"; 2: "(the Cartesian, or rather, the Malebranchian system, and, more broadly, the system of occasional causes)"; 3ff "(the ... assistance)"

131 2ff.: sentence inserted

132 4ff.: "unless ... influence" placed in parantheses

133 1: different sentence. "The system of occasional causes denies neither the universal harmony nor the universal mutual influence of the substances of this world (§452, 448), but denies that the latter is physical and that the former is pre-established."

134 3ff.: "all" inserted

135 1: "The systems of pre-established harmony, physical influence, and assistance"; 2ff.: "The systems ... physical influence"

136 2ff.: "(1)" inserted

137 1: §453

138 1: The sentence end here, and a new sentence begins with "The system of universal pre-established harmony is similar to the system of universal physical influence (§70) in the world, in that ..."

139 2ff.: "and (2)" inserted

140 1f.: "The system of universal pre-established harmony and universal assistance"; 3ff.: "The ... causes"

141 2: "GENERAL"; 3ff "UNIVERSAL"

142 1: "The harmony of a world's substances mutually influencing one another is the COMMERCE of these among one another. Philosophical hypotheses invented for explaining this commerce are called GENERAL SYSTEMS, which, ..."; 2: "GENERAL ... SUBSTANCES"; 3ff.: "UNIVERSAL ... SUBSTANCES"

143 1f.: "Therefore, the system of universal pre-established harmony, of universal physical influence, and of universal assistance"; 3ff.: "Therefore ... causes"

144 1–3: "(§448–56)"

145 1f.: "GENERAL"; 3ff.: "UNIVERSAL"

146 1f.: "Aside from the general systems of universal pre-established harmomy, physical influence, and assistance"; 3ff.: "Aside ... causes"

147 3ff.: "universal" inserted

148   1: §450
149   2ff.: §248 inserted
150   1f.: "Through assistance, or the real influence of infinite substance alone"; 3ff.: "Through ... alone"
151   3ff.: "whatever they suffer" inserted
152   1f.: "however, the influencing substance"; 3ff.: "however ... interaction"
153   1f.: "assistance"; 3ff.: "the influence ... alone"
154   2ff.: "according to" inserted
155   2ff.: rest of the paragraph inserted
156   3ff.: "given" inserted
157   2: "[and] assistance and its system"; 3ff.: "and ... causes"
158   1: "Now, monads constituting bodies are more connected than those not constituting such (§407, 414), and bodies are possible in a world (§57). Therefore there are bodies in the most perfect world, and there are spirits (§440), and hence the greatest mechanical nexus, pneumatic nexus, and pneumatico-mechanical nexus (the greatest harmony of the kingdom of nature and grace)." 2ff.: "Therefore, if ... 403)."
159   1: §464
160   1: different sentence. "Hence the most perfect world is such as the dualist conceives it (§464)."
161   1f.: "Section II"
162   2ff.: "(natured nature, cf. §859)" inserted
163   1f.: "is maximally contingent"; 3ff.: "has ... contingency"
164   1: §347
165   1: "was actualized"; 2ff.: "is to be actualized"
166   1: "ABSOLUTELY, or UNQUALIFIEDLY NATURAL"
167   2ff.: reference inserted
168   1: "was actualized"; 2ff.: "is to be actualized"
169   1: "RESPECTIVELY (relatively) NATURAL AS SUCH"
170   1: rest of the paragraph is different. "Hence SOMETHING NATURAL WITH RESPECT TO A SPECIFIC BODY is something actualized by its determined nature, and WITH RESPECT TO A SPECIFIC CORPOREAL WORLD, it is that which is actualized through the universal nature of the bodies of a specific world (§4)." 2ff: "(cf. §474)" inserted
171   3ff : "(merely, entirely, utterly)" inserted
172   3ff : "(now and in this manner)" inserted
173   1: different text. "SOMETHING NATURAL WITH RESPECT TO A SPECIFIC CONTINGENT SPIRIT is something actualized through its determined nature. SOMETHING NATURAL WITH RESPECT TO A SPECIFIC PNEUMATIC WORLD is that which is actualized through the universal nature of the spirits of a specific world (§469). Hence, it is clear what is NATURALLY or physically POSSIBLE and IMPOSSIBLE (§16, 17)."
174   1: rest of the paragraph is different. "Hence, the succession of natural beings absolutely as such is the COURSE OF NATURE ABSOLUTELY AS SUCH; the succession of natural beings respectively as such is the COURSE OF NATURE RESPECTIVELY AS SUCH; the succession of natural beings with respect to a specific body is the course of nature with respect to that body; the succession of natural beings with respect to a specific corporeal world is the course of nature with respect to that world (§469). The succession of natural beings with respect

to a specific contingent spirit is the course of nature with respect to that spirit; the succession of natural beings with respect to a specific pneumatic world is the course of nature with respect to that nexus (§470)."

175   1: "and it is either unqualified or respective with respect to a specific body or specific material world (§469), and with respect to a specific spirit or specific pneumatic world (§469)"; 2ff.: "opposed ... nature (§466)"

176   1: rest of the paragraph is slightly different: "Of the complex of these, the RIGHT OF NATURE is the BROADEST whose parts are the laws and rules of motion (§432) and the laws of the nature of spirits, which are generally called the LAWS OF ALTERATION."

177   1: "either unqualifiedly or respectively"

178   2ff.: "even" inserted

179   2ff.: "or... (§466)" inserted

180   2ff.: "even" inserted

181   2ff.: "or ... (§466)" inserted

182   1: §372

183   1: "Something natural with respect to a specific body or a specific material nexus in the world"; 2ff.: "Something ... world"

184   1: §432

185   1f.: Section III

186   3ff.: sentence inserted

187   3ff.: "The supernatural and" inserted

188   1f.: "not"; 3ff.: "neither"

189   3ff.: "supernatural, nor is it" inserted

190   2: "determinate" inserted

191   2ff.: §384 inserted

192   3ff.: sentence inserted

193   1: different text. "An extraordinary event whose natural cause we do not know is a nevertheless natural if it is called a MIRACLE FOR US; a miracle for us is not a strict miracle (§474)."

194   3ff.: "the supernatural and" inserted

195   3ff.: "supernatural and" inserted

196   3ff.: "supernatural and" inserted

197   1: different sentence "What is preternatural with respect to a specific body, or a specific corporeal world, or a specific spirit, or a specific pneumatic world comes about contrary to the respective course of nature (§474, 471)."

198   3ff.: "supernatural, or" inserted

199   3ff.: "The supernatural and" inserted

200   3ff.: "things that are supernatural and" inserted

201   2ff.: this and the previous sentence inserted

202   3ff.: "The supernatural and" inserted

203   1: "unqualified"; 2ff.: "universal"

204   2ff.: "such ... (§384)" inserted

205   1: "not"; 2ff.: "neither"

206   2ff.: "nor ... order" inserted

207   3ff.: "much less a miracle" inserted

208   3ff.: section heading inserted

209   1: "stricter law of the best"; 2ff.: "law of the best"

210   2ff.: rest of paragraph inserted

211   1: "hence extraordinary with respect to the unqualified order of nature"; 2ff.: "hence … nature"
212   3ff.: "e.g. miraculous" inserted
213   1: §87
214   1: "unqualified"; 2ff.: "universal"
215   2ff.: reference inserted
216   1: "even unqualified"; 2ff.: "both … universal"
217   2ff.: "in the world" inserted
218   3ff.: "something … correctly," inserted
219   3ff.: "The supernatural and" inserted
220   3ff.: "no supernatural things" inserted
221   3ff.: "the supernatural, and" inserted
222   3ff.: "The supernatural and" inserted
223   3ff.: "a supernatural and" inserted
224   3ff.: "a supernatural event, and" inserted
225   3ff.: "given supernatural event, or" inserted
226   3ff.: "the supernatural event, or" inserted
227   2ff.: §378 inserted
228   3ff.: "nothing supernatural" inserted
229   3ff.: "every supernatural thing" inserted
230   2ff.: reference inserted
231   3ff.: "supernatural event or" inserted
232   1: §28
233   3ff "instead of a supernatural event, or" inserted
234   3ff.: "supernatural, or" inserted
235   3ff; "when a supernatural effect" inserted
236   3ff.: "the supernatural effect, or" inserted
237   3ff.: "supernatural effect, or" inserted
238   2ff.: reference inserted
239   3ff.: "the supernatural, and" inserted
240   3ff.: "something supernatural, and" inserted
241   1: "IN THE MORE GENERAL SENSE"; 2ff.: "IN THE BROADER SENSE"
242   2ff.: reference inserted
243   1f.: different text. "Since the universal nature of the most perfect world is the greatest among the natures of the possible worlds (§466, 437), it will be the most fecund (§166, 430). Therefore as many and as great natural beings as there can be in any possible world, there will be that many and that great natural beings in the most perfect (§469)."
244   2ff.: "in the world" inserted
245   1: *quae*; 2ff.: *quas*
246   3ff.: "the supernatural, or" inserted
247   2ff.: §445 inserted
248   1: *eventum reliquis in mundo optimo compossibilem admodum bonum*; 2–6: *eventum reliquis in mundo optimo compossibilem optimis optimum*; 7: *eventum reliquis in mundo optimo optimis compossibilem optimum*
249   3ff.: "the supernatural, or more correctly," inserted
250   3ff.: "of the best things" inserted
251   3ff.: "supernaturally and" inserted
252   3ff.: "miracles" inserted

253	3ff.: sentence inserted
254	3ff.: "of supernatural events, and" inserted
255	3ff.: "and ... nature" inserted
256	6f.: §459
257	2ff.: "even" inserted
258	1f.: *sensu*; 3ff.: *significatu*
259	1f.: *sensu*; 3ff.: *significatu*
260	1: §473
261	2ff.: "prodigies, and" inserted
262	1: "respective"; 2ff.: "some"

Part III: Psychology

1	1: "C[hapter] I,"
2	1: "C[hapter] II,"
3	2ff.: capitals added
4	1: "The complex of representations in the soul which are simultaneous at any instant is a TOTAL PERCEPTION,"; 2ff.: "The whole ... PERCEPTION"
5	1: different text. "The representations in my soul are either smaller or greater (§214). The former are called WEAKER, and the latter, STRONGER. The weaker ones that emerge change the state of the soul less, and stronger ones, more (§208, 214)."
6	2: this and the previous sentence set in italics
7	1f.: "extension"; 3ff.: "abundance ... vastness"
8	3ff.: "nobility ... majesty" enclosed in parentheses
9	1: "coexisting with partial representations, or"; 2ff.: "that ... are"
10	1: "or rules over the soul" 2ff.: "or" deleted, and "it rules over the soul" placed in parentheses
11	1: §214
12	2ff.: rest of paragraph inserted
13	2ff.: "(the intellect in the broad sense, cf. §402)" inserted
14	1: "The FACULTY of knowing something obscurely and confusedly, or indistinctly, is the INFERIOR COGNITIVE FACULTY"; 2ff.: "Therefore, all else being equal ... FACULTY"
15	1: §821
16	1f.: *vel*; 3ff.: *aut*
17	1f.: *vel*; 3ff.: *aut*
18	2: paragraph set in italics
19	1: "sensation"; 2ff.: "perception"
20	2ff.: rest of paragraph inserted (except as indicated below)
21	3ff.: sentence inserted
22	3ff.: sentence inserted
23	1–5: *Tam intensive quam extensive*; 6: *Tam intensive quam intensive*; 7: *Tam extensive quam intensive*
24	1: "[the science] of sensitive meditation or eloquence that either aims at a lesser perfection, RHETORIC, or a greater, THE UNIVERSAL POETIC ARTS"; 2–3 "(the logic of the inferior faculty of cognition)"; 4ff.: "(the logic ... reason)."
25	2ff.: "(apparitions)" inserted
26	1: "in the more strict sense"; 2ff.: "more strictly considered"

27   2ff.: this and the previous sentence inserted
28   2ff.: "from the point of sensation" inserted
29   2ff.: "to the point of sensation" inserted
30   2: paragraph in italics
31   1f.: "most obscurely"; 3ff.: "with … certitude"
32   1: §338; 2: §538; 3ff.: §531, 538
33   2ff.: §539
34   3ff.: sentence inserted
35   2ff.: sentence inserted
36   2ff.: "of the whole world" inserted
37   2ff.: reference inserted
38   2ff.: "i.e. the PREJUDICE OF THOMAS" inserted
39   2ff.: "*(i.e. the sophism: after this, therefore because of this)*" inserted
40   2ff.: reference inserted
41   1: §542
42   2ff.: this and the previous sentence inserted
43   3ff.: period inserted
44   1f.: "Hence EPILEPSY (the epileptic sickness, the falling sickness, the Herculean sickness), a convulsive sickness notably impeding external sensations through a paroxysm, is not ecstasy."
45   1: §473
46   3ff.: "and … 500)" inserted
47   1f.: "a minor degree of epilepsy (§552, 247)"
48   2ff.: "generally" inserted
49   2ff.: "generally" inserted
50   1: *lypothymia, lypopsychia*; 2ff.: *lipothymia, lipopsychia*
51   2ff.: section heading inserted
52   1: *phantasian*; 2–5: set in capitals; 6f.: *PHANTASIAM*
53   1f.: first part of the sentence is different. "The parts of the brain whose motion coexists as much with sensation as with imagination"
54   6f.: §539
55   AA: §357
56   1: §557
57   1: §529
58   1f.: *priorum*; 3ff.: *illorum*
59   1f.: *posteriora*; 3ff.: *horum*
60   2ff.: this and the previous sentence inserted
61   2: paragraph in italics
62   1f.: "most clearly"; 3ff.: "most strongly"
63   3ff.: "truly" inserted
64   3ff.: "certainly" inserted
65   1f.: "more obscurely"; 3ff.: "more weakly"
66   1: *obscurius*; 2ff.: *obscurior*
67   1: *clarius*; 2ff.: *clarior*
68   2ff.: this and the previous sentence inserted
69   1f.: "that which is not to be imagined"; 3ff.: "that which is not to be partially or entirely imagined"
70   2ff.: sentence inserted
71   1: §538

72	2ff.: section heading inserted
73	1f.: "most obscurely"; 3ff.: "most weakly"
74	1f.: "most clearly"; 3ff.: "most strongly"
75	2ff.: "and ... PROPORTIONS" inserted
76	2: this and the previous sentence italicized
77	1f.: "most obscurely"; 3ff.: "least intensely"
78	1f.: "most clearly"; 3ff.: "most strongly"
79	1f.: "the more clearly"; 3ff.: "the more strongly"
80	2ff.: "and ... DISPROPORTIONS" inserted
81	2ff.: sentence inserted
82	2ff.: "and perspicaciousness" inserted
83	2ff.: sentence inserted
84	2ff.: "and hence perspicaciousness" inserted
85	1: §559
86	1: "Someone noticeably lacking wit is STUPID"; 2ff.: "Someone ... (dullard)"
87	2ff.: sentence inserted
88	2ff.: reference inserted
89	2ff.: section heading inserted
90	6f.: §557
91	6f.: §558
92	1: §432
93	2: paragraph in italics
94	1f.: "most obscurely"; 3ff.: "least intensely"
95	1f.: "most clearly"; 3ff.: "most intensely"
96	1f.: "more clearly"; 3ff.: "more intensely"
97	1f.: "most obscurely"; 3ff.: "least intensely"
98	1f.: "VAST"; 3ff.: "EXTENSIVE"
99	3ff.: "(rich, vast)" inserted
100	1f.: "more obscurely"; 3ff.: "less intensely"
101	1f.: "something very clearly"; 3ff.: "something more intensely"
102	1: "The collection of rules for perfecting memory is called the MNEMONIC ART, the part of aesthetics that prescribes ..."; 2ff.: The sentence is broken in two, and second sentence begins: "The mnemonics of sensitive memory (§579) is ..."
103	2ff.: section heading inserted
104	2ff.: "POETIC" inserted
105	1: §511
106	2: paragraph in italics
107	1f.: "clearest"; 3ff.: "strongest"
108	1f.: "most obscurely"; 3ff.: "least intensely"
109	1f.: "clear"; 3ff.: "strong"
110	1f.: "more clearly"; 3ff.: "more strongly"
111	1: §572
112	6: §549
113	2ff.: "more observable" inserted
114	2ff.: "habitually" inserted
115	1: Section V
116	2: paragraph in italics
117	1f.: "most obscurely"; 3ff.: "least intensely"
118	1f.: "most clearly"; 3ff.: "most strongly"

119   1f.: "more clearly"; 3ff.: "more strongly"
120   1f.: "more obscurely"; 3ff.: "least intensely"
121   2ff.: sentence inserted
122   1: §97
123   1–3, AA: §597
124   1: §597
125   AA: §349
126   2ff.: sentence inserted
127   2ff.: section heading inserted
128   1f.: "most obscurely"; 3ff.: "least intensely"
129   1f.: "most clearly"; 3ff.: "most strongly"
130   1f.: "more clearly"; 3ff.: "more strongly"
131   1f.: "most obscurely"; 3ff.: "least intensely"
132   1: §522
133   2ff.: "(flavour… (§533)" inserted
134   2ff.: "JUDGMENT" inserted
135   2ff.: sentence inserted
136   1: §578
137   2ff.: section heading inserted
138   1: §522
139   2ff.: sentence inserted
140   2: paragraph in italics
141   1f.: "most obscurely"; 3ff.: "least intensely"
142   1f.: "most clearly"; 3ff.: "most strongly"
143   2: paragraph in italics
144   1f.: "more obscurely"; 3ff.: "less intensely"
145   1f.: "clearer"; 3ff.: "stronger"
146   1: "or a prophesy. The mantic arts are the collection of rules for completing the natural faculty of foretelling (§349)"; 2ff.: "(a prophesy)"
147   1: §571
148   2ff.: section heading inserted
149   1: "FACULTY OF USING SIGNS"; 2ff.: "FACULTY OF CHARACTERIZATION"
150   1: "of the faculty of using signs"; 2ff.: "of the faculty of characterization"
151   1: "faculty of using signs"; 2ff.: "faculty of characterization"
152   1: "either I attend more to the sign, and such COGNITION will be called SYMBOLIC, or more to the signified, and such"; 2ff.: "and the perception … the"
153   1: "of the faculty of using signs"; 2ff.: "of the faculty of characterization"
154   1: "faculty of using signs"; 2ff.: "faculty of characterization"
155   1f.: "most obscurely"; 3ff.: "least intensely"
156   1: "faculty of using signs"; 2ff.: "faculty of characterization"
157   2: this and the previous sentence in italics
158   1: different sentence. "The complex of rules for perfecting the faculty of using signs is characterization"; 2ff.: rest of the paragraph inserted
159   1-6: "The collection of these four disciplines"; 7: "The collection of these disciplines"
160   1: "Section VI. The superior cognitive faculty"
161   2ff.: "(the mind)" inserted
162   1: §538–62; 2-3: §538–600; 4ff.: §538, 600
163   1: §512
164   2: this and the previous sentence in italics

165   3ff.: sentence inserted
166   2: paragraph in italics
167   1–4: "conceivable"; 5–7: "inconceivable"
168   1: "perceive"; 2ff.: "distinguish"
169   1: "represents"; 2ff.: "distinguishes"
170   2: this and the previous sentence in italics
171   2ff.: sentence inserted
172   4ff.: "to the extent that it is required for speaking" inserted
173   1f.: "PSYCHOLOGICALLY"; 3ff.: "NATURALLY"
174   1f.: "PSYCHOLOGICALLY"; 3ff.: "NATURALLY"
175   1: Section VII
176   1: "designation"; 2ff.: "characterization"
177   1: "designation"; 2ff.: "characterization"
178   1: "distinctly"; 2ff.: "clearly"
179   3ff.: "C," inserted
180   1: "distinctly"; 2ff.: "clearly"
181   1: "distinctly"; 2ff.: "clearly"
182   3ff.: "and connected" inserted
183   1f.: "BEYOND that REASON"; 3ff.: "OUTSIDE … REASON"
184   3ff.: parenthetical comment inserted
185   1f.: "beyond the reason"; 3ff.: "outside the sphere of reason"
186   1: §248; 2ff.: §631, 640
187   2: this and the previous sentence in italics
188   2ff.: references inserted
189   2ff.: reference inserted
190   3ff.: "and the wit … NUMB" inserted
191   1: "and"; 2ff.: replaced with a comma
192   3ff.: "EMPIRICAL" inserted
193   1f.: "NUMBED" (capitals)
194   1f.: "i.e. changed from lively to slow" inserted and reference placed after "excited";
          3ff.: reference placed after "numbed"
195   1: "Section VIII. The appetitive faculty"; 2ff.: "Section XIIII. Indifference"
196   1f.: *RELATIVE*; 3ff.: *RESPECTIVE*
197   1: "know"; 2ff.: "apperceive"
198   1: "know"; 2ff.: "am most conscious of it"
199   2ff.: "clearly" inserted
200   2ff.: "to the extent that it is observed" inserted
201   1f.: *relative*; 3ff.: *respective*
202   1: "or"
203   2ff.: "clearly" inserted
204   1f.: *RELATIVELY*; 3ff.: *RESPECTIVELY*
205   2ff.: new section heading
206   2ff.: "(intellectual)" inserted
207   1: §522
208   1: *minus placentibus*; 2ff.: *non placentibus*
209   1: *minus displicentibus*; 2ff.: *non displicentibus*
210   1: *minus placentia*; 2ff.: *non placentia*
211   1: *minus displicentia*; 2ff.: *non displicentia*
212   2ff.: "cf. §661" inserted

213 1: "obscurest"; 2ff.: "smallest"
214 2ff.: "i.e. the least true, clear, and specific (§531, 620)" inserted
215 1: "clearer"; 2ff.: "greater"
216 2ff.: "i.e. ... (§531)" inserted
217 3ff.: this and the previous sentence inserted
218 1: "most clear"; 2ff.: "clearer"
219 2ff.: "(§542) ... (§531)" inserted
220 2ff.: "i.e. ... (§531)" inserted
221 2ff.: "(cf. §656)" inserted
222 1–3, AA: §658
223 2ff.: "brief, fluctuating" set in parentheses
224 2ff.: section heading inserted
225 2ff.: "(will ... §690)" inserted
226 1: "any endeavour of mine"; 2ff.: "any power of mine"
227 1: "endeavour"; 2ff.: "effort"
228 1: "endeavour"; 2ff.: "effort"
229 1: "endeavour"; 2ff.: "effort"
230 1: "endeavour"; 2ff.: "effort"
231 AA: §620
232 1f.: "(§665), desire and aversion"; 3ff.: "these"
233 1: §666
234 1: "is called ALIVE, insofar as it is not dead and hence symbolic cognition, which is dead as such (§652); only intuitive [cognition] is alive (§652)"; 2ff.: "is MOVING ... hollow)."
235 1: "dead"; 2ff.: "inert"
236 1: "alive"; 2ff.: "moving"
237 2ff.: sentence inserted
238 1: "the pleasure stemming from a specific object were wholly the same as the disgust from the same"; 2ff.: "the knowledge moving someone ... object"
239 1: "Because I expect that which will exist through any endeavour of mine"; in 2, replaced with: "Everything being equal (§664, 665)"
240 3ff.: "and indeed ... (§665)" inserted
241 2ff.: "at the same time" inserted
242 2ff.: "(§331)" inserted
243 2ff.: rest of the paragraph inserted
244 AA: §220
245 AA: §220
246 1, 2, 3, 4: "and"; 5ff.: "or"
247 2: "equal in foresight and expectation" inserted; in 3ff, changed to: "following foresight and expectation"
248 1f.: "along with effective desire, there would be also be effective aversion of the same thing; along with complete aversion there would also be complete desire of the same thing (§671), and at the same time, ineffective desire along with effective aversion, ineffective aversion along with effective desire (§81, 663); incomplete desire while the aversion of the same the would be complete, and incomplete aversion"; 3ff.: "there would be a complete aversion ... aversion"
249 1f.: sentence begins with "Therefore, if I would have desired or averted efficiently in a state of equilibrium, at the same time I would have desired or averted the same thing inefficiently; if in the same state"; 3ff.: "Therefore ... equilibrium"

250 1: "nor effectively"; 2: "with equal foresight and expectation, nor effectively"; 3ff.: "following foresight and anticipation"

251 1f.: *Quod si*; 3ff.: *Quodsi*

252 1f.: "if I desire or avert effectively"

253 1f.: "with the equal foresight and expectation"; 3ff.: "following the foresight and anticipation"

254 3ff.: "or must be impeded" inserted

255 2ff.: "that is about to exist or must be impeded by my determined effort" inserted

256 1f.: "in an equal foresight and expectation of an object and its opposite"

257 3ff.: sentence inserted

258 1: "either"; 2ff.: "(1)"

259 1: "or"; 2ff.: "(2)"

260 AA: ENTIRELY

261 1f.: "effective; while the non-efficacious are ineffective, the efficacious will either be complete, or incomplete; (3) {1: "or again"} complete; while the non-efficacious are incomplete, the efficacious will either be effective, or not (§672)"; 3ff.: "(2) ... (§671)."

262 2: "in an equal foresight and anticipation"; 3ff.: "remaining following the foresight and anticipation"

263 1f.: "in the second or third sense"; 3ff.: "to that degree that we have considered a means"

264 1f.: different sentence: "Therefore in the state of pure pleasure or mere disgust, or in the state of preponderance, I only desire or avert efficiently in the second or third sense (§661, 674)."

265 1: Section VIIII

266 2ff.: sentence inserted

267 2ff.: "(sympathy, love)" inserted

268 2ff.: "(natural antipathy, natural hate)" inserted

269 3ff.: "The (stronger)" inserted

270 2ff.: "and to this ... (§622)" inserted

271 1: §676

272 1–3, AA: §529; 5ff.: §19

273 1: §652

274 2ff.: "all else being equal" inserted

275 1: GAUDIUM (*laetitia*); 2ff.: GAUDIUM

276 2ff.: sentence inserted

277 2ff.: reference inserted

278 1–5: *IRRISIO*; 6: *PERISIO*; 7: *DERISIO*

279 1: "(mournfulness)"

280 2ff.: "MOURNING ... is" inserted

281 1: *MOESTITIA*; 2ff.: *MAESTITIA*

282 1: sentence ends

283 2ff.: "and" inserted

284 1: "mourning" starts new sentence

285 1–3: *sunt* ; deleted in 4ff as superfluous in Latin

286 1: SECTION X

287 2ff.: "(mind)" inserted

288 1: §607

289 1–3, 5ff, AA: §641

290   1: *non nisi*; 2–7 *non, nisi*; AA.: *nonnisi*
291   2ff.: "(a conflict … reason)" inserted
292   2ff.: "intellectual" inserted
293   2ff.: reference inserted; 5ff.: §616
294   1–3: *nec*; 4ff.: *non*
295   2: "with still equal foresight and expectation of an object and its opposite" inserted;
       3ff.: "that still … opposite"
296   2ff.: "then" inserted
297   1: "The perceptions of an IMPELLING CAUSE"; 2ff.: "The IMPELLING CAUSES"
298   2ff.: reference inserted
299   1f.: "and sometimes even"; 3ff.: "and"
300   3ff.: "although … volition" inserted
301   2ff.: "(a …sense)" inserted
302   1f.: "and hence they are efficacious in the third, although not always the second,
       sense of §675"; 3ff.: "and … §675"
303   2ff.: "not just unqualifiedly, but also qualifiedly (§469)?" inserted
304   1–3, AA: *iudicat*; 4ff.: *indicat*
305   2ff.: "(a joyful person)" inserted
306   2ff.: "(considerate)" inserted
307   2ff.: "or MAXIMS" inserted
308   1f.: "not strenuous'"; 3ff.: "WEAK (exceedingly impotent)"
309   1: "SECTION XI. FREEDOM"; 2ff.: " SECTION XVIIII. SPONTANEITY"
310   2: paragraph in italics
311   2: reference inserted
312   1: "intrinsic and"
313   2ff.: section heading inserted
314   1: different paragraph. "The ACTIONS for which the powers of an agent are sufficient
       are POSITED in its COMMAND. The opposite of the actions that are posited within
       the command of some agent is either posited within the command of the same agent,
       or not (§9). The former are FREELY EXECUTED (physically indifferent in terms of
       the exercise of the act), and the latter are MERELY NATURAL."
315   2: *supra*; 3ff.: *extra*
316   2–4, 7: PHYSICE; 6: PHYSICA
317   1: different sentence. "Merely natural actions are such that once the specific
       nature of a specific being has been posited, their opposite becomes impossible
       through the positing of this nature (§708, 52), and their opposite is also
       physically impossible (§470); hence merely natural actions can be said to be
       naturally necessary."
318   1: §101
319   3ff.: "which would then be ABSOLUTE (essential)" inserted
320   1: "through that nature"; 2ff.: "for it … qualifiedly"
321   1: §709
322   3ff.: "and this … (natural)" inserted
323   2ff.: references inserted
324   2ff.: reference inserted
325   1: "the physical indifference of the exercise, along with freedom"; 2ff.: "freedom"
326   2ff.: "thus" inserted
327   1: "endeavour"; 2ff.: "effort"
328   1: *nec*; 2ff.: *non*

329   1: "without preference and against preference"; 2ff.: "(without preference, against preference)"
330   1f.: *sensu*; 3ff.: *significatu*
331   2ff.: reference inserted
332   1f.: "VIOLENCE"; 3ff.: "CONSTRAINT"
333   1f.: "VIOLENCE or"
334   1f.: "violence"; 3ff.: "constraint"
335   2: paragraph in italics
336   2ff.: section heading inserted
337   1: "free choice or FREEDOM"; 2ff.: "FREEDOM (free choice)"
338   2ff.: "cf. §707, 708, 710 (moral freedom in the unqualified sense)" inserted
339   2ff.: reference inserted
340   1: (§719)
341   1: "[it is] mixed"; 2ff.: "my freedom is mixed"
342   2ff.: reference inserted
343   1: (§719)
344   2ff.: reference inserted
345   1: different sentence. "That which more closely depends on freedom is MORAL."
346   1: rest of paragraph is different. "Therefore MORAL NECESSITY (certitude) will be that which depends more closely on freedom, and that which produces it will be MORAL NECESSITATION or OBLIGATION. Obligation to a reluctant action will be MORAL COERCION. Therefore, that which is MORALLY NECESSARY is (1) that whose opposite is impossible in a free substance as such; (2) that whose opposite is impossible, i.e. IMPERMISSIBLE, through freedom in conformity with moral laws."
347   2: different sentence. "Hence the MORALLY POSSIBLE is (1) what is possible through freedom in kind, or in free substance as such; it is (2) what is possible through the freedom determined in conformity with moral laws, or the PERMISSIBLE."
348   2: "The MORALLY IMPOSSIBLE is (1) what is impossible through freedom in kind, or in a free substance as such"; 3ff.: "The MORALLY ... substance"
349   1: §733
350   2ff.: reference inserted
351   2: paragraph italicized
352   1: §724
353   1: "Of things that are indifferent in terms of the exercise of the act"; 2ff.: "*From ... execution*"
354   1: §414
355   1: §723
356   1f.: "violence"; 3ff.: "constraint"
357   1f.: "violence"; 3ff.: "power"
358   3ff.: capitals
359   1: "noble and LIBERAL"; 2ff.: "LIBERAL (noble)"
360   1: "or mediately" ; 2ff.: "(mediately)"
361   1: "immediately facing <*contra*> and DIRECTLY UNDER it"; 2ff.: "however ... it"
362   2ff.: capitals
363   1: *nihilo tamen minus*; 2ff.: *tamen*
364   2ff.: "whose ... ADDICTION" inserted
365   1: Section XII
366   1–3, AA: §210

367   1: capitals
368   2ff.: reference inserted
369   3ff.: §79 inserted
370   1f.: "alters"; 3ff.: "endures"
371   3ff.: reference inserted
372   2ff.: "human" inserted
373   1: §737
374   1: "Therefore it acts (§210). Therefore it is the power for representing its own body (§210)." 2ff.: sentences combined into one.
375   1: §254
376   1: *cur haec, non alia, anima humana obscure, clare, distincte repraesentet*; 2ff.: *cur anima humana obscure, clare, distincte repraesentet haec, non alia*
377   1: §512
378   1: different paragraph. "The human soul is a substance (§741, 198). Therefore it can exist even if it is not the determination of another (§191). Hence, it can exist even if it is not part of an actual man (§740). The SOUL that exists even if it is not part of an actual animal is SEPARATE. Therefore the existence of the separate human soul does not involve (§15) [*sic*]." There is no obvious direct object in the final sentence; perhaps we can supply "an animal." Also, uncharacteristically, Baumgarten places a period before the reference.
379   4ff.: "[although] … this," inserted
380   2–3: "only if these same"; 4ff.: "(1) this substance … they"
381   1f.: paragraph begins differently (text between curly braces added in 2). "The human soul is a monad (§744, 234) and hence a simple being (§230). Therefore it does not have parts outside of parts (§224). Now, if it were a whole of many powers {strictly speaking}, some of its parts would be substances posited mutually outside of one another (§198). Hence the human soul does not have many powers {strictly speaking}; {strictly and unqualifiedly}, there is only one power of the human soul (§77, 74)." Rest of paragraph is the same in 1–7, with the exceptions noted below.
382   1: "accurately"; 2ff.: "strictly"
383   6–7: comma instead of hyphen
384   3ff.: "much … sense (§521–720)" inserted
385   AA: §742
386   1: *potest oriri (§229, 133), sed non nisi ex nihilo*; 2ff : *non potest oriri, nisi ex nihilo*
387   1: *potest interire (§229, 133), sed non nisi ex nihilo*; 2ff : *non potest interire, nisi ex nihilo*
388   1f.: "a coexisting human soul has a seat in its body (§409)"; 3ff.: "then … (§409)."
389   1: §16
390   6f.: §705
391   1: §741
392   1f.: §303
393   1: §737
394   6f.: §210
395   1f.: (text inside curly braces deleted in 2): "{a faculty that is either real or ideal (§217)}, to be actualized by its unique power (§744). Therefore the locomotive faculty of the human soul is actualized through its power of representing the universe according to the position of the body (§741)"; 3ff.: "which, just … body (§741, 417)"
396   1: §367

397   1: §396
398   1: §834
399   2ff.: "i.e." inserted
400   1: §757
401   1: (§4, 744, 216)
402   1: §200
403   1: "or" inserted
404   2ff.: "personality (§641, 754)" inserted
405   1: *eiusmodi*; 2ff.: *eius modi*
406   1: this and the previous sentence form one sentence
407   2ff.: "that loses … freedom" inserted
408   3ff.: "that is composed … another" inserted
409   2ff.: reference inserted
410   1: "natural with respect"; 2ff.: "natural"
411   3ff.: "insofar … (§469)" inserted
412   3ff.: rest of paragraph inserted
413   1f (text in curly brackets deleted in 2): "The preternatural {with respect} to the human soul, those occurrences in the human soul that"; 3ff.: "The preternatural … that"
414   1: "philosophical hypotheses invented" 2ff.: "doctrines … well-suited"
415   1f.: "assistance"; 3ff.: "occasional causes"
416   1–5: *systematis*; 6f.: *systematibus*. *Systematibus* seems preferable.
417   2ff.: sentence inserted
418   1f.: "assistance"; 3ff.: "occasional causes"
419   1f.: "assistance"; 3ff.: "occasional causes"
420   1f.: "assistance"; 3ff.: "infinite power alone"
421   1: *sit*; 2ff.: *esset*
422   1: *nequit*; 2ff.: *non posset*
423   1f.: "assistance"; 3ff.: "occasional causes"
424   1f.: "assistance"; 3ff.: "occasional causes"
425   1: "The HARMONIC ALTERATIONS of the parts of the world posited in commerce are those for which a sufficient ground of the alterations occuring in one part of the commerece can be known according to the power of the other part of the commerce."
426   1: (§353, 757)
427   2ff.: "whenever … body" inserted
428   2ff.: §448 inserted
429   1: §764
430   1: "a composite"; 2ff.: "its"
431   1: §215
432   1f.: "assistance"; 3ff.: "occasional causes"
433   1: different title. "The origination and immortality of the human soul"
434   1: "It is the wont of the body, of the kind human beings have on this earth, to originate and die. Provided that a body of this sort originates, the soul that will be in the closest commerce with the body either existed beforehand, or it originates at the same time that the body is born, or it originates directly after the body has originated (§298)"; 2ff.: "When … afterward."
435   1: "Those who posit that the human soul originates when its body originates, or not until after it has originated"; 2ff.: "Those … afterward"

436   1: "only then"; 2: " first"
437   1: "originates"; 2ff.: "is actualized"
438   2ff.: "in the world by … apart" inserted
439   2ff.: sentence inserted
440   1: *fuisse*; 2ff.: *exstitisse*
441   1: §773
442   2ff.: section heading inserted
443   1: different text. "DEATH IN GENERAL is the cessation of all actions and sufferings that depend on the specific nature of some being. Therefore the DEATH OF THE HUMAN BODY will be the cessation of all its alterations that depend on its nature, as far as it exerts power <*qua pollet*> as a human body. Now, its vital motions are alterations that depend on its specific nature, as far as it exerts power. Hence the total cessation of vital motions is the death of the human body. Therefore the death defined in §556 is the death of the human body. When all the vital motions of a body cease, all the chosen motions of the body likewise cease (§733). And since they also depend on the specific nature of the body (§469), the death of the body is the cessation of all its vital and chosen motions. LIFE IN GENERAL is the state of a being whereby some actions or sufferings that depend on its specific nature exist in that being. Therefore, as long as there is even one vital or chosen motion in the human body, it is alive."
444   2ff.: §448 inserted
445   2ff.: "(a … animal)" inserted
446   2ff.: §777 inserted
447   1: "The death of the body that we experience there to be for men on this earth, if it is conceived as only respective, is called ANIMAL TRANSFORMATION."
448   1: different paragraph. "The DEATH OF THE HUMAN SOUL is the cessation of all its actions and sufferings that depend on its specific nature, hence the cessation of its spiritual actions and sufferings (§754). The human soul can perish by annihilation (§745). Therefore its spiritual actions and sufferings can also cease. Therefore the death of the human soul, considered in itself, is possible (§228, 15). The LIFE OF THE HUMAN SOUL is its state in which some actions and sufferings that depend on its specific nature exist in that soul."
449   3ff.: "insofar as it is a human soul" inserted
450   3ff.: "which … distinct (§741)" inserted
451   1: different text. "The IMMORTALITY OF THE HUMAN SOUL is called (1) the impossibility of perishing together with its body through corruption. In this sense, the soul is immortal because it is indestructible (§746). (2) Its duration that is to be continued without end, and hence after the death of the body. In this sense the human soul, which is not to be annihilated (§780), is immortal (§746, 299). (3) The personality that is to be preserved after the death of its body. This is the meaning most accepted by philosophers. (4) The life after the death of the human body."
452   3ff.: references inserted
453   2: (§228, 354)
454   2ff.: section heading inserted
455   1: different paragraph. "The faculty of conceiving its own past states and the present one, and itself in these, is sufficiently determined through the spirituality of the human soul and the faculty of representing the universe (§754, 753). But this is personality (§641, 579). Therefore personality is natural for an actual human soul (§759), and pertains to its specific nature (§758). Also natural is a possibility of a

mode, namely that of a distinct recognition (§579). And therefore, an attribute of
the human soul (§63). Now, the attributes of things are absolutely and internally
inalterable. Hence personality in a human soul is inalterable. Therefore, the human
soul, enduring even after the death of its body, preserves its personality, and is
immortal in the most accepted sense of immortality (§781). The human soul
that survives its body but with its personality destroyed is a chimera (§590)." The
reference to §781 pertains only to the text of the first edition. The reference to §63
seems mistaken; §64 is more logical.

456 1: different paragraph. "The human who endures after the death of its body
preserves its own life (§199, 198). Therefore it acts (§179, 210). Among these
actions there are some for which its own powers <*vires*> are sufficient such that it
determines itself through freedom (§756, 730), indeed, for which it is posited within
its command to determine itself through freedom (§708). Therefore, some of the
actions of the human soul enduring after the death of its body are free (§719). Free
actions are those that depend on the specific nature of a human soul (§758, 754).
Therefore, enduring after the death of its body, the human soul lives (§780), and is
also immortal in the fourth sense of §782." The last reference, §782, is somewhat
puzzling; Baumgarten must have meant §781. This reference pertains only to the
text of the first edition.

457 1: "The state of the human soul after death (of the body and of the human being,
such as we experience on this earth) can be considered (1) as the state of the separate
soul when the absolute death of the human being is maintained (§778)"; 2ff.: "can
… maintained (§778)."

458 1–4: *missae*; 5, 6, 7: *missa*
459 3ff.: "improbably" inserted
460 2ff.: this and the previous two sentences inserted.
461 2ff.: reference inserted
462 1: §783
463 1: §457
464 1: (§742, 784)
465 2ff.: rest of paragraph inserted
466 2: (§784, 783)
467 1: §755
468 2ff.: "and … same" inserted
469 1f.: different text. "Those things that are physically GOOD for the spirit, in the broad
sense, either (1) depend more closely on its freedom, and are MORALLY GOOD
(§723). Perfection based on the morally good is BLESSEDNESS. Or (2) they do not
depend more closely on its freedom, and they are PHYSICALLY GOOD, TAKEN
STRICTLY (§147). Perfection based on the physically good, strictly considered, is
PROSPERITY. The collection of prosperity and blessedness is HAPPINESS."
470 1f.: different text. "Those things that are physically EVIL for the spirit, in the broad
sense, either depend more closely on its freedom, and are MORALLY EVIL (the
evils of guilt, sins) (§723), and imperfection based on the morally evil is MORAL
CORRUPTION; or, they do not depend more closely on its freedom, and they
are PHYSICALLY EVIL, TAKEN STRICTLY (§147). Imperfection based on the
physically evil, strictly considered, is MISERY. The collection of moral corruption
and misery is UNHAPPINESS."
471 1: §280
472 2ff.: "as … (§264)" inserted

473   1: §87
474   1: §87
475   1: no capitals
476   3ff.: rest of paragraph inserted
477   1: Section IIII
478   1f.: "The souls different from the soul of the human being"
479   1: §742
480   1: §747
481   1: different text. "The soul of brutes are the coexisting characters (§793) that have been described (§519–623, 676–88). Therefore they are compossible (§57). Therefore the soul of a brute is possible (§8). The monads in these are the greatest in the world, after spirits (§793, 440). Therefore the souls of brutes compossible with the spirits of the best world in the same are in the same (§436)."
482   2: "known bodies"; 3ff.: "bodies appearing"
483   1–4: *sint*; 6,7: *sit*
484   1–4: *sunt*; 6,7: *sint*
485   6,7: §939
486   3ff.: Section heading inserted
487   3ff.: "finite" inserted
488   2ff.: §796 inserted
489   3ff.: rest of paragraph inserted
490   1–3: *potest*; 4ff.: *possit*
491   2ff.: "physically" inserted
492   1: "and liberty, which are to be extended by free actions"; 2ff.: "by increasing … forgetfulness"
493   3ff.: rest of paragraph inserted

Part IIII: Natural Theology

1   1: "(C[hapter] I),"
2   1: "(C[hapter] II)"
3   3–6: *necessario*; 7: *necessaria*
4   3ff.: sentence inserted
5   1f.: different sentence. "Whatever is in the most perfect being can be called its perfection."
6   2ff.: rest of paragraph inserted
7   2ff.: §190 inserted
8   3ff.: rest of paragraph inserted
9   1f.: "no metaphysical evil, no physical evil, whether broadly (§146) or strictly considered, no moral evil"; 3ff.: "nor … sense"
10   3ff.: rest of paragraph inserted
11   1f.: "The perfections of God, considered in themselves, are either representable in him without any being thought outside of God, and are ABSOLUTE, or they cannot be represented without some being thought outside of God, and they are RESPECTIVE"; 3ff.: "The … perfections (§37)."
12   1: *aut*; 2ff.: *vel*
13   1: *aut*; 2ff.: *vel*

14 1: different text "Any given perfection of God is as great as can be in any being (§712). Now, it is a ground (§23). Therefore it is a ground that is as great as can be in any being. Now, the greatest ground in a being is essence (§40, 166). Therefore, any given perfection of God is his essence."

15 3ff.: "since ... (§171)" inserted

16 3ff.: "Although ... (§876)" inserted

17 1: "one can"; 2ff.: "it is preferable to"

18 3ff.: sentence inserted

19 3ff.: rest of paragraph inserted

20 3, AA: §302

21 3ff.: "(1)" inserted

22 3ff.: "(2) ... (§74)" inserted

23 1f.: "supreme rationality (§19)"; 3ff.: "supreme nexus (§817)" inserted

24 3: §176 inserted; 4ff.: §179

25 1: "more broadly"; 2ff.: "in general"

26 2ff.: sentence inserted

27 3ff.: rest of paragraph inserted; 6f.: §106

28 3–6: *salva*; 7: *salvo*

29 1: different text. "Thus, the same thing is clear: Every internal perfection of God is his essence (§116). Every essence is absolutely necessary (§806). Therefore every internal perfection of God is absolutely necessary. All of these taken together, beyond the one that is taken as his essence, constitute the existence of God (§55). Therefore the existence of God is absolutely necessary, and God is a necessary being (§109)."

30 1f.: "and by way of negation"; 3ff.: "by way of negation"

31 1f.: sentence ends with "or eminence, analogy, and excellence," which is deleted in 3ff; 2ff.: "EMINENTLY ... reign" inserted

32 1: §816

33 1: "they are the counterpart of attributes"; 2ff.: "they are attributes"

34 2ff.: rest of paragraph inserted

35 4ff.: "truly" inserted

36 1: §107

37 2ff.: §121 inserted

38 AA: §808

39 3ff.: §822 inserted

40 2ff.: "in the strict sense" inserted

41 1: §196

42 1: "Substance is capable of something if its power suffices for that which is to be actualized"

43 2ff.: "absolutely" inserted

44 2ff.: reference inserted

45 1: "And finally, that which is IMPOSSIBLE FOR SOMETHING is called"; 2ff.: "That ... is"

46 2ff.: reference inserted

47 1: §828

48 6f.: §306

49 3ff.: rest of paragraph inserted

50 1: §82

51 1: §385

52   3–5: sentence was printed twice
53   2ff.: rest of paragraph inserted
54   6f.: §250
55   1f.: different paragraph, text in curly brackets added in 2. "Many gods are impossible. For, as long as each ought to be a substance (§830), they would exist mutually outside of one another (§282, 811), and they would either be totally the same, or only partially (§267, 265). If they were posited to be totally the same, they would be impossible (§269). If they were posited to be partially different, something would be in one that would not be another (§38). This would either be a reality or a negation (§36). If it were a reality, that which lacked it would not be God (§807). If it were a negation, that which it belonged to would not be God (§808). {If one reality were posited in one god, but another of equal value in another god, (1) such gods would be posited outside of one another and yet they would be totally equal, which contradicts §272; (2) in neither would there be the totality of realities, and hence neither would be God (§807).} Therefore, since there is a God and because there are not more than one, God is unique (§77). {POYTHEISM is the doctrine that holds there to be many gods, and is in error}."
56   1: "God did not originate (§837); therefore he follows nothing (§124). He cannot perish (§837); therefore nothing follows him (§124). Hence he is called the first and last being, the A and Ω, by reduction (§826, 300)"
57   1: "In that sense"; 2ff.: "Thus"
58   1: "its eternity differs from eternity in many distinctions"; 2ff.: "its ... God"
59   1: "(1) Such an eternal being does not originate, but on the other hand it could have originated (§227, 837). (2) Such an eternal being does not perish, but on the other hand it can nevertheless perish at any given moment (§227, 837)."
60   1: "(3)"
61   1: §219
62   1: "(4)"
63   1: "(5)"
64   3ff.: "because ... be (§259)" inserted
65   1: §381
66   1f.: "infinite beings"; 3ff.: "really infinite"
67   1: §843
68   2ff.: §310 inserted
69   3ff.: rest of paragraph inserted
70   2ff.: sentence inserted
71   1: §736
72   1: "and in that world, it is spirits (§440), and among its spirits it is those"; 2ff.: "in the world ... spirits"
73   1f.: "not only physical but also"; 3ff.: "any and especially"
74   2ff.: "(naturing, cf. §466) nature" inserted
75   1: "every single one of which is his essence (§816)"; 2ff.: "through ... suffering"
76   1: "Hence the things pertaining to the nature of God are actualized by his essence (§470)"; 2ff.: "Therefore .... (§833)"
77   2ff.: rest of paragraph inserted
78   2ff.: §859 inserted
79   3ff.: rest of paragraph inserted
80   2ff.: "and ... (§816)" inserted
81   1: no capitals

82   2ff.: rest of paragraph inserted
83   2: "Therefore" starts a new sentence; 3ff.: "although"
84   4ff.: "and to all finite beings" inserted
85   3ff.: §806 inserted
86   1: §36
87   1: §160
88   1f.: "Cognition of God"; 3ff.: "Cognition concerning God"
89   1f.: ARCHETYPE; 3ff.: "EXEMPLARY (ἀρχέτυπος)"
90   1: §385
91   3ff.: rest of paragraph inserted
92   1: different sentence. "However, he never pays greater attention to signs than to the signified, or vice versa (§870)."
93   1: different paragraph. "God knows every truth most distinctly (§864), in every nexus (§872). Therefore his cognition is certain. He knows all certain principles, everything founded by them, and every nexus of principles and that which is founded by them (§864, 872); therefore, his cognition is supreme knowledge <scientia>. God knows most distinctly what is false (§87), and all moral certitudes, probabilities, doubts, improbabilities, opinions, and errors of the souls (§869)."
94   3ff.: "superficial ... speculative (§669, 671)" inserted
95   6f.: "probabilities, doubts, improbabilities" deleted
96   3ff.: "as well ... speculations" inserted
97   1: §873
98   1: "(1)"
99   1: "of all souls"; 2ff.: "of all things"
100 1: "(2)"
101 1: ordinals instead of α, β, γ
102 2ff.: sentence inserted
103 1: §323
104 1: "next"
105 1: §885
106 1: §852
107 1: paragraph begins with "Someone who errs confuses the false with the true. God can confuse nothing with something different (§870, 843). Therefore God cannot err."
108 2ff.: "and ... confusion" inserted
109 2: "The smallest ... is" italics
110 1: paragraph begins with "SUBJECTIVE CERTITUDE is the clear cognition of the truth in something. Hence"
111 2: "The smallest ... be" italics
112 6f.: §979
113 1: "WISDOM is the knowledge of the final nexus"; 2ff.: "WISDOM ... means (§872)"
114 3ff.: "and most ardently" inserted
115 1: *medium*; 2ff.: *remedium*
116 6f.: §582
117 1: "known"; 2ff.: "established"
118 2ff.: §873 inserted
119 2ff.: "and ... possess (§882)" inserted
120 3ff.: "and the ... souls (§873)" inserted
121 2ff.: reference inserted

122   3ff.: §873 inserted
123   1f.: "Archetypal"; 3ff.: "Exemplary"
124   2ff.: "TO THE INTELLECT" inserted
125   2ff.: "distinctly" inserted
126   2ff.: "distinctly" inserted
127   2ff.: sentence inserted
128   5ff.: 700
129   1: §833
130   2ff.: "because ... (§844)" inserted
131   2ff.: sentence inserted
132   1: "infinite love"; 2ff.: "love"
133   1–5: *universalia*; 6f.: *universalis*
134   2ff.: "(3)" inserted
135   1–5: "(§874–76)"; 6: "(§874 876)" [sic]; 7: "(§874, 876)"; 3ff.: rest of paragraph inserted
136   2: sentence in italics
137   1: no italics
138   6f.: §631
139   1f.: *alteri benefaciendum*; 3ff.: *faciendum alteri bene*
140   2: rest of paragraph in italics
141   1: "volition"; 2ff.: "propensity ... will"
142   1f.: "conferring the smallest good on a being"; 3ff.: "the smallest ... being"
143   3ff.: "and worthier" inserted
144   2ff.: reference inserted
145   1: §161
146   1: §872
147   1f.: "physical"; 3ff.: "contingent"
148   1: "hence he does not wish to confer"; 2ff.: "according ... conferring"
149   1f.: "physical"; 3ff.: "contingent"
150   1f.: "physical"; 3ff.: "contingent"
151   2ff.: "Nemesis" inserted
152   2ff.: sentence inserted
153   1–3, 5ff, AA: *arbitrio* 4, *arbitrario*
154   1f.: "physical"; 3ff.: "contingent"
155   2ff.: "and only the objects of divine love (§899)"
156   2ff.: §909 inserted
157   1f.: "physical"; 3ff.: "contingent"
158   1: §903
159   1–3, AA: (§884–8)
160   1: different text. "Since whatever God can be, in terms of his internal perfections, he actually is (§845), and since whatever is possible for him through essence is that which is also possible for him through a perfect nature (§859), the greatest life must be attributed to God (§776)."
161   1: different text. "Since the greatest life of God indeed cannot be destroyed through annihilation (§837), not only does he have whatever is a reality in the immortality of a finite spirit (§787), but also for the very reason that annihilation in itself is not repugnant to any finite spirit (§780), he alone has absolutely necessary immortality (§110)."
162   1: §806

163   1: §873
164   1: "did not originate"; 2ff.: "would ... beginning"
165   1: §9
166   1: §876
167   AA: §370
168   1: §227
169   1: §833
170   1: §857
171   1: §671
172   1: §193
173   2ff.: italics
174   1–6: *mirabilem ecstasin*; 7: *per mirabilem ecstasin*
175   1: "Those who ... ecstasy (§552)" joined with previous sentence
176   1f.: "physical"; 3ff.: "contingent"
177   2ff.: "them" inserted
178   1f.: "physical"; 3ff.: "contingent"
179   1f.: "or moral evil"; 3ff.: "and ... evil"
180   1f.: "physical"; 3ff.: "contingent"
181   1f.: "physical"; 3ff.: "contingent"
182   1f.: "physical"; 3ff.: "contingent"
183   3ff.: section heading inserted
184   1: *Cognitio*; 2ff.: *Agnitio*
185   2ff.: reference inserted
186   1: *imperfectissima*; 2ff.: *in perfectissima*
187   1f.: "physical"; 3ff.: "contingent"
188   1: §353
189   1: no capitals in this sentence
190   1: "or the worship of God"; 2ff.: "(the worship of God)"
191   3ff.: "is" inserted
192   1: §946
193   1–6: *haec*; 7: *hinc*
194   1: §941
195   1f.: "physical"; 3ff.: "contingent"
196   1–5: *in eodem*; 6f.: *in eadem*
197   1: different text. "In that very moment in which a monad of this world acts, God actualizes its force by conservation (§953). Therefore he concurs with all the actions of all the substances of this world (§314). And since he immediately concurs as the cause without whose action the proximate sufficient ground would not even exist (§27), God immediately concurs with all the actions of all the substances of this world."
198   1: §876
199   2ff.: "and insofar as" inserted
200   1: §540
201   1, 2, 3, AA, 7: *hinc*; 4, 5, 6: *hunc*
202   1: this and the previous sentence merged into one sentence; 2: sentence in italics
203   3ff.: rest of paragraph inserted
204   1: "Such would be annihilation (§228, 967). Therefore the physical impedition of the fall is possible in itself. Therefore also possible for divine omnipotence"; 2ff.: "The fall ... physically (§833)"

205   1: §969
206   1: §969
207   6f.: §909
208   1: §801
209   3ff.: "is" inserted
210   1f.: "forcing that very spirit to observe certain laws in its free actions (§971 {1: §973}). Whoever has the right of forcing a person to [observe] certain moral laws is a LEGISLATOR; 3ff.: "obliging … LEGISLATOR."
211   1: different text "Whoever alone among the many spirits is their legislator is a MONARCH. Now God alone has legislative command over all created spirits (§973). Therefore he is the supreme and greatest monarch. Whence the spirits subject to his full power are called the city of God, and indeed every created spirit is a citizen subordinated to God."
212   1: no capitals
213   2ff.: rest of paragraph inserted
214   3ff.: "and … NATURE" inserted
215   3ff.: section heading inserted
216   1: §943
217   3ff.: "and … 222)" inserted
218   1–3, AA: *mali in iisdem*; 4ff.: *mali iisdem*
219   3ff.: rest of paragraph inserted
220   2ff.: "to its objects" inserted
221   2ff.: rest of paragraph inserted
222   2ff.: sentence inserted
223   1f.: "non-ending"; 3ff.: "eternal"
224   2ff.: "IN … future"
225   1f.: "non-ending"; 3ff.: "eternal"
226   2ff.: sentence inserted
227   3ff.: section heading inserted
228   2ff.: "IN THE BROAD SENSE (cf. §986, 989)" inserted
229   1: "God reveals his mind"; 2ff.: "The divine mind is revealed"
230   1: *se*; 2ff.: *animam*
231   1: "his own ends"; 2ff.: "the ends of God"
232   1: "his own"; 2ff.: "his"
233   2ff.: reference inserted
234   1: *tantum*; 2ff.: *solam*
235   1f.: "vast"; 3ff.: "fecund"
236   2ff.: "noble" inserted
237   2ff.: reference inserted
238   1: *suppeditans*; 2ff.: *suppeditat*
239   1f.: "vast"; 3ff.: "fecund"
240   2ff.: "more vast {3ff.: fecund}, noble" inserted
241   1–3, AA: §986
242   1: §989
243   3ff.: "HOLY" inserted
244   2ff.: "just … SUBJECTIVELY" inserted
245   2ff.: §986 inserted
246   2ff.: "through faith taken subjectively" inserted
247   1f.: "theological"; 3ff.: "holy"

248   1: "subjectively"; 2ff.: "objectively"
249   1f.: "theological"; 3ff.: "holy"
250   3ff.: "HOLY" inserted
251   1f.: "theological"; 3ff.: "holy"
252   3ff.: reference set in brackets
253   2ff.: "(theoretical)" inserted
254   1: *errans*; 2ff.: *errat*
255   1f.: "theological"; 3ff.: "holy"
256   1: no italics

General Index